HANDBOOK OF

CHILDHOOD BEHAVIORAL ISSUES

Evidence-Based Approaches to Prevention and Treatment

HANDBOOK OF
CHILDHOOD BEHAVIORAL ISSUES

Evidence-Based Approaches to Prevention and Treatment

Edited by
Thomas P. Gullotta
Gary M. Blau

Research Assistant
Jessica M. Ramos

Routledge
Taylor & Francis Group
New York   London

Routledge
Taylor & Francis Group
270 Madison Avenue
New York, NY 10016

Routledge
Taylor & Francis Group
2 Park Square
Milton Park, Abingdon
Oxon OX14 4RN

© 2008 by Taylor & Francis Group, LLC
Routledge is an imprint of Taylor & Francis Group, an Informa business

Printed in the United States of America on acid-free paper
10 9 8 7 6 5 4 3 2 1

International Standard Book Number-13: 978-0-415-95461-7 (Hardcover)

Library of Congress Cataloging-in-Publication Data

Handbook of childhood behavioral issues : evidence-based approaches to prevention and treatment / edited by Thomas P. Gullotta and Gary M. Blau; research assistant, Jessica M. Ramos.
    p. ; cm.
    Includes bibliographical references.
    ISBN-13: 978-0-415-95461-7 (alk. paper)
    ISBN-10: 0-415-95461-4 (alk. paper)
    1. Behavior disorders in children. 2. Child psychopathology. 3. Children--Health and hygiene. 4. Child development. 5. Evidence-based pediatrics. I. Gullotta, Thomas, 1948- II. Blau, Gary M. III. Ramos, Jessica M.
    [DNLM: 1. Child Behavior Disorders--prevention & control. 2. Child Development. 3. Child. 4. Evidence-Based Medicine. 5. Mental Disorders--prevention & control. WS 350.6 H2364 2007]

RJ506.B44H2485 2007
618.92'89--dc22
        2007019087

**Visit the Taylor & Francis Web site at
http://www.taylorandfrancis.com**

**and the Routledge Web site at
http://www.routledge.com**

Contents

About the Editors

Gary M. Blau, PhD is a clinical psychologist and is currently the chief of the Child, Adolescent, and Family Branch of the Center for Mental Health Services. In this role he provides national leadership for children's mental health and is responsible for developing and implementing programs designed to improve the lives of children and families. Prior to this, Dr. Blau was the bureau chief of Quality Management and Director of Mental Health for the Connecticut Department of Children and Families (DCF), and the director of Clinical Services at the Child and Family Agency of Southeastern Connecticut. He received his PhD from Auburn University (Auburn, Alabama) in 1988.

Thomas P. Gullotta, MA, MSW is CEO of Child and Family Agency and a member of the psychology and education departments at Eastern Connecticut State University. He is the senior author of the 4th edition of *The Adolescent Experience*, coeditor of *The Encyclopedia of Primary Prevention and Health Promotion*, and editor emeritus of the *Journal of Primary Prevention*. He is the senior book series editor for *Issues in Children's and Families' Lives*. Tom holds editorial appointments on the *Journal of Early Adolescence*, *The Journal of Adolescent Research*, and the *Journal of Educational and Psychological Consultation*. He has published extensively on adolescents and primary prevention. Tom was honored in 1999 by the Society for Community Research and Action, Division 27 of the American Psychological Association with their Distinguished Contributions to Practice in Community Psychology Award.

Contributors

Jill Antonishak received her doctorate from the Department of Psychology at the University of Virginia in 2005 and her bachelor's degree from Goucher College. Her research focuses on adolescent risk taking and problem behavior, with an emphasis on peer relations. Other research interests include the application of developmental psychology to law and public policy, especially juvenile justice and media issues. She is currently a Society for Research in Child Development (SRCD) Congressional Fellow.

Nancy Cantey Banasiak is an assistant professor in the Pediatric Nurse Practitioner Specialty. She has been a faculty member of Yale University School of Nursing since 1998 and practices at Yale-New Haven Hospital Primary Care Center with a focus on asthma. She holds her master's degree of science from Catholic University of America.

Brian Bishop is an associate professor and community psychologist. He teaches community and cross-cultural psychology at Curtin University, Perth, Western Australia. Brian conducts research on community-based interventions and community health. He is particularly interested in the impact of community risk and protective factors on mental health and mental health with indigenous communities.

Martin Bloom retired from teaching at the University of Connecticut School of Social Work to a life devoted to art, primary prevention, and research. He coedited (with Tom Gullotta) *The Encyclopedia of Primary Prevention and Health Promotion;* the fifth edition of *Evaluating Practice* (with Joel Fischer and John Orme); along with other books on human behavior (with Carel Germain) and aging (with Waldo Klein). He works alone on his art.

Edward S. Brodkin is assistant professor of Psychiatry at the University of Pennsylvania School of Medicine. He graduated from Harvard College and Harvard Medical School and completed training in psychiatry at Yale. He treats adults with autism spectrum disorders. His research is focused on the genetics and neurobiology of social behaviors and autism. He has received grant support from agencies including the Burroughs Wellcome Fund, NIMH, and the Cure Autism Now Foundation.

Jeanne Brooks-Gunn is the Virginia and Leonard Marx Professor of Child Development at Teachers College and the College of Physicians and Surgeons, Columbia University. She codirects the National Center for Children and Families at Teachers College. Dr. Brooks-Gunn's specialty is policy-oriented research focusing on family and community influences upon the development of children and youth. She also designs and evaluates interventions aimed at enhancing the well-being of children living in poverty and associated conditions.

Paul J. Brounstein received his doctorate in Experimental Social Psychology from the University of Maryland (1977). He currently serves as a senior public health advisor in the Center for Mental Health Services (CMHS). His assignments include assisting CMHS and SAMHSA to translate effective, evidence-based practice to broad-based local implementation; assisting in the efforts to evaluate violence and suicide prevention initiatives. He is also working with colleagues in the European Union to collaborate on an international registry of effective mental health promotion and mental illness prevention and treatment programs. This last assignment builds directly upon the work he pioneered while at the Center for Substance Abuse Prevention for which he received the HHS Secretary's Distinguished Service Award in 2003.

Kevin R. Bush is an associate professor of Family Studies at Miami University, Oxford, Ohio. His research interests focus on child and adolescent development in the contexts of family and culture. He has conducted studies with U.S. and international (e.g., Chinese, Mexican, South Korean, and Russian) samples of children, adolescents, and families. His work has been published in several scholarly journals and books. He received his doctorate in Human Ecology from Ohio State University.

Sucheta D. Connolly is director of the Pediatric Stress and Anxiety Disorders Clinic and associate professor of Clinical Psychiatry at the University of Illinois at Chicago (UIC). Her research interests include risk and protective factors in childhood anxiety disorders and selective mutism. She graduated from Washington University Medical School in St. Louis, completed her residency in general psychiatry at UIC, and her residency in child and adolescent psychiatry at the University of Chicago.

David de Voursney is currently a presidential management fellow at the Substance Abuse and Mental Health Services Administration working on the Safe Schools/Healthy Students program. Originally from Charlottesville, Virginia, he has a bachelor's degree in psychology from Earlham College and a master's degree in public policy from the University of Michigan. He has worked with youth as a case manager for families with children and as a residential counselor with youth involved in the justice system.

Raymond W. DuCharme is the founder and director of The Learning Clinic, Inc. (TLC), a private nonprofit education and treatment program for children and adolescents. TLC has provided day education and residential services since 1980. He has been a researcher and teacher, an adjunct professor at the University of Connecticut and assistant professor at Brown University, a national consultant and author of numerous papers, book chapters, and articles on the subjects of treating and educating students with autistic spectrum disorders and associated comorbid conditions.

Janet F. Gillespie is an associate professor and the graduate program director in the Department of Psychology at SUNY Brockport, where she also chairs the Institutional Review Board. Dr. Gillespie received her doctorate from Southern Illinois University at Carbondale with concentrations in clinical child and community psychology. Her publications include articles on children's quality of life, research ethics, school-based prevention, and social problem solving and social skills training with children. Her research interests also include positive psychology and child and family social competence. She is a member of the American Psychological Association and the Association for Psychological Science.

Patricia A. Graczyk is an assistant professor of Clinical Psychology in Psychiatry at the University of Illinois at Chicago (UIC) and a school psychologist in Indian Prairie School District 204 in Naperville, Illinois. She completed her doctorate in clinical and school psychology at Northern Illinois University in 1998 and a NIMH Postdoctoral Prevention Research Fellowship at UIC in 2001. Her research interests include pediatric anxiety disorders, school-based mental health services, and children's social and emotional competence.

Elaine M. Gustafson an assistant professor in Nursing at Yale University School of Nursing in the Pediatric Nurse Practitioner Specialty has been practicing as a PNP since the early 1990s at Fair Haven Community Health Center in New Haven, CT. Her research has focused on coping skills training for youth with asthma and prevention of type 2 diabetes in overweight youth. She has presented nationally and internationally on these topics.

E. Wayne Holden is the executive vice president of Social and Statistical Sciences at RTI International, the nation's second largest nonprofit, independent research organization. He is also an adjunct Professor in the Department of Psychiatry and Behavioral Sciences at Duke University School of Medicine. He has directed national, multisite program evaluations of children's mental health services and has over 20 years of experience as a pediatric/clinical child psychologist.

Elizabeth A. Holden is a graduate student in the Clinical/Community Psychology program at the University of North Carolina at Charlotte. Her specialty area is the treatment of adolescents with co-occurring substance abuse and mental health disorders.

Korey K. Hood is a staff clinician and research associate at the Joslin Diabetes Center and Instructor of Psychiatry at Harvard Medical School. He specializes in clinical and health psychology with a focus on pediatric chronic disease. He is part of a multidisciplinary team aimed at promoting optimal diabetes management and health outcomes. He is federally funded to conduct clinical research on the interaction of diabetes management and behavioral and emotional outcomes.

Theresa Kruczek is an associate professor in the Department of Counseling Psychology and Guidance Services at Ball State University, where she is director of the Counseling Practicum Clinic. She is a licensed health services provider in Psychology whose clinical specialty is working with children and adolescents who are survivors of abuse. Her primary research focus is family violence, more specifically identifying ways to promote adaptive coping and resiliency in child abuse survivors.

David S. Mandell is assistant professor of Psychiatry and Pediatrics at the University of Pennsylvania School of Medicine. His research focuses on the organization, financing, and delivery of healthcare and education services to children with autism. He is especially interested in how federal, state, and local policies affect service delivery and outcomes for children with autism.

Danyelle Mannix is currently working as an evaluator for Educational Services, Inc. She has over 10 years experience in mental health and substance abuse services research; serving as an analyst on several state and multisite national evaluations involving children and families. She has a bachelor's degree in psychology from American University and is a doctoral candidate in behavioral neuroscience at American University. She resides in Maryland with her partner and three children.

Kathleen A. McGrady has been the clinical director of The Learning Clinic, Inc. (TLC) since 1994. TLC is a private nonprofit education and treatment program for children and adolescents. She is a neuropsychologist and has been a researcher and author of numerous papers and presentations on assessment, diagnosis, and treatment of children and adolescents with autistic spectrum disorders, and the associated comorbid conditions.

Mikki Meadows-Oliver is a lecturer at Yale University School of Nursing in the Pediatric Nurse Practitioner Program. Her clinical practice is with the Yale Asthma Outreach Program where, in collaboration with the Yale Pediatric Asthma Care Team, she conducts home visits to children with persistent asthma. She has participated on coalitions and committees to improve pediatric asthma care. She has presented nationally and has published articles related to caring for children with asthma.

Miriam Mulsow is an associate professor and director of Human Development and Family Studies Graduate Programs at Texas Tech University. Her doctorate in child and family development is from the University of Georgia. She studies family stress and resiliency, parenting stress, attention deficit hyperactivity disorder, and addictions. Her current research is in Cambodia and includes studies of trauma from war and genocide, postnatal alcohol consumption among breastfeeding mothers, and program evaluation.

Tonja R. Nansel is an investigator at the National Institute of Child Health and Human Development, Prevention Research Branch. Her research focuses on behavioral interventions to improve management of diabetes in children and their families. Current research includes a multisite study testing the efficacy of a clinic-integrated family-based intervention targeting diabetes management behaviors, as well as research on promoting healthy dietary choices among youth with diabetes.

Heather M. Pederson received her bachelor's degree in psychology from the University of Texas at Austin. She is currently a doctoral student of counseling psychology at Indiana University. She is a researcher at the Center for Adolescent and Family Studies (CAFS), working particularly on a project to create a web-based clearinghouse of evidence-based practices for child and adolescent behavior and learning problems. Her research interests include family-based treatment outcomes with at-risk youth.

Gary W. Peterson is professor and chair of the Department of Family Studies and Social Work at the University of Miami, Oxford, Ohio. His areas of research are parent–child/adolescent relations, cross-cultural influences on adolescent development, and family theory. His current research focuses most prominently on how parental qualities influence the development of social competence by adolescents in several societies around the globe.

Nina Philipsen is a second-year doctoral student in developmental psychology and a graduate research fellow at the National Center for Children and Families. She has a bachelor's degree in psychology from the University of Texas and a master's degree from Purdue University in child development and family studies. She works on the Fragile Families Project and with the Early Childhood Longitudinal Study—Birth dataset. Her primary research interests include early childhood policy and health issues.

Jessica M. Ramos received her bachelor's degree in psychology from Eastern Connecticut State University. She is a research assistant at Child and Family Agency of Southeastern Connecticut. She has assisted in the editorial process of books on primary prevention,

prevention and treatment of behavioral problems in children and adolescents, Asperger Syndrome, promotion of prosocial behavior, and interpersonal violence in the African American community. She is involved in agency research and reviews cases for Quality Assurance.

N. Dickon Reppucci has been professor of Psychology and director of Community Psychology Training at the University of Virginia since 1976. He received his doctorate from Harvard University in 1968 and was an assistant and associate professor at Yale University from 1968 to 1976. He is an author, coauthor, or editor of more than 150 books, chapters, and articles. His major research interests include children, families, and the law, especially juvenile justice and adolescent development, and the prevention of child abuse and neglect.

Clare Roberts is an associate professor of Clinical Psychology and coordinator of Clinical Psychology Training at Curtin University in Perth, Western Australia. She has been practicing as a clinical child psychologist since 1990. Clare set up the Curtin Child Psychology Clinic and was director of this clinic for five years. Her current research interests include school and family-based interventions to prevent anxiety, depression, and behavior problems in children.

Rosanna Rooney is a clinical psychologist who works as a senior lecturer at Curtin University in Perth, Western Australia. She also conducts a clinical psychology practice where she specializes in child and adult internalizing problems. Rosie's research interests include the prevention of internalizing disorders in children, as well as child and adult cross-cultural psychology. She has recently worked extensively on an international project spanning 13 countries, related to mental health in migrant youth.

Jill Salsman is working toward her doctoral degree in counseling psychology at Ball State University, Muncie, IN. Her research interests are in the areas of eating disorders and childhood sexual abuse. Her clinical focus is the adolescent population. She received her bachelor's degree in psychology from Augustana College in Rock Island, IL, and a master's degree in counseling from Ball State University.

Lora M. Scagliola is a graduate student in the doctoral program in school psychology at the University of Rhode Island. She received her bachelor's degree in psychology from the University of Central Florida in Orlando and a master's degree in psychology from the State University of New York (SUNY) College at Brockport. She has completed externships in research at SUNY and at the University of Rochester's Mt. Hope Family Center, in addition to a master's level practicum at Unity Mental Health Systems in Rochester, NY. She continues practicum experience in the Rhode Island public schools. Her research interests include character strengths in children, quality of life issues, educational and mental health policy, and cultural awareness.

Rachael A. Schuster received her bachelor's degree in psychology from the University of Wisconsin—Madison. She is currently a doctoral student in the counseling psychology program at Indiana University. She is a researcher at the Center for Adolescent and Family Studies (CAFS) in Bloomington, Indiana. Her research interests include the influence of risk and protective factors on therapeutic outcome, disruptive behavior problems in childhood, and acculturation/enculturation experiences of Hmong living in the United States.

Adam J. Schwebach completed his master's degree from Eastern Kentucky University. He is a doctoral candidate at the University of Utah pursuing a doctorate degree in school psychology with an emphasis in neuropsychology. He currently works as a doctoral resident at the Neurology Learning and Behavior Center in Salt Lake City, Utah. He is also a certified school psychologist with the Weber County School District in Ogden, Utah. His research interests include evaluating cognitive processing deficits in children with attention deficit hyperactivity disorder. He conducts evaluations and treatment interventions for children and adolescents with ADHD, learning disabilities, traumatic brain injuries, and emotional and behavioral disorders.

Derek J. Schwebach has a master's of social work degree from the University of Utah. His interests include work with families and children experiencing issues related to child abuse, juvenile justice, domestic violence, mental health, and substance abuse. Currently, he is working as a certified social worker for the Utah County Division of Substance Abuse, and is an on-call social worker for Primary Children's Hospital in Salt Lake City.

Thomas L. Sexton is a professor in the Department of Counseling Psychology at Indiana University. He is on the faculty of the nationally accredited doctoral program in counseling psychology, and he directs the Center for Adolescent and Family Studies (CAFS), a national research center for the study and dissemination of research based practices for the treatment of at-risk adolescents and their families. He has presented workshops on functional family therapy and consulted with systems of care attempting to integrate evidence-based practices both nationally and internationally. He is coauthor of the FFT clinical manual, author of all of the most recent theoretical chapters on FFT, and the designer of the FFT Clinical Services System. His interest in family psychology and psychotherapy research have resulted in over 40 journal articles, 25 book chapters, and four books. His most recent book is *The Handbook of Family Therapy*, a major reference for family psychology. He is a licensed psychologist (IN), a Fellow of the American Psychological Association, and a board certified family psychologist (ABPP).

Aubyn C. Stahmer is a research scientist at Children's Hospital and UC San Diego. Her research involves examining the effectiveness of early intervention in young children with autism, individualizing early intervention to meet the specific needs of children and families, and better understanding community early intervention systems. She has worked in the area of autism for over 15 years. Her clinical expertise is in the areas of early identification, parent education, and early intervention.

Stephanie Vitanza is an associate professor at Argosy University-Phoenix, Arizona. Her clinical specialty is working with families, and children and adolescents who have been sexually abused. She also treats children and teens who have been physically abused or neglected or who may have witnessed homicide or violence. Her publications and presentations focus on trauma, violence in relationships, and group treatment for adolescents who have been sexually abused.

Introduction

Thomas P. Gullotta and Gary M. Blau

By opening this book we believe we know something about you. You are a practicing mental health professional who is expected to justify your helping efforts to managed care providers, grantors, and most importantly the client you have partnered with to assist him or her achieve desired life changes. You are a graduate or advanced undergraduate student checking out the book that will occupy your interest for the next semester. You are a family member who has a child, sibling, or relative with issues discussed in this volume, or you have experienced one or more of these problems on a personal basis. First, welcome. Now, knowing you, shouldn't you know something about us and our beliefs that influenced the development of this book.

We are husbands and fathers. Gary has a biological daughter and son. Tom has an adopted son. We have both known joy and sorrow with our children—not just the normal "on-time" developmental issues of childhood but for Tom's son the issues of Asperger's syndrome and childhood bipolar disorder. Gary has other relatives who have experienced issues such as Down's syndrome and depression. The reality is that each of us, whether writing or reading, is touched in some way by issues affecting mental health.

We have both worked as clinicians and administrators in a variety of settings: municipal, state, and federal government, psychiatric hospital, community mental health center, and nonprofit children's social service agencies. Over the decades we have witnessed dramatic changes in how the issues discussed in this book are conceptualized and how helping services are delivered.

HOW ISSUES ARE CONCEPTUALIZED

Not long ago parents were thought to be responsible for their children's disorders. For example, mental health clinicians were taught that the psychological basis for schizophrenia was a "schizophrenogenic mother"; that is, a mother who was rejecting and cold, yet overprotective and controlling. Today, we know that schizophrenia is rooted mostly in genetics and neurobiology. Similar inferences can be traced to other maladies such as attention deficit hyperactivity disorder, the affective disorders, and disorders on the autism spectrum. Certainly, some parenting styles are more successful than others. However, we have learned that most all parents love their children and want nothing more than to see them happy, healthy, and full of life. So, the question becomes not one of blame, but how best to partner with parents so that their children reach this potential.

Maybe more important for the therapist is the question of how to realign our perceptions, judgments, and beliefs to be able to even entertain the possibility that parents want the best for their children. Obvious you say? According to many families who receive services and are involved with the latest family-driven reform efforts, it is not as obvious as one might think or wish.

What is taught and reinforced in practice is the concept of disorder and dysfunction. We define the person by their illness or disability. Emotions and behavior are viewed in the context of a medical model. This book even has an element of the medical model at its core—separated into chapters that reflect diagnostic categories that have underlying etiologies. This is what we are trained to do and what is familiar to us. We are trained to diagnose pathology and treat symptoms, to look for what is inherently wrong with a child and a family. The problem with this approach is that it focuses too much attention on individual frailties and faults. Simply put, sick people have to be fixed and then adapt to the rest of the world. We tend to gravitate toward looking for the bad. If you don't believe us then just watch the evening news. The challenge is not simply to become a diagnostician and focus on dysfunction; it is to find a way to focus on what is right with a child and family. We must find strengths in each and every person, and determine what is inherently good. Indeed, we dare you to look at your own children, siblings, nieces, and nephews and not find something of which to be proud. This is the way we must look at every child and family. We must find their competencies and nurture them.

This leads us to how we conceptualize the mental health issues and problems in living examined in this volume. Our approach is biopsychosocial-environmental: First, not one but many factors interact in differing degrees for each person to continually invent and reinvent that individual. Think of yourself as a potato in a stew pot: Frankly, alone (as a potato, that is) you're rather bland tasting and pale in complexion. But immersed in the stew we've prepared you'll soak up the biopsychosocial-environmental flavors that follow. *Bio* is an abbreviation of biology and equates to not only genes but the neurochemicals, hormones, and so on that sometimes dictates or influences our physical, mental, and emotional development. *Psycho* is an abbreviation for psychology and refers to traits such as self-esteem and locus of control and such states of behavior as self-concept or ability. *Social* encompasses the relationships with others that influence behavior. Parents, relatives, siblings, peers, teachers, clergy, neighbors, and others have the power to strengthen or weaken psychological states and traits by their interactions with us. These same people and others may not be able to alter heredity but they can minimize to the extent possible the script our genes hand us, and they are essential in helping us avoid or minimize the toxic elements in the environment. The environment is an external condition like lead that can seriously damage a child's intellectual development. Environment is also action that removes lead from gasoline and contaminated painted surfaces in older homes. Environment can be airborne pollutants that aggravate a child's asthma, or it can mean the development of standards for the exchange of air in a building to lessen those pollutants. It is fat laden food and sugar loaded snacks that contribute to childhood obesity and diabetes, and it is the removal of trans fat from foods and soda machines from schools. It is poverty and ghettoes, euphemistically called neighborhoods, that discourage a child's spirit and teach violent behavior, and it is community development efforts that give rebirth to these areas. Given this conceptualization of multiple pathways to encourage good and not-so-good behavior, and the importance of each pathway for each individual, our task was to convey this complexity in this book. But before we do that let's revisit your status as a potato. From bland and pasty, this set of ingredients has imparted to you a different color, texture, and a complexity of flavors represented by the herbs, spices, vegetables, meat, or fish added to your particular stew. You are no longer simply a potato or to return you to humanity two sets of intermingling genes. You are the result of a complex set of interactions that continues across your lifespan.

HOW HELPING SERVICES ARE DELIVERED

Encouragingly, this biopsychosocial-environmental view has gained increased popularity in recent years. Whether referred to as an ecological model (Bronfenbrenner, 1979), or person-in-the-environment approach (Germaine & Bloom, 1999), since the 1950s services have shifted away from residential institutions to community locations. Theoretical conceptualizations increasingly acknowledge the multitude of factors influencing the development of behavior. That in turn has resulted in more complex helping interventions being developed to assist children and their families in need. Importantly and following an older movement in medicine, these efforts are being viewed critically. It is no longer enough to believe an effort works, it must be shown to work. This is the essence of evidence-based practice.

Perhaps, this is the point where a good clinician begins to ask, "So what do I do?" The good news to be found in this book is that there is empirical evidence supporting helping treatment strategies. However, we encourage you to maintain a critical eye. Much of the current research about treatment effectiveness does not account for cultural variations and differences, or real-world realities. For example, while an intervention is promising in an experimental clinic delivered by highly trained experts, how does this work if a person lives 100 miles away from the nearest facility or needs to take a train and two buses to get there? Consider also, how many of you readers have actually learned to provide one of the evidence-based practices discussed in this book?

Finally, we remind the reader that the goal in human services should not be just to provide intervention and treatment (some might say, facilitating recovery). Rather, we must promote positive mental health, and whenever the opportunity presents itself, prevent the onset of the mental health issue or problem in living. Mental health workers call this primary prevention and health promotion. Our biopsychosocial-environmental worldview offers numerous opportunities to intervene for good. Here are just a few examples. Genetic tests are being used in experimental interventions in utero to prevent spina bifada from developing (http://www.spinabifadamoms.com). Prenatal screenings can now identify congenital defects such as heart or lung problems, which can then be corrected through prenatal surgery (http://www.health.enotes.com/childrens-health-encyclopedia/prenatal-surgery). The universal application of silver nitrate or penicillin to the eyes of infants at the time of birth prevents blindness due to infection from gonorrhea.

Programs that utilize all or nearly all of prevention's technology of education, competency promotion, natural caregiving, and community organization/systems intervention reduce aggressive behavior in childhood (Shure, 1992) and promote prosocial behavior in preschoolers (Chesebrough, King, Gullotta, & Bloom, 2004). Other programs like the

Prenatal/Infancy Project increase child rearing skills and strengthen the attachment be-tween parent and child (Olds, 1997). Mentoring efforts bring this social connectedness beyond the immediate family (Taylor & Bressler, 2000). Lastly, correcting dysfunctional institutional practices can lessen a child's trauma from receiving cancer treatment (Tadmor, 2003), and community mobilization, such as the Civil Rights Movement or Mothers Against Drunk Driving (MADD) can address dysfunctional societal behavior (Albee, 2003).

Compared to the past, we live in an exciting time for service delivery made all the more interesting by the discovery of naturally occurring substances such as lithium salt and the herb St. John's Wort, or the development of new chemical compounds leading to treatments for the affective disorders and other serious mental health issues. As prac-titioners or consumers or policy makers we must continually educate ourselves about what is possible.

THE CHAPTERS AHEAD

In order to share our understanding with you, we have organized this book as follows. Part I is foundational and provides the reader with a broad and necessary understanding of childhood development and its theories. Part II examines the family and community's influence on the child's development and assesses treatment and prevention measures with this population. Part III deals with physical health issues and the important con-nection between physical and mental health. Part IV speaks to behavioral health issues. The authors of these sections have formatted their chapters to provide the reader with a succinct comprehensive overview of the issue under discussion. Each author has reviewed risk and resiliency issues, genetic, family, and community factors. Against this backdrop, authors were then asked to identify "What Works." These are treatment strategies with three or more successful trials. "What Might Work" represents less than three successful trials, mixed trial results, or the absence of evidence good theory. And "What Doesn't Work" are practices that should be discontinued, if that has not already taken place. Next, and when appropriate, follows a discussion of medications that are in use. This is followed by an examination of prevention/health promotion strategies that work, might work, or don't work. The authors conclude their chapter with direct specific best advice on the treatment and prevention of the topic under discussion.

As we conclude this introduction, we must acknowledge the good humor and hard work of a group of scholars who in many cases have worked with us for several years as we have explored the extent to which evidence-based practice exists in prevention/health promotion, adolescence, and now early childhood. We offer this ensemble work as our collective attempt to improve services for children and their families. For practitioners, it is a clear and decisive view of best practice. For administrators and policy makers, it is a blueprint for implementing services that matter. For families, it is hope.

REFERENCES

Albee, G. W. (2003). The contributions of society, culture, and social class to emotional disorder. In T. P. Gullotta & M. Bloom (Eds.), *The encyclopedia of primary prevention and health promotion* (pp. 97–103). New York: Kluwer Academic.

Bronfenbrenner, U. (1979). *The ecology of human development.* Cambridge, MA: Harvard University Press.

Chesebrough, E., King, P., Gullotta, T. P., & Bloom, M. (2004). *A blueprint for the promotion of prosocial behavior in early childhood.* New York: Kluwer Academic.

Germaine, C. B., & Bloom, M. (1999). *Human behavior in the social environment: An ecological view.* New York: Columbia University Press.

Olds, D. (1997). The prenatal/early infancy project: Fifteen years later. In G. W. Albee & T. P. Gullotta (Eds.), *Primary prevention works* (pp. 41–67). Thousand Oaks, CA: Sage.

Shure, M. (1992). *I can problem solve: An interpersonal cognitive problem-solving program.* Champagne, IL: Research Press.

Tadmor, C. P. (2003). Perceived personal control. In T. P. Gullotta & M. Bloom (Eds.), *The encyclopedia of primary prevention and health promotion* (pp. 812–820). New York: Kluwer Academic.

Taylor, A. S., & Bressler, J. (2000). *Mentoring across generations: Partnerships for positive youth development.* New York: Kluwer Academic.

Part I

FOUNDATIONAL CHAPTERS

Chapter One

From Theory to Practice

Treatment and Prevention Possibilities

Thomas P. Gullotta[1]

INTRODUCTION

This chapter discusses theories that explain childhood behavior and give rise to interventions that ideally help children to cope with and adapt to distress, and when possible, to avoid it. By necessity, this chapter paints an impressionistic landscape of a vast, detailed area rich in nuances. The reader is encouraged to seek out the primary sources referenced to explore that theoretical landscape in depth.

Every behavioral theory begins with an observation that is followed by a suspicion. Better theories have multiple observations of the same occurrence and continued confirmation of that explanatory suspicion. The best theories entertain numerous other suspicions to explain the observation before replacing the word *suspicion* with the words *suspected cause*. The latter term is used because theories are not laws but merely assumptions of why certain behaviors occur, reoccur, or fail to occur in a given predictable manner.

It must be remembered that theories are influenced by the period in which they are developed. The term *social reality* refers to the commonly held beliefs of a particular period regardless of their ultimate truth. Thus, Galileo found himself declared a heretic for suggesting that the earth was not the center of the universe, and Joseph Langley was ridiculed by his colleagues at the Smithsonian Institution for imagining that the day was near when man would travel in a heavier-than-air flying machine powered by an internal combustion gasoline engine (Pauwels & Bergier, 1988). Or, as shall be seen, a theorist can interpret clients' statements that they were sexually misused in childhood by their fathers not as factual recollections but fantasies.

Any clinical, preventive, or health promotion intervention worth using must be able to identify its roots. Those roots are the one or more theoretical frameworks from which the intervention emerges. Better behavioral theories have a body of juried, published clinical case studies, program examples, or qualitative research that describes the application of techniques emerging from those theories. The best behavioral theories give birth to interventions that have been tested repeatedly through an experimental design.

Surprisingly, only recently have the helping sciences paid attention to the question: Does this intervention improve the client's health? The answer to this question has fueled the transformation of physical health care from an art (i.e., in my professional judgment) to a science (i.e., my decision to do this procedure is based on the results of 3,000 similar cases). Since the mid-1990s, this simple question has dampened interest in some theoretical schools and given impetus to others in the behavioral sciences.

HOW THEORY INFLUENCES THERAPY

Before outlining several theories and the interventions that derive from their tenets, it is necessary to put a wash on this academic canvas. This wash is the necessary ingredient for a successful therapeutic relationship (Rogers, 1965). For a helping relationship to succeed, five conditions must develop between the client and the helper. The first is trustworthiness, which is a difficult condition to achieve in relationships where the client is not a willing participant. The next is genuineness, a condition complicated by racial, ethnic, and socioeconomic status (SES) differences between client and helper. Third is empathy, which is not to be confused with sympathy that implies agreement and commiseration with the client's situation. The fourth condition is honesty without which the relationship is a sham.

Like the straw man in the *Wizard of Oz*, how simple these ingredients are to achieving a successful helping relationship. Why, indeed, you and I could have thought of these fundamental conditions ourselves! Without trustworthiness, genuineness, empathy, and honesty, therapeutic change cannot occur. But there remains one final factor vital to achieving change; namely, the client's *perception* of the helper as trustworthy, genuine, empathic, and honest. Without this leap of faith on the client's part, change is not possible.

Interestingly, what remains unanswered is whether the presence of these five conditions is enough for life changing events to occur. Does the makeup of the intervention really matter, or is it the conditions under which it is delivered? We know that in drug trials the "placebo effect" can be as powerful a curative agent as the new drug. The resolution of this issue waits further testing.

PSYCHOANALYTIC THEORY

For more than one hundred years, Sigmund Freud and psychoanalysis have been interchangeable terms. From shortly after the turn of the last century to the early 1960s, his construction of human behavior dominated the delivery of mental health services in the United States and elsewhere. His understanding of human behavior offered a pathway to health for his "neurotic patients" (Freud, 1920/1949, p. 17). As an interesting aside, Freud did not recommend psychoanalysis for delusional (psychotic) behavior. He felt that, "it is just as powerless as any other therapy to heal these sufferers" (p. 227).

Theoretical Tenets of Psychoanalytic Theory

To understand psychoanalytic theory, one must appreciate that Freud understood that two instinctual urges were at the base of all behavior. The first was the sexual urge, and the second was the death urge (Freud, 1935/1920, p. 133). The second urge emerged in Freud's writings after the First World War in response to the unimaginable slaughter that occurred, and it has been reinterpreted to refer to mankind's aggressive urges.

Freud postulates that the psyche is comprised of three parts that emerge as the child ages. The id is present at birth and represents the wishes that derive from the instinctual urges. The ego develops at approximately age 2: It is understood as the source of neurotic behavior because it wishes to satisfy the needs of the id while simultaneously avoiding punishment for the id's desires. Lastly, the superego (conscience) emerges as the judge of all behavior.

Concurrent with the development of the psyche is a primitive developmental process beginning at birth and concluding "about the sixth or eighth year" in a "latency period" (Freud, 1920/1949, p. 286). This developmental process contains three distinct erotogenic stages. The first, occurring at birth, is the oral stage where the mouth is the sexual organ that receives nourishment and satisfaction from mother's breast.

The second is the anal stage. Here, the child is striving toward mastery of the environment, "which easily passes over into cruelty" (Freud, 1920/1949, p. 287) and sadistic-anal behavior. Behavior may be passive or active. It entails curiosity, exploration, and gazing. The sexual orifices of mouth, anus, vagina, and penis evolve from pregenital or single organ pleasures to genital zone pleasures.

These genital zone pleasures are associated with the male and female child's first "love object"—mother or father. In the third, oedipal stage, Freud (1920/1949) writes that,

> the little man wants his mother all to himself, finds his father in the way, be-comes restive when the latter takes upon himself to caress her, and shows his satisfaction when the father goes away or is absent.... When the little boy shows the most open sexual curiosity about his mother, wants to sleep with her at night, insists on being in the room while she is dressing, or even attempts physical acts of seduction...the erotic nature of this attachment to her is established without a doubt. (pp. 291–292)

Likewise, the process is repeated between daughter and father. "The loving devotion to the father, the need to do away with the superfluous mother and to take her place," mirrors the sexual desires of the boy (Freud, 1920/1949, p. 292).

For Freud (1920/1949), "the little human being is frequently a finished product in his fourth or fifth year, and only gradually reveals in later years what lies buried in him" (p. 310). Here, Freud is referencing the role of the ego's defense mechanisms in insulating the individual from the desire of the id expressed by the libido's fixation. Freud (1920/1949, p. 316) expresses dysfunctional behavior (neurosis) in the following formula:

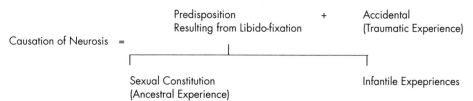

Thus, dysfunctional behavior results when one or more distressful (traumatic) experiences trigger earlier oral, anal, or oedipal experiences that were not successfully resolved before the fourth or fifth year of the child's life.

The Use of Analytically Oriented Therapy

The need of the ego to shelter the individual from his or her instinctual urges gives rise to a series of protective actions that Freud labeled defense mechanisms. These mechanisms transform the instinctual urges into more socially acceptable but potentially problematic behaviors. In the process these urges are pushed from conscious awareness into the unconscious. Psychoanalysis seeks to uncover this unconscious anxiety. Through free association (uncensored talk) and retelling dreams, the client with the help of the therapist peels away the protective layers to reveal the early childhood events that are the cause of the client's distress. It is an interpretative process in which all is not what it appears to be. That is, a cigar may be a phallic symbol, or as Freud once remarked to a colleague, "Sometimes a good cigar is just a good cigar" (Meltzer, 1987, p. 215). It is a lengthy process,

> When we undertake to treat a neurotic psycho-analytically we proceed...to explain to him the difficulties of the method, its long duration, the trials and sacrifices which will be required of him; and, as to the result, we tell him that we can make no definite promises, that success depends upon his endeavors, upon his understanding, his adaptability and his perseverance. (Freud, 1920/1949, p. 17)

In this model, change is an educational event involving transference as an essential element. Change takes place as the client with the assistance of the therapist achieves insight into her or his behavior. That insight provides the impetus for attitudinal and ultimately behavioral change. It is a process that requires a higher level of cognitive operations.

The term *cognitive operations* is associated with Jean Piaget. Observing the behavior of his own and other children, this remarkable scholar developed a four-stage developmental theory to explain the emergence of cognition in childhood.[2] What is of interest to us in this model is the emergence of formal operational thought, which takes place between the ages 12 and 15. Formal operational processing involves the capacity to think about thoughts, to hypothesize, to understand that actions taken today have consequences at a distant time, and to be reflective (Piaget, 1950; Piaget & Inhelder, 1958). These are the required intellectual processes needed to achieve the understanding necessary in Freud's theory to achieve insight and therapeutic change. Piaget's critics properly note that the partial development of formal operations may occur earlier or later than age 12; that it may take much longer than age 15 to be established; and that formal operation is not a universal event. That is, a majority of the adult population may not develop the capacity for formal operations (Byrnes, 2001).

Let us now consider the use of analytically oriented therapy with children ages 5 to 12. From Piaget's writings a child between the ages of 5 and 12 is unlikely to demonstrate formal operational capabilities. Indeed, if the child is between the ages of 5 and 7, she or he may still be preoperational. If the child is between the ages of 7 to 11, Piaget would contend that the child is cognitively operating from a concrete perspective. In either event, with a majority of the adult population never developing formal operational thought and with formal operations developing, when it does, over years, is it unrealistic to assume that a child can benefit from this intervention?

For example, are you asking young children to relate their dreams and to free associate at that early age? No, that is not the methodology in use. Rather, the child's intrapsychic world is uncovered through the child's play. It is believed that the child's actions during play with the therapist reveal the unresolved issues interfering with the child's successful adjustment. But a few words of caution are in order. To successfully address the child's issues requires that the language of play be correctly interpreted. But now here's a dilemma. Recall the earlier example that the cigar may represent a phallic symbol or it may be simply a cigar. Consider, as Freud (1935/1920) did early in his formulation of this theoretical perspective, that a client's report that she or he was sexually molested by a person may be real or fantasy:

> Under the pressure of the technical procedure which I used at the time, the majority of my patients reproduced from their childhood scenes in which they were sexually seduced by some grown-up person. With female patients the part of seducer was almost always assigned to their father. I believed these stories, and consequently supposed that I had discovered the roots of the subsequent neurosis in these experiences of sexual seduction in childhood…. When, however, I was at last obliged to recognize that these scenes of seduction had never taken place, and that they were only phantasies which had made up or which I myself had perhaps forced upon them, I was…at a loss…(Now I realize) I had in fact stumbled for the first time upon the Oedipus complex. (pp. 60–61)

Today, many would contend that Freud had it right but wrongly chose existing "social reality" over the truth. In too many instances children are sexually abused. In addition, while Vygotsky's (1978) theory of cognitive development, in particular the zone of proximal development, which notes that knowledge development is contingent on guidance and assistance from others, was decades away from articulation, Freud was correct in fearing that his clinical work might have unknowingly led his clients to express memories that may not have been real. These dilemmas have focused attention away from analytically oriented approaches to other theoretical interventions. Child's play remains a language. Interpreting that language correctly is the challenge. What one then does with that interpretation is the therapeutic intervention that can be insight oriented or not.

BEHAVIORAL THEORIES

The behaviorist is concerned with the obvious. It is the overt problem behaviors that need to be replaced with more functional behaviors. Development plays no essential role in the early construction of this theory. It is the environment that matters. Environmental exposure to language and experiences will either hasten or retard the speed of the child's ability to learn. Despite its mechanistic construction, learning theory is optimistic in its belief that all behavior can be reshaped. As one of its strongest proponents once expressed:

> Behaviorism is the scientific study of human behavior. Its real goal is to provide the basis for the prediction and control of human beings…. We can say that

the behaviorists' job is—given the stimulus, to predict the response—given the response, to predict the stimulus…. We hope someday to attain such proficiency that we can take the worst adult social failure (provided he is biologically sound), pull him apart, psychologically speaking, and give him a new set of works. (Watson, 1928, p. 2, 20)

Theoretical Tenets of Behaviorism

The origin of behaviorism is credited to the Russian physiologist Ivan Pavlov whose research on dog salivation led to the discovery of classical conditioning. That is, a response to a stimulus, such as salivating at the sight and smell of a favorite food (unconditioned stimulus), can be paired with an unconnected item or occurrence such as a picture, sound, or other entity (conditioned stimulus) to eventually elicit the same response when it is presented (salivation).

B. F. Skinner (1953) is credited with the next step in the evolution of this model—operant conditioning. Simply put, the response following a behavior either will increase or decrease the probability of that behavior reoccurring. Thus, if a child asks, "Mom, would you please pass the milk." And Mom responds by saying, "That was very nice asking, Jimmy, using the word *please*. Here is the milk." There is an increased likelihood that Jimmy will use the word *please* again in his demands for milk. With additional reinforcement for using the word *please* in other situations, the word *please* should generalize to everyday usage. Clearly, this is a powerful learning technique and is the basis for the majority of educational interventions currently in use.

With the latest development in learning theory, social learning theory and social cognitive theory, the popularity of this model has grown. Albert Bandura (1977, 1986) maintains that learning occurs as we model our behavior after others. Learning occurs as we observe the consequences of our behavior and that of others. Learning is environmental meaning that the reinforcement following a response will increase or decrease the probability of its reoccurrence. Lastly, we are active participants rather than passive recipients in this process, which means that we partially control our environment by our reaction to it.

The Use of Behavioral Therapy

Depending upon the client population, classical, operant, and increasingly social cognitive learning approaches are in use. The higher the intellectual functioning of the individual is a factor in the choice of the model. Given the straightforwardness of the explanatory principles, each approach lends itself to manualization. An advantage of manualization is that fidelity and dosage are easier to determine. Fidelity is the degree to which one adheres to following a set of directions and dosage refers to the amount of intervention necessary to achieve change. Fidelity and dosage, in either instance, are recommendations rather than hard and fast rules.

As the reader examines this book further, she or he cannot help but notice that social cognitive interventions dominate the sections on "What Works" and "What Might Work." There are two principle reasons for this. The first is the comparative ease of administration noted in the previous paragraph. The second is the recognition of the client as an active participant in the change process. This recognition gives cause for encouraging client motivation and self-determination. In this model, it is not the external stimulus in the environment in isolation that matters, rather, it is the individual's internal processing of that stimulus—in other words the meaning the individual gives to that stimulus is what matters.

How does cognitive development affect the application of behavioral interventions? Recall, that in this model all behavior is learned. Imagine the process to unfold gradually with the infant ordering his or her world on the basis of priority needs such as food and warmth (sensorimotor). As the child constructs an understanding of the world (Piaget uses the term *mental schema*), he or she incorporates new information that either reaffirms previous learning (assimilation) or creates new understandings (accommodation). Thus, the child, the adolescent, or the adult has only as much behavioral repertoire as has been previously learned. The less learning there is the more fundamental is the intervention. The social learning intervention increases in complexity as knowledge increases.

HUMANISTIC THEORY

While Freud's theory places heavy emphasis on biological instinctual urges and behaviorism contends that nearly all behavior is learned, the humanists celebrate the belief that humankind have been blessed with the capacity to choose, to be responsible for that choice, and to achieve their potential. Humanism encompasses several schools of thought including logotherapy, gestalt, and client-centered therapy. For this purpose, I will limit discussion to client-centered therapy and three individuals who made significant contributions to humanism: Charlotte Buhler (1935), Abraham Maslow (1970), and Carl Rogers (1961, 1965).

Theoretical Tenets

Buhler's, Maslow's, and Rogers's contributions to humanistic theory are many. To Buhler (1935), we attribute the concept of self-actualization. This is the individual's effort to grow, improve, and achieve a satisfying life potential. To Maslow (1970), we ascribe a universal individual hierarchy of needs. The foundation of this pyramid begins with physiological necessities such as food, water, and shelter and then progresses to satisfying safety needs. Only after these fundamental levels are achieved do we see emotional needs emerging. The first is the need for love and belonging followed by the need for esteem. As each need is met, the next level of potentialities is accessible such that the last self-actualization might be ultimately realized. It is Carl Rogers (1961, 1965) who operationalized these concepts into the therapeutic approach of client-centered therapy.

THE USE OF CLIENT-CENTERED THERAPY

A minister, Rogers's belief in the goodness potential of humankind led to the formulation of a principle tenet of client-centered therapy. That is, if encouraged, individuals will resolve issues blocking their development. Once those issues are removed the opportunity for optimal development is achievable. Encouragement in this sense means a nondirective approach without criticism.

Assuming physical and safety needs have been met, the barrier to love, belonging, esteem, and realizing one's potential is a lifetime of conditional positive regard which is expressed by the "I" or "me" (the real self). To reach the "ideal self" (what I want to be) requires unconditional positive regard. Unconditional positive regard is the valuing of a person, regardless of behavior, because that person is a human being. This ability to look beyond people's flaws and imperfections to their potential enables change to occur. Change in this model involves the balancing of the real self with the ideal self to achieve a place where one is comfortable with who and what one is.

How does cognitive development affect the application of humanistic interventions? For the child operating from a preoperational (2 to 7) context, client-centered therapy requires a capacity for logical operations that is not yet evident in the 5- to 7-year-old child. As concrete operations develop in the child between 7 and 11 years of age, the possibility of a client-centered approach increases slightly. It is with the 12- to 15-year-old, and the hopeful development of partial formal operations that this approach, which needs self-reflection to succeed, is potentially useful.

The interest in maximizing one's potential is a recurrent theme in Western society. Certainly, it is attractive to see ourselves as not being instinctually or mechanically driven. Indeed, this chapter begins with one of Rogers's important contributions to the field. Namely, for therapeutic change to occur the client–therapist relationship must be trusting, genuine, empathic, and honest. Whether, this is enough is still to be determined.

TRANSPERSONAL THEORY

What do a shaman, yoga, traditional, and alternative religious belief systems have to do with helping theories? They represent a few of the many non-Western methodologies for enabling client change to occur. Transpersonal approaches are growing as the immigrant population of the United States shifts from Western Europe to Latin America, Asia, and elsewhere across the globe. These immigrants have brought with them not only their cuisine, their cultural view of the family and its members, their cultural practices (e.g., alcohol is frowned upon in Islamic cultures), but also their methods for addressing physical and emotional illnesses. Some U.S. evangelical churches believe in the power to cure illness and to exorcise evil from their parishioners. St. John's Wort, a herb known to Western society for a millennium, relieves depression, and alcoholism is rare in Islamic and Judaic cultures in contrast to non-Islamic cultures within the United States (Gullotta, Adams, & Markstrom, 2000).

While there is scant evidence for transpersonal approaches, immigrant populations are reticent to embrace much of the "science" to be found within the pages of this volume. If Carl Rogers is right, and I suspect he is, that the client must perceive the helper as indeed being helpful in order for the helping act to be helpful, then our evidence-based practice matters for naught. Instead, the placebo effect that the client believes this herb, chant, or prayer will work triggers the release of brain chemicals that indeed may do well for the client.

GENES AND BEHAVIOR

Genes are comprised of long strings of deoxyribose nucleic acid (DNA), the chemical building block of all living matter. Each gene contains a set of instructions that permit the replication of one kind of protein molecule. Proteins exist in thousands of variations, each of which has a specific function. Once correctly assembled and working harmoniously, these proteins result in life.

Structural genes generally ignore the environment and perform their specific function of producing proteins or enzymes. The regulator gene is sensitive to the environment, and the activity of these genes can be widely influenced by a variety of factors including heat, exposure to heavy metals like lead, or viruses.

Flawed DNA, missing some vital information or providing misinformation, is believed by some to explain behavioral and emotional problems. The question is whether this flaw is solely genetic or genetic and environmental. Selectionists like Michael Gazzaniga (1992) believe that all behavior is hardwired; that is, genetic. As he writes:

> For the selectionist, the absolute truth is that all we do in life is discover what is already built into our brains. While the environment may shape the way in which any given organism develops, it shapes it only as far as preexisting capacities in that organism allow. Thus, the environment selects from the built-in options; it does not modify them. (p.3)

Representative of the interplay between environment and genes is Robert Plomin's work (1994). Instructionists favor a dialogue between nature and nurture. For example, some human characteristics such as height are highly inheritable. Ninety percent of one's height can be attributed to the genes we received from our parents. But other characteristics or behaviors do not have this effect size.

As Plomin (1994), states:

> [Genetic research] provides the strongest available evidence for the importance of environmental influence. That is, twin and adoption studies usually find more than half the variance in behavioral development cannot be accounted for by genetic factors. For example, if identical twins are 40% concordant for schizophrenia, as recent studies suggest, no genetic explanation can account for the 60% discordance between these pairs of genetically identical individuals. (p. 28)

To Plomin's example of schizophrenia, let me add this example. Some young people experience epilepsy to such an extent that it cannot be controlled through medication. To reduce the severity of damage to their brain, a heroic operation is performed that removes parts of the brain responsible for their seizures. Regrettably, this operation can result in damage to areas of the brain affecting speech, coordination, and movement. If Gazzaniga is correct then once these areas of the brain have been destroyed their function should be lost forever. Fortunately, that is not the case. Other parts of the brain appear to reprogram to imperfectly compensate for this loss. The younger the child the greater the compensatory effect appears to be. The brain is malleable within certain parameters that diminish with age. This is further evidence that environment matters from partially reconstructing a damaged brain to triggering the release of chemicals that determine behavior.

BRAIN CHEMICALS AND BEHAVIOR

How is chocolate similar to running or sex like a turkey sandwich? Each of these activities stimulates the release of brain chemicals that in some people bring pleasure. These and other activities like progressive relaxation, laughter, or anger, in fact any activity, will produce brain chemicals such as dopamine, norepinephrine, serotonin, and others that influence our mood and behavior for good and bad.

This discovery has revolutionized the treatment of individuals with serious and not so serious mental health issues. From this perspective a chemical imbalance explains the behavior problem. Once that imbalance has been corrected the problem behavior disappears. This imbalance may be the result of solely genetic factors, solely environmental factors, or an interplay between the two.

Psychopharmacology, and researchers' interest in understanding brain functioning, is an exciting and promising development in both the prevention and treatment of those with concerning behaviors. It is a field in its infancy with only a beginning understanding of the brain and the effects of drugs on the brain. This is especially true for children and adolescents where virtually no evidence-based testing has occurred, despite the fact that these medications are prescribed for both.

As the reader of this volume soon discovers, the human touch is essential to achieving the desired outcome of improved behavior. So the future of helping is very unlikely to reside in a pill. The human touch is capable of exciting the same neural pathways and chemical transmitters to encourage healthier behavior.

THE PREVENTION OF ILLNESS
AND THE PROMOTION OF HEALTH

The value of health promotion and illness prevention is self-evident. Health is a desired state that allows for a fuller, more joyful, and productive life, and it is significantly less expensive than illness! Using stress theory as its theoretical framework, prevention acts before the development of illness to avoid or modify the stressor. (Recently, some scholars have preferred to use the word *trauma*.) Health promotion seeks to strengthen the individual to either resist or reduce the severity of the stressor's impact. Given the attention to brain chemicals and genes, it is important to remember this observation by the former U.S. Surgeon-General C. Evert Koop (1995, p. 760), "diseases are of two types: those we develop inadvertently and those we bring upon ourselves by failure to practice preventive measures. Preventable illness makes up approximately 70% of the burden of illness and associated costs."

Albee's Incidence Formula

There are numerous useful models for identifying the risks and protective factors that contribute to and inoculate one from the development of behavioral or emotional disorders. One, of the most useful, was developed by George Albee.

Albee's (1980, 1985) formula is expressed in the following equation:

$$\text{Incidence} = \frac{\text{Organic factors \& stress \& exploitation}}{\text{Coping skills \& self - esteem \& support groups}}$$

Enlarging the size of the numerator increases the incidence of behavior problems while activities that reduce, modify, or eliminate these factors decrease the incidence of behavior problems. Correspondingly, increasing the size of the denominator decreases incidence. Let's look at each factor in this equation.

The Numerators: Organic Factors

The degree to which genetic factors determine emotional health and their contribution to such serious mental issues as schizophrenia, the major affective disorders, and alcoholism continue to be heatedly debated. It is likely that genetic factors influence some specific dysfunctions, but work in this area has been disappointingly inconclusive and even the more thorough twin studies suggestive of genetic factors in schizophrenia have not escaped severe criticism. This has led Plomin (1990, p. 187) to observe that, "Heritabilities for behavior [in the best of studies] seldom exceed 50%," providing enormous opportunities for living situations to affect the ultimate outcome.

Still, not all organic factors are hidden in the mysteries of DNA. A number of conditions exist (Tay-Sachs disease, phenylketonuria, galactosemia, tuberous sclerosis, and Huntington's chorea, for example) whose origin is genetic. "Organic" in the sense Albee uses it also refers to environmental factors that have an impact on the organism. For example, the ingestion of lead, exposure to mercury, infection by such pathogenic microorganisms as treponema pallidum and neisseria gonorrhea, or the HIV retrovirus can cause brain damage or psychosis. A strep infection can result in the development of a type of OCD behavior known as pediatric autoimmune neuropsychiatric disorder associated with a group streptococcal infection (PANDAS). Pregnant women who smoke, use drugs, or consume excessive amounts of alcohol expose the fetus to such risks as prematurity, low birth weight, and fetal alcohol syndrome. Denied an adequate diet, an expectant mother will deliver a low-birth-weight infant who if also denied an adequate diet is at considerable risk of falling at least 250 grams below the normal 1400 grams in brain weight by age 6: simply put, environmental interventions matter.

STRESS

There are several models to explain the human response to stress. All include the concept that stress can be either positive or not and that stress is any change in life, from a breath or a heartbeat to a tear or a laugh. Fundamental among these explanations is that offered by Hans Selye (1936, 1982). He suggests that regardless of the nature of the stressor it activates the general adaptation syndrome with the body responding in a predictable sequence of alarm, resistance, and, if adaptation does not occur, ultimately exhaustion.

In the state of alarm the body assesses the magnitude of the stressor and whether it is beneficial, neutral, or harmful, and responds accordingly. Because no organism can remain in a state of alarm for long either the next stage, resistance, or death occurs. With resistance, the body engages the stressor. If the stressor is perceived as distressful, it is fought. If the stressor is neutral or beneficial, it is tolerated. It is in the stage of resistance that the body displays its "adaptive" energy. No organism can remain in a constant struggle with the stressor, so it must ultimately either accept or defeat the stressor or enter into the stage of exhaustion in which illness, and even death may result.

Selye (1982, pp.10–11) believed that the adaptive energy found in the stage of resistance, "might be compared to an inherited bank account from which we can make withdrawals but to which we apparently cannot make deposits." He suggested that every activity, "causes wear and tear [leaving] some irreversible chemical scars, which accumulate to constitute the signs of aging. Thus, adaptability should be used wisely and sparingly rather than squandered."

For intervention purposes the issues are determining which factors contribute to an accelerated rate of withdrawal of adaptive energy and which slow, stem, or alter this withdrawal process. Finally, could Selye be mistaken? Can we promote resiliency and in so doing make a wellness deposit?

EXPLOITATION

Albee has written extensively on his belief that the powerlessness that results from exploitation is a principal factor in the higher incidence of psychopathology among women and minority groups (Albee, 1985, 1995; Joffe & Albee, 1981; Kessler & Albee, 1977; Albee & Gullotta, 1986). Kessler and Albee (1977) in their review of the literature on primary prevention state that:

> Everywhere we looked, every social research study we examined, suggested that major sources of human stress and distress generally involve some form of excessive power.... It is enough to suggest the hypothesis that a dramatic reduction and control of power might improve the mental health of people. (pp. 380–381)

THE DENOMINATORS: COPING SKILLS

Coping is the management of expected and unexpected stresses in life in ways that allows a person to remain healthy in body and mind without causing ill health in another person. It involves mustering the resources necessary in the stage of resistance to either defeat or tolerate some stressor. It is problem solving under conditions in which it is not clear what actions are best taken. This ability to change and adapt is enhanced in people who are open to new experiences and who are able to use their cognitive skills to place events in perspective. In short it is being able to view the world as manageable, and when a situation cannot be conquered, being able to accept it and continue living.

Self-Esteem

Positive self-esteem encompasses self-love, self-acceptance, and a belief in one's personal competence. Belonging to society, being valued by that society, and having the opportunity to make a meaningful contribution to that society is necessary for healthy self-esteem (Gullotta, Adams, & Montemayor, 1990).

Support Groups

The last factor in Albee's equation is an antidote to a "pathogenic triad; that is, 1. a fateful life event, 2. an event likely to exhaust the individual physically, [and the] 3. Loss of social support," leading to illness (Dohrenwend, Krasnoff, Askensy, & Dohrenwend, 1982, p. 339). Research is clear that people with lasting, meaningful, trusting, and supportive relationships are less likely to suffer adverse health outcomes and exhibit more positive mental health (Gullotta & Bloom, 2003a).

The Use of Preventive/Promotive Interventions

The application of Albee's equation involves the use of prevention's four tools. These tools are: education, social competency enhancement, community organization/systems intervention (CO/SI), and natural caregiving (Gullotta & Bloom, 2003b). These tools are less successful when used alone and more successful when used in groups of two, three, and ideally four.

  The first tool of education is printed, heard, or seen informational material. It is prevention's most commonly used tool and yet its weakest because education increases knowledge, occasionally changes attitude, but rarely, if ever, changes behavior. To be effective it needs to be partnered with other tools. Commonly, it is paired with efforts to enhance competency; that is, encourage positive self-esteem, promote an internal locus of control, and develop a community-focused perspective. These efforts are enhanced further with nurturing natural caregiving. I coined the term *natural caregiving* in a paper for the prevention office at NIMH many years ago in reaction to the then prevalent belief that counseling approaches and psychopharmacology were the future tools for addressing behavior problems (Gullotta, 1980). Is it "unnatural caregiving" to pop a pill or speak to a stranger about an emotional pain or hurt? Consider that the last person on the list of people to see if one is distressed is the mental health clinician or pill dispenser. Rather, it is a friend, minister, teacher, or coach to whom the child turns. Strengthening these natural occurring and potentially nurturing relationships promotes the ability to cope and adapt successfully. Lastly, CO/SI recognizes that exploitation is best addressed through political social change. It understands all institutions are to varying degrees dysfunctional and in need of intervention to alter that dysfunctional organizational pattern of behavior.

Does prevention/health promotion work? As the reader, explores other chapters in this volume it is important to pay attention to the sections on prevention and health promotion. Notice that successful or promising developmentally appropriate interventions use multiple tools in their effort to achieve the desired outcome of improved functioning. So, the answer is yes. Prevention works when done correctly.

CONCLUSION

Theory has influenced the development of counseling services for children in need of help for better than a century and childhood preventive interventions for more than 50 years. With the advent of evidence-based practice new questions concerning the tenets and developmental appropriateness of these schools of thought have spurred the increased use of some theories while others have languished. With proper funding for research, the day might soon come when a formulary of optimal practice would be available. Then again, if Carl Rogers is correct that the client–therapist relationship is the essence necessary for therapeutic change to occur then that formulary will forever remain unwritten.

In contrast, preventive interventions relying as they do on populations rather than a child or family likely will continue to refine its ability to deliver interventions to improve the health or prevent the onset illness of groups in childhood.

NOTES

1. A portion of this chapter is adapted from T. P. Gullotta et al. (2000) *The Adolescent Experience*, and T. P. Gullotta (1997) *Operationalizing Albee's Incidence Formula*.
2. Recall that Piaget (Piaget & Inhelder, 1958) proposes a developmental model for the gradual construction of understanding. Beginning at birth, the sensorimotor stage focuses on sensory experiences and their interplay with motor actions. From roughly 2 to 7, the child in the preoperational stage acquires language but cannot perform mental operations that are reversible. In concrete operations, a child from 7 to 11 years of age and many adults can arrange objects into hierarchical classifications, understand class inclusion relationships, serialize, and the principle of conservation. It is, however, in formal operations that individuals are able to think abstractly, relate to symbols, theorize, and hypothesize.

REFERENCES

Albee, G. W. (1980). A competency model must replace the defect model. In L. A. Bond & J. C. Rosen (Eds.), *Competence and coping during adulthood* (pp. 75–104). Hanover, NH: University Press of New England.

Albee, G. W. (1985). The argument for primary prevention. *Journal of Primary Prevention, 5*, 213–219.

Albee, G. W. (1995). Ann and me. *Journal of Primary Prevention, 15*, 331–350.

Albee, G. W., & Gullotta, T. P. (1986). Facts and fallacies about primary prevention. *Journal of Primary Prevention, 6*, 207–218.

Bandura, A. (1977). *Social learning theory*. Englewood Cliffs, NJ: Prentice-Hall.

Bandura, A. (1986). *Social foundations of thought and action: A social cognitive theory*. Englewood Cliffs, NJ: Prentice-Hall.

Buhler, C. (1935). The curve of life as studied in biographies. *Journal of Applied Psychology, 19*, 405–409.

Byrnes, J. P. (2001). *Minds, brains and learning*. New York: Guilford.

Dohrenwend, B. S., Krasnoff, L., Askensy, A. R., & Dohrenwend, B. P. (1982). The psychiatric epidemiology research interview life events scale. In L. Goldberger & S. Breznitz (Eds.), *Handbook of stress* (pp. 332–363). New York: Free Press.

Freud, S. (1935). An autobiographical study. In J. Strachey (Ed. & Trans.), *The standard edition of the complete psychological works of Sigmund Freud* (Vol. 26). London: Hogarth Press.

Freud, S. (1949). *A general introduction to psychoanalysis.* New York: Perma Giants. (Original work published 1920).

Gazzaniga, M. S. (1992). *Nature's mind: The biological roots of thinking, emotions, sexuality, language, and intelligence.* New York: Basic Books.

Gullotta, T. P. (1980). *Primary prevention's technology.* Paper written for National Institute of Mental Health Department of Prevention, Rockville, MD.

Gullotta, T. P. (1997). Operationalizing Albee's incidence formula. In G. W. Albee & T. P. Gullotta (Eds.), *Primary prevention works* (pp. 23–40). Thousand Oaks, CA: Sage.

Gullotta, T. P., Adams, G. R., & Markstrom, C. A. (2000). The adolescent experience (4th ed.). New York: Academic Press.

Gullotta, T. P., Adams, G. R., & Montemayor, R. (Eds.). (1990). *Developing social competency in adolescence.* Newbury Park, CA: Sage.

Gullotta, T. P., & Bloom, M. (2003a). *Encyclopedia of primary prevention and health promotion.* New York: Kluwer Academic.

Gullotta, T. P., & Bloom, M. (2003b). Primary prevention at the beginning of the 21st century. In T. P Gullotta & M. Bloom (Eds.), *Encyclopedia of primary prevention and health promotion* (pp. 116–122). New York: Kluwer Academic.

Joffe, J. M., & Albee, G. W. (1981). Powerlessness and psychopathology. In J. M. Joffe and G. W. Albee (Eds.), *Prevention through political action and social change* (pp. 53–57). Hanover, NH: University Press of New England.

Kessler, M., & Albee, G. W. (1977). An overview of the literature of primary prevention. In G. W. Albee & J. M. Joffe (Eds.), *Primary prevention of psychopathology: The issues* (pp. 351–400). Hanover, NH: University Press of New England.

Koop, C. E. (1995). A personal role in health care reform. *American Journal of Public Health, 85*(6), 759–760.

Maslow, A. H. (1970). *Motivation and personality.* New York: Harper & Brothers.

Meltzer, F. (1987). Editor's introduction: Partitive plays, pipe dreams. *Critical Inquiry, 13,* 215–221.

Pauwels, L., & Bergier, J. (1988). *The morning of the magicians.* New York: Dorset Press.

Piaget, J. (1950). *The psychology of intelligence.* London: Routledge & Kegan.

Piaget, J., & Inhelder, B. (1958). *The growth of logical thinking: From childhood to adolescence.* New York: Basic Books.

Plomin, R. (1990). *Nature and nurture.* Pacific Grove, CA: Brooks/Cole.

Plomin, R. (1994). *Genetics and experience.* Thousand Oaks, CA: Sage.

Rogers, C. R. (1961). *On becoming a person.* Boston: Houghton Mifflin.

Rogers, C. R. (1965). The therapeutic relationship: Recent theory and research. *Australian Journal of Psychology, 17,* 95–108.

Selye, H. A. (1936). A syndrome produced by diverse nocuous agents. *Nature, 138,* 32.

Selye, H. A. (1982). History and present status of the stress concept. In L. Goldberger & S. Breznitz. (Eds.), *Handbook of stress* (pp. 7–20). New York: Free Press.

Skinner, B. F. (1953). *Science and human behavior.* New York: Macmillan.

Vygotsky, L. S. (1978). *Mind in society: The development of higher psychological processes.* Cambridge, MA: Harvard University Press.

Watson, J. B. (1928). *The ways of behaviorism.* New York: Harper & Brothers.

Chapter Two

Childhood Growth and Development

David de Voursney, Danyelle Mannix, Paul J. Brounstein, and Gary M. Blau[1]

Genetic and biological factors, familial, social, and environmental influences all play important and varying roles across the life span. These factors have interactive effects on development, impacting growth at the same time as they influence each other.

As fetuses form in the womb, genetic factors play a dominant role in development. At the same time a combination of environmental variables such as maternal nutrition, prenatal care, and the presence of chemical contaminants can hinder or support prenatal development. After birth, the scope of influence on development widens. Biological influences on development meld with social and emotional influences. As children's temperaments emerge, their initial formative relationships with their families set the stage for future relationships and emotional growth. The social skills developed in these first years of life are the key to successful relationships outside the family setting.

During these first years of life, children also grow in the way that they learn and think about the world. Most salient among a newborn's skills are reflexes and the ability to cry. From this point infants rapidly gain new behavioral controls, language ability, and problem solving skills. While much of this development is biologically determined, children's physical and social environments play an important role in providing stimulation that will result in the development of important cognitive skills and abilities.

Through early childhood, children interact with a broader set of environments as they develop relationships with other toddlers and nonfamilial adults. As they grow, children move into increasingly complex social situations with larger peer groups and reduced levels of adult supervision, including childcare, preschool, and eventually kindergarten. With the foundation they receive at home and in early social settings, children must learn to interact with others, regulate their emotions, and build the skills that will enable them to succeed along the path of developmental responsibilities.

The idea that children's development is formed as they pass through interrelated systems is not a new one. Since the 1960s, Uri Bronfenbrenner has been a major proponent of a bioecological understanding of human development (Lerner, 2004). In his view the individual exists in this series of nested systems like a Russian doll. The individuals' active interaction with these systems determines the path of their development.

Bronfenbrenner categorized the world into microsystems, mesosystems, exosystems, and macrosystems (Bronfenbrenner, 1977). Microsystems are systems that directly impact individual development, such as a child's classes in school. Mesosystems are the group of microsystems that directly affect an individual's development at a given period of time. Exosystems are systems that influence an individual's development even though they do not directly interact with that person's life. For example, a school district administrator might decide to remove free coffee from teachers' lounges to cut down on costs. In this way the administrator may negatively impact the development of many school children at the exosystem level by angering their teachers, without setting foot in a classroom. The final level is the macrosystem, which is the level that incorporates the influence of the wider culture, upper levels of government, and public policy. While we will not use Bronfenbrenner's taxonomy in this chapter, it is helpful to understand the various levels at which individuals are affected by society, and to realize that levels of influence are nested within each other.

Kurt Lewin, a predecessor of Bronfenbrenner's who had great influence on his work, developed field theory, which held that individual behavior had to be understood in the context of the person's total situation, or the "field" in which he or she existed (Danziger, 2000). This early ecological viewpoint provides us with a valuable kernel of truth. By viewing individuals outside of the contexts in which they grow we ignore many of the mechanisms that will determine their success or failure. As mental health professionals, policymakers, or human beings, ignoring the wider environment or any of the contexts of human experience will lead us to an incomplete and ineffective view of the issues surrounding human development.

Today field theory has grown more complex and is better articulated. Advances in statistical analysis and the availability of data have made it easier to assess and understand many of the interactions between factors affecting development. We are far away from understanding all that goes into an individual system level and further away from understanding fully how different systems interact to influence development. However, understanding and embracing ecological models moves us closer to measuring key indicators and their ultimate impact on developmental and behavioral milestones. By looking across individual biological, family, community, and broader social systems we are learning a great deal about the precursors and determinants of observed outcomes. The adoption of an ecological model that incorporates the physical and social sciences together will allow for a more complete understanding of the various factors that shape development.

A conception of this framework based on a model proposed by Thomas Glass and William McAtee (2006), can be seen in Figure 2.1. This model recognizes that we are constrained both by our temporary physical states and by the resources and conditions currently available in our environment. However, we have the ability to interact with and affect our ecological system from the global to the molecular level, and increasingly the genomic level. Understanding the determinants of social, environmental, and biological states at these different levels is central to designing interventions, such as broader preventative programs that will improve the health of individuals, communities, and society as a whole.

Within this ecological framework, the concept of risk and protective factors plays a

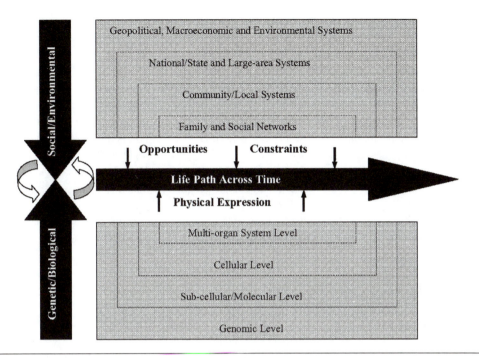

Figure 2.1 The Nested Ecological System. Adapted from Glass and McAtee (2006).

vital role in our understanding of the influence that different variables have on development. Risk factors are those factors that have been identified as having a high correlation with observed negative developmental outcomes. One commonly cited risk factor is social isolation. Children who are socially isolated are more likely to experience a range of negative outcomes including school dropout, youth delinquency, depression, and other emotional cognitive and behavior disorders (Hawkins, Catalano, & Miller, 1992). While it is difficult to identify a specific causal mechanism for most risk factors, many make sense within an ecological understanding of development. It seems plausible that children without the social skills necessary to form personal connections are more likely to experience social isolation and therefore may also be likely to experience these negative outcomes. Socially isolated children may miss out on cognitive stimulation, and therefore suffer from less robust cognitive development. Policy makers and mental health professionals hope to improve the chances of addressing the developmental potential of children across the population, by targeting programs to children at high risk and designing programs to address risk factors.

Table 2.1 lays out the risk factors explored in this chapter. Though not exhaustive, this list demonstrates the range of factors that exist cross the different domains of development. Each of these factors is complex and will likely have varied influences on the individuals it affects. Many of these factors cross the lines between the physical, cognitive, and socioemotional domains. For example, maternal depression has been shown to be a risk factor not only for cognitive development, but also for socioemotional development. Other factors also have obvious connections to one another. For instance prenatal exposure to alcohol leads to fetal alcohol syndrome, which is in turn a risk factor for cognitive development.

Table 2.1 Risk factors associated with negative developmental outcomes

Physical development	Cognitive development	Socioemotional development
Prenatal exposure	Down syndrome	Early social deficits
Viral infection—Group B strep infection (GBS)	Fetal alcohol syndrome and spectrum disorder	Maladaptive temperament
Alcohol exposure	Negative genetic inheritance	Insecure parent–child attachment
Malnutrition—Iron deficiency	Low maternal education	Low ability to regulate emotion and attention
Harmful hormonal exposure	Low socioeconomic status	Marital conflict
Premature birth	Coming from a single-parent family	Maternal depression
Low birth weight	Stressful life events	Negative genetic inheritance
Postnatal exposure	Maternal anxiety	Low birth weight
Trauma/nerve damage	Low maternal IQ	
Early or late onset of puberty	Large household size	
Deviation from normal physical maturation	Single-parent families	
Stressful environment	Poor parenting style Maternal depression Bad quality of childcare Premature birth	

Protective factors are conditions that enable individuals to overcome the negative effects of risk factors in their environment. Researchers have noticed a pattern that some people seem to experience generally positive outcomes across many areas of their lives despite facing significant challenges. This ability to overcome risky or adverse environments is called resilience. Identifying the unique qualities of resilient individuals may help to identify protective factors for use in interventions and supports that will support resilience across the population. One important protective factor is the quality of interaction children have with their parents. Children who have better relationships with their parents are more likely to be socially competent, and exhibit more appropriate interpersonal behaviors (Hawkins et al., 1992; Mrazek & Haggerty, 1994).

As with risk factors, protective factors require careful study to understand how exactly they influence development. A simple correlation between a particular factor and resilience or a positive outcome does not mean that there is a causal relationship. While it seems plausible that having a close relationship with a parent would give a child a stable emotional base to support that child's development, it is also possible that socially competent children are able to maintain better relationships with their parents, and that it is this competence that enables their positive development as much as the support they receive from their parents (see Table 2.2),

Genetic and biological influences, familial influences, and social and societal risk and protective factors do not exist in vacuums, but have interactive effects on each other. Mothers living in depressed communities are more likely to suffer from poor nutrition and the effects of environmental contaminants. These contaminants will in turn affect the prenatal biological development of their children. In this way the physi-

Table 2.2 Protective factors shown to promote resilience

Above average intelligence	Good sibling relationships
Adequate rule setting	Having a close relationship with a responsive parent
Appealing sociable easygoing disposition	Internal locus of control
Attending effective schools	Positive temperament
Authoritative parenting: Warmth, structure, and high expectations	Self-efficacy, self-confidence, high self-esteem
Bonds to prosocial adults outside of the family	Sense of coherence
Close relationships to a caring parent figure	Smaller family structure
Connections to prosocial organizations	Social competence
Connections to supportive extended family networks	Socioeconomic advantages
Faith	Supportive parents
Good intellectual functioning	Talents

Source: Adapted from Masten and Coatsworth (1998) and Mrazek and Haggerty (1994).

cal development of children is shaped by their wider social environment even before they are born. Similarly, societal and economic factors may force parents to spend less time with their children, and lead them to rely on childcare settings which add more complexity in the development of social skills. Children's social development will be influenced when they enter childcare settings, preschools, and schools by the social skills that their playmates have developed in their respective family settings. If a child's peers lack appropriate social skills then that child will have a harder time engaging in healthy play and learning.

In short, these systems are complex and interrelated. While this web of factors makes the task of understanding human development more difficult, it can also be utilized to support healthy child development. A positive change in one environment is likely to have echoes through other settings. When children develop the proper social and emotional skills it not only benefits their own development, but may also have positive effects that reverberate in that child's school and community.

In this chapter, we introduce development in the context of three major domains: physical, cognitive, and socioemotional development. In each of these categories, we lay out a set of developmental milestones, based on normative development. As with all normative descriptions, the reader should recognize that no two people follow the same path through life, and that individuals may reach developmental milestones at different ages. We then introduce and discuss briefly some of the factors that affect development in each of these three domains.

PHYSICAL DEVELOPMENT

In humans, the genetic commands are contained in 23 pairs of chromosomes. One of these pairs determines the sex of the organism. For example, if female, it is an XX pair; if male, an XY pair. Every chromosome contains thousands of genes, some dominant and some recessive. Genes only tell part of the story because they determine an individual's genotype, but not its phenotype (which corresponds to its visible structure and behavior). A phenotype is any detectable characteristic of an *organism* (i.e., structural, biochemical, physiological, and behavioral) determined by an interaction between its *genotype* and environment. Phenotypes may be determined by multiple *genes* and influenced by *environmental* factors, and this determination begins in the womb (Maturana & Varela, 1980).

Prenatal Growth

Embryological development involves a progressive process of anatomical differentiation. These changes are produced by the interaction of genetic endowment and environmental factors as noted above.

The major stages of prenatal development in humans correspond closely to those of other mammals. Shortly after conception a fertilized cell undergoes a rapid process of cell division, resulting in a cluster of proliferating cells, called the blastocyst. Within a few days, the blastocyst differentiates into a three-layered structure, with each of these layers subsequently differentiating into major parts of the body. Around the time of birth, the vast majority of cells are in their appropriate adult locations, and all of the major landmarks of the brain are in place. However, this does not mean that brain development is complete. It is important to stress that prenatal brain development does not consist simply of the unfolding of a rigid "genetic plan." Many of the architectural features of the brain are the result of complex interactions at the cellular level, and remain malleable throughout childhood into adulthood. This experience-dependent brain development is the source of the brain's lifelong plasticity.

The milestones of brain development involve: the development and migration of brain cells to where they belong in the brain; additions of nerve cells through the sprouting of new axons or by expanding the dendritic surface; the formation of connections, or synapses, between nerve cells; and the postnatal addition of other types of cells, notably glia. Once the nerve cells are formed and finish migrating, they rapidly extend axons and dendrites and begin to form connections (synapses) with each other, often over relatively long distances. During these prenatal months, the developing brain is highly vulnerable to internal risks (such as errors of neural migration) and external hazards resulting from drug or alcohol exposure, infection (e.g., strep or viruses), malnutrition, and other environmental harms. Such risk factors may lead to future cognitive impairments and the potential for impairments in emotional and behavioral functioning. Malnutrition, for example, may particularly impact the hippocampus and cerebellum (Levitsky & Strupp, 1995), and such early prenatal influences may then reduce a child's future ability to adapt to stressful situations (Keller, Cuadra, Molina, & Orsingher, 1990).

Prenatal Environment

In embryology the meaning of the term *environment* changes as development proceeds. In early embryonic development, the environment of a given cell is the other cells with which it makes contact. Somewhat later, the embryonic environment includes hormonal exposure. An example of this is the formation of external genitals, which differentiate into those of a male in the presence of androgen, and those of a female when androgen is absent. The presence of testosterone in the third trimester organizes the physiological characteristics of brain regions such as the hypothalamus in the male direction, so that release of hormones that govern sexual and reproductive functions follows the noncyclic pattern seen in the postadolescent male (Cooke, Hegstrom, Villeneuve, & Breedlove, 1998).

Alcohol exposure in utero is one on the most well-documented environmental risk factors for the unborn fetus. Fetal alcohol syndrome (FAS) was first described in 1973 (Jones & Smith, 1973). It has recently been suggested that the term *alcohol-related neurodevelopmental disorder* be used to focus specifically on brain dysfunctions in the presence of significant prenatal alcohol exposure but without physical deformities. Fetal alcohol syndrome is estimated to occur at a rate of 1 to 3 per 1,000 live births; alcohol-related neurodevelopmental disorder is estimated to be at least 10 times more prevalent. Even early in utero exposure to alcohol can have severe developmental consequences. In mice, the effects of fetal exposure to alcohol as early as the seventh day of gestation results in not only the typical dysmorphy of facial features of fetal alcohol syndrome but also brain anomalies, such as small overall size and deficiencies in cerebral hemispheres, striatum, olfactory bulbs, limbic structures, the corpus callosum, and lateral ventricles. Because FAS severity can vary with exposure levels, it is now referred to as fetal alcohol spectrum disorder (FASD); with the FAS referring only to the most severe cases.

Prenatal nutritional deficiencies can also create an unhealthy environment for fetal growth. Although sufficient nutrient intake is important throughout life, certain nutrients have a more profound effect on the developing brain than others. A fair amount of research has focused on the vulnerability of the hippocampus to early iron deficiency (Erikson, Pinero, Connor, & Beard, 1997). Preliminary evidence from a study of infants of diabetic mothers (who are at risk for lower levels of iron), has revealed impaired recognition memory despite normal iron status in infants at 6 to 8 months of age (Nelson et al., 2000). Disruptions in recognition memory, in turn, may be a subtle early effect that could contribute to learning disabilities later on. Biological risks, such as iron deficiency, often do not occur in isolation. They are typically found in greater numbers among infants who grow up in disadvantaged environments (Lozoff, Jimenez, Hagen, Mollen, & Wolf, 2000) where mothers may not enjoy adequate nutrition or prenatal care. Therefore, it can be very difficult to disentangle poor development and behavioral outcomes due to biological exposure, from those due to environmental risk factors.

Premature Birth and Low Birthweight

The percentage of low-birth-weight babies (due to premature birth) increased in each of the 50 states between 1990 and 1997 (Annie E. Casey Foundation, 2000). Improvement in neonatal intensive care units means that most infants born after 28 weeks of gestation and more than 50% of infants born at 24 to 28 weeks survive (National Research Council and Institute of Medicine 2000). However, a large number of infants who survive a premature birth have sustained damage to developing neurological structures and have significant neurological morbidity (Allen, Donohue, & Dusman, 1993). Recent research with toddlers suggests that even low-risk preterm infants (those born between 27 and 34 weeks gestational age) cannot be assumed to have caught up with their full-term counterparts in all aspects of cognitive development (de Haan, Bauer, Georgieff, & Nelson, 2000).

Premature birth has two primary effects on brain development. First, prematurity predisposes the infant to pathological events that may directly injure the brain. Second, premature birth interrupts the normal process of intrauterine brain development by denying expected intrauterine stimuli and factors important for growth. This disruption in brain development is due to the early omission of factors such as folate and vitamin B6 that are critical for normal development, and can lead to problems in learning and social interactions. Ultimately, the morbidity seen at any gestational age is the result of the combination of the number and severity of exposure to both types of influence.

In addition to a disruption in early brain development, premature babies are also almost always of low-birth weight. Babies with low birth weight are more likely than babies with normal birth weight to have a range of health and developmental problems, including lower IQ, cerebral palsy, less emotional maturity, less social competence, and attention difficulties. Many low-birth-weight premature infants are especially vulnerable because they are more likely to experience environmental risks such as living in poverty, having a single parent, or being the child of a teenage mother (National Research Council and Institute of Medicine, 2000). The challenges that the increasing number of low-birth-weight babies present to society are only beginning to be known, as is the broader impact that proper prenatal care and early intervention may have on reducing the number of premature births.

Postnatal Growth

Almost two-thirds of the mass of the cerebral cortex is added after birth. This comparatively long phase of postnatal development is a unique feature of human brain development. Therefore in humans there is an increased extent to which the later stages of brain development can be influenced by the physical and social environments of the child. Some degree of plasticity is even retained into adulthood. For example, important forebrain regions, such as the hippocampal dentate gyrus (which is involved in establishing new memories), continue to receive new nerve cells into adulthood (e.g., Eriksson et al., 1998). Growth factors are present in different quantities and locations at different points in development of the brain, and are regulated by genes involved in normal brain development. However, they can also change in their concentration in response to nerve damage, playing a role in the brain's attempts to adapt to and restore functioning following trauma.

Some aspects of the orderly progression of a child's physical development are determined by maturation, which can be thought of as genetically preprogrammed and is somewhat independent of specific environmental conditions. An example of this is walking where such steps as creeping, crawling, and walking occur in much the same sequence for all babies. The sequence of behavioral milestones is also analogous to the ordered progression that characterizes physical growth. The particular rate of this behavioral schedule may vary somewhat from one baby to the next, but the steps in that schedule are essentially the same for all (i.e., crawling precedes walking). These and other early sensory and motor achievements seems to be relatively unaffected by specific practice, but are primarily a result of growth and development on the infant's brain and musculature.

The preadolescent period marks the beginning of the biological changes associated with puberty and physical growth. Puberty is the period of life during which reproductive capability is acquired. It is characterized clinically by the acquisition of secondary sexual characteristics associated with a growth spurt, and on average takes 3 to 4 years. There is variation in the timing and onset of puberty due to variations in genetic, biological, and environmental factors. However, the normal ages are 9 to 12 for girls and 11 to 13 for boys (Tanner & Davies, 1985). Early maturation is defined as the development of sexual characteristics before the age of 8 years in girls and 9 years in boys. Delayed puberty is defined when there are no signs of puberty at the age of 13½ years in girls and 14 years in boys (Herman-Giddens, Slora, & Wasserman, 1997). Growth and development that occurs during puberty affects all body organs and systems. The pubertal "growth spurt" is the only postnatal period in which there is normally an acceleration in the increase of both stature and weight. The growth spurt in stature has an onset that is highly variable from individual to individual, and is affected by genetic, gender, and nutritional influences (Tanner & Davies, 1985).

The most dramatic changes during puberty relate to the reproductive organs. The male and female sex hormones produced at the onset and during puberty cause breast development and menstruation in girls, and enlargement of the penis and testicles in boys. There are several forms of premature sexual maturation in both girls and boys. Puberty may be delayed for several years and still occur normally. This delay could occur for a variety of reasons including poor nutrition, many forms of systemic disease, or be due to defects of the reproductive system (hypogonadism) or the body's responsiveness to sex hormones. Early or late onset of puberty, or any deviation from the natural order of maturation, may impact the child during this emotionally and socially sensitive developmental period. In late onset puberty, a low dose of testosterone or estrogen for a few months is sometimes used to bring about the first reassuring changes of normal puberty. If the delay is due to systemic disease or poor nutrition, the preferred therapeutic intervention is likely to focus mainly on those conditions (Traggiai & Stanhope, 2003).

Postnatal Environment

Although an organism's genetic instructions dictate the biological maturation of many of its early achievements, maturation cannot occur without a proper environment. Animal studies have shown that sensory deprivation can retard development; environmental enrichment can help it along. After birth, the key environmental events that affect development are those that occur in the physical and social world. It is clear that what we call "environment" is not the same at all ages. For example, how an infant would perceive a loud noise at a concert is very different from how a teenager would perceive the same sound. There is clearly agreement that what is important at one stage in life may not be important at another. However, most believe that there are critical or sensitive periods in development during which certain events would have a different impact depending on whether they occur at earlier or later times (Almli & Finger, 1987; Montessori, 1949, 1972). The hypothesis of critical periods was derived from embryological development where there is great plasticity in cell development (Debanne, Daoudal, Sourdet, & Russier, 2003; Song & Huganir, 2002).

Research on premature infants has provided substantial evidence of the importance of the caregiving environment for the baby's later progress. This theme is also supported by animal research studying the effects of stress on the developing brain. Current understanding of how psychological stimuli, such as experiences of fear and anxiety, give rise to the physiological manifestations of stress is centered on the amygdala. This area communicates with other areas of the brain involved in attention, memory, planning, and behavior control. In rats, alterations to the nest that result in better organized maternal behavior result in infant rats that develop into less fearful, less stress-reactive adults, whereas changes that disrupt maternal behavior result in more fearful and stress-reactive adult rats. Alternatively, supportive and nurturing caregiving can protect offspring from these consequences (Kimmel, Rees, & Francis, 1990; Morgane et al., 1993).

Most of the research on how experience affects the developing brain explores the detrimental consequences of harmful experiences, but enriched environments also impact postnatal development. For example, rats placed in complex environment cages have outperformed those raised alone, or placed in typically barren laboratory cages, on a variety of learning and problem-solving tasks as adults. The brains of the rats reared in the complex environments also showed more mature synaptic structure, more dendritic spines, larger neuronal dendritic fields, more synapses per neuron, more supportive glial tissue, and increased capillary branching that increases blood volume and oxygen supply to the brain. In humans, much of the later postnatal brain development can be viewed as an active process to which both the child and his or her caregivers contribute. Thus, studying the postnatal emergence of cortical specialization for different cognitive functions offers the possibility of new perspectives not only on the study of perceptual and cognitive development, but also for social development, education, and atypical developmental pathways.

Summary

From the prenatal period through childhood, youth in environments that fail to provide them with adequate nutrition and prenatal care, expose them to biological risks, and subject them to nonstimulating or neglectful care are at higher risk for a range of negative outcomes. Heredity, biology, and the environment are each sources of normal development and plasticity in a growing child. For example, the development of antisocial behavior in children may be influenced by heritable characteristics, and by family influences that arose independently of the child. A child with an inherited vulnerability to inattention and impulsivity is much less likely to develop a formal disorder in supportive, nonstressful family, school, and community environments (Lemery & Goldsmith, 1999).

COGNITIVE/LANGUAGE DEVELOPMENT

The study of cognitive development explores the way that a person thinks, learns, solves problems, and makes decisions across the life span. Here we look at cognitive development separately from physical development even though the two impact each other. Since the early twentieth century our understanding of cognitive development has grown significantly. In recent years, the field of cognitive development has become highly specialized with researchers focusing on specific aspects of cognitive development such as language, perception, intelligence, learning, and memory. In this section, we summarize some of the commonly accepted cognitive milestones, and discuss factors that influence cognitive development.

Jean Piaget, the French psychologist, is often referred to as the father of cognitive psychology. Piaget used his observations of his own and other children to infer conclusions about their internal cognitive states. Piaget identified a set of cognitive stages based on these inferences claiming that these were universal patterns to human cognitive development. According to Piaget, children evolve along a path of sequential cognitive stages with distinct patterns of cognitive activity at different ages. While Piaget recognized individual variation in moving between stages he felt that environmental factors could only play a minor role in affecting the speed at which people moved along this predetermined cognitive path. Although some of Piaget's theories have been called into question, his methods and the attention he brought to cognitive development represent a significant contribution to our understanding of human development (Lutz & Sternberg, 1999). By forming testable hypotheses about cognitive development Piaget set the stage for the insights and science that provide the basis for our current understanding of cognitive development.

Theories of cognitive development have traditionally been categorized as "nativist", or "behavioral" in nature. "Nativist" approaches claim that genetic factors determine the path of development, while "behavioral" approaches explain development in terms of environmental factors. A complete view of cognitive development considers neither approach exclusively. Interaction between the environment and genetic factors provides a more satisfactory explanation of development (Goswami, 2001). The ecological model moves past this debate by recognizing the influence of genetic and environmental factors, and then attempting to map out the varied and interactive pathways through which these factors contribute to development.

Tracking the cognitive development of individuals across the life path is not an easy task. Newborn infants are notoriously bad at returning questionnaires, and are only slightly more responsive to interviews. Even young children who have rudimentary verbal skills have a limited ability to participate in complex mental testing. While there have been advances in scanning technology such as the magnetic resonance imaging (MRI), positron emission tomography (PET), and computed tomography (CT) scans, these approaches are problematic with young children because they often require the subject to be still for an extended period of time, or they involve exposure to radiation, which researchers fear may have adverse effects on the developing brains of infants and young children.

As a result, researchers must often follow in Piaget's footsteps and make inferences based on observations and experiments designed to parse out the cognitive states of children. This approach has led to some interesting methodologies. For example, one group of researchers used a specially designed mechanical nipple to measure the sucking patterns of newborns. They found that children 12 hours after birth exhibit different sucking patterns when they are exposed to the sound of their mother's voice or the sound of a story that has been read to them consistently during the last six weeks of pregnancy (DeCasper & Fifer, 1980; DeCasper & Spence, 1986). These findings suggest that, even directly after birth, infants have the ability to form mental representations of familiar voices and patterns.

The Path of Childhood Cognitive Development

Newborn babies have a very limited set of skills. Those skills they do possess are geared toward ensuring survival by making connections to caregivers and signaling when something is not right by crying. After birth, babies have fully mature hearing and may respond to familiar sounds. While newborns have poorly developed sight they will focus on images close to them, preferring human faces to other forms. By 1 to 2 months babies begin cooing. By 3 months, infants focus on objects more intently, follow moving objects with their gazes, and recognize familiar people and objects. At this time, children are able to temporarily learn to activate an electronic spinning mobile by kicking their feet (Rovee-Collier, Sullivan, Enright, Lucas, & Fagen, 1980). Around 6 months babbling begins. By 7 months, babies have full color vision, and become more active in their interactions with the world, exploring with their hands and mouth. Experiments show that children at this age are able to find partially hidden objects. By 8 to 12 months, an infant starts to gesture, by pointing and showing, and infants begin to comprehend words (American Academy of Pediatrics, 1998; National Research Council and Institute of Medicine, 2000; Santrock, 2004).

At the end of their first year, infants will test objects in a variety of ways such as shaking, banging, tossing, and dropping. By this time, babies also find hidden objects more easily. Infants at this age begin to look at images when they hear the corresponding word. They imitate gestures, and begin to use objects for their intended use, drinking from cups and dialing on phones. Around 13 months babies say their first word, and by 18 months they begin to learn several new words every day. After their second year children can find objects hidden behind multiple covers, and have the ability to sort items by color or shape and play make believe. By 18 to 24 months, children often use two word expressions such as "give toy" or "dad walk," and their understanding of language and their vocabulary increases rapidly. Between ages 2 and 3 children can remember 2-digit strings of numbers in the short term (American Academy of Pediatrics, 1998; Dempster, 1981; National Research Council and Institute of Medicine, 2000; Santrock, 2004).

Between the ages of 3 and 7 years, children rapidly develop language and memory skills in addition to forming reasoning ability. By the age of 3, children often speak in complete sentences. They also display an increased ability to talk about objects that are not physically present. By 4 and 5, children seem to have mastered the grammatical fundamentals of their native languages. At this age, children are capable of simple deductive reasoning by syllogism if the syllogisms presented are realistic (Hawkins, Pea, Glick, & Schribner, 1984). By age 6, children often have a speaking vocabulary of 8,000 to 14,000 words, and are still learning new words at a rapid rate as high as 22 new words a day. As they grow older, children increasingly use strategies for enhancing their memory such as rehearsing. By age 7, children can remember a string of five digits in the short term (American Academy of Pediatrics, 1998; Dempster, 1981; National Research Council and Institute of Medicine, 2000; Santrock, 2004).

While the foundation for reading is laid through the preschool years, children in elementary school are expected to master reading. Reading is an important step in children's development. In addition to the negative academic consequences, children who don't become literate are at risk for a host of conduct problems and psychiatric disorders (Maughan & Carroll, 2006). Beyond that children who fail to read and thrive at school may lose a sense of self-efficacy which is very important to building resilience (Mrazek & Haggerty, 1994). Through elementary school children also begin to master the fundamentals of mathematics. Unlike earlier phases of cognitive development such as verbal language learning, reading and math ability are more dependent on formal instruction.

Factors in Cognitive and Language Development

A number of factors, including biological and genetic factors, affect cognitive development. Children who suffer from physical disorders such as Down syndrome or fetal alcohol syndrome have cognitive deficits when compared with the general population. In addition genetic inheritance plays a role in cognitive development and intelligence. Studies of the intelligence of identical and fraternal twins placed in different environments show that there is a link between genetics and intelligence, though the estimates of this effect vary (Plomin & Spinath, 2004).

A number of researchers have looked at the influence of environmental factors on cognitive development. These studies usually map the presence of risk factors in children's environment and then look at the relationship between those risk factors and cognitive development as measured by cognitive tests, or school performance. A common theme of these studies is the recognition that risk factors are associated with one another. This means that a subset of children disproportionately experience a number of risk factors. It is hardly surprising that risk factors for reduced cognitive development like low maternal education, low socioeconomic status, coming from a single parent family, and experiencing stressful life events, are correlated with one another (Burchinal, Roberts, Hooper, & Zeisel, 2000). This presents researchers with a problem. Parsing out the effects of individual risk factors is often difficult because they frequently co-occur with other related risk factors.

Risk factors are often closely associated with negative outcomes, but this does not mean there is a causal relationship. There are a number of reasons why one factor may be related to another without having a direct causal relationship. Maternal anxiety is an example of a cited risk factor for academic performance (Gutman, Sameroff, & Cole, 2003). While it seems plausible that maternal anxiety could affect the academic performance of children, most parents will attest that the academic performance of their children can also lead to a certain amount of maternal anxiety.

A number of factors are associated with lower levels of cognitive and academic ability. Children coming from backgrounds with low maternal IQ, large household size, minority ethnic status, single-parent families, stressful life events, or authoritarian child rearing environments are at higher risk of poor cognitive and language performance during childhood (Burchinal et al., 2000). Maternal depression is also associated with weaker cognitive and language development (NICHD Early Child Care Research Network, 1999). The amount of responsiveness and stimulation of childcare settings is also related to the strength of cognitive development (NICHD Early Child Care Research Network, 2000).

As we look at this research we should be careful in how we interpret the results. Certainly the data seem to show that an accumulation of risk factors is associated with lower levels of cognitive language and academic development. As noted earlier, these factors don't exist in a vacuum. While you might expect robust mental health and high IQ to have universally positive effects on academic achievement, some data show that the positive effect of these individual qualities is negated by the level of environmental risk (Gutman et al., 2003). Instead of focusing on one risk factor or another, examining the fluid nature of risk should allow professionals to identify those children in need of increased services and supports, and provide us with an avenue to understand the dynamics that lead to poor cognitive outcomes.

Summary

While we consider the factors that affect and hinder cognitive development we should remember that cognitive development is closely related to physical and socioemotional development. Environmental insults in the womb affect both physical structures and cognitive abilities. Likewise rich and supportive environments support robust cognitive and physical development. Cognitive development also plays a role in young children's ability to interact with peers as they grow and become able to engage in more complex activity (National Research Council and Institute of Medicine, 2000). While it can be helpful to consider cognitive development separate from these other domains, a deeper understanding can be reached by examining cognitive development in its ecological context.

SOCIOEMOTIONAL DEVELOPMENT

Socioemotional development has two components: Social development follows the ability to build and maintain relationships with others, including family, peers, and adults across the lifespan. Emotional development refers to an individual's ability to understand his or her own emotions and the emotional states of others, and the ability to regulate his or her own emotions along the path of development (Commonwealth Fund, 2004).

These are important skills because they are directly related to an individual's ability to thrive across a number of settings. Children who fail to develop proper socioemotional skills are likely to face serious challenges in the years ahead. Research shows that these skills enable children to form relationships (Denham & Holt, 1993). Children who don't interact appropriately with their peers early during childhood are more likely experience a range of negative outcomes such as school dropout and criminal behavior (Parker & Asher, 1987).

The Path of Childhood Socioemotional Development

The socioemotional development of children begins with a basic connection to caregivers at the time in their lives when children are only able to communicate the most basic of needs. A month after birth, a baby will recognize and focus on human faces. The baby will also show a preference for its mother's voice. By 3 months, the infant begins to develop a social smile, enjoying contact with others, and sometimes crying when that contact ends. The baby will become more expressive, and may even imitate the movements and facial expressions of others. By 7 months, the baby will enjoy social play, and respond to the emotional expression of others. By 9 months, babies seem to try to get the attention of other infants. By the end of the first year, infants become shy around strangers, and will cry when their caregivers leave. At this age, the child will also enjoy imitation and will show a preference for certain toys and people, repeating sounds or gestures to attract attention. The child will also begin to test parental reactions, by refusing food or crying after parents have left the room (American Academy of Pediatrics, 1998; National Research Council and Institute of Medicine, 2000).

By the end of 2 years, children become increasingly aware of their own identity and more enthusiastic about the presence of other children. Children at this age will also become more independent and, to the delight of parents, will also begin to act defiant. By the end of 3 years, children will be able to take turns in play, and will spontaneously show affection for playmates. By this time children will express a wide range of emotions, and will be far more independent. By their fourth birthday, children will cooperate with other children, and be able to negotiate solutions to conflicts. Continuing their movement toward independence, they will engage in more imaginative pretend play and show interest in new experiences. By the age of 5, children want to please and act like their friends, and are more likely to agree to rules (American Academy of Pediatrics, 1998).

Through the elementary school years emotional and moral development continues as children gain an understanding of complex emotions like shame and pride (Kuebli, 1994). At this age, children also begin to understand that more than one emotion can be experienced at once. Elementary age children also gain a fuller understanding of the way that life events impact emotion. In addition children at this age become better at regulating their emotions (Winter & Vallance, 1994).

Certainly, emotional development continues into the preteen and teenage years and into adulthood. As the demands of society on youth increase, so to must their ability to regulate their emotions and behavior. In addition to increasing responsibilities teens must navigate new social situations, such as romantic relationships, at a time when they receive less supervision and guidance than ever before. While family relationships are still important, peer relationships become vital for teenagers, and teens will develop intense relationships that place a high value on trust and intimacy. Those who fail to develop socially and become isolated are more likely to experience depression and delinquency (Gullotta & Adams, 2005).

Factors in Socioemotional Development

While socioemotional risk factors exist along the span of development, a secure emotional base and the development of appropriate social skills early on in life will help individuals proceed down a positive developmental path. If children begin their social lives with deficits, this may lead them to rely on maladaptive short term strategies to solve their problems. If, for example, children come to depend on adult intervention to solve their problems, they will not develop the skills necessary to negotiate conflict on their own. Furthermore children who follow this path are likely to alienate peers by inviting unwanted intervention of authority figures. Children may also become oppositional with peers and overcompensate for social shortcomings by relying on aggressive or inappropriate behavior. While in the short term this strategy may result in accomplishing a goal, getting others to agree with a desired outcome, in the long term the result will be isolation as peers avoid undesirable interaction.

While a number of successful interventions address social and emotional problems later in life, focusing on healthy development early in life may minimize outcomes that are painful for those affected and costly for society. Children who develop maladaptive temperaments early on are more likely to exhibit problem behavior later in life (e.g., attention deficit hyperactivity disorder, oppositional defiant disorder), have limited access to peer groups, and reduced educational and employment opportunities (Tschann, Kaiser, & Chesney, 1996; Wachs, 1999). Likewise children who fail to form healthy early attachments with caregivers are also at higher risk of straying from the path of successful social development. Developing the proper social and self-regulation skills early is another step in the right direction that enables children to build positive social relationships as they enter daycare and school settings. Without these pieces in place, children are less likely to succeed socially.

One commonly cited factor in youth social and emotional development is temperament, which is conceptualized as the stable set of individual personality traits that emerge early in life. Temperament seems to stabilize by the first three or four months after birth (National Research Council and Institute of Medicine, 2000). Negative temperament has been linked to undesirable social outcomes for children. Infants who react to new intense stimulation fearfully at 4 months of age are more likely to be shy and withdrawn when they are toddlers, while children that react positively to the same stimulation are more likely to be active and busy later in life (Kagan, Snidman, & Arcus, 1998). Wary 12-month-old children have been found to rely on more passive strategies to deal with stressful situations, like retreating to their caregiver or self-soothing, whereas more active children use more active strategies, like distraction when confronted with stressful situations (Mangelsdorf, Shapiro, & Marzolf, 1995). Findings like this show that temperament may interact with other environmental factors to determine the skills and strategies children use as they navigate their world and develop socially.

In a 1999 review of the literature, Theodore Wachs suggested that a number of factors determine temperament. According to Wachs, biological factors such as genetics and brain function play a role in determining temperament. In addition social factors, such as culture and the social context in which children are reared, play an important role. Other factors that play less significant roles include nutrition, gender, intelligence, parental characteristics, and the level of chaos in the child's environment. With many of these factors, such as the social environment of the child, it is difficult to measure specific effects as a child's temperament will impact that child's social environment and the environment will shape the child's temperament. Children who receive more teaching from their mothers between the ages of 12 and 18 months display a more positive temperament than those who experience less teaching. At the same time mothers of children with difficult temperaments at 12 months exhibit less teaching behavior by 18 months (Maccoby, Snow, & Jacklin, 1984).

One factor that is often seen as an aspect of a child's temperament is the ability to regulate emotions and attention. It is a child's ability to regulate his or her emotions that enables that child to succeed in a number of settings. A range of literature has linked children's ability to self-regulate to social competence (Belsky, Friedman, & Hsieh, 2001; Colder & Chassin, 1997; Colder & Stice, 1998; Eisenberg, Fabes, Guthrie, & Reiser, 2000). In order to be socially competent children must learn to control emotions to such an extent that they do not resort to aggressive or avoidant strategies that are likely to alienate their peers (Calkins & Fox, 2002). Children who do not develop these skills may be pushed away from their peers for a number of reasons. Besides using aggressive behavior, children who react with inappropriate levels of emotion may violate social norms and set themselves apart from other children, damaging their prospects for healthy social interaction.

In addition to regulation of emotions, children's ability to regulate attention also plays a role in the development of social competence. Children must learn to focus their attention in order to achieve school readiness (Belsky et al., 2001). Youth who are diagnosed with attention deficit hyperactivity disorder are at a higher risk for a range of negative outcomes including social difficulties, lower grades, poor grade retention, and school dropout (DuPaul & Weyandt, 2006).

Families play an important role in the development of children. For children to establish a healthy attachment pattern they must have a responsive parent to attach to. In addition, parents play an important role in acculturating their children and instilling a sense of right and wrong. Parents are also important because they teach their children appropriate social skills and model appropriate ways for children to manage conflicts and frustrations (National Research Council and Institute of Medicine 2000). Social skills are not only transmitted through individual interaction, but also through the family environment. Marital discord is a factor that has been connected with undesirable outcomes for children. Children who live in families with higher levels of marital discord are more likely to exhibit inappropriate social behaviors (Cummings, Mark, & Davies, 2002).

Parents play important roles in the emotional development of their children. Children of parents with affective disorders are more likely to have an affective disorder of their own (Zahn-Waxler, Klimes-Dougan, & Slattery, 2000). Children of women facing depression also have higher rates of depression and increased rates of psychopathology (Beck, 1999; Hammen et al., 1987; Nomura, Wickramaratne, Warner, Mufson, & Weissman, 2002). This relationship is probably due to a combination of genetic inheritance and the environmental impact of having a depressed mother. Siblings also play a role in development, not only do they provide children with social practice, they may also provide children with opportunities to build empathy, and teach each other social behavior (Dunn & Kendrick, 1982).

An important concept in childhood development is attachment. Children who are securely attached to a caregiver look to that caregiver for care and attention, and will retreat to that caregiver between periods of exploration for reassurance and stability. Attachment is generally measured using a process pioneered by Mary Ainsworth called the "strange situation," in which children are temporarily separated from their parents and then monitored to gauge their reactions. Based on these reactions children are classified according to various attachment patterns based on previously established norms such as secure, insecure, avoidant, resistant, and disorganized.

Children classified as securely attached are more likely to be socially competent as toddlers (Pastor, 1981) and preschoolers (Erickson, Sroufe, & Egeland, 1985). Securely attached children are also more likely to be popular as preschoolers (LaFreniere & Sroufe,

1985) and develop less discordant and supportive relationships with other preschoolers (Park & Waters, 1989). Infants that don't display secure attachment as infants are
more likely to be hostile with other children, or are whiny and easily frustrated during
preschool play (Erickson et al., 1985; LaFreniere & Sroufe, 1985). Attachment may determine the quality of early social interactions, as affected children tend to have social
skill deficits and maladaptive behavior patterns.

Like other skills, social skills must be learned. Much of this learning takes place as
children interact with their peers. Toddlers who frequently participate in supervised
play with groups of children engage in more complex interactions with their peers
(Holmberg, 1980; Howes, Rubin, Ross, & French, 1988; Mueller & Brenner, 1977). Evidence also suggests that children who have spent more time in childcare settings at a
young age interact better with their peers, so long as this time in childcare settings does
not interrupt early attachment with parents (National Research Council and Institute
of Medicine, 2000).

Summary

Within the domain of socioemotional development none of the factors mentioned above
exerts a purely independent influence. While temperament, attachment, and family
influences are all listed as separate factors, temperament certainly plays a role in the
ability of a child to regulate his or her emotions, and other family dynamics influence
and react to temperament. Likewise, socioemotional development cannot be fully understood without considering the influence of genetic, biological, and cognitive realities.
In some ways the separation of these factors, like the separation between the physical
cognitive and socioemotional, is artificial. However, it is important to understand how
these factors influence both healthy and maladaptive functioning.

CONCLUSION

In this chapter we reviewed normative child development across three domains, and
explored the concept of risk and protective factors and their effect on development.
By moving beyond individual variables towards an understanding of the interaction
of multiple factors, the scientific community continues to refine its understanding of
development.

The following chapters go into greater depths, explaining the dynamics that sur-
round issues such as pervasive developmental disorders and ADHD. Within each of
these subjects a range of factors play important roles. The interactions of these factors
determine to a large extent a child's ability to succeed in life. As a result, a holistic understanding of these factors is our best route to addressing these issues and improving
the lives of children.

NOTE

1. The views expressed in this paper are those of the authors, and do not necessarily represent the views
    of the institutions and organizations with which they are affiliated.

REFERENCES

Allen, M. C., Donohue, P. K., & Dusman, A K. (1993). The limit of viability: Neonatal outcome of infants born at 22 to 25 weeks of gestation. *New England Journal of Medicine, 329*, 1597–1601.

Almli, C., & Finger, S. (1987). Neural insult and critical period concepts. In Marc H. Bornstein (Ed.), *Sensitive periods in development: Interdisciplinary perspectives* (pp. 123–143). Hillsdale, NJ: Lawrence Erlbaum.

American Academy of Pediatrics. (1998). *Caring for your baby and young child: Birth to Age 5.* (Steven P. Shevlov, Ed.). New York: Bantam Books.

Annie E. Casey Foundation. (2000). *Kids count data book: State profiles of child well-being.* Baltimore: Author.

Beck, C. T. (1999). Maternal depression and child behaviour problems: A meta-analysis. *Journal of Advanced Nursing, 29*(3), 623–629.

Belsky, J., Friedman, S. L., & Hsieh, K. (2001). Testing a core emotion-regulation prediction: Does early attentional persistence moderate the effect of infant negative emotionality on later development? *Child Development, 72*(1), 123–133.

Bronfenbrenner, U. (1977). Lewinian space and ecological substance. *Journal of Social Issues, 33*(4), 199–212.

Burchinal, M. R., Roberts, J. E., Hooper, S., & Zeisel, S. A. (2000). Cumulative risk and early cognitive development: A comparison of statistical risk models. *Developmental Psychology, 36* (6), 793–807.

Calkins, S. D., & Fox, N. A. (2002). Self-regulatory processes in early personality development: A multilevel approach to the study of childhood social withdrawal and aggression. *Development and Psychopathology, 14*, 477–498.

Colder, C., & Chassin, L. (1997). Affectivity and impulsivity: Temperament risk for adolescent alcohol involvement. *Psychology of Addictive Behaviors, 11*(2), 83–97.

Colder, C., & Stice, E. (1998). A longitudinal study of the interactive effects of impulsivity and anger on adolescent problem behavior. *Journal of Youth and Adolescence, 27*, 255–274.

Commonwealth Fund. (2004). Early childhood development in a social context. *Child Trends and Center of Health Research.* Vol 17.

Cooke, B, Hegstrom, C. D., Villeneuve, L. S., & Breedlove, S. M. (1998). Sexual differentiation of the vertebrate brain: Principles and mechanisms. *Frontiers in Neuroendocrinology, 91*, 323–362.

Cummings, E., Mark, D., & Davies, P. T. (2002). Effects of marital conflict on children: Recent advances and emerging themes in process-oriented research. *Journal of Child Psychology and Psychiatry, 43*(1), 31–63.

Danziger, K. (2000). Making social psychology experimental: A conceptual history, 1920–1970. *Journal of the History of the Behavioral Sciences, 36*(4), 329–347.

Debanne, D., Daoudal, G., Sourdet, V., & Russier, M. (2003). Brain plasticity and ion channels. *Journal of Physiology-Paris, 97*(4–6), 403–414.

DeCasper, A.J., & Fifer, W. P. (1980). Of human bonding: Infants prefer their mothers' voices. *Science, New Series, 208*(4448). 1174–1176.

DeCasper, A. J., & Spence, M. J. (1986). Prenatal maternal speech influences newborns' perception of speech sounds, *Infant Behavior and Development, 9*(2), 133–150.

de Haan, M., Bauer, P. J., Georgieff, M. K., & Nelson, C. A. (2000). Explicit memory in low-risk infants aged 19 months born between 27 and 42 weeks of gestation. *Developmental Medicine & Child Neurology, 42*, 304–312.

Dempster, F. N. (1981). Memory span: Sources of individual and developmental differences. *Psychological Bulletin, 89*(1), 63–100.

Denham, S. A., & Holt, R. W. (1993). Preschoolers' likeability as cause or consequence of their social behavior. *Developmental Psychology, 29*, 271–275.

Duncan, G. J., & Brooks-Gunn, J. (Eds.). (1997). *Consequences of growing up poor.* New York: Russell Sage Foundation.

Dunn J., & Kendrick, C. (1982). *Siblings: Love, envy, and understanding.* Cambridge, MA: Harvard University Press.

DuPaul, G. J., & Weyandt, L. L. (2006). School-based intervention for children with attention deficit hyperactivity disorder: Effects on academic, social, and behavioral functioning. *International Journal of Disability, Development and Education, 53*(2), 161–176.

Eisenberg, N., Fabes, R. A., Guthrie, I. K., & Reiser, M. (2000). Dispositional emotionality and regulation: Their role in predicting quality of social functioning. *Journal of Personality and Social Psychology, 78*,136–157.

Erikson, K. M., Pinero, D. J., Connor, J. R., & Beard, J. L. (1997). Regional brain iron, ferritin and transferrin concentrations during iron deficiency and iron repletion in developing rats. *Journal of Nutrition, 127,* 2030–2038.

Erickson, M. F., Sroufe, L. A., & Egeland, B. (1985). The relationship between quality of attachment and behavior problems in preschool in a high-risk sample. *Monographs of the Society for Research in Child Development, 50*(1/2), 147–166.

Eriksson, P., Perfileva, E., Bjork-Eriksson, T., Alborn, A., Nordborg, C., Peterson, D., & Gage, F. (1998). Neurogenesis in the adult human hippocampus. *National Medicine, 4,* 1313–1317.

Glass, T. A., & McAtee, M. J. (2006). Behavioral social science at the crossroads in public health: Extending horizons, envisioning the future. *Social Science and Medicine, 62,* 1650–1671.

Goswami, U. (2001). Cognitive development: No stages please—we're British. *British Journal of Psychology, 92*(1), 257–277.

Gullotta, T. P., & Adams, G. (Eds.). (2005). *Handbook of adolescent behavioral problems: Evidence-based approaches to prevention and treatment.* New York: Springer.

Gutman, L. M., Sameroff, A. J., & Cole, R. (2003). Academic growth curve trajectories from 1st Grade to 12th Grade: Effects of multiple social risk factors and preschool child factors. *Developmental Psychology, 39*(4), 777–790.

Hammen, C., Gordon, D., Burge, D., Adrian, C., Jaenicke, C., & Hiroto, D. (1987). Maternal affective disorders, illness, and stress: Risk for children's psychopathology *American Journal of Psychiatry, 144,* 736–741.

Hawkins, J. D., Catalano, R. F., & Miller, J. Y. (1992). Risk and protective factors for alcohol and other drug problems in adolescence and early adulthood: Implications for substance abuse prevention. *Psychological Bulletin, 112*(1), 64–105.

Hawkins, J., Pea, R. D., Glick, J., & Scribner, S. (1984). "Merds that laugh don't like mushrooms": Evidence for deductive reasoning by preschoolers. *Developmental Psychology, 20*(4), 584–594.

Herman-Giddens, M. E., Slora, E. J., & Wasserman, R. C. (1997). Secondary sexual characteristics and menses in young girls seen in office practice: A study from the pediatric research in office settings network. *Pediatrics, 99,* 501–512.

Holmberg, M. C. (1980). The development of social interchange patterns from 12 to 42 months *Child Development, 51*(2), 448–456.

Howes, C., Rubin, K. H., Ross, H. S., & French, D. C. (1988). Peer interaction of young children. *Monographs of the Society for Research in Child Development, 53*(1), i–92.

Jones, K. L., & Smith, D. W. (1973). Recognition of fetal alcohol syndrome in early infancy. *Lancet,* (2), 999–1001.

Kagan, J., Snidman, N., & Arcus, D. (1998). Childhood derivatives of high and low reactivity in infancy. *Child Development, 69,* 1483–1493.

Keller, E. A., Cuadra, G. R., Molina, V. A., & Orsingher, O. A. (1990). Perinatal under-nutrition affects brain modulatory capacity of beta-adrenergic receptors in adult rats. *Journal of Nutrition, 120,* 305–308.

Kimmel, C. A., Rees, D. C., & Francis, E. Z. (1990). Qualitative and quantitative comparability of human and animal developmental neurotoxicity. *Neurotoxicology and Teratology, 12,* 173–292.

Kuebli, J. (1994). Young children's understanding of everyday emotions. *Young Children, 49,* 36–47.

LaFreniere, P. J., & Sroufe L. A. (1985). Profiles of peer competence in the preschool: Interrelations between measures, influence of social ecology, and relation to attachment history. *Developmental Psychology, 21,* 46–69.

Lemery, K. S., & Goldsmith, H. H. (1999). Genetically informative designs for the study of behavioral development *International Journal of Behavioral Development, 23,* 293–317.

Lerner, R. M. (2004). Foreword: Urie Bronfenbrenner: Career contributions of the consummate developmental scientist. In U. Bronfenbrenner, *Making human beings human* (pp. ix–xxvi). Thousand Oaks, CA: Sage.

Levitsky, D. A., & Strupp B. J. (1995). Malnutrition and the brain: Changing concepts, changing concerns. *Journal of Nutrition, 125*(8). 2212S–2220S.

Lozoff, B., Jimenez, E., Hagen, J., Mollen, E., & Wolf, A. W. (2000). Poorer behavioral and developmental outcome more than 10 years after treatment for iron deficiency in infancy. *Pediatrics, 105,* E51.

Lutz, D. J., & Sternberg, R.J. (1999). Cognitive development. In M. H. Bornstein & M. E. Lamb (Eds.), *Developmental psychology and advanced textbook* (4th ed., pp. 275–312). Mahwah, NJ: Lawrence Erlbaum.

Maccoby, E. E., Snow, M. E., & Jacklin, C. N. (1984). Children's dispositions and mother–child interaction at 12 and 18 months: A short-term longitudinal study. *Developmental Psychology, 20*(3), 459–472.

Mangelsdorf, S., Shapiro, J., & Marzolf, D. (1995). Developmental and temperamental differences in emotion regulation in infancy. *Child Development, 66,* 1817–1828.

Masten, A. & Coatsworth, D. (1998). The development of competence in favorable and unfavorable environments: Lessons from research on successful children. *American Psychologist, 53,* 205–220.

Maturana, H. R., & Varela, F. G. (1980b). Autopoiesis: The organization of the living. In H. R. Maturana & F. G. Varela (Eds.), *Autopoiesis and cognition.* (Original work published 1972; in Spanish)

Maughan, B., & Carroll, J. (2006). Literacy and mental disorders. *Current Opinion in Psychiatry, 19*(4), 350–354.

Montessori, M. (1972). *The secret of childhood.* New York: Ballantine Books.

Morgane, P. J., Austin-LaFrance, R. J., Bronzino, J., Tonkiss, J., Diaz-Cintra, S., Cintra, L., Kemper, & T., Galler, J. R. (1993). Prenatal malnutrition and development of the brain. *Neuroscience and Biobehavioral Reviews, 17,* 91–128.

Mueller, E., & Brenner, J. (1977). The origins of social skills and interaction among playgroup toddlers. *Child Development, 48*(3), 854–861.

Mrazek, P. J., & Haggerty, R. J. (Eds.).(1994). *Reducing risks for mental disorders: Frontiers for preventive intervention research.* Washington, D.C.: National Academy Press.

National Research Council and Institute of Medicine. (2000). From neurons to neighborhoods: The science of early childhood development. Committee on Integrating the Science of early Childhood Development. In J. P. Shonkoff & D. A. Phillips (Eds.), *Board on Children, Youth Families, Commission on Behavioral and Social Sciences and Education.* Washington, D.C.: National Academy Press.

Nelson, C. A., Wewerka, S., Thomas, K. M., Tribby-Walbridge, S., deRegnier, R., & Georgieff, M. (2000). Neurocognitive sequelae of infants of diabetic mothers. *Behavioral Neuroscience, 114,* 950–956.

NICHD Early Child Care Research Network. (1999). Chronicity of maternal depressive symptoms, maternal sensitivity, and child functioning at 36 months. *Developmental Psychology, 35*(5), 1297–1310.

NICHD Early Child Care Research Network. (2000). The relation of child care to cognitive and language development. *Child Development, 71,* 960–970.

Nomura, Y., Wickramaratne, P. J., Warner, V., Mufson, L. & Weissman, M. (2002). Family discord, parental depression and psychopathology in offspring: 10-year follow-up. *Journal of the American Academy of Child and Adolescent Psychiatry, 41*(4), 402–409.

Park, K. A., & Waters, E. (1989). Security of attachment and preschool friendships. *Child Development, 60,* 1076–1081.

Parker, J. G., & Asher, S. R. (1987). Peer relations and later personality assessment: Are low accepted children at risk? *Psychological Bulletin, 102,* 357–389.

Pastor, D. L. (1981). The quality of mother–infant attachment and its relationship to toddlers' initial sociability with peers. *Developmental Psychology, 17*(3), 326–335.

Plomin, R., & Spinath, F. (2004). Intelligence: Genetics, genes and genomics *Journal of Personality and Social Psychology, 86*(1), 112–129.

Rovee-Collier, C. K., Sullivan, M. W., Enright, M., Lucas, D., & Fagen J. W. (1980). Reactivation of infant memory. *Science, 208*(4448), 1159–1161.

Santrock, J. W. (2004). *Life span development* (10th ed.). Boston: McGraw-Hill.

Song, I., & Huganir, R. L. (2002). Regulation of AMPA receptors during synaptic plasticity. *Trends in Neurosciences, 25*(11), 578–589.

Tanner, J. M., & Davies, P. S. (1985). Clinical longitudinal standards for height and weight velocity for North American children. *Journal of Pediatrics, 107,* 317–329.

Traggiai, C., & Stanhope, R. (2003). Disorders of pubertal development. *Best Practice & Research Clinical Obstetrics & Gynaecology, 17*(1), 41–56.

Tschann, J., Kaiser, P., & Chesney, M. A. (1996). Resilience and vulnerability among preschool children: Family functioning temperament, and behavior problems. *Journal of the American Academy of Child and Adolescent Psychiatry, 35,*184–192.

Wachs, T. (1999). The what, why, and how of temperament: A piece of the action. In Laurence Balter (Ed.), *Child psychology: A handbook of contemporary issues* (pp. 23–44). Philadelphia: Taylor and Francis.

Winter, M. G., & Vallance, D. D. (1994). A developmental sequence in the comprehension of emotions: Intensity, multiple emotions, and valence. *Developmental Psychology, 30,* 509–514.

Zahn-Waxler, C., Klimes-Dougan, B., & Slattery, M. J. (2000). Internalizing problems of childhood and adolescence: Prospects, pitfalls, and progress in understanding the development of anxiety and depression. *Development and Psychopathology, 12,* 443–466.

Part II

FAMILY AND COMMUNITY INFLUENCES

Chapter Three

Family Influences on Child Development

Kevin R. Bush and Gary W. Peterson

The topic, family influences on child development, elicits popular images of parents shaping their children through setting limits based on parental knowledge/values. Although the family certainly serves as an important social context for shaping and guiding child development, the relationship is not simply unidirectional. Children are not passive beings simply shaped by their social environments without exerting any influence themselves. As children interact with parents, siblings, and other significant family members, meaning is cocreated, significant symbols are exchanged, and roles are reciprocally determined and constantly negotiated. Besides common patterns, developmentally the influence of children on their parents and family interactions in general has significant variation across individuals as well as across time. That is, while infants and preschool children certainly influence parents' behavior and family interactions, the bidirectionality is somewhat less obvious compared to middle childhood and adolescence. More specifically, older children and adolescents typically have more readily apparent influence on their social environments, such as when they interact with siblings (usually their first peer relationships) as well as parents as they negotiate autonomy as children develop.

This chapter provides an overview of the prominent aspects of diverse family forms that influence the development of prosocial as well as problematic outcomes among children during middle childhood (aged 5–13). Theoretical and empirical work regarding the influence of family structural variations (i.e., family SES, poverty, maternal employment, divorce, remarriage, and the presence of siblings), parental styles, dimensions of parental behavior, parent–child conflict, and interparental or marital conflict on child development are reviewed.

SOCIALIZATION IN FAMILIES

Following a general social science perspective, families influence children through the socialization process. That is, the social dynamics created within families provide methods of transferring important values, constructing shared meanings, and participating in relationships where important social skills are modeled and learned.

Families provide a continual evolving social context for socialization. Traditional conceptions of socialization within family relationships has followed a unidirectional or social mold approach, in which parents are viewed as influencing and shaping children (who are seen as passive recipients of parental influence) to internalize and become responsive to societal expectations (Inkeles, 1968; Parsons & Bales, 1955; Peterson & Hann, 1999). A more accurate view of socialization recognizes that children are also active participants in this process. Recent theoretical and empirical work recognizes the complex nature of socialization and asserts that the process is at least bidirectional, if not more complex (Kuczynski, 2003; Peterson & Hann, 1999). Children both influence and are influenced by many social agents in their ecological social context (e.g., parents, siblings, peers, teachers, extended family). However, most of this theorizing and empirical work has been conducted within the context of U.S. families or other populations within other "Western" or individualistic countries. Therefore, although we cannot be sure how the notion of bidirectionality applies to parent–child relationships within non-Western or collectivistic countries, or even within all cultural groups in the United States, it is probably safe to assume that more complex models of socialization operate within these contexts as well.

Socialization is a complex multidirectional process involving the family as the focal influence, but also involves many other ecological systems within which children and families are embedded (Bronfenbrenner 1979, 1994) such as neighborhoods, schools, and larger social systems (e.g., culture, religion). While an ecological view is imperative, it is also important to emphasize that the family still has some influence and regulation on many of the socialization sources outside the family, such as through the impact on selection of neighborhoods, schools, and peers (Rutter, 2002). It is difficult to isolate specific socialization influences (e.g., family, peer, biological) as sole effects that drive development; rather, it is recognized that a combination of socialization, genetic, and maturational factors form the overall structure of child development (Lerner, 2002).

Parent–child socialization is a dialectical process in which continuity, creativity, and change are complementary components of a larger whole (Kuczynski, 2003; Peterson & Hann, 1999). Consequently, the parent–child relationship is a process of continuity and change in which both the parent and the child increasingly share meanings, influence one another, and are constantly changing in respect to each other. Moreover, there are multiple levels of analyses that must be considered when conceptualizing family socialization, including the individual (e.g., parent or child), dyad (e.g., parent–child, parent–parent, or sibling–sibling), and family system. For most children the family remains the primary context for social influence and security, fostering both positive and negative outcomes.

CHILDREN'S SOCIAL COMPETENCE AND PROBLEM BEHAVIOR: OUTCOMES OF SOCIALIZATION

Although more complex conceptions of socialization exist, the most dominant tradition prevalent in parent–child research is the "social mold" or "parental influence" perspective. In this approach, the extent to which parental styles, behaviors, and characteristics contribute to various social and psychological child outcomes are explored. From this social mold perspective, parents are viewed as conveyors of social reality who shape children into functional or deviant participants in society (Maccoby & Martin, 1983; Peterson & Bush, 2003; Peterson & Hann, 1999). That is, parents serve as social agents who teach and guide the young as they learn appropriate behavior, conduct, and expectations through parental support and control attempts, as well as modeling.

Before examining the methods of parental influence, it is important to consider the goals or values that parents seek either to foster or inhibit in their offspring. Specifically, most parents intend to foster social competence in their young by expecting them to follow and adopt the behaviors and values considered to be normative in their social ecology and thus serve to increase adaptation in relationships with others (Bloom, 1990; Gillespie, 2003; Peterson & Bush, 2003; Peterson & Leigh, 1990). Social competence is defined as a set of attributes or psychological resources that help children adapt and cope with the various social situations they are likely to encounter (Baumrind, 1991; Peterson & Bush, 2003). Recent conceptualizations of social competence identify several subdimensions, including: (1) psychological or cognitive resources (e.g., self-regulation, problem solving skills); (2) an achievement orientation; (3) social skills and prosocial behavior with peers and other interpersonal relationships; and (4) a balance between age appropriate independence and connectedness in references to parents.

The inverse of social competence is risk or problem behavior, such as externalizing or internalizing attributes. Externalizing behaviors refer to "acting out" behaviors such as aggression, violence, conduct or behavioral problems at home, school, or other social contexts (Meyer, 2003). Internalizing attributes refer to difficulties that are manifest psychologically or internally resulting in problems such as anxious or depressive thoughts/disorders. Self-regulation, social skills, and other dimensions of children's social competence, along with aspects of family socialization processes that foster such outcomes (e.g., parental support) are sources of social-psychological resilience that assist children in successfully coping with situations that can challenge adaptation and lead to risk behavior (Gillespie, 2003; Hauser, 1999). In contrast, the lack of social competence, or the prevalence of internalizing or externalizing attributes increases the chances of children experiencing other problems during development such as school failure, parent–child conflict, and poor peer relationships.

THE FAMILY SYSTEM AND CHILD DEVELOPMENT

A useful means of conceptualizing the role of children within families is that most are members of family systems. Despite the structural variation of families, following a family systems perspective allows for continuity without placing constraints for particular structural qualities of families. All families are viewed as operating as systems and thus following the properties of a system regardless of composition, SES, ethnicity, or other possible structural variations. Highlighting the systemic qualities of children's lives entails that family systems are complex entities whose members are tied together as part of a larger relationship whole (Broderick, 1993). Following this approach, all elements of the family system are interrelated through dynamic, mutual, and circular processes that link together the constituent individuals and relationships within families.

There are several assumptions of systems theory. One major assumption of systems theory is that of isophorphism, which refers to an equivalence of form. That is, aspects of the larger system (e.g., family) are reflected in interactions among the parts of the system; for example, between subsystems or between members within a subsystem (Whitchurch & Constantine, 1993). Through observing interactions between family members and subsystems, patterns can be identified which reflect or represent the rules and boundaries of the family system. Another important major assumption of systems theory is that of nonsummativity, or holism; this refers to viewing the whole system as more than simply the sum of its components or parts (Broderick, 1993). Following this view, a family is more than simply a parent plus a child; rather, the interaction between each of the components and the resulting meaning(s) and structure(s) that emerge out of this interaction must be considered. That is, the focus is on the emergent qualities of the system as a whole, versus the qualities of any particular individual or subsystem within the larger family system (Broderick, 1993). Another important assumption is that human systems are self-reflexive, and as a result are able to examine their systems and establish their own goals (Whitchurch & Constantine, 1993). The goal oriented focus of family systems theory underscores the multiple and reciprocal directionality of family influences, and the potential for conflict with divergent views between individual members and family subsystems.

Each family develops unique patterns of communication that define their relationships, goals, roles, and strategies for accomplishing goals, all of which provide structure for daily life. That is, patterns of interaction through carrying out of roles and the accomplishment of goal oriented tasks create rules through repeated patterns of interaction. A systemic view of family relationships involving children often focuses on the degree of openness in information exchange that occurs between members (e.g., parents and children). Such a focus on communication is important, as open communication between parents and children facilitates close and supportive relationships, which in turn, are related to negotiation of conflict, autonomy, and positive growth in family relationships.

FAMILY STRUCTURAL VARIATION

Structural variations in family life refer to differences across families in the composition (number of people), types of relationships (e.g., biological relationship between child and parent), and resources available (e.g., income and education level). An ongoing debate exists regarding the impact of structural family variations versus processes within families on child outcomes, parent–child relationships, parenting, and marriage. Although the debate continues to rage on with no end in sight, growing evidence suggests that only modest differences in child outcomes can be directly traced to particular structural variation within families. Rather, the impact of structural variations is typically indirect through influences on specific family processes and social psychological variables (e.g., patterns of communication and parental behavior) on childhood development (Demo & Cox, 2000; Teachman, 2000; Wilson, Peterson, & Wilson, 1993). The structural characteristics of family life impact the quality of interaction or processes that take place during socialization. Thus, the key point is to examine the impact of the structural characteristics of families on the functioning or processes occurring within family systems (Rutter, 2002).

FAMILY SES

Socioeconomic status (SES) refers to a family's particular social and economic standing in society based on indices of parental education, income, and resources. SES has been found to be related to parenting beliefs, values, and behaviors as well as to child outcomes, although most of the effect of SES on childhood outcomes is through its impact on parents and family processes. For example, lower SES is associated with parental stress, depression, poor neighborhoods, and poor living conditions. In turn these effects of SES on the parents and the family environment are associated with more punitive and inconsistent parenting behavior as well as exposure to acute and chronic stressors which are associated with poor child outcomes such as lower academic achievement and internalizing or externalizing attributes (e.g., McLoyd, 1998).

Parents of different socioeconomic status often have distinctive conditions of life as well as values and priorities that reflect these conditions. These values and priorities, in turn, influence parental demands on their offspring for forms of social competence that are perceived as adaptive in their particular context. Most of the studies in this area follow Kohn's (1963, 1977; Pearlin & Kohn, 1966) pioneering work on the relationships between parental education, occupation, values, and parenting beliefs and practices. For example, parents in blue-collar occupations have been found to emphasize obedience and conformity in their parenting values, which are related to success within blue-collar occupations. In contrast, parents of white-collar occupations (i.e., higher educational levels) are more likely to emphasize and value independence, creativity, and initiative seeking with their children (which in turn, are related to values facilitating success in the parents' occupations).

The social context in which parenting and socialization occur, such as the quality of neighborhood, nutrition, home learning environment, access to schools and education, as well as underlying parental beliefs and socialization goals are all related to the social and economic resources of parents (Leyendecker, Harwood, Comparini, & Yalcinkaya, 2005). Moreover, the specific components of SES are likely to have differential effects on family dynamics and childhood development. For example, human capital (nonmaterial resources such as parental education) has been found to be the most robust aspect of SES in regard to predicting parenting behavior among young children (e.g., Richman, Miller, & Levine, 1992). However, with development, social capital (e.g., social connections and networks with supportive others outside the family), and financial capital (e.g., ability to provide for basic necessities such as food and clothes) are likely to become more salient influences on parenting and socialization of children (e.g., as fathers and other caregivers exert more influence on the young) (Leyendecker et al., 2005). The relationship between SES and parenting and childhood outcomes does not, however, appear to be a simple linear relationship. That is, the effects of changes in SES are more pervasive at the lower ends of the continuum, such as for families living at or below the poverty line, whereas the same amount of change in education or income at the other end of the continuum (upper-class families) is not as likely to have a similar effect (Duncan & Magnuson, 2003; McLoyd, 1998). Moreover, social capital is especially helpful for families with low financial capital and low human capital, as supportive social networks can serve to buffer the effects of poverty on the parenting environment and child outcomes (e.g., Field, Widmayer, Adler, & De Cubas, 1990).

The effects of poverty on child development occur as a result of few resources being available and thus less enriched learning environments in the home (e.g., fewer books and educational toys) as well as stressors associated with living in poor neighborhoods. The detrimental effects of poverty appear to be greater among families with young children compared to those with older offspring (Leyendecker et al., 2005). That is, exposure to poverty in middle childhood appears to have less negative consequences than exposure to poverty in early childhood (e.g., Duncan & Brooks-Gunn, 1997; Hao & Matsueda, 2006). This is related to the greater impact of poor nutrition on school achievement in early childhood, and the greater impact of neighborhood disadvantage on older children and parents.

MATERNAL EMPLOYMENT

The increasing prevalence of women in the work force and the coincidental rise in dual-earner families over recent decades is one of the most influential changes that U.S. families and society have faced (Baum, 2004; Riggio, 2006). Approximately 75% of mothers with minor children work outside of the home (U.S. Bureau of Labor Statistics, 2001). The research evidence regarding the effects of maternal employment on parents, parenting, and child outcomes is inconclusive at best. For example, studies have found negative effects (e.g., Han, Waldfogel, & Brooks-Gunn, 2001); positive effects (e.g., Alessandri, 1992; Barnett, Marshall, Raudenbush, & Brennan, 1993; Baruch & Barnett, 1986; Makri-Botsari & Makri, 2003; Vandell & Ramanan, 1992); and the lack of long term negative effects (Gottfried, Gottfried, Bathurst, & Killian, 1999; Harvey, 1999; Hoffman, 2000). More specifically, on the positive side, maternal employment directly facilitates positive child outcomes by providing positive role models, especially for girls. Additionally, maternal employment increases family income, which in turn increases positive child outcomes such as cognitive development and academic performance (e.g., Baum, 2004), presumably through increased access to educational and related resources (e.g., higher quality neighborhoods and schools). On the other hand, early maternal employment has been negatively related to children's behavioral adjustment (Belsky & Eggebeen, 1991), cognitive development (Baydar & Brooks-Gunn, 1991), and academic performance (Baum, 2004).

Reasons for excluding previous studies include the lack of control for influential factors such as quality of child care and quality of parent–child interactions (Brooks-Gunn, Han, & Waldfogel, 2002). There does seem to be some evidence for differential effects of maternal employment based on ethnicity, SES, type of employment, and children's developmental stage. For example, several studies have found negative effects of maternal employment on child outcomes among European-American samples but not for African-American samples (Han et al., 2001; Waldfogel, Han, & Brooks-Gunn, 2002). The detrimental effects of maternal employment are also more amplified among families living in poverty, compared to those in the middle and upper classes.

The impact of maternal employment on child outcomes and family processes varies with children's developmental stage. By middle childhood, nonfamily influences such as peers, teachers, and schools play a greater role in children's lives, thus maternal employment may have less impact for children in the latter portion of middle childhood than in earlier periods (e.g., Baum, 2004). For example, the increases in family income from maternal employment is likely to be more salient during middle childhood, as family income will impact the quality of children's schools and neighborhoods (Baum, 2004). Moreover, older children are more likely to perceive their parents as potential role models, and thus benefit from having employed mothers, especially girls (cf., Haveman, Wolfe, & Spaulding, 1991).

The quality of the mother's job or her satisfaction with it also has an important impact. Although work can have positive effects on mental health such as lowering financial strain and the experience of psychological rewards, not all employment situations will have positive outcomes. Employment characterized by long hours, stressful, menial, or physically taxing work is more likely to contribute to mothers' feeling of frustration, stress, fatigue, and possibly psychological symptoms which in turn have a negative impact on the parenting environment and child outcomes. For example, mothers employed in low prestige jobs are more likely to exhibit coercive parenting (Raver, 2003). Employed mothers who work longer hours have been found to spend less time (Sayer, Bianchi, & Robinson, 2004), engage in less monitoring (Muller, 1995), talk less, express less affection (Repetti & Wood, 1997), and engage in more arguments with their children (Crouter, Bumpus, Maguire, & McHale, 1999).

DIVORCE

Most children experience important family structural and process changes when their parents divorce. It is estimated that approximately one million children experienced their parents' divorce during each year of the 1990s (U.S. Bureau of the Census, 1999). Two meta-analyses of studies of children and divorce found that offspring of divorced parents experienced more problematic outcomes compared to children of continuously married parents (Amato, 2001; Amato & Keith, 1991). More specifically, children of divorced parents scored significantly higher on measures on problematic outcomes (e.g., depression and conduct problems) and significantly lower on positive measures of well-being (e.g., academic achievement, self-concept, social relations, and quality of relationships with parents) compared to children with continuously married parents (Amato, 2000, 2001; Amato & Keith, 1991). However, despite these differences in adjustment, it is important to remember that the majority of children from divorced families do well (Amato, 2003; Hetherington & Stanley-Hagen, 1999; Kelly & Emery, 2003; O'Conner, 2003).

Children's adjustment to divorce can be enhanced through factors that decrease interparental conflict (or shield children from this conflict), and increase the provision of adequate involvement (monitoring along with emotional and economic support from parents, extended family members), and other sources of formal and informal support (Chen & George, 2005). More specifically, the parent–child relationship has been found to be an important mediator of children's adjustment to parental divorce (Hetherington & Stanley-Hagen, 1999; Kelly & Emery, 2003; O'Conner, 2003), with children who experience a positive parent–child relationship and positive parenting environment being more likely to have positive adjustment (Hetherington & Stanley-Hagen, 1999; O'Conner, 2003).

Several potential mechanisms exist through which parental divorce may influence negative consequences among children. One method of exploring possible ways that divorce impacts parents and children is through the theoretical perspectives that have been developed over the years. Although many family, sociological, and psychological theories have been applied to children and divorce, two main approaches have been the divorce–stress–adjustment perspective and the selection perspective (Amato, 2000).

Selection Perspective

Following a selection perspective, it is assumed that adjustment problems cause marital disruption (Amato, 2000). The main premise is that poorly adjusted people are "selected out" of marriage because these individuals possess problematic personal or social characteristics. These problematic characteristics thus predispose individuals to poor relationships and increase their likelihood of divorcing, as well as experiencing low levels of well-being after the divorce (Amato, 2000). Following the selection perspective, it is assumed that at least some of children's problems observed during or after the divorce process were actually present during the marriage (e.g., Amato & Booth, 1996; Cherlin et al., 1991). Another assumption from this perspective is that the poor personal and social characteristics of parents (e.g., antisocial personality traits) are direct causes of poor family functioning, divorce, and negative child outcomes (Amato, 2000). Thus, this perspective also raises the issues of children of divorce inheriting genetic traits from their poorly adjusted parents which predispose the children for poor personal and social outcomes (Amato, 2000).

Divorce–Stress-Adjustment Perspective

Following a divorce–stress perspective, it is assumed that marital disruption causes adjustment problems. However, the actual event of the divorce itself is not necessarily viewed as a direct cause of negative consequences for children (Amato, 2000). Rather, marital dissolution is viewed as a process instead of a discrete event (which begins while the couple is still living together and typically ends long after the legal divorce is over), which in turn, brings about other events and possible stressors that impact children and parents. Specifically, the process can be experienced as stressful that couples go through as they "uncouple" their marriage (Amato, 2000). These stressful developments redefine a parent as single and lead to financial and emotional independence from one's ex-spouse. Stressors of this kind increase the risk for family members to experience decreased emotional well-being and behavioral functioning (Amato, 2000). More specifically, events and processes emerge that have the potential to affect the emotions, behavior, health, and relationships of parents, children, and other family members who experience the divorce process. Several mediators that can impact parental health, parenting behaviors, parent–child relationships, and children's outcomes have been identified in the literature, such as (1) child custody, (2) coparenting, (3) emotional support, and (4) economic stability (e.g., Amato, 2000; Chen & George, 2005).

The negotiation of custody arrangements, as well as the continuous interaction involved in maintaining custody arrangements (e.g., dropping children off and picking them up and arranging schedules around these processes) can be very stressful for parents, children, as well as extended family members (Grych, 2005). Disagreements between parents about child-related issues are more strongly associated with children's adjustment problems than conflict topics not related to children (e.g., Synder, Klien, Gdowski, Faulstich, & LaCombe, 1988) and are more likely to elicit children's efforts to intervene in the conflict, as well as self-blame. Although the physical separation of divorce may reduce the frequency with which children actually witness their parents engaged in conflict, disagreements that do occur between divorced parents are likely to be more intense compared to interparental conflict within married families (Buchanan & Hieges, 2001). Some parents may find themselves suddenly having sole custody and needing to change their roles in their newly formed single-parent family system in order to meet changing work, financial, and childcare responsibilities. On the other side, some parents find themselves losing shared or constant contact/custody of their children. Obviously situations such as these can be very distressing for parents, as well as for children, who must now adjust to less time and interaction with each other than they were accustomed to when both parents and the children lived under the same roof.

The ability of ex-spouses to coparent their children together, regardless of feelings toward one another, or the level of satisfaction with the custody arrangement or divorce settlement, can have a huge impact on the well-being and adjustment of children (Grych, 2005). Supportive parenting functions as an important protective factor for children experiencing parental divorce (Wolchik et al., 1993). Thus, parenting serves as an important mediator between interparental conflict and children's outcomes (Grych, 2005) as conflict between parents can undermine supportive and consistent parenting. Moreover, following family systems theory, children can easily be drawn into parental conflict (i.e., triangulation or coalitions). Such as when the focus of parents on a child's behavior may serve as a distraction away from parental conflict, or parents may unite together to blame their child for their conflict (e.g., Minuchin, 1974). Similarly, divorced parents can easily fight through their children, such as having their child convey messages, especially contemptuous information, to the other parent. Actions such as these put children in the middle of a parental war, and may leave children feeling forced to take sides or withdraw from one or both parents.

In order for successful reorganization of the family system to occur postdivorce, both parents will need to agree on such elements as parenting strategies or discipline, or at least agree to respect and not undermine each parent's rules and parenting behaviors with the children during their custody times (Grych, 2005). Parents who are able to put aside differences and agree on parenting children together versus continuing to engage in conflict through children will increase their chances of establishing a functional coparenting relationship. This increases the likelihood that children will experience a consistent environment and not get caught up in the conflict between their parents.

The emotional support system of each ex-spouse is an extremely important factor in predicting the well-being of each parent, as well as the well-being of their children. For example, most parents are likely to experience changes in their support systems, such as a loss of support from in-laws, and joint friends/neighbors of the former couple. Emotional support for children from adults outside of the family (e.g., teachers), as well as from their peers, has also been found to increase children's positive adjustment to divorce (Barnes, 1999; Rodgers & Rose, 2002).

The economic stability of each ex-spouse and their respective newly formed single-parent household, as well as their combined "binuclear family system" is extremely important during and after the transition from a two-parent married household. For example, many custodial mothers typically experience downward mobility, in contrast to noncustodial fathers who on average experience an increase in their economic stability.

Several other disruptive events can also mediate the influence of divorce on parents and children, such as changes in employment, housing, and need for childcare. Many parents may find themselves needing to enter (or reenter) the workforce or needing to find affordable childcare for the first time. Similarly, many parents may discover that they need to find additional employment in order to maintain the same standard of living they experienced within a two-parent marriage. For example, a noncustodial parent struggling to pay her or his own bills in addition to alimony, child-support, and the house payment on the home that the ex-spouse now occupies with their children may find themselves needing to file for bankruptcy, move back in with parents, or take on additional employment to meet all of the additional financial obligations. A custodial parent, on the other hand, is likely to face similar struggles as she or he attempts to support children on one income and balance working full-time with being a full-time parent. For example, many custodial mothers and their children end up moving to less expensive neighborhoods after divorce and have to cope with changing to schools that have fewer resources than the schools the children had previously attended or are located in more dangerous neighborhoods.

Siblings

Another important structural variation that influences child development within families is the presence and number of siblings as well as the quality of sibling relationships. Sibling relationships typically serve as the models for peer relations and a "practice" ground for developing social skills and peer relationships. Positive sibling relationships are particularly beneficial for engaging in cooperative and pretend play, which in turn provide opportunities to develop children's understanding of one another. For example, having one or two siblings instead of none is related to enhanced social skills in peer group interactions (Downey & Caldron, 2004).

Sibling relationships are unique in several ways. First, most siblings spend a great deal of time together, in fact by middle childhood, young siblings spend more time with one another than they spend with parents or peers (McHale & Crouter, 1996). Second, sibling relationships tend to be emotionally uninhibited, which increases the chance of siblings influencing one another (Dunn, 2002). Third, the quality of sibling relationships is highly variable across time, as well as across and between siblings. For example, one sibling could exert positive influences on his younger brother by teaching him how to play sports, and practicing and modeling prosocial behavior. This same older sibling, on the other hand, might get involved in substance abuse and thus influence his younger sibling to do so also, either by direct encouragement, or through modeling or shared peer influences. Additionally, sibling relationships during middle childhood are likely to be more egalitarian (Buhrmester & Furman, 1990), and be characterized by high intensity and extensive emotionality. Moreover, middle childhood is a time that siblings will typically experience less pull from relationships outside of the family that might weaken the close and intimate bonds of siblings (Dunn, 2002).

Research findings continue to note direct negative influences of siblings such as the association between poor quality sibling relationships and children's current and later externalizing and internalizing attributes. More specifically, studies have found that sibling conflict in middle childhood is predictive of deviant and problem behavior in adolescence and early adulthood (Bank, Patterson, & Reid, 1996; Paterson, 1982; Richman et al., 1982). Recent studies have also found several positive effects of sibling relationships on child development (Pike, Coldwell, & Dunn, 2005; Richmond et al., 2005). For example, Richmond et al. found that as sibling relationships increased in quality (e.g., more warmth and less conflict) over time, children's depressive symptoms decreased.

Another important influence on child development and sibling relationships is the extent of differential parental treatment. Children are typically very well aware of the differences in the behavior of their parents toward them compared to their siblings (Dunn & Munn, 1985). Researchers have consistently reported that perceptions of receiving less favorable parental treatment compared to one's sibling is positively related to externalizing and internalizing problems (Dunn, Stocker, & Plomin, 1990; McHale, Crouter, McGuire, & Updegraff, 1995; McHale, Updegraff, Jackson-Newson, Tucker, & Crouter, 2000). Richmond et al.'s study (2005) examined the combined influences of differential parental treatment and quality of sibling relationships on externalizing behavior and depressed mood across time. Richmond et al. found that sibling relationship quality was not as salient as a predictor for children's externalizing problems, although it was for depressed mood. Thus it appears that the experience of being treated unfairly by parents is more salient in predicting the behavioral problems of children than the quality of sibling relations. Of course, it is important to keep in mind the complex relationships between sibling relationship quality, differential parental treatment, and children's outcomes.

Other studies have also concluded that parental differential treatment is more strongly related to children's externalizing problems than to children's internalizing attributes (e.g., Boyle et al., 2004; Kowal, Kramer, Krull, & Crick, 2002). That is, children who display externalizing problems are more likely to elicit more parental control compared to siblings without behavioral problems. Thus the child who is acting out and receiving more negative attention than their sibling is likely to notice the difference in parental treatment, which might in turn, lead to more acting out behavior, followed by more parental control. In contrast, parents might be less likely to notice children's depressed mood and less likely to respond to children's depressive symptoms with increased parental control (Richmond et al., 2005).

Although sibling relationships can serve as both positive and negative influences on child development, it is important to note the complexity of the impact of siblings. It is not simply the quality of sibling relationships nor the extent of differential parental treatment, but rather the complex interaction of changes in the sibling context that are associated with changes in children's adjustment (Richmond et al., 2005).

In summary, the influence of family structural variations on child development occurs primarily through the impact of these differing structural organizations on family processes and interactions such as parenting behaviors, goals, and parent–child relationships. That is, structural variations in families (e.g., divorce, SES, siblings) have consequences for child development by influencing interaction and relationships as well as resources and opportunities, which in turn impact child development directly or indirectly through family processes.

FAMILY PROCESS AND RELATIONSHIP VARIABLES

As mentioned previously, the aspects of family life that have the strongest direct influences on child development (socially competent and problematic outcomes) are family processes and relationships rather than structural dimensions of families. The subsequent sections review the most prominent parental and family process dimensions of the parent–child relationship that have either negative or positive consequences for social competence development in children. More specifically, two broad methods of conceptualizing parental socialization of children from both bidirectional (parent–child conflict and interparental conflict) and social mold perspectives (i.e., parenting styles and behaviors) are examined.

Parenting Styles and Behaviors

Researchers have developed several methods of examining how parents either foster or inhibit desired outcomes in children (Peterson & Hann, 1999).

Parental Styles

The term *parenting styles* refers to constellations of childrearing behaviors that operate in combination to influence behaviors and attitudes in the young (Baumrind, 1991; Baumrind & Black, 1967; Dornbusch et al., 1987; Maccoby & Martin, 1983; Steinberg, Mounts, & Lamborn, 1991). The most prominent researcher in the parenting styles literature is Diana Baumrind (1971, 1978, 1991), who has conceptualized several childrearing typologies. Although changing somewhat over time, Baumrind's most commonly identified typology includes the three categories: authoritarian, authoritative, and permissive parenting.

Authoritarian Parenting Style

This style appears to be associated with the most problematic psychosocial outcomes among children and adolescents, at least among middle-class European-American samples (Baumrind, 1978, 1991; Dornbusch et al., 1987; Peterson & Hann, 1999). This style consists of parenting behaviors characterized as punitive, demanding, overly strict, and uncompromising. Authoritarian parenting also consists of lower levels of support, communication, and reasoning (Baumrind, 1978, 1991; Peterson & Hann, 1999). Parents who fit into this category are described as using harsh punishment in an arbitrary manner to gain compliance, without tolerating much input from the young. A common objective is to shape and control the behavior and attitudes of children in accordance with an absolute set of standards. Authoritarian parents value obedience from children, with punitive or arbitrary measures being used to ensure compliance. Researchers examining U.S. samples have reported that parents whose parenting practices fall into the authoritarian style tend to foster lower levels of social competence (e.g., self-concept and school performance) and higher levels of problematic outcomes such as conduct disorder, externalizing behavior, and noncompliance in the young (Baumrind, 1971, 1978, 1991; Dornbusch et al., 1987; Steinberg et al., 1991).

Permissive Parenting Style

Baumrind (1978, 1991) describes the permissive parenting style as being tolerant and accepting of children's impulsive behavior. She describes these parents as using little punishment and as avoiding the implementation of firm controls or restrictions. Parenting behaviors composing this typology include high levels of acceptance and autonomy granting, along with low levels of discipline and behavioral control. Moreover, this category has been divided further into (1) permissive-indulgent and (2) permissive-neglectful. Parents falling into the permissive-neglectful style of parenting convey low levels of support and low levels of parental control. Children living with permissive-neglectful parents typically experience too much autonomy and without the context of a supportive relationship or secure base. This is a type of autonomy characterized more as "separation" from a parent, than a negotiated process of establishing a healthy balance between managing one's own affairs and remaining connected to parents. Children in permissive-neglectful homes are more likely to associate with deviant peers, especially as they enter adolescence and young adulthood, and to be deviant in reference to authority, since they have not been exposed sufficiently to rules or consistent discipline (e.g., monitoring) from their parents.

The permissive-indulgent parenting style is characterized by low levels of parental control, but high levels of parental support and nurturance. Some children with permissive-indulgent parents may experience high levels of self-esteem/confidence and autonomy. However, the lack of parental control by permissive parents can override the positive impact of their frequent use of nurturance. Consequently, the potential exists for autonomy granting to occur in the context of few if any parental rules or discipline, with the results being that children are granted too much autonomy. That is, the impact of permissive-indulgent parenting may be similar to that of permissive-neglectful parenting in the sense that associations with deviant peers, lack of motivation or engagement in school, and externalizing behavior problems from the lack of parental rules and consistent discipline are predicted (Maccoby & Martin, 1983).

Authoritative Parenting Style

This style of parenting is characterized by high levels of support, warmth, clearly defined rules, effective communication (promoting psychological autonomy), and moderate to high levels of behavioral control (Baumrind, 1991; Steinberg et al., 1991). Research with U.S. samples has found authoritative parenting to predict desirable psychosocial outcomes among children and adolescents, at least most strongly among middle-class European-American children (Baumrind, 1991; Dornbusch et al., 1987; Steinberg et al., 1992). For example, authoritative parenting has been associated with high levels of self-esteem, school performance, social skills, and fewer problems with antisocial behaviors and substance abuse (Baumrind, 1971, 1978, 1991; Dornbusch et al., 1987; Maccoby & Martin, 1983; Steinberg, Dornbusch, & Brown, 1992; Steinberg et al., 1991).

Parenting Behaviors

An alternative strategy to the use of global conceptions of parenting, such as parenting styles, is to focus on specific dimensions of parental behaviors (Barber, 1997; Linver

& Silverberg, 1997; Peterson & Hann, 1999). Because parenting styles are composed of combinations of parenting behaviors, it is difficult to determine how specific dimensions of parenting are predictive of particular developmental outcomes among children and adolescents (Barber, 1997, 2002a; Herman, Dornbusch, Herron, & Herting, 1997; Linver & Silverberg, 1997).

In contrast, the examination of specific dimensions of parenting behavior allows researchers to isolate relationships between specific parenting behaviors and child and adolescent outcomes (Barber, 1997; Linver & Silverberg, 1997; Peterson & Hann, 1999). That is, this strategy permits researchers to establish whether a specific dimension of parenting is the primary predictor of particular psychosocial outcomes among children and adolescents (Barber, 1997, 2002b; Linver & Silverberg, 1997; Peterson & Hann, 1999). An important objective of research that focuses on individual dimensions of parenting behavior, therefore, is to examine specific aspects of parenting styles to more precisely define the primary predictors of various negative and positive psychosocial outcomes (e.g., Barber, 1997; Herman et al., 1997). Researchers who use this approach may be able to more precisely identify which dimensions of parental behavior are contributing to specific child and adolescent outcomes (e.g., externalizing versus internalizing disorders). Studies examining the relationships between specific parental behaviors and child outcomes among diverse cultural groups have found significant positive relationships between parental support, behavioral control, autonomy granting and (1) self-concept and (2) academic achievement (Bean, Bush, McKenry, & Wilson, 2003; Bush, Peterson, Cobas, & Supple, 2002; Herman et al., 1997; Lau & Cheung, 1987; Linver & Silverberg, 1997). Similarly, studies have also found significant negative relationships between parental support, behavioral control, autonomy granting, and externalizing and internalizing problems (e.g., Hill & Bush, 2001; Hill, Bush, & Roosa, 2003).

Another limitation regarding global conceptualizations of parenting, such as Baumrind's parenting styles typology, is the lack of these configurations to predict some child outcomes as strongly within ethnic minority populations or non-Western cultural groups. Several studies have concluded that the parenting style typologies are not as predictive of similar outcomes across ethnic groups (Dornbusch et al., 1987; Steinberg et al., 1991). For example, Dornbusch et al. reported that authoritative parenting was a positive predictor of academic achievement among European Americans, but was not significantly related to the academic achievement of Asian Americans. Authoritarian parenting was the only parenting style significantly related (negatively) to the academic achievement of Asian Americans. Findings such as these have led some researchers to prematurely conclude that Asian-American parents are authoritarian. However, despite these findings, Asian Americans in this sample had significantly higher academic achievement in comparison to adolescents from the other ethnic groups. A more recent conclusion by Steinberg et al. (1992) points to the differential contribution and importance of peer support across ethnic groups to explain this paradox. Steinberg et al. suggest that among Asian Americans, peer support for academic achievement offsets the negative influence of authoritarian parenting.

Other scholars assert that parenting style typologies do not capture the aspects of Asian (e.g., Chinese) parenting, such as forms of control like the strong emphasis on child training, and the different methods used by Asian parents to convey love and caring to their children (Chao, 1994). That is, cultural influences among Asian-American parents and other non-Western cultural groups perhaps are not captured, and therefore overlooked, in the conceptualization of parenting style typologies (Chao, 1994, 2000, 2001). By focusing on the identification of relationships between distinctive dimensions of parenting (i.e., support, behavioral control, autonomy granting and psychological control) and specific child outcomes, a more accurate model of socialization among ethnically diverse families can be developed (Barber, 1997; Chao, 2001; Herman et al., 1997).

Parental Support

Specific parenting behaviors that express support include verbal expressions of love and caring as well as physical affection in the form of hugs and kisses (Peterson & Hann, 1999). Parental support includes affection, warmth, nurturance, companionship, and responsiveness (Barber, 1997; Peterson & Hann, 1999). In other words, supportive behaviors express confidence, love, acceptance, and feelings of value for the young. Parental support is especially useful for fostering close relationships between parents and children (Peterson & Hann, 1999) and a positive predictor of children's social competence (Baumrind, 1978, 1991). Supportive behavior by parents encourages secure attachment (Karavasilis, Doyle, & Markiewicz, 2003; Kerns, Tomich, Aspelmeier, & Contreras, 2000), academic achievement, self-concept (Bean et al., 2003; Bush et al., 2002), and inhibits the development of internalizing and externalizing attributes (Atzaba-Poria, Pike, Deater-Deckard, 2004; Caron, Weiss, Harris, & Catron, 2006; Hill & Bush, 2001; Hill et al., 2003).

Parental Behavioral Control

Methods of firm parental control refer to parents' efforts aimed at supervising children through consistent rules, regulations, and restrictions imposed on children, as well as parental knowledge or awareness of children's activities obtained through observation and inquiry. In other words, parental behavioral control focuses on control over daily activities and consists of clearly communicated expectations, enforced rules, and consistent discipline during the monitoring of children's activities (Baumrind, 1971; Bugental & Grusec, 2006; Peterson & Hann, 1999).

During early childhood, behavioral control involves more direct supervision by parents or others in authority, whereas, among older children and adolescents, behavioral control involves more distal forms. During middle childhood, the young continue to require parental supervision as a means of fostering social competence, but also to guard against any drift toward delinquent behavior as they begin to establish and maintain peer relationships, and interact with more people outside of the family and home (Kerns, Aspelmeier, Gentzler, & Grabill, 2001; Peterson & Hann, 1999). Parental behavioral control may indicate parents' interest, involvement, and concern with their children. As children progress from early to middle childhood, they assume more responsibility for self-regulation, thus behavioral control is mutually negotiated, as parents still need to ensure that their child complies with family and societal standards. A major issue in parent–child relationships during middle childhood is how parents and children negotiate appropriate levels of parental behavioral control over the developing autonomy of children (Kerns et al., 2001; Peterson & Hann, 1999).

Parents use behavioral control attempts to communicate and enforce a clear set of standards for children. When used in a consistent and nonarbitrary manner, children will have clear sets of standards against which to evaluate themselves and, thereby, foster the development of social competence (Barber, 1997; Baumrind, 1991; Crouter & Head, 2002;

Peterson & Hann, 1999). Positive feelings about oneself are best facilitated when the rules are clear as opposed to when rules are either unclear or arbitrarily imposed (Peterson & Hann, 1999). In addition, parents who monitor the activities of their children are more likely to facilitate engagement in school and academic achievement (Chao, 1994; Herman et al., 1997; Linver & Silverberg, 1997; Steinberg et al., 1992) as well as to guard against the development of externalizing problems (Caron et al., 2006). Moreover, several aspects of parental behavioral control, such as (1) parents' awareness of their children activities and (2) children's cooperation and willingness to check in with parents are significantly related to secure attachments within parent–child relationships during middle childhood (Kerns et al., 2001). In contrast, parenting behavior characterized as permissive, or low in behavioral control, has been found to predict such adverse outcomes as conduct problems and drug use (Baumrind, 1991; Dornbusch et al., 1987).

Parental Psychological Control
Excessive, arbitrary, and coercive parental behaviors that inhibit the development of psychological autonomy among children are referred to as psychological control (Barber, 1997, 2002a, 2002b). Psychological control attempts include parental intrusiveness, guilt induction, and love withdrawal or a variety of socialization practices that can have different consequences on child development (Bugental & Grusec, 2006). More specifically, psychological control can be manifest through the suppressing of children's development of psychological autonomy; through inducing guilt in children; or through overprotectiveness. For example, parents, who use intrusive psychological control, value compliance and do not negotiate with their children, thus providing them with little choice. However, intrusiveness can be perceived as indicating parental caring and has been associated with some positive outcomes (Bugental & Grusec, 2006). In contrast, the use of guilt induction or love withdrawal involves emotional manipulation and is less likely to lead to positive child outcomes or be perceived by them as an indication of parental caring.

Controlling parental behavior that relies on psychological manipulation is not responsive to the psychological needs and emotions of children and fails to communicate clear expectations. Thus, children are not provided with a clear or positive rationale against which to evaluate themselves. These arbitrary control attempts serve to devalue children's sense of self as parents communicate rejection and a lack of respect for the young, thus interfering with their establishment of a sense of identity (Barber, 1996, 2002a, 2002b). Studies among diverse samples have supported the view that psychological control is a negative predictor of self-esteem and academic achievement (Bean et al., 2003; Bush et al., 2002; Herman et al., 1997; Linver & Silverberg, 1997) as well as a positive predictor of internalizing and externalizing attributes (Bugental & Grusec, 2006; Caron et al., 2006).

Psychological Autonomy Granting
Autonomy granting does not suggest lack of parental control or involvement; but rather, extensive involvement is at the heart of granting autonomy as one of the most positive psychological and social outcomes developed by children (e.g., Bugental & Grusec, 2006; Herman et al., 1997). The basis of successful socialization is a positive relationship that fosters willingness on the part of the child to be influenced or to be receptive to parental socialization. An important socialization goal is for parents to balance controlling

children's behavior with their growing need for autonomy (e.g., Bugental & Grusec, 2006). That is, parents should recognize the importance of children's need to develop independence, and administer discipline and support in such a way that encourages the child's feelings of autonomously directed behavior. A key aspect of autonomy granting is allowing children to make choices (Grolnick, 2003) while balancing this with the maintenance of authority. It is a complex process to provide opportunities for choice and autonomy while maintaining hierarchical authority and close relationship that involves gradual renegotiation over time (Peterson & Hann, 1999).

Parents who grant psychological autonomy as part of their parenting behavior provide opportunities and encouragement of the young to express their growing independence within a supportive parent–child relationship (Gray & Steinberg, 1999). Parental psychological autonomy granting fosters positive self-worth, academic achievement (Barber, 2002a; Bush et al., 2002), and secure attachment in children (Karavasilis et al., 2003).

FAMILY CONFLICT: PARENT–CHILD AND INTERPARENTAL CONFLICT

Typically, when one mentions parent–child conflict, the developmental period of adolescence comes to mind. This transitional time is likely to produce and or bring to light, differences in goals and age expectations for behaviors between teens and their parents. However, parent–child conflict also occurs during middle childhood as children enter school and associate with a more complex array of peers and make more bids for autonomy. Early parent–child conflict can be an important predictor of later developmental outcomes. For example, early parent–child conflict is associated with the "early starter" pathway and with antisocial behavior across development (Brennan, Hall, Bor, Najman, & Williams, 2003; Ingoldsby, Shaw, Winslow, Schonberg, Gilliom, & Criss, 2006; Loeber, Farrington, Strouthamer-Loeber, Moffit, & Caspi, 1998).

Parent–Child Conflict

As children mature during middle childhood, especially as they become more involved with peers and begin to enter adolescence, the negotiation of independence with their parents may serve as fuel for parent–child conflict. That is, as children make bids for more autonomy, parents who are not responsive to these bids, or at least not perceived to be fair, are likely to face conflict with their children. Moreover, children who are not responsive to their parents' efforts to grant or encourage increased independence also are likely to face conflict with their parents. Consequently, parent–child conflict is very much a bidirectional process and does not necessarily indicate maladjustment, as long as the conflict is moderate, negotiated, and managed to some degree. Thus, the quality of communication and closeness within the parent–child relationship are important predictors of conflict resolution between parents and children. Other potential causes of parent–child conflict include influences outside of the parent–child relationship, such as interparental or marital conflict. Several studies have found that parent–child conflict mediates the relationship between marital conflict and children's adjustment (Acock & Demo, 1999; Buehler & Gerard, 2002; Gerard, Krishnakumar, & Buehler, 2006). That is, the frustrations associated with marital conflict may spill over into the parent–child relationship.

Interparental Conflict

At least some conflict occurs in all intimate relationships; thus, all interparental conflict is not necessarily harmful to parents or children. A key determining factor is how the conflict is managed, including the adequacy of resolution and the extent to which children are shielded from exposure. That is, all conflict between parents does not have the same impact on children. An analysis of interparental conflict must take into account several factors including: parental conflict management strategies, parental coping abilities, children's coping strategies, the frequency and severity of conflict, and children's exposure/involvement in the conflict. All of these factors play important roles regarding the impact of conflict on parents, parent–child relationships, and children's' outcomes (Grych, 2005). Based on such analyses, researchers have identified parental disagreements that are hostile, aggressive, poorly resolved, and those that pertain to the child as being the most detrimental to the adjustment of the young (e.g., Cummings, Goeke-Morey, & Papp, 2001).

Theoretical and empirical work has documented the high risk that children who are exposed to interparental conflict face for developing psychological, social, and behavioral problems both during childhood as well as later in life (Gerard et al., 2006; Grych, 2005; Grych & Fincham, 2001; Kelly, 2000). Children exposed to interparental conflict have a higher likelihood of developing internalizing problems such as depression and anxiety, in addition to externalizing problems such as disruptive behavior and aggression during childhood. Moreover, during adolescence and adulthood, children who witnessed their parents' hostility and aggression are more likely to perpetrate acts of violence toward their intimate partners during their own adolescence and adulthood (Wekerle & Wolf, 1999), experience higher rates of divorce, as well as become less socially and behaviorally adjusted during adulthood (Amato & Keith, 1991).

Marital or interparental conflict can influence children's adjustment either directly on a variety of child outcomes or indirectly by disrupting the socialization behaviors of parents that promote children's well-being. The theoretical notion of "spillover" guides most of the research that examines the indirect influences of martial conflict on child development. That is, children's psychosocial development can be detrimentally affected when marital conflict leads to parents' use of psychologically controlling parenting behavior, decreased involvement/support, and negative interaction between parents and children. For example, parental involvement (Buehler & Gerard, 2002) and harsh parental discipline (Gerard et al., 2006) have been identified as significant mediators of the relationship between marital conflict and children's adjustment during middle childhood.

Marital conflict has also been found to have direct influences on children's maladjustment (Buehler & Gerard, 2002) as well as increasing parent–child conflict (Gerard et al., 2006), which in turn predicts internalizing and externalizing problems of children (Gerard et al., 2006). A recent meta-analysis of the link between marital conflict and parenting behaviors found that the association between harsh discipline and marital conflict was stronger than the relationships found between marital conflict and other parenting behaviors (Krishnakumar & Buehler, 2000).

Findings from several longitudinal studies indicate that the effect of divorce on children varies according to the level of interparental conflict prior to divorce (for review see Amato, 2001; Amato & Keith, 1991). Children whose parents engaged in relatively low levels and frequencies of overt conflict appear to experience decreased adjustment following divorce (Amato, Loomis, & Booth, 1995; Hanson, 1999; Jekielek, 1998; Morrison & Coiro, 1999). Conversely, children whose parents engage in chronic, overt, intense, and unresolved conflict seem to have better adjustment if the parents divorce. Children whose parents did not engage in overt and chronic conflict are likely to experience the divorce as unexpected and thus an event that itself seems to start a series of stressors (Amato, 2001). Children whose parents engaged in chronic and overt conflict would be less likely to see the divorce as shocking and unexpected, and more likely to experience less exposure to conflict and stress, and might even feel relieved. In summary, children's exposure to chronic, overt, and unresolved interparental conflict is likely to have undesirable short-term and long-term outcomes for children. How parents handle interparental conflict is likely to be a large determinant of the impact that such family strife has on children's development, including the impact of parental divorce on the young.

CONCLUSION

A primary conclusion of this review is that the family context provides a complex array of influences on development during middle childhood. Although structural variations in families (e.g., family composition, SES, and divorce) can serve as powerful influences on child development, many of these effects are indirect predictors of development, such as through direct impact on parenting behavior or other family process variable, which, in turn, affect child outcomes.

Another conclusion is the need for more research that expands beyond the social mold perspective and simultaneously assesses bidirectional influences, genetic influences, and the impact of siblings, peers, and other socialization agents both within and outside the family (e.g., Kuczynski, 2003; Peterson & Hann, 1999). Part of this complexity involves examining how multiple contexts of socialization operate either in conjunction; or at odds with each other. More research attention is needed on bidirectional and multidirectional influences that children, their parents, and their siblings experience in families. An emphasis on more complex socialization models also will require greater efforts to disentangle genetic from family and other social and environmental influences. Greater emphasis on twin studies and other behavioral genetic designs is needed to more precisely identify aspects of child development that are truly a product of nurture rather than nature.

Despite the growth of influences from social agents beyond families during middle childhood, families remain sources of complex, complementary, and contradictory influences on the young during middle childhood. An important goal for future research is to demonstrate how family influences are distinctive from, contradictory, or complementary with the influence of other social agents such as schools, peer groups, neighborhoods, churches, and relevant organizations/institutions. Research of this kind is needed to examine the efficacy of human ecological models that convey more realistic conceptions of the complex social world that child and families face each day (Bronfenbrenner, 1979; Lerner, 2002).

Lastly, an important implication of the current research on families and children indicates that family-based prevention/intervention models should be focused primarily on the interaction processes which occur within families rather than various structural dimensions. Family-based prevention/intervention approaches should be applied as part of a larger strategy involving components implemented across social contexts such as of the family, school, peer group, and community. Such a broad-based strategy recognizes that no single strategy can promote socially competent outcomes and help prevent the development of problem behaviors when social contexts contradict each other in addressing multiple influences. Instead, greater success will be attained through a major public health effort that provides a coordinated package of approaches designed to address both general issues across contexts but also having sufficient flexibility for varied community circumstances.

REFERENCES

Acock, A. C., & Demo, D. H. (1999). Dimensions of family conflict and their influence on child and adolescent maladjustment. *Sociological Inquiry, 69*, 641–658.

Alessandri, S. M. (1992). Effects of maternal work status in single-parent families on children's perception of self and family and school achievement. *Journal of Experimental Child Psychology, 54*, 417–433.

Amato, P. R. (2000). The consequences of divorce for adults and children. *Journal of Marriage & Family, 62*(4), 1269–1987.

Amato, P. R. (2001). Children of divorce in the 1990s: An update of the Amato and Keith (1991) meta-analysis. *Journal of Family Psychology, 15*(3), 355–370.

Amato, P. R. (2003). Reconciling divergent perspectives: Judith Wallerstein, quantitative family research, and children of divorce. *Family Relations, 52*(4), 332–339.

Amato, P. R., & Booth, A. (1996). A prospective study of divorce and parent–children relationships. *Journal of Marriage & Family, 58*(2), 356–365.

Amato, P. R., & Keith, B. (1991). Parental divorce and the well-being of children: A meta-analysis. *Psychological Bulletin, 110*(1), 26–46.

Amato, P. R., Loomis, L. S., & Booth, A. (1995). Parental divorce, marital conflict, and offspring well-being during early adulthood. *Social Forces, 73*, 985–915.

Atzaba-Poria, N., Pike, A., & Deater-Deckard, K. (2004). Do risk factors for problem behaviour act in a cumulative manner? An examination of ethnic minority and majority children through an ecological perspective. *Journal of Child Psychology and Psychiatry, 45*(4), 707–714.

Bank, L., Patterson, G. R., & Reid, J. B. (1996). Negative sibling interaction patterns as predictors of later adjustment problems in adolescent and young adult males. In G. Brody (Ed.), *Sibling relationships: Their causes and consequences* (pp. 197–229). Norwood, NJ: Ablex.

Barber, B. K. (1996). Parental psychological control: Revisiting a neglected construct. *Child Development, 67*, 3296–3319.

Barber, B. K. (1997). Introduction: Adolescent socialization in context—The role of connection, regulation, and autonomy in the family. *Journal of Adolescent Research, 12*, 5–11.

Barber, B. K. (2002a). *Intrusive parenting: How psychological control affects children and adolescents.* Washington, D.C.: American Psychological Association Press.

Barber, B. K. (2002b). Re-introducing psychological control. In B. K. Barber (Ed.), *Intrusive parenting: How psychological control affects children and adolescents* (pp. 8–23). Washington, D.C.: American Psychological Association Press.

Barnes, G. G. (1999). Divorce transitions: identifying risk and promoting resilience for children and their parental relationships. *Journal of Marital and Family Therapy, 25*, 425–441.

Barnett, R. C., Marshall, N. L., Raudenbush, S. W., & Brennan, R. T. (1993). Gender and the relationship between job experiences and psychological distress. A study of dual-earner couples. *Journal of Personality and Social Psychology, 64*, 794–806.

Baruch, G. K., & Barnett, R. C. (1986). Role quality, multiple role involvement, and psychological well-being in midlife women. *Journal of Personality and Social Psychology, 51*, 578–585.

Baum, C. L. (2004). The long-term effects of early and recent maternal employment on a child's academic achievement. *Journal of Family Issues, 25*(1), 29–60.

Baumrind, D. (1971). Harmonious parents and their preschool children. *Developmental Psychology, 4*(1), 99–102.

Baumrind, D. (1978). Parental disciplinary patterns and social competence in children. *Youth and Society, 9*, 239–276.

Baumrind, D. (1991). Effective parenting during the early adolescent transition. In P. A. Cowan & M. Hetherington (Eds.), *Family transitions* (pp. 111–163). Hillsdale, NJ: Lawrence Erlbaum.

Baumrind, D., & Black, A. E. (1967). Socialization practices associated with dimensions of competence in preschool boys and girls. *Child Development, 38*(2), 291–326.

Baydar, N., & Brooks-Gunn, J. (1991). Effects of maternal employment and child-care arrangements on preschoolers' cognitive and behavioral outcomes: Evidence from the children of the National Longitudinal Survey of Youth. *Developmental Psychology 27*, 932–945.

Bean, R. A., Bush, K. R., McKenry, P. C., & Wilson, S. (2003). The impact of parental support, behavioral control, and psychological control on the academic achievement and self-esteem of African-American and European-American adolescents. *Journal of Adolescent Research, 18*(5), 523–542,

Belsky, J., & Eggebeen, D. (1991). Early and extensive maternal employment and young children's socioemotional development: Children of the National Longitudinal Survey of Youth. *Journal of Marriage & Family, 53*(4), 1083–1098.

Bloom, M. (1990). The psychosocial constructs of social competency. In T. P. Gullotta, G. R. Adams, & R. Montemayor (Eds.), *Developing social competency in adolescence* (pp. 5–25). Newbury Park, CA: Sage.

Boyle, M. H., Jenkins, J. M., Georgiades, K., Cairney, J., Duku, E., & Racine, Y. (2004). Differential-maternal parenting behavior: Estimating within- and between-family effects on children. *Child Development, 75*, 1457–1476.

Brennan, P. A., Hall, J., Bor, W., Najman, J. M., & Williams, G. (2003). Integrating biological and social processes in relation to early-onset persistent aggression in boys and girls. *Developmental Psychology, 39*, 309–323.

Broderick, C. B. (1993). *Understanding family process: Basics of family systems theory.* Newbury Park, CA: Sage.

Bronfenbrenner, U. (1979). *The ecology of human development: Experiments by nature and design.* Cambridge, MA: Harvard University Press.

Bronfenbrenner, U. (1994). Ecological models of human development. In T. Husen & T. N. Postlethwaite (Ed.), *The international encyclopedia of education* (2nd ed., pp. 1643–1647). New York: Elsevier Science.

Brooks-Gunn, J., Han, W., & Waldfogel, J. (2002). Maternal employment and child cognitive outcomes in the first three years of life: The NICHD study of early child care. *Child Development, 73*(4), 1052–1072.

Buchanan, C. M., & Hieges, K. L. (2001). When conflict continues after the marriage ends: Effects of post-divorce conflict on children. In J. Grych & F. Fincham (Eds.), *Interparental conflict and child development* (pp. 337–362). New York: Cambridge University Press.

Buehler, C., & Gerard, J. M. (2002). Marital conflict, ineffective parenting, and children's and adolescent's maladjustment. *Journal of Marriage and the Family, 64*, 78–92.

Bugental, D. B., & Grusec, J. (2006). Socialization theory. In N. Eisenberg (Ed.), *Handbook of Child Psychology, Vol. 3: Social, Emotional and Personality Development* (pp. 366–428). Hoboken, NJ: Wiley.

Buhrmester, D., & Furman, W. (1990). Perceptions of sibling relationships during middle childhood and adolescence. *Child Development, 61*, 1387–1398.

Bush, K. R., Peterson, G. W., Cobas, J., & Supple, A. J. (2002). Adolescents' perceptions of parental behaviors as predictors of adolescent self-esteem in mainland China. *Sociological Inquiry, 72* (4), 503–526.

Caron, A., Weiss, B., Harris, V., Catron, T. (2006). Parenting behavior dimensions and child psychopathology: Specificity, task, dependency, and interactive relations. *Journal of Clinical Child and Adolescent Psychology, 35*(1), 34–45.

Chao, R. (1994). Beyond parental control and authoritarian parenting style: Understanding Chinese parenting through the cultural notion of training. *Child Development, 65*, 1111–1119.

Chao, R. K. (2000). Cultural explanations for the role of parenting in the school success of Asian-American Children. In R. Taylor & M. C. Wang (Ed.), *Resilience across contexts: Family, work, culture, and community* (pp. 333–363). Temple University: Center for Research in Human Development

Chao, R. K. (2001). Extending research on the consequences of parenting style for Chinese Americans and European Americans. *Child Development, 72*, 1832–1843.

Chen, J., & George, R. A. (2005). Cultivating resilience in children from divorced families. *The Family Journal: Counseling and Therapy for Couples and Families, 13*(4), 452–455.

Cherlin, A. J., Furstenberg, F. F., Jr., Chase-Lansdale, P. L., Kiernan, K. E., Robins, P. K., Morrison, D. R., et al. (1991). Longitudinal studies of effects of divorce on children in Great Britain and the United States. *Science, 252*(5011), 1386–1389.

Crouter, A. C., Bumpus, M. F., Maguire, M. C., & McHale, S. M. (1999). Linking parents' work pressure and adolescents' well-being: Insights into dynamics in dual-earner couples. *Developmental Psychology, 35*(6), 1453–1461.

Crouter, A. C., & Head, M. R. (2002). Parental monitoring and knowledge of children. In M. H. Bornstein (Ed.), *Handbook of parenting* (Vol. 3, pp. 461–483). Mahwah, NJ: Lawrence Erlbaum.

Cummings, E. M., Goeke-Morey, M. C., & Papp, L. M. (2001). Couple conflict: It's not just you and me, babe. In A. Booth, A. C. Crouter, & M. Clements (Eds.), *Couples in conflict* (pp. 117–148). Mahwah, NJ: Lawrence Erlbaum.

Demo, D. H., & Cox, M. J. (2000). Families with young children: A review of research in the 1990s. *Journal of Marriage and the Family, 62*, 876–895.

Dornbusch, S. M., Ritter, P. L., Leiderman, P. H., Roberts, D. F., & Fraleigh, M. J. (1987). The relation of parenting style to adolescent school performance. *Child Development, 56*, 326–341.

Downey, D. B., & Caldron, D. J. (2004). Playing well with others in kindergarten: The benefit of siblings at home. *Journal of Marriage and Family, 66*, 333–350.

Duncan, G. J., & Brooks-Gunn, J. (1997). Income effects across the life span: Integration and interpretation. In G. Duncan & J. Brooks-Gunn (Eds.), *Consequences of growing up poor* (pp. 596–610). New York: Russell Sage Foundation.

Duncan, G. J., & Magnuson, K. A. (2003). Off with Hollingshead: Socioeconomic resources, parenting, and child development. In M. H. Bornstein (Ed), *Socioeconomic status, parenting, and child development* (pp. 83–106). Mahwah, NJ: Lawrence Erlbaum.

Dunn, J. (2002). Sibling relationships. In P. K. Smith & C. H. Hart (Eds.), *Blackwell handbook of childhood social development* (pp. 223–237). Oxford: Blackwell.

Dunn, J., & Munn, P. (1985). Becoming a family member: Family conflict and the development of social understanding in the second year. *Child Development, 56*(2), 480–492.

Dunn, J., Stocker, C. M., & Plomin, R. (1990). Nonshared experiences within the family: Correlates of behavior problems in middle childhood. *Development and Psychopathology, 2*, 113–126.

Field, T., Widmayer, S., Adler, S., & De Cubas, M. (1990). Teenage parenting in different cultures, family constellations, and caregiving environments: Effects on infant development. *Infant Mental Health Journal, 11*(2), 158–174.

Gerard, J. M., Krishnakumar, A., & Buehler, C. (2006). Marital conflict, parent–child relations, and youth adjustment: A longitudinal investigation of spillover effects. *Journal of Family Issues, 27*(7), 951–975.

Gillespie, J. F. (2003). Social competency, adolescence. In T. P. Gullotta & M. Bloom (Eds.), *Encyclopedia of primary prevention and health promotion* (pp. 1004–1009). New York: Kluwer Academic/Plenum.

Gottfried, A. E., Gottfried, A. W., Bathurst, K., & Killian, C. (1999). Maternal and dual-earner employment: Family environment, adaptations, and the developmental impingement perspective. In M. E. Lamb (Ed.), *Parenting and child development in "nontraditional" families* (pp. 15–37). Mahwah, NJ: Lawrence Erlbaum.

Gray, M., & Steinberg, L. (1999). Adolescent romance and the parent-child relationship: A contextual perspective. In W. Furman, B. Brown, & C. Feiring (Eds.), *Contemporary perspectives on adolescent romantic relationships* (pp. 235–265). New York: Cambridge University Press.

Grolnick, W. S. (2003). *The psychology of parental control: How well-meant parenting backfires.* Mahwah, NJ: Lawrence Erlbaum.

Grych, J. H. (2005). Interparental conflict as a risk factor for child maladjustment. *Family Court Review, 43*(1), 97–108.

Grych, J. H., & Fincham, F. D. (2001). *Interparental conflict and child development: Theory, research, and applications.* New York: Cambridge University Press.

Han, W.-J., Waldfogel, J., & Brooks-Gunn, J. (2001). The effects of early maternal employment on later cognitive and behavioral outcomes. *Journal of Marriage and Family, 63*, 336–354.

Hanson, T. L. (1999). Does parental conflict explain why divorce is negatively associated with child welfare? *Social Forces, 77*, 1283–1316.

Hao, L., & Matsueda, R. (2006). Family dynamics through childhood: A sibling model of behavior problems. *Social Science Research, 35*(2), 500–524.

Harvey, E. (1999). Short-term and long-term effects of early parental employment on children of the National Longitudinal Survey of Youth. *Developmental Psychology, 35*, 445–459.

Hauser, S. T. (1999). Understanding resilient outcomes: Adolescent lives across time and generations. *Journal of Research on Adolescence, 9*, 1–24.

Haveman, R., Wolfe, B., & Spaulding, J. (1991). Childhood events and circumstances influencing high school completion. *Demography, 28*, 133–157.

Herman, M. R., Dornbusch, S. M., Herron, M. C., Herting, J. R. (1997). The influence of family regulation, connection, and psychology autonomy on six measures of adolescent functioning. *Journal of Adolescent Research, 12*(1), 34–67.

Hetherington, E. M., & Stanley-Hagen, M. (1999). The adjustment of children with divorced parents: A risk and resiliency perspective. *Journal of Child Psychology and Psychiatry, 40*, 129–140.

Hill, N. E., & Bush, K. R. (2001). Relationships between parenting environment and children's mental health among African American and European American mothers and children. *Journal of Marriage and the Family, 63*, 954–966.

Hill, N. E., Bush, K. R., & Roosa, M. R. (2003). Parenting and family socialization strategies and children's mental health: Low income, Mexican American and European American mothers and children. *Child Development, 74*(1), 189–204.

Hoffman, L. W. (2000). Maternal employment: Effects of social context. In R. D. Taylor & M. C. Wang (Eds.), *Resilience across contexts: Family, work, culture, and community* (pp. 147–176). Mahwah, NJ: Lawrence Erlbaum.

Ingoldsby, E. M., Shaw, D. S., Winslow, E., Schonberg, M., Gilliom, M., & Criss, M. M. (2006). Neighborhood disadvantage, parent-child conflict, neighborhood peer relationships, and early antisocial problem trajectories. *Journal of Abnormal Child Psychology, 34*(3), 303–319.

Inkeles, A. (1968). Society, social structure, and child socialization. In J. A. Clausen (Ed.), *Socialization and society* (pp. 73–129). Boston: Little, Brown.

Jekielek, S. M. (1998). Parental conflict, marital conflict and friendship networks. *Journal of Social and Personal Relationships, 9*, 219–935.

Karavasilis, L., Doyle, A. B., Markiewicz, D. (2003). Associations between parenting style and attachment to mother in middle childhood and adolescence. *International Journal of Behavioral Development, 27*(2), 153–164.

Kelly, J. B. (2000). Children's adjustment in conflicted marriages and divorce: A decade review of research. *Journal of American Academy of Child and Adolescent Psychiatry, 39*, 963–972.

Kelly, J. B. & Emery, R. E. (2003). Children's adjustment following divorce: Risk and resilience perspectives. *Family Relations: Interdisciplinary Journal of Applied Family Studies, 52*, 352–362.

Kerns, K. A., Aspelmeier, J. E., Gentzler, A. L., & Grabill, C. M. (2001). Parent–child attachment and monitoring in middle childhood. *Journal of Family Psychology, 15*(1), 69–81.

Kerns, K., Tomich, P., Aspelmeier, J., & Contreras, J. (2000). Attachment based assessments of parent–child relationships in middle childhood. *Developmental Psychology, 36*, 614–626.

Kohn, M. L. (1963). Social class and parent–child relationships: An interpretation. *American Journal of Sociology, 68*(4), 471–480.

Kohn, M. L. (1977). *Class and conformity: A study in values* (2nd ed.). Chicago: University of Chicago Press.

Kowal, A., Kramer, L., Krull, J. L., & Crick, N. R. (2002). Children's perceptions of the fairness of parental preferential treatment and their socioemotional well-being. *Journal of Family Psychology, 7*, 515–528.

Krishnakumar, A., & Buehler, C. (2000). Interparental conflict and parenting behaviors: A meta-analytic review. *Family Relations, 49*, 25–44.

Kuczynski, L. (2003). Beyond bidirectionality: Bilateral conceptual frameworks for understanding dynamics in parent–child relations. In L. Kuczynski (Ed.), *Handbook of dynamics in parent–child relations* (pp. 3–24). Thousand Oaks, CA: Sage.

Lau, S., & Cheung, P. C. (1987). Relations between Chinese adolescents' perceptions of parental control and organization and their perception of parental warmth. *Developmental Psychology, 23*, 726–729.

Lerner, R. M. (2002). *Concepts and theories of human development* (3rd ed.). Mahwah, NJ: Lawrence Erlbaum.

Leyendecker, B., Harwood, R. L., Comparini, L., & Yalcinkaya, A. (2005). Socioeconomic status, ethnicity, and parenting. In T. Luster & L. Okagaki (Eds.), *Parenting and ecological perspective: Monographs in parenting series* (pp. 319–342). Mahwah, NJ: Erlbaum.

Linver, M. R., & Silverberg, S. B. (1997). Maternal predictors of early adolescent achievement related outcomes. *Journal of Early Adolescence, 17*(3), 294–318.

Loeber, R., Farrington, D. P., Strouthamer-Loeber, M., Moffit, T. E., & Caspi, A. (1998). The development of male offending: Key findings from the first decade of the Pittsburgh youth study. *Studies on Crime and Crime Prevention, 7*, 141–171.

Maccoby, E. E., & Martin, J. A. (1983). Socialization in the context of the family: Parent–child interaction. In P. H. Mussen (Series Ed.) and M. E. Hetherington (Ed.), *Handbook of child psychology: Vol. 4. Socialization, personality, and social development* (pp. 1–101). New York: Wiley.

Makri-Botsari, E., & Makri, E. (2003). Maternal employment: Effects on her mental health and children's functional status. *Psychological Studies, 48*, 36–46.

McHale, S. M., & Crouter, A. C. (1996). The family contexts of children's sibling relationships. In G. H. Brody (Ed.), *Sibling relationships: Their causes and consequences* (pp. 173–196). Norwood, NJ: Ablex.

McHale, S. M., Crouter, A. C., McGuire, S. A., & Updegraff, K. A. (1995). Congruence between mother's and father's differential treatment of siblings. *Child Development, 66*, 116–128.

McHale, S. M., Updegraff, K. A., Jackson-Newsom, J., Tucker, C. J., & Crouter, A. C. (2000). When does parents' differential treatment have negative implications for siblings? *Social Development, 9*, 149–172.

McLoyd, V. C. (1998). Socioeconomic disadvantage and child development. *American Psychologist, 53*, 185–204.

Meyer, A. L. (2003). Risk-taking, adolescence. In T. P. Gullotta & M. Bloom (Eds.), *Encyclopedia of primary prevention and health promotion* (pp. 895–900). New York: Kluwer Academic/Plenum.

Minuchin, S. (1974). *Families and family therapy*. Cambridge MA: Harvard University Press.

Morrison, D. R., & Coiro, M. J. (1999). Parental conflict and marital disruption: Do children benefit when high conflict marriages are dissolved? *Journal of Marriage and Family, 61*, 626–637.

Muller, C. (1995). Maternal employment, parental involvement, and mathematics achievement among adolescents. *Journal of Marriage and Family, 57*(4), 85–100.

O'Conner, T. G., (2003). Vulnerability and resilience in children in divorced and remarried families. In R. M. Gupta & D. S. Parry-Gupta (Eds.), *Children and parents: Clinical issues for psychologists and psychiatrists* (pp. 180–206). London: Whurr.

Parsons, T., & Bales, R. (1955). *Family socialization and interaction process*. New York: Free Press.

Paterson, G. R. (1982). *A social learning approach: Vol. 3. Coercive family process*. Eugene, OR: Castalia.

Pearlin, L. I., & Kohn, M. L. (1966). Social class, occupation, and parental values: A cross-national study. *American Sociological Review, 31*(4), 466–479.

Peterson, G. W., & Bush, K. R. (2003). Parenting, adolescence. In T. P. Gullotta & M. Bloom (Eds.), *Encyclopedia of primary prevention and health promotion* (pp. 780–788). New York: Kluwer Academic/Plenum.

Peterson, G. W., & Hann, D. (1999). Socializing parents and children in families. In M. B. Sussman, S. K. Steinmetz, & G. W. Peterson (Eds.), *Handbook of marriage and the family* (pp. 327–370). New York: Plenum Press.

Peterson, G. W., & Leigh, G. K. (1990). The family and social competence in adolescence. In T. P. Gullotta, G. R. Adams, & R. Montemayor (Eds.). *Developing social competency in adolescence: Advances in adolescent development* (Vol. 3, pp. 97–138). Newbury Park, CA: Sage.

Pike, A., Coldwell, J., & Dunn, J. F. (2005). Sibling relationships in early/middle childhood: Links with individual adjustment. *Journal of Family Psychology, 19*(4), 523.

Raver, C. (2003). Does work pay psychologically as well as economically? The role of employment in predicting depressive symptoms and parenting among low-income families. *Child Development, 74*(6), 1720–1736.

Repetti, R. L., & Wood, J. (1997). Effects of daily stress at work on mothers' interactions with preschoolers. *Journal of Family Psychology, 11*, 90–108.

Richman, A. L., Miller, P. M., & Levine, R. A. (1992). Cultural and educational responsiveness in maternal responsiveness. *Developmental Psychology, 4*, 614–621.

Richman, N., Stevenson, J., & Graham, P. (1982). *Preschool to school: A behavioral study*. London: Academic Press.

Richmond, M. K., Stocker, C. M., & Rienks, S. L. (2005). Longitudinal associations between sibling relationship quality, parental differential treatment, and children's adjustment. *Journal of Family Psychology, 19*(4), 550–559.

Riggio, H. R. (2006). The adaptive response of families to maternal employment: Part II—Family perspectives. *American Behavioral Scientist, 49*(10), 1303–1309.

Rodgers, K. B., & Rose, H. A. (2002). Risk and resiliency factors among adolescents who experience marital transitions. *Journal of Marriage and family, 64*(4), 1024–1037.

Rutter, M (2002). Family influences on behavior and development: Challenges for the future. In J. P. McHale & W. S. Grolnick, (Eds.), *Retrospect and prospect in the psychological study of families* (pp. 321–351). Mahwah, NJ: Lawrence Erlbaum.

Sayer, L. C., Bianchi, S. M., & Robinson, J. P. (2004). Are parents investing less in children? Trends in mothers' and fathers' time with children. *American Journal of Sociology, 110*, 1–43.

Steinberg, L., Dornbusch, S. M., & Brown, B. B. (1992). Ethnic differences in adolescent achievement: An ecological perspective. *American Psychologist, 47*, 723–729.

Steinberg, L. D., Lamborn, S. D., Dornbusch, S. M., & Darling, N. (1992). Impact of parenting practices on adolescent achievement: Authoritative parenting, school involvement, and encouragement to succeed. *Child Development, 63*, 1266–1281.

Steinberg, L. D., Mounts, N. S., & Lamborn, S. D. (1991). Authoritative parenting and adolescent adjustment across varied ecological niches. *Journal of Research on Adolescence, 1*(1), 19–36.

Snyder, D. K., Klein, M. A., Gdowski, C. L., Faulstich, C., & LaCombe, J. (1988). Generalized dysfunction in clinic and nonclinic families: A comparative analysis. *Journal of Abnormal Child Psychology, 16*, 97–109.

Teachman, J. D. (2000). Diversity of family structure: Economic and social influences. In D. H. Demo, K. R. Allen, & M. A. Fine (Eds.), *Handbook of family diversity* (pp. 32–58). New York: Oxford University Press.

U.S. Bureau of the Census. (1999). *Statistical abstract of the United States 1999*. 119th edition. Washington, DC: U.S. Government Printing Office.

U.S. Bureau of Labor Statistics. (2001). *Statistical tables: Employment and the labor force*. Retrieved August 27, 2006, from: http://www.bls.gov/opub/rtaw/stattab2.htm

Vandell, D. L., & Ramanan, J. (1992). Effects of early and recent maternal employment on children from low-income families. *Child Development, 63*, 938–949.

Waldfogel, J., Han, W. J., & Brooks-Gunn, J. (2002). The effects of early maternal employment on child cognitive development. *Demography, 39*(2), 369–392.

Wekerle, C., & Wolfe, D. A. (1999). Dating violence in mid-adolescence: Theory, significance, and emerging prevention initiatives. *Clinical Psychology Review, 19*, 435–456.

Whitchurch, G. G., & Constantine, L. L. (1993). Systems theory. In P. G. Boss, W. J. Doherty, R., Larossa, W. R. Schumm, & S. K. Steinmetz (Eds.), *Source book of family theories and methods* (pp. 385–411). New York: Plenum Press.

Wilson, S. W., Peterson, G. W., & Wilson, P. (1993). The process of educational and occupational attainment of adolescent females from low-income, rural families. *Journal of Marriage and the Family, 55*, 158–175.

Wolchik, S. A., West, S. G., Westover, S., Sandler, I. N., Martin, A., Lustig, J., et al. (1993). The children of divorce parenting intervention: Outcome evaluation of an empirically-based program. *American Journal of Community Psychology, 21* 293–331.

Chapter Four

Ecological and Community Level Influences on Child Development

Jill Antonishak and N. Dickon Reppucci

Communities are a key social setting for the development of social and psychological wellness (Cowen, 1994), and yet they can be defined by social, political, geographic, or economic boundaries. For example, the terms *neighborhood* and *community* are often used interchangeably, but these two constructs are not synonymous. Neighborhoods are often described in terms of geographic boundaries and physical proximity (Aber & Nieto, 2000), while communities are traditionally defined as settings in which there are common connections, bonds, or attachments between people in them. For example, people who participate in an online support group may share more interests and created sense of community than those living on the same neighborhood block.

For the purposes of this chapter, we cast a wide net with our definition of community to capture the complex and intertwined ecological influences that create shared bonds and experiences that influence children. Child development is influenced by multiple proximal and distal contexts, and these contexts influence each other. Researchers in psychology and other disciplines have acknowledged the importance that multiple contexts can play in individual development, as evidenced by the increasing use of theoretical frameworks that incorporate multiple social settings as important contributors to development, such as Bronfenbrenner's (1979) ecological theory, transactional–ecological theory (Lynch & Cicchetti, 1998), and dynamic systems theory (Ford & Lerner, 1992). These theories advocate for a framework in which individual development is nested in the context of the family, neighborhoods, schools, and political, cultural, and societal milieus.

Felner and his colleagues (Felner, Kasak, Mulhall, & Flowers, 1997) have argued that the "community both defines the problem to be solved and tests the adequacy of the answer" (p. 527). If the problem is defined at an individual level, the solution would be remediated by individual methods, such as, counseling or medication. Yet research and interventions focusing solely on individual level factors are likely to miss the contribution of other contexts to the problem. Shinn and Toohey (2003) have labeled this the "context minimization error." Considering contextual influences can serve as a catalyst to help redefine the problem and suggest interventions that target either or both system-level and individual change.

We cast a wide net with our definition of *community* in an effort to present a wide range of factors; however, this approach limits our ability to be exhaustive. As community and developmental psychologists, we consider our role to highlight the necessity of considering social contexts and forces larger than individual and family level factors. Given that the remaining chapters of this book are focused on specific topics related to primary prevention, health promotion, and intervention, we provide information on the ways in which communities influence development, shape the definition of social problems, and impact the implementation and evaluation of prevention and intervention programs. First, we provide an overview of ecological analysis by focusing on the influence of social structures and social processes. We describe aspects of the community that enhance or inhibit healthy development and emphasize the importance of social capital and collective efficacy in promotion of community and child wellness and the risk factors associated with lack of community resources. Next, general systems theory has suggested two processes that represent particular challenges to researchers—multifinality and equifinality (Cicchetti, 1993; Cicchetti & Rogosch, 1996), particularly when examining problem behavior outcomes. We review the implications of these phenomena on the development of intervention programs. We also examine the theoretical and methodological challenges when focusing on community level influences. Since much of this book examines evidence-based programs to promote healthy development and prevent maladaptive behaviors, we conclude with a discussion of community conditions that facilitate the successful implementation of programs and the importance of community capacity.

ECOLOGICAL INFLUENCES ON DEVELOPMENT

Ecological theory emphasizes the importance of the development of individuals within embedded, interconnected contexts. We borrow from Kelly and colleagues' approach to ecological analysis (Kelly, Ryan, Altman, & Stelzner, 2000), which emphasizes two core components: (1) social structures and (2) social processes. *Social structures* are settings for social interactions and patterns of social exchange, and are nested within other social contexts. Moving from proximal to distal, these contexts include home environments, geographic residence, schools, churches, neighborhoods, parental work environments, social policies, economic and cultural forces. Although not an exhaustive list, these settings exemplify influences on child development above and beyond individual and family level constructs. For example, schools are situated within neighborhoods, which are embedded within cultural and economic contexts. Within the school setting there are multilevel influences, including individual child and teacher characteristics, classroom influences, and school culture that provide varying opportunities for interaction and patterns of social exchange.

Social processes are the activities within the various structures, as well as the interactions between them. The process component refers to the interactions that children have with other individuals and systems within their particular settings that occur on a regular basis. While most research focuses on individual level factors, such as the psychological, biological, and behavioral characteristics of children, there are structures and processes within communities that can serve as risk factors, which can increase the likelihood of problem outcomes (such as lack of community or institutional resources), or as protective factors, which can decrease the likelihood of a problem outcome or buffer the effect of a risk factor (such as presence of supportive adults).

Social structures are commonly included in the study of social phenomena. Although explicit characteristics of these structures may not be captured, researchers frequently include setting variables, such as type of geographic location (rural, urban) as covariates in quantitative analyses. However, processes are less frequently included in research designs, partly because of the difficulty of operationally defining process, but also because processes vary by structure and the interactions between process and structure often create complex phenomena. Yet, processes are essential in understanding how social structures influence the individual, and what promotes or inhibits positive development.

While many interventions are designed to prevent or change maladaptive trajectories, having a better understanding of the interplay between social structures and processes enhances the likelihood of creating contexts that foster healthy development. Utilizing an ecological perspective enables researchers to consider the multiple entry points for intervention. For example, reading skills can be researched at multiple levels. At the individual level, researchers can consider a child's cognitive abilities, skills, temperament, and family resources and support. At the systems level, they can focus on reading curriculums, teaching techniques and style, or classroom setting. Yet it is also important to examine how individual and system level factors interact with each other. How do children of specific abilities and skills learn with different teaching styles (e.g., do certain teaching styles work better for children with learning disabilities)? How does family support influence classroom level variables (e.g., do more involved parents shape availability of resources within the classroom)? These research questions involve examination of nested social structures and complex processes.

COMMUNITY LEVEL RISK AND PROTECTIVE FACTORS

Despite the amorphous nature of communities, research has demonstrated key community components that serve as risk and protective factors. Most community level protective factors are related to creating a psychological sense of community or feelings of belonging. We focus on social capital and collective efficacy as key protective factors for children because they enable communities to mobilize resources to protect children and promote healthy development, while a lack of economic and institutional resources serves as a risk factor for poor developmental outcomes.

Social Capital, Psychological Sense of Community, and Collective Efficacy

While physical capital is composed of the monetary and physical resources within a community or family, *social capital* represents the network of relationships and connections among individuals, and these relationships serve as social resources. Economists, policymakers, and sociologists tend to use the term *social capital* (Coleman, 1988), while community psychologists use the term *psychological sense of community* (PSC; Sarason, 1974). Represented broadly, these concepts can also be the nontangible assets within groups, such as academic achievement and connection to institutions (Coleman,

1988). Inherent in social capital/PSC is a process of reciprocity, in which relationships are mutually beneficial, fulfill members' needs, and offer a sense of social support and connections (McMillan & Chavis, 1986). Gorman-Smith, Tolan, and Henry (2000) found that supportive social processes protected youth from chronic delinquency compared to children from similar neighborhoods without social support. The protective nature of these relationships is likely to vary based on the presence and quality of social networks, and the degree of personal responsibility that residents assume within the neighborhood (Wilson, 1995). Hagan, MacMillan, and Wheaton (1996) found that when families move out of a community, it may be the loss of social capital/PSC that influences poor educational achievement outcomes and antisocial behavior. For some families, support and involvement from within the family may provide a buffer against the external stress and negative effects of the loss of community level social capital.

While school structural characteristics, such as school size or location, are often implicated in healthy development, school processes related to students', parents', teachers', and other personnel's sense of community may play a more important role. The sense of belonging and shared purpose that matters in neighborhoods also matters in schools (Roeser, Midgley, & Urdan, 1996). Theorists suggest that schools which emphasize the creation of a community of learning, set high academic standards, and give parents, teachers, and staff a role in governance may have stronger academic and social outcomes for students (Gruber & Trickett, 1986; Slavin et al., 1996; Trickett, McConahay, Phillips, & Ginter, 1985). For example, research has consistently confirmed that teachers' expectations of student abilities play a role in academic and social outcomes by creating self-fulfilling prophecies that perpetuate education inequalities. Instead, by focusing on targeting multiple abilities, cooperative learning can create an inclusive learning context and foster a sense of belonging for students, which has been linked to higher achievement (Weinstein, 2002; Weinstein, Gregory, & Strambler, 2004;).

Collective efficacy represents an important form of social capital within neighborhoods and communities. In communities with high collective efficacy, members are involved and have networks of mutual trust and shared norms, which translate into a collective sense of responsibility for the community. Residents are involved in community organizations and willing to intervene for the common good of the neighborhood. Collective efficacy represents more than just provision of social support. Increasing social support is a common intervention strategy (Weiss & Halpern, 1991). Although social support alone may be adequate in alleviating some family stressors, permanent change within a community is unlikely unless it is accompanied by a sense of empowerment and the building of collective efficacy, rather than dependency. Aspects of the community can often serve as what Kelly (1987) refers to as "activating qualities." These can be individuals, organizations, or events that serve as springboards for action. Community leaders or policymakers can mobilize the energy and enthusiasm of other community members to create change.

In neighborhoods with high collective efficacy, residents are more likely to monitor children and have lower rates of crime and community violence (Sampson, Raudenbush, & Earls, 1997). Parents in cohesive neighborhoods may be less restrictive toward their children because of the availability of neighborhood resources and high levels of neighborhood monitoring (Chavis and Wandersman, 1990). Although most work on collective efficacy has focused on communities with low socioeconomic resources, Luthar (2003) suggests that children from affluent neighborhoods may be at risk for problematic outcomes such as internalizing problems or substance use. Residents' relative indepen-dence and lack of a clear set of pressing issues within the community, such as gangs and drugs, may fail to activate a sense of collective efficacy.

Lack of Opportunity and Institutional Resources

Just as social capital and collective efficacy serve as protective factors, a lack of these characteristics presents a risk for healthy child development (Leventhal & Brooks-Gunn, 2000). Demographic characteristics of communities, such as racial composition and percentage of female-headed households, are often implicated in increasing risk for problem behaviors. A focus on individual characteristics, such as race or family level poverty, represents another example of the context minimization error (Shinn & Toohey, 2003), because these variables often mask the contributions of community characteristics (Leventhal & Brooks-Gunn, 2000). The majority of studies also examine demographic characteristics of residents, such as family level socioeconomic status (SES) as aggregate variables to represent neighborhood risk factors, and research has almost exclusively focused on low-income urban areas. As a result, we know very little about how communities may influence child development in rural, suburban, or high-income areas. Moreover, the focus on poor, urban areas presents a methodological challenge in untangling the effects of poverty and neighborhood and isolating causal variables from SES (Duncan & Raudenbush, 1999).

Interventions have also demonstrated that raising income alone may not be adequate to change developmental trajectories (Mayer, 1997; Yeung, Linver, & Brooks-Gunn, 2002), because the effects of family income go beyond the family level, and low SES families are often living in high stress, poor neighborhoods. Providing in-kind services that sup-port families, such as formal child care and after school programs, are likely to represent more meaningful change for families (Currie, 1997; Fuligni & Brooks-Gunn, 2000). One reason additional income alone may be unlikely to change trajectories for low-income families is because they reside in high poverty neighborhoods. A multilevel perspective is likely to be more appropriate for alleviating some of this stress. For example, the New Hope intervention program which provided job search assistance and a modest earn-ings supplement with health and childcare opportunities was more effective than just increasing family level income. The combination of multiple aspects was necessary to reduce parental stress and improve parent–child relations, which resulted in positive outcomes for children (Morris, 2002).

Although some communities have a high mobility rate for residents, it appears that the essential characteristics of a neighborhood are greater than the individuals living there (Aber, Gephart, Brooks-Gunn, and Connell, 1997). Usually, a set of values and beliefs exist in a neighborhood and remain stable, regardless of who is moving in or out. This is not to say that communities do not change; housing policies or employ-ment opportunities may alter a neighborhood and its values, but the effect of these shifts usually unfold slowly over time. Regardless, transient communities often lack social organization, which prevents the formation of social capital and collective efficacy. The factors that accompany social disorganization, such as vacant housing, neighborhood violence, or crime, can serve as risk factors for poor child outcomes.

A lack of community resources has also been linked to poor outcomes for children. Resources, or lack thereof, within a community often represent more important influences than family level SES. Spencer, McDermott, Burton, and Kochman (1997) examined the qualities of neighborhoods and crime rates and found that crime statistics were more closely related to poor institutional resources, such as poor housing quality or lack of social meeting places, than to individual family economic characteristics, such as single-parent households or family income.

The unemployment rate, frequency of vacant housing, inadequate health care, poor schools, population loss, and residential instability have all been linked to high rates of violent crime and delinquency, child maltreatment, antisocial behavior, and teenage pregnancy (Coulton, Korbin, Su, & Chow, 1995; Hill, Levermore, Twaite, and Jones, 1996). Youth from low-resource, chaotic communities are often more likely to witness community violence, which has been linked to anxiety and symptoms similar to post-traumatic stress disorder (Horn & Trickett, 1998), and is one of the strongest predictors of future use of violence (DuRant, Cadenhead, Pendergrast, Slavens, & Linder, 1994).

The stress and social isolation that often accompanies neighborhood poverty has been linked to several important developmental outcomes. While neighborhood poverty has been linked to rates of violence, it is not usually an isolated causal factor. Rather, when poverty is combined with economic and racial inequality, population density, frequency of vacant housing, and residential fluidity, this results in the creation of a socially disorganized setting, which fosters frustration and anger (Coulton et al., 1995; Hill, Soriano, Chen, & LaFromboise, 1994). Such communities tend to be unable to maintain positive social institutions, such as businesses and community interest groups (Furstenberg, 1993), which feeds into a cycle of worsening conditions.

A lack of employment opportunities or lack of voice in the decision-making process has also been linked to poor child outcomes. Steinberg, Catalano, and Dooley (1981) compared two urban areas and found child abuse was significantly related to changes in employment rates and opportunities for parents. Even controlling for neighborhood and individual risk factors, lack of community involvement and resources have been linked to poor outcomes. Caughy, O'Campo, and Brodsky (1999) found that mothers living in neighborhoods with poor institutional involvement (such as voting) and a limited number of resources (public agencies and health care facilities) were more likely to have higher rates of premature deliveries and low birth weights, even after controlling for individual level risk factors and neighborhood SES. Wilson (1995) suggests that poor environmental conditions in the neighborhood lead to feelings of isolation for families, which can lead to strained parenting and negative outcomes for children and youth.

Lack of resources in schools also plays a role in academic and social outcomes for children. The quality of school staff, such as the number of mental health professionals and teachers with advanced credentials represent invaluable resources. For example, Raudenbush and Willms (1991, 1995) found that student achievement was the result of individual characteristics, but also of teacher characteristics (e.g., previous experience and training) and school characteristics (e.g., size and community socioecomomic status). Tuerk (2005) found that by high school, performance on standardized tests in Virginia mandated by the federal No Child Left Behind Act was differentially related to quality of teachers, and less qualified teachers were more likely to be in schools in lower SES neighborhoods.

Similarly, low resource schools suffer from many of the same issues as low resource neighborhoods (violence, disorganization, student and staff fluidity). Overly focusing on individual academic ability in schools has been linked to declining value of education and achievement, while a focus on effort, expectations that all students can learn and master material, and improvement are more strongly related to less frustrated students who place higher value on learning (MacIver, Reuman, & Main, 1995).

In summary, research related to communities represents a challenge for researchers due to the complexity of modeling community level variables and effects. However, bolstering community level protective factors and encouraging social capital, as well as working to ameliorate the lack of resources in communities, represent important contexts for intervention.

PRINCIPLES OF SYSTEMS THEORY

The principle of *multifinality* suggests that a range of developmental outcomes is likely to occur from a given set of social structures and processes (Cicchetti & Rogosch, 1996), while the principle of *equifinality* stipulates that there are multiple pathways to the same outcome.

Multifinality

The same early experiences in childhood will not result in the same outcomes for all youth. For example, for some children, exposure to community violence may be a risk factor for perpetration of future violence and aggression (more externalizing behaviors), while for others exposure to the same level of violence may result in anxiety and depressive symptomology (internalizing behaviors) (Horn & Trickett, 1998).

Examining how early experiences result in different outcomes has given rise to the study of *resilience,* a process in which some children demonstrate adaptation and competence despite adverse developmental contexts (Luthar, 1993; Masten, Best, & Garmezy, 1990; Rutter, 1987). For example, not all children growing up in low resource neighborhoods will exhibit either internalizing or externalizing behaviors; many will be able to adapt and experience healthy developmental outcomes. Wyman, Cowen, Work, and Parker (1991) found that resilient children were more likely to have close caregiver–child relationships with consistent discipline practices, optimistic views of the future, and experience greater support from their extended family. Resilience processes are also strongly linked to emotional support from adults outside of the family (Werner, 1993).

The construct of resilience has garnered much attention, as have interventions designed to foster resilience in children. Because they are focused at individual level change, resilience promotion interventions can seem like quick and easy fixes for problems. Defining resilience as a static individual level construct often results in short-term, piecemeal programs designed to promote resiliency. The results of such programs targeting high-risk children are often disappointing because they focus only on individual level factors, rather than on how individual characteristics interact with social settings (Luthar & Cicchetti, 2000). Not surprisingly, attempts to empower children to be resilient in highly chaotic environments are likely to fail without coordinating efforts at the classroom, school, or community levels (Pianta & Walsh, 1998). Most researchers agree that resilience is a process, an interaction between individual characteristics and environmental factors, rather than a fixed temperamental characteristic or trait (Luthar & Cicchetti, 2000; Luthar, Cicchetti, & Becker, 2000; Masten, 1994). Resiliency programs that are likely to be the most successful appear to be those designed to create resiliency by promoting social structures at the community level (Luthar & Cicchetti, 2000).

Equifinality

Aggression and antisocial behaviors have been linked to a range of social influences and processes. Risk factors within families, schools, peer groups, neighborhoods, and media have all been implicated in the development of aggressive and antisocial trajectories. We provide brief examples of risk factors within these multiple levels with potential intervention strategies to demonstrate the multiplicity of social influences on a given pathway. This is not to say that any one of these risk factors is sufficient in it and of itself to cause aggressive and antisocial outcomes, but rather each may be one contributory factor among many.

Within the family context, Patterson and colleagues (1989) have suggested the development of antisocial behavior results from a coercive interaction cycle within families, with parental discipline representing one of the most powerful predictors of antisocial behavior. Coercive parenting styles, ineffective discipline, and lack of monitoring reinforce a cycle of problem behaviors in children, which often results in rejection by prosocial peers, academic difficulties, and amplifying psychopathology over time. Family level interventions designed to encourage consistent and positive parenting are likely to help prevent child aggression.

At the peer group level, Thornberry and Krohn (1997) postulate an interactional theory to explain peer effects on delinquency and drug use among adolescents, in which peers reinforce problem behaviors while providing a supportive context for such behavior. In middle childhood, both victims of aggression (e.g., Parker & Asher, 1987; Roecker Phelps, 2001; Schwartz, McFadyen-Ketchum, Dodge, Pettit, & Bates, 1998) and high status children (Hawley, 2002; Hawley & Little, 1999) are more likely to be physically aggressive, suggesting multiple peer processes supporting aggressive behavior. Peer-based interventions are relatively common for delinquent and problem behaviors among youth, but Dishion, McCord, and Poulin (1999) found iatrogenic effects for adolescents who had participated in a peer-based intervention focusing on problem-solving skills, peer support, and resisting negative influences. They found that the youths' rule-breaking talk, usually outside the actual treatment group, predicted an increase in problem behaviors. These findings suggest caution in the development of peer-based interventions, but do not rule out peers as an important prosocial influence. Interventions that give youth an opportunity to interact with positive peer models may have more positive effects by hindering or preventing aggressive outcomes. By providing information and support and modeling positive social behaviors, peers can serve as prosocial influences (Berndt, 1996). For example, Hudley and Graham (1993) found a reduction in aggressive boys' hostile attributions after participation in an intervention program that targeted both aggressive and nonaggressive boys. Programs in which socially rejected children are partnered with average or popular youth may increase the target child's likeability and protect him or her against victimization within the social network.

Within the school context, teacher or classroom structures and processes may be linked to aggressive outcomes. For example Kellam and colleagues (Kellam, Ling, Merisca, Brown, & Ialongo, 1998) found that after randomly assigning children to first grade classrooms, the classrooms differed in the level of aggression and that the degree of classroom aggression influenced children's trajectory of aggression into middle school. The investigators administered the Good Behavior Game intervention, designed to reduce aggressive and maladaptive behaviors through a reward system to teams of children, and found that this group level intervention influenced long-term individual effects on aggression, with reductions for the most aggressive boys by sixth grade.

At the neighborhood level, social disorganization and lack of social control contribute to antisocial and aggressive behavior. Families in high stress neighborhoods are likely to have less parental monitoring and more inconsistent parenting styles (Steinberg, Darling, & Fletcher, 1995). In highly chaotic, low-resource neighborhoods, children are more likely to witness community violence, which has been linked to higher rates of perpetration of violence (Horn & Trickett, 1998). Given this evidence, programs designed to increase social support and mobilize collective efficacy may have the potential to increase safety and social monitoring of neighborhood children

Media depicting violence and aggression have consistently been linked to perpetration of such acts (for reviews see Anderson et al., 2003; Huesmann, Moise-Titus, Podolski, & Eron, 2003). Exposure to violence and physical aggression primes aggression-related attitudes and behaviors. Each time a person is exposed to such media, it may create or tap into existing aggressive social scripts. With repeated exposure, children are likely to carry these detrimental social orientations into social interactions.

Each of the levels we have discussed represents an opportunity for intervention. At the family and individual level, parental and anger management skills training may be helpful in breaking the cycle. At the peer level, promotion of social skills may shield youth from the negative influence of peers. At the classroom level, interventions promoting cooperation and prosocial interactions appear likely to reduce aggressive actions between students. Reductions in portrayals of media violence or decreasing amount of time children view violent media are likely to reduce aggressive and violent outcomes.

Interventions are typically designed to intervene at one contextual level, but children navigate among multiple contexts each day, and often there is little coordination between systems. To understand community level changes that may result from community based interventions, researchers need to conduct setting level evaluations in order to elucidate how settings can promote healthy development. Such an evaluation strategy requires a shift away from solely examining individual level change (Tseng, Seidman, & Granger, 2005). The effectiveness of any intervention is likely to depend on the support (or lack thereof) in other contexts. The most successful interventions for antisocial and aggressive behavior in children, such as Family and Schools Together (FAST; McDonald et al., 1997) and Multisystemic Therapy (MST; Bourdin et al., 1995) programs, target multiple levels for intervention.

An ecological perspective suggests that an intervention at one level may have positive implications for other contexts. For example, what effect does a school-based intervention have on the surrounding community? Many school-based programs encourage parental involvement as a core component. If parents are more actively involved, they may also perceive greater social support and opportunities to build social networks and connections in the community. Moreover, parents may then be able to provide greater supervision of neighborhood activities and mobilize resources for community change as well. This may translate into social capital and a sense of collective efficacy; thus, the effects of a program started at one level may shape neighborhood resources in other contexts.

METHODOLOGICAL AND CONCEPTUAL CHALLENGES IN UNDERSTANDING THE INFLUENCE OF COMMUNITY

Determining unbiased community effects and causal relationships between community characteristics and child outcomes is complicated by potentially confounding variables (Duncan & Raudenbush, 1999) and multiple pathways of community influence. Communities can serve as direct influences on child development. For example, the availability of public spaces, such as playgrounds can affect child and parental patterns of social congregation and concentrated neighborhood disadvantage and instability have been directly linked to crime (e.g., Morenoff et al., 2001; Sampson et al., 1997). However, community variables represent complex social phenomena and frequently have indirect influences on development. For example, social policies rarely directly affect children, but they do influence contexts within which children are embedded (Yoshikawa & Hsueh, 2001). Time limits on receipt of welfare benefits require that parents find employment, and increased working hours are likely to play a large influence in parental stress and supervision and time spent in child care, all factors which influence child development. While government policies related to divorce, marriage, and birth control have little to do with changing family structure (Bane & Jargowsky, 1988), policies can improve the structures and process that influence families and children. For example, state childcare regulations mandate staff–child ratios in day care centers, which influence the quality of care within childcare settings (Philips, Howes, & Whitebook, 1992).

Community level factors may also serve to mediate or moderate individual, family, or other community characteristics (Boyce et al., 1998). Similarly, parenting styles may be differentially successful depending on the neighborhood (Steinberg, Darling, & Fletcher, 1995), and parents living in high-risk neighborhoods may adapt different strategies (Furstenberg, 1993). For some parents, the stress associated with high crime rates and disorganized neighborhoods could result in lower levels of parental monitoring, while for other parents, it may result in highly restrictive efforts to shield children from exposure to community stress. As an adaptive strategy, some parents may rely on other neighborhood parents as a protective resource, creating an extended social support network. These phenomena suggest the range of ways in which community level factors can serve as indirect influences on child development.

Researchers are faced with decisions about categorizing community contexts as either a single measure or constructing multivariate indices based on cumulative risk factors. Most likely, contexts both independently and jointly contribute to development, but research isolating these relationships is lacking. Cook, Herman, Phillips, and Settersten (2002) examined the effects of high-quality parenting, peer relationships, school, and neighborhoods, and found that independently, each had a relatively modest effect on child outcomes. The combination of all four contexts, however, resulted in a large effect size, suggesting an additive effect for contextual contributions. Youth in high-quality contexts were protected from risk, while low-quality contexts contributed to poor developmental outcomes. This study is particularly exemplary because it included processes within each of the contexts, rather than just structural variables.

Parental divorce represents an event in which there are independent and joint effects on development. While traditionally considered a family level and direct influence, divorce usually coincides with significant changes in social structures and processes beyond the family level. Divorce is likely to be accompanied by a residential move (or in the case of shared custody, the introduction of an additional neighborhood setting), changes in parental social support networks or employment status, and introduction to new peer groups. While studies often account for these factors as covariates in analyses, these contextual changes represent independent and interlinked influences on development and highlight the complexity of examining developmental issues from a multiple systems level.

While capturing direct, indirect, and joint influences on development represents a continuing challenge for research, new statistical and methodological advances have helped researchers better understand processes and influences. Methods, such as hierarchical linear modeling, allow for an analysis of nested contexts, as well as change within individuals or structures (see Raudenbush & Bryk, 2002 for a comprehensive review of this method). This approach has been particularly helpful in examining classroom or school effects because individual students are nested in classrooms (Bryk & Raudenbush, 1987), or classrooms situated in schools (e.g., Lee, 2000). Recent methodological and statistical advances have made modeling the complexity of transactional processes more feasible. Structural equation models enable researchers to examine the transactional processes and study changes within individuals and contexts (Collins & Sayer, 2001). For example, latent difference score models offer promising ways to examine how change within one context or individual affects changes within another context or individual (McArdle & Hamagami, 2001; Nesselroade & Ram, 2004).

Understanding these mechanisms and the interplay between an individual and the environment provides valuable information for designing interventions. Unfortunately there is little research examining the functional dynamics and organizational structures that may inhibit or promote healthy development because of the methodological and conceptual challenges these processes present. Just as communities have direct, indirect, and joint effects on development, interventions are likely to function in similar ways. Research on joint influences suggests that any intervention efforts must include multiple contexts of influence to strengthen setting congruence and to be well-coordinated for meaningful impact. Setting congruence is how well the values and social expectations within one setting match the surrounding influences for children. Children's developmental contexts, however, do not appear to be strongly related. Cook et al. (2002) found that the quality of children's peer group, family, school, and neighborhoods were only moderately correlated. Such findings suggest that children could have a supportive family environment and peer group, but still attend a disorganized school in a chaotic neighborhood. For example, while schools may provide the message that academics is critical, children often receive contradictory input from peer groups (Fordham & Ogbu, 1986; Luthar & McMahon, 1996). In sum, programs may not be as effective when targeting only one level, and can be strengthened by incorporating multiple processes (e.g., neighborhoods coupled with schools, peers coupled with families).

COMMUNITY AS A CONTEXT FOR INTERVENTION

The remaining chapters of this book examine what programs are likely to work and have evidence to support effectiveness. However, without accounting for community level variation and capacity in a new setting, programs are less likely to succeed. Problems often emerge when programs designed for one setting are transitioned into new settings. One of the biggest challenges for intervention research is extending programs that have demonstrated effectiveness into new communities (Miller & Shinn, 2005; Wandersman, 2003), which may have their own unique characteristics. Initial assessment of each community, a process often neglected by interventionists, should be a required part of the intervention. Although an intervention program may be tested in one community, questions regarding whether another community has the appropriate capacity to implement the program or the willingness to tailor the program to its resources and unique nature merit careful analysis. Capacity, in and of itself, is a multilevel context that represents variables that allow for the successful implementation of a program, such as individuals, organizations, infrastructure, and political and economic considerations. This capacity can facilitate or inhibit the implementation of any given program no matter how effective it has been elsewhere (for a review, see Chinman et al., 2005). Failing to consider how interventions interact with setting characteristics can be detrimental to determining program effectiveness, which requires a well-designed needs assessment and process evaluation of the unique circumstances within the community.

Communities must have adequate resources to implement a program that does not sacrifice program integrity. Failure to address basic community conditions will hamper successful programming. Homer and Milstein (2004) found that implementing programs in communities with inadequate resources *reinforced* community weaknesses. Some degree of community organization is necessary to ensure that the program not only has the resources for implementation, but also that basic needs are not compromised and are being met. For example, in schools where staff and student safety is compromised or a large percentage of the students come to school hungry every day will find that adding an intervention component to increase academic achievement is unlikely to be successful if these other needs are not being met.

Programs are unlikely to be successful without "community buy-in". Working with representatives of the larger community as well with the setting personnel increases the likelihood of buy-in and that the community has the capacity to appropriately adapt the program. This is an essential aspect of any intervention (Kelly et al., 2000). If communities fail to support the program, the program is unlikely to have adequate participation for meaningful change or to be implemented with fidelity. Communities may not buy-in to the program if it fails to coincide with the values of the community; for example, high school sex education programs that include discussion of condom use rather than abstinence only are unlikely to be acceptable in conservative communities, even though there is no data to support the idea that sexual behavior will increase (Rosario & Schrimshaw, 2006). Moreover, if teachers are running an intervention program, it is important to remember that they are nested in schools with differing social policies and cultures, and that teachers may differentially value the program. Kallestad and Olweus (2003) found more variation in the implementation of a bullying prevention program at the classroom than the school level, which could have resulted from different degrees of buy-in from teachers.

Considering community capacity is essential to any discussion of generalizability and transportability of existing evidence-based programs. Are basic needs being met? Is there a likelihood of participation? Is the intervention likely to be viewed as a replication of existing services? What is the likelihood of easily incorporating it into existing programs? Are staff and personnel appropriately trained? Is there invested leadership? Is the current organizational infrastructure adequate to implement the program? Will the culture of the surrounding community be accepting? All of these questions must be examined to ensure that the program is being implemented with fidelity. Without adequate answers, program success is more challenging.

CONCLUSION

In this chapter we highlighted the need to look beyond the individual and family level influences on child development. Children are embedded within multiple contexts of influences and are affected by social structures and social processes that cannot be ignored (Bronfenbrenner, 1979). Most successful interventions operate on multiple ecological levels. *Multilevel* interventions represent efforts to incorporate community influences, and programs targeting multiple contextual levels are strengthened by incorporating multiple processes. Researchers have found that comprehensive community-based programs are effective at alleviating multiple problem behaviors, such as delinquency (Tate, Reppucci, & Mulvey, 1995), cigarette smoking (Jason, Pokorny, Curie, & Townsend, 2002), and conduct disorder (Henggeler, Schoenwald, & Pickrel, 1995) to name but a few. These programs offer a promising opportunity for intervention and prevention of problem behaviors (see Reppucci, Woolard, & Fried, 1999; Wandersman and Florin, 2003). In summary, several key concepts are helpful for understanding how community influences development and the importance of considering systems level settings and processes in the design and implementation of prevention and intervention programs:

- Individual development is nested in the context of the family, neighborhoods, schools, and political, cultural, and societal milieus. Understanding the interplay between these social structures and processes of development is critical in understanding the creation of contexts to foster healthy development. Considering contextual influences can serve as a catalyst to help redefine the problem and suggest interventions that target either or both system level and individual change.
- Utilizing an ecological perspective broadens the entry points for intervention. While interventions are typically designed to intervene at one contextual level, children navigate among multiple contexts each day, and often there is little coordination between systems. The effectiveness of any intervention is likely to depend on the support (or lack thereof) in other contexts.
- The promotion of social assets, such as social capital and collective efficacy, is a meaningful intervention strategy that targets multiple poor developmental outcomes. While a lack of economic and institutional resources serve as a risk factor for children and families, facilitating social capital and collective efficacy enables communities to mobilize resources to protect children and promote healthy development.
- Programs are unlikely to be successful without an understanding of community

readiness and buy-in from key players. Assessing the assets and deficits within a community setting can ensure a smooth transition for the intervention efforts and increase likelihood of program success.

Community contexts represent important influences in the lives of children. The inclusion of both proximal and distal influences in research about child development, in conjunction with individual level characteristics, enhances our ability to understand the mechanisms that affect the development of problem behaviors and how to utilize the potential within the community to promote healthy development.

REFERENCES

Aber, J. L., Gephart, M., Brooks-Gunn, J., & Connell, J. (1997). Development in context: Implications for studying neighborhood effects. In J. Brooks-Gunn, G. Duncan, & J. L. Aber (Eds.), *Neighborhood poverty: Vol. 1. Context and consequences for children* (pp. 44–61). New York: Russell Sage Foundation.

Aber, M. S., & Nieto, M. (2000). Suggestions for the investigation of psychological wellness in the neighborhood context: Toward a pluralistic neighborhood theory. In D. Cicchetti, J. Rappaport, I. Sandler, & R. P. Weissberg (Eds.), *The promotion of wellness in children and adolescents* (pp. 185–219). Washington, D.C.: CWLA Press.

Anderson, C. A., Berkowitz, L., Donnerstein, E., Huesmann, L. R., Johnson, J., Linz, D., Malamuth, N., & Wartella, E. (2003). The influence of media violence on youth. *Psychological Science in the Public Interest, 4,* 81–110.

Bane, M. J., & Jargowsky, P. A. (1988). The links between government and family structure: What matters and what doesn't. In A. Cherlin (Ed.), *The changing American family and public policy* (pp. 219–261). Washington, D.C.: Urban Institute Press.

Berndt, T. J. (1996). Exploring the effects of friendship quality on social development. In W. M. Bukowski, A. F. Newcomb, & W. W. Hartup (Eds.), *The company they keep: Friendship in childhood and adolescence* (pp. 346–365). New York: Cambridge University Press.

Bourdin, C. M., Mann, B. J., Cone, L. T., Henggeler, S. W., Fucci, B. R., Blaske, D. M., et al. (1995). Multisystemic treatment of serious juvenile offenders: long-term prevention of criminality and violence. *Journal of Consulting and Clinical Psychology, 63,* 569–578.

Boyce, W. T., Frank, E., Jensen, P. S., Kessler, R. C., Nelson, C. A., & Steinberg, L. (1998). Social context in developmental psychopathology: Recommendations for future research from the MacArthur Network on Psychopathology and Development. *Development and Psychopathology, 10,* 143–164.

Bronfenbrenner, U. (1979). *The ecology of human development.* Cambridge, MA: Harvard University Press.

Bryk, A. S., & Raudenbush, S. W. (1987). Application of hierarchical linear models to assess change. *Psychological Bulletin, 101,* 147–158.

Caughy, M. O., O'Campo, P. J., & Brodsky, A. E. (1999). Neighborhoods, families, and children: Implications for policy and practice. *Journal of Community Psychology, 27,* 679–699.

Chavis, D. M., & Wandersman A. (1990). Sense of community in the urban environment: A catalyst for participation and community development. *American Journal of Community Psychology, 18,* 55–81.

Chinman, M., Hannah, G., Wandersman, A., Ebener, P., Hunter, S. B., Imm, P., et al. (2005). Developing a community science research agenda for building community capacity for effective preventive interventions. *American Journal of Community Psychology, 35,* 143–157.

Cicchetti, D. (1993). Developmental psychopathology: Reactions, reflections, projections. *Developmental Review, 13,* 471–502.

Cicchetti, D., & Rogosch, F. (1996). Equifinality and multi-finality in developmental psychopathology. *Development and Psychopathology, 8,* 597–600.

Coleman, J. (1988) Social capital in the creation of human capital. *American Journal of Sociology, 94,* 95–120.

Collins, L. M, & A. Sayer (2001). *Methods for the analysis of change.* Washington, D.C.: American Psychological Association.

Cook, T. D., Herman, M. R., Phillips, M., & Settersten, R. A. (2002). Some ways in which neighborhoods, nuclear families, friendship groups, and schools jointly affect changes in early adolescent development. *Child Development, 73,* 1283 1300.

Coulton, C., Korbin, J., Su, M., & Chow, J. (1995). Community level factors and child maltreatment rates. *Child Development, 66,* 1262–1276.

Cowen, E. (1994). The enhancement of psychological wellness: Challenges and opportunities. *American Journal of Community Psychology, 22,* 149–180.

Currie, J. (1997). Choosing among alternative programs for poor children. *The Future of Children, 7,* 113–131.

Dishion, T. J., McCord, J., & Poulin, F. (1999). When interventions harm: Peer groups and problem behavior. *American Psychologist, 54,* 755–764.

Duncan, G. J., & Raudenbush, S. W. (1999). Assessing the effects of context in studies of child and youth development. *Educational Psychologist, 34,* 29–41.

DuRant, R. H., Cadenhead, C., Pendergrast, R. A., Slavens, G., & Linder, C. W. (1994). Factors associated with the use of violence among urban black adolescents. *American Journal of Public Health, 84,* 612–617.

Felner, R. D., Kasak, D., Mulhall, P., & Flowers, N. (1997). The Project on High Performance Learning Communities: Applying the land-grant model to school reform. *Phi Delta Kappan, 78,* 520–527.

Ford, D. H., & Lerner, R. M. (1992). *Developmental system theory.* Thousand Oaks, CA: Sage.

Fordham, S., & Ogbu, J. U. (1986). Black students' school success: Coping with the burden of "acting white." *Urban Review, 18,* 176–206.

Fuligni, A. S., & Brooks-Gunn, J. (2000). The healthy development of young children: SES disparities, prevention strategies, and policy opportunities. In B. D. Smedley & S. L. Syme (Eds.), *Promoting health: Intervention strategies and behavioral research* (pp. 170–216). Washington, D.C.: National Academy of Sciences.

Furstenberg, F. F. (1993). How families manage risk and opportunity in dangerous neighborhoods. In W. J. Wilson (Ed.), *Sociology and the public agenda* (pp. 231–258). Newbury Park, CA: Sage.

Gorman-Smith, D., Tolan, P. H., & Henry, D. B. (2000). A developmental-ecological model of the relation of family functioning to patterns of delinquency. *Journal of Quantitative Criminology, 16,* 169–198.

Gruber, J., & Trickett, E. (1986). Can we empower others? The paradox of empowerment in the governing of an alternative public school. *American Journal of Community Psychology, 15,* 353–372.

Hagan, J., MacMillan, R., & Wheaton, B. (1996). New kid in town: Social capital and the lifecourse effects of family migration on children. *American Sociological Review, 61,* 368–385.

Hawley, P. H. (2002). Social dominance and prosocial and coercive strategies of resource control in preschoolers. *International Journal of Behavioral Development, 26,* 167–176.

Hawley, P. H., & Little, T. D. (1999). Winning some and losing some: A social relations approach to social dominance in toddlers. *Merrill-Palmer Quarterly, 45,* 185–214.

Henggeler, S. W., Schoenwald, S. K., & Pickrel, S. G. (1995). Multisystemic therapy: Bridging the gap between university- and community-based treatment. *Journal of Consulting and Clinical Psychology, 63,* 709–717.

Hill, H., Levermore, M., Twaite, J., & Jones, L. (1996). Exposure to community violence and social support as predictors of anxiety and social and emotional behavior among African American children. *Journal of Child and Family Studies, 5,* 399–414.

Hill, H. M., Soriano, F. I., Chen, S. A., & LaFromboise, T. D. (1994). Sociocultural factors in the etiology and prevention of violence among ethnic minority youth. In L. Eron, J. Gentry, & P. Schlegel (Eds.), *Reason to hope: A psychosocial perspective on violence and youth* (pp. 59–97). Washington, D.C.: American Psychological Association.

Homer, J., & Milstein, B. (2004) *Optimal decision making in a dynamic model of poor community health.* Proceedings of the 37th Hawaii International Conference on System Science; Big Island, Hawaii. Retrieved January 2006 from: http://csdl.computer.org/comp/proceedings/hicss/2004/2056/03/205630085a.pdf

Horn, J., & Trickett, P. (1998). Community violence and child development: A review of the research. In P. Trickett & C. Schellenbach (Eds.), *Violence against children in the family and the community* (pp. 103–138). Washington, D.C.: American Psychological Association.

Hudley, C., & Graham, S. (1993). An attributional intervention to reduce peer-directed aggression among African-American boys. *Child Development, 64,* 124–138.

Huesmann, L. R., Moise-Titus, J., Podolski, C. L., & Eron, L. D. (2003). Longitudinal relations between children's exposure to TV violence and their aggressive and violent behavior in young adulthood: 1977–1992. *Developmental Psychology, 39,* 201–221.

Jason, L. A., Pokorny, S. B., Curie, C. J., & Townsend, S. M. (2002). Introduction: Preventing youth access to tobacco. *Journal of Prevention & Intervention in the Community, 24,* 1–13.

Kallestad, J. H., & Olweus, D. (2003). Predicting teachers' and schools' implementation of the Olweus Bullying Prevention Program: A multilevel study. *Prevention and Treatment, 6,* 3–21.

Kellam, S. G., Ling, X., Merisca, R., Brown, C. H., & Ialongo, N. (1998). The effect of the level of aggression in the first grade classroom on the course and malleability of aggressive behavior into middle school. *Development and Psychopathology, 10,* 165–185.

Kelly, J. (1987). An ecological paradigm: Defining mental health consultations as a prevention service. In J. Kelly & R. Hess (Eds.), *The ecology of prevention: Illustrative mental health consultation* (pp. 1–36). Hillsdale, NJ: Erlbaum.

Kelly, J. G., Ryan, A. M., Altman, B. E., & Stelzner, S. (2000). Understanding and changing social systems: An ecological view. In J. Rappaport & E. Seidman (Eds.), *The handbook of community psychology* (pp. 133–159). New York: Plenum.

Lee, V. E., (2000). Using hierarchical linear modeling to study social contexts: The case of school effects. *Educational Psychologists, 35,* 125–141.

Leventhal, T., & Brooks-Gunn, J. (2000). The neighborhoods they live in: The effects of neighborhood residence on child and adolescent outcomes. *Psychological Bulletin, 126,* 309–337.

Luthar, S. S. (1993). Methodological and conceptual issues in research on child resilience. *Journal of Child Psychology and Psychiatry, 34,* 441–453.

Luthar, S. S. (2003). The culture of affluence: Psychological costs of material wealth. *Child Development, 74,* 1581–1593.

Luthar, S. S., & Cicchetti, D. (2000). The construct of resilience: Implications for interventions and social policies. *Development and Psychopathology, 12,* 857–885.

Luthar, S. S., Cicchetti, D., & Becker, B. (2000). The construct of resilience: A critical evaluation and guidelines for future work. *Child Development, 71,* 543–562.

Luthar, S. S., & McMahon, T. J. (1996). Peer reputation among inner-city adolescents: Structure and correlates. *Journal of Research on Adolescence, 6,* 581–603.

Lynch, M., & Cicchetti, D. (1998). An ecological–transactional analysis of children and contexts: The longitudinal interplay among child maltreatment, community violence, and children's symptomatology. *Development and Psychopathology, 10,* 235–257.

MacIver, D. J., Reuman, D. A., & Main, S. R. (1995). Social structuring of schools: Studying what is, illuminating what could be. *Annual Review of Psychology, 46,* 375–400.

Masten, A.S. (1994). Resilience in individual development: Successful adaptation despite risk and adversity. In M. Wang & E. Gordon (Eds.), *Risk and resilience in inner city America: Challenges and prospects* (pp. 3–25). Hillsdale, NJ: Erlbaum.

Masten, A. S., Best, K. M., & Garmezy, N. (1990). Resilience and development: Contributions from the study of children who overcome adversity. *Development and Psychopathology, 2,* 425–444.

Mayer, S. E. (1997). *What money can't buy: Family income and children's life chances.* Cambridge, MA: Harvard University Press.

McArdle, J. J., & Hamagami, F. (2001). Linear dynamic analyses of incomplete longitudinal data. In L. Collins & A. Sayer (Eds.), *Methods for the analysis of change* (pp. 137–176). Washington, D.C.: American Psychological Association.

McDonald, L., Billingham, S., Conrad, P., Morgan, A., Nina. O., & Payton, E. (1997). Families and schools together (FAST): Integrating community development with clinical strategy. *Families in Society, 78,* 140–155.

McMillan, D. W., & Chavis, D. M. (1986). Sense of community: A definition and theory. *American Journal of Community Psychology, 14,* 6–23.

Miller, R. L. & Shinn, M. (2005). Learning from communities: Overcoming difficulties in dissemination of prevention and promotion efforts. *American Journal of Community Psychology, 35,* 169–183.

Morenoff, J. Sampson, R. J., & Raudenbush, S. W. (2001). Neighborhood inequality, collective efficacy and the spatial dynamics of homicide. *Criminology, 39,* 517–560.

Morris, P. A. (2002). The effects of welfare reform policies on children. *Society for Research on Child Development Social Policy Report, 16,* 4–18.

Nesselroade, J. R. & Ram, N. (2004) Studying intraindividual variability: What we have learned that will help us understand lives in context. *Research in Human Development, 1,* 9–29.

Parker, J. G., & Asher, S. R. (1987). Peer relations and later personal adjustment: Are low-accepted children at risk? *Psychological Bulletin, 102,* 357–389.

Patterson, G. R., & Bank, L. (1989). Some amplifying mechanisms for pathologic processes in families. In M. R. Gunnar & E. Thelan (Eds.), *Systems and development: Minnesota symposium on child psychology* (Vol. 22, pp. 167–210). Hillsdale, NJ: Erlbaum.

Patterson, G. R., DeBaryshe, B. D., & Ramsey, E. (1989). A developmental perspective on antisocial behavior. *American Psychologist, 44,* 329–335.

Philips, D. A., Howes, C., & Whitebook, M. (1992). The social policy context of child care: Effects on quality. *American Journal of Community Psychology, 20,* 25–51.

Pianta, R. C. & Walsh, D. J. (1998). *High-risk children in schools: Constructing sustaining relationships.* New York: Routledge.

Raudenbush, S. W., & Bryk, A. S. (2002). *Hierarchical linear models: Applications and data analysis methods.* Thousand Oaks, CA: Sage.

Raudenbush, S. W., & Willms, J. D. (1991). *Pupils, classrooms, and schools: International studies of schooling from a multilevel perspective.* New York: Academic Press.

Raudenbush, S. W., & Willms, J. D. (1995). The estimation of school effects. *Journal of Educational and Behavioral Statistics, 20,* 307–335.

Reppucci, N. D., Woolard, J. L., & Fried, C. S. (1999). Social, community and preventive interventions. *Annual Review of Psychology, 50,* 387–418.

Roecker Phelps, C. E. (2001). Children's responses to overt and relational aggression. *Journal of Clinical Child Psychology, 30,* 240–252.

Roeser, R. W., Midgley, C. M., & Urdan, T. C. (1996). Perceptions of the school psychological environment and early adolescents' psychological and behavioral functioning in school: The mediating role of goals and belonging. *Journal of Educational Psychology, 88,* 408–422.

Rosario, M, & Schrimshaw, E. W. (2006). Sexual behavior among adolescents: The role of the family, school, and media in promoting sexual health. In K. Freeark & W. Davidson (Eds.), *The crisis in youth mental health: Critical issues and effective programs* (pp. 197–218). Westport, CT: Praeger.

Rutter, M. (1987). Psychosocial resilience and protective mechanisms. In J. Rolf, A. Masten, D. Cichetti, K. Nuechterlein, & S. Weintraub (Eds.), *Risk and protective factors in the development of psychopathology* (pp. 181–214). New York: Cambridge University Press.

Sampson, R. J., Raudenbush, S. W., & Earls, F. (1997). Neighborhoods and violent crime: A multilevel study of collective efficacy, *Science, 277,* 918–924.

Sarason, S.B. (1974). *The psychological sense of community: Prospects for a community psychology.* San Francisco: Jossey-Bass.

Schwartz, D., McFadyen-Ketchum, S. A., Dodge, K. A., Pettit, G. S., Bates, J. E. (1998). Peer group victimization as a predictor of children's behavior problems at home and in school. *Development and Psychopathology, 10,* 87–99.

Shinn, M., & Toohey, S. (2003). Community contexts of human welfare. *Annual Review of Psychology, 54,* 427–459.

Slavin, R. E., Madden, N. A., Dolan, L. J., Waski, B. A., Ross, S., Smith, L., & Dianda, M. (1996). Success for all: A summary of research. *Journal of Education for Students Placed at Risk, 1,* 41–76.

Spencer, M. B., McDermott, P., Burton, L., & Kochman, T. (1997). An alternative approach to assessing neighborhood effects on early adolescent achievement and problem behavior. In J. Brooks-Gunn, G. Duncan, & J. L. Aber (Eds.), *Neighborhood poverty: Vol. 2. Policy implications for studying neighborhoods* (pp. 145–163). New York: Russell Sage Foundation.

Steinberg, L, Catalano, R., & Dooley, D. (1981). Economic antecedents of child abuse and neglect. *Child Development, 52,* 260–267.

Steinberg, L., Darling, N., & Fletcher, A. (1995). Authoritative parenting and adolescent adjustment: An ecological journey. In P. Moen, G. H. Elder, & K. Luscher (Eds.). *Examining lives in context: Perspectives on the ecology of human development* (pp. 423–466). Washington, D.C.: American Psychological Association.

Tate, D. C., Reppucci, N. D., & Mulvey, E. P. (1995). Violent juvenile delinquents: Treatment effectiveness and implications for future action. *American Psychologist, 50,* 777–781.

Thornberry, T. P., & Krohn, M. D. (1997). Peers, drug use, and delinquency. In D. M. Stoff, J. Brieling, & J. D. Maser (Eds.), *Handbook of antisocial behavior* (pp. 218–233). New York: Wiley.

Trickett, E., McConahay, J., Phillips, D., & Ginter, M. (1985). Natural experiments and the educational context: The environment and effects of an alternative inner-city public school on adolescents. *American Journal of Community Psychology, 13,* 617–643.

Tseng, V., Seidman, E., & Granger, R. (2005). *A discussion of the field's current capacity for conducting group-level experiments to improve schools and other youth-serving organizations.* New York: W.T. Grant Foundation.

Tuerk, P. W. (2005). Research in the high-stakes era: Achievement, resources, and No Child Left Behind. *Psychological Science, 16,* 419–425.

Wandersman, A. (2003). Community science: Bridging the gap between science and practice with community-centered models. *American Journal of Community Psychology, 31,* 227–242.

Wandersman, A., & Florin, P. (2003). Community interventions and effective prevention. *American Psychologist, 58,* 441–448.

Weinstein, R. S. (2002). *Reaching higher: The power of expectations in schooling.* Cambridge, MA: Harvard University Press.

Weinstein, R. S., Gregory, A., & Strambler, M. J. (2004). Intractable self-fulfilling prophecies fifty years after Brown v. Board of Education. *American Psychologist, 59,* 511–520.

Weiss, H., & Halpern, R. (1991). *Community-based family support and education programs: Something old or something new?* New York: Columbia University School of Public Health, National Center for Children in Poverty.

Werner, E. (1993). Risk, resilience, and recovery: Perspectives from the Kauai Longitudinal Study. *Development and Psychopathology, 5*, 503–515.

Wilson, W. J. (1995). Jobless ghettos and the social outcome of youngsters. In P. Moen, G. Elder, & K. Luescher (Eds.), *Examining lives in context: Perspectives on the ecology of human development* (pp. 527–543). Washington, D.C.: American Psychological Association.

Wyman, P. A., Cowen, E. L., Work, W. C., & Parker, G. R. (1991). Developmental and family milieu correlates of resilience in urban children who have experienced major life stress. *American Journal of Community Psychology, 19,* 405–426.

Yeung, W. J., Linver, M, & Brooks-Gunn, J. (2002.) How money matters for young children's development: Parental investment and family processes. *Child Development, 73,* 1861–1879.

Yoshikawa, H., & Hsueh, J. (2001). Child development and public policy: Toward a dynamic systems perspective. *Child Development, 72*, 1887–1903.

Chapter Five

The Evidence Base for Treating Children's Mental Health Disorders

E. Wayne Holden and Elizabeth A. Holden

This chapter provides an overview of the evidence base for the psychosocial treatment of children's mental health disorders. This is a daunting task despite the fact that targeted approaches for addressing children's mental health problems are just over a century old—a relatively short period of time when one considers the lengthy history of general health care. During this period of time, however, multiple conceptual and theoretical models have emerged that have had a significant influence on the development of psychosocial treatment approaches, preventive interventions, and the preferred evidence upon which they are based.

Developments in the treatment of children's mental health disorders have often been driven by the dynamic tension between the constrained amount of scientific evidence available and the real world pressures of clinical decision making, rather than pure scientific advances and direct technology transfer to the field. This has resulted in a complex current day situation with divergent viewpoints on what constitutes evidence for specific treatment approaches (Drake, Latimer, Leff, McHugo, & Burns, 2004) and the relative roles of science and independent clinical decision making in determining which treatment approaches should be applied to specific problems and how the application of treatment approaches should evolve in the field (American Psychological Association, Presidential Task Force on Evidence-Based Practice, 2006).

Adding to the complexity of determining evidence for treatments has been significant advances in highly related areas such as diagnostic categories for children and adolescents (American Psychiatric Association, 1994), clearer understanding of the etiological underpinnings of child and adolescent disorders (Egger & Angold, 2006; Wilmshurst, 2005), and advances in psychiatric epidemiology that have underscored the high prevalence rates and attendant negative consequences of mental health disorders among youth (U.S. DHHS, 1999, 2001a). These advances have been driven largely by improved data collection and data analysis technologies that have helped to support the broadening of conceptual and theoretical perspectives from individually oriented approaches to family systems and eventually to social ecological models that fit well with broader public health perspectives. Accompanying these advances has been an expanding interest in prevention as well as the refinement of treatment approaches. This has resulted in the rapid development of a substantial literature base supporting the efficacy of specific psychosocial treatments for children and adolescents (American Psychological Association, Presidential Task Force on Evidence-Based Practice, 2006; Burns and Hoagwood, 2002, 2004; Hibbs & Jensen, 2005; Weisz, Jensen-Doss, & Hawley, 2006; Weisz, Sandler, Durlak, & Anton, 2005).

This chapter utilizes five different theoretical and conceptual frameworks for discussing the lens through which the evidence base for treating children's mental health disorders is viewed: psychodynamic and psychoanalytic; behavioral and cognitive-behavioral; family systems; social ecological approaches.; and public health approaches

PSYCHODYNAMIC AND PSYCHOANALYTIC MODELS

Psychoanalytic models initially emerged in the late 19th century and represent one of the oldest approaches to formally conducting psychotherapy in general, and specifically treating children (Fonagy, 2004). Psychoanalytic approaches yielded some of the initial published case studies that documented the successful psychosocial treatment of children with psychiatric disorders. These approaches target underlying psychodynamic constructs as the locus of treatment with changes in these constructs theoretically resulting in symptom reduction.

Psychoanalysis and the broader associated psychodynamic tradition were primarily developed within the context of clinical inquiry and observation. Theory and practice were developed and refined as a function of clinical observation and case description. During their initial development, rigorous research protocols were not used to test the efficacy of these approaches or to inform their development. This type of therapeutic approach was the predominant mode of intervention with children in the first half of the 20th century and variants of this approach continue to be practiced widely in clinical settings today.

Play therapy is currently the most frequently used psychodynamic approach to the treatment of children (Landreth, Sweeney, Ray, Homeyer, & Glover, 2005). This intensive form of treatment involves the establishment of a therapeutic relationship through nondirective play in which the child overtly projects his or her underlying conflicts. Within a nonjudgmental atmosphere, responses by the therapist serve to reinterpret these conflicts and reduce underlying emotional issues resulting in observable symptom reduction. This form of outpatient psychotherapy typically occurs on a regular basis and can be continued for a lengthy period of time. A popular variation of this approach termed filial therapy has been used to train and monitor parents as play therapists. Although popular in the field (Landreth et al., 2005) and still considered to be a viable treatment approach, play therapy has been criticized for its lack of development through systematic research. Randomized trials attesting to the efficacy of this intervention approach have been less routinely pursued than is the case with other approaches to treating children. In the past, much of the evidence for this intervention strategy rested on uncontrolled group studies and extensive case study reports that were rich with clinical information, but less useful in judging efficacy and effectiveness (Landreth et al., 2005).

The evidence base for those choosing to implement psychodynamic approaches such as play therapy has been primarily based upon clinical observation and accumulated clinical experience. Specific components of the approach were refined through clinical application and practice rather than transfer of research refined methods into the field. Much of the emphasis in this area is on nonspecific relationship components as essential to promoting therapeutic change. This experiential evidence base develops directly within the clinical context and avoids some of the problems associated with generalizing from potentially contrived research contexts to applied clinical settings. However, the lack of objective evaluation of these approaches through research protocols is problematic. The absence of evidence on the degree of improvement obtained from psychodynamic treatment and the maintenance of these changes across time has been the subject of criticism, making it difficult for clinicians to judge the effectiveness of their approaches and to make appropriate clinical decisions regarding the course or termination of therapy. This lack of information could result in longer than necessary courses of therapy with minimal progress in producing symptom reduction, overdependence upon the therapeutic relationship, or other potentially problematic side effects.

It is important to note that a review paper on the efficacy of play therapy with children (Bratton, Ray, Rhine, & Jones, 2005) used meta-analytic strategies to summarize the results of the controlled accumulated outcome literature, consisting of 43 published and 50 unpublished studies. Only studies with at least a pretest–posttest design and a control group were included, with approximately 70% of the studies reporting random assignment to groups. The overall treatment effect reported by this study was .80 (a large effect size) which is quite consistent with other meta-analytic reviews of child psychotherapy that included a broader set of intervention approaches such as cognitive-behavioral and behavioral therapies (Casey & Berman, 1985; Kazdin, Bass, Ayers, & Rodgers, 1990; Weisz, Weiss, Alicke, & Klotz, 1987; Weisz, Weiss, Han, Granger, & Morton, 1995). Larger effect sizes were associated with humanistic play therapy approaches as opposed to more directive play approaches and filial models that utilized parents as therapists. Effect sizes were not directly related to child characteristics such as presenting problems or demographics, although the mean age of the children treated in this review was lower than for other meta-analytic studies of child treatment approaches. Optimal effects were obtained in studies with 35 to 40 treatment sessions although treatment context and approach moderated this effect. The authors suggested that the evidence from the review should be used to advocate for changes in managed care policy to support longer durations and intensity of outpatient therapy. These data, however, can also be interpreted to indicate that play therapy may be inefficient relative to other forms of intervention for children requiring substantially more resources long term and lacking specific positive effects for individual disorder categories.

This meta-analytic review provides evidence that a significant number of studies have been completed on the efficacy of play therapy and its conclusions offer a number of data-based recommendations for conducting play therapy in the field. Active use of information from this research database is more consistent with other theoretical models underlying approaches to child therapy. It will be interesting to see how evidence like this will affect the developmental trajectory of play therapy as a treatment modality for children in the future. As discussed previously, one emerging trend is the development and testing of shorter term implementation of play therapy (Kaduson & Schaefer, 2006), which fits well with managed health care and concerns regarding the cost effectiveness of intervention packages. It is also important to determine the relative effectiveness of play therapy for different disorder categories (i.e., internalizing versus externalizing disorders). This will require more specific and targeted research protocols in the future.

BEHAVIORAL AND COGNITIVE-BEHAVIORAL APPROACHES

Behavioral and cognitive-behavioral approaches to the treatment of children's mental health disorders emerged initially from experimental psychology with a focus on observation and the application of learning theory to the understanding and modification of behavior. The initial application of this approach to children consisted of the use of operant and classical conditioning to address specific behavior problems (Lock, 2004). Over time, this developed into a comprehensive set of behavior change strategies commonly referred to as behavior modification, which had a significant impact on teacher training and classroom approaches as well as parent education (Lock, 2004). These types of intervention strategies, which create and maintain consistency in environmental contingencies operating on children's behavior, have remained a mainstay of this approach across time. The evidence base supporting these approaches ranges from experimental case studies to randomized clinical trials. The recent positive behavioral intervention and support movement (Gresham et al., 2004) that is rapidly being implemented in school settings is a popular outgrowth of this model.

Concerns regarding the generalization and maintenance of change associated with behavioral approaches and the emergence of cognitive science in the 1960s prompted the integration of cognitive and behavioral models. In addition to focusing on environmental contingencies, this more expanded approach includes a focus on identifying and modifying cognitive factors that may exert an influence on internal constructs as well as moderating observable behavior (Kazdin, 2004). From a theoretical perspective, this more comprehensive and integrated model based on expanded learning theory perspectives has allowed for a broader integration of factors influencing change and greatly expanded the potential targets for therapeutic interventions. This has resulted in a plethora of fully integrated and operationalized treatment packages which have been quite amenable to scientific research. In fact, reviews of child therapy outcome research indicate that the most extensive literature base is on cognitive-behavioral models (Burns & Hoagwood, 2002; Hibbs & Jensen, 2005; Weisz, Jensen, & McLeod, 2005). It also appears that, at least from a self-report perspective, cognitive-behavioral therapy is the most frequently practiced approach with children and adolescents in community settings (Walrath, Sheehan, Holden, Hernandez, & Blau, 2006). The evidence base for this approach is dependent upon research innovations for developing and modifying interventions and fairly rigorous ongoing assessment and monitoring protocols that are implemented concurrent with treatment in the field.

In practice, this approach begins with a fairly extensive behavioral and cognitive-behavioral assessment to identify factors that are maintaining problematic cognitions and behaviors that result in observable symptoms. Once conceptualized, these assessment results lead to the formulation of an intervention approach that often includes close monitoring and reassessment to determine if change has occurred in the expected direction and to identify modifications that need to be made in the intervention approach. A wide range of treatment packages have been developed for implementing cognitive-behavioral therapy with children and adolescents (Hibbs & Jensen, 2005).

For example, trauma focused cognitive-behavioral therapy (TF-CBT; Cohen, Mannarino, & Deblinger, 2006) is a well-recognized cognitive-behavioral approach to treating children who have experienced various forms of trauma. Although this approach is relatively systematized with training and support available through web-based education (http://www.tfcbt.musc.edu), it is applied in a flexible manner to meet the specific needs of children and their families. TF-CBT is a short term treatment that involves parent and child education about trauma, emotional identification, stress management, innovative methods for sharing and reliving traumatic experiences, cognitive modification, and more general parent education. Multiple, randomized controlled trials have been completed supporting the efficacy of this intervention method (Cohen, 2005; Cohen, Goodman, Brown, & Mannarino, 2004; Cohen, Mannarino, & Knudsen, 2005), and it has been adopted as a model program by the National Registry of Evidence-based Programs and Practices sponsored by the U.S. Substance Abuse and Mental Health Services Administration.

Cognitive-behavioral models are well suited to manualization which makes them excellent candidates for testing within research protocols such as randomized clinical trial designs, training both professionals and paraprofessionals, and dissemination into the field. The evidence base for this set of interventions is the research literature supplemented by ongoing assessment and observation during the application of treatment protocols. Effect sizes associated with behavioral and cognitive-behavioral interventions are large in meta-analytic reviews (Compton, March, Brent, Albano, Weersing, & Curry, 2004; Sukhodolsky, Kassinove, & Gorman, 2004; Weisz, Sandler, et al., 2005), and a wide range of literature is available for understanding factors that may need to be modified to enhance transportability into the field (Kendall & Choudhury, 2003).

FAMILY SYSTEMS THERAPIES

Family systems therapies broaden the conceptual–theoretical framework from the individual to include other family members. The focus here is on a complex set of the most powerful interpersonal relationships in a child or adolescent's life as the most important factor influencing development and maintaining maladaptive behavior. Symptomatic behavior in any one family member reflects underlying interpersonal and system dynamics that once corrected and changed should result in symptom reduction or complete alleviation of the presenting problem. Similar to the psychodynamic approach, initial work in this area was based primarily on clinical applications and development of therapeutic strategies in the field (Barker, 2006). Unlike behavioral and cognitive-behavioral approaches and more consistent with psychodynamic models, the scientific evidence base for family systems therapies followed the development of these models in the field.

By expanding significantly beyond the individual, the degree of conceptual complexity increased substantially with the emergence of family therapy. Rather than being based upon a well-articulated set of universal principles, theoretical models from a wide range of areas such as biology, information processing, and systems dynamics were used to guide the initial development of what has become a broad set of therapy approaches. Hence, family therapies are available that reflect varying foci of attention on underlying theoretical frameworks, mechanisms of change, and specific intervention strategies. Many of these approaches, such as behavioral family systems therapy (Wood, Piacentini, Southam-Gerow, Chu, & Sigman, 2006), have also incorporated other theories and models of individual behavior so that the individual therapy approaches described previously can be fully integrated into family systems interventions. In many community settings family therapy is the standard approach to addressing the problems that children and adolescents present for treatment, and various forms of individual therapy are applied as adjunct or secondary interventions within treatment plans. Given the broader focus on family members, this perspective has hastened attention on factors such as cultural competence (Chaiklin, 2006) and the empowerment of parents and youth as change agents (U.S. DHHS, New Freedom Commission on Mental Health, 2003).

Clinical application of this approach requires initial assessment of family dynamics and relationship parameters followed by the application of specific intervention strategies. Although the evidence base for evaluating change often focuses on improvement in the identified patient, underlying these changes are improvements in systems functioning that may be subtle and difficult to track. Observational methods are typically used to evaluate change although self-report and other report measures have been developed to evaluate family systems parameters. The typical length of treatment varies substantially depending upon the type of family therapy that is implemented and the degree of presenting problems that are being addressed.

Brief strategic family therapy (BSFT; Szapocznik & Williams, 2000; http://www.brief-strategic-family-therapy.com) is one example of the current evolution of family therapies. This approach has been developed since the mid-1970s based upon a careful scientific process with multiple randomized trials and other research studies supporting effectiveness. It has been adopted as an evidence based intervention and best practice that is being used in large federally sponsored trials to treat teenagers with substance abuse disorders (Szapocznik, Perez Vidal, Brickman, et al., 1988) and externalizing or conduct problems (Szapocznik, Robbins, Mitrani, et al., 2002). Systematic training and certification for therapists is an important part of the model, based upon an intensive and structured training approach and detailed observational feedback from videotaped therapy sessions. This model is based upon sequential staging as therapy unfolds and a series of principles that guide decision making for therapists. It is also a brief approach that fits well within the current managed mental health care system. In addition, it is one of the few outpatient therapy models that has targeted and actively considered the importance of cultural competence as an underlying concept that influences mechanisms of change and the applications of therapeutic principles (Santisteban, Suarez-Morales, Robbins, & Szapocznik, 2006; Soo-Hoo, 1999). Even more expanded application and use of BSFT is highly likely in the future given the importance of culture in addressing mental health disorders (U.S. DHHS, 2001b) and significant changes in population demography that are predicted to accelerate in the future.

Functional family therapy (FFT; http://www.fftinc.com) is another empirically supported phase based family therapy approach that is targeted toward families with teenagers who primarily display conduct disorder or substance abuse disorders (Onedera, 2006). This well-tested model incorporates a systematic training and implementation package with a model of integrated assessment and intervention across engagement-motivation, behavior change, and generalization phases. Utilizing evidence-based approaches, therapist skills are enhanced to reduce risk and enhance protective factors in families referred for services. This intervention approach has received recognition from multiple federal agencies addressing the needs of youth, especially those youth who are displaying delinquency problems and interacting with the juvenile justice system (Hinton, Sheperis, & Sims, 2003; Kashani, Jones, Bumby, & Thomas, 1999).

A substantial research base is now available on family therapy and the integration of family systems constructs into the child development literature. Family therapy appears to be an effective intervention for childhood emotional and behavioral disorders (Northey, Wells, Silverman, & Bailey, 2003), especially externalizing disorders and behavioral systems family therapy methods. Reviews that include meta-analytic findings (Dowden & Andrews, 2003) have provided support for the effectiveness of family therapy with populations of children who are involved in the juvenile justice system. Efficacy research is generally more advanced than research documenting the process of therapeutic change in family therapy (Heatherington, Friedlander, & Greenberg, 2005).

SOCIAL ECOLOGICAL APPROACHES

Social ecological approaches build upon the foundation created by the family systems movement to include broader environmental perspectives. The genesis of these approaches as applied to children can be traced to the seminal work of Bronfenbrenner (1977). His ecology of human development framework is often referred to as a concentric series of circles that begins with the individual and extends outwards to include the family, other organizational systems that directly influence children and families (e.g., day care, school, primary health care, church, other community groups), community level factors, and finally broader constructs such as culture and public policy. Interactions between these layers of the social ecological context are also included in this conceptual framework. This model has had a significant influence on expanding the conceptual and research base for children's development and concurrently on the development and application of approaches to mental health promotion and treatment.

The application of this model to the treatment of children's mental health disorders has occurred during an era where deinstitutionalization and broader changes in the health care system, such as managed care, have offered the opportunity for innovative community-based models. Stroul and Friedman (1986) applied this perspective to children with serious and chronic mental health disorders (frequently referred to as serious emotional disturbance). Since the mid-1980s, their systems of care framework has provided a template for reorganizing services in communities across multiple agencies involved in the child serving sector (i.e., mental health, child welfare, juvenile justice, substance abuse, education, and health care) to decrease fragmentation, improve efficiency, and produce improved outcomes. This generic set of system of care approaches is designed to involve multiple community members using traditional and nontraditional service delivery methods to produce service delivery systems that are child and family focused, culturally competent and competence based. Rather than being focused on specific disorders or sets of disorders, systems of care target children who are at risk for out of home placement and who often display complex, comorbid conditions. More recent evolution of these systems has focused on extending into early intervention and prevention services as well as treatment (Huang et al., 2005; Kutash, Duchnowski, & Friedman, 2005).

The systems of care approach has had a major and sustained impact on public policy, with substantial federal resources through the Comprehensive Community Mental Health Services for Children and their Families Program supporting the development of these programs across the United States (Holden et al., 2003; Holden, Stephens, & Santiago, 2005). Concurrently, child welfare, foundation, and state level funding have been provided to promote the reorganization of community-based services that follow the systems of care model. Accumulating scientific evidence for this type of approach, however, has been a daunting task over the last two decades. This is primarily a function of the fact that these very complex community-based models do not fit well within traditional research paradigms that are rooted in experimental, randomized clinical trial designs. Broader perspectives including quasi-experimental designs, qualitative approaches, and health services methods focused on analyzing data from community sources to understand the programmatic effects of policy changes (Epstein, Kutash & Duchnowski, 2005; Lyons, 2004; Pumariega & Winters, 2003) have been implemented to develop an understanding of these complex treatment approaches.

The Surgeon-General's Report on Mental Health (U.S. DHHS, 1999) concluded that this approach was promising, but that evidence for differential outcomes was lacking primarily as a result of the absence of significant differences in outcomes for children in systems of care as compared to treatment as usual reported in the Fort Bragg and Stark County studies (Bickman, Guthrie, et al., 1995; Bickman, Noser, & Summerfelt, 1999). More recent evidence (Stephens, Holden, & Hernandez, 2004; Stephens, Connor, et al., 2005) has provided support for the relationship between system of care principles in community settings and differential outcomes as well as differences in emotional and behavioral outcomes for children participating in systems of care as compared to treatment as usual in matched comparison communities. Significant reductions in juvenile justice recidivism (Foster, Qaseem, & Connor, 2004) and significant community costs offsets (Foster & Connor, 2005) have been documented.

An important and promising specific treatment approach that has developed in conjunction with the systems of care framework has been wraparound services (Bruns, Burchard, Suter, Leverentz-Brady, & Force, 2004; http://www.rtc.pdx.edu/nwi). The hallmark of this model is the use of child and family teams that include family members and representatives from other community support systems who work in a collaborative and coequal manner to fashion and implement comprehensive and strengths based plans for supporting children and adolescents with serious mental health disorders. A series of principles guides the conduct of this approach which is intended to leverage traditional, evidence-based interventions and nontraditional community supports in an innovative, strengths based fashion. Incremental data from the field have suggested that this is an effective approach for addressing the needs of children with the most severe and persistent mental health problems (Burchard, Bruns, & Burchard, 2002) and methods for evaluating fidelity to wraparound principles have been developed (Epstein, Nordness, et al., 2005; Bruns et al., 2004), yet randomized controlled trials of this approach are just now beginning after nearly 15 years of development in the field.

Multisystemic therapy has its roots in social ecological theory and has developed and proliferated concurrently with the systems of care framework (Henggeler, Schoenwald, Rowland, & Cunningham, 2002; Schoenwald & Rowland, 2002; http://www.mstservices.com). This model was developed as a result of careful, controlled and systematic research with multiple, randomized clinical trials attesting to its effectiveness (Curtis, Ronan, & Borduin, 2004; Henggeler, 2004). The targeted group for this intervention was initially adolescents with conduct problems that resulted in juvenile justice involvement (Schaeffer & Borduin, 2005). More recently, MST has been successfully applied to adolescents with comorbid substance abuse disorders and individuals at risk for psychiatric hospitalization (Curtis et al., 2004; Schoenwald & Rowland, 2002). Essentially, MST is based on a set of principles that guide the conduct of relatively short-term, comprehensive intervention plans that include the best available evidence based treatments and extend across the multiple systems that children participate in on a daily basis. One hallmark of MST is maintaining intervention fidelity which has resulted in extensive training, monitoring, and certification protocols designed to maintain integrity of the intervention in community settings. Fidelity to intervention has been documented as a critical factor promoting effectiveness of MST in community settings (Schoenwald, Sheidow, Letourneau, & Liao, 2003). This has produced an intervention approach that has become commercialized with training, monitoring, and rights to using the approach provided to private and public organizations on a cost basis. This treatment model has proliferated across most states and is being implemented in other countries (Ogden & Halliday-Boykins, 2004).

The successful use of the above interventions in community settings requires that clinicians adopt a program evaluation or total clinical outcomes management (TCOM; Lyons, 2004) perspective. In addition to typical individual assessment and outcomes data, adoption of this perspective requires collecting and analyzing information on intervention fidelity and evaluating the effectiveness of interventions on functioning in multiple community settings such as school, community organizations, juvenile justice programs, and child welfare programs (Schoenwald, Sheidow, & Letourneau, 2004). Programmatic concerns beyond the treatment of individual children and families heighten the need for aggregation of information at the group and program levels. Given this level of involvement in creating and sustaining a local evidence base, service delivery personnel will likely find themselves actively participating in crafting and implementing effective programs that enhance the development of children, adolescents, and their families. This can represent a substantial challenge for those who were trained in and have actively practiced therapies that are based upon more individually oriented theoretical models.

PUBLIC HEALTH MODELS

Public health approaches to the prevention and treatment of children's mental health disorders have received increased attention since the mid-1980s. This is due primarily to the recognition of a relatively high prevalence rate of children's mental health disorders in the United States (U.S. DHHS, 1999) and predictions that the prevalence of children's neuropsychiatric disorders will increase by 50% worldwide by 2025 (WHO, 2001). These statistics suggest that children's mental health disorders are at near epidemic proportions and that broad public health models are needed to accurately understand etiology and risk factors. In addition, these high prevalence rates indicate that multiple levels of prevention and treatment will be needed to effectively combat these problems in the future. Public health models offer a broader orientation for crafting and sustaining integrated service delivery systems within community settings that ensure healthy development and positive outcomes for all children and adolescents (Tolan & Dodge, 2005).

Utilizing epidemiology as its underlying scientific discipline, public health models seek to broadly understand the distribution of children's mental health disorders and the determinants of these disorders at multiple levels. This involves initially conducting cross-sectional research that employs sampling strategies to derive prevalence estimates that are generalizable to large populations. Once prevalence is determined, case control and longitudinal cohort studies are conducted to determine the incidence of cases and to identify risk and protective factors. Interventions that are constructed based on risk and protective factor models are eventually tested in the community through large scale effectiveness trials. In comprehensive approaches, these trials can involve universal interventions targeted to the population as a whole, selected interventions targeted to high risk populations and indicated interventions targeted to incident cases. Intervention strategies can be broad ranging and may vary from regulatory and policy changes to communication campaigns to interventions that directly alter health care practice.

Ongoing surveillance systems are often utilized to determine if incidence and prevalence are reduced by these intervention programs. Furthermore, program evaluation either on a local level or aggregated into national level data is frequently employed to monitor the implementation of intervention programs and to inform modifications that need to be made to enhance effectiveness.

The public health model is consistent with biopsychosocial perspectives on mental health disorders (Friedman et al., 2004; Holden & Black, 1999; Holden & Nitz, 1995) and allows for the simultaneous identification of multiple risk factors and exposures related to the incidence and prevalence of children's mental health conditions. Historically, most of the funding in the public health arena, however, has been directed toward conditions that contributed directly to mortality with less attention paid to those more prevalent conditions that create substantial morbidity across the lifespan (i.e., chronic mental health disorders, substance abuse, associated behavioral risk factors). Although behavioral risk factors have received more attention, particularly since the mid-1990s, the lack of investment in psychiatric epidemiology, particularly in the children's area, has resulted in an incomplete public health knowledge base. From a public health perspective, this has produced a more fragmented set of universal, selected, and indicated interventions than is optimal at the current point in time. On a broader level, this constrains the effectiveness of interventions to decrease the incidence and prevalence of disorders.

One might question why those involved in traditional clinical services provision with children should or would be concerned with the public health approach and concepts like prevalence and incidence of disorders. Are these issues so far removed from clinical practice settings that they constitute irrelevant evidence to consider in day-to-day decision making regarding practice approaches and the implementation of interventions? Perhaps it is a scientific obligation to understand those factors influencing the emergence and sustaining of epidemics within populations so that contextual factors can be included within individual treatment decision making. It might also be important to have a broad conceptualization of risk factors to identify early emerging problems and to promote the use of preventive interventions on universal and selected levels. In the past few years, some have argued that developmental epidemiology (Walker-Barnes, 2003) should be a core discipline underlying clinical interventions with children and that public health represents a much broader and potentially more effective model for conceptualizing the solutions to the current children's mental health epidemic (Holden & Blau, 2006). Indeed, many of the interventions that are initially formulated and tested within public health models eventually become standard clinical practice.

The Fast Track project (Conduct Problems Prevention Research Group, 1999a, 1999b; Greenberg, Lengua, Coie, Pinderhughes, & the Conduct Problems Prevention Research Group, 1999; http://www.fasttrackproject.org) is currently one of the best examples of a comprehensive, public health approach to addressing children's mental health.

As conceptualized in the early 1990s, the model focused on developing and testing a comprehensive set of selected and indicated interventions designed to prevent and treat conduct disorder in children.

Approximately 10,000 children were sampled and screened across four communities with 891 selected as being at high risk for conduct disorder and followed with high response rates across time. An adaptive intervention design and delivery model with multiple components was used within a complex multisite, multicohort design. Those in the intervention group participated in an intervention package with classroom, family, and individual child components designed to decrease risk factors and enhance protective factors in elementary school. Interventions during early adolescence were based upon individualized planning to promote strengths and reduce risks and included tutoring, mentoring, home visits, and involvement in community based programs. Significant positive differences in social, cognitive, and academic skills and decreased aggression and harsh discipline by parents have been reported (Nix, Pinderhughes, Bierman, Maples, & the Conduct Problems Prevention Research Group, 2005). It is anticipated that this study will provide substantial information on the prevention of conduct disorder and the development of youth as the sample is followed into adulthood.

THE FUTURE OF EVIDENCE IN CHILD BEHAVIORAL HEALTH

Given the rapid pace of change across multiple areas impacting upon children's services, it is almost certain that significant changes will occur over the next few years that will continue to transform the landscape of behavioral health services provision in community settings. Many of these changes are occurring at a broad level within health and human services systems and are driven by rapid advances in science and technology, implementation of public policy, and concerns regarding the costs and cost effectiveness of interventions. These changes will have implications for workforce training across child serving systems as well as for those with a more specialized focus on children's mental health in the future.

One of the most important recent scientific advances affecting health care has been in the area of genomics. Completion of the human genome project has resulted in the identification of marker genes that indicate risk for various diseases, and a broad constellation of genetic information that is now being used to predict differential responses to medical interventions (Collins, Green, Guttmacher, & Guyer, 2003; Guttmacher & Collins, 2005). We are now entering the age of personalized medicine where individual characteristics such as a genetic footprint will be increasingly relied upon to make decisions regarding the full spectrum of care from preventive interventions to full blown treatment protocols. Complex patterns of marker genes for those who are at risk for developing substance abuse disorders have already been identified (Foroud & Li, 1999; Foroud, Edenburg, Goate, et al., 2000), and it is conceivable that progress could accelerate in other disorder areas relevant to children's mental health. The initial impact of this work is most likely to occur in the development and application of pharmacotherapy for children's mental health disorders, resulting in much more finely tuned medications and pharmacotherapy protocols. This should accelerate our ability to integrate pharmacotherapy and psychosocial interventions in the future. It is conceivable that genetic markers could also be used to identify at-risk children who may benefit from early psychosocial interventions or genetic markers may be used to identify those who are more likely to respond to specific psychosocial interventions as part of their personalized health care.

The complex unfolding of genomics throughout health care raises significant ethical and humanistic issues. Gene–environment interactions ultimately determine the extent of phenotypical expression and an overemphasis on the use of sophisticated genotyping technology risks the effects of stigma and labeling as well as the inappropriate application of treatments that may not be necessary in the absence of clear environmental triggers. Advances in the use of genomics in mental health services will need to be approached cautiously with an appropriate appreciation for the evidence base underlying a very complex set of decision making processes and the humanistic–ethical context within which services are delivered.

The age of information technology has to a large extent benefited children's mental health. The volume and pace at which we can collect and analyze information to develop, implement, and understand the outcomes of psychosocial interventions has expanded exponentially, improving science as well as clinical application. Indeed, much of the discussion in the previous sections of this chapter documents our enhanced ability to collect, aggregate, and analyze information to support the scientific evidence base for interventions in children's mental health. Accompanying this explosion in information technology has been an increased emphasis on accountability, both at the levels of outcomes of clinical interventions and policy. These accountability standards will create pressure for systematization and documentation of effectiveness as well as efficacy of interventions. Comprehensive electronic health records linked with other electronic data systems in community settings will decrease fragmentation of service delivery in the future and allow for the accurate tracking of multiple indicators of health and development across the contexts that influence the day to day lives of children and adolescents. Fully linked and comprehensive management information systems in community settings that are accessible by families as well as professionals will provide real time information to coordinate packages of interventions, communicate effectively, and promote accurate decision making and a community evidence base for evaluating effectiveness.

Increased information technology has been accompanied by improved access in the general population to information for making informed decisions regarding health care. Security and confidentiality of health care records have improved with increased access to health care records for consumers. Direct consumer health care marketing has accelerated with a primary focus on pharmaceutical options, but also an emerging emphasis on psychosocial and preventive interventions. More informed consumers require a reconceptualization of the therapist–client relationship to focus on greater collaboration regarding the options that are available for therapeutic intervention, the application of these options, and the ultimate outcomes that are targeted from interventions. These trends are only likely to increase in the future with one outcome being that Internet access will provide the same access to health care information, technology, and personal data for professionals as well as families.

In addition, information technology has created areas such as telemedicine (Fortney, Pyne, Edlund, et al., 2006; Harper, 2006) that improves access to the best possible care for those in isolated, rural areas. In the past several years, we have begun to witness the use of therapeutic intervention packages through the Internet. For example, a family problem solving intervention delivered through the Internet was recently tested against an information only Internet condition for families whose children had experienced traumatic brain injury (Wade, Carey, & Wolfe, 2006). Significantly, less emotional distress and improved problem solving skills were found for the intervention group following this innovative treatment application. The use of the Internet for intervention delivery and support will accelerate in the future with more well-articulated and complex knowledge management and delivery systems.

Information technology has been used to link large networks of individuals together who are focusing on innovative approaches to specific problem areas in children's behavioral health. For example, the National Child Traumatic Stress Network (NCTSN) has utilized a web based system (http://www.ncstn.org) for linking together a national coordinating center, intervention development centers, and community treatment centers with the overall goal of improving the standard of care for children who have experienced trauma. This network provides access points for professionals and consumers to obtain information about trauma and cutting edge evidence based practices that are under development. More importantly, this system expands beyond information exchange to provide a mechanism for linking individuals and organizations into the network for ongoing dialogue and communication. Similar approaches are being used to improve the dissemination of information regarding the building of systems of care (http://www.systemsofcare.samhsa.gov) in community settings. Innovation and creativity in this area will accelerate in the future resulting in web based systems that provide even more sophisticated approaches to network development.

The future of interventions with children will likely rely increasingly on the use of frequent information technology interactions and less on the standard mode of in-person therapy sessions. This will improve the ability to implement and coordinate intervention strategies across community contexts and sectors that are involved in supporting the development of children. Specialized mental health interventions will be disseminated and implemented through the many community members who are invested in supporting children's development. Furthermore, in addition to rapid and extensive communication networks for supporting programs and intervention packages, the ability to collect, analyze, and respond to data about children's behavior and the outcomes of interventions will become a real time phenomenon. It is quite possible that in the not too distant future nanotechnology will create extremely small, personalized data collection systems that are fully linked with information networks to provide ongoing moment-to-moment health data (Ferrante, 2005; Heinzelmann, Lugn, & Kvedar, 2005). It is conceivable that behavioral health data could be collected with these systems. One of the implications for the mental health workforce is to understand the importance of integrating information technology and principles from communication science into the development of health promotion and treatment strategies.

Within the context of rapid and sometimes overwhelming scientific and information technology changes, it is important to consider more humanistic and interpersonal perspectives on the evidence base for the treatment of children's mental health disorders in the future. Nonspecific relationship factors have always been an important component of therapy approaches, and some have argued that they account for significantly more variance in outcomes with children than the specific strategies that are implemented (Karver, Handelsman, Fields, & Bickman, 2006; Shirk & Karver, 2003). Recent work in the area of therapeutic alliance suggests that the relationship between therapist and client may be the most important factor mediating successful outcomes (Kazdin, 2006). A balanced perspective in the future will continue to give equal weight to the importance of interpersonal relationships with trusted adults who provide guidance and mentoring within the health promotion and treatment interventions that are developed for children and adolescents. These issues are much more difficult to operationalize and place within a scientific paradigm that objectifies and categorizes evidence for decision making. They may never fit neatly within an increasingly data driven and technology efficient society, but will always occupy a central role in framing our viewpoints and approach to the difficulties that are confronted by children and adolescents.

Equally important related issues are our sensitivity to cultural differences on what constitutes evidence for appropriate and accepted interventions, our approach to how stigma influences the community's perceptions of and response to mental health disorders, and the continued empowerment of family members and youth themselves who often experience blame for their struggles and problems. Increasing globalization and multiculturalism, especially in the United States, suggests that nontraditional approaches such as transpersonal therapies and culture-specific approaches will receive greater attention at the services level and within the context of research regarding the development and application of mental health services.

One final note with respect to future trends relates to public policy regarding the support for and direction of children's mental health services. The costs basis for services has shifted from inpatient and residential services to community based services (Ringel & Sturm, 2001), and managed behavioral health care will continue to exert a significant influence on the funding for and development of integrated service delivery systems. A sustained focus on quality improvements in general health care prompted by Institute of Medicine reports on mortality linked to medical errors (Institute of Medicine [IOM], 1999, 2001) has resulted in a specific report on quality improvement in services for mental health and substance use disorders (IOM, 2005). This report provides a series of recommendations for improving safety, effectiveness, patient centered care, timeliness, efficiency, and the equitable nature of mental health services. The recommendations and agenda for change from this report are likely to spur advances in quality improvement at multiple levels that will affect the information that we focus upon in the future for determining the evidence for behavioral health interventions with children, adolescents and their families. This information will be integrated into federal policy that will impact both public sector and private sector organizations that are involved in the behavioral health care of children.

CONCLUSIONS

Behavioral health services for children have evolved substantially at the level of theory, application, and supporting evidence. The active use of multiple theoretical frameworks, intervention models, and experience-based as well as research-based evidence, has driven progress in this area. The remaining chapters in this book provide specific information on the current applications of interventions to disorder classes that can be used to address important questions regarding disorder specific safety, efficacy, effectiveness and equity. This greater level of specificity carries important weight in determining the outcome of current intervention decision making in addition to progress in developing new intervention strategies.

Sustained momentum in the future will ensure that innovations continue to occur that improve the effectiveness of services in community settings, ultimately reducing the unacceptably high prevalence rates and related negative consequences of chronic childhood mental health conditions. One hopes that the dynamic tensions between an increasingly information and technology based society and the more humanistic aspects of interpersonal interaction will combine to create an appreciation for utilizing broadly construed evidence to continually spur this momentum. Continued success will require broad community perspectives that not only provide the best possible care to individuals, but also transform care systems and the broader community context in which children develop. The transformation agenda (SAMHSA, U.S. DHHS, 2005) resulting from the reports by the President's New Freedom Commission on Mental Health (U.S. DHHS, New Freedom Commission on Mental Health, 2003) provides a template for comprehensively improving the mental health care system in the future. An enhanced evidence base is an important part of that agenda as well as innovative uses of information technology and a balanced humanistic perspective that fully includes family members in the transformational process (U.S. DHHS, New Freedom Commission on Mental Health, 2005a). Creating communities that provide direct access to the best possible screening, prevention, and treatment that is supported by theory, evidence, and stakeholder inclusion is the ultimate goal of this transformation effort in the future. Those who are actively involved in promoting children's mental health have both an opportunity and a responsibility to fully participate in this challenge as we continually refine and improve our approaches to improving the lives of children, adolescents, and their families.

REFERENCES

American Psychiatric Association. (1994). *Diagnostic and statistical manual for mental health disorders* (4th ed.). Washington, D.C.: Author.

American Psychological Association, Presidential Task Force on Evidence-Based Practice (2006). Evidence-based practice in psychology. *American Psychologist, 61*(4), 271–285.

Barker, P. (2006). Family therapy: An intimate history. *Journal of the Canadian Academy of Child and Adolescent Psychiatry, 15*(1), 40–41.

Bickman, L., Guthrie, P., Foster, E. M., Lambert, E. W., Summerfelt, W. T., Breda, C., et al. (1995). *Managed care in mental health: The Fort Bragg experiment.* New York: Plenum.

Bickman, L., Noser, K., & Summerfelt, W. T. (1999). Long-term effects of a system of care on children and adolescents. *Journal of Behavioral Health Services & Research, 26*(2), 185–202.

Bratton, S. C., Ray, D., Rhine, T., & Jones, L. (2005). The efficacy of play therapy with children: A meta-analytic review of treatment outcomes. *Professional Psychology: Research and Practice, 36*(4), 376–390.

Bronfenbrenner, U. (1977). Toward an experimental ecology of human development. *American Psychologist, 32*(7), 513–531.

Bruns, E. J., Burchard, J. D., Suter, J. C., Leverentz-Brady, K., & Force, M. M. (2004). Assessing fidelity to a community-based treatment for youth: The Wraparound Fidelity Index. *Journal of Emotional and Behavioral Disorders, 12*(2), 79–89.

Burchard, J. D., Bruns, E. J., & Burchard, S. N. (2002). The wraparound approach. In B. J. Burns & K. E. Hoagwood (Eds.), *Community treatment for youth: Evidence-based interventions for severe emotional and behavioral disorders.* New York: Oxford University Press.

Burns, B. J., & Hoagwood, K. E. (Eds.). (2002). *Community treatment for youth: Evidence-based interventions for severe emotional and behavioral disorders.* New York: Oxford University Press.

Burns, B. J., & Hoagwood, K. E. (Eds.). (2004). Evidence-based practice, Part I: Research update. *Child and Adolescent Psychiatric Clinics of North America, 13*(4).

Casey, R. J., & Berman, J. S. (1985). The outcome of psychotherapy with children. *Psychological Bulletin. 98*(2), 388–400.

Chalklin, H. (2006). Ethnicity and family therapy. *Journal of Nervous and Mental Disease, 194*(6), 458–459.

Cohen, J. A. (2005). Treating traumatized children: Current status and future directions. *Journal of Trauma and Dissociation, 6*(2), 109–121.

Cohen, J. A., Goodman, R. F., Brown, E. J., & Mannarino, A. (2004). Treatment of childhood traumatic Grief: Contributing to a newly emerging condition in the wake of community trauma. *Harvard Review of Psychiatry, 12*(4), 213–216.

Cohen, J. A., Mannarino, A. P., & Deblinger, E. (2006). *Treating trauma and traumatic grief in children and adolescents.* New York: Guilford.

Cohen, J. A., Mannarino, A. P., & Knudsen, K. (2005). Treating sexually abused children: 1 year follow-up of a randomized controlled trial. *Child Abuse and Neglect, 29*(2), 135–145.

Collins, F. S., Green, E. D., Guttmacher, A. E., & Guyer, M. S. (2003). A vision for the future of genomics research. *Nature, 422*, 1–13.

Compton, S. N., March, J. S., Brent, D., Albano, A. M., Weersing, V. R., & Curry, J. (2004). Cognitive-behavioral psychotherapy for anxiety and depressive disorders in children and adolescents: An evidence-based medicine review. *Journal of the American Academy of Child and Adolescent Psychiatry, 43*(8), 930–959.

Conduct Problems Prevention Research Group. (1999a). Initial impact of the Fast Track prevention trial for conduct problems: I. The high-risk sample. *Journal of Consulting and Clinical Psychology, 67*, 631–647.

Conduct Problems Prevention Research Group. (1999b). Initial impact of the Fast Track prevention trial for conduct problems: II. Classroom effects. *Journal of Consulting and Clinical Psychology, 67*, 648–657.

Curtis, N. M., Ronan, K. R., & Borduin, C. M. (2004). Multisystemic treatment: A meta-analysis of outcome studies. *Journal of Family Psychology, 18*, 411–419.

Dowden, C., & Andrews, D. A. (2003). Does family intervention work for delinquents: Results of a meta-analysis. *Canadian Journal of Criminology and Criminal Justice, 45*(3), 327–342.

Drake, R. E., Latimer, E. A., Leff, H. S., McHugo, G. J., & Burns, B. J. (2004). What is evidence? In B. J. Burns & K. E. Hoagwood (Eds.), Evidence-based practice, Part I: Research update. *Child and Adolescent Psychiatric Clinics of North America, 13*(4), 717–728.

Egger, H. L., & Angold, A. (2006). Common emotional and behavioral disorders in preschool children: Presentation, nosology, and epidemiology. *Journal of Child Psychology and Psychiatry, 47*(3–4), 313–337.

Epstein, M., Kutash, K., & Duchnowski, A. (Eds.). (2005). *Outcomes for children and youth with behavioral and emotional disorders and their families: Programs and evaluation best practices.* Austin, TX: Pro-Ed.

Epstein, M. H., Nordness, P. D., Gallagher, K., Nelson, J. R., Lewis, L., & Schrepf, S. (2005). School as the entry point: Assessing adhering to the basic tenets of the wraparound approach. *Behavioral Disorders, 30*(2), 85–93.

Ferrante, F. E. (2005). Evolving telemedicine/ehealth technology. *Telemedicine Journal and e-Health, 11*(3), 370–383.

Fonagy, P. (2004). Psychodynamic therapy with children. In H. Steiner (Ed.), *Handbook of mental health interventions in children and adolescents: An integrated developmental approach* (pp. 621–658). San Francisco: Jossey-Bass.

Foroud, T., Edenberg, H. J., Goate, A., Rice, J., Flury, L., Koller, D. L., et al. (2000). Alcoholism susceptibility loci: Confirmation studies in a replicate sample and further mapping. *Alcoholism: Clinical and Experimental Research, 24*, 933–945.

Foroud, T., & Li, T-K. (1999). Genetics of alcoholism: A review of recent studies in human and animal models. *The American Journal on Addictions, 8*(4), 261–278.

Fortney, J. C., Pyne, J. M., Edlund, M. J., Robinson, D. E., Mittal, D., & Henderson, K. L. (2006, January–February). Design and implementation of the Telemedicine-Enhanced Antidepressant Management Study. *General Hospital Psychiatry, 28*(1), 18–26.

Foster, E. M., & Connor, T. (2005). Public costs of better mental health services for children and adolescents. *Psychiatric Services, 56*(1), 50–55.

Foster, E. M., Qaseem, A., & Connor, T. (2004). Can better mental health services reduce the risk of juvenile justice system involvement? *American Journal of Public Health, 94*(5), 859–865.

Friedman, R. M., Best, K. A., Armstrong, M. I., Duchnowski, A. J., Evans, M. E., Hernandez, M., Hodges, S., & Kutash, K. (2004). Chhild mental health policy. In B. L. Levin, J. Petrila & K. Hennessy (Eds.), *Mental health services: A public health perspective* (pp. 129–153). New York: Oxford University Press.

Greenberg, M. L., Lengua, L. J., Coie, J., Pinderhughes, E. E., & the Conduct Problems Prevention Research Group. (1999). Predicting developmental outcomes at school entry using a multiple-risk model: Four American communities. *Developmental Psychology, 35*, 403–417.

Gresham, F. M., McIntyre, L. L., Olson-Tinker, H., Dolstra, L, McLaughlin, V., & Van, M. (2004). Relevance of functional behavioral assessment research for school-based interventions and positive behavioral support. *Research in Developmental Disabilities, 25*(1), 19–37.

Guttmacher, A. E., & Collins, F. S. (2005). Realizing the promise of genomics in biomedical research. *Journal of the American Medical Association, 294*, 1399–1402.

Harper, D. C. (2006). Telemedicine for children with disabilities. *Children's Health Care, 35*(1), 11–27.

Heatherington, L., Friedlander, M. L., & Greenberg, L. (2005). Change process research in couple and family therapy: Methodological challenges and opportunities. *Journal of Family Psychology, 19*(1), 18–27.

Heinzelmann, P. J., Lugn, N. E., & Kvedar, J. C. (2005). Telemedicine in the future. *Journal of Telemedicine and Telecare, 11*(8), 384–390.

Henggeler, S. W. (2004). Decreasing effects sizes for effectiveness studies—Implications for the transport of evidence-based treatments: Comment on Curtis, Ronan, and Borduin (2004). *Journal of Family Psychology, 18*, 420–423.

Henggeler, S. W., Schoenwald, S. K., Rowland, M. D., & Cunningham, P. B. (2002). *Serious emotional disturbance in children and adolescents: Multisystemic therapy.* New York: Guilford.

Hibbs, E. D., & Jensen, P. S. (Eds.). (2005). *Psychosocial treatments for child and adolescent disorders* (2nd ed.). Washington, D.C.: American Psychological Association.

Hinton, W. J., Sheperis, C., & Sims, P. (2003). Family-based approaches to juvenile delinquency: A review of the literature. *Family Journal: Counseling and Therapy for Couples and Families, 11*(2), 167–173.

Holden, E. W., & Black, M. M. (1999). Theory and concepts of prevention science as applied to clinical psychology. *Clinical Psychology Review, 19*(4), 391–401.

Holden, E. W., & Blau, G. N. (2006). An expanded perspective on children's mental health. *American Psychologist, 61*, 642–643.

Holden, E. W., & Nitz, K. (1995). Epidemiology of adolescent health disorders. In J. L. Wallander & L. J. Siegel (Eds.), *Adolescent health problems: Behavioral perspectives. Advances in pediatric psychology* (pp. 7–21). New York: Guilford.

Holden, E. W., Santiago, R. L., Manteuffel, B. A., Stephens, B. L., Soler, R., Liao, Q., et al. (2003). System of care demonstration projects: Innovation, evaluation and sustainability. In A. Pumariega & N. Winters (Eds.), *Handbook of community systems of care: The new child and adolescent community psychiatry* (pp. 432–458). San Francisco: Jossey-Bass.

Holden, E. W., Stephens, R. L., & Santiago, R. L. (2005). Methodological challenges in the national evaluation of the Comprehensive Community Mental Health Services for Children and Their Families Program. In R. G. Steele & M. C. Roberts (Eds.), *Handbook of mental health services for children, adolescents, and families: Issues in clinical child psychology* (pp. 387–401). New York: Kluwer Academic/Plenum.

Huang, L., Stroul, B., Friedman, R., Mrazek, P., Friesen, B., Pires, S., et al. (2005). Transforming mental health care for children and their families. *American Psychologist, 60*, 615–627.

Institute of Medicine (IOM). (1999). *To err is human.* Washington, D.C.: National Academies Press.

Institute of Medicine. (IOM). (2001). *Crossing the quality chasm: A new health system for the 21st century.* Washington, D.C.: National Academies Press.

Institute of Medicine (IOM). (2005). *Improving the quality of health care for mental and substance-use conditions.* Washington, D.C.: The National Academies Press.

Kaduson, H. G., & Schaefer, C. E. (Eds.). (2006). *Short term play therapy for children.* New York: Guilford.

Karver, M. S., Handelsman, J. B., Fields, S., & Bickman, L. (2006). Meta-analysis of therapeutic relationship variables in youth and family therapy: The evidence for different relationship variables in the child and adolescent treatment outcome literature. *Clinical Psychology Review, 26*(1), 50–65.

Kashani, J. H., Jones, M. R., Bumby, K. M., & Thomas, L. A. (1999). Youth violence: Psychsocial risk factors, treatment, prevention, and recommendations. *Journal of Emotional and Behavioral Disorders, 7*, 200–210.

Kazdin, A. E. (2004). Cognitive-behavior modification. In J. M. Wiener & M. K. Dulcan (Eds.), *The American psychiatric publishing textbook of child and adolescent psychiatry* (3rd ed., pp. 985–1006). Washington, D.C.: American Psychiatric Press.

Kazdin, A. E. (2006). Arbitrary metrics: Implications for identifying evidence-based treatments. *American Psychologist, 61*(1), 42–49.

Kazdin, A. E., Bass, D., Ayers, W. A., Rodgers, A. (1990). Empirical and clinical focus of child and adolescent psychotherapy research. *Journal of Consulting and Clinical Psychology, 58*(6), 729–740.

Kendall, P. C., & Choudhury, M. S. (2003). Children and adolescents in cognitive-behavioral therapy: Some past efforts and current advances and the challenges in our future. *Cognitive Therapy and Research, 27*(1), 89–104.

Kutash, K., Duchnowski, A. J., & Friedman, R. M. (2005). The system of care twenty years later. In M. Epstein, K. Kutash, & A. J. Duchnowski (Eds.), *Outcomes for children and youth with behavioral and emotional disorders and their families: Program and evaluation best practices* (2nd ed.). Austin, TX: Pro-Ed.

Landreth, G. L., Sweeney, D. S., Ray, D. C., Homeyer, L. E., & Glover, G. J. (2005). *Play therapy interventions with children's problems: Case studies with DSM-IV-TR diagnoses* (2nd ed.). New York: Jason Aronson.

Lock, J. (2004). Psychotherapy in children and adolescents: An overview. In H. Steiner (Ed.). *Handbook of mental health interventions in children and adolescents: An integrated developmental approach* (pp. 485–497). San Francisco: Jossey-Bass.

Lyons, J. S. (2004*). Redressing the emperor: Improving our children's mental health system*. Westport, CT: Praeger.

Nix, R. L., Pinderhughes, E. E., Bierman, K. L., Maples, J. J., & the Conduct Problems Prevention Research Group. (2005). Decoupling the relation between risk factors for conduct problems and the receipt of intervention services: Participation across multiple components of a prevention program. *American Journal of Community Psychology, 36,* 307–325.

Northey, W. F., Wells, K. C., Silverman, W. K., & Bailey, C. E. (2003). Childhood behavioral and emotional disorders. *Journal of Marital & Family Therapy, 29*(4), 523–545.

Ogden, T., & Halliday-Boykins, C. A. (2004). Multisystemic treatment of antisocial adolescents in Norway: Replication of clinical outcomes outside of the U.S. *Child and Adolescent Mental Health, 9*(2), 77–83.

Onedera, J. D. (2006). Functional family therapy: An interview with Dr. James Alexander. *Family Journal: Counseling and Therapy for Couples and Families, 14,* 306–311.

Pumariega, A. J., & Winters, N. C. (Eds.). (2003). *The handbook of child and adolescent systems of care.* San Francisco: Jossey-Bass.

Ringel, J. S., & Sturm, R. (2001). National estimates of mental health utilization and expenditures for children in 1998. *Journal of Behavioral Health Services & Research, 28*(3), 319–333.

Santisteban, D. A., Suarez-Morales, L., Robbins, M. S., & Szapocznik, J. (2006). Brief strategic family therapy: Lessons learned in efficacy research and challenges to blending research and practice. *Family Process, 45*(2), 259–271.

Schaeffer, C. M., & Borduin, C. M. (2005). Long-term follow-up to a randomized clinical trial of multisystemic therapy with serious and violent juvenile offenders. *Journal of Consulting and Clinical Psychology, 73,* 445–453.

Schoenwald, S. K., & Rowland, M. D. (2002). Multisystemic therapy. In B. J. Burns & K. E. Hoagwood (Eds.), *Community treatment for youth: Evidence-based interventions for severe emotional and behavioral disorders* (pp. 91–116). New York: Oxford University Press.

Schoenwald, S. K., Sheidow, A. J., & Letourneau, E. J. (2004). Toward effective quality assurance in evidence-based practice: Links between expert consultation, therapist fidelity and child outcomes. *Journal of Clinical Child and Adolescent Psychology, 33*(1), 94–104.

Schoenwald, S. K., Sheidow, A. J., Letourneau, E. J., & Liao, J. G. (2003). Transportability of multisystemic therapy: evidence for multi-level influences. *Mental Health Service Research, 5*(4), 223–239.

Shirk, S. R., & Karver, M. (2003). Prediction of treatment outcome from relationship variables in child and adolescent therapy: A meta-analytic review. *Journal of Consulting and Clinical Psychology, 71*(3), 452–464.

Soo-Hoo, T. (1999). Brief strategic family therapy with Chinese Americans. *American Journal of Family Therapy, 27*(2), 163–179.

Stephens, R. L., Holden, E. W., & Hernandez, M., (2004). System-of-care practice review scores as predictors of behavioral symptomatology and functional impairment. *Journal of Child and Family Studies, 13*(2), 179–191.

Stephens, R. L., Connor, T., Nguyen, H., Holden, E. W., Greenbaum, P. E., & Foster, E. M. (2005). The longitudinal comparison study of the national evaluation of the Comprehensive Community Mental Health Services for Children and their Families Program In M. Epstein, K. Kutash, & A. Duchnowski (Eds.), *Outcomes for children and youth with behavioral and emotional disorders and their families: Programs and evaluation best practices* (pp. 525–550). Austin, TX: Pro-Ed.

Stroul, B. A., & Friedman, R. M. (1986). *A system of care for children and youth with severe emotional disturbances* (Rev. ed.). Washington, D.C.: Georgetown University Child Development Center, CASSP Technical Assistance Center.

Sukhodolsky, D. G., Kassinove, H., & Gorman, B. S. (2004). Cognitive-behavioral therapy for anger in children and adolescents: A meta-analysis. *Aggression and Violent Behavior, 9*(3), 247–269.

Szapocznik, J., Perez Vidal, A., Brickman, A., Foote, F. H., Santisteban, D., Hervis, O. E. et al. (1988). Engaging adolescent drug abusers and their families into treatment: A strategic structural systems approach. *Journal of Consulting and Clinical Psychology, 56*(4), 552–557.

Szapocznik, J., Robbins, M. S., Mitrani, V. B., Santisteban, D., Hervis, O. E., & Williams, R. A. (2002). Brief strategic family therapy with behavior problem Hispanic youth. In F. Kaslow & J. Lebow (Eds.), *Comprehensive handbook of psychotherapy* (Vol. 4). Hoboken, NJ: Wiley.

Szapocznik, J., & Williams, R. A. (2000, June). Brief strategic family therapy: Twenty-five years of interplay among theory, research and practice in adolescent behavior problems and drug abuse. *Clinical Child and Family Psychology Review, 3*(2), 117–134.

Tolan, P. H., & Dodge, K. A. (2005). Children's mental health as a primary care and concern: A system for comprehensive support and service. *American Psychologist, 60,* 601–614.

U.S. Department of Health and Human Services, Office of the Surgeon-General. (1999). *Mental health: A report of the Surgeon-General.* Washington, D.C.: U.S. Government Printing Office.

U.S. Department of Health and Human Services, Office of the Surgeon-General. (2001a). *Youth violence: A report of the Surgeon-General.* Rockville, MD: Author.

U.S. Department of Health and Human Services, Office of the Surgeon-General. (2001b). *Mental health: Culture, race and ethnicity—A supplement to mental health: A report of the Surgeon-General.* Rockville, MD: Author.

U.S. Department of Health and Human Services, New Freedom Commission on Mental Health. (2003). *Achieving the promise: Transforming mental health care in America. Final report* (DHHS Pub. No. SMA-03-3832.). Rockville, MD: Author.

U.S. Department of Health and Human Services, New Freedom Commission on Mental Health (2005a). *Subcommittee on evidence-based practices: Background paper* (DHHS Pub. No. SMA-05-4007). Rockville, MD: Author.

U.S. Department of Health and Human Services, Substance Abuse and Mental Health Services Administration. (2005b). *Transforming mental health care in America. Federal action agenda: First steps* (DHHS Pub. No. SMA-05-4060). Rockville, MD: Author.

Wade, S. L., Carey, J., & Wolfe, C. R. (2006). An online family intervention to reduce parental distress following pediatric brain injury. *Journal of Consulting and Clinical Psychology, 74*(3), 445–454.

Walker-Barnes, C. J. (2003). Developmental epidemiology: The perfect partner for clinical practice. *Journal of Clinical Child and Adolescent Psychology, 32,* 181–186.

Walrath, C. M., Sheehan, A. K., Holden, E. W., Hernandez, M., & Blau, G. (2006). Evidence-based treatments in the field: a brief report on provider knowledge, implementation, and practice. *Journal of Behavioral Health Services Research, 33*(2), 244–253.

Weisz, J. R., Jensen, A. L., & McLeod, B. D. (2005). Development and dissemination of child and adolescent psychotherapies: Milestones, methods, and a new development-focused model In E. D. Hibbs & P. S. Jensen (Eds.), *Psychosocial treatment for child and adolescent disorders* (2nd ed., pp. 9–40). Washington, D.C.: American Psychological Association.

Weisz, J. R., Jensen-Doss, A., & Hawley, K. M. (2006). Evidence-based youth psychotherapies versus usual clinical care. *American Psychologist, 61,* 671–689.

Weisz, J. R., Sandler, I. N., Durlak, J. A., & Anton, B. S. (2005). Promoting and protecting youth mental health through evidence-based prevention and treatment. *American Psychologist, 60,* 628–648.

Weisz, J. R., Weiss, B., Alicke, M. D., & Klotz, M. L., (1987). Effectiveness of psychotherapy with children and adolescents: A meta-analysis for clinicians. *Journal of Consulting and Clinical Psychology, 55*(4), 542–549.

Weisz, J. R., Weiss, B, Han, S. S., Granger, D. A., & Morton, T. (1995). Effects of psychotherapy with children and adolescents revisited: A meta-analysis of treatment outcome studies. *Psychological Bulletin, 117,* 450–468.

Wilmshurst, L. (2005). *Essentials of child psychopathology.* Hoboken, NJ: Wiley.

Wood, J. J., Piacentini, J. C., Southam-Gerow, M., Chu, B. C., & Sigman, M. (2006). Family cognitive behavioral therapy for child anxiety disorders. *Journal of the American Academy of Child & Adolescent Psychiatry, 45*(3), 314–321.

World Health Organization. (2001). *The world health report 2001: Mental health: New understanding, new hope.* Geneva, Switzerland: World Health Organization.

Chapter Six

Principles and Approaches to Primary Prevention

Martin Bloom

INTRODUCTION

First, I want to share a "sense" of the nature of primary prevention. Nobel prize winner Barbara McClintock referred to this "sense," in relation to her biological field of study, as a sense of the organism, a feeling *for* and a feeling *into* the object of study so as to grasp its fundamental meaning (Keller, 1983). For me, that sense began with words by George Albee (2003, 2005), one of the founders of contemporary primary prevention. In the middle of a discussion Albee once said words to the effect that, "You can't stop an epidemic by treating one person at a time. Taking preventive actions before the epidemic occurs is the only way." I kept thinking about this point in relation to my graduate education and my then-current work that involved a research project where social workers treated one person at a time—so much time and effort, so few people served. There had to be another way to help large numbers of people and make use of the years of graduate education that I had been privileged to obtain. Albee's clear and simple statement was what I was looking for: "You can't stop an epidemic by treating one person at a time... [prevention]...is the only way." And so I began my own search in primary prevention. I would encourage the reader to be open to a similar watershed experience in her or his own life and career. It will be a fabulous moment of enlightenment.

Unfortunately, having these watershed insights does not prevent one from going overboard, loving the idea too much, and assuming that Jesus, Moses, Mohammed, and Buddha are sitting on one's shoulder nodding in agreement with one's righteous ideas. So make it tough love, make your ideas and practices show real success, not blind hope. As Hippocrates says, sitting on the other shoulder: Help if you can, but do no harm. And as Louis Pasteur said, "Nature favors the prepared mind."

THE SCIENTIFIC ENDEAVOR RELATED TO PRIMARY PREVENTION

Primary prevention is the term used for two different activities: One is a helping enterprise that takes place before a problem emerges, in contrast with various treatment and rehabilitation activities that deal with a problem after it has occurred, or after treatment has gone as far as it can go. The second is a scientific endeavor, which identifies what primary prevention means in general, and with regard to a specific helping enterprise. It offers general ways to evaluate primary prevention programs, and refers us to specific studies where the general terms are translated into specific programs. This chapter reflects both aspects, beginning with the scientific endeavor, including a discussion of core concepts, whole networks of concepts and propositions, and the growing empirical base for the application of these in helping practice, along with some ethical issues.

The contemporary use of the term *primary prevention* began within the public health and medical areas, and then expanded to include a wide range of domains such as education and social work where a predictable problem or concern could be addressed to prevent it from occurring, while at the same time, support for current states of health and healthy functioning could be provided. More recently, an equivalent effort is going into identifying desirable possibilities and taking suitable actions to have them come to be (Durlak, 2003). It is worth reviewing this history because different helping paradigms were involved in defining primary prevention, which have bedeviled the field.

Problems, according to the disease-medical model, involve a microorganism that causes specific pathologic changes that have characteristic signs visible through special instruments, and later symptoms visible to the patient, that go through sequential stages. Medical specialists are needed for treatment and cure, in relationship to a single passive patient, often involving the use of expensive procedures and medications (Mausner & Bahn, 1974). When the societal medical system does not provide for basic medical services for all citizens, then those with limited funds do not get basic medical services, to the detriment of the society as a whole.

A public health model emerged in order to expand the boundaries of possible causal factors, from biological–genetic ones ("causal agents"), to social and physical environmental factors ("environments"). It introduced the idea that victims ("hosts") may contribute to their own problems. Thus, a line of preventive action might be taken with any or all of these three factors, and new types of personnel might be involved in the solution, including parents, teachers, and the would-be client, who might be trained to deliver limited but useful services, rather then depending on an expert at the point when the problem has fully emerged (Leavell & Clark, 1953).

A third model emerged that did not assume, as the disease-medical and the public health models did, that there was a known causal agent which followed a clear developmental history. The sociocultural and social learning model recognized the complexity of life, where multiple causation and multiple teachers are the rule, and where no clear etiology or natural history is necessarily present (Albee & Joffe, 2004). There may not be any "underlying" condition, such as a twisted gene or a warped psyche or an immoral society that causes an individual to do as he or she does. What is "bad" behavior in one sociocultural context may be defined as "good" in another context. For example, "delinquent behavior" is viewed as "bad" by police and citizens at large, while it may be positive and status-enhancing behavior at the "street" level.

People are biological–genetic beings, but there is little that can be done after the fact of their birth at that level, except to prevent possible repeats of inherited pathological conditions through genetic counseling, or to structure the environment to minimize biological risk factors (Fishbein, 2000). This means that the role of biological–genetic research in practical human affairs is limited, even while this basic research may eventually have profound implications for future preventive or promotive procedures. For example, let's imagine that biological sciences one day permit us to select characteristics of our future offspring, their intelligence, physical features, gender, and the like. Can you imagine the mountain of related ethical and practical problems this would unleash? For several decades, China has had a "one child" rule for most of its citizens, except farmers, which has led to the demographic outcome of female infanticide. As the Chinese proverb suggests, be careful what you wish for because it may come true.

The social learning model offered many criticisms of the disease-medical model, especially when professionals sought "underlying" mental or social conditions in relationship to some psychological condition. Those who extended the disease-medical model into social affairs offered widely differing treatments, usually without empirical evidence that their technique worked any better than other methods or no treatment at all (Albee, 2003). Others criticized the importation of the medical model into social affairs, because it gave undue power and control to "experts" with little input from clients who wanted to be more active in their own situation. Class, gender, and cultural–ethnicity issues emerged to cause more confusion, with some groups getting more of expensive (but often ineffective) methods and others more of relatively less expensive (but about as ineffective) methods (Albee, 2005).

Few of these psychosocial and cultural factors fit into a disease-medical model; rather, a public health model, and later, a social learning model emerged that involved changes in the understanding of what causes mental or social problems. These factors included socioeconomic, cultural, and physical environmental forces and pressures that individuals incorporate into their being through social learning if they are aware of these factors, or by environmental pressures regardless of whether or not the host/ victims are aware.

There are two major implications of these public health and social learning models: first, if a potential problem is due to learning, then there ought to be ways to unlearn the problematic lesson and learn a healthy one instead, and to establish educational institutions that make positive lessons possible. Moreover, the "teachers" of these healthy (and unhealthy) lessons are local: parents, neighbors, teachers, among others. This means that there are several avenues by which to reach young children, through parents, teachers, ministers, and even TV or comic book characters. Indeed, the greater the number of helpful teachers available to deliver comparable messages, the more likely are children to learn and act on them. This is a basis for the optimism that seems to pervade professionals in the primary prevention field—working with well- functioning people and offering positive enhancing programs related to the strengths of these participants.

Second, if untoward environmental factors are the cause of problems, then it takes collective action, sometimes on an international level, to avert the problems. This is the basis for the pessimism that seems to pervade professionals in the primary prevention field. Solutions to problems, even empirically supported research on effective preventive–promotive solutions, are difficult to apply, collectively, in the real world. (Think about global warming and the resistance to facing known solutions.) And even when we have what we think are effective solutions, they are often not adopted in practice, in part because there is often no financial payoff to societal power brokers.

We have to remember that there are many "teachers" of unhealthful lessons as well; many sources of temptation for overeating, and the like; and every prevention–promotion program has to take into account the whole environment of forces pushing and pulling on people over the course of their development. Don't assume the game has ever ended, even if the score may be favorable to your side. Moreover, remember that every program has effects beyond itself, and oftentimes, these effects may be unexpected and unwelcome. For example, say you want to reduce cigarette smoking, a most preventable cause of premature death for hundreds of thousands of people. Good, now figure out how to prevent weight gain, possibly obesity, by former smokers (among others), another highly preventable cause of many serious illnesses and premature death.

This transition, especially in social and educational fields, has led to many changes in basic strategy, techniques, and the audiences involved. It was in this context that we offered a general definition of primary prevention, as well as an extended discussion of the terms (Gullotta & Bloom, 2003):

> Primary prevention as the promotion of health and the prevention of illness involves actions that help participants (or to facilitate participants to help themselves) (1) to prevent predictable and interrelated problems, (2) to protect existing states of health and healthy functioning, and (3) to promote psychosocial wellness for identified populations of people. These consist of (a) whole populations in which everyone requires certain basic utilities of life; (b) selected groups of people at risk or with potential; and (c) indicated subgroups at very high risk. Primary prevention may be facilitated by increasing individual, group, organizational, societal, cultural, and physical environmental strengths and resources, while simultaneously reducing the limitations and pressures from these same factors. (pp. 13–14)

We will discuss some of the basic issues involved in this definition of primary prevention. Every time primary prevention is defined all three elements have to be present—prevention, protection, and promotion—so that the bad guys don't slip in the back door just as we are locking the front door. We have made plans to involve all three aspects at the same time (even though different people and professions may be involved in cooperative efforts).

Time

Notice that the three forms of primary prevention (prevention, protection, and promotion) involve timed factors. We act to prevent and protect now so that some *future* untoward condition will not occur, which will be a difficult question for evaluation—how do we know that the problem would ever have occurred? One possibility is the random assignment from the same population to an experimental and a control group. If the problem happened to the untreated control group, and not to the treated experimental group, we have a basis for inferring causality of the treatment condition, all other things being equal.

We also act now to promote some positive condition that currently does not exist for the client. It is important to keep the promotion idea active because we not only have to prevent some problem from occurring; we also have to substitute something positive in its place. Otherwise, our clients will wander off looking for other forms of excitement (trouble).

There are some other important time considerations. When should we do all of this wondrous prevention work? There are arguments for doing it *far* in advance of the expected problem when the young client is more easily influenced and the forces opposing our prevention program are fewer in number. Or, should prevention programs be conducted *shortly before* the expected problem when the client is primed for some action, like a sex education program to be delivered shortly before puberty? There are some answers to these questions, based on empirical experience, but it is still a difficult matter when you are actually facing the situation. "What? Teach my 10-year-old about sexual intercourse, condoms, and the like? Sorry, I have to drive him to soccer practice; I have no time."

Other writers suggest that the best time to begin a prevention program is *shortly after* early manifestations of the problem emerge, because now we know quite exactly which persons will be victims and we can spend our limited money on those who will actually need it (Cowen, 1973). For example, working with obese children in school would be a form of preventive treatment, if these children actually were able to slim down and remain so into adulthood when life-threatening issues of obesity are likely to increase in severity.

TARGETS OF PREVENTIVE INTERVENTION

Since writing that encyclopedia definition, we have had the opportunity to study systems models more extensively and would add the following thoughts to the preceding definition. First, as ecologists and Buddhists note, everything in the world is connected with everything else, to a greater or lesser degree (reflected in our as-yet limited knowledge). Thus, to separate events and elements of the world so as to distinguish existing or potential problems, states of health, or future possibilities, may be an act of hubris in making distinctions that do not exist for the sake of a science and helping professions that seek to change what exists. Although our values may be in the "right" place—few preventionists have ever thought that what they were doing was anything less that the "right" thing to do—we are led to a second thought:

Every aspect of every primary preventive action contains some positive and some negative elements from the perspectives of the people involved—the recipients as well as the initiators. An important parallel dimension to helping, as I mentioned earlier (after Hippocrates) is to do no harm, even while one is seeking to help, if one can. This recognition of the complexity of life with its positive and negative elements for different people involved is not intended to paralyze workers in primary prevention, but simply to recognize that everything has an up- and a downside, if we observe closely enough. Primary prevention is thus an effort in trying to optimize the former, while minimizing the latter, at the same time as we are dealing with the interlocking cluster of slippery systems that are directly and indirectly affected by our actions.

WHO IS THE AUDIENCE FOR PRIMARY PREVENTION?

Another implication of systems thinking in connection with the term *primary prevention* involves the nature and size of its audience. Early definitions spoke of reducing the incidence of new cases of dysfunctional behavior (reflecting the medical and public health origins of primary prevention). In this sense, it was necessary to focus on populations at risk because this is where public health measures could be undertaken and empirical evidence for the reduction in incidence (and hence, "success" in helping) could be documented. However, it is more difficult to speak of an increased incidence of moral behavior, of interpersonal skills, of happiness, or of insight. Thus, we are led to rethinking what are appropriate audiences for preventive–promotive efforts.

Surely, incidence of medical and public health concerns remain important, and probably will be used as evidence to seek legislative appropriations in support of prevention programming. However, every population of people is engaged one by one. Vaccinate a thousand school pupils, but inject the medicine into the arms of children one by one, and observe the individual public reactions to the shot as well as the biochemical reactions in which each child brings his or her own life history into interaction with the vaccination. Moreover, notice the group character of reactions, as a norm of mild hysteria emerges in some classes of students, but not in others, thus initiating copycat responses. This leads us to suggest that with increasing knowledge of populations, groups, and individual reactions, it is becoming possible to consider customized preventive efforts that optimize the effectiveness of the intervention. As Gullotta (1994) wrote more than a decade ago:

> By equipping teachers, clergy, youth leaders, bartenders, hairdressers, media reporters, students, parents, friends, and others with the ability, skill, and knowledge to promote functional behaviors in themselves and others, prevention happens. (p. 7)

Prevention happens, one person at a time, in one group at a time, in one community at a time, but we have to recognize conceptually that all of these happen to 6 billion people in effect at the same time.

So, where does this leave us with regard to the specific question: Do we address primary prevention practices to large populations at risk (and with potential)? Or do we address specific subpopulations known to have a high incidence of a problem, or specific individuals who currently are showing signs of, or manifesting full-blown problems? It is cheaper to provide large numbers of people with inexpensive preventive devices, even though we do not know who will actually need them (think of ready condom availability to the entire population of teenagers), than delivering expensive treatments to a much smaller number of victims of the problem that has emerged in their lives. So everyone is the audience for primary prevention, whether individually, in groups, or as large populations taken as a whole. And everyone is involved, directly or indirectly, with the healthy functioning of these audiences. So if everyone is involved, then, sometimes, no one gets involved and goes to work to do what needs to be done. Primary prevention may be its own minefield.

If only the problem were as simple as even this statement leads one to believe. The ethical issues alone, of delivering condoms or any device to all members of some class are horrendous. Will giving youth with hormones operating in overdrive a handful of condoms push them into premature sex? The answer is no, in this instance; there is ample empirical evidence that this does not occur (Christopher, 1995). What would religious groups say? The answer is that there are many different religious groups, some of whom frown on any expression of sexuality in other-than married couples composed of one male and one female. Other religious groups are more practical in terms of sexual education and the availability of protective devices, although no religion purposely intends to put youth in harm's way.

In general, there are few good simple solutions to complex problems; on the other hand, there are some poor complex solutions to simple (and complex) problems. The question is how to distinguish the one from the other.

ACTIONS THAT COMPOSE PRIMARY PREVENTION

The problem here is that there are many words for the same action, and sometimes there are similar terms for different actions. Most basic are actions taken by individuals or groups to *promote* some positive target event, in contrast to those actions that seek to *obviate or forestall* other negative target events.

This basic definition means that prevention and protection belong to the obviating category, while promotion belongs to the promoting category, most of the time. I am sure you will think of exceptions. All right, I'll tell you one exception: What may be positive to one group may be negative to another. So which should it be called? The answer is to select a reference point, say the target group of persons, and use promotion or obviation from their point of view—if they have a collective point of view.

Interventions are the general class name for any actions in treatment, rehabilitation, or primary prevention. Unfortunately, researchers speak of treatment groups, meaning groups receiving planned interventions of some sort, including prevention, protection, or promotion. Live with it; the researchers are not going to change to suit us. Context will provide information on what they really mean to say.

Another sort of problem in talking about actions is that an action is a complex set of behaviors and events, and we should probably be thinking about the preponderant effect, and not assume that every element is in agreement with the whole. This helps to explain why seemingly perfect projects come up with some negative results.

Active and Passive Strategics

This important distinction largely addresses whether you intend to have the recipients of your service perform actions on their own behalf—this is the active strategy, like buckling a seat belt—or whether the action is performed on the recipients—a passive strategy, like having air bags that operate whether or not the driver performs some action to inflate them. Research has shown that passive strategies are more effective than active ones in achieving desired results (Robertson, 1986), which doesn't speak well for human beings in performing preventive/promotive acts. That said, look for passive strategies where possible, and fall back to active ones when necessary (Boyce & Geller, 2003).

ETHICS OF PRIMARY PREVENTION

There are many ethical issues in this field. Let's talk about a few of them. Suppose your would-be clients don't *want* your preventive/promotive services. Then what? Can you force them to be healthy, good, wise, educated, safe sexually, sober, unpregnant, svelte, happy, well-exercised, and the like? The answers are, of course, yes and no. Suppose your clients want to smoke and drink while they are pregnant. You know that there is a probability that these actions will harm the unborn child in serious and life-long ways. And you can try to convey this knowledge to a woman as clearly and forcefully as possible—while she stares at you as she puffs on a cigarette and happily swigs a bottle of beer. In immediate enjoyment versus long-term probability, enjoyment generally wins.

Or, take this ethical example; a sex worker plies his or her trade. A customer wishes a service without any protective device, and is willing to pay more for this act. You know that this increases the sex worker's chances of getting the life-threatening virus for AIDS, and in fact, there are some exact probabilities for this (Germain & Bloom, 1999):

> If the sexual partner is HIV seronegative, with no history of high-risk behavior, and uses condoms, then one sexual encounter leads to a 1 in 5 billion risk of contracting AIDS. However, if the sexual partner's HIV serostatus is unknown but the person is in a high risk group (such as homosexual men, intravenous drug users, etc.) and does not use condoms, than the risk increases dramatically to 1 in 50,000 encounters.
>
> If the sexual partner is HIV seropositive and does not use condoms, then if there are 500 sexual encounters, the risk of contracting AIDS is 2 in 3. (pp. 25–26)

So, professionally and ethically, what should you do with regard to your sex worker client? One issue for the sex worker is a sustainable livelihood versus a safe and healthy life. Another issue is the power contest between the paying customer (usually male), and the fee-for-service worker (usually female). Is having (paid) sex an organic release or a power ploy that deprecates the sex worker? If these questions are disquieting, then consider a job in a less hectic, less pressuring field, like traders of stock futures or sky divers.

The multiple implications of these issues highlight the complexity of making any ethical decision regarding human affairs, because every action affects events in unpredictable ways far beyond the immediate situation, some of which may be harmful. But as Hippocrates said, help if you can. I would add that we can't be paralyzed into inaction by a future unknown harm; we have to act on a preponderant good over an unknown evil, while taking due precautions to address problems, should any arise. Back to the personal versus professional values issues: There are two sides to this issue at least. The first is when the helping professional has strong values that run counter to the actions of clients. It is hard to keep one's perspective and honor the client's wishes, when the helper is convinced that these wishes are wrong, harmful, and the like. Fortunately, helpers in primary prevention have a number of options. Remember the host, agent, environment trilogy in public health where action with any of the three may help to prevent predictable problems and promote desired ends—to help clients, directly or indirectly—so it becomes more nearly possible to act on one's values. For example, professionals who personally hate the idea of abortions should be active in preventive education on sexual health long before the issue of abortions ever surfaces. Given that more than 90% of people will eventually be sexually active, and that there is evidence that sex education does not drive young people into having sex, doesn't it make good sense to teach them about this as young children along with the responsibilities for all of their actions, sexual and otherwise? All right, this may make sense, but is it equally axiomatic that schools should do the teaching, rather than parents? Everything in values is fuzzy, and if you think you absolutely know the right, good, and true answer, a little humility would be suggested.

The second issue related to personal and professional values is when the helper is too strongly convinced of the rightness of his or her preventive–promotive position. This kind of professional helper is often parodied in the popular literature and arts as not listening to what would-be clients want, can accept, and are willing to perform. Stereotypes invade the professions whenever helpers think that "these people" are not capable of controlling their own behavior, let alone raising children adequately (i.e., according to my suggestions). With such opinions, we may gloss over gaps in our knowledge, assert more that we can defend (if asked), and feel good—when we should be worried about the outcomes of our preventive interventions.

In general, ethical issues occur continuously, whenever helping professionals seek to make changes in the lives or circumstances of others, however benignly and humanely the service is offered. The issues may be momentous; they may also be subtle. We have to be on the lookout for these issues in every plan we make and every action we take, as these valued perspectives may bias the direction of our prevention program in ways that are untoward.

Primary prevention can be proud of its record of achievements, especially in documentation of cost–benefit analyses across many areas, from the wearing of seat belts, condoms, and motorcycle helmets, to the engaging in exercise, stopping (or never starting) of smoking, and the practice of stress reduction. The "great advances in medicine" are mostly in public health inoculation and good hygiene, both aspects of primary prevention. However, this past record of achievement falls short of what remains to be done. The American public tends toward the hedonic, in spite of relevant information of limited natural resources, the ingestion of supersize takeout and processed foods, and the collective buying of much more than we sell in the world. Prevention is needed on a scale more vast than anything we had entertained to do in the past.

THEORIES OF PRIMARY PREVENTION

Let me begin with some metatheory, that is, an abstract statement of terms for which any given theory has to account. This model is derived from Albee's (1983) formula on the incidence of problems in mental health, which I have generalized to a metatheory for any significant social behavior.

First, let's examine Albee's formula:

$$\text{The incidence of mental disorders} = \frac{\text{Organic factors} + \text{stress} + \text{exploitation}}{\text{Coping skills} + \text{self-esteem} + \text{support groups}}$$

This formula follows the public health model by offering several entry points to reduce the harmful events stemming from personal organic factors+social stress+social and cultural exploitation, by using personal coping skills+self-esteem built out of constructive social interactions+social support groups. Thus, if an individual is weak on coping skills and self-esteem, then support groups can compensate to a degree to deal with negative personal factors and social stresses. We can also teach better coping skills and help to improve the individual's self-esteem. I believe Albee also intended that the factors in the numerator could be addressed independently from the denominators. For example, we could decrease factors that produce organic problems in individuals (such as reducing second-hand smoke so it will not harm children). Thus, while Albee names specific factors, I believe that we can generalize these individual, interpersonal, and sociocultural conditions to construct a more general formulation. In simple terms, social behavior is the result of interactions between positive factors in the individual, small group, large collective institutions, culture, society, and the physical environment, as reduced by the interaction of negative factors in the same categories. Put another way, each individual has strengths and weaknesses relevant to the preventive issue, as do involved primary groups, local and distant institutions, and so forth. The planner's task is to examine each factor for its possible relevance to the presenting situation, and to figure out which of the factors might be most easily and successfully modified, with the fewest emergent ethical or other problems. This is a kind of mental cost–benefit analysis over the whole ecology of a preventive–promotive situation. I would also add that the relationship among these many variables is an interactive one, not merely an additive one, which makes the formulation immensely complicated. Preventionists have to deal in probabilities, not certainties, even when they have a large number of facts at hand.

There are a lot of potentially relevant factors in any situation. Ignore any portion of this formulation at your own risk, because each portion may be an important causal factor in a given case. But in most cases, there are probably a handful of variables that are predominantly responsible for outcomes, and to these variables you should be giving special attention. Read the literature to see what others have thought about relevant factors, and consider these, as well as other insights you may have that may extend the scope of knowledge. Don't be afraid to be wrong; be concerned, rather, with not taking some interesting chances where we lack knowledge. Every tested hypothesis is a way to advance understanding and improve delivery of future preventive services.

In his contribution to the *Encyclopedia of Primary Prevention and Health Promotion*, Silverman (2003, pp. 33–38) reviewed a number of theories of primary prevention. These included: The *deficit reduction model* (derived from clinical thinking), which assumes that the problem resides within the individual. Thus, efforts must be made to provide people with basic skills, such as cognitive skills (e.g., problem solving in academic situations); interpersonal skills (e.g., self-regulation and assertiveness); and behavioral skills (such as refusal skills when offered problematic substances). These competence-building skills provide a kind of social inoculation against life's problems.

Silverman also discusses the *enhancement–wellness model*, which shifts the focus away from existing deficits toward people's strengths. He speaks of a conceptual continuum running from health-destroying behaviors (like nicotine dependence), health-defeating behaviors (such as overwork), to health-maintaining behaviors (diet and exercise, for instance), to health-protective behaviors (seat belts, immunizations), to health promoting behaviors (creative thinking, regular physical exams).

Silverman's *antecedent conditions model* focuses on predisposing conditions (e.g., poor cognitive skills, poor family functioning) and precipitating conditions (such as poor affective skills, frustration, hopelessness) that place people at risk of untoward outcomes. There are two points where interventions can take place. The first uses societal forces to diminish predisposing conditions (for instance, better schools, family services), while the second point of intervention tries to diminish precipitating factors that are close to the expression of the problem. This model recognizes that a person's negative behavior may be functional in disordered contexts, as when a hungry but poor person steals bread for his family.

By reading the current literature in such journals as *The Journal of Primary Prevention, Prevention Science, American Journal of Public Health, American Journal of Community Psychology, Journal of Safety Research, American Journal of Preventive Medicine, Health Education Quarterly*, readers will discover particular theories that belong to one or another of Silverman's broad models. For example, Bandura's (1986) social cognitive theory can be considered an antecedent conditions model but with elements of enhancement and wellness. Csikszentmihalyi's (1996) flow model is mainly about enhancement and wellness. Dale Johnson's (2006) approach to skills training and refusal skills may belong to the deficits model.

TRANSLATING PRIMARY PREVENTION THEORY INTO PRACTICE: THE HELPING ENDEAVOR

Imagine a world where there is ample evidence for all of the things you would like to do as a helping professional in primary prevention. I mean good evidence, not just opinions or pilot research projects—although ideas and hunches are the starting points of all science. Wouldn't that be wonderful?

Now, don't get your hopes up, because the following is merely a shadow of that wonderful world. In the *Encyclopedia of Primary Prevention and Health Promotion*, several hundred experts from around the world wrote entries that summarized what we know about 146 topics, including their judgment of research findings that are sufficiently strong so as to represent "strategies that work"—in contrast to promising strategies and strategies that do not work. In the following table, I have extracted a dozen topics with summaries of strategies that work to give you an idea of the range and depth of knowledge that we currently have.

STRATEGIES OF PRACTICE

Having a list of empirical findings from projects is one thing. Translating these findings into terms and actions that are relevant to one's project is another. I want to discuss translation of theory and empirical findings into action statements for a project. To do this, I will take one study from those listed in Table 6.1, and go from the stated theory and the presented research results to a strategy for practice. Then, I will generalize on this process so that readers may be able to make optimal use of any of the other studies.

First, consider the study by Bierman, Greenberg, and Conduct Problems Prevention Research Group (CPPRG; 1996). I'll quote an excerpt by Smith and Furlong (2003) to give the flavor of the project, which is

a comprehensive, multicomponent primary prevention and early intervention program targeting students in grades 1–5 who are at-risk for development of

Table 6.1 **Primary prevention strategies that work: Selected topics from entry authors in the** *Encyclopedia of primary prevention and health promotion* **(Gullotta & Bloom, 2003)**

Aggressive behavior in children and adolescents (Bierman, Greenberg, & Conduct Problems Prevention Research Group, 1996)

"FAST Track is a school-based program that teaches students effective conflict resolution skills, interpersonal problem solving skills, emotional competence, and prosocial skills. Teachers are trained in classroom management, while parents receive parent education. This comprehensive, multicomponent program has been tested at many sites across the United States, and shows decreases in peer ratings of aggressive behavior and observed improvements in overall classroom environment" (Smith & Furlong, 2003, p. 178).

Attention deficit hyperactivity disorder (Dulcan et al., 1997) "At times, the most appropriate response to a behavioral problem is behavior modification, a change in classroom placement, or modification in the teacher's classroom management style…. "(Dulcan et al., 1997, p. 915)

"Token economies help to improve specific behaviors; also useful are daily report cards, homework notebooks that are reviewed and signed by parents…." (Mulsow & Lee, 2003, p. 210)

Bullying behavior (Horne & Orpinas, 2003) Several strategies: 1) strong support from administrators, with teachers and staff training to be aware of, and responsive to, aggressive actions; 2) clear code of conduct statement; 3) student training in assertiveness, empathy, problem solving, anger management, and relaxation.

Cancer prevention (Fintor, 2003) "Successful, cost-effective, adolescent cancer programs using a comprehensive, integrated approach to promote a variety of healthy behaviors has been described in the literature. The majority of these studies have involved reducing the use of tobacco products…studies involving nutrition, exercise, and reducing exposure to cancer-associated viral agents have also been successful" (p. 251).

Promoting creativity in adolescence (Reis & Renzulli, 2003) The Schoolwide Enrichment Model (SEM) is one of the most widely used enrichment models in the USA, in which a talent pool is located, curricula modified to focus on student strengths and eliminate already-mastered materials; then enrichment experiences are offered to encourage creative productivity applied to their particular topic. Evidence that the SEM approach works is supported by numerous studies (pp. 351–352).

Depression in adolescence (Roberts & Bishop, 2003) Studies using cognitive behavior models in afterschool programs with 10- to 13-year-olds who reported elevated levels of depression were shown to maintain more optimistic attribution styles, compared to a control group, 3 years after completing the program (Gillham & Reivich, 1999; Jaycox, Reivich, Killham, & Seligman, 1994).

Environmental health in children (Herne, 2003) Herne discusses a wide variety of methods that work to improve the environmental health of children and others, including (1) reducing indoor air pollution by preventing exposure to combustion products; volatile organic compounds; and asthma exacerbaters like smoke and mold. Outdoor air pollutants may be prevented by reducing exposure to lead and mercury, to contaminated water, and to pesticides (pp. 465–467).

Family strengthening (Gavazzi, 2003). A representative study by Kumpfer and Tait (2000) was "designed to assist families of adolescents in deterring substance use and improving parent–adolescent relationships. Program activities include parent skill development (anger and stress management, discipline, etc.); adolescent skills development (social skills, coping, communication, etc.) and family skill development (problem solving, family meetings, etc.). This program has been rigorously studied in 12 summative evaluation studies [with reports of significant increases in family functioning and decreases in teen substance use]" (Gavazzi, 2003, p. 488).

Unintentional injuries in adolescence (Tuchfarber, Garcia, & Zins, 2003) Environmental injury prevention approaches have been effective in reducing adolescent unintentional injury mortality due to automobile accidents, but the magnitude is hard to assess. Removal of unforgiving structures (trees, bounders) from roadways, energy-absorbing highway barriers, improved lighting on dark roadways has contributed to fewer serious crashes among all drivers (Robertson, 1998). Safety engineering involving passive restraints (air bags, seat belts) also provide protection. Legislative interventions (such as when full driving privileges can be assumed) may also be effective.

School dropout among adolescents (Dowrick, 2003, pp. 926–927) Comprehensive strategies are best, including when school, family, community, and individual elements are combined to address three overlapping categories: (1) improve school climate by affecting teacher–student relationships, school–family relationships, school–family relationships, or (smaller) school size; (2) improve school outcomes by schoolwide academic overhaul, improvement of social behavior, and after-school and recreational programs; and (3) address risk and protective factors.

School violence (Furlong, Sharkey, & Jimenez, 2003) The U.S. Department of Education's expert panel selected exemplary programs based on rigorous empirical data, such as the Second Step program (Frey, Hirschstein, & Guzzo, 2000), which is a school-based, social skills curriculum for students from preschool through junior high school. It aims to teach effective social skills in order to reduce impulsive and aggressive behavior, while increasing students' social competence. The 20-lesson program emphasizes empathy, impulse control, and anger management. Evaluative research suggests successful outcomes.

Self-esteem (DuBois, 2003) Self-esteem in adolescence is a multidimensional topic that reflects how the individual customarily regards him- or herself positively or negatively across multiple domains. Programs that attempted to enhance self-esteem using well-defined theory and based on prior research achieved better overall adjustment scores than programs with more general goals. Big Brothers/Big Sisters, for example, used one-to-one connections over more than one year, and have shown positive outcomes. School restructuring programs to facilitate entrance into new school environments, and programs emphasizing physical activities, have also been effective.

---

aggressive behavior. The school-based portion of the program focuses on teaching students effective conflict resolution/interpersonal problem solving skills, emotional competence (including empathy, communication), and prosocial skills. This is supplemented by teacher training in classroom management, remedial academic instruction for students, and consultation involving counselors, psychologists, and other mental health professionals. The home-based portion of the program includes parent education and modeling and training of appropriate interpersonal skills for both students and their families. (p. 178)

This is the kind of brief summary of the study that many readers will first encounter. Let's see what we can make of it: *Comprehensive* it is, with portions directed at students and peers in the school setting, together with their teachers who receive special training, and who may use an array of helping professionals to deal with complex issues. On top of that, parents are involved in educational programs at home, possibly including direct training of parents and children on dealing with problems that might escalate into aggression.

Multicomponent it is. We might interpret the remedial instruction as a kind of rehabilitation, and the early intervention as a kind of treatment of existing interpersonal problems, along with the rest of the program directed toward primary prevention before some serious problems occurred in children who were "at-risk"; that is, doing something to a population of persons. In fact, there were many students in multiple sites across the United States involved in this project. This means that there must have been reason for selecting just these at-risk children—some behaviors that were not what was formally expected at school. It may push our definition of primary prevention as happening *before* problems exist, but people have to show some indicator of a potential problem in order to have a group on which to test primary prevention methods.

Each of the component parts of the program was presumably chosen based on *theoretical or empirical reasons*, plus the *common sense* to select likely elements in a situation. Is there any serious alternative? Not if you are held responsible for the outcome of your preventive interactions. If you think you know the perfect answer immediately, you're in the wrong business.

So, "effective conflict resolution" was named first, and indeed, there are programs directed to these issues. It is likely they involved becoming aware that there was a conflict (it takes two to tango) and that this conflict has serious implications for one or both parties; that is, someone is going to get hurt, maybe both parties, or maybe innocent bystanders. There has to be some mechanism to cool down the potential combatants, even temporarily, and there has to be some alternative mechanism to resolve the conflict between them. This last point assumes a rational world where parties will seek some kind of fair resolution, even if they recognize that they won't get their own way entirely. This might involve enhancement of skills that lead both parties to new positive goals. There usually has to be a third party to the conflict, who will organize and conduct all of the above. There are theories that support this line of reasoning, to which I will return.

Smith and Furlong (2003, p. 178) reported that a large sample of first-grade students at multiple sites across the country did show decreased peer ratings of their aggressive behavior. Classrooms in which this project was being conducted also showed observed improvements in overall classroom environment, presumably as a result of the experimental program. Other findings showed improvements with high-risk students on interpersonal skills, and reduced aggressive and disruptive behaviors. Furthermore, relationships with both parents and peers improved over many outcome measures. These other findings take us beyond the conflict resolution idea, so I'll not discuss them further, other than to point out that these might be the enhancements I spoke of earlier. Overall, these findings are positive, so much so that Smith and Furlong chose the project as having strategies that work. What are these strategies?

Reading what they have summarized, I would suggest the following strategies: First, aggression in young children arises for many reasons, so be comprehensive in employing the major players in the children's world, such as teachers, peers, and parents. Second, we might wish to do many things to prevent aggression, but only some things are in our power to do (ethically, practically, and based on empirical evidence). So, in order to translate a theory into a strategy of practice we need to find *those elements of the theory and its empirical evidence, which the researchers found potent in their study that we can ethically employ in our own context.*

Third, we need to pull together what elements we can employ that have some record of being effective with like participants, and make this program compatible with relevant participants—the powers that be in the school system, the teachers, the parents, and by no means least, the students themselves. Very few people want to be evil; raising hell may be the easiest path in an evil world. If reasonable alternatives are provided, equally as much fun as the proscribed actions, and even laudable, they might move people otherwise labeled as evil (probably for good reason from society's point of view). No guarantees, by the way. Every real research project may turn up negative as well as positive findings. When we find studies, such as those of Bierman, Greenberg, and the CPPRG, treasure them as points of departure on a quest to prevent predictable problems, protect existing states of healthy functioning, and promote desired goals for populations of people.

REFERENCES

Albee, G. W. (1983). Psychopathology, prevention, and the just society. *Journal of Primary Prevention, 4*(1), 5–40.

Albee, G. W. (2003). The contributions of society, culture, and social class to emotional disorder. In T. P. Gullotta & M. Bloom (Eds.), *Encyclopedia of primary prevention and health promotion* (pp. 61–69). New York: Kluwer Academic/Plenum.

Albee, G. W. (2005). Call to revolution in the prevention of emotional disorders. *Ethical Human Psychology and Psychiatry, 7*(1), 37–44.

Albee, G. W., & Joffe, J. M. (2004). Mental illness is NOT "an illness like any other." *Journal of Primary Prevention, 24*(4), 419–436.

Bandura, A. (1986). *Social foundations of thought and action: A social cognitive theory.* Englewood Cliffs, NJ: Prentice-Hall.

Bierman, K. L., Greenberg, M. T., & Conduct Problems Prevention Research Group. (1996). Social skills training in the FAST Track Program. In R. DeV. Peters & R. J. McMahon (Eds.), *Preventing childhood disorders, substance abuse, and delinquency* (pp. 65–89). Thousand Oaks, CA: Sage.

Boyce, T. E., & Geller, E. S. (2003). Accident, motor vehicle, adulthood. In T. P. Gullotta & M. Bloom (Eds.), *Encyclopedia of primary prevention and health promotion* (pp. 146–153). New York: Kluwer Academic/Plenum.

Christopher, R. S. (1995). Adolescent pregnancy prevention. *Family Relations, 44,* 384–391.

Cowen, E. (1973). Social and community intervention. *Annual Review of Psychology, 24,* 423–472.

Csikszentmihalyi, M. (1996). *Creativity: Flow and the psychology of discovery and invention.* New York: HarperCollins.

Dowrick, P. W. (2003). School drop-out, adolescence. In T. P. Gullotta & M. Bloom (Eds.), *Encyclopedia of primary prevention and health promotion* (pp. 924–929). New York: Kluwer Academic/Plenum.

DuBois, D. L. (2003). Self-esteem, adolescence. In T. P. Gullotta & M. Bloom (Eds.), *Encyclopedia of primary prevention and health promotion* (pp. 953–961). New York: Kluwer Academic/Plenum.

Dulcan, M., Dunne, J. E., Ayers, W., Arnold, V., Benson, S., Bernet, W. et al. (1997). Practice parameters for the assessment and treatment of children, adolescents, and adults with attention-deficit/hyperactivity disorder: AACAP Official Action. *Journal of the American Academy of Child and Adolescent Psychiatry, 36*(Suppl.) 85S–121S.

Durlak, J. A. (2003). Effective prevention and health promotion programming. In T. P. Gullotta & M. Bloom (Eds.), *Encyclopedia of primary prevention and health promotion* (pp. 61–69). New York: Kluwer Academic/Plenum.

Fintor, L. (2003). Cancer, adolescence. In T. P.Gullotta & M. Bloom (Eds.), *Encyclopedia of primary prevention and health promotion* (pp. 248–255). New York: Kluwer Academic/Plenum.

Fishbein, D. (2000). The importance of neurobiological research to the prevention of psychopathology. *Prevention Science, 1*(2), 89–106.

Frey, K. S., Hirschstein, M. K., & Guzzo, B. A. (2000). Second step: Preventing aggression by promoting social competence. *Journal of Emotional and Behavioral Disorders, 8,* 102–112.

Furlong, M. J., Sharkey, J. D., & Jimenez, T. C. (2003). School violence, adolescence. In T. P. Gullotta & M. Bloom (Eds.), *Encyclopedia of primary prevention and health promotion* (pp. 929–937). New York: Kluwer Academic/Plenum.

Gavazzi, S. M. (2003). Family strengthening, adolescence. In T. P. Gullotta & M. Bloom (Eds.), *Encyclopedia of primary prevention and health promotion* (pp. 486–492). New York: Kluwer Academic/Plenum.

Germain, C. B., & Bloom, M. (1999). *Human behavior in the social environment: An ecological view* (2nd ed.). New York: Columbia University Press.

Gillham, J. E., & Reivich, K. (1999). Prevention of depressive symptoms in school children: A research update. *Psychological Science, 10,* 461–463.

Gullotta, T. P. (1994). The what, who, why, where, when, and how of primary prevention. *Journal of Primary Prevention, 15*(1), 5–14.

Gullotta, T. P., & Bloom, M. (Eds.). (2003). *Encyclopedia of primary prevention and health promotion.* New York: Kluwer Academic/Plenum.

Hearne, S. (2003). Environmental health, childhood. In T. P. Gullotta & M. Bloom (Eds.), *Encyclopedia of primary prevention and health promotion* (pp. 462–470). New York: Kluwer Academic/Plenum.

Horne, A. M., & Orpinas, P. (2003). Bullying, childhood. In T. P. Gullotta & M. Bloom (Eds.), *Encyclopedia of primary prevention and health promotion* (pp. 233–240). New York: Kluwer Academic/Plenum.

Jaycox, L. H., Reivich, K. J., Gillham, J., & Seligman, M. E. P. (1994). Prevention of depressive symptoms in school children. *Behavior Research and Therapy, 32*(8), 801–816.

Johnson, D. L. (2006). Parent–child development center follow-up project: Child behavior problem results. *Journal of Primary Prevention, 27*(4), 391–407.

Keller, E. F. (1983). *A feeling for the organism: The life and work of Barbara McClintock*. San Francisco: Freeman.

Kumpfer, K. L. & Tait, C. M. (2000). *Family skills training for parents and children*. Washington, D.C.: U.S. Department of Justice, Office of Justice Programs, Office of Juvenile Justice and Delinquency Prevention.

Leavell, H. R., & Clark, E. G. (Eds.). (1953). *Textbook in preventive medicine*. New York: McGraw-Hill.

Maslow, A. H. (1971). *The further reaches of human nature*. New York: Viking.

Mausner, J. S., & Bahn, A. K. (1974). *Epidemiology: An introductory text*. Philadelphia: W. B. Saunders.

Mulsow, M., & Lee, J. R. (2003). Attention deficit hyperactivity disorder (ADHD), childhood. In T. P. Gullotta & M. Bloom (Eds.), *Encyclopedia of primary prevention and health promotion* (pp. 207–212). New York: Kluwer Academic/Plenum.

Reis, S., & Renzulli, J. (2003). Creativity, adolescence. In T. P. Gullotta & M. Bloom (Eds.), *Encyclopedia of primary prevention and health promotion* (pp. 348–355). New York: Kluwer Academic/Plenum.

Roberts, C., & Bishop, B. (2003). Depression, adolescence. In T. P. Gullotta & M. Bloom (Eds.), *Encyclopedia of primary prevention and health promotion* (pp. 403–410). New York: Kluwer Academic/Plenum.

Robertson, L. S. (1986). Injury. In B. Edelstein & L. Michelson (Eds.), *Handbook of prevention* (pp. 343–360). New York: Plenum.

Robertson, L. S. (1998). *Injury epidemiology: Research and control strategies* (2nd ed.). New York: Oxford University Press.

Silverman, M. M. (2003). Theories of primary prevention and health promotion. In T. P. Gullotta & M. Bloom (Eds.), *Encyclopedia of primary prevention and health promotion* (pp. 27–42). New York: Kluwer Academic/Plenum.

Smith, D. C., & Furlong, M. J. (2003). Aggressive behavior, childhood. In T. P. Gullotta & M. Bloom (Eds.) *Encyclopedia of primary prevention and health promotion* (pp. 175–182). New York: Kluwer Academic/Plenum.

Tuchfarber, B., Garcia, V. F., & Zins, J. (2003). Injuries, unintentional, adolescence. In T. P. Gullotta & M. Bloom (Eds.), *Encyclopedia of primary prevention and health promotion* (pp. 621–627). New York: Kluwer Academic/Plenum.

Part III

PHYSICAL HEALTH ISSUES

Chapter Seven

Overweight and Obesity in Childhood

Nina Philipsen and Jeanne Brooks-Gunn

INTRODUCTION

In recent years, rates of childhood overweight have increased so rapidly, not only in the United States but also in other parts of the world, that the problem has been called an epidemic (Flegal, Carroll, & Johnson, 2002). While policymakers, parents, and pediatricians are eager to uncover the most effective policies, programs, and practices, no consensus has reached. Pin-pointing the reason for the increase in obesity rates is difficult to do because there are many likely contributors, including increased television viewing and media exposure, fast food and convenience store availability, the low cost of calorie dense foods, increased child-aimed advertising, and decreases in school physical education programs, amongst others. With so many possible explanations for the cause, the most effective solution remains unclear. For now, the best solutions and preventive measures are those that approach the problem from many angles. A multifaceted approach that coordinates the federal and local governments, communities, schools, and families is needed in order to successfully address this problem and achieve the goal of healthy weight in childhood.

DEFINITION AND MEASUREMENT OF OVERWEIGHT AND OBESITY

Although slightly different, measures of overweight and obesity in children and adults are both based on the body mass index (BMI). BMI is defined as weight in kilograms divided by height in meters squared (kg/m^2). The Centers for Disease Control (CDC) categorizes adults as "overweight" if BMI is 25 or above, "obese" if BMI is 30 or above. Adults with a BMI over 35 are categorized as severely obese (Sturm, 2003). For children and adolescents ages 2 to 19, if BMI is greater than or equal to the 85th percentile, but less than the 95th percentile (for children of the same age and gender, based on pediatric growth charts developed by the CDC and the National Center for Health Statistics), children are deemed "at risk for overweight." In addition, "overweight" is defined as at or above the 95th percentile. The CDC does not use the term *obese* for children and adolescents.

However, both the American Obesity Association and many published articles use the word *obese* and apply it to children at or above the 95th percentile. The term *overweight* is then used to describe children between the 85th and 95th percentiles. These are the definitions used in this chapter.

Age specific percentiles are used instead of BMI to classify children into weight categories because children's body fat changes as they grow. Median BMI decreases from ages 2 to 6 and then increases again into adulthood. For example, the 95th percentile of BMI for boys is 19.3 at age 2, 17.8 at age 4, 21 at age 9, and 25.1 at age 13. At age 20, it is slightly over 30, which is the adult cut-off for obesity. Percentiles are based, however, on the particular growth charts used to calculate them. One drawback of this method is that as the childhood population weight increases, so will the weight at the 95th percentile, rendering cohort comparisons difficult (Paxson , Fink, & Brooks-Gunn, in press).

PREVALENCE OF OVERWEIGHT AND OBESITY

Since the mid-1970s, overweight and obesity rates have been climbing steadily for both males and females across all age groups. Between 1971 and 1974, about 5% of all 2- to 19-year-olds were classified as obese. The rapid increase is especially evident if one compares those rates to the 15% of children classified as obese between 1999 and 2002 (Anderson & Butcher, 2006). Logically, child and adult obesity rates tend to increase together because children who are obese (even very young children) are likely to become obese adults (Whitaker, Wright, Pepe, Seidel, & Dietz, 1997). Also of concern are the rapidly rising rates of clinically severe obesity, which are rising faster than those of obesity (Sturm, 2003). Determining the exact time when obesity rates began to increase is important in identifying the causes of the increase. Obesity rates in the United States for both adults and children seemed to be stable through 1980. After 1980 the rates began to increase, implying an environmental or societal change (Anderson & Butcher, 2006).

Obesity rates are generally higher among minority and low-income children and rates are increasing more rapidly in these populations (Anderson & Butcher, 2006). However, prevalence is similar for both boys and girls.

CONSEQUENCES OF CHILDHOOD OVERWEIGHT AND OBESITY

Childhood overweight poses two kinds of risk: overweight children are more likely to suffer immediate consequences during early childhood, and they run a greater risk of adult overweight or obesity, which is associated with its own set of risk factors (Daniels, 2006). During childhood, high BMI can lead to high blood pressure (Falkner & Daniels, 2004), which is a major risk factor for heart attack for adults (Chobanian et al., 2003). BMI in childhood as well as the increase of BMI from childhood to adulthood has been linked to adult high blood pressure (Lauer & Clarke, 1989). Childhood overweight has also been linked to left ventricular hypertrophy, the increased thickness of the heart's main pumping chamber (Yoshinaga et al., 1995), which is another condition likely to lead to a heart attack. However, the greatest risk results from a hardening of the arteries, know as atherosclerosis. Overweight, obesity, high blood pressure, and high cholesterol increase the risk for atherosclerosis. Normally, these processes take many years before they result in a heart attack or stroke. However, if the problems begin early, during childhood, then there is a likelihood that the progression will be accelerated and that a stroke or heart attack may occur earlier (Daniels, 2006).

Childhood overweight and obesity are also linked to a host of metabolic disorders such as insulin resistance, metabolic syndrome (Cook, Weitzman, Auinger, Nguyen, & Dietz, 2003), dyslipidemia (abnormal levels of fat in the blood; The National Cholesterol Education Program Expert Panel on Detection, 2002), and type II diabetes (Pinhas-Hamiel, 1996). Cross-sectional studies have also linked asthma with childhood overweight and obesity, although it is unclear as to how the two are associated. It is possible that overweight and obesity can lead to inflammation of the airways in the lungs, thus increasing risk for asthma. On the other hand, children who have asthma are also less likely to participate in physical activities and may be treated with corticosteroids, both predictors of overweight and obesity in children (Daniels, 2006).

Childhood overweight and obesity are also likely to have an effect on the gastrointestinal tract: as many as 50% of obese children have fat deposits on their livers (Kinugasa et al., 1984). Although this disease has not been studied extensively in children, in adults, weight loss has been found to improve weight related fatty liver disease.

Additionally, extra strain on the skeletal system can lead to orthopedic problems. Hip problems and abnormal growth of the tibia (the main bone of the lower leg) are the most common problems experienced by young people (Daniels, 2006).

Lastly, children who are overweight or obese are also more likely to experience depressive symptoms (Stice, Hayward, Cameron, Killen, & Taylor, 2000), poor peer relationships (Strauss & Pollack, 2003), and an overall lower quality of life (Schwimmer, Burwinkle, & Varni, 2003). Body dissatisfaction, dietary restraint, and bulimic symptoms are associated with depression among adolescent girls (Stice et al., 2000). In addition, despite self-reporting similar numbers of friends as normal-weight adolescents, overweight children are less likely to be "nominated" as a friend by peers. Overweight children may be socially marginalized, which can increase the social and emotional consequences, such as depression, they may already be experiencing, or could be the reason for the initial depression (Strauss & Pollack, 2003). It has been difficult for researchers to discern whether obesity leads to depression, or whether depression leads to obesity. Evidence has been found supporting both hypotheses (Erickson, Robinson, Haydel, & Killen, 2000; Goodman & Whitaker, 2002), but more longitudinal and cross-lag research designs are needed. On the whole, childhood and adult obesity are both linked with a shorter life expectancy; however, these associations are modest (Olshansky et al., 2005; Preston, 2005).

BIOLOGICAL AND GENETIC FACTORS

Obesity and overweight result from a complex interaction of genetic and environmental factors. On an individual level, not everyone is equally susceptible to weight gain and the adverse consequences associated with it. The evidence suggests that genetic factors may play an important role in determining the response of body mass and body fat stores to changes in energy balance. It is likely that genetic variation in several genes contributes to response and thus to the susceptibility to obesity (Perusse & Bouchard, 1999). Recent research has yielded a range of estimates of the degree of familial correlation in weight due to shared genetics. Twin studies generally yield heritability estimates of BMI between 50% and 90%, while adoption or general family studies yield estimates between 25% and 50% (Maes, Neale, & Eaves, 1997). The twin study estimates include genetic as well as gene by environment interaction effects, perhaps explaining why these studies yield a larger heritability estimate. In other words, the estimates may be higher because monozygotic twins may share more environmental factors than dizygotic twins. However, studies of monozygotic twins who were raised separately yield estimates around 70% (Allison et al., 1996).

The twin studies also provide an opportunity to study the gene by environment interaction via an intervention method (Perusse & Bouchard, 1999). Both members of a monozygotic twin pair are exposed to an environmental standardized treatment and then compared to other twin pairs who are not genetically related to them. The within- and between-twin pair comparisons are made on the variance of the response to the treatment. If a significantly higher variance is found *between* versus *within* the twin pairs, it suggests that the changes induced by treatment are different in genetically dissimilar people and similar in genetically similar people. Since the treatment is the same across all twin pairs, the gene by environment interaction can be analyzed with the differences between the twin pairs.

This method was used in a study called The Long-Term Overfeeding Study, which was done with 12 pairs of healthy monozygotic twin pairs (Bouchard et al., 1990). The participants ingested a 1,000 kcal surplus six days a week for 100 days. At the end of the intervention period, there was three times more variance in weight gain and six times more variance in abdominal visceral fat between pairs than within pairs, which suggests a significant genotype-overfeeding interaction. Due to the variation in genes between twin pairs, there was a difference in how the participants reacted to the intervention. A second study, The Negative Energy Balance Study, was designed the same way, but involved an opposite kind of intervention (Bouchard et al., 1994). Seven pairs of adult male twins exercised on cycle ergometers nine out of 10 days over a period of 93 days while maintaining a constant daily energy and nutrient intake. As before, between-twin pair variance in loss of body fat was significantly greater than within-twin pair variance. Thus, the susceptibility of individuals to environmental factors is likely to vary across individuals of diverse genetic makeup implying that the effectiveness of prevention and intervention programs is likely to vary as well.

INDIVIDUAL FACTORS INFLUENCING RISK AND RESILIENCY

Gender and ethnic differences and prenatal and birth weight are the main individual factors that influence risk and resiliency.

Gender and Ethnic Differences

Rates of obesity are similar for boys and girls but vary across racial and ethnic groups. Group comparisons were made using data from the 1999 to 2000 National Health and Nutrition Examination Survey (NHANES; Ogden, Flegal, Carroll, & Johnson, 2002). The NHANES is a series of cross-sectional, nationally representative surveys conducted by the National Center for Health Statistics and the Centers for Disease Control and Prevention. Comparisons between racial and ethnic groups revealed that the rates of obesity among 12- to 19-year-old non-Hispanic black children and Mexican-American children were significantly higher than among non-Hispanic white children; 24%, 23%, and 13% respectively (see Table 7.1). Among infants from birth to 23 months of age, there were also differences between racial and ethnic groups. About 10% of the non-Hispanic white children were at or above the 95th percentile cut-off, compared to 19% of non-Hispanic black children.

An analysis of the Fragile Families and Child Wellbeing Survey indicates that Hispanic 3-year-olds were nearly twice as likely as white children to be overweight or obese. Hispanic children also had twice the odds of overweight or obesity as black children, despite similar family socioeconomic profiles. Additionally, these racial and ethnic differences were only slightly decreased by including maternal health and health behaviors, and children's opportunity for exercise in the models, indicating that other, unmeasured factors must account for these differences (Kimbro, Brooks-Gunn, & McLanahan, 2007). The exact reason for the differences among racial and ethnic groups and whether this trend will persist is unclear.

Table 7.1 **Prevalence of overweight (BMI ≥ 85th percentile) and obesity (BMI ≥ 95th percentile) by sex, age, and ethnicity: NHANES 1999–2000.**

	Age	All	Non-Hispanic white	Non-Hispanic black	Mexican American
Percent Overweight or Obese (BMI ≥ 85th percentile)					
Both sexes	2–5	20.6 (1.8)	20.5 (2.7)	19.3 (3.5)	22.7 (3.0)
	6–11	30.3 (2.4)	26.2 (3.6)	35.9 (3.0)	39.3 (3.0)
	12–19	30.4 (1.9)	26.5 (2.4)	40.4 (2.2)	43.8 (2.6)
Male	2–5	20.9 (2.4)	21.4 (3.7)	12.6 (3.1)	26.0 (4.9)
	6–11	32.7 (3.7)	29.4 (5.7)	43.5 (3.6)	43.0 (4.2)
	12–19	30.5 (2.1)	27.4 (3.0)	35.7 (2.8)	44.2 (3.0)
Females	2–5	20.4 (3.0)	19.7 (4.1)	26.6 (6.4)	19.5 (4.0)
	6–11	27.8 (3.2)	22.8 (4.7)	37.6 (3.6)	35.1 (4.4)
	12–19	30.2 (2.8)	25.4 (3.3)	45.5 (3.0)	43.5 (4.2)
Percent obese (BMI ≥ 95th percentile)					
Both sexes	2–5	10.4 (2.4)	10.1 (2.4)	8.4 (2.3)	11.1 (2.5)
	6–11	15.3 (1.7)	11.8 (2.4)	19.5 (2.0)	23.7 (2.0)
	12–19	15.5 (1.2)	12.7 (1.7)	23.6 (2.1)	23.4 (2.1)
Male	2–5	9.9 (2.2)	8.8 (3.2)	5.9 (2.4)	13.0 (3.9)
	6–11	16.0 (2.3)	12.0 (3.0)	17.1 (2.8)	27.3 (3.1)
	12–19	15.5 (1.6)	12.8 (2.4)	20.7 (2.6)	27.5 (3.0)
Females	2–5	11.0 (2.5)	11.5 (3.3)	11.2 (3.8)	9.2 (2.9)
	6–11	14.5 (2.5)	11.6 (3.5)	22.2 (3.3)	19.6 (3.1)
	12–19	15.5 (1.6)	12.4 (2.1)	26.6 (2.7)	19.4 (2.8)

Notes: Standard errors in parentheses. All Races includes groups not shown separately (i.e., Other).
Source: Ogden, C. L., Flegal, K. M., Carroll, M. D., & Johnson, C. L. (2002). Prevalence and trends in overweight among US children and adolescents, 1999–2000. *Journal of the American Medical Association, 288,* 1728 1702.

The Prenatal Environment and Birth Weight

The prenatal environment is partially determined by the mother's genetic makeup and partially by her actions, experiences, and decisions during pregnancy. In this section, the influence that the prenatal environment has on the child's birth weight will be discussed.

A host of previously conducted research studies have reported a positive association between birth weight and BMI in childhood and early adulthood (Barker, Robinson, Osmond, & Barker, 1997; Braddon, Rogers, Wadsworth, & Davies, 1986; Parsons, Powers, & Manor, 2001). Generally, infants weighing more than 4,000 grams are considered to have high birth weight (Polhamus, Thompson, Dalenius, Borland, Smith, & Grummer-Strawn, 2006). Altered maternal-fetal glucose metabolism and maternal hyperglycemia can lead to excess fetal insulin, a growth hormone for the fetus. This is the case for mothers with gestational diabetes mellitus (GDM). A survey called the Growing Up Today Study, conducted with 7,981 girls and 6,900 boys, ages 9 to 14, revealed that among the 465 participants whose mothers had GDM, 17% were overweight and 10% were obese in early adolescence compared to 14% and 7%, respectively, for the group without maternal diabetes. These trends remained similar even after controlling for age, gender, physical activity, television watching, energy intake, breastfeeding duration, and other maternal and family variables. However, adjustment for the mother's own BMI weakened the GDM associations. The study results modestly supported an association between maternal GDM and obesity in the child (Gillman, Rifas-Shiman, Berkey, Field, & Colditz, 2003).

A second influential aspect of the prenatal environment is the amount of maternal weight gain during pregnancy. High maternal weight gain has been suggested to contribute to high birth weight and high BMI later in childhood and adolescence. Some studies have shown that weight gain is positively associated with birth weight (Simpson, Lawless, & Mitchell, 1975), and that this association is stronger for women who are underweight (Abrams & Parker, 1990). One study showed a link between increased risk of child obesity at age 17 for those children born to mothers with the highest pregnancy weight gain. This result persisted after controlling for mother's prepregnancy weight, infant birth weight, birth order, and gestational age (Seidman, Ever-Hadani, & Gale, 1989). Overall, the research in this area is inconclusive and the topic needs further investigation.

Low birth weight (less than 2,500 grams) has also been considered a risk factor for overweight or obesity in childhood and adolescence due to the possibility of overcompensation which can lead to rapid weight gain. Early research on the Dutch famine reported that 19-year-old men who were fetuses during the famine period were more likely to be obese than those men who were conceived earlier or later (Ravelli, Stein, & Susser, 1976).The authors of the study hypothesized that nutritional deprivation affected the differentiation of hypothalamic centers regulating food intake and growth. Subsequently, when food availability increased, an accumulation of excess fat was produced. Another study demonstrated that young children who display rapid "catch up" growth in the first few years of life, after weighing less than their peers at birth, have higher BMI by age 5 (Ong et al., 2002). Research based on data from the National Collaborative Perinatal Project (CPP) also suggests that rapid weight gain in early life is associated with childhood obesity. However, in this study, the association seemed to be independent of birth weight. In this cohort the children born at full-term with a weight appropriate for gestational age still displayed childhood overweight status associated with rapid weight gain in infancy, independent of birth weight. It could be argued that these findings may be explained by the occurrence of any excessive weight gain over time (Stettler, Zemel, Kumanyika, & Stallings, 2002).

A study has assessed the impact of maternal smoking using data on 4,974 German children aged 5 to 6 years. A dose-dependent association between overweight and obesity and maternal smoking during pregnancy was observed after controlling for a wide range of confounders including maternal education, parental obesity, the child's birth weight, breastfeeding, snacking behavior, and television and videogame use. This finding suggests that prenatal exposure to inhaled smoke products, rather than lifestyle factors, associated with maternal smoking accounts for this finding, although unobserved differences between smokers and nonsmokers may still exist (von Kries, Toschke, Koletzko, & Slikker, 2002). In the same sample of parents and children, no statistically significant difference in obesity risk was found between maternal smoking in the first trimester compared to maternal smoking throughout pregnancy (Toschke, Montgomery, Pfeiffer, & von Kries, 2003). In addition, smoking after pregnancy was not associated with childhood obesity. Since intrauterine exposure was associated with obesity in children at school entry, but postpregnancy smoking was not, the authors again concluded that maternal smoking during pregnancy rather than family lifestyle factors associated with smoking appears to be affecting child weight (Toschke, Koletzko, Slikker, Hermann, & von Kries, 2002).

FAMILY FACTORS INFLUENCING RISK AND RESILIENCY

Parents and families are key influences on the home environments of children and adolescents. They take part in determining the food available in the house, the routine of meals, and the availability of both sedentary and physical activities. Parents serve as models for their children, and parents' knowledge of nutrition as well as their daily habits will largely influence the knowledge and habits of their children. Through the family environment that they establish, parents have many avenues through which they can influence a child's BMI and likelihood of being overweight or obese.

Family Socioeconomic Status

Data from the NHANES III illustrate that among U.S. children there is a significant inverse association between SES and obesity for children age 12 years and older, meaning low SES groups have a higher risk of obesity (Wang, 2001). The difference is not due to location of families because in the NHANES III sample, no difference between families from rural and urban communities emerged.

Maternal Employment

Research on maternal employment provides some insight into why the association between SES and childhood obesity may be difficult to explain. One study using data from the National Longitudinal Survey of Youth (NLSY) produced results that indicated higher prevalence of overweight for children whose mothers worked more hours per week over the child's life. Subgroup analyses showed that maternal employment was associated with obesity in children ages 3 to 11 and that high SES mothers who worked many hours had children who were the most likely to be overweight (Anderson, Butcher, & Levine, 2003). The authors hypothesize that the rise in maternal employment may have led to an increase in child obesity, since children with working mothers may consume more prepared or fast foods; receive less supervision after school (possibly increasing TV viewing or snack food consumption); have less time for outdoor play; or receive low-quality foods in childcare settings. However, it is unclear as to why this association would be greater in high SES families. This research suggests that the factors leading to greater obesity and overweight among children and adolescents may vary across socio-economic groups and age groups.

Family Influence on Food

The work status of parents is only one part of a complicated web of ways in which parents influence the diet and habits of their children. A parent's influence on what a child consumes begins during infancy, when the parent has almost full control over the diet. Later, as the child gets older, the parent has control by providing the food and establishing the family routines and habits.

Many researchers believe that breastfeeding infants can have a protective effect against obesity (for a review Arenz, Ruckerl, Koletzko, & von Kries, 2004). In a study using data from the NHANES III, breastfeeding initiation was associated with reduced risk of being overweight, while there was no clear effect of the duration of breastfeeding on being at risk for overweight, and no threshold effect. The strongest predictor of child overweight status was the mother's concurrent weight. The rate of overweight children nearly tripled with maternal overweight status and more than quadrupled with maternal obesity status (Hediger, Overpeck, Kuczmarski, & Ruan, 2001). A second project using data from the Growing Up Today Study found similar results, but additionally found an effect for duration. Children who had been breastfed for three months or less, compared to those who had been breastfed for at least seven months, were more likely to be overweight (Gillman, Rifas-Shiman, Camargo, et al., 2001). In addition, several other studies have found similar effects for both initiation and duration, indicating that any amount of breastfeeding provides some benefit, but, in general, the longer the child is breastfed, the less likely they are to be obese or overweight later (Toschke, Koletzko, et al., 2002; von Kries, Koletzko, et al., 1999).

Since the weight of the mother is such a strong predictor of childhood overweight and obesity, most studies control for mother's weight, but then still find that breastfeeding is a significant predictor. One study examined whether breastfeeding was more important for children with mothers who were obese than for those mothers who were not. Like the previous studies, the researchers found clear differences in the odds of both overweight and obesity for children by mother's weight status. The risk of obesity doubled for all racial and ethnic groups for children of obese mothers compared to the children of normal-weight mothers. Interestingly, breastfeeding seemed to be protective for the children of obese mothers but not for the children of nonobese mothers. This could indicate that obese mothers should be especially encouraged to breastfeed their babies (Kimbro et al.,

2007). Similar protective effects were found in a study with low-birth-weight infants. The smaller and thinner infants showed dramatic catch-up in weight and length that perhaps overcompensated for their birth size and resulted in larger childhood size, even after controlling for the weight of the mother. However, marked differences in growth rates between infants who were breastfed or bottle-fed at three months were observed, in that breast-feeding had growth-limiting effects (Ong et al., 2002). These results taken together suggest that breastfeeding can function as a protective factor for infants who are otherwise exposed to other forms of risk.

In addition to breastfeeding, parents also influence the development of their children's eating habits after infancy. Research suggests that differences in physiologic regulation of energy intake begins as early as preschool, and is influenced by exposure to and repeated experience with food (Birch, 1998). Therefore early exposure to fruits and vegetables and other foods that are high in energy and low in calories should lead to preference and consumption of these foods. However, overcontrolling a child's food choices may be counterproductive, because it may undermine their self-regulation abilities (Hill, 2002).

Children are also susceptible to the context in which foods are offered. Studies have found that children develop preferences for foods offered in positive contexts and are likely to dislike foods offered in negative contexts (Hursti, 1999). Interestingly, even small habits make a difference for child outcomes. Families who eat regular meals together are more likely to have children who consume a wider variety of healthy foods and are less likely to consume foods high in sugar and fat (Neumark-Sztainer, Hannan, Story, Croll, & Perry, 2003). These data, however, are correlational and not experimental, so these associations may be due to unmeasured differences in families and children. Decreasing sugar intake is important because children who consume drinks such as sugar sweetened fruit juices, even if only once or twice during the day, are at increased risk for becoming overweight (Welsh et al., 2005). In conclusion, it appears that parents have the potential to have an influence by providing a wide variety of healthy foods under a positive context, where the option to choose among the food provided is left up to the child.

Family Influence on Physical Activity

Physical activity is an important part of maintaining a healthy weight. Studies show that children with active mothers are twice as likely to be active as children with inactive mothers. Children with two active parents are almost six times more likely to be active than children with two inactive parents (Hood et al., 2000). There is some evidence that indicates that children who spend excessive amounts of time watching television or participating in other media activities may be decreasing the amount of time that they participate in physical activities. A study using data from 49 New York State WIC agencies on 2,761 adults with children aged 1 to 5 years found that having a TV in the bedroom was linked with the prevalence of child overweight (Dennison, Erb, & Jenkins, 2002). Similar results have been found for older children (Lindsay, Sussner, Kim, & Gortmaker, 2006). Parents who are themselves active and limit accessibility to television, are likely to have children with lower risk of overweight and obesity. Again, these differences may be due to unmeasured characteristics of the families and children because the data are correlational and not experimental.

SOCIAL AND COMMUNITY FACTORS INFLUENCING
RISK AND RESILIENCY

Influential factors include neighborhood facilities, childcare, school, television and advertising.

Neighborhood

Access to safe parks and other recreational facilities, functional sidewalks and trails, and access to supermarkets with fresh produce and other healthy foods are three ways in which a neighborhood can potentially influence childhood overweight and obesity. A clear association exists between access to recreational facilities and programs and child activity levels (Sallis, Prochaska, & Taylor, 2000). However, whether the link extends from neighborhoods to child weight is inconclusive (Burdette & Whitaker, 2004). Children living in low-income neighborhoods are less likely to have parks, sports fields, fitness clubs, and trails than children in more affluent areas (Estabrooks, Lee, & Gyurcsik, 2004). Children living in low-income neighborhoods face additional barriers because in those areas facilities like this are often not as safe. Physical activity can be encouraged on a neighborhood level through the accessibility of sidewalks and bike trails, thus encouraging people to use active forms of transportation. Residents of these "high-walkable" neighborhoods get one hour more of physical activity each week and are almost two and a half times more likely to meet physical activity recommendations when compared to residents of "low-walkable" neighborhoods (Frank, Schmid, Sallis, Chapman, & Saelens, 2005). Lastly, the lower availability of supermarkets and other healthy food options within low-income communities may explain some of the racial, ethnic, and SES differences in overweight and obesity (Sherry, Mei, Scanlon, Mokdad, & Grummer-Strawn, 2004).

Child Care

The Child and Adult Care Food Program (CACFP) is a federal program that provides funds for meals and snacks served to 2.8 million children in private or public nonprofit childcare centers. One study was done in 1995 with a nationally representative sample of 1,962 CACFP-participating childcare sites. Most sites offered breakfast, lunch, and one or two snacks. The food provided to the children was often short of daily energy needs and recommended dietary allowance for key nutrients. In addition the meals often exceeded guidelines for saturated fat content. However, on average 90% of the breakfasts and 87% of the lunches included all required components of the meal pattern requirements. The food component most often missing from meals was fruits and veg-etables (Fox, Glantz, Geitz, & Burstein, 1997). Several other studies have addressed the nutritional inadequacy in childcare settings (Briley, Roberts-Gray, & Rowe, 1993; Briley, Roberts-Gray, & Simpson, 1994). The link between these practices and child weight has not been addressed, but clearly merits investigation as increasing numbers of children spend time in childcare centers.

School

Most children eat at least one, and sometimes two or more meals during their time at school each day. The food, services, and nutrition education provided in schools serve as a vehicle for influencing childhood overweight and obesity. In 2000, 26% of states required schools to conduct height and weight or BMI screening. Of these schools, 61% were required to notify parents of the results. Screening such as this provides an opportunity for monitoring and for early intervention if necessary (Story, Kaphingst, & French, 2006). School lunches are also an opportunity to provide students with nutritious foods that they may not be receiving at home. For the low-income children, school meals were implemented to reduce hunger. Since 1995 federally funded school breakfasts and lunches have had to meet the requirements set in the Dietary Guidelines for Americans, in which limits are set for total saturated fat and percent of calories from fat. As of 1999, 75% of schools had not met the recommendations for amount of fat per meal (Fox, Crepinsek, Connor, & Battaglia, 2001). A second source of excessive calories in the schools is the availability of competitive foods that are not federally funded. This includes foods and beverages sold in snack bars, student stores, vending machines, and fundraisers. These foods are mostly beverages, fruit drinks (not 100% juice), salty snacks, and baked goods, while only 18% contain vegetables (Story et al., 2006). Consumption of these foods is displacing the consumption of more nutritious foods such as fruits, vegetables, and low-fat milk (Cullen & Zakeri, 2004). The trends in food available to children, paired with trends of decreasing physical education periods and recess time, apply a negative impact on children's weight and overall health. Interventions based on these school characteristics are discussed later in the chapter.

Television Commercials and Advertising

Especially for the group of children who watch excessive amounts of television, the content that they view is believed to have an effect on their food choices, although the evidence is not strong. In order to investigate the link between exposure to types of televised food messages and children's actual food selection, a longitudinal study was conducted with 5- to 8-year-olds attending summer camp. During their two-week stay at camp, the only television viewed by the children was a half-hour cartoon program each afternoon. The program contained 4.5 minutes of either candy commercials, fruit commercials, public service announcements, or no commercials. Children exposed to the fruit commercials were more likely to select orange juice during a snack period following the cartoon program. Those exposed to candy commercials were least likely to choose orange juice (Gorn & Goldberg, 1982). This study reflects real-life television because commercials broadcast during children's Saturday morning programming promote foods predominantly high in fat and/or sugar, many of which have relatively low nutritional value (Kotz & Story, 1994). This trend seems to be especially extreme during shows popular among the African-American population (Tirodkar & Jain, 2003).

EVIDENCE-BASED TREATMENT INTERVENTION
AND PREVENTION FOR CHILDHOOD OBESITY

Most intervention programs are not limited to overweight and obese children, but include a wide range of children at the baseline measurement. For this reason, these programs are not strictly interventions for overweight and obese children, but could also be implemented in order to prevent childhood overweight and obesity from an early age. Therefore prevention and intervention in response to the challenge of childhood overweight and obesity are considered together.

What Works

A review of the literature did not uncover any intervention that met the criteria of three successful trials.

What Might Work

Although there is no intervention for childhood overweight and obesity that has been implemented repeatedly, a host of elegantly implemented interventions have been tried and have resulted in varying levels of success. Many of these interventions target one point of influence such as the community, the school, the family, or the individual in order to intervene on one of the processes leading to overweight and obesity. The best approaches act on two or more of these influences; for example, changing some aspect of the nutritional environment at school and providing parent education in order the decrease the risk factors at home as well.

Community-Based Treatment

As reviewed earlier in this chapter, access to parks, sidewalks, trails, and supermarkets are community approaches to altering obesity rates. Although recent research has identified a link between these elements of a community and physical activity, the intervention research in this area is extremely limited. Examples of community initiatives do exist, one being the Learning Landscapes Project in Denver, Colorado. The project is a partnership between professors and graduate students of landscape architecture from the University of Colorado at Denver and local public elementary schools. The project began in 1992, with a primary goal being to provide a space for children to participate in physical play and education (Brink & Yost, 2004). However, the effect these new environments have on changing children's physical activity levels, and or on childhood overweight and obesity, have not been evaluated.

A different kind of community campaign called VERB was initiated by the Centers for Disease Control and Prevention. A series of paid advertisements combined with community promotions and Internet activities were implemented within the schools and communities to promote physical activity for children ages 9 to 13. A longitudinal, quasi-experimental evaluation was developed to assess the impact of the commercial marketing methods that ran nationally between June 2002 and June 2003. Included in the study were 3,120 parent–child dyads from the United States who were interviewed before the VERB campaign was launched in April to June of 2002 and then again in April to June of 2003. After one year 74% of the children surveyed reported being aware of the VERB campaign. The children most likely to increase their physical activity levels as a result of the campaign were young children (those under 10 years old), those with parents who had less than a high school education, children from urban areas, and children with a low active baseline (Huhman et al., 2005).

School-Based Treatment

A common approach to combating obesity is to change some aspect of the school environment. Interventions include having healthier foods in the cafeteria, reducing or banning snack food availability, increasing opportunities for exercise during or after school, increasing teaching about healthy eating, and providing take-home assignments for parents and children. Four programs which have been approached intervention through schools are discussed here: the Child and Adolescent Trial for Cardiovascular Health (CATCH), Sports, Play, and Active Recreation for Kids (Project SPARK), Pathways, and Kiel Obesity Prevention Study (KOPS).

After-school programs can provide a safe and nurturing environment for children to spend time and present opportunities for academic and health promotion. In 2002, 439 first- through third-graders participated in a two-year longitudinal study designed to determine the effectiveness of after-school program participation and its effect on BMI. Although the BMI of after-school program participants and nonparticipants was no different at baseline, after controlling for ethnicity and family income, participants showed a significantly lower BMI than nonparticipants at the follow-up (Mahoney, Lord, & Carryl, 2005).

A program entitled the Child and Adolescent Trial for Cardiovascular Health (CATCH) offered a slightly different intervention approach, targeting different aspects of the child's life simultaneously (Hoelscher et al., 2001; Webber et al., 1996). The intervention included 4,019 kindergarten through fifth graders from 24 public schools in four states. The schools were randomly assigned to one of three groups: 10 schools to a control group, seven schools to a school-based intervention group, and seven schools to a school-plus-family-based intervention group. The objectives of the intervention included reducing total fat, saturated fat, and sodium content in food served in the school, increasing the amount of time that students spend doing rigorous physical activity during physical education class, and reducing total individual cholesterol levels. In the intervention groups, physical education teachers received special training, and school lunches were improved. For the intervention group with the family component, students also completed take-home assignments with parents. At the follow-up, changes in obesity, blood pressure, and serum lipids were not significantly different between the treatment and control groups. However, total cholesterol decreased significantly more in the intervention groups than in the control group. Although there were no other changes in the short-term as a result of this intervention, the sustained implementation of these important behavior changes may influence long term health outcomes.

Sports, Play, and Active Recreation for Kids (Project SPARK) targeted children's physical activity both in and out of school (Sallis et al., 1993). Five hundred and fifty fourth- and fifth-graders from seven elementary schools in Southern California were assigned to one of three conditions, a teacher-led intervention, a specialist-led intervention, and a control group (who participated in existing physical education classes). Students in both intervention groups received 30-minute physical education classes per week as well as a self-managed curriculum to encourage physical activity outside of school. No significant group differences were seen in skin fold thickness; however, after two years, there was a trend (though not significant) for the children exposed to the intervention to have lower levels of body fat. This result may be due to a lack of intensity of the intervention because supervised physical activity was limited to 30 minutes per week.

Pathways, a multicomponent, randomized, controlled, school-based intervention, involved 1704 third- to fifth-graders in 41 schools over three consecutive years (Caballero et al., 2003). The intervention focused on schools serving American-Indian communities in Arizona, New Mexico, and South Dakota and had four components: change in dietary intake, increase in physical activity, a classroom curriculum focused on healthy eating and lifestyle, and a family-involvement program. The amount of fat was reduced in school meals and a physical education program was implemented for at least three 30-minute sessions per week of moderate to vigorous physical activity. In addition, the classroom curriculum consisted of two 45-minute lessons delivered by the teacher each week for 8 to 12 weeks. Lastly, families were given take-home packets that introduced them to the Pathways program and provided with low-fat foods and ideas for healthful snacks. Families were also invited to cooking demonstrations and other activities at school. No differences in change in BMI were seen between the intervention and control groups. However, children in the intervention schools reported lower daily caloric intake and percentage of energy from total fat. School lunches in the intervention schools did contain less fat, but the caloric values were similar.

A fourth school-based intervention program is the Kiel Obesity Prevention Study (KOPS), an intensive program initiated with 2,400 German 5- to 7-year-olds (Muller, Asbeck, Mast, Langnase, & Grund, 2001). The teachers in intervention schools were trained in a nutrition education program. The families participating with overweight or obese children or obese parents were targeted to receive three to five counseling sessions, and a six-month sports program was offered twice a week. The primary behavioral and educational messages to children and their parents were to eat fruits and vegetables, reduce the intake of high fat foods, be active at least an hour per day, and decrease TV viewing to less than one hour per day. On alternating years, the control schools became the intervention schools and vice versa. The increase in skin fold thickness was lower for the intervention than the control classrooms as was the percentage of fat mass for the overweight children. In the intervention classrooms, significant increases in daily physical activity, daily fruit and vegetable consumption, and nutrition knowledge were found. In addition, daily hours of television viewing decreased.

Taken together these school-based interventions produced varying results. Pathways, Project SPARK, and CATCH did not result in BMI or skin fold thickness changes. KOPS, on the other hand, provided more intensive services for those families with obese or overweight children and did show weight reductions. Mixed results have also emerged in intervention programs implemented in middle and high schools (Gortmaker et al., 1999; Neumark-Sztainer, Story, Hannan, & Rex, 2003). More intensive interventions need to be implemented in order to establish both long- and short-term improvements in children's BMI.

Family-Based Treatment

Many of the aforementioned studies contained a family intervention component in addition to a school-based intervention. In contrast, the primary focus of the following studies was on the out-of-school aspects of children's lives.

The Girls Health Enrichment Multi-Site Program (GEMS) included 1,080 African-American, 8- to 10-year-old girls and their parents who were randomized into treatment and control groups across four sites (Rochon et al., 2003). Here pilot data are presented with 54 8- to 10-year-old African-American girls from one of the four sites (Story et al., 2003). Measures were taken at baseline and at 12 weeks following the intervention, "Girlfriends for KEEPS" (Keys to Eating, Exercising, Playing, and Sharing). The after-school intervention was conducted twice a week for 12 weeks, and focused on increasing physical activity and healthy eating. Family packets were sent home each week and two family night events were held during the course of the 12-week program. The control group met once a month for Saturday morning and participated in art and crafts, self-esteem, and other workshops, excluding nutrition and physical activity components. No difference between the treatment and control group's BMI was found at the follow-up. However, physical activity levels and their behavioral intention for healthy eating and nutrition knowledge were higher in the intervention group. Physical activity differences and dietary intake differences between the two groups were not statistically significant.

Hip-Hop to Health Jr. is a five-year randomized controlled intervention targeting 3- to 5-year-old minority children enrolled in 24 Head Start programs. Although this program was administered through Head Start, it had a large family-based component. Included in the sample were 416 black children, 337 black parents, 362 Hispanic children, and 309 Hispanic parents (Fitzgibbon, Stolley, Dyer, VanHorn, & Kaufer Christoffel, 2002). At baseline, 15% of the black children and 28% of the Hispanic children were overweight in addition to more than 75% of the parents who were either overweight or obese (Stolley et al., 2003). Participants were randomly assigned to a 14-week parent and child focused dietary and physical activity intervention, or a general health intervention. Children participated in nutrition classes for 45 minutes three times a week for 14 weeks. The parent component of the intervention consisted of a weekly newsletter, homework assignments, and aerobics classes twice a week. At the two-year follow-up intervention children had significantly smaller increases in BMI compared with control children. There were no significant differences between intervention and control children in food intake/physical activity (Fitzgibbon, Stolley, Schiffer, et al., 2005).

A different family-oriented approach to combating childhood obesity was taken in a Swedish clinical trial of family therapy combined with dietary counseling and medical checkups (Flodmark, Ohlsson, Ryden, & Sveger, 1993). Unlike the other studies, this intervention included only participants who were classified as obese based on BMI. Forty-four 13-year-old children were randomly assigned to one of the two treatment groups, one receiving conventional treatment and the second receiving family therapy. A demographically matched group of 48 children also classified as obese, made up the comparison group. The conventional treatment consisted of dietary counseling by a dietitian and regular visits to an experienced pediatrician with an interest in weight problems. The family therapy group received the same dietary counseling and medical checkups by another pediatrician. In addition, the pediatrician and a psychologist offered six family therapy sessions spread over one year. The therapy sessions focused on a brief solution-based therapy. At the one-year follow-up, the increase of BMI in the family therapy group was less than in the conventional treatment group and the comparison group. Perhaps the success of this intervention can be attributed to the individualization of the treatment or the multifaceted approach including both medical attention as well as therapy.

The most well-known family-based treatments were conducted by Epstein and colleagues who compared four family-based behavioral treatment interventions. Across the four studies, 185 families with children who were 20% to 100% over their average weight for their age and sex were included. Both 5- and 10-year follow-ups were conducted (Epstein, McCurley, Wing, & Valoski, 1990; Epstein, Valoski, Wing, & McCurley, 1990). In all studies, families were randomized to treatments that lasted from 8 to 12 weeks, with monthly meetings from 6 to 12 months. The four studies provided families with dietary information and measurement based on the stop light diet. This diet categorizes foods according to the colors on a traffic light. (green foods: low calorie; yellow foods: moderate calorie; red foods: high calorie). Study 1 compared groups based on varying family members targeted for reinforcement. The parent–child group received $5 back each week contingent on either parent or child losing weight for the week, the child-only group received $5 back contingent on the child's weight loss, and the control group received $5 back contingent on attendance (Epstein, Wing, Koeske, & Valoski, 1987). Study 2 compared groups based on diet and lifestyle exercise with a diet–exercise group, a diet-alone group, and a no-treatment control group. Rewards were oriented toward the child in the diet–exercise and diet-alone groups, with reinforcement for exercise change and child weight loss. The diet-alone group was instructed in calisthenics and stretching but was not reinforced for exercise changes, only child weight loss. The diet-exercise and the diet-only groups decreased overweight more than the control group at follow-up (Epstein, Wing, Koeske, & Valoski, 1984). Study 3 compared children based on family history of obesity, one group in which at least one parent was obese and one in which both parents were not obese. The children were reinforced for habit change. During treatment, children with no obese parent had a greater decrease in percent overweight than children with an obese parent (Epstein, Wing, Valoski, & Gooding, 1987). Study 4 compared varying types of exercise randomized to three groups: the lifestyle exercise group, the programmed aerobic exercise group, or the calisthenics control group. Behavior change based on physical activity was reinforced. Parents and children had reciprocal reinforcement contingencies, meaning they were instructed to support the behavior change of one another. The lifestyle exercise group decreased overweight significantly more than the calisthenics control group, while the programmed aerobic exercise group fell between the other two groups (Epstein, Wing, Koeske, & Valoski, 1985).

Results from the five-year follow-up showed that the best child outcomes were associated with both conjoint targeting and reinforcement of child and parent behavior or reciprocal targeting and reinforcement of children and parents. The child's success was predicted by self-monitoring, changing eating behavior, praise, and change in parent percent overweight. Parental successes were predicted by self-monitoring weight, baseline parent percent overweight, and participation in fewer subsequent weight control programs (Epstein, McCurley, et al., 1990). At the 10-year follow-up, the results of the four studies were combined. Outcomes revealed that 34% of participants in the treatment groups had decreased percentage overweight by 20% or more while 30% were no longer obese (Epstein, Valoski, et al., 1990).

What Doesn't Work

There are no (reasonable) interventions that should not be used at the present time. However, some parenting and feeding practices should not be supported. Practices in this category include giving newborn infants supplements (water, glucose water, formula, and other fluids) if the mother is planning on breastfeeding; putting juice or cereal in bottles (American Academy of Pediatrics, 2004); and young children taking a bottle to bed (Kimbro et al., 2007).

Prevention

As noted earlier, teasing differences between prevention and intervention is not possible. Thus these sections have been combined.

Psychopharmacology and Childhood Obesity

Generally, pharmacological treatments are not prescribed for children, mainly because most drugs made for the treatment of obesity are not tested on children, and are therefore not known to be safe. Four experimental drugs have produced weight loss in studies involving children; however, these drugs are designed for very specific cases. Metformin has been used for treating obese adolescents with insulin resistance and hyperinsulinae-mia, octreotide for hypothalamic obesity, growth hormone in children with Prader-Willi syndrome, and leptin for congenital leptin deficiency (Paxson et al., 2005).

Pharmacological treatments are generally reserved for children with a biological cause of obesity or those presenting with severe obesity-related complications. When possible, it is best to treat obesity, especially in children, without the use of drugs. However, for cases where the obesity is a result of a genetic mutation, children and adolescents need drugs along with multiple other strategies, to be applied in combination with a carefully designed and monitored treatment program (Caprio, 2006).

Recommended Best Practice

The best interventions of childhood over weight and obesity are those that approach lifestyle changes from many angles. The interventions which are most effective usually include changes in diet, behavior, and physical activity, and incorporate the child's school, family, and sometimes community, in the process. Most treatments that prove to be effective can also be implemented as effective prevention strategies. Recommendations for best practices for both prevention and intervention at the community, school, and family levels, are summarized here:

Community
- Allocate community resources to developing and maintaining "walkable" neighborhoods with parks, open spaces, and trails and paths to encourage physical activity.
- Increase public transportation to and from low-income neighborhoods to provide access to supermarkets, fresh foods, and other community resources.

- Increase regulation prohibiting commercials for foods high in calories, sugar, and fat, during television programming for children.
- Strengthen regulatory requirements for both federally and privately funded meals and snacks served in day care.

School

- Increase early detection of overweight children through in-school screenings and mandatory reports to parents.
- Increase physical education periods and recess time as well as an increase in the amount of time spent physically active during the period.
- Limit competitive foods high in calories, sugar, and fat sold now in schools.

Family

- Avoid first- and second-hand smoke and other behaviors that can put the fetus at risk for low birth weight.
- Attend regular prenatal care in order to monitor appropriate weight gain during pregnancy.
- Breastfeed as a protective precaution against childhood obesity, especially if a child's mother is overweight or obese or if the child is either low or high birth weight.
- Avoid giving routine supplements such as water, glucose water, formula, and other fluids to breastfeeding newborns.
- Avoid putting children to bed with a bottle.
- Avoid giving children, juice, water, or cow's milk before six months of age.
- Provide a healthy example for children through parent diets and activities.
- Limit pharmacological treatments of obesity to extreme cases, based in biological causes.
- Increase the availability of a variety of healthy food options for children, while letting the child make decisions on what to eat in a positive context.
- Restrict televisions and computers to communal portions of the house instead of in children's bedrooms.
- Encourage physical activity.

REFERENCES

Abrams, B., & Parker, J. D. (1990). Maternal weight gain in women with good pregnancy outcome. *Obstetrics and Gynecology, 76*, 1–7.

Allison, D. B., Kaprio, J., Korkeila, M., Koskenvuo, M., Neale, M. C., & Hayakawa, K. (1996). The heritability of body mass index among an international sample of monozygotic twins reared apart. *International Journal of Obesity and Related Metabolic Disorders, 20*, 501–506.

American Academy of Pediatrics. (2004). Breastfeeding and the use of human milk. *Pediatrics, 155*, 496–506.

Anderson, P. M., & Butcher, K. E. (2006). Childhood obesity: Trends and potential causes. *Future of Children, 16*, 19–45.

Anderson, P. M., Butcher, K. F., & Levine, P. B. (2003). Maternal employment and overweight children. *Journal of Health Economics, 22*, 477–504.

Arenz, S., Ruckerl, R., Koletzko, B., & von Kries, R. (2004). Breast-feeding and childhood obesity—A systematic review. *International Journal of Obesity & Related Metabolic Disorders: Journal of the International Association for the Study of Obesity, 28*, 1247–1256.

Barker, M., Robinson, S., Osmond, C., & Barker, D. (1997). Birth weight and body fat distribution in adolescent girls. *Archives of Disease in Childhood, 77*, 381–383.

Birch, L. (1998). Development of food acceptance patterns in the first years of life. *Proceedings of the Nutrition Society, 57*, 617–624.

Bouchard, C., Tremblay, A., Despres, J. P., Nadeau, A., Lupien, P. J., Theriault, G., et al. (1990). The response to long-term overfeeding in identical twins. *The New England Journal of Medicine, 322*, 1477–1482.

Bouchard, C., Tremblay, A., Despres, J. P., Theriault, G., Nadeau, A., Lupien, P. J., et al. (1994). The response to exercise with constant energy intake in identical twins. *Obesity Research, 2*, 400–410.

Braddon, F. E., Rogers, B., Wadsworth, M. E., & Davies, J. M. (1986). Onset of obesity in a 36 year birth cohort study. *British Medical Journal, 293*, 299–303.

Briley, M. E., Roberts-Gray, C., & Rowe, S. (1993). What can children learn from the menu at the child care center? *Journal of Community Health, 18*, 363–377.

Briley, M. E., Roberts-Gray, C., & Simpson, D. (1994). Identification of factors that influence the menu at child care centers: A grounded theory approach. *Journal of the American Dietetic Association, 94*, 276–281.

Brink, L., & Yost, B. (2004). Transforming inner-city school grounds: Lessons from learning landscapes. *Children, Youth and Environments, 14*, 208–232.

Burdette, H. L., & Whitaker, R. C. (2004). Neighborhood playgrounds, fast-food restaurants, and crime: Relationships to overweight in low-income preschool children. *Preventive Medicine, 38*, 57–63.

Caballero, B., Clay, T., Davis, S. M., Ethelbah, B., Rock, B. H., Lohman, T., et al. (2003). Pathways: A school-based, randomized controlled trial for the prevention of obesity in American Indian schoolchildren. *American Journal of Clinical Nutrition, 78*, 1030–1038.

Caprio, S. (2006). Treating child obesity and associated medical conditions. *Future of Children, 16*, 209–224.

Chobanian, A. V., Bakris, G. L., Black, H. R., Cushman, W. C., Green, L. A., Izzo, J. L. J., et al. (2003). The seventh report of the Joint National Committee on Prevention, Detection, Evaluation, and Treatment of High Blood Pressure: The JNC 7 Report. *Journal of the American Medical Association, 289*, 2560–2572.

Cook, S., Weitzman, M., Auinger, P., Nguyen, M., & Dietz, W. H. (2003). Prevalence of a metabolic syndrome phenotype in adolescents: Findings from the Third National Health and Nutrition Examination Survey, 1988–1994. *Archives of Pediatric and Adolescent Medicine, 157*, 821–827.

Cullen, K. W., & Zakeri, I. (2004). Fruits, vegetables, milk, and sweetened beverages consumption and access to à la carte/snack bar meals at school. *American Journal of Public Health, 94*, 463–467.

Daniels, S. R. (2006). The consequences of childhood overweight and obesity. *Future of Children, 16*, 47–67.

Dennison, B. A., Erb, T. A., & Jenkins, P. L. (2002). Television viewing and television in bedroom associated with overweight risk among low-income preschool children. *Pediatrics, 109*, 1028–1035.

Epstein, L. H., McCurley, J., Wing, R. R., & Valoski, A. (1990a). Five-year follow-up of family-based behavioral treatments for childhood obesity. *Journal of Consulting & Clinical Psychology, 58*, 661–664.

Epstein, L. H., Valoski, A., Wing, R. R., & McCurley, J. (1990b). Ten-year follow-up of behavioral, family-based treatment for obese children. *Journal of the American Medical Association, 264*, 2519–2523.

Epstein, L. H., Wing, R. R., Koeske, R., & Valoski, A. (1984). The effects of diet plus exercise on weight change in parents and children. *Journal of Consulting and Clinical Psychology, 52*, 429–437.

Epstein, L. H., Wing, R. R., Koeske, R., & Valoski, A. (1985). A comparison of lifestyle exercise, aerobic exercise and calisthenics on weight loss in obese children. *Behavior Therapy, 16*, 345–356.

Epstein, L. H., Wing, R. R., Koeske, R., & Valoski, A. (1987). Longterm effects of family-based treatment of childhood obesity. *Journal of Consulting and Clinical Psychology, 55*, 91–95.

Epstein, L. H., Wing, R. R., Valoski, A., & Gooding, W. (1987). Long-term effects of parent weight on child weight loss. *Behavior Therapy, 18*, 219–226.

Erickson, S. J., Robinson, T. N., Haydel, K. F., & Killen, J. D. (2000). Are overweight children unhappy? Body mass index, depressive symptoms, and overweight concerns in elementary school children. *Archives of Pediatrics & Adolescent Medicine, 154*, 931–935.

Estabrooks, P. A., Lee, R. E., & Gyurcsik, N. C. (2004). Resources for physical activity participation: Does availability and accessibility differ by neighborhood Socioeconomic status? *Annals of Behavioral Medicine and Science in Sports and Exercise, 25*, 100–104.

Falkner, B., & Daniels, S. R. (2004). Summary of the fourth report on the diagnosis, evaluation, and treatment of high blood pressure in children and adolescents. *Hypertension, 44*, 387–388.

Fitzgibbon, M. L., Stolley, M. R., Dyer, A. R., VanHorn, L., & Kaufer Christoffel, K. (2002). A community-based obesity prevention program for minority children: Rationale and study design for Hip-Hop to Health Jr. *Preventive Medicine, 34*, 289–297.

Fitzgibbon, M. L., Stolley, M. R., Schiffer, L., Van Horn, L., Kaufer Christoffel, K., & Dyer, A. (2005). Two-year follow-up results for Hip-Hop to Health Jr.: A randomized controlled trial for overweight prevention in preschool minority children. *The Journal of Pediatrics, 146*, 618–625.

Flegal, K. M., Carroll, M. D., & Johnson, C. L. (2002). Prevalence and trends in obesity among US Adults: 1999–2000. *Journal of the American Medical Association, 288*, 1723–1727.

Flodmark, C. E., Ohlsson, T., Ryden, O., & Sveger, T. (1993). Prevention of progression to severe obesity in a group of obese schoolchildren treated with family therapy. *Pediatrics, 91*, 880–884.

Fox, M. K., Crepinsek, M. K., Connor, P., & Battaglia, M. (2001). *School nutrition dietary assessment study II: Summary of findings.* Alexandria, VA: U.S. Department of Agriculture, Food and Nutrition Service, Office of Analysis, Nutrition, and Evaluation.

Fox, M. K., Glantz, F. B., Geitz, L., & Burstein, N. (1997). *Early childhood and child care study: Nutritional assessment of the CACFP: Vol.2. Final REPORT.* Washington, D.C.: U.S. Department of Agriculture, Food and Consumer Service.

Frank, L. D., Schmid, T. L., Sallis, J. F., Chapman, J., & Saelens, B. E. (2005). Linking objectively measured physical activity with objectively measured urban form: Findings from SMARTRAQ. *American Journal of Preventive Medicine, 28*, 117–125.

Gillman, M. W., Rifas-Shiman, S., Berkey, C. S., Field, A. E., & Colditz, G. A. (2003). Maternal gestational diabetes, birth weight, and adolescent obesity. *Pediatrics, 111*, e221–226.

Gillman, M. W., Rifas-Shiman, S. L., Camargo, C. A., Jr., Berkey, C. S., Frazier, A. L., Rockett, H. R. H., et al. (2001). Risk of overweight among adolescents who were breastfed as infants. *Journal of the American Medical Association, 285*, 2461–2467.

Goodman, E., & Whitaker, R. C. (2002). A prospective study of the role of depression in the development and persistence of adolescent obesity. *Pediatrics, 110*, 497–504.

Gorn, G. J., & Goldberg, M. E. (1982). Behavioral evidence of the effects of televised food messages on children. *Journal of Consumer Research, 9*, 200–205.

Gortmaker, S. L., Peterson, K., Wiecha, J., Sobol, A. M., Dixit, S., Fox, M. K., et al. (1999). Reducing obesity via a school-based interdisciplinary intervention among youth: Planet Health. *Archives of Pediatrics & Adolescent Medicine, 153*, 409–418.

Hediger, M. L., Overpeck, M. D., Kuczmarski, R. J., & Ruan, W. J. (2001). Association between infant breastfeeding and overweight in young children. *Journal of the Amercian Medical Association, 285*, 2453–2460.

Hill, A. J. (2002). Developmental issues in attitudes to food and diet. *Proceedings of the Nutrition Society, 61*, 259–266.

Hoelscher, D. M., Kelder, S. H., Murray, N., Cribb, P. W., Conroy, J., & Parcel, G. S. (2001). Dissemination and adoption of the Child and Adolescent Trial for Cardiovascular Health (CATCH): A case study in Texas. *Journal of Public Health Management & Practice, 7*, 90–100.

Hood, M. Y., Moore, L. L., Sundarajan-Ramamurti, A., Singer, M., Cupples, L. A., & Ellison, R. C. (2000). Parental eating attitudes and the development of obesity in children: The Framingham Children's Study. *International Journal of Obesity & Related Metabolic Disorders: Journal of the International Association for the Study of Obesity, 24*, 1319–1325.

Huhman, M., Potter, L. D., Wong, F. L., Banspach, S. W., Duke, J. C., & Heitzler, C. D. (2005). Effects of a mass media campaign to increase physical activity among children: Time 1 results from the VERB campaign. *Pediatrics, 116*, e277.

Hursti, U. K. K. (1999). Factors influencing children's food choice. *Annals of Medicine, 31*, 26–32.

Kimbro, R. T., Brooks-Gunn, J., & McLanahan, S. (2007). Racial and ethnic differentials in overweight and obesity among three-year-old children. *American Journal of Public Health, 97*, 298– 05.

Kinugasa, A., Tsunamoto, K., Furukawa, N., Sawada, T., Kusunoki, T., & Shimada, N. (1984). Fatty liver and its fibrous changes found in simple obesity of children. *Journal of Pediatric Gastroenterology & Nutrition, 3*, 408–414.

Kotz, K., & Story, M. (1994). Food advertisements during children's Saturday morning television programming: Are they consistent with dietary recommendations? *Journal of the American Dietetic Association, 94*, 1296–1300.

Lauer, R. M., & Clarke, W. R. (1989). Childhood risk factors for high adult blood pressure: The Muscatine Study. *Pediatrics, 84*, 633–641.

Lindsay, A. C., Sussner, K. M., Kim, J., & Gortmaker, S. (2006). The role of parents in preventing childhood obesity. *Future of Children, 16*, 169–186.

Maes, H. H., Neale, M. C., & Eaves, L. J. (1997). Genetic and environmental factors in relative body weight and human adiposity. *Behavior Genetics, 27*, 325–351.

Mahoney, J. L., Lord, H., & Carryl, E. (2005). Afterschool program participation and the development of child obesity and peer acceptance. *Applied Developmental Science, 9*, 202–215.

Muller, M. J., Asbeck, I., Mast, M., Langnase, K., & Grund, A. (2001). Prevention of obesity—More than an intention. Concept and first results of the Kiel Obesity Prevention Study (KOPS). *International Journal of Obesity & Related Metabolic Disorders: Journal of the International Association for the Study of Obesity, 25*(Suppl. 1), S66–S74.

Neumark-Sztainer, D., Hannan, P. J., Story, M., Croll, J., & Perry, C. (2003). Family meal patterns: Associations with socio-demographic characteristics and improved dietary intake among adolescents. *Journal of the American Dietetic Association, 103*, 317–322.

Neumark-Sztainer, D., Story, M., Hannan, P. J., & Rex, J. (2003). New moves: A school-based obesity prevention program for adolescent girls. *Preventive Medicine, 37*, 41–51.

Ogden, C. L., Flegal, K. M., Carroll, M. D., & Johnson, C. L. (2002). Prevalence and trends in overweight among US children and adolescents, 1999–2000. *Journal of the American Medical Association, 288*, 1728–1732.

Olshansky, S. J., Passaro, D. J., Hershow, R. C., Layden, J., Carnes, B. A., Brody, J., et al. (2005). Special report: A potential decline in life expectancy in the United States in the 21st century. *The New England Journal of Medicine, 352*, 1138–1145.

Ong, K. K., Preece, M. A., Emmett, P. M., Ahmed, M. L., Dunger, D. B., & Team, A. S. (2002). Size at birth and early childhood growth in relation to maternal smoking, parity and infant breast-feeding: Longitudinal birth cohort study and analysis. *Pediatric Research, 52*, 863–867.

Parsons, T. J., Powers, C., & Manor, O. (2001). Fetal and early life growth and bodymass index from birth to early adulthood in 1958 British cohort: Longitudinal study. *British Medical Journal, 323*, 1331–1335.

Paxson, C., Fink, C., & Brooks-Gunn, J. (2005). Growing up overweight: Causes, consequences and treatment. In T. P. Gullotta & G. R. Adams (Eds.). *Handbook of evidence-based approaches for the treatment and prevention of challenging behaviors in adolescence* (pp. 387–412). New York, NY: Springer.

Perusse, L., & Bouchard, C. (1999). Genotype-environment interaction in human obesity. *Nutrition Reviews, 57*, 31–38.

Pinhas-Hamiel, O. (1996). Increased incidence of non-insulin-dependent diabetes mellitus among adolescents. *Journal of Pediatrics, 128*, 608–615.

Polhamus, B., Thompson D., Dalenius K., Borland E., Smith B., & Grummer-Strawn L. (2006). *Pediatric nutrition surveillance 2004 report*. Atlanta, GA: U.S. Department of Health and Human Services, Centers for Disease Control and Prevention.

Preston, S. H. (2005). Deadweight?—The influence of obesity on longevity. *New England Journal of Medicine, 352*, 1135–1137.

Ravelli, G. P., Stein, Z. A., & Susser, M. W. (1976). Obesity in young men after famine exposure in utero and early infancy. *New England Journal of Medicine, 295*, 349–353.

Rochon, J., Klesges, R. C., Story, M., Robinson, T. N., Baranowski, T., Obarzanek, E., et al. (2003). Common design elements of the Girls' Health Enrichment Multi-site Studies (GEMS). *Ethnicity & Disease, 13*(Suppl. 1), S6–14.

Sallis, J. F., McKenzie, T. L., Alcaraz, J. E., Kolody, B., Hovell, M. F., & Nader, P. R. (1993). Project SPARK. Effects of physical education on adiposity in children. *Annals of the New York Academy of Sciences, 699*, 127–136.

Sallis, J. F., Prochaska, J. J., & Taylor, W. C. (2000). A review of correlates of physical activity of children and adolescents. *Medicine and Science in Sports and Exercise, 32*, 963–975.

Schwimmer, J. S., Burwinkle, T. M., & Varni, J. W. (2003). Health-related quality of life of severely obese children and adolescents. *Journal of the American Medical Association, 289*, 1813–1819.

Seidman, D. S., Ever-Hadani, P., & Gale, R. (1989). The effect of maternal weight gain in pregnancy on birth weight. *Obstetrics & Gynecology, 74*, 240–246.

Sherry, B., Mei, Z., Scanlon, K. S., Mokdad, A. H., & Grummer-Strawn, L. M. (2004). Trends in state-specific prevalence of overweight and underweight in 2- through 4-Year-old children from low-income families from 1989 through 2000. *Archives of Pediatric and Adolescent Medicine, 158*, 1116–1124.

Simpson, J. W., Lawless, R. W., & Mitchell, A. C. (1975). Responsibility of the obstetrician to the fetus. II. Influence of pre-pregnancy weight and pregnancy weight gain in birth weight. *American Journal of Obstetrics and Gynecology, 45*, 481–487.

Stettler, N., Zemel, B. S., Kumanyika, S., & Stallings, V. A. (2002). Infant weight gain and childhood overweight status in a multicenter cohort study. *Pediatrics, 109*, 194–199.

Stice, E., Hayward, C., Cameron, R. P., Killen, J. D., & Taylor, C. B. (2000). Body-image and eating disturbances predict onset of depression among female adolescents: A longitudinal study. *Journal of Abnormal Psychology, 109*, 438–444.

Stolley, M. R., Fitzgibbon, M. L., Dyer, A., Van Horn, L., Kaufer Christoffel, K., & Schiffer, L. (2003). Hip-Hop to Health Jr., an obesity prevention program for minority preschool children: Baseline characteristics of participants. *Preventive Medicine, 36*, 320–329.

Story, M., Kaphingst, K. M., & French, S. (2006). The role of schools in obesity prevention. *Future of Children, 16*, 109–142.

Story, M., Sherwood, N. E., Himes, J. H., Davis, M., Jacobs, D. R., Jr., Cartwright, Y., et al. (2003). An after-school obesity prevention program for African-American girls: The Minnesota GEMS pilot study. *Ethnicity & Disease, 13* (Suppl. 1) , S54–64.

Strauss, R. S., & Pollack, H. A. (2003). Social marginalization of overweight children. *Archives of Pediatrics and Adolescent Medicine, 157*, 746–752.

Sturm, R. (2003). Increases in clinically severe obesity in the United States, 1986–2000. *Archives of Internal Medicine, 163*, 2146–2148.

The National Cholesterol Education Program (NCEP) Expert Panel on Detection. (2002). Third report of the National Cholesterol Education Program (NCEP) Expert Panel on Detection, Evaluation, and Treatment of High Blood Cholesterol in Adults (Adult Treatment Panel III), final report. *Circulation, 106*, 3143–3421.

Tirodkar, M. A., & Jain, A. (2003). Food messages on African American television shows. *American Journal of Public Health, 93*, 439–441.

Toschke, A. M., Koletzko, B., Slikker, W., Jr., Hermann, M., & von Kries, R. (2002). Childhood obesity is associated with maternal smoking in pregnancy. *European Journal of Pediatrics, 161*, 445–448.

Toschke, A. M., Montgomery, S. M., Pfeiffer, U., & von Kries, R. (2003). Early intrauterine exposure to tobacco-inhaled products and obesity. *American Journal of Epidemiology, 158*, 1068–1074.

von Kries, R., Koletzko, B., Sauerwald, T., von Mutius, E., Barnert, D., Grunert, V., et al. (1999). Breast feeding and obesity: Cross sectional study. *British Medical Journal, 319*, 147–150.

von Kries, R., Toschke, A. M., Koletzko, B., & Slikker, W., Jr. (2002). Maternal smoking during pregnancy and childhood obesity. *American Journal of Epidemiology, 156*, 954–961.

Wang, Y. (2001). Cross-national comparison of childhood obesity: The epidemic and the relationship between obesity and socioeconomic status. *International Journal of Epidemiology, 30*, 1129–1136.

Webber, L. S., Osganian, S. K., Feldman, H. A., Wu, M., McKenzie, T. L., Nichaman, M., et al. (1996). Cardiovascular risk factors among children after a 2 1/2-year intervention—The CATCH Study. *Preventive Medicine, 25*, 432–441.

Welsh, J. A., Cogswell, M. E., Rogers, S., Rockett, H., Mei, Z., & Grummer-Strawn, L. M. (2005). Overweight among low-income preschool children associated with the consumption of sweet drinks: Missouri, 1999–2002. *Pediatrics, 115*, e223–229.

Whitaker, R. C., Wright, J. A., Pepe, M. S., Seidel, K. D., & Dietz, W. H. (1997). Predicting obesity in young adulthood from childhood and parental obesity. *New England Journal of Medicine, 337*, 869–873.

Yoshinaga, M., Yuasa, Y., Hatano, H., Kono, Y., Nomura, Y., Oku, S., et al. (1995). Effect of total adipose weight and systemic hypertension on left ventricular mass in children. *The American Journal of Cardiology, 76*, 785–787.

Chapter Eight

Diabetes in Childhood

Tonja R. Nansel and Korey K. Hood

INTRODUCTION

Type 1 diabetes (previously called insulin-dependent or juvenile-onset diabetes) is a common pediatric chronic disease, occurring in approximately 1 in every 400 to 600 children (National Institute of Diabetes and Digestive and Kidney Diseases, 2005). Onset is commonly in middle childhood, but the disease may develop as early as infancy and as late as middle adulthood. Type 1 diabetes results from autoimmune destruction of the insulin-producing beta cells of the pancreas (also called the islets of Langerhans). This results in a complete loss of the ability to produce insulin, a hormone necessary for survival. Normally, ingested food is broken down into glucose, which is circulated through the blood and used by the cells for energy, growth, and brain functioning. Without insulin, glucose cannot be transported into the cell. Instead, it remains in the blood, resulting in hyperglycemia (high blood sugar) while the cells literally starve. In addition to this vital role in carbohydrate metabolism, insulin is essential for storage of both fats and amino acids.

Type 2 diabetes (previously called non-insulin-dependent or adult-onset diabetes) involves different physiological processes, but has similar symptoms and physical effects. Type 2 diabetes is not immune-mediated, and is characterized by insulin resistance rather than insulin deficit. That is, the body is able to make insulin, but the cells cannot properly use it. Type 2 diabetes is highly associated with obesity, diet, and a sedentary lifestyle. With obesity, particularly visceral fat, the amount of insulin produced increases, while the sensitivity to insulin decreases. Until recently, type 2 diabetes was rare to nonexistent in childhood. However, with the dramatic increase in obesity in the U.S. population, a concomitant increase of type 2 in adults, and the emergence of type 2 diabetes in children has occurred (Fagot-Campagna et al., 2000; Kaufman, 2002). Because type 2 diabetes has only recently been diagnosed in the pediatric population, relatively little research addressing emotional health in this population has been conducted. While findings from research with the type 1 population may well be relevant to those with type 2, there are substantial demographic differences in the populations. Type 1 diabetes has the highest prevalence among Caucasians and occurs with similar frequency across socioeconomic lines; however, type 2 diabetes is most prevalent in minority groups, particularly Hispanic and African-American populations, and among those of lower socioeconomic status. Thus, generalization of findings from the type 1 population to those with type 2 diabetes must be done with caution. Because inadequate research findings on the type 2 population are currently available, this chapter will address only type 1 diabetes.

Treatment of type 1 diabetes involves providing insulin through multiple daily injections or through the use of an insulin pump, which infuses insulin through an indwelling catheter placed under the skin. Because insulin is broken down in the stomach, it cannot be given orally. Inhaled insulin became available in 2006; however, as of the writing of this chapter, it has not been approved for use in children and adolescents. The amount of insulin required by the body at any given time is variable, depending on foods eaten, activity, and other factors. The specific dose of insulin taken is based primarily on the amount of carbohydrate consumed; thus children with diabetes typically either consume a specified amount of carbohydrate at each meal or match their insulin dose to the amount of carbohydrate chosen. Even with careful matching of insulin dose to carbohydrate consumption, however, the delivery of insulin is not as precisely matched to the body's needs as a healthy pancreas would be able to do, and as a result, the body's blood sugar level may become excessively high or low. A person with diabetes must check his or her blood sugar level multiple times a day in order to correct for these blood sugar fluctuations. This is generally done by pricking the finger and placing a drop of blood on a special reagent strip, which is then read by a pager-sized device. The maintenance of blood sugar in a near-normal range is the goal of the diabetes management regimen. A person with diabetes, then, must learn to "think like a pancreas," anticipating the effects of food, physical activity, and other factors such as illness and stress, on their blood sugar levels, and correcting for fluctuations in blood sugar as they occur. While physical activity may require additional adjustment to the insulin dose or carbohydrate consumption, regular physical activity is desirable for optimal diabetes management: it improves insulin sensitivity, reduces overall insulin requirement, and promotes cardiovascular health and optimal body weight.

Excessively low blood sugar, or hypoglycemia, results in impaired cognitive functioning, because the brain can only use glucose to function. Symptoms of hypoglycemia include trembling, dizziness, sweating, and confusion. If not recognized and treated immediately by consumption of fast-acting carbohydrate (e.g., sugar, juice), it can progress to loss of consciousness and seizure, requiring treatment by an injection of glucagon, which releases stored glucose from the liver. Thus, the occurrence of hypoglycemia can be a frightening event for parents and children, and its ever-present possibility a source of worry, especially when the child is not under the parent's supervision. High blood sugar (hyperglycemia), on the other hand, may not result in immediately perceivable symptoms. However, if prolonged, it can result in a dangerous state called diabetic ketoacidosis. Due to the insulin deficit accompanying prolonged high blood sugar, the body must use only fat for its energy needs. The by-products of fat metabolism, ketones, cause excessive acidity in the blood. This acidity is accompanied by dehydration from the body's attempt to eliminate the excess blood sugar through urination. Hospitalization is generally required for treatment of diabetic ketoacidosis. If untreated, diabetic ketoacidosis results in diabetic coma and death. Importantly, high blood sugar also results in gradual damage to the body over time; thus the extent and frequency of high blood sugar is directly related to the risk of long-term complications of diabetes, including cardiovascular disease, blindness (due to retinopathy), kidney failure (nephropathy), and painful nerve damage (neuropathy).

Given the complexity and intensity of diabetes management, it is not surprising that the quality of life in children with diabetes tends to be worse than that of children without a chronic illness. Children with diabetes report lower overall life satisfaction and greater interference with activities, while their parents experience the negative emotional impact of the illness (Faulkner, 2003; Sawyer et al., 2005). However, quality of life in children with diabetes appears to be no worse than that of children with asthma and cystic fibrosis (Sawyer et al., 2005). There is some evidence that optimal management of diabetes promotes greater quality of life. Though research findings are not completely consistent, in the largest study assessing quality of life in children with diabetes, including 2,101 youth from 17 countries, greater quality of life was observed in youth whose diabetes was under better control (Hvidore Study Group on Childhood Diabetes, 2006).

The risk for depression is increased in the presence of chronic diseases occurring in childhood and adolescence (Lavigne & Faier-Routman, 1992). It is estimated that depression in children and adolescents with type 1 diabetes occurs at 2 to 3 times the rate of depression in children without diabetes (Kokkonen, Taanila, & Kokkonen, 1997). Recent reports showed that a significant percentage (17–21%) of youths with type 1 diabetes had substantial depressive symptoms (Grey, Wittemore, & Tamborlane, 2002; Hood et al., 2006), twice the rate of the most liberal estimate of depression in youths without diabetes (Lewinsohn, Clarke, Seeley, & Rohde, 1994). Upon the initial diagnosis of diabetes, children demonstrate an increase in depression and adjustment; these generally resolve by one year postdiagnosis (Grey et al., 2002; Kovacs et al., 1990; Northam, Anderson, Adler, & Werther, 1996). However, by two years after diagnosis, greater rates of depression, dependency, and withdrawal are again observed (Grey, Cameron, Lipman, & Thurber, 1995). This likely reflects the reality of the self-care burden imposed by diabetes, which may engender more dependency conflicts and hostility (Hauser et al., 1990). Correlates of depression in youths with type 1 diabetes include individual, diabetes-specific, and family functioning variables. In some studies, age and gender have been associated with depression in youths with type 1 diabetes (Jacobson et al., 1997; LaGreca, Swales, Klemp, Madigan, & Skyler, 1995). Other correlates include lower family cohesion and less warm and caring family behaviors (i.e., parental or family support for diabetes management) (Grey et al., 2002).

Depression in children and adolescents with type 1 diabetes has been associated with poorer diabetes outcomes (Littlefield et al., 1992), recurrent hospital admissions for diabetic-ketoacidosis (Smaldone, Judy, Raymond, & Weinger, 2004; Stewart, Rao, Emslie, Klein, & White, 2005), and a 10-fold increase in suicidal ideation (Goldston, Kovacs, Ho, Parrone, & Stiffler, 1994). However, these themes are not consistently found across studies on depression and type 1 diabetes in youths. In fact, the entire sample of studies from which these results are drawn is less than 20, indicating a serious need for further documentation of the link between depression and diabetes in youths. Typical comorbid conditions such as anxiety rarely have been examined alongside depression (Grey et al., 2002). Further, much of the groundbreaking work done on depression in youths with type 1 diabetes by Kovacs and colleagues (Kovacs, Goldston, Obrosky, & Iyengar, 1992; Kovacs, Brent, Steinberg, Paulauskas, & Reid, 1986; Kovacs, Feinberg, et al., 1985; Kovacs et al., 1990) occurred before the focus on intensive insulin therapy (Diabetes Control and Complications Trial Research Group, 1994a). Current rates may be higher, given the increased emphasis on achieving normoglycemia and intensification of the treatment regimen (Silverstein et al., 2005).

The promotion of emotional health in children with diabetes involves addressing "traditional" emotional health outcomes such as depression, anxiety, and adjustment problems, as well as overall quality of life. In addition, the complexity of managing type 1 diabetes underscores the need for emotional and behavioral health to maximize the child or adolescent's diabetes self-management. A certain level of cognitive ability, emotional maturity, and long-term perspective are necessary to interpret blood glucose levels appropriately and integrate carbohydrate intake along with physical activity levels into the selection and timing of appropriate insulin doses. Recent advances in diabetes care have greatly improved potential health outcomes; but at the same time have increased the daily effort involved in the diabetes management regimen. Therefore, this chapter will address adherence to the diabetes treatment regimen and resulting metabolic control as relevant outcomes for understanding risk and resiliency, as well as for evaluating the effectiveness of behavioral intervention.

BIOLOGICAL/GENETIC FACTORS

The autoimmune destruction of insulin-producing beta cells that causes type 1 diabetes is a process influenced by genetic and environmental factors (Hattersley, 1997; Sadeharju, Knip, Hiltunen, Akerblom, & Hyoty, 2003). The recent increase in type 1 diabetes prevalence of 3% per year from 1990 to 1996 suggests an important environmental role in its development. However, there is considerable scientific inquiry about the nature of this gene–environment interaction and many aspects are still not understood (Atkinson & Eisenbarth, 2001; Knip, 1998; Morales, She, & Schatz, 2001). Environmental factors that may play a role in triggering this autoimmune process in genetically susceptible individuals include exposure to a specific virus group (enterovirus), consumption of cow's milk protein, vitamin D deficiency, and various toxins (Akerblom, Vaarala, Hyoty, Ilonen, & Knip, 2002).

INDIVIDUAL FACTORS INFLUENCING RISK AND RESILIENCY

Individual adaptation to the demands imposed by diabetes is influenced by the cognitive and behavioral capacities of the child, as well as personal demographic factors. Girls typically show a poorer quality of life (Faulkner, 2003; Hvidore Study Group on Childhood Diabetes, 2006) and higher rates of depression (Grey et al., 2002) than do boys, and older youths tend to demonstrate poorer quality of life (Hvidore Study Group on Childhood Diabetes, 2006), greater depression (Grey et al., 2002), and poorer adherence (Jacobson et al., 1990; Johnson et al., 1992; LaGreca, Follansbee, & Skyler, 1990; Weissberg-Benchell et al., 1995) than their younger counterparts. This may be related to greater perceived impact of diabetes management as the youth takes on greater responsibility for management tasks while also experiencing normal developmental changes of adolescence, with accompanying school, extracurricular, and social activities. Feelings of being "different" may be accentuated during this time, as adolescents are developing a sense of identity. Racial differences in adherence are also present. Poorer adherence and metabolic control have been observed in African-American youths (Auslander, Anderson, Bubb, Jung, & Santiago, 1990; Auslander, Thompson, Dreitzer, White, & Santiago, 1997; Harris, Greco,

Wysocki, Elder-Danda, & White, 1999; Faulkner, 2003; Weissberg-Benchell et al., 1995), though at least some of this difference may be accounted for by family structure and socioeconomic status.

Adaptation to the daily demands imposed by diabetes management may be understood from the perspective of a stress-adaptation model (Lazarus & Folkman, 1984; Pollack, 1993), in which the individual's psychological response to a situation and ensuing coping responses impact adjustment and subsequent outcomes (including quality of life, adherence, and metabolic control). Support for this model has been found across both cross-sectional and longitudinal studies. In newly diagnosed children, the use of avoidance behaviors for coping was associated with poorer metabolic control one year later (Grey, Lipman, Cameron, & Thurber, 1997). Among preadolescents and adolescents with established diabetes, the use of cognitive restructuring was associated with greater emotional well-being (Edgar, Psychol, & Skinner, 2003). In studies spanning up to four years, avoidant coping, aggressive coping, and behavioral disengagement were associated with poorer metabolic control (Graue, Wentzel-Larsen, Bru, Hanestad, & Sovik, 2004; Seiffge-Krenke & Stemmler, 2003), while active coping skills promoted greater adherence (Jacobson et al., 1990) and metabolic control (Delamater, Kurtz, Bubb, White, & Santiago, 1987; Graue et al., 2004). In addition, adolescents' level of social competence has been found to buffer the negative effect of stress on metabolic control, such that youth with low social competence show poorer metabolic control associated with stress, while for those with high social competence, increased stress was not associated with poorer control (Hanson, Henggeler, & Burghen, 1987).

Constructs grounded in social cognitive theory (Bandura, 1986) provide further insight into individual factors influencing risk and resiliency. Perceptions regarding the expected positive and negative outcomes of the diabetes management regimen (termed outcome expectations in social cognitive theory) influence the degree to which children and adolescents adhere to the regimen (Bond, Aiken, & Somerville, 1992; Brownlee-Duffeck et al., 1987; Iannotti et al., 2006; Palardy, Greening, Ott, Holderby, & Atchison, 1998). For example, beliefs that diabetes management behaviors will interfere with social activities or cause interpersonal discomfort create a substantial barrier to regular adherence, while beliefs that adhering to one's regimen will enhance the ability to engage in sports or bring about parental approval and praise will promote greater adherence. These beliefs reflect both external reality as well as internal cognitive processes, and so indicate several possible routes that behavioral intervention may be used to improve diabetes management. In addition, beliefs about one's ability to engage in the requisite diabetes management tasks, or self-efficacy, further influences behavior (Griva, Myers, & Newman, 2000; Grossman, Brink, & Hauser, 1987; Iannotti et al., 2006; Ott, Greening, Palardy, Holderby, & DeBell, 2000; Palardy et al., 1998). Self-efficacy may develop out of past experience with the desired behavior, as well as personal beliefs about ones capabilities. Self-efficacy may be enhanced through skill development and subsequent positive behavioral experiences.

FAMILY FACTORS INFLUENCING RISK AND RESILIENCY

The great majority of work regarding risk and resiliency among youth with diabetes has addressed the role of the family in promoting emotional health and adaptation to the demands of the diabetes regimen. Diabetes is a life-altering event for families, who rapidly transition from dealing with typical developmental and parenting issues in a healthy child to facing the many emotional, cognitive, and behavioral issues inherent in diabetes management. Parents are faced with the knowledge that their child has an irreversible chronic disease, which carries the threat of both short- and long-term complications. They deal with the constant possibility of the effects of both low and high blood sugar. With low blood sugar comes the threat of loss of consciousness or seizure. Episodes of high blood sugar, on the other hand, may evoke the fear of future long-term complications. Daily blood glucose monitoring, insulin administration, meal planning, carbohydrate counting, and anticipating and responding to low and high blood sugar values, as well as making frequent health care visits and communicating with the health care team as needed impose a considerable burden on families. Thus, it is not only the individual with diabetes who adapts to the demands and stress of the illness, but the entire family.

Given the burden of care associated with diabetes management, it is perhaps not surprising that children from two-parent families demonstrate significantly better metabolic control than those from single-parent families (Auslander, Anderson, et al., 1990; Auslander, Thompson, et al., 1997; Hanson, Henggeler, Rodrigue, Burghen, & Murphy, 1988b; Harris et al., 1999). With two parents comes a greater ability to share the work associated with managing the illness, as well as the potential social and emotional support afforded by a partner.

Greater than the effect of the family structure on promoting emotional health in diabetes, however, is the level of family functioning. Healthy adaptation to the demands associated with diabetes management is greatly facilitated by an environment of healthy, positive family functioning. A family's general level of warmth, cohesion, support, communication, problem solving, and conflict resolution skills is consistently associated with quality of life, adherence, and metabolic control (Auslander, Bubb, Rogge, & Santiago, 1993; Bobrow, Avruskin, & Siller, 1985; Davis et al., 2001; Gustafsson, Cederblad, Ludvigsson, & Lundin, 1987; Hanson, DeGuire, Schinkel, & Kolterman, 1995; Hanson, Henggeler, Harris, & Moore, 1989; Hauser et al., 1990; Leonard, Jang, Savik, & Plumbo, 2005; Schafer, McCaul, & Glasgow, 1986; Whittemore, Urban, Tamborlane, & Grey, 2003; Wysocki, 1993). Such an environment promotes emotional support, adaptive coping skills, motivation, self-efficacy, and positive outcome expectations, as well as teamwork and appropriate levels of assistance and autonomy. Conversely, family conflict, both general (Hauser et al., 1990; Miller-Johnson et al., 1994) and that specifically related to diabetes (Anderson, Vangsness, et al., 2002; Laffel, Connell, et al., 2003; Wysocki, 1993), is associated with impaired quality of life, adherence, and metabolic control. Family conflict may adversely affect diabetes adjustment by impairing family communication and problem solving, diminishing emotional support and teamwork, and setting up diabetes management tasks as an area for rebellion or power struggles.

An important challenge facing youth with diabetes and their parents is the negotiation and sharing of diabetes management responsibilities. When children are initially diagnosed with diabetes, parents typically assume most or all of the responsibility for its day-to-day management. Normal developmental processes, however, result in a transition of responsibility from parent to youth that occurs over a period of several years, with the youth assuming progressively more responsibility over time. However, there is substantial evidence that youth who are given excessive responsibility, such as that exceeding their level of cognitive and social maturity, experience poorer adherence and metabolic control, and increased frequency of hospitalizations (Anderson, Auslander, Jung, Miller, & Santiago, 1990; Anderson, Ho, Brackett, Finkelstein, & Laffel, 1997; Anderson, Vangsness, et al., 2002; Ingersoll, Orr, Herrold, & Golden, 1986; Wysocki, Taylor, et al., 1996). In addition, even as youth assume greater responsibility for specific diabetes management tasks, the support and assistance of their parents remains critical. While youth ratings of parent support are consistently associated with well-being, adherence, and metabolic control across ages (Hanson et al., 1987; Lewin et al., 2005; McKelvey et al., 1993; Skinner, John, & Hampson, 2000), the way in which support and assistance are provided must evolve. The parental role changes from a directive role to one that is more collaborative and consultative. Indeed, regardless of the specific amount of assistance provided, collaborative involvement is associated with better outcomes across age, while intrusive or controlling involvement is associated with worse outcomes among older youth (Anderson & Coyne, 1991; Wiebe et al., 2005).

SOCIAL AND COMMUNITY FACTORS INFLUENCING RISK AND RESILIENCY

Given the demanding nature of the diabetes management regimen and its constant presence in day-to-day life, it seems evident that diabetes management and emotional adaptation to the illness would be influenced by broader social and community factors. Socioeconomic status has consistently been found to be associated with poorer adherence (Auslander et al., 1997; Glasgow et al., 1991; White, Kolman, Wexler, Polin, & Winter, 1984). This may be due to multiple factors, including the many stressors and competing demands faced by these families, as well as potential greater difficulty in accessing health care and obtaining needed medical supplies and resources. Not surprisingly, the health care system that youth and their families are able to access influence subsequent health outcomes. Those who receive care at pediatric endocrinology specialty centers demonstrate more favorable health outcomes than those receiving care by adult endocrinology or general practitioners. These centers not only are more specialized in the medical care of children and adolescents, but also are better able to address both the developmental needs of the youth and management of diabetes within the family system. They typically employ a multidisciplinary approach, with routine access to diabetes educators and dietitians, as well as referral for psychological care when needed. Finally, parents' and youths' satisfaction with health care provider competence are related to greater adherence, and fewer hospitalizations (Hanson, Henggeler, Harris, et al., 1988).

For children and adolescents, the most immediate and salient environment after the family is the peer network. Surprisingly, little research has addressed this area. The studies that have been conduced indicate that, while family is the primary source of tangible support and assistance for diabetes management tasks, peers play an important role in the provision of emotional support, possibly surpassing that of the family (LaGreca, 1992; LaGreca, Auslander, et al., 1995). This emotional support is provided in various forms, including acceptance (e.g., helping the youth to not feel different because of diabetes), companionship support (such as adjusting plans to accommodate the child's meal plan or exercising with the child), helping the youth to maintain a positive outlook, and praising or encouraging the youth regarding diabetes management. This support is important not only for youths' emotional health (Skinner et al., 2000), but may positively impact adherence as well (Bearman & LaGreca, 2002).

EVIDENCE-BASED TREATMENT INTERVENTIONS FOR EMOTIONAL HEALTH IN CHILDHOOD DIABETES

Children and adolescents with type 1 diabetes and their families are faced with the difficult task of managing a chronic disease with a complex, intensive, daily regimen. Worldwide, diabetes management and control remains largely suboptimal in many pediatric diabetes centers (Danne et al., 2001; Mortensen & Hougaard, 1997). While suboptimal glycemic control is in part due to the imperfect nature of the treatment regimen, as well as physiological changes during puberty that increase insulin need and unpredictability, it is also linked to poor adherence to the diabetes management regimen (Anderson, Ho, et al., 1997; Weissberg-Benchell et al., 1995). For example, approximately 30% of adolescents report missing prescribed blood glucose monitoring and making up results to appear to be in better control. One-quarter also report missing insulin injections. In addition, parents significantly underestimated the degree to which mismanagement occurs. Poor adherence and suboptimal glycemic control are related to an array of demographic, diabetes-specific, emotional (e.g., depression), and family functioning factors that inhibit the youth's and family member's ability to manage diabetes optimally (Amiel, Sherwin, Simonson, Lauritano, & Tamborlane, 1986; Moreland et al., 2004). Thus, clinical researchers and practitioners continue to search for ways to improve diabetes management and control, mindful of the physiologic, behavioral, and emotional challenges of managing diabetes.

In a review of behavioral assessment and treatment in pediatric diabetes, Wysocki (2006) notes that treatment of suboptimal diabetes management and control should follow thorough assessment of family, personal, and contextual factors. Treatment is often aimed at improving adherence behaviors and should consider family factors as either promoting or putting up barriers to effective management. Improving family management processes (e.g., diabetes-specific communication, problem solving, conflict) can be helpful in achieving better diabetes outcomes. However, a systematic review and meta-analysis concluded that overall, psychological interventions in children and adolescents with diabetes show weak evidence of improving diabetes control (Winkley, Ismail, Landau, & Eisler, 2006). These mixed messages are not surprising given the variety of outcomes targeted in psychological intervention trials. Many studies suggest improvements in processes linked to diabetes control, as highlighted by Wysocki (2006); however, they may not always translate to improved diabetes control.

As noted, interventions designed for children and adolescents with type 1 diabetes target several different outcomes. In this chapter, we focus on all outcomes (diabetes control as defined by percentage of hemoglobin A1c in the blood; diabetes management as defined by adherence; and individual and family factors as evidenced by quality of life, emotional distress, or conflict) because they are all either directly or indirectly related. The links between psychological interventions and emotional outcomes in youths with a chronic disease such as diabetes are nearly impossible to separate.

What Works

Regardless of the outcome of interest (management, control, or adjustment), no psychological interventions meet the criteria for this category. There are promising evidence-based interventions, but none has been successfully replicated three times. It is very typical for these interventions to be carried out and reported by only one group of researchers, which also limits "evidence-based practice."

What Might Work

There are many promising psychological interventions aimed at improving family processes around diabetes management, adherence, and diabetes control. These interventions are not presented in any particular order as they all have merit. We highlight previous studies that may have served as the foundation or starting point for some of the more refined treatment packages. Note that we also focus on research conducted since the mid-1990s, as diabetes management has experienced a dramatic shift in the way it is prescribed and conducted due to advances in insulin therapy and the encouraging results of the Diabetes Control and Complications Trial (Diabetes Control and Complications Trial Research Group, 1993, 1994b, 1996) demonstrating the clear effect of optimal blood glucose control on the prevention or delay of long-term complications. For each intervention, the conceptual framework (e.g., cognitive-behavioral vs. behavioral), the format with which they were delivered (group, family-based, individual), and the target group (age range, family members included or not) are reviewed.

Behavioral Family Systems Therapy for Diabetes

Behavioral Family Systems Therapy (BFST) is a family-focused intervention that employs flexible, multidimensional methods of treatment to improve family communication and problem solving skills (Robin & Foster, 1989). The BFST model has been adapted to the treatment of youths with type 1 diabetes to promote these family-based skills in an effort to improve diabetes management and control (Wysocki, Harris, Greco, et al., 2000). Wysocki and colleagues conducted a randomized, controlled trial of BFST that included 10 sessions over a 3-month period and found subsequent improvements in these family processes (e.g., improved communication, reduced conflict). These effects were observed for up to one year post-treatment (Wysocki, Greco, Harris, Bubb, & White, 2001). However, it was not until the investigators adapted the intervention to be more diabetes-specific (BFST-Diabetes; BFST-D) that improvements in adherence and diabetes control occurred (Wysocki et al., 2006).

In BFST-D, families receive 12 sessions across six months from a psychologist trained in the BFST model. Sessions focus on problem solving, communication, cognitive restructuring, and functional-structural family therapy (Wysocki, Harris, Buckloh, et al., 2006). Additional components of BFST-D have previous empirical support and include behavioral contracting around diabetes management tasks, goal setting, diabetes education, psychoeducation, parental participation in simulated diabetes tasks (e.g., testing and treating simulated hypoglycemia), and possible extension into the social networks of the youth.

Coping Skills Training

Coping Skills Training (CST) is a group-based approach to teaching problem solving and communication skills to youths with type 1 diabetes (Grey, Boland, Davidson, Li, & Tamborlane, 2000). The theoretical approach to CST is consistent with a cognitive-behavioral model and a goal of this intervention is to increase the competence of the adolescent. Groups of two to three teens participate in six weekly sessions and then are followed for monthly visits across the remainder of the year. The trainer is typically a master's level nurse practitioner with training in pediatric psychiatry. CST, combined with intensive insulin management, has been shown to produce better diabetes control and promote improvements in quality of life up to one year later (Grey, Boland, Davidson, Yu, & Tamborlane, 1999; Grey et al., 2000).

Previous studies have indicated some benefit from coping and problem solving skills training (Cigrang et al., 1991; Satin, LaGreca, Zigo, & Skyler, 1989; Warren-Boulton, Anderson, Schwartz, & Dreyer, 1981). However, these studies were largely conducted with smaller sample sizes, and all were done prior to the aforementioned major shift in diabetes management due to the results of the Diabetes Control and Complications Trial.

Family-Focused Teamwork Interventions

Family-focused teamwork (TW) interventions focus on parent–child interactions and seek to improve diabetes sharing of responsibility while reducing conflict. Ultimately, better functioning in these areas has led to improved diabetes outcomes and quality of life (Anderson et al., 1997; Anderson, Brackett et al., 1999; Svoren, Butler, Levine, Anderson, & Laffel, 2003). Conducted within the context of a pediatric diabetes clinic, these interventions are integrated into the existing model of care. Typically, a trained research assistant works with families at the time of their clinic visit and covers various topics ranging from education about diabetes management to family processes (e.g., strategies to minimize conflict). As a "care ambassador," the research assistant also works with the family to schedule appointments and relay concerns to the medical staff. These interventions have been shown to improve adherence (Anderson, Brackett, et al., 1999) and reduce acute complications (e.g., emergency room visits) for those participating in the teamwork intervention (Svoren et al., 2003).

Multisystemic Therapy

Multisystemic Therapy (MST) is an intensive form of family therapy that takes place in home and community settings and has traditionally targeted youths with serious mental health issues and their families. The approach has recently been applied to treating youths with suboptimal or poorly controlled diabetes (Ellis, Naar-King, et al., 2004; Ellis, Frey, et al., 2005). The specific focus in MST is on improving the mental health of the adolescent by targeting individual needs within the context of the family system and the broader community (school, health care system). As noted, this is an intensive program that involves a primary therapist and supervisor. The MST therapist meets two to three times weekly with families until treatment goals are met, although there is an attempt to keep families in MST for six months. In a large, randomized, controlled trial of MST, intent-to-treat analyses revealed positive outcomes in adherence and metabolic control as well as a decrease in diabetes-related stress (Ellis, Frey, et al., 2005). These findings suggest promise for this intervention.

What Doesn't Work

A literature review did not reveal any interventions that clearly did not work. This is likely due to the "file drawer" phenomenon, but also to the relative infancy of this area of research. It should be noted, however, that clinical experience suggests that "scare tactics" such as threats that one will experience long-term complications due to poor adherence or exposure to people experiencing poor diabetes outcomes (e.g., on dialysis, amputation, blindness) does not motivate children and adolescents to do better with diabetes management and in fact is more likely to impair emotional adjustment and behavioral management.

Comment

Common to each of these promising intervention approaches is attention to the individual, family, and social contexts of diabetes management. Processes addressed across approaches, at least to some degree, include behavioral skills such as coping and problem solving, the development of adaptive family processes, and a consideration of the broader social context in which diabetes management occurs. In addition, consideration is given to the interface of diabetes management with normal developmental challenges, including parent–child sharing of responsibility, as well as the management of peer and social situations. Finally, while the interventions are not primarily educational in nature, all address various diabetes-specific issues as they juncture with the behavioral, emotional, and family process challenges that arise in the management of this illness.

PSYCHOPHARMACOLOGY AND CHILDHOOD DIABETES

A review of the available literature revealed few indicators of the best psychopharmacologic approaches to treating children and adolescents with diabetes who also have emotional problems. There are no randomized, controlled trials of medication treatment versus psychological treatment or placebo for children and adolescents with type 1 diabetes who also have a psychological disorder (e.g., major depressive disorder). This is concerning given the two-to threefold increase in risk of depression in youths with diabetes. However, given the low prevalence of type 1 diabetes in youths (~ 1 in 500 youths) and only a fraction of those with depression, there may be limited numbers to conduct such a study. Clinical experience suggests that many children and adolescents with diabetes are treated as they would be if they did not have diabetes (e.g., prescribed antidepressant medication if clinically depressed). Further, there do not appear to be contraindications to the use of typical childhood medications for such conditions as depression, anxiety, or ADHD. However, each case should be considered individually.

There are indications that some of the atypical antipsychotics are associated with hyperglycemia and possible onset of diabetes (Koller, Cross, & Schneider, 2004; Sernyak, Gulanski, & Rosenheck, 2005). When considering use of these medications in youths with diabetes, it appears that much caution is warranted and close follow-up is an absolute must.

EVIDENCE-BASED STRATEGIES TO PREVENT EMOTIONAL PROBLEMS IN YOUTHS WITH DIABETES

An extensive literature review yielded no trials with the primary aim of preventing the development of emotional problems in youths with diabetes. However, the findings from several studies suggest that targeting diabetes outcomes early may have a beneficial effect on emotional outcomes. Across the few studies reported here, the targeted participants were largely those with recently diagnosed diabetes, with the aim of preventing the difficulties that can arise as diabetes management begins.

What Works

As with treatment interventions for emotional health in children with diabetes, a review of the literature did not uncover any preventive intervention that met the criteria of three successful trials. There are promising evidence-based interventions, but none has been successfully replicated three times.

What Might Work

Promising options for preventing emotional problems in youth with diabetes include family-focused teamwork intervention, self-management training, and peer based interventions.

Family-Focused Teamwork Intervention

Family-focused teamwork (TW) interventions were addressed earlier in this chapter. Within the area of prevention of difficulties related to adjustment, diabetes management, or control, TW interventions aim to establish effective parent–child communication patterns and realistic sharing of diabetes responsibilities (Laffel, Vangsness, et al., 2003). In this framework, the care ambassador met with families around the time of their clinic visit and reviewed a plan for a responsibility-sharing agreement. Families received four educational modules around management, with the care ambassador tailoring their plans to the apparent needs of the particular family. Laffel, Vangsness, and colleagues (2003) targeted children and adolescents with relatively newly diagnosed diabetes, but also included a subset of participants with diabetes duration from three to six years. At the end of the intervention, approximately one year later, there was improvement in diabetes control for the group that received the TW intervention. In addition, family involvement in diabetes tasks increased significantly in the TW intervention. Both of these findings suggest that early intervention is an effective strategy for prevention.

Self-Management Training

Self-management training (SMT) extends the traditional diabetes education provided after diagnosis, with the goal for families to master self-management information and skills over time in the context of a collaborative relationship with the health care team. Soon after the standard education that families received in the hospital at the time of diabetes diagnosis, SMT was delivered to a subset of participants (Delamater, Bubb, et al., 1990). SMT consisted of seven visits with a medical social worker within the first 4 months after diagnosis and then booster sessions at 6 and 12 months postdiagnosis. The session content was adapted from models of behavioral parent training. All participants, including those in standard care groups, improved diabetes control across the first six months; however, only those in the SMT group had significantly better diabetes control at one and two years postdiagnosis. While there were no indicators of emotional functioning reported in this study, these results do suggest that intervening early prevents the deterioration in diabetes control that often comes with childhood and adolescence. A limitation of this study is the small sample size (n = 36 total).

Peer Based Interventions

Several interventions for youths with type 1 diabetes have focused on peer relationships (Anderson, Wolf, Burkhart, Cornell, & Bacon, 1989; Greco, Shroff Pendley, McDonell, & Reeves, 2001). Greco and colleagues (2001) targeted adolescents with newly diagnosed diabetes in an intervention aimed at increasing diabetes knowledge and social support of diabetes care by including these adolescents' best friends. Both the adolescent and best friend attended four two-hour sessions that consisted of group education and therapy delivered by a licensed psychologist. Another group received standard diabetes care during this time. Some of the skills addressed during this intervention included problem solving, reflective listening, social support, and stress management, in addition to the basics of diabetes management. While the study sample was small (21 participant-friend dyads in each group), those in the peer-intervention group showed more diabetes knowledge and support, the friends demonstrated better self-perception, and parents reported less diabetes-related conflict. These findings are promising and highlight the potential of intervening early with peers to both teach and normalize diabetes care, and provide concrete ways to offer social support.

What Doesn't Work

A review of the literature did not uncover any intervention that should not be used at the present time due to ineffectiveness or adverse outcomes. Interestingly, we found no research addressing support or self-help groups as a potential route for the promotion of emotional health in youths with type 1 diabetes. Clinical experience seems to indicate that, while youth value the support of peers with diabetes in the diabetes camp setting, they do not generally show an interest in potential peer support from a regular organized group setting of youth with diabetes. This may related to the developmental needs of youths in the areas of identity development and peer relationships, possibly creating a desire by the youth to not identify themselves by their illness.

Comment

This collection of interventions aimed at preventing future deterioration of diabetes management and control are promising in their potential for a positive impact on emotional outcomes. However, there is a clear need for much more work in this area before these interventions are considered the gold standard for prevention. Several keys for prevention appear to be early intervention that cuts across family functioning and the social networks of these youths, as well as the specific challenges created by the complex and intensive nature of diabetes management.

RECOMMENDED BEST PRACTICE

We have reported on a handful of promising approaches for prevention and treatment in the emotional health of children and adolescents with type 1 diabetes. A unifying feature of these interventions is that they target both physical and emotional health outcomes and all show evidence and future promise for promotion of both. With these findings in mind, we make the following recommendations when implementing an intervention for youths with type 1 diabetes, whether primarily preventive or treatment focused.

- Each of the intervention approaches reviewed in this chapter offers a potentially efficacious means for promoting the emotional health of children with diabetes. Further, each approach has potential application to both prevention and treatment. Indeed, in this area, there is often not a clear delineation between prevention and treatment. Individual and family adaptation to diabetes, maintenance of emotional health and quality of life, and adherence to the behavioral demands of the illness are all interrelated and dynamic processes that must be addressed comprehensively.
- Regardless of the specific approach selected, an intervention promoting emotional health in children with diabetes must address the individual, family, and social contexts of diabetes management. The demands of the illness create added demands on individual, family, and social interaction, coping, and problem solving, potentially magnifying existing maladaptive patterns and creating the need for a greater level of skill than might be required otherwise. Thus, the comprehensiveness of each intervention approach must be maintained in order to be effective.
- The diabetes-specific nature of the intervention needs to be emphasized. There is evidence to suggest that the interventions reviewed can improve family processes in general, but the key processes for effective management and control appear to be those that are diabetes-specific. Because diabetes is embedded in to the daily lives of these youths and their families, even interventions specifically targeting family processes such as communication, conflict, and problem solving need to addresses these processes as they interface with diabetes management.
- The approach chosen should be consistent with the resources available. The studies reported here include individual, family, group, and system interventions, and all show effectiveness in improving physical and emotional health outcomes. The most effective intervention may be one that includes all of these components, but cost, personnel, and other resources are practical considerations. The most suit-

able method of delivery is one that fits bests with the available resources and can be practically sustained over time.

- Hands-on activities are a must. Every intervention reviewed here includes practical, behavioral strategies that are both practiced during the intervention and outside of the clinic. Developing plans for solving diabetes-specific problems, behavioral contracting, and setting up links in the broader system are all examples of hands-on activities that can be conducted in an effective intervention.

- It is important to remain flexible while maintaining integrity of the approach. All of these effective interventions cover certain content areas, whether the development of more adaptive family functioning in BFST-D, the development of coping skills in CST, goal-setting and achievement in MST, or the basics of diabetes in each intervention package. However, all approaches emphasize the flexible nature of the intervention and work with families if they need additional help or more focused help. Diabetes management and the nature of children and adolescents can throw many twists and turns in to an intervention. The effective intervention will be one that is responsive to those ups and downs while still maintaining fidelity.

- Relevant sociocultural factors that may affect intervention selection or implementation should be considered. It should be noted that little research has addressed differential needs or the effectiveness of intervention approaches across racial/ethnic/cultural or socioeconomic groups. This is likely due to the difficulty in obtaining sufficient numbers of subjects in any one minority group from a single clinical site for comparative analyses. Thus, practitioners working with these populations should build needs assessment and formative evaluation into their work to ensure that the intervention approach taken is implemented in a way that is culturally relevant and sensitive to the unique needs and challenges of the target population.

In summary, the field of behavioral intervention in diabetes management is not yet sufficiently advanced to provide a singular, clear "best practice" approach. Nonetheless, we have obtained a good understanding of the myriad factors influencing emotional health and behavioral management in children with diabetes, and there exist multiple promising approaches that share important commonalities in their theoretical underpinnings and target processes. A compilation of the findings from these varying approaches suggest that behavioral intervention offers an efficacious means for promoting the emotional and physical health of children with diabetes.

REFERENCES

Akerblom, H. K., Vaarala, O., Hyoty, H., Ilonen, J., & Knip, M. (2002). Environmental factors in the etiology of type 1 diabetes. *American Journal of Medical Genetics, 115,* 18–29.

Amiel, S. A., Sherwin, R. S., Simonson, D. C., Lauritano, A. A., & Tamborlane, W. V. (1986). Impaired insulin action in puberty. A contributing factor to poor glycemic control in adolescents with diabetes. *New England Journal of Medicine, 315,* 215–219.

Anderson, B. J., Auslander, W. F., Jung, K. C., Miller, P., & Santiago, J. V. (1990). Assessing family sharing of diabetes responsibilities. *Journal of Pediatric Psychology, 15,* 477–492.

Anderson, B., Brackett, J., Ho, J., & Laffel, L. (1999). An office-based intervention to maintain parent–adolescent teamwork in diabetes management: Impact on parent involvement, family conflict, and subsequent glycemic control. *Diabetes Care, 22,* 713–721.

Anderson, B. J., & Coyne, J. C. (1991). "Miscarried helping" in the families of children and adolescents with chronic diseases. In J. H. Johnson & S. B. Johnson (Eds.), *Advances in Child Health Psychology* (pp. 167–177). Gainesville, FL: J. Hillis Miller Health Science Center.

Anderson, B., Ho, J., Brackett, J., Finkelstein, D., & Laffel, L. (1997). Parental involvement in diabetes management tasks: Relationships to blood glucose monitoring adherence and metabolic control in young adolescents with insulin-dependent diabetes mellitus. *The Journal of Pediatrics, 130,* 257–265.

Anderson, B. J., Vangsness, L., Connell, A., Butler, D., Goebel-Fabbri, A., & Laffel, B. (2002). Family conflict, adherence, and glycaemic control in youth with short duration type 1 diabetes. *Diabetic Medicine, 19,* 635–642.

Anderson, B. J., Wolf, F. M., Burkhart, M. T., Cornell, R. G., & Bacon, G. E. (1989). Effects of a peer group intervention on metabolic control of adolescents with IDDM: Randomized outpatient study. *Diabetes Care, 12,* 184–188.

Atkinson, M. A., & Eisenbarth, G. S. (2001). Type 1 diabetes: New perspectives on disease pathogenesis and treatment. *Lancet, 358,* 221–229.

Auslander, W. F., Anderson, B., Bubb, J., Jung, K. C., & Santiago, J. V. (1990). Risk factors to health in diabetic children: A prospective study from diagnosis. *Health & Social Work,15,* 133–142.

Auslander, W. F., Bubb, J., Rogge, M., & Santiago, J. V. (1993). Family stress and resources: Potential areas of intervention in children recently diagnosed with diabetes. *Health & Social Work, 18,* 101–113.

Auslander, W. F., Thompson, S., Dreitzer, D., White, N. H., & Santiago, J. V. (1997). Disparity in glycemic control and adherence between African-American and Caucasian youths with diabetes. *Diabetes Care, 20,* 1569–1575.

Bandura, A. (1986). *Social foundations of thought and action: a social cognitive theory.* Englewood Cliffs, NJ: Prentice-Hall.

Bearman, K. J., & LaGreca, A. M. (2002). Assessing friends' support of adolescents' diabetes care: The Diabetes Social Support Questionnaire—Friends' version. *Journal of Pediatric Psychology, 27,* 417–428.

Bobrow, E. S., Avruskin, T. W., & Siller, J. (1985). Mother–daughter interaction and adherence to diabetes regimens. *Diabetes Care, 8,* 146–151.

Bond, G. G., Aiken, L. S., & Somerville, S. C. (1992). The health belief model and adolescents with insulin-dependent diabetes mellitus. *Health Psychology, 11,* 190–198.

Brownlee-Duffeck, M., Peterson, L., Simonds, J. F., Kilo, C., Goldstein, D., & Hoette, S. (1987). The role of health beliefs in the regimen adherence and metabolic control of adolescents and adults with diabetes mellitus. *Journal of Consulting and Clinical Psychology, 55,* 139–144.

Cigrang, J. A., Shuster, M. L., Hanson, C. L., Burghen, G. A., Harris, M. A., & Schinkel, A. M. (1991). Psychosocial intervention for youths with IDDM: A controlled study of the metabolic and psychological effects of group therapy. *Diabetes, 40*(Suppl. 1), 536A.

Danne, T., Mortensen, H. B., Hougaard, P., Lynggaard, H., Aanstoot, H. J., Chiarelli, F., et al. (2001). Persistent differences among centers over 3 years in glycemic control and hypoglycemia in a study of 3,805 children and adolescents with type 1 diabetes from the Hvidore Study Group. *Diabetes Care, 24,* 1342–1347.

Davis, C. L., Delamater, A. M., Shaw, K. H., La Greca, A. M., Eidson, M. S., Perez-Rodriguez, J. E., et al. (2001). Parenting styles, regimen adherence, and glycemic control in 4- to 10- year-old children with diabetes. *Journal of Pediatric Psychology, 26,* 123–129.

Delamater, A. M., Bubb, J., Davis, S. G., Smith, J. A., Schmidt, L., White, N. H., et al. (1990). Randomized prospective study of self-management training with newly diagnosed diabetic children. *Diabetes Care, 13,* 492–498.

Delamater, A. M., Kurtz, S. M., Bubb, J., White, N. H., & Santiago, J. V. (1987). Stress and coping in relation to metabolic control in adolescents with type 1 diabetes. *Developmental and Behavioral Pediatrics, 8,* 136–140.

Diabetes Control and Complications Trial Research Group (1993). The effect of intensive treatment of diabetes on the development and progression of long-term complications in insulin-dependent diabetes mellitus. *The New England Journal of Medicine, 329,* 977–985.

Diabetes Control and Complications Trial Research Group (1994a). Effect of intensive diabetes treatment on the development and progression of long-term complications in adolescents with insulin-dependent diabetes mellitus: Diabetes Control and Complications Trial. *Journal of Pediatrics, 125,* 177–188.

Diabetes Control and Complications Trial Research Group (1994b). Effect of intensive diabetes treatment on the development and progression of long-term complications in adolescents with insulin-dependent diabetes mellitus: Diabetes Control and Complications Trial. *The Journal of Pediatrics, 125,* 177–188.

Diabetes Control and Complications Trial Research Group (1996). The absence of a glycemic threshold for the development of long-term complications: The perspective of the Diabetes Control and Complications Trial. *Diabetes, 45,* 1289–1298.

Edgar, K. A., Psychol, D., & Skinner, T. C. (2003). Illness representations and coping as predictors of emotional well-being in adolescents with type 1 diabetes. *Journal of Pediatric Psychology, 28*(7), 485–493.

Ellis, D. A., Frey, M. A., Naar-King, S., Templin, T., Cunningham, P. B., & Cakan, N. (2005). The effects of multisystemic therapy on diabetes stress among adolescents with chronically poorly controlled type 1 diabetes: Findings from a randomized, controlled trial. *Pediatrics, 116,* 826–832.

Ellis, D. A., Naar-King, S., Frey, M., Templin, T., Rowland, M., & Greger, N. (2004). Use of multi-systemic therapy to improve regimen adherence among adolescents with type 1 diabetes in poor metabolic control: A pilot investigation. *Journal of Clinical Psychology in Medical Settings, 11,* 315–324.

Fagot-Campagna, A., Pettitt, D., Engelgau, M., Burrows, N., Geiss, L., Valdez, R., et al. (2000). Type 2 diabetes among North American children and adolescents: an epidemiologic review and a public health perspective. *The Journal of Pediatrics, 136,* 664–672.

Faulkner, M. S. (2003). Quality of life for adolescents with type 1 diabetes: Parental and youth perspectives. *Pediatric Nursing, 29,* 362–368.

Glasgow, A. M., Weissberg-Benchell, J., Tynan, W. D., Epstein, S. F., Driscoll, C., Terek, J., et al. (1991). Re-admissions of children with diabetes mellitus to a children's hospital. *Pediatrics, 88,* 98–104.

Goldston, D. B., Kovacs, M., Ho, V. Y., Parrone, P. L., & Stiffler, L. (1994). Suicidal ideation and suicide attempts among youth with insulin-dependent diabetes mellitus. *Journal of the American Academy of Child and Adolescent Psychiatry, 33,* 240–246.

Graue, M., Wentzel-Larsen, T., Bru, E., Hanestad, B. R., & Sovik, O. (2004). The coping styles of adolescents with type 1 diabetes are associated with degree of metabolic control. *Diabetes Care, 27,* 1313–1317.

Greco, P., Shroff Pendley, J., McDonell, K., & Reeves, G. (2001). A peer group intervention for adolescents with type 1 diabetes and their best friends. *Journal of Pediatric Psychology, 26,* 485–490.

Grey, M., Boland, E., Davidson, M., Li, J., & Tamborlane, W. V. (2000). Coping skills training for youth on intensive therapy has long-lasting effects on metabolic control and quality of life. *Journal of Pediatrics, 137,* 107–113.

Grey, M., Boland, E. A., Davidson, M., Yu, C., & Tamborlane, W. V. (1999). Coping skills training for youths with diabetes on intensive therapy. *Applied Nursing Research, 12,* 3–12.

Grey, M., Cameron, M. E., Lipman, T. H., & Thurber, F. W. (1995). Psychosocial status of children with diabetes in the first 2 years after diagnosis. *Diabetes Care, 18,* 1330–1336.

Grey, M., Lipman, T., Cameron, M. E., & Thurber, F. W. (1997). Coping behaviors at diagnosis and in adjustment one year later in children with diabetes. *Nursing Research, 46,* 312–317.

Grey, M., Wittemore, R., & Tamborlane, W. (2002). Depression in type 1 diabetes in children: natural history and correlates. *Journal of Psychosomatic Research, 53,* 907–911.

Griva, K., Myers, L. B., & Newman, S. (2000). Illness perceptions and self efficacy beliefs in adolescents and young adults with insulin dependent diabetes mellitus. *Psychology and Health, 15,* 733–750.

Grossman, H. Y., Brink, S., & Hauser, S. T. (1987). Self-efficacy in adolescent girls and boys with insulin-dependent diabetes mellitus. *Diabetes Care, 10,* 324–329.

Gustafsson, P., Cederblad, M., Ludvigsson, J., & Lundin, B. (1987). Family interaction and metabolic balance in juvenile diabetes mellitus: A prospective study. *Diabetes Research and Clinical Practice, 4,* 7–14.

Hanson, C. L., DeGuire, M. J., Schinkel, A. M., & Kolterman, O. G. (1995). Empirical validation for a family-centered model of care. *Diabetes Care, 18,* 1347–1356.

Hanson, C. L., Henggeler, S. W., & Burghen, G. A. (1987). Social competence and parental support as mediators of the link between stress and metabolic control in adolescents with insulin-dependent diabetes mellitus. *Journal of Consulting and Clinical Psychology, 55*(4), 529–533.

Hanson, C. L., Henggeler, S. W., Harris, M. A., Mitchell, K. A., Carle, D. L., & Burghen, G. A. (1988a). Associations between family members' perceptions of the health care system and the health of youths with insulin-dependent diabetes mellitus. *Journal of Pediatric Psychology, 13,* 543–554.

Hanson, C. L., Henggeler, S. W., Harris, M. A., & Moore, M. (1989). Family system variables and the health status of adolescents with insulin-dependent diabetes mellitus. *Health Psychology, 8,* 239–253.

Hanson, C. L., Henggeler, S. W., Rodrigue, J. R., Burghen, G. A., & Murphy, W. D. (1988b). Father-absent adolescents with insulin-dependent diabetes mellitus: a population at risk? *Journal of Applied Developmental Psychology, 9,* 243–252.

Harris, M. A., Greco, P., Wysocki, T., Elder-Danda, C., & White, N. H. (1999). Adolescents with diabetes from single-parent, blended, and intact families: Health-related and family functioning. *Families, Systems & Health, 17,* 181–196.

Hattersley, A. T. (1997). Genes versus environment in insulin-dependent diabetes: The phoney war. *Lancet, 349,* 147–148.

Hauser, S. T., Jacobson, A. M., Lavori, P., Wolfsdorf, J. I., Herskowitz, R. D., Milley, J. E., et al. (1990). Adherence among children and adolescents with insulin dependent diabetes mellitus over a four year longitudinal follow-up: II. Immediate and long-term linkages with the family milieu. *Journal of Pediatric Psychology, 15*, 527–542.

Hvidore Study Group on Childhood Diabetes. (2006). Good metabolic control is associated with better quality of life in 2,101 adolescents with type 1 diabetes. *Diabetes Care, 24*, 1923–1928.

Hood, K., Huestis, S., Maher, A., Bulter, D., Volkening, L., & Laffel, L. (2006). Depressive symptoms in children and adolescents with type 1 diabetes: Assocation with diabetes-specific characteristics. *Diabetes Care, 29*, 1389–1391.

Iannotti, R. J., Schneider, S., Nansel, T. R., Haynie, D. L., Plotnick, L. P., Clark, L. M., et al. (2006). Self-efficacy, outcome expectations, and diabetes self-management in adolescents with type 1 diabetes. *Journal of Developmental and Behavioral Pediatrics, 27*, 98–105.

Ingersoll, G. M., Orr, D. P., Herrold, A. J., & Golden, M. P. (1986). Cognitive maturity and self-management among adolescents with insulin-dependent diabetes mellitus. *Behavioral Pediatrics, 108*, 620–623.

Jacobson, A. M., Hauser, S. T., Lavori, P., Wolfsdorf, J. I., Herskowitz, R. D., Milley, J. E., et al. (1990). Adherence among children and adolescents with insulin-dependent diabetes mellitus over a four-year longitudinal follow-up: I. the influence of patient coping and adjustment. *Journal of Pediatric Psychology, 15*, 511–526.

Jacobson, A. M., Hauser, S. T., Willett, J. B., Wolfsdorf, J. I., Dvorak, R., Herman, L., et al. (1997). Psychological adjustment to IDDM: 10-year follow-up of an onset cohort of child and adolescent patients. *Diabetes Care, 20*, 811–818.

Johnson, S. B., Kelly, M., Henretta, J. C., Cunningham, W., Tomer, A., & Silverstein, J. (1992). A longitudinal analysis of adherence and health status in childhood diabetes. *Journal of Pediatric Psychology, 17*, 537–553.

Kaufman, F. R. (2002). Type 2 diabetes mellitus in children and youth: A new epidemic. *Journal of Pediatric Endocrinology & Metabolism, 15*, 737–744.

Knip, M. (1998). Prediction and prevention of type 1 diabetes. *Acta Paediatrica*, 87(Suppl. 425), 54–62.

Kokkonen, J., Taanila, A., & Kokkonen, E. (1997). Diabetes in adolescence: The effect of family and psychologic factors on metabolic control. *Nordic Journal of Psychiatry, 51*, 165–172.

Koller, E., Cross, J., & Schneider, B. (2004). Risperidone-associated diabetes mellitus in children. *Pediatrics, 113*, 421–422.

Kovacs, M., Brent, D., Steinberg, T. F., Paulauskas, S., & Reid, J. (1986). Children's self-reports of psychological adjustment and coping strategies during first year of insulin-dependent diabetes mellitus. *Diabetes Care, 9*, 472–479.

Kovacs, M., Feinberg, T. L., Paulauskas, S., Finkelstein, R., Pollock, M., & Crouse-Novak, M. (1985). Initial coping responses and psychosocial characteristics of children with insulin-dependent diabetes mellitus. *Journal of Pediatrics, 106*, 827–834.

Kovacs, M., Goldston, D., Obrosky, D. S., & Iyengar, S. (1992). Prevalence and predictors of pervasive non-compliance with medical treatment among youths with insulin-dependent diabetes mellitus. *Journal of the American Academy of Child and Adolescent Psychiatry, 31*, 1112–1119.

Kovacs, M., Iyengar, S., Goldston, D., Stewart, J., Obrosky, D. S., & Marsh, J. (1990). Psychological functioning of children with insulin-dependent diabetes mellitus: A longitudinal study. *Journal of Pediatric Psychology, 15*, 619–632.

Laffel, L. M. B., Connell, A., Vangsness, L., Goebel-Fabbri, A., Mansfield, A., & Anderson, B. J. (2003). General quality of life in youth with type 1 diabetes: Relationship to patient management and diabetes-specific family conflict. *Diabetes Care, 26*, 3067–3073.

Laffel, L. M., Vangsness, L., Connell, A., Goebel-Fabbri, A., Butler, D., & Anderson, B. J. (2003). Impact of ambulatory, family-focused teamwork intervention on glycemic control in youth with type 1 diabetes. *Journal of Pediatrics, 142*, 409–416.

LaGreca, A. M. (1992). Peer influences in pediatric chronic illness: An update. *Journal of Pediatric Psychology, 17*, 775–784.

LaGreca, A. M., Auslander, W. F., Greco, P., Spetter, D., Fisher, E. B., Jr., & Santiago, J. V. (1995). I get by with a little help from my family and friends: Adolescents' support for diabetes care. *Journal of Pediatric Psychology, 20*, 449–476.

LaGreca, A. M., Follansbee, D. M., & Skyler, J. S. (1990). Developmental and behavioral aspects of diabetes management in youngsters. *Children's Health Care, 19*, 132–139.

LaGreca, A. M., Swales, T., Klemp, S., Madigan, S., & Skyler, J. (1995). Adolescents with diabetes: Gender differences in psychosocial functioning and glycemic control. *Children's Health Care, 24*, 61–78.

Lavigne, J. & Faier-Routman, J. (1992). Psychological adjustment to pediatric physical disorders: A meta-analytic review. *Journal of Pediatric Psychology, 17*, 133–157.

Lazarus, R. S., & Folkman, S. (1984). Coping and adaptation. In W. D.Gentry (Ed.), *The handbook of behavioral medicine* (pp. 282–325). New York: Guilford.

Leonard, B. J., Jang, Y.-P., Savik, K., & Plumbo, M. A. (2005). Adolescents with type 1 diabetes: Family functioning and metabolic control. *Journal of Family Nursing, 11*, 102–121.

Lewin, A. B., Geffken, G. R., Heidgerken, A. D., Duke, D. C., Novoa, W., Williams, L. B., et al. (2005). The Diabetes Family Behavior Checklist: A psychometric evaluation. *Journal of Clinical Psychology in Medical Settings, 12*, 315–322.

Lewinsohn, P. M., Clarke, G. N., Seeley, J. R., & Rohde, P. (1994). Major depression in community adolescents: Age at onset, episode duration, and time to recurrence. *Journal of the American Academy of Child and Adolescent Psychiatry, 33*, 809–818.

Littlefield, C. H., Craven, J. L., Rodin, G. M., Daneman, D., Murray, M. A., & Rydall, A. C. (1992). Relationship of self-efficacy and binging to adherence to diabetes regimen among adolescents. *Diabetes Care, 15*, 90–94.

McKelvey, J., Waller, D. A., North, A. J., Marks, J. F., Schreiner, B., Travis, L. B., et al. (1993). Reliability and validity of the diabetes family behavior scale (DFBS). *The Diabetes Educator, 19*, 125–132.

Miller-Johnson, S., Emery, R. E., Marvin, R. S., Clarke, W., Lovinger, R., & Martin, M. (1994). Parent–child relationships and the management of insulin-dependent diabetes mellitus. *Journal of Consulting and Clinical Psychology, 62*, 603–610.

Morales, A. E., She, J. X., & Schatz, D. A. (2001). Prediction and prevention of type 1 diabetes. *Current Diabetes Reports 1*, 28–32.

Moreland, E. C., Tovar, A., Zuehlke, J. B., Butler, D. A., Milaszewski, K., & Laffel, L. M. (2004). The impact of physiological, therapeutic and psychosocial variables on glycemic control in youth with type 1 diabetes mellitus. *Journal of Pediatric Endocrinology and Metabolism, 17*, 1533–1544.

Mortensen, H. B. & Hougaard, P. (1997). Comparison of metabolic control in a cross-sectional study of 2,873 children and adolescents with IDDM from 18 countries. The Hvidore Study Group on Childhood Diabetes. *Diabetes Care, 20*, 714–720.

National Institute of Diabetes and Digestive and Kidney Diseases. (2005). *National diabetes statistics: Prevalence of diagnosed diabetes in people aged 20 years or younger, United States.* Bethesda, MD: U.S. Department of Health and Human Services, National Institutes of Health.

Northam, E., Anderson, P., Adler, R., & Werther, G. (1996). Psychosocial and family functioning in children with IDDM at diagnosis and one year later. *Journal of Pediatric Psychology, 21*, 699–717.

Ott, J., Greening, L., Palardy, N., Holderby, A., & DeBell, W. (2000). Self-efficacy as a mediator variable for adolescents' adherence to treatment for insulin-dependent diabetes mellitus. *Children's Health Care, 29*, 47–63.

Palardy, N., Greening, L., Ott, J., Holderby, A., & Atchison, J. (1998). Adolescents' health attitudes and adherence to treatment for insulin-dependent diabetes mellitus. *Developmental and Behavioral Pediatrics, 19*, 31–37.

Pollack, S. E. (1993). Adaptation to chronic illness: A program of research for testing nursing theory. *Nursing Science Quarterly, 6*, 86–92.

Robin, A. L., & Foster, S. L. (1989). *Negotiating parent–adolescent conflict: A behavioral family systems approach.* New York: Guilford.

Sadeharju, K., Knip, M., Hiltunen, M., Akerblom, H. K., & Hyoty, H. (2003). The HLA-DR phenotype modulates the humoral immune response to enterovirus antigens. *Diabetologia, 46*, 1100–1105.

Satin, W., LaGreca, A. M., Zigo, M. A., & Skyler, J. S. (1989). Diabetes in adolescence: Effects of multifamily group intervention and parent simulation of diabetes. *Journal of Pediatric Psychology, 14*, 259–275.

Sawyer, M. G., Reynolds, K. E., Couper, J. J., French, D. J., Kennedy, D., Martin, J., et al. (2005). A two-year prospective study of the health-related quality of life of children with chronic illness—The parents' perspective. *Quality of Life Research, 14*, 395–405.

Schafer, L. C., McCaul, K. D., & Glasgow, R. E. (1986). Supportive and nonsupportive family behaviors: Relationships to adherence and metabolic control in persons with type I diabetes. *Diabetes Care, 9*, 179–185.

Seiffge-Krenke, I., & Stemmler, M. (2003). Coping with everyday stress and links to medical and psychosocial adaptation in diabetic adolescents. *Journal of Adolescent Health, 33*, 180–188.

Sernyak, M., Gulanski, B., & Rosenheck, R. (2005). Undiagnosed hyperglycemia in patients treated with atypical antipsychotics. *Journal of Clinical Psychiatry, 66*, 1463–1467.

Silverstein, J., Klingensmith, G., Copeland, K., Plotnick, L., Kaufman, F., Laffel, L., et al. (2005). Care of children and adolescents with type 1 diabetes: A statement of the American Diabetes Association. *Diabetes Care, 28*, 186–212.

Skinner, T. C., John, M., & Hampson, S. E. (2000). Social support and personal models of diabetes as predictors of self-care and well-being: A longitudinal study of adolescents with diabetes. *Journal of Pediatric Psychology, 25,* 257–267.

Smaldone, A., Judy, H., Raymond, A., & Weinger, K. (2004). Comorbid hospitalizations for children with single and recurrent ketoacidosis. *Diabetes, 53*(Suppl.2), A425.

Stewart, S. M., Rao, U., Emslie, G. J., Klein, D., & White, P. C. (2005). Depressive symptoms predict hospitalization for adolescents with type 1 diabetes mellitus. *Pediatrics, 115,* 1315–1319.

Svoren, B., Butler, D., Levine, B., Anderson, B., & Laffel, L. (2003). Reducing acute adverse outcomes in youths with type 1 diabetes: a randomized, controlled trial. *Pediatrics, 112,* 914–922.

Warren-Boulton, E., Anderson, B. J., Schwartz, N. L., & Dreyer, A. J. (1981). A group approach to the management of diabetes in adolescents and young adults. *Diabetes Care, 4,* 620–623.

Weissberg-Benchell, J., Glasgow, A. M., Tynan, W. D., Wirtz, P., Turek, J., & Ward, J. (1995). Adolescent diabetes management and mismanagement. *Diabetes Care, 18,* 77–82.

White, K., Kolman, M. L., Wexler, P., Polin, G., & Winter, R. J. (1984). Unstable diabetes and unstable families: A psychosocial evaluation of children with recurrent diabetic ketoacidosis. *Pediatrics, 73,* 749–755.

Whittemore, R., Urban, A. D., Tamborlane, W. V., & Grey, M. (2003). Quality of life in school-aged children with type 1 diabetes on intensive treatment and their parents. *The Diabetes Educator, 29,* 847–854.

Wiebe, D. J., Berg, C. A., Korbel, C., Palmer, D. L., Swinyard, M. T., & Donaldson, D. L. (2005). Children's appraisals of maternal involvement in coping with diabetes: Enhancing our understanding of adherence, metabolic control, and quality of life across adolescence. *Journal of Pediatric Psychology, 30,* 167–178.

Winkley, K., Ismail, K., Landau, S., & Eisler, I. (2006). Psychological interventions to improve glycaemic control in patients with type 1 diabetes: Systematic review and meta-analysis of randomized controlled trials. *British Medical Journal, 333,* 65–69.

Wysocki, T. (1993). Associations among teen-parent relationships, metabolic control, and adjustment to diabetes in adolescents. *Journal of Pediatric Psychology, 18,* 441–452.

Wysocki, T. (2006). Behavioral assessment and intervention in pediatric diabetes. *Behavior Modification, 30,* 72–92.

Wysocki, T., Greco, P., Harris, M. A., Bubb, J., & White, N. H. (2001). Behavior therapy for families of adolescents with diabetes: Maintenance of treatment effects. *Diabetes Care, 24,* 441–446.

Wysocki, T., Harris, M. A., Buckloh, L. M., Mertlich, D., Sobel Lochrie, A., Taylor, A., et al. (2006). Effects of behavioral family systems therapy for diabetes on adolescents' family relationships, treatment adherence, and metabolic control. *Journal of Pediatric Psychology, 31,* 928-938.

Wysocki, T., Harris, M. A., Greco, P., Bubb, J., Danda, C. E., Harvey, L. M., et al. (2000). Randomized, controlled trial of behavior therapy for families of adolescents with insulin-dependent diabetes mellitus. *Journal of Pediatric Psychology, 25,* 23–33.

Wysocki, T., Taylor, A., Hough, B. S., Linscheid, T. R., Yeates, K. O., & Naglieri, J. A. (1996). Deviation from developmentally appropriate self-care autonomy: Association with diabetes outcomes. *Diabetes Care, 19,* 119–125.

Chapter Nine

Asthma in Childhood

Elaine M. Gustafson, Mikki Meadows-Oliver, and Nancy Cantey Banasiak

INTRODUCTION

Asthma remains a major public health concern and the most common chronic illness of childhood; it afflicts 5 million children in the United States (Redd, 2002). When not properly managed, asthma can be a life threatening disease. Deaths due to asthma are rare in children but increase with age. In 2002, 170 children died from asthma (National Center for Health Statistics [NCHS], 2002). According to the American Lung Association (ALA), hospitalizations due to asthma have decreased as has asthma mortality in recent years. It is believed that asthma prevalence has stabilized possibly due to improved disease management (ALA, 2005).

It is important to note that asthma is a complex disease that is somewhat challenging to diagnose in childhood. Symptoms may be nonspecific and may include wheezing, cough, shortness of breath, and chest tightness. All of these symptoms can be attributed to many other diseases as well. Childhood asthma leads to decreased participation in school and play activities. It is characterized by excessive sensitivity of the lungs to various stimuli. These may include viral respiratory illness, indoor and outdoor allergens, vigorous exercise, cold exposure or sudden temperature change, cigarette smoke, or stress and excitement (ALA, 2005).

In order to evaluate asthma and to initiate appropriate treatment, a thorough understanding of the disease and its causes is imperative. This paper focuses primarily on health promotion and on the prevention and treatment of asthma in school-age children.

MAJOR THEORETICAL PERSPECTIVES

Studies in the United States, Europe, Australia, and New Zealand have established that allergy plays a significant role in the development of asthma and that immune globulin E (IgE), which mediates sensitization to indoor allergens, is a major risk factor (Clark et al., 1999). Findings of a recent U.S. study of over 5,500 children, 6 to 8 years old, comparing African-American and European-American children, suggest that the former group may be predisposed to asthma (Joseph, Ownby, Peterson, & Johnson, 2000); the hypothesis was based on significant racial differences found between total serum IgE and airway responsiveness and between serum IgE and asthma status.

Sensitization to indoor aeroallergens (airborne allergens) is a more likely factor in the development of asthma than is sensitization to outdoor aeroallergens. Indoor aeroallergens would include house dust mites, pet dander, especially cat dander, and exposure to cockroaches (Becker, 2000). Cat dander appears to pose a greater problem than does house dust mites in that it is present in very small particles and is more widely distributed in the home and community than are house dust mites, which settle quickly after being distributed (Rosenstreich et al., 1997). Nevertheless, house dust mites are found in all homes built in temperate climates (Jones, 1998) and evidence suggests that exposure to dust mite allergen, particularly in infants, may be an important factor in the onset of asthma (Holt, Macaubas, Prescott, & Sly, 2000). However, a systematic review of 23 studies on controlling house dust mites, involving 686 adults and children, found that reduction in exposure to house dust mite antigen does not lead to clinical improvement in patients with asthma who are sensitive to mites (Gotzsche et al., 2004)).

Environmental tobacco smoke (ETS) is a serious environmental hazard for children. It is estimated that up to 1 million children have their asthma condition worsened due to ETS (Etzel, 1995). A report from the U.S. Surgeon-General supports this claim that children exposed to second hand smoke are at greater risk for various respiratory illnesses, especially asthma (USHHS, Surgeon-General's Report, 2006).

The most common presentation of asthma is symptoms associated with viral respiratory illness resulting in an intermittent, episodic pattern of disease (Weinberger, 2003). Viral respiratory infection in very young children is often manifested as bronchiolitis. This condition is frequently due to respiratory syncytial virus (RSV) and causes lower respiratory symptoms with cough and wheezing, especially in infants. One episode of this nature in infancy, however, is not sufficient to diagnose asthma, as chronic or recurring lower respiratory illness is necessary to make a diagnosis (Weinberger, 2003). In a study by Martinez et al. (1995), it was found that of children who wheeze in the first few years of life, only a very small percentage (approximately 15%) actually develop persistent wheezing and asthma and the majority of these early intermittent wheezers outgrow their symptoms by age 6.

Asthma usually begins in childhood often with an inherited susceptibility to environmental allergens. The severity of episodes or *exacerbations* ranges from mild to life threatening. These may be triggered by exposures and conditions such as respiratory illness, presence of house dust mites or cockroaches, animal dander, mold, pollen, exposure to cold air, exercise, stress, tobacco smoke, and indoor and outdoor air pollutants (Williams, Goldberg, Kaluzny-Petroff, Luna, & Majer, 1995). The frequency and severity of asthma symptoms can be decreased by the use of medications and reduced exposure to environmental pollutants. Asthma cannot be cured; it can, however, be controlled by both pharmacologic and nonpharmacologic means.

DEFINITIONAL ISSUES

As a more complete understanding of the pathophysiology of the disease of asthma has emerged since the late 1950s, a clearer definition of asthma has been developed. The redefinition of asthma in the Expert Panel report of the National Heart Lung and

Blood Institute/National Asthma Education and Prevention Program in 1997 described asthma as,

> a chronic inflammatory disorder of the airways in which many cells and cellular elements play a role, in particular, mast cells, eosinophils, T lymphocytes, neutrophils, and epithelial cells. In susceptible individuals, this inflammation causes recurrent episodes of wheezing, breathlessness, chest tightness, and cough, particularly at night and in the morning. These episodes are usually associated with widespread but variable airflow obstruction that is often reversible either spontaneously or with treatment. The inflammation also causes an associated increase in existing bronchial hyper responsiveness to a variety of stimuli. (p. 3)

Numerous techniques to diagnose asthma have been developed in recent years. These include pre- and postbronchodilator spirometry, exercise spirometry, and methacholine challenge. Tests under investigation for use in the early identification of asthma in children include inflammatory markers in blood, urine, or sputum and testing of biomarkers such as exhaled nitric oxide (Guilbert & Krawiec, 2003).

INCIDENCE RATES

A review of five national data sources from the National Center for Health Statistics was used to describe trends in childhood asthma from 1980 to 1996. Prevalence among 0 to 17-year-old children was found to have increased from 36 per 1,000 children to 75 per 1,000 children from 1980 to 1995. This was an increase of 4.3% per year during that time period (Akinbami & Schoendorf, 2002).

In a longitudinal retrospective study using medical and school linked records in Rochester, MN estimates were as high as 17.6% of a population of kindergarten through 12th grade children having physician-diagnosed asthma (Yawn, Wollen, Kurland, & Scanlon, 2002). In another study of 230 urban predominantly black school children, the prevalence of undiagnosed asthma was estimated to be 14.3%. These children also reported more symptoms of atopic disease than did nonasthmatic children. Findings from this study also revealed that children who actually had symptoms of asthma also had more days absent from physical education, as well as more bronchitis and sleep disturbance (Joseph, Foxman, Leickly, Peterson, & Ownby, 1996).

DSM-IV CRITERIA

Studies by Villa et al. (1999) on the prevalence of DSM-IV anxiety and affective disorders in a population of children with asthma compared to healthy controls revealed more anxiety symptoms in the asthmatic group. Self-esteem was found to be good among the asthmatic children and depression was not found to be significant in this group. Of the 82 subjects studied, 24 were found to have generalized anxiety disorder with boys and girls and adolescents and young children equally affected. A further study by this group and others comparing children with asthma and those with insulin dependent diabetes mellitus (IDDM) found that the asthmatic children had more psychiatric symptoms compared to those with diabetes, with anxiety disorders predominating. They conclude that asthma appears to be associated with higher overall incidence of particular psychiatric problems compared to diabetes (Villa et al., 2000).

BIOLOGICAL/GENETIC FACTORS

Asthma is a multifactorial disease process with genetic, allergic, environmental, infectious, emotional, and nutritional components (Miller, 2001). It has been classified as a complex genetic disorder with genetic susceptibility and an appropriate environmental stimulus necessary for the expression of the disease (Huss & Huss, 2000). Asthma may begin early in life in genetically predisposed children exposed to individually specific environmental stimuli (Foley, 2002).

The genetic component of asthma was suggested through observations that allergic subjects had significantly higher incidence of family histories of disease as compared with controls. Asthma is widely considered a "polygenic" or multifactorial illness in which family history is a consistent risk factor (McCunney, 2005). A dominant or recessive model of inheritance for asthma has not been supported. Asthma has numerous contributing genes, each having variable degrees of involvement in any given individual (Steinke & Borish, 2006).

The genetic component of asthma represents the cumulative influence of many genes (Steinke & Borish, 2006). There is a great amount of heterogeneity underlying asthma. At least 64 genes have been associated with asthma (Hoffjan, Nicolae, & Ober, 2003). Variations in eight genes were revealed in a comprehensive review of studies that researched genetic bases for asthma; five or more studies reviewed associated those variations with asthma phenotypes. They include: Interleukin-4 (IL4), Interleukin-13 (IL13), β2 adrenergic receptor (ADRB2), human leukocyte antigen DRB1 (HLA-DRB1), tumor necrosis factor (TNF), lymphotoxin-alpha (LTA), high affinity IgE receptor (FCER1B), and IL-4 receptor (IL4RA) (Hoffjan et al., 2003).

Certain genes control distinct aspects of asthma. For example, polymorphisms in the asthma susceptibility gene ADAM33 on chromosome 20p13 have been associated with compromised lung function in early childhood. Polymorphisms in the T-bet gene were found to be associated with airway hyperresponsiveness in Caucasian children with asthma. Polymorphisms in the GPRA gene on chromosome 7p have been associated with asthma, airway hyperresponsiveness, and allergic predisposition in children (Wenzel & Covar, 2006).

There are confounding influences of genetic heterogeneity (mutations in different genes that result in the same phenotype) and the incomplete penetrance of genetic phenotypes that reflects both the importance of gene–gene interaction and gene–environment interactions (Steinke & Borish, 2006). For a complex disease such as asthma, the necessity for these gene–gene interactions is not surprising. Research has shown that some genetic abnormalities have not been associated with asthma in isolation but when they were observed with an additional gene, an impact on asthma was revealed (Wenzel & Covar, 2006).

Identification of genes that make an individual susceptible to asthma is difficult and has been hampered by variability in the clinical phenotype, genetic heterogeneity among human populations, and a failure to sometimes consider important environmental influences (i.e., gene–environment interactions) (Barnes, 2006). In addition to specific genes, other factors have been recognized to contribute to the development of asthma through their ability to influence gene expression. Examples of gene–environment interactions include the requirement of exposures to cigarette smoke and air pollution before certain genotypes manifest themselves (Steinke & Borish, 2006). Just as the environment is a powerful factor in selecting for genetic variation, the environment is also important in determining whether certain traits associated with variants are ever expressed. It is not sufficient to have genetic susceptibility alone but environmental exposure is essential for expression or manifestation of the disease (Barnes, 2006).

In addition to specific genes and environmental factors playing a role in the pathogenesis of asthma, certain biological factors may play a role. Asthma symptoms are more common and severe in young males, but after puberty, the disease seems to be more common and severe in females (Guilbert & Krawiec, 2003). Other biological factors that may influence the expression of asthma include findings that the incidence of asthma was higher in babies with low birth weight and prematurity. Also, the risk of asthma increased with maternal age (Dik, Tate, Manfreda, & Anthonisen, 2004).

In summary, asthma is a complex disease caused by the interaction of genetic, biologic, and environmental factors. The exact mode of inheritance of asthma remains elusive. The genetic and environmental factors that mediate asthma risk and expression have been shown to be intricately linked. The genetic and environmental factors interact pre- and postnatally to determine asthma phenotype in the child. No single gene has been identified that causes asthma. While it is appreciated that asthma is a polygenic disease, the exact number of genes contributing to asthma within the human population is unknown. The study of the genetics of asthma has been hampered by its complexity and heterogeneity (Carroll, 2005).

INDIVIDUAL FACTORS INFLUENCING RISK AND RESILIENCY (ETHNICITY, GENDER, AND RACE)

In recent decades, the prevalence and severity of asthma has affected many different populations. A disproportionate number of African Americans and Latinos living in poverty in the United States are affected (Lucas & Platts-Mills, 2005).

Age of onset is a significant predictive factor for the persistence of asthma. Persistent severe asthma in a young infant poses a greater risk for development of chronic airflow limitation and continued severe symptoms. Of infants who develop respiratory syncytial virus (RSV) approximately 20% will develop lower respiratory illness and of these, one quarter to one half will experience acute asthma associated with viral respiratory illnesses (VRI) (Weinberger, 2003).

Asthma has been shown to be more severe in boys than in girls in several studies; however, this increased risk seems to disappear around puberty, and after age 20 asthma incidence is greater in women (Guilert & Krawiec, 2003). Many children who develop severe symptoms that persist throughout their life have a family history of asthma. These children often experience atopy in childhood and have airway hyperreactivity (Guilert & Krawiec, 2003). Rationale for the association with family history is not clear; however, twin studies suggest that 50% of an individual's susceptibility to asthma may be genetic (Duffy et al., 1990).

FAMILY FACTORS INFLUENCING RISK AND RESILIENCY

There is no doubt that asthma has a heritable component. A family history of asthma and allergy, especially if both parents are affected, is associated with the development of asthma (Slezak, Persky, Kviz, Ramakrishnan, & Byers, 1998). Lux, Henderson, and Pocock (2000) note that among infants, the highest incidence of early wheezing occurred if the mother herself had asthma and if the infant was preterm.

SOCIAL AND COMMUNITY FACTORS INFLUENCING RISK AND RESILIENCY

A large study of suburban children aged 6 to 8 years found significant racial differences in the relationship between serum IgE and airway hyperresponsiveness and IgE and asthma status. These findings by Joseph, Ownby, et al. (2000) support the hypothesis that African-American children may be predisposed to more severe asthma or that racial factors may predispose children to more severe asthma. Asthma prevalence data from 1980 to 1996 further supports this hypothesis. From 1980 to 1981 there was a 15% higher incidence rate among black non-Hispanic children. This gap further increased to 26% between 1995 and 1996, and widened further in 2000 to 44%. Between 1981 and 1995 national statistics revealed a dramatic increase in asthma prevalence among Hispanic children as well (Akinbami & Schoendorf, 2002).

There is speculation that rising asthma rates may be associated with the increase in obesity in children. A study by Sulit, Storfer-Isser, Rosen, Kirchner, & Redline (2005) of 788 children aged 8 to 11 years attempted to assess the extent to which sleep disordered breathing (SDB) could explain the association between obesity and wheezing/asthma. They found that children with wheeze were significantly more likely to be male, black, obese, and to have a maternal history of asthma (Sulit et al. 2005). Their findings suggest that obesity, defined as BMI in the 95th percentile or greater for age and sex, is associated with asthma and wheezing. These findings further support the need to assess snoring as a consequence of obesity and its relationship to asthma/wheeze in primary care, and they raise the question as to whether sleep disordered breathing exacerbates asthma symptoms and whether treatment for SDB may improve both asthma and SDB (Sulit et al. 2005).

EVIDENCE-BASED TREATMENT INTERVENTIONS FOR CHILDREN WITH ASTHMA

Inflammation of the airways continues to be the key component of asthma, causing recurrent symptoms of wheeze, cough, shortness of breath, and chest tightness. Often the symptoms vary from patient to patient and are reversed partially or completely with or without treatment (National Asthma Education and Prevention Program [NAEPP], 2003). Early diagnosis and treatment is the key to improving quality of life. After a comprehensive history, physical examination, laboratory studies, and exclusion of other diagnoses (see Table 9.1), a diagnosis of asthma is made. Treatment consists of a combination of short acting and long acting medications, depending on the patient's asthma classifica-

Table 9.1 Differential diagnosis

Allergic rhinitis and sinusitis
Foreign body
Vocal cord dysfunction
Vascular ring or laryngeal webs
Laryngotracheomalacia, tracheal stenosis, or bronchiostenosis
Enlarged lymph nodes or tumor
Viral bronchiolitis or obliterative bronchiolitis
Cystic fibrosis
Bronchopulmonary dysplasia
Heart disease
Recurrent cough not due to asthma
Aspiration from swallowing mechanism dysfunction or gastroesophageal reflux

Source: Adapted from NAEPP (1997).

tion. Environmental controls are essential in reducing exposure to triggers exacerbating asthma symptoms. Under- or inappropriate treatment, along with disparities in health care, are a major contributor in increased morbidity and mortality that affects the health and well-being of children (Swartz, Banasiak, & Meadows-Oliver, 2005).

The goals of asthma therapy include maintaining normal activity, prevention of asthma symptoms, maintaining normal pulmonary function testing, prevention of asthma exacerbations, minimizing side effects of medications, and patient and family satisfaction (NAEPP, 1997). The National Asthma Education and Prevention Program Expert Panel Report from 1997 recommended a stepwise approach for treating patients with asthma. Appropriate therapy can be initiated after classification of patient's symptoms is made. Classification depends on severity of symptoms, forced expiratory volume in one second (FEV1), and peak expiratory flow (PEF) (see Table 9.2).

Environmental factors are a major contributor to asthma symptoms and exacerbations and providers need to identify triggers. Triggers may include viral infections, pet dander, dust mites, cockroach feces, mold, indoor and outdoor pollutants (i.e., environmental tobacco smoke, perfumes, cleaning agents and sprays, and pollens from tress, grass and weeds) (see Table 9.3). If allergies are associated with asthma symptoms, a referral to an allergist should be considered. Management of allergens includes pharmacology, allergy avoidance, and immunotherapy.

Table 9.2 Asthma classification

Classification	Daily symptoms	Nighttime symptoms	Lung function
Mild intermittent	≤ 2 times a week	≤ 2 times a month	FEV1 or PEF ≥80% predicted PEF variability <20%
Mild persistent	≥ 2 times a week	> 2 times a month	FEV1 or PEF ≥80% predicted PEF variability 20-30%
Moderate persistent	Daily	> 1 time a week	FEV1 or PEF >60-80% predicted PEF variability >30%
Severe persistent	Persistent	Frequent	FEV1 or PEF ≤60% predicted PEF variability >30%

FEV1 = Forced expiratory volume in 1 second
PEF = Peak expiratory flow
Adapted from NAEPP (1997)

Table 9.3 Trigger avoidance and environmental controls

Animal allergens

Remove the animal and products made of feathers from home
Keep pets out of child's bedroom
Keep bedroom door closed
Provide filtering materials over forced air vents to collect dust and dander
Remove carpet if possible or a least from child's bedroom
Wash pets weekly to reduce dander
Remove upholstered furniture from home or avoid sleeping on it

Cockroach control

Avoid leaving food or garbage exposed
Cockroach reduction with poison baits, traps, or boric acid

House dust mites

Encase mattress and pillow in allergen impermeable covers
Wash sheets and bed covers weekly in hot water >130ºF
Remove or minimize stuffed toys from bed or wash weekly
Vacuum twice a week to reduce dust
Reduce humidity in home to less than 50%

Mold control

Decrease humidity
Control mold growth

Avoid outdoor environmental allergens: pollen, glass, flowers, and trees

Use air conditioner during warm weather to control humidity and decrease amount of outdoor allergens
    entering home
Stay inside when there are high pollen counts
Refer to allergist

Exercise

Medicate before exercise or playing, if exercise induces symptoms

Food and food additives

Avoid food products with sulfites if asthma symptoms are associated with eating processed foods

Avoid irritants

Avoid cigarette smoke, strong odors, air pollutants, chemicals, wood burning stoves, fumes from gas, oil or
    kerosene stoves

Medicines

Avoid aspirin and nonsteroidal anti-inflammatory drugs if they cause an increase in asthma symptoms
Avoid beta-blockers

Emotional expressions

Refer to a mental health expert if needed

Evaluate for other factors affecting asthma

VRI/Rhinitis
Sinusitis
Gastroesophageal reflux
Infections
Annual influenza vaccine

Consider exposure outside home

Evaluate symptoms only occurring at daycare, school, or work
Evaluate chemical exposure

Source: Adapted from NAEPP (1997).

What Works

In order to control asthma, pharmacologic therapy is initiated to prevent exacerbations, minimize symptoms, and promote healthy living. Therapy is based on the patient's classification and tailored to his or her symptoms. Asthma medications are divided into two categories: quick relief medications and long-term control medications. Quick relief medications are used for acute situations of broncho-constriction and associated symptoms of wheezing, coughing, and chest tightness. Short acting β2-agonists and anticholinergics are considered quick relief medications. Systemic corticosteroids are also considered important in acute exacerbations to prevent hospitalizations, increase recovery time, and prevent relapses (NAEPP, 1997).

Quick Relief Medications

β2-adrenergic agonists (β-agonists) are the first line of medications in acute asthma therapy. β-agonists are available for delivery via metered dose inhaler (MDI), dry powder inhaler (DPI), and nebulized therapy. Multiple studies have compared MDI and nebulized therapy. An integrated literature review by the Cochrane Collaboration concluded that MDI/spacers produced the same results as nebulized therapy when evaluating time in the emergency department (ED), peak flow measurements, and with added benefit of decrease oxygen use, lower heart rates, and the cost advantage of the MDI/spacer (Cates, Bara, Crilly, & Rowe, 2006). A review of the literature by Travers et al. (2001) found no clear evidence to support the use of intravenous β2-agonists for severe asthma exacerbations.

Anticholinergics

Ipratropium bromide in combination with β-agonists improved outcomes with children with acute severe asthma exacerbations when multiple doses of anticholinergics were administered (Plotnick & Ducharme, 2000; Rodrigo & Rodrigo, 2002). In children with mild to moderate asthma exacerbations, a single dose of anticholinergics added to a β-agonist had no effect on rates of hospital admission (Rodrigo & Rodrigo, 2002).

Systemic Corticosteroids

Early treatment with systemic corticosteroids has proven to be effective in the treatment of acute asthma. A review by Rowe, Spooner, Ducharme, Bretzloff, and Bota, (2001) concluded that the administration of corticosteroids (IV or PO) within one hour of admission to the emergency department reduced the admission rate of children with acute asthma. There is little evidence to suggest inhaled corticosteroids are as effective as oral steroids in acute exacerbations (Edmonds, Camargo, Pollack, & Rowe, 2003). The recommended dose of oral corticosteroids is 1 to 2 mg/kg/day for 3 to 10 days with a maximum dose of 60 mg daily (NAEPP, 2003).

Long-Term Control Medications

Long-term control medications include inhaled corticosteroids and leukotriene modifiers.

Inhaled Corticosteroids

Inhaled corticosteroids (ICS) are the mainstay of treatment for children with persistent asthma. Studies have shown that patients using inhaled corticosteroids require fewer bursts of systemic corticosteroids and less use of β2-agonists (Calpin, MacArthur, Stephens, Feldman, & Parkin, 1997). An expert panel from different medical organizations convened to review adverse effects of corticosteroids (Leone, Fish, Szefler, & West, 2003). They found inhaled corticosteroids in children had a short-term effect on growth, bruising, and skin thinning but were not associated with cataracts, a reduction in bone density, or final height (Leone et al., 2003).

Cromolyn is a nonsteroidal asthma medication used as an alternative treatment for children with mild, persistent, and exercise-induced asthma. Over 30 years, treatment with cromolyn has shown a decrease in frequency and severity of exacerbations and an increased number of symptom free days (Storms & Kaliner, 2005). Multiple studies have concluded ICS were superior to cromolyn when measuring lung function and control of asthma (Guevara, Ducharme, Keren, Nihtianova, & Zorc, 2006).

Leukotriene Modifiers

Leukotriene modifiers are recommended for use as an alternative therapy to inhaled corticosteroids and as step-up therapy for children with moderate or severe asthma (NAEPP, 2003). A systematic review by Ducharme (2003) found inhaled corticosteroids were more effective then leukotriene modifiers in monotherapy. They are the first classification of mediator-specific drug therapy (Krawiec &Wenzel, 1999). Leukotriene modifiers are divided into two classes: leukotriene-receptor antagonists and leukotriene-receptor inhibitors. Leukotrienes are not recommended during acute exacerbations.

What Might Work

At the time of writing, the field has interventions that either do or do not work.

What Doesn't Work

Long-acting β2-agonists and methylzanthines do not work alone as therapies for pediatric asthma. Rather in both adults and children long acting β2 agonists are recommended in combination with inhaled corticosteroids.

Long Acting β2-Agonist Monotherapy

The use of long acting β2-agonists *alone* is not recommended in pediatrics (Courtney, McCarter, & Pollart, 2005). In adults, multiple studies have examined the combination therapy of long-acting β2-agonists with inhaled corticosteroids and have shown a reduction in exacerbations (O'Byrne, Barnes, et al., 2001; Pauwels et al., 1997). In a study by O'Byrne, Bisgaard, et al. (2005), patients aged 4 to 80 years were treated with combination therapy of long-acting β2-agonists with inhaled corticosteroids. A reduction was seen in the number of severe exacerbations, use of reliever medication, and nighttime symptoms. Many also had milder daytime symptoms and improvement in lung function.

Methylxanthines

A systematic review of 34 studies by the Cochrane Collaborative in 2006 concluded that patients on xanthine had more symptom free days but it was less effective than ICS (Seddon, Bara, Ducharme, & Lasserson, 2006). The need for continuous monitoring of blood levels and frequent side effects makes xanthines less favorable (Courtney et al., 2005; Seddon et al., 2006).

PSYCHOPHARMACOLOGY AND ASTHMA IN CHILDREN

A review of the literature did not uncover any psychotropic medications that are used in the treatment of asthma. However, the literature did reveal that asthma has been associated with several psychological conditions and that many of the medications used to treat asthma may have psychologically related side effects. Chen and colleagues (2006) have noted that psychological stress was associated with poor asthma outcomes in a sample of 37 school-aged children with physician-diagnosed asthma. These results support previous study findings of psychological conditions being present in children with asthma. A study of 74 inner city children aged 5 to 11 years of age showed that nearly 25% of pediatric asthma patients in an inner-city asthma clinic met criteria for a probable diagnosis of current anxiety disorders or depression. The findings provide preliminary evidence that mental health problems are somewhat common among pediatric asthma patients (Goodwin, Messineo, Bregante, Hoven, & Kairam, 2005). In addition to anxiety disorders, it has been shown that children with asthma (ages 9–17 years) were significantly more likely to have suicidal ideation when compared with youth without asthma, even after controlling for the effects of comorbid mental disorders (Goodwin & Marusic, 2004). Psychological morbidities and asthma are associated, but there is no evidence that one leads to the other. Researchers have noted that psychological difficulties in children with asthma may result from poor health rather than from asthma itself (Calam, Gregg, & Goodman, 2005).

Chronic illnesses such as asthma may not only affect the mental health of the child with asthma but may affect close family members as well. For example, Holmes and Deb (2003) noted that the negative impact of chronic illness on the psychological health of family members is sometimes larger than their direct psychological impact on the patient. Mental health conditions in caregivers can adversely impact the care of children with asthma. Researchers have found that children were more likely to have increased asthma morbidity if they had caregivers with depression and who had experienced negative life stressors (Shalowitz, Berry, Quinn, & Wolf, 2001). Subsequent studies have supported this finding. Wood, Smith, Romero, Bradshaw, Wise, and Chavkin (2002) reported that poorer mental health in parents was associated with increased asthma symptoms.

While there were no psychotropic medications found in the literature to treat asthma, a systematic review of evidence by the Cochrane library noted that many psychologically related conditions in children with asthma have improved when the children received cognitive behavioral therapy (CBT) (Yorke, Fleming, & Shuldham, 2006). The review reported a significant increase in self-efficacy and coping among children with asthma who received CBT. Also, asthma specific anxiety, in extremely anxious children, was reduced significantly in those children receiving CBT (Yorke et al., 2006).

Medications used to treat asthma have the potential to cause psychologically related side effects in children. Albuterol (Proventil, Ventolin) is a short-acting bronchodilator used to relieve bronchospasm in patients with asthma. Hyperactivity and insomnia are possible reactions to taking this medication. It has been noted that these side effects occur more frequently in children than in adults. Nervousness was also listed as an adverse reaction (Taketomo, Hodding, & Kraus, 2005).

Salmeterol and formoterol are both long-acting β2-adrenergic agonists. Formoterol (Foradil) is a bronchodilator used in the maintenance treatment of asthma. Psychologically related side effects of formoterol include nervousness, hyperactivity, insomnia, and fatigue. Similarly, as a long-acting bronchodilator, salmeterol (Serevent) may cause nervousness, hyperactivity, and insomnia. With both salmeterol and formoterol, monoamine oxidase (MAO) inhibitors and tricyclic antidepressants may potentiate cardiovascular effects such as increased heart rate and blood pressure abnormalities. It is recommended that providers wait at least two weeks after discontinuation of these therapies before initiating therapy with long-acting beta agonists (Taketomo et al., 2005).

Beclomethasone (Qvar) is an inhaled corticosteroid used in the long-term treatment of asthma. There were no reported psychological side effects of beclomethasone and no reported drug interactions with medications used to treat psychological conditions (Taketomo et al., 2005). Budesonide (Pulmicort®) is another inhaled corticosteroid that is used in the long-term treatment of persistent asthma. Nervousness, insomnia, and fatigue are listed as possible psychologically related adverse effects of budesonide. Similar side effects of fatigue and insomnia have been noted with other inhaled corticosteroids such as Fluticasone (Flovent). There were no drug interactions with psychotropic medications reported for either budesonide or fluticasone (Taketomo et al., 2005).

Both prednisone (Deltasone) and prednisolone (Orapred, Pediapred, Prelone) are oral systemic corticosteroids used in the treatment of asthma. There were no reported drug interactions with psychotropic medications. Psychoses have been reported as a side effect of both prednisone and prednisolone (Taketomo et al., 2005). Case reports of steroid-induced psychoses have been reported in the literature. A case report of a 5-year-old girl, with no previous psychiatric history, revealed that she developed a temporary steroid-induced psychosis after three days of systemic steroid therapy for an asthma exacerbation. The young girl developed a short term, acute psychotic reaction with visual hallucinations, delusions, panic reactions, and myoclonic movements of her hands (Lee, Lin, & Huang, 2001). Koh et al. (2002) noted that while steroid induced psychosis is a well-known but infrequent side effect of steroid therapy, there is no reliable way to predict who will suffer this adverse event.

Montelukast (Singulair) is a leukotriene receptor antagonist that is approved for use in the prophylaxis and chronic treatment of asthma. Several psychologically related short term adverse effects of montelukast have been noted. Irritability, restlessness, insomnia, dream abnormalities, hallucinations, and agitation have been reported. There were no drug interactions with psychotropic medications listed for montelukast (Taketomo et al., 2005).

Omalizumab (Xolair) is an injectable antiasthmatic medication, given every two to four weeks, used to treat moderate to severe, persistent allergic asthma that cannot be adequately managed with inhaled steroids. Fatigue has been noted as a possible side effect of omalizumab. There have been no drug interactions reported (Taketomo et al., 2005). Omalizumab (Xolair) is the newest drug introduced to inactivate IgE. IgE-mediated response has been associated with asthma exacerbations when patients are exposed to allergens

(Briars & Diaz, 2005). It is recommended for patients 12 years and older with moderate to severe allergic asthma whose symptoms are difficult to control with other medications.

Immunotherapy

Allergen immunotherapy is an important consideration in patients with asthma when the allergen is unavoidable, the symptoms occur most of the year, and medications are unable to control the allergy (NAEPP, 1997). Immunotherapy has been shown to reduce asthma symptoms and medication use and bronchial reactivity (Abramson, Puy, & Weiner, 2003).

THE PREVENTION OF ASTHMA IN CHILDREN

The effective prevention of asthma, from the perspective of public health, involves primary, secondary, and tertiary prevention. In primary prevention of asthma, reductions in the incidence of asthma are the key. In secondary prevention involves disease detection, management, and control of asthma. The reduction of complications caused by severe disease is the focus of tertiary prevention of asthma (Joseph, Williams, Ownby, Saltzgaber, & Johnson, 2006). This section focuses on primary and secondary prevention.

What Works

A review of the literature did not uncover any intervention that met the criteria of three successful trials in the primary prevention of asthma (i.e., the reduction in the incidence of asthma in children).

What Might Work

A review of the literature revealed randomized control trials from two cohorts that were successfully able to prevent the development of asthma in children at high risk for developing the condition. Arshad, Batesman, and Matthews (2003) followed a group of 120 infants for eight years to determine the effectiveness of an intervention to prevent asthma. Fifty-eight children were in the intervention group and the remaining children comprised the control group. Allergy avoidance measures were started at birth in the intervention group. These measures included reducing exposures to household dust, providing a low-allergen diet for the infants, such as being breastfed or receiving a hydrolyzed formula. Results revealed that at 8 years of age, those children in the intervention group were at significantly reduced risk of developing asthma.

In a longitudinal study, Becker, Watson, Ferguson, Dimich-Ward, & Chan-Yeung, (2004) sought to determine the effectiveness of a multifaceted intervention for the primary prevention of asthma in high-risk children. Intervention measures such as avoidance of house dust, pets, and environmental tobacco smoke (ETS) were put in place before birth. The authors also encouraged breastfeeding with delayed introduction of solids. At 2 years of age significantly fewer children in the intervention group were diagnosed with asthma when compared to children in the control group (Becker et al., 2004). A follow-up study of this same cohort revealed similar findings. At 7 years of age, the children in the intervention group had a significantly lower rate of physician-diagnosed asthma (Chan-Yeung et al., 2005). These results of the longitudinal studies show the continued effectiveness of allergen reduction interventions that commenced prenatally.

The U.S. Environmental Protection Agency report, *Indoor Air, Second Hand Smoke: Setting the Record Straight* (2006), notes that the harmful respiratory effects of second hand smoke are undisputed. In children under 18 years of age, ETS exposure results in more coughing and wheezing as well as a small but significant decrease in lung function. Children with asthma have more frequent and severe attacks when exposed to ETS, and ETS is a risk factor for the onset of asthma in children.

An ongoing study by Borrelli et al. (2002) to determine motivating factors that may assist parents of asthmatic children to quit smoking contrasts two theory-based smoking cessation interventions. They hypothesize that enhancing the perception of risk to self and the child will motivate smoking cessation more than standard approaches. They intend to identify which treatment produces behavior change and the processes by which behavior change occurs. The interventions will be incorporated into medical visits for asthma education and will potentially enhance the health of both the parent and the child with asthma.

The trigger-avoidance and environmental controls, shown in Table 9.3, are known to be effective in the management and control of asthma in children.

Yearly influenza immunization is recommended for all children with chronic illnesses, especially those with asthma or reactive airway disease. Yet it is reported that less than 10% of these children receive the influenza vaccine. The use of a computerized staged reminder strategy consisting of a computerized reminder letter followed by an autodial recall telephone message six weeks later was successful in improving immunization rates for influenza vaccine among children with asthma from 5.4% to 32% in all age groups regardless of the insurance status (Gaglani, Riggs, Kamenicky, & Glezen, 2001).

Massage therapy given by parents to asthmatic children for 20 minutes at bedtime has resulted in improvement in pulmonary function tests in one study when compared to standard relaxation exercises (Field et al., 1998). Although the authors note that the long-term benefits of massage therapy remain unknown, when done by parents costs and side effects are minimal and this complementary therapy can be safely recommended for parents to try.

Exercise, including yoga and breathing exercises should be encouraged for children with asthma because it is easier to control asthma in well-conditioned individuals, and asthma symptoms triggered by exercise can easily be controlled. Many world class athletes with asthma have set records for athletic performance (Kemper & Lester, 1999).

Psychologically related conditions in children with asthma have been noted to improve when children receive cognitive behavioral therapy (CBT). Children were noted to have significant increase in self-efficacy and coping after receiving CBT and studies revealed that asthma specific anxiety, in extremely anxious children, was reduced in those children receiving CBT.

What Doesn't Work

At the present time, a review of the literature did not uncover any intervention that should not be used in the primary prevention of asthma. However, there are numerous complementary and alternative therapies (CAM) under study. The use of elimination diets has not been shown to be effective in the prevention of asthma. Yet, many adults report reduction in asthma symptoms when on restrictive diets. Children with documented food allergies require food restricted diets, but there is no evidence that they are helpful in reducing asthma symptoms (Kemper & Lester, 1999).

Deep breathing exercises in which patients are trained to "breathe less" using a technique developed by a Russian physician, Konstantin Buteyko, is described as nonsense by Kemper and Lester (1999) in spite of reported testimonials. In addition, they note that homeopathy is expensive and has not been tested adequately in children.

According to the expert panel of the National Asthma Education and Prevention Program, antibiotics are not recommended for treatment in acute asthma unless there is evidence of pneumonia or sinusitis (NAEPP, 2003). A systematic review by Marra, et al. (2006) examined eight studies and concluded that exposure to one course of antibiotics in the first 12 months of life may be a risk factor in the development of asthma.

Recommended Best Practices

Early diagnosis and treatment of asthma is the key to improving the quality of life of children with asthma. Prompt medical care employing recommended guidelines for diagnosis and treatment from the National Health Lung and Blood Institute, Expert Panel 2 (National Asthma Education and Prevention Program, NAEPP) are essential for control of asthma in children.

Pharmacology

"Underdiagnosis and inappropriate therapy are the major contributors of asthma morbidity and mortality" (NAEPP, 2003, p. 17). Inflammation of the airways continues to be the component of asthma that causes recurrent symptoms of wheeze, cough, shortness of breath, and chest tightness. Goals of asthma therapy include:

- Prevention of chronic symptoms
- Maintenance of "normal pulmonary function"
- Maintenance of normal activity levels, including physical activity
- Prevention of exacerbations and emergency room visits
- Use of optimal pharmacotherapy with minimal or no side effects
- Patient and family's expectations for asthma care are met
- Patient and family are satisfied with asthma care. (NAEPP, 1997)

Medications are categorized into two general classes. They are quick relief medications used to treat acute symptoms and exacerbations and long-term control medications used to achieve and maintain control of persistent asthma.

Early treatment with systemic corticosteroids has proven to be effective in the treatment of acute asthma, reducing the hospital admission rate of children seen in emergency rooms. Inhaled corticosteroids (ICS) are the mainstay of treatment for children with persistent asthma. Their use results in limiting the amount of systemic corticosteroids and β-agonist medication needed. ICS are the most effective anti-inflammatory therapy available for mild, moderate, or severe persistent asthma. They are well tolerated and safe at recommended dosages. The NAEPP (2003) recommends the following to reduce potential for adverse events with the use of ICS:

- Administer with spacers or holding chambers;
- Advise patients to rinse mouth (rinse and spit) after use;
- Use lowest possible dose of ICS to maintain control;
- Add long acting inhaled β-agonist to control symptoms rather than increasing dose of ICS;
- Monitor growth of children.

The Panel notes that the majority of studies have not demonstrated an effect on growth of children and the use of ICS has significantly less potential to effect growth than systemic corticosteroids. Early treatment of asthma exacerbations is the best management strategy.

Elements of early treatment include:

- A written action plan: the purpose of this is to guide patient self-management of exacerbations at home, especially for patients with moderate to severe persistent asthma.
- Recognition of early or worsening signs of asthma.
- Appropriate intensification of therapy.
- Prompt communication between patient and clinician about any serious increase in symptoms or decreased responsiveness to current therapy.

Prevention

Identification of genes that increase susceptibility of an individual to asthma is a process complicated by many issues including environmental influences on gene expression. Some genes in fact only express themselves with exposure to tobacco smoke or air pollution. Genetic susceptibility along with environmental exposure is necessary for the manifestation of disease.

Lifestyle approaches to address the environment of the asthmatic child are essential in the prevention of exacerbations of disease. Identification of triggers that result in asthma symptoms should be noted and those specific triggers avoided:

- Indoor and outdoor allergens
- ETS
- Viral respiratory illness

Other Known Contributing Causes of Asthma Symptoms

It is also important to consider risk factors in the potential development of asthma. These may include:

- Family history of asthma
- Ethnic background—mainly African American
- Socioeconomic status, poor inner city
- Lack of access to quality health care

For children with asthma, education is a key component and should begin at the time of diagnosis and be integrated into every aspect of asthma care. Key components of a partnership in asthma care include:

- Teaching asthma self-management by all members of the health care team based on needs of each patient, maintaining sensitivity to cultural beliefs and practices;
- Joint development of treatment goals;
  - Teach and reinforce:
  - Basic facts about asthma
  - Roles of medications
  - Skills: use of inhaler/spacer/holding chamber/self-monitoring
  - Environmental control measures
  - When and how to take rescue actions
- Written daily self-management plan and action plan for exacerbations;
- Support adherence by promoting open communication, using an individualized approach adjusted as needed, emphasizing goals and outcomes, and encouraging family involvement. (NAEPP, 1997)

Also, yearly influenza vaccine for children with asthma may prevent respiratory illnesses, a leading cause of asthma symptoms in children.

Finally, according to the U.S. Surgeon-General Richard Carmon, avoidance of second hand smoke is critical in the prevention of asthma symptoms. He notes in his 2006 report on the effects of second hand smoke that children are especially vulnerable, leading to more severe symptoms than originally thought, especially frequent and severe asthma attacks (USHHS, Surgeon–General's Report, 2006).

REFERENCES

Abramson, M. J., Puy, R. M., & Weiner, J. M. (2003) Allergen immunotherapy for asthma. *The Cochrane Database of Systematic Reviews, 4*, Art. No.: CD001186. http://www.mrw.interscience.wiley.com/cochrane/clsys-rev/articles/CD001186/frame.html (retrieved 6/16/07).

Akinbami, L. J., Schoendorf, K. C. (2002). Trends in childhood asthma: Prevalence, health care utilization, and mortality. *Pediatrics, 110*(2), 315–322. http://pediatrics.aappublications.org/cgi/content/full/110/2/315 (retrieved 5/15/07).

American Lung Association (ALA), *Asthma and allergy fact sheet,* http://www.lungusa.org/site/pp.asp?c=d vLUK9O0e&b=44352 (retrieved 4/16/07).

Arshad, S., Bateman, B., & Matthews S. (2003). Primary prevention of asthma and atopy during childhood by allergen avoidance in infancy: A randomised controlled study. *Thorax, 58*, 489–493.

Barnes, K. (2006). Genetic epidemiology of health disparities in allergy and clinical immunology. *Journal of Allergy and Clinical Immunology, 117*, 243–254.

Becker, A., Watson, W., Ferguson, A., Dimich-Ward, H., & Chan-Yeung, M. (2004). The Canadian primary prevention study: Outcomes at 2 years of age. *Journal of Allergy & Clinical Immunology, 113*, 650–656.

Becker, A. B. (2000). Is primary prevention of asthma possible? *Pediatric Pulmonology, 30*(1), 63–72.

Borrelli, B., McQuaid, E. L., Becker, B., Hammond, K., Papandonatos, G., Fritz, G., et al. (2002). Motivating parents of kids with asthma to quit smoking: The PAQS project. *Health Education Research, 17*(5), 659–669. http://her.oxfordjournals.org/cgi/reprint/17/5/659 (retrieved 4/16/07).

Briars, L. A., & Diaz, A. (2005) Omalizumab: A steroid-sparing option for improving pediatric asthma management? *Journal of Pediatric Health Care, 19*(6), 386–391.

Calam, R., Gregg, L., & Goodman, R. (2005). Psychological adjustment and asthma in children and adolescents: The UK nationwide mental health survey. *Psychosomatic Medicine, 67*, 105–110.

Calpin, C., MacArthur, C., Stephens, D., Foldman, W., & Parkin, P. C. (1997). Effectiveness of prophylactic inhaled steroids in childhood asthma: A systemic review of the literature. *Journal of Allergy & Clinical Immunology, 100*, 452–457.

Carroll, W. (2005). Asthma genetics: Pitfalls and triumphs. *Paediatric Respiratory Reviews, 6*, 68–74.

Cates, C. J., Bara, A., Crilly J. A., & Rowe, B. H. (2006). Holding chambers (spacers) versus nebulisers for beta-agonist treatment of acute asthma. *The Cochrane Database of Systematic Reviews, 2*, Art. No.: CD000052. http://www.mrw.interscience.wiley.com/cochrane/clsysrev/articles/CD000052/frame.html

Chan-Yeung, M., Ferguson, A., Watson, W., Dimich-Ward, H., Rosseau, R., Lilley, M., et al. (2005). The Canadian Childhood Asthma Primary Prevention Project: Outcomes at 7 years of age. *Journal of Allergy & Clinical Immunology, 116*, 49–55.

Chen, E., Hanson, M., Paterson, L., Griffin, M., Walker, H., & Miller, G. (2006). Socioeconomic status and inflammatory processes in childhood asthma: The role of psychological stress. *Journal of Allergy and Clinical Immunology, 117,* 1014–1020.

Clark, N. M., Brown, R. W., Parker, E., Robins, T. G., Remick, D. G., Jr., Philbert, M. A., et al. (1999). Childhood asthma. *Environmental Health Perspectives, 107*(Suppl. 3), 421–429.

Courtney, A. U., McCarter, D. F., & Pollart, S. M. (2005). Childhood asthma: Treatment update. *American Family Physicians, 71*(10), 1959–1968.

Dik, N., Tate, R., Manfreda, J., & Anthonisen, N. (2004). Risk of physician-diagnosed asthma in the first six years of life, *Chest, 126*, 1147–1153.

Ducharme, F. (2003). Inhaled glucocorticoids versus leukotriene receptor antagonists as single agent asthma treatment: Systematic review of current evidence. *British Medical Journal, 326*, 621–626.

Duffy, D. L., Martin, N. G., Battistutta, D., Hopper, J. L., & Mathews, J. D. (1990). Genetics of asthma and hay fever in Australian twins. *American Review Respiratory Diseases. 142*(6 part 1), 1331–1358.

Edmonds, M. L., Camargo, C. A., Pollack, C. V., & Rowe, B. H. (2003). Early use of inhaled corticosteroids in the emergency department treatment of acute asthma. *The Cochrane Database of Systematic Reviews, 3*, Art. No.: CD002308. http://www.mrw.interscience.wiley.com/cochrane/clsysrev/articles/CD002308/frame.html

Etzel, R. A. (1995). Indoor air pollution and childhood asthma: Effective environmental interventions. *Environmental Health Perspectives, 103*(6), http://www.pubmedcentral.nih.gov/articlerender.fcgi?tool=pubmed&pubmedid=8549490 (retrieved 6/30/06).

Field, T., Henteleff, T., Hernandez-Reif, M., Martinez, E., Mavunda, K., Kuhn, C., et al. (1998). Children with asthma have improved pulmonary function after massage therapy. *Journal of Pediatrics, 132*, 854.

Foley, S. (2002). Infant asthma: Genetic predisposition and environmental influences. *Newborn and Infant Nursing Reviews, 2*, 200–206.

Gaglani, M., Riggs, M., Kamenicky, C., & Glezen, W. P., (2001). A computerized reminder strategy is effective for influenza immunization of children with asthma or reactive airway disease. *The Pediatric Infectious Disease Journal, 20*(12),1155–1160.

Goodwin, R., & Marusic, A. (2004). Asthma and suicidal ideation among youth in the community. *Crisis: The Journal of Crisis Intervention and Suicide Prevention, 25*, 99–102.

Goodwin, R., Messineo, K., Bregante, A., Hoven, C., & Kairam, R. (2005). Prevalence of probable mental disorders among pediatric asthma patients in an inner-city clinic. *Journal of Asthma, 42*, 643–647.

Gotzsche, P. C., Johansen, H. K., Schmidt, L. M., Burr, M. L. (2004). House dust mite control measures for asthma. Cochrane Database of Systematic Reviews, 2, Art. No: CD001187. http://www.mrw.interscience.wiley.com/cochrane/clsysrev/articles/CD001187/frame.htm (retrieved 6/15/07).

Guevara, J. P., Ducharme, F. M., Keren, R., Nihtianova, S., & Zorc, J. (2006). Inhaled corticosteroids versus sodium cromoglycate in children and adults with asthma. *The Cochrane Database of Systematic Reviews, 2*, Art. No.: CD003558. http://www.mrw.interscience.wiley.com/cochrane/clsysrev/articles/CD003558/frame.html

Guilbert, T., & Krawiec, M. (2003). Natural history of asthma. *The Pediatric Clinics of North America, 50*, 523–538.

Hoffjan, S., Nicolae, D., & Ober, C. (2003). Association studies for asthma and atopic diseases: A comprehensive review of the literature. *Respiratory Research, 4*, 1–12. http://www.respiratory-research.com/content/4/1/14 (retrieved 6/4/06).

Holmes, A. & Deb, P. (2003). The effect of chronic illness on the psychological health o f family members. *Journal of Mental Health Policy and Economics, 6*, 13–22.

Holt, P. G., Macaubas, C., Prescott, S. L., & Sly, P. D. (2000). Primary sensitization to inhalant allergens. *American Journal of Respiratory & Critical Care Medicine, 162*(3 Pt 2), S91–94.

Huss, K., & Huss, R. (2000). Genetics of asthma and allergies. *Nursing Clinics of North America, 35*, 695–705.

Jones, A. P. (1998). Asthma and domestic air quality. *Social Science & Medicine, 47*(6), 755–764.

Joseph, C. L., Foxman, B., Leickly, F. E., Peterson, E., & Ownby, D., (1996). Prevalence of possible undiagnosed asthma and associated morbidity among urban school children. *The Journal of Pediatrics, 129*(5), 735–742.

Joseph, C. L., Ownby, D. R., Peterson, E. L., & Johnson, C. C. (2000). Racial Differences in physiologic parameters related to asthma among middle-class children. *Chest, 117*(5), 1336–1344.

Joseph, C., Williams, L., Ownby, D., Saltzgaber, J., & Johnson, C. (2006). Applying epidemiologic concepts of primary, secondary, and tertiary prevention to the elimination of racial disparities in asthma. *Journal of Allergy & Clinical Immunology, 117*, 233–240.

Kemper, K. J., & Lester, M. R., (1999). Alternative asthma therapies: An evidence-based review. *Contemporary Pediatrics, 16*(3), 162–195,

Koh, Y., Choi, I., Shin, I., Hong, S., Kim, Y., & Sim, S. (2002). Steroid-induced delirium in a patient with asthma: A report of one case. *Korean Journal of Internal Medicine, 17*, 150–152.

Krawiec, M. E., & Wenzel, S. E. (1999). Use of leukotriene antagonist in childhood asthma. *Current Opinion in Pediatrics, 11*(6), 540–554.

Lee, K., Lin, Y., & Huang, F. (2001). Steroid-induced acute psychosis in a child with asthma: Report of one case. *Acta Paediatrica Taiwanica, 42*, 169–171.

Leone, F. T., Fish, J. E., Szefler, S. J., & West, S. L. (2003) Systematic review of the evidence regarding potential complications of inhaled corticosteroid use in asthma. *Chest, 124*, 2329–2340.

Lucas, S., & Platts-Mills, A. E., (2005). Physical activity and exercise in asthma: Relevance to etiology and treatment. *Journal of Allergy and Clinical Immunology, 115*(5), 928–934.

Lux, A. L., Henderson, A. J., & Pocock, S. J. (2000). Wheeze associated with prenatal tobacco smoke exposure: A prospective, longitudinal study. ALSPAC Study Team. *Archives of Disease in Childhood, 83*(4), 307–312.

Marra, F., Lynd, L., Coombes, M., Richardson, K., Legal, M., Fitzgerald, J. M., et al. (2006). Does antibiotic exposure during infancy lead to development of asthma? A systematic review and meta-analysis. *Chest, 129*(3), 610–618.

Martinez, F. D., Wright, A. L., Taussig, L. M., Holberg, C. J., Halonen, M., & Morgan, W. J. (1995). Asthma and wheezing in the first six years of life. The Group Health Medical Associates. *New England Journal of Medicine, 332*(3), 133–138.

McCunney, R. (2005). Asthma, genes, and air pollution. *Journal of Occupational and Environmental Medicine, 47*, 1285–1291.

Miller, A. (2001). The etiologies, pathophysiology, and alternative treatment of asthma. *Alternative Medicine Review, 6*, 20–47.

National Center for Health Statistics (2002). *Report of final mortality statistics*. US Department of Health and Human Services, Centers for Disease Control and Prevention, Hyattsville, MD, http://www.cdc.gov/nchs/deaths.htm (retrieved 6/15/07).

National Asthma Education and Prevention Program (NAEPP) (1997). *Expert panel report 2: Guidelines for the diagnosis and management of asthma.* (NIH Publication No. 97-4051). Bethesda, MD: National Heart Lung and Blood Institute, U.S. Department of Health and Human Services. http://www.nhlbi.nih.gov/guidelines/asthma/asthgdln.pdf (retrieved 6/15/07).

National Asthma Education and Prevention Program (NAEPP). (2003). *Expert panel report: Guidelines for the diagnosis and management of asthma: Update on selected topics 2002.* (NIH Publication No. 02-5074). Bethesda, MD: National Heart Lung and Blood Institute, U.S. Department of Health and Human Services.

O'Byrne, P. M., Barnes, P. J., Rodriquez-Roisin, R., Runnerstrom, E., Sandstrom, T., Svensson, K., et al. (2001). Low dose inhaled budesonide and formoterol in mild persistent asthma: The OPTIMA randomized trial. *American Journal of Respiratory and Critical Care Medicine, 164*, 1392–1397.

O'Byrne, P. M., Bisgaard, H., Godard, P. P., Pistolesi, M., Palmquist, M., Zhu, Y., et al. (2005). Budesonide/formoterol combination therapy as both maintenance and reliever medication in asthma. *American Journal of Respiratory and Critical Care Medicine, 171*, 129–136.

Pauwels, R. A., Lofdahl, C-G., Postma, D. S., Tattersfield, A. E., O'Byrne, P. M., Barnes, P. J., et al. (1997). Effects of inhaled formoterol and budesonide on exacerbations of asthma. *The New England Journal of Medicine, 337*, 1405–1411.

Plotnick, L. H., & Ducharme, F. M. (2000). Combined inhaled anticholinergics and beta2-agonist for initial treatment of acute asthma in children. *The Cochrane Database of Systematic Reviews, 3*, Art. No.: CD000060. http://www.mrw.interscience.wiley.com/cochrane/clsysrev/articles/CD000060/frame.html (retrieved 6/16/07).

Redd, S. C., (2002). Asthma in the United States: Burden and current theories. *Environmental Health Perspectives, 110*, 557–560.

Rodrigo, G. J., & Rodrigo, C. (2002). The role of anticholinergics in acute asthma treatment: An evidence-based evaluation. *Chest, 121*, 1977–1987.

Rosenstreich, D. L., Eggleston, P., Kattan, M., Baker, D., Slavin, R. G., Gergen, P., et al. (1997). The role of cockroach allergy and exposure to cockroach allergen in causing morbidity among inner-city children with asthma. *New England Journal of Medicine, 336*(19), 1356–1363.

Rowe, B. H., Spooner, C., Ducharme, F. M., Bretzlaff, J. A., & Bota, G. W. (2001). Early emergency department treatment of acute asthma with systemic corticosteroids. *The Cochrane Database of Systematic Reviews*, 1, Art. No.: CD002178. http://www.mrw.interscience.wiley.com/cochrane/clsysrev/articles/CD002178/frame.html (retrieved 6/15/07).

Seddon, P., Bara, A., Ducharme, F. M., & Lasserson, T. J. (2006). Oral xanthines as maintenance treatment for asthma in children. *The Cochrane Database of Systematic Reviews*, 2, Art. No.: CD002885. http://www.mrw.interscience.wiley.com/cochrane/clsysrev/articles/CD002885/frame.html (retrieved 6/15/07).

Shalowitz, M., Berry, C., Quinn, K., & Wolf, R. (2001). The relationship of life stressors and maternal depression to pediatric asthma morbidity in a subspecialty practice. *Ambulatory Pediatrics, 1*, 185–193.

Slezak, J. A., Persky, V. W., Kviz, F. J., Ramakrishnan, V., & Byers, C. (1998). Asthma prevalence and risk factors in selected Head Start sites in Chicago. *Journal of Asthma, 35*(2), 203–212.

Steinke, J., & Borish, L. (2006). Genetics of allergic disease. *The Medical Clinics of North America, 90*, 1–15.

Storms, W., & Kaliner, M.A. (2005). Cromolyn sodium: Fitting an old friend into current asthma treatment. *Journal of Asthma, 42*, 79–89.

Sulit, L. G., Storfer-Isser, A., Rosen, C. L., Kirchner, L., & Redline, S. (2005). Association of obesity, sleep-disordered breathing, and wheezing in children. *American Journal of Respiratory and Critical Care Medicine, 171*, 659–664.

Swartz, M. K., Banasiak, N. C., & Meadows-Oliver, M. (2005). Barriers to effective pediatric asthma care. *Journal of Pediatric Health Care, 19*(2), 71–79.

Taketomo, C., Hodding, J., & Kraus, M. (2005). *Lexi-Comp's Pediatric Dosage Handbook* (12th ed.) Hudson, OH: Lexi-Comp.

Travers, A., Jones, A. P., Kelly, K., Barker, S. J. Camargo, C. A., & Rowe, B. H. (2001). Intravenous beta2-agonist for acute asthma in the emergency department. *The Cochrane Database of Systematic Reviews*, 1, Art. No.: CD002988. http://www.mrw.interscience.wiley.com/cochrane/clsysrev/articles/CD002988/frame.html (retrieved 6/15/07).

U.S. Environmental Protection Agency. Indoor air , second hand smoke: Setting the record straight: Secondhand smoke is a preventable health risk. http://www.hhs.gov/news/press/2006pres/20060627.html (retrieved 6/28/06).

U.S. Health and Human Services. (2006, June 27). The *health consequences of exposure to secondhand tobacco smoke*: A report of the Surgeon-General. http://www.surgeongeneral.gov/library/secondhandsmoke/ (retrieved 6/28/06).

Villa, G., Nollet-Clemencon, C., Vera, M., Robert, J. J., deBlic, J., Jouvent, R., et al. (1999). Prevalence of DSM-IV disorders in children and adolescents with asthma versus diabetes. *Canadian Journal of Psychiatry, 44*(6), 562–569.

Villa, G., Nollet-Clemencon, C., Vera, M., Robert, J. J., deBlic, J., Jouvent, R., et al. (2000). Prevalence of DSM-IV anxiety and affective disorders in a pediatric population of asthmatic children and adolescents. *Journal of Affective Disorders, 58*(3), 223–231.

Weinberger, M. (2003). Clinical patterns and natural history of asthma. *Journal of Pediatrics, 142*, S15–S20.

Wenzel, S. & Covar, R. (2006). Update in asthma 2005. *American Journal of Respiratory and Critical Care Medicine, 173*, 698–706.

Williams, P., Worstell, M., Goldberg, E., Kaluzny-Petroff, S., Golding, J., Luna, P., et al. (1995). *Asthma and physical activity in the school: Making a difference*. National Heart, Lung and Blood Institute. http://www.nhlbi.nih.gov/health/public/lung/asthma/phy_asth.pdf (retrieved 9/11/06).

Wood, P., Smith, L., Romero, D., Bradshaw, P., Wise, P., & Chavkin, W. (2002). Relationships between welfare status, health insurance status, and health and medical care among children with asthma. *American Journal of Public Health, 92*, 1446–1452.

Yawn, B. P., Wollan, P., Kurland, M., & Scanlon, P., (2002). A longitudinal study of the prevalence of asthma in a community population of school-age children. *The Journal of Pediatrics, 140*(5), 576–581.

Yorke, J., Fleming, S., & Shuldham C. (2006). *Psychological interventions for children with asthma... Cochrane Database of Systematic Reviews*, 4, Art. No.: CD003272. http://www.mrw.interscience.wiley.com/cochrane/clsysrev/articles/CD003272/frame.html (retrieved 6/15/07).

Chapter Ten

Quality of Life in Children with Cancer[1]

Janet F. Gillespie and Lora M. Scagliola

INTRODUCTION

The diagnosis of cancer presents a uniquely stressful and challenging crisis which affects all aspects of a child's life, all issues of development, and all who care for the child. Many writers (e.g., Eiser, 2001, 2004; Kupst, 1992; Phipps, Larson, Long, & Rai, 2006) describe the cancer diagnosis as one of the most traumatic events possible for a child, and one that affects everything and everyone in his or her family. In a text devoted to child disorders, it must be noted that the "disorder" of cancer is unique among diagnoses that influence children's emotional health. This single term really encompasses a variety of illnesses, all involving a disruption in normal cell development and a proliferation of cells which becomes uncontrolled (Altman & Sarg, 1992). While there are obvious commonalities, different types of cancer may bring different stressors, depending on the type of malignancy and the course of treatment (e.g., side effects and after effects of surgery versus chemotherapy or radiation therapy). Understanding the array and scope of life tasks and areas affected in pediatric cancer, and outlining ways to promote emotional health and quality of life in juvenile cancer patients, requires that several overarching issues be outlined. First, it is important to view the diagnosis through a framework of the affected child's existence in multiple life domains (e.g., school, home). Second, the issue of disruption of typical developmental tasks must be addressed, both during and after treatment. Moreover, the impact of the diagnosis on others in the child's world (parents, siblings, teachers/peers in the school setting, and caregivers in the health field) should be acknowledged. Also important is the biopsychosocial perspective (Engel, 1977), recognizing physical, socioemotional, and cognitive aspects of adaptation to cancer, which has been underscored by several authors (Bearison, 1998; Eiser, 2001; L. Peterson, Reach, & Grabe, 2003). Finally, the concepts of emotional health and quality of life must be defined. All of these points are addressed in this chapter.

The incidence of cancer in children is fortunately rare. While rates of pediatric cancer vary to a certain extent around the world, rates are relatively stable across industrialized nations, and fewer than 1% of all cases of cancer in these countries occur in children (Stiller & Draper, 2005). The incidence of all types of pediatric cancers in the United States is estimated to be approximately 13 in every 10,000 children (Eiser, 2001).

As Dragone, Bush, Jones, Bearison, and Kamani (2002) note, this incidence of pediatric cancer amounts to a total of nearly 9,000 new cases per year.

The most common forms of childhood cancers appear to be blood-, brain-, or soft tissue-related, witheukemias, lymphomas, and cancers of the central nervous system comprising the majority of pediatric cases (Stiller & Draper, 2005). For example, cases of acute lymphoblastic leukemia (ALL), a blood disorder of excess white blood cells (lymphoblasts), comprise approximately 25% of all diagnosed childhood cancers, and three-fourths of all cases of childhood leukemia (Butler & Mulhern, 2005). Similarly, non-Hodgkin lymphoma (NHL) comprises nearly half of all diagnoses of lymphoma in those under 20 (Lanzkowsky, 2005). Other possible cancer diagnoses seen in children include sarcomas, such as osteosarcoma (cancer of the bone tissue), and nephroblastoma of the kidney (Wilms' Tumor), the fourth most common type of pediatric cancer in the United States (Lanzkowsky, 2005). Survival rates of childhood cancers have increased dramatically since the 1970s, from an approximate 56% five-year survival rate to one that now averages nearly 80% (Tercyak, Donze, Prahlad, Mosher, & Shad, 2006). However, mortality rates widely vary based upon the exact type of cancer diagnosis, and this improvement is not uniform among all types of malignancy (DeClerq, DeFruyt, Koot, & Benoit, 2004). Nonetheless, improvements in diagnosis and treatment have led some authors cautiously to express the optimistic view that the time may have come to begin to consider some pediatric cancers as chronic illnesses rather than fatal disorders. In fact, pediatric cancer is almost always included in child psychopathology texts in chapters enumerating chronic health-related conditions (e.g., Mash & Wolfe, 1999).

BIOLOGICAL/GENETIC FACTORS IN CHILDHOOD CANCER

The biological and genetic factors in pediatric cancer, like the diagnosis itself, are multifaceted. In terms of etiology, a great number of potential influencing factors have been studied, but precise answers remain elusive. Many in the field (Bearison, 1998; Butler & Mulhern, 2005; Margolin, Steuber, & Poplack, 2001) feel that the specific causal pathways to most cases of childhood cancers are still unknown. Haas (2005) notes that over 600 potential "genetic predisposition factors" (p. 22) have been suggested as playing a role in cancer's development in children. One current theory is that individual and sporadic genetic differences arise (or begin to arise even prenatally) for selected children. Precisely how these individualized or random genetic differences occur is unclear, but Versteeg (2005) notes that the rapid pace of cell division in infants may selectively present a "window of opportunity" (p. 39) for cancer via improper or abnormal activity in *oncogenes*. These genetic variations then act so as to influence an individual child's probability of developing cancer; for example, by differentially affecting a child's susceptibility to the effects of environmental carcinogens. This is significant because it has also been noted that, due to children's lesser body weights compared to adults, the relative impact upon children of exposure to toxins in the air, water, or food they ingest is proportionately greater (Haas, 2005; Steingraber, 1997). Stiller and Draper (2005) note that the study of "clusters" of diagnosed cases of cancer in children has led, for example, to the examination of families living in proximity to nuclear reactor sites as well as investigation of cancer rates in children of fathers employed in the nuclear energy industry. Moore (2002) suggested a connection between cancer cases and fathers employed in the metal/chemical industries. However, no precise link has been clearly established in either of these examples. Other writers, in contrast (e.g., Eiser, 2004; Pinkerton, Cushing, & Sepion, 1994) have posed an alternative possibility for explanation of these clusters or "pockets" of cases. They note that when new industrial sites are developed, workers who relocate there for employment bring new viruses/pathogens with them, and in that way introduce potential immune system risks to vulnerable children. Other risk factors that may relate to a child's parent(s) are detailed elsewhere in this chapter.

There is also evidence that at least some pediatric cancers are heritable and occur due to genetic factors. Chantada and Schvartzman (2005) cite retinoblastoma as prototypic of this type of cancer. They additionally note Knudson's (1971) "two hit" causal model, which explains that the emergence of this cancer hinges upon the occurrence of two genetic events (i.e., the result of both germ cell and also retinal cell mutations that happen before birth). Several sources identify more than a dozen recessive or dominant gene disorders, including neurofibromatosis and tuberous sclerosis that can predispose some children to certain types of pediatric cancer (e.g., Day & Henry, 2002; Pinkerton et al., 1994).

There is another set of significant biological factors in childhood cancer which relates to the child's functioning postdiagnosis, in terms of changes in normal biological functioning and development that may occur as sequelae of treatment. Authors have noted for some time (e.g., Barakat et al., 2003; Mulhern, 1994) that children who have been treated for brain tumors are more likely to develop neuropsychological/neurocognitive difficulties resulting from cranial radiation-induced damage to brain matter. These difficulties may include effects on intellectual performance (i.e., lowered IQ scores posttreatment), memory, and a myriad of possible differences in social and emotional competence with peers, such as skill in information processing and planfulness, adaptation to novel situations, and ability to communicate effectively. Moreover, children who survive cancer may face eventual changes in their reproductive capacity. Although this risk is not as common for children as for adults, the possibility of changes in fertility after radiation therapy has been noted as a salient fear for youthful cancer survivors (e.g., Bearison, 1998). It is reassuring to note that new discoveries in pelvic radiation with adults may lead to potential solutions in pediatric oncology; for example, via administration of gonadotropin releasing hormone to temporarily alter (i.e., make dormant) gonad glands and thus counteract that risk (Mishell, 2001). Kliesch, Behre, Jurgens, and Nieschlag (1996) also addressed this concern in a study of young adolescent male survivors of cancer (aged 14–17 years). Their findings indicated that cryopreservation of semen may be a realistic option for young males at risk for infertility. In contrast, the possibility for young female survivors of cancer preserving ova via freezing or other methods is a less viable option; this technology is still being developed (He, Liu, & Rosenwaks, 2003).

PHARMACOLOGY IN CHILDHOOD CANCER

Pharmacology plays a vital role in the treatment of pediatric cancer. Since the initial groundbreaking reports of remission using methotrexate in the 1950s (Holland, 2002), chemotherapy has been a cornerstone of most types of cancer treatment. It is beyond the scope of this chapter to describe in entirety this aspect of cancer treatment, but reviews in the literature of pediatric oncology (e.g., Fox & Adamson, 2005; Lanzkowsky, 2005) list over 30 different chemotherapy drugs commonly used for the cancers of childhood. The most common types are *cytotoxic*, and act via "poisoning" and destroying malignant cells. Examples of these kinds of drugs include mercaptopurine, vincristine, and methotrexate, which is still used (Fox & Adamson, 2005). Additionally, combination therapy is the "gold standard" in cancer treatment; several childhood cancers require radiation, chemotherapy, and surgery in order to facilitate a remission. Pharmacological interventions in childhood cancer that are not specifically associated with the cancer itself have been for the most part used to reduce the pain associated with medical procedures. In these cases, tranquilizing drugs (e.g., Valium), sedation (e.g., short-acting anesthetics such as halothane and propofol), and analgesic (pain-reducing) agents (e.g., premedicating agents such as lidocaine) have been most commonly used (Jay, Elliott, Fitzgibbons, Woody, & Siegel, 1995; Peterson et al., 2003). None of these is considered a perfect solution to procedural pain, however, due to possible side effects (Jay, Elliott, Fitzgibbons, Woody, & Siegel, 1995). Finally, several authors have recently addressed the issue of the use of psychotropic medication in treatment of neuropsychological effects in cancer survivors. Butler and Mulhern (2005) summarized four studies of use of methylphenidate (Ritalin) to address attentional problems in childhood cancer survivors. The results, taken together, indicated that some childhood cancer survivors may benefit from use of stimulant medication, and that their behavioral response is similar to that of children diagnosed with ADHD.

INDIVIDUAL FACTORS INFLUENCING RISK AND RESILIENCY

Enumeration of individual risk factors in pediatric cancer is a twofold task, as these factors can be classified first on the basis of a child's risk for the cancer diagnosis itself; and second, in terms of risk of emotional maladaptation secondary to the cancer diagnosis. In terms of risk factors for a diagnosis of cancer that are individual in nature, there have been cases noted of emergence of cancer in children and adolescents following viral infections, such as in the case of the Epstein-Barr virus, and heightened risk of Hodgkin lymphoma (Stiller, 2002) or Burkitt lymphoma (Haas, 2005). Also, it has long been noted that the diagnosis of acute lymphoblastic leukemia is more prevalent in boys than in girls (e.g., Krajinovic, Labuda, Richer, Karimi, & Sinnett, 1999), and in Caucasian than African-American children (Dragone et al., 2002). It is also noted that there are some genetic developmental factors that appear to correlate with increased risk of cancer for individual children. Hasle, Clemmensen, and Mikkelsen (2000, as cited in Stiller, 2002) reported that children and adolescents with Down syndrome face a risk for some types of leukemia that is 10 times higher than that of their non-Down syndrome peers.

Other risk factors for cancer that are solely a matter of the child's individual characteristics or of any child behaviors (unrelated to family or environmental factors) have not been well identified. This is presumably due to the fact that the behavioral health and lifestyle factors proven to be of significance in adults' development of cancer (smoking, excessive alcohol use) are not pertinent for young children. Steingraber (1997), in fact noted that

> The lifestyle of toddlers has not changed much over the past half century. Young children do not smoke, drink alcohol, or hold stressful jobs. Children

do, however, receive a greater dose of whatever chemicals are in air, food, and water because, pound for pound, they breathe, eat and drink more than adults do...they are also affected by parental exposures before conception, as well as by exposures in the womb. (p. 39)

These sentiments—that children are in essence completely innocent in development of cancer—make the disorder even more emotionally difficult. While there may be a few isolated case examples of youth behavior and cancer consequences (e.g., excessive exposure to sun or tanning salons, and skin cancer in late adolescence) those kinds of outcomes tend to be long-term, are rare, and are not solely the result of choices made by the child, but rather are presumably influenced by parental decisions. In sum, as suggested above, many cases of pediatric cancer may be idiopathic but not brought about by individual factors. There is no evidence that anything children themselves do or choose to do plays a part in their diagnosis of cancer.

Identifying protective factors for prevention of pediatric cancer is an area currently as diverse as the speculations about its cause; it is not yet known how to prevent cancer in children. Advice that exists in the form of what is usually suggested by physicians for an overall healthy lifestyle for adults, for example, maintenance of a healthy weight, regular exercise, a diet low in fat and high in fiber and antioxidants, and avoidance of tobacco, could benefit children and adolescents as well, but this conclusion cannot be extrapolated to presume it will prevent pediatric cancer as little follow-up research of this type has been accomplished. Nonetheless, some general suggestions provided by professionals have stressed the importance of breastfeeding, vitamin supplements, and ensuring that children exercise and eat fruits, vegetables, and high-fiber foods (Canadian Association of Physicians for the Environment, 2000).

Factors that promote emotional resilience in pediatric cancer patients have been studied as well. Kazak (1994) and others have noted that several reviews in the 1980s and 1990s suggested that children who have survived cancer will have ongoing emotional difficulties. However, these difficulties tend to take the form of internalizing rather than externalizing disorders, and pediatric cancer survivors are not generally reported to present noticeable behavioral problems for their teachers. Kazak and colleagues (1997) evaluated the presence of the diagnosis of posttraumatic stress disorder among survivors of leukemia aged 8 to 20 and found that, compared to a noncancer comparison group of similarly aged youth, the levels of *diagnosable* PTSD were not different. However, some child cancer survivors do show some posttraumatic stress symptoms. Phipps et al. (2006) suggest that the occurrence of such symptoms varies with the child's level of anxiety before diagnosis. Finally, it is interesting to note that children with cancer, collectively, have consistently been described as showing less emotion (for example, fewer depressive symptoms) than might be predicted given the seriousness of their situation. This stoicism has been referred to as "repressor adaptation" (Bearison, 1998; Canning, Canning, & Boyce, 1992), and "defensive denial" (Shedler, Mayman, & Manis, 1993). Alternatively, a positive psychology view might yield a different possibility, namely that children with cancer are given a far greater opportunity than the rest of us to develop the "signature strengths" (Peterson & Seligman, 2004; Seligman, 2002) of valor, bravery, and perseverance.

FAMILY FACTORS INFLUENCING RISK AND RESILIENCY

Significant bodies of scientific proof support a genetic or heritable risk for cancer in offspring of parents who themselves have been diagnosed; but these findings are in large part pertinent only to the development of malignancies emerging in their children's *adulthood* (e.g., breast, colon, and lung cancers). In contrast, few data are available which speak to whether or not a parent's previous cancer diagnosis plays a part in a *child's* risk for pediatric cancers. Some other parental risk factors that may have an effect on pediatric cancer (i.e., by affecting one child at a time) have been suggested, however, and these factors appear to relate to children's exposure in utero to known carcinogens. For example, a child who has been directly exposed to radiation during the fetal period (e.g., from extensive multiple CT scans during maternal pregnancy) carries a risk of cancer that is higher than average. Even this causal pathway from exposure to diagnosis, however, is not well understood. Radiation usually works toxic effects only through very high or repeated exposures, and "dose-time" relationships (Pinkerton et al., 1994) can be very hard to predict. Moreover, this example, more common in previous generations, would today be of much lower probability as medical precautions in radiography (and the availability of improved technology) have decreased this risk (Newcomb, 2003). Another parental risk factor that is well documented is that males and females (in late adolescence to early adulthood) show greater rates of testicular and cervical and vaginal cancer respectively if their mothers ingested diethylstilbestrol (DES) during pregnancy (Mishell, 2001).

Stiller and Draper (2005) caution that some maternal risk factors that appear physical in nature may in fact be related to maternal differences in socioeconomic status, thus affecting both the risk of events such as miscarriage and the accuracy of early diagnosis of child illness. Indeed, there are documented differences in pediatric cancer's prevalence in different ethnic groups (Dragone et al., 2002). Data from the National Cancer Institute's Center for the Reduction of Cancer Health Disparities attest to the fact that patients from families from underserved populations are more likely than others in the United States to have their cancer diagnosed in later stages, to lack access to adequate treatments, and to be diagnosed with and die from those cancers that are preventable or curable (National Cancer Institute, 2005).

Parents' and siblings' relationships with children who are coping with cancer have also been studied. Not surprisingly, family function and child function are closely related. Houtzager et al. (2004) evaluated the psychological functioning of siblings of cancer patients and found that brothers and sisters of children with cancer are affected most in the initial months following diagnosis.

SOCIETAL AND COMMUNITY FACTORS INFLUENCING RISK AND RESILIENCY

Community and societal factors influencing risk and resiliency in childhood cancer presumably vary in part with governmental policies and funding that promote and support (1) an environment free of carcinogens, and (2) access to specialized pediatric oncology centers for all affected children (regardless of socioeconomic status). In terms of the first issue, however, while potential carcinogens abound in the daily life of an average

American family, it has been very difficult to verify cause and effect in suspicions of risk for cancer, and pinpointing which children are most vulnerable is even more difficult. Where communities have existed in proximity to sites containing large amounts of known carcinogens (such as those discovered in Love Canal, a community near Niagara Falls, New York in the 1980s), case reports of miscarriages and pediatric cancers suggested to citizens a relationship attributable to toxic chemicals that had leached into the soil (Orford, 1992). Pinkerton et al. (1994) noted that exposure to radioactive fallout from the nuclear bombs in Hiroshima and Nagasaki produced a significant increase in leukemia diagnoses for five years after the event; but that the offspring of bomb survivors were fortunately not similarly affected. More recently, the atomic energy plant disaster at Chernobyl, Ukraine, has been the subject of speculation about environmental risk for later cancer (Davies & Ross, 1998).

There are also several significant societal factors in the greater society that will influence the way in which cancer will be experienced once it has developed. One of the primary factors, as mentioned, is children's access to pediatric hospitals that have specialized oncology centers. First, regional and geographic differences exist, in that children in rural areas of the United States face a greater challenge in terms of availability of appropriate medical care, pediatric oncology services, and pediatric psycho-oncology services. These differences in access can also be related to the socioeconomic status of the child's family (National Cancer Institute, 2005). Furthermore, as the majority of children who are diagnosed with cancer are assigned to a treatment protocol that is part of an experimental clinical trial, their survival may literally depend on whether or not there exists an open slot for them in a given study at a given children's medical center (Bognar & Reichert, 2006; Fisher, 2005). Finally, a significant risk factor exists for children in the form of the medical community's awareness of the prevalence of child cancers. Even medical professionals may not initially evaluate the risk of a malignancy when children present with specific symptoms. For example, Noonan (Personal communication, May 18, 2006) noted that juvenile and adolescent lymphomas can at first be misdiagnosed as mononucleosis.

UNIQUE ISSUES FACED BY CHILDREN WITH CANCER

Table 10.1 lists some of the possible psychosocial issues and stressors, as well as the physical challenges related to these issues faced by children with cancer. These factors are classified by the dimensions of the child's life in which these occur, the span of influence (short- versus long-term), and the type of intervention (i.e., treatment versus preventive efforts) that is indicated for each. Every psychosocial issue or physical challenge that is faced by a child with cancer is relevant to one or more developmental tasks of childhood or adolescence; and these are in all likelihood interrelated. Assuming that this is the case, then previous reviews relevant to child and adolescent adjustment (e.g., Durlak & Wells, 1997) would suggest that efforts to promote emotional health at one level or in one domain can have effects in others. In presenting this table, Durlak's (1997, 2000) models of multiple domains of child and adolescent problems and competencies are extremely helpful, as is Bronfenbrenner's (1977) ecological model, as these models note multiple levels of influence that may relate to children and adolescents.

Table 10.1 Unique issues and interventions needed for children with cancer

Shorter term

Possible physical challenges that are the focus of treatment interventions

Distress (pain, discomfort, fear) during venipuncture, lumbar puncture, bone marrow aspiration
Postsurgical pain
Nausea, weight loss, lethargy, and other side effects resulting from chemo- or radiation therapy
Hair loss, surgical scars, edema, and other physical appearance changes

Possible psychological/social challenges that are the focus of preventive interventions

Self

Embarrassment or self-consciousness about cancer diagnosis
Anxiety about prognosis
Ambivalence over attention received

Family-Related

Diagnosis-associated stress (e.g., waiting for confirmation of diagnosis, remissions, recurrences)
Disruption of daily routine and relationships to siblings, parents
Worry over parents' financial and emotional states
Loneliness experienced from separation from some or all family members

School- and peer-related

Isolation/separation from friends due to cancer treatment
Stigmatization by teachers, peers, others
Excessive absences
Academic difficulties

Longer term

Possible physical challenges

Neurocognitive late effects
Bone density loss
Secondary cancers
Infertility

Possible psychological/social challenges

Self

Feelings of "differentness" from others
Anxiety over recurrence or secondary diagnosis

Family-related

Separation from parents
Loss of parent as primary advocate for health maintenance

Peer-related

Intimate relationship issues (e.g., fertility concerns)
Anxiety over disclosure of medical history

Career and finance related

Insurability/health care access
Availability of adequate long-term survivorship care
Health care provider transitions while in college or relocating families as they react and adapt to a cancer
    diagnosis.

Extensive discussion of every possible child or family issue in childhood cancer is beyond the scope of this chapter; for a comprehensive review, see Eiser (2004).

Physical Challenges

First and foremost from a purely physical standpoint, the challenge facing children with cancer is daunting. They must simultaneously marshal the energy to endure stressful, often intensely painful medical procedures, carry on as well as possible with their daily life tasks at school and home, and also deal with the normal developmental tasks of their ongoing physical and psychological development—as well as cope with the side effects of cancer treatment. They are expected to strive to function as, and be treated as, a "normal" (nondiagnosed) child and also stay aware of their "differentness" in medical status (e.g., for safety reasons). Eiser (2004) sums it up well in noting that children with cancer can be thought of as needing to "function in two worlds" (p. 32), in that they must simultaneously live in the worlds of both "well" and "ill" persons. Taken together, the effect of these issues can be staggering.

Jay, Elliott, Ozolins, Olson, and Pruitt (1985) noted that two of the most painful interventions that are implemented with children who have cancer are bone marrow aspiration (BMA), and lumbar punctures (LP), both of which require needle insertion into bone or nerve tissue respectively. Bone marrow aspiration additionally involves suctioning bone marrow from the patient once the needle is inserted. Not surprisingly, children's parents have reported finding these procedures the most stressful to observe and endure, particularly since effective treatment utilizing these procedures are never singular occurrences but rather ones that may take several years, repeated frequently up to several dozen times (Jay & Elliott, 1990). Fortunately, as described later in this chapter, effective interventions for both parents' and children's distress during these procedures have been developed. It should be noted that the term *distress* has been recommended as the preferred term to describe effects of invasive procedures, as the stress associated is both with physical pain as well as the fear, anxiety, and anticipation of same (Wicks-Nelson & Israel, 2006).

A second issue closely related to dealing with the pain of essential medical procedures exists in the form of tasks children may have to experience in dealing with side effects of their treatment. Bognar and Reichert (2006) vividly portray in a documentary film a 12-year-old's courageous willingness to insert his own nasogastric feeding tube twice daily to counter the weight loss from his chemotherapy for lymphoma. Third, adolescents who are diagnosed with cancer are confronted with the illness precisely at the time when puberty begins and their reproductive systems are developing, and thus may face the possibility that essential treatments could impact their ability to have children of their own (Bearison, 1998). Furthermore, children and adolescents for whom treatment is successful in eliminating their cancer must learn to cope with neuropsychological and physical changes that can be the result of the treatment (Kiltie, Lashford, & Gattamaneni, 1997). These potential consequences, collectively termed *late effects*, have been described in reviews of the long-term effects of cancer (e.g., Eiser, 1998; Lanzkowsky, 2005; Mulhern, 1994).

Socioemotional Challenges

Children with cancer face a number of emotional issues that are associated with their diagnosis. They must confront the stress created by disruption of their normal daily routine during treatment, recuperation, and recovery. Moreover, this stress may be worst for some children (such as those with other, preexisting mental health diagnoses) for whom changes in routine, or transitions, are already quite challenging. Another prominent challenge may be a sense of loneliness or of being misunderstood, as they may experience changes in their relationships (even with those closest to them) given that cancer raises sensitive issues of life-threatening illness, still considered a difficult topic to address by many in U.S. society . Indeed, for those children for whom a bone marrow transplant may be part of their treatment, the isolation and sense of being removed from daily life (quarantined) may also add to their stress or anxiety over separation from parents (Last & Grootenhuis, 2005). Peer relationships are also inevitably affected, as younger and older children alike deal with the stigmatization or avoidance that may occur when peers become aware of their illness (Wicks-Nelson & Israel, 2006). Also, children and adolescents with cancer often experience repeated separations from their peers and friends at school (Prevatt, Heffer, & Lowe, 2000). They may even lose to cancer friends whom they met in the hospital.

Testimonials from children living with cancer provide poignant examples of some of these feelings. "Tim," diagnosed with Hodgkin's lymphoma, shrugged his shoulders when asked if he sees his friends often, wistfully remarking, "What's left of them." He also recalled his teacher's question about his extensive knowledge of body function and structure during a class discussion. Tim remarked that he chose to say he didn't know how he had acquired the knowledge rather than reveal his medical history ("Why get into all that?") (Bognar & Reichert, 2006). Finally, even if children with cancer make a successful recovery, they face challenges that persist into late adolescence and adulthood. A pediatric survivor lives with the omnipresent fear of a relapse, recurrence, or a secondary diagnosis (e.g., of another cancer) in the future, one that may have been precipitated by the treatments he or she received in battling the first cancer. The fear that cancer may recur has been described as the "sword of Damocles" hanging over one's head (Koocher & O'Malley, 1981). Finally, childhood cancer survivors need to be able to have some confidence that their long-term health care needs will be adequately served, through follow-up care, and a greater awareness of this need on the part of health care providers, as the population of adult survivors of pediatric cancer is now more than 270,000 U.S. adults (Institute of Medicine, 2006). Park et al. (2005) reported findings from The Childhood Cancer Survivor Study (CCSS) which suggest that ability to obtain health insurance is remains a challenge for adult survivors of pediatric cancer. For example, survivors were less likely to have health insurance than their siblings who had not been treated for cancer (83.9 percent versus 88.3 percent), and were far more likely to have faced difficulties obtaining coverage (29 percent for survivors versus 3 percent for siblings).

EVIDENCE-BASED TREATMENT INTERVENTIONS FOR CHILDREN EXPERIENCING CANCER

Children with cancer face a unique physical health stressor, but their quality of life in emotional and social areas can be maintained throughout their cancer with the right support. With this point in mind, the next sections present both strategies designed to ameliorate the distress of cancer itself (treatment interventions), and also strategies intended to prevent as effectively as possible the emotional maladjustment that the stress of cancer can bring (preventive interventions).

Several techniques have been shown to be effective in reducing children's distress (both physical and psychological) during painful medical procedures, including those procedures that are more routine in nature (such as venipuncture for blood draws or intravenous catheter insertion) and also those more invasive (surgery; lumbar puncture [LP]; bone marrow aspiration [BMA]). Collectively, these techniques appear to be primarily cognitive behavioral in nature, developed out of behavioral literature on stress inoculation training (Meichenbaum, 1985); coping skills training (Barlow, 1985), and modeling and rehearsal (Masters, Burish, Hollon, & Rimm, 1987). One cautionary note is necessary in presenting and evaluating these procedures, however. Namely, while there is clear evidence of their efficacy in the pediatric literature, it can be somewhat difficult to find and compare the results of successful attempts. The reason for this seems to be for the most part semantic, because different writers have referred to highly similar techniques by different terms. Just one example of this is use of modeling-rehearsal strategies, in which the child cancer patient is allowed to see, touch, or "practice" his or her treatment with actual or model medical instruments (e.g., Jay, Elliott, Woody, & Siegel, 1991). Most psychologists would label this a CBT method, whereas other writers (e.g., Favara-Scacco, Smirne, Schiliro, & DiCataldo, 2001; Pinkerton et al., 1994) referred to it as "play" and "art therapy." What also may vary is that different clinicians may also implement the technique at different time points during treatment.

Treatment Intervention Strategies That Work

The psychotherapeutic strategies that work best in reducing children's distress during medical procedures most typically utilize one or more of the following elements: (1) informational/educational intervention; (2) attention distraction (also called simply distraction); (3) coping skills training (such as guided self-dialogue); and (4) visual imagery. Excellent commentaries on the success of these types of therapy packages are available (e.g., Beale, 2006; Kazak, 2005; L. Peterson, Reach, & Grabe, 2003). Brief descriptions of each are below, along with information on which combinations appear most efficacious.

Information Sharing

There is clear evidence that information sharing works. Slavin, O'Malley, Koocher, and Foster (1982) found higher levels of positive psychological adjustment in child cancer patients who were directly told of their diagnosis compared to that of children who were not told but found out about it at a later time. Last and van Veldhuizen (1996) measured levels of anxiety and depression in 8- through 16-year olds following their being informed about their cancer by parents, and found that those who received accurate and honest information about their illness and prognosis fared far better in levels of symptomatology. Bearison (1998) noted, however, that there is a complex relationship between information provision and children's anxiety. In some cases (e.g., Jacobsen et al., 1990, as cited by Bearison, 1998), the information that parents provide their children could serve to increase distress where there had been none. Finally, it should be noted that L. Peterson (1989) cautioned that the positive impact of provided information is not uniform, as that impact will vary with different children's coping styles. Information sharing has also been effectively accomplished by using films. Since Melamed and Siegel's groundbreaking 1975 film illustrating a child's operation, pediatric and health psychologists have assisted children by showing them films or videos, usually didactic in nature, sharing with the child information about his or her illness/treatment. Additional examples of film-based information sharing will be provided in the description below of combined treatments.

Attention Distraction

Distracting (or refocusing) children's attention as a way of helping them cope has been attempted using a wide variety of methods, including counting, playing with soap "bubbles", or giving children contact with companion therapy animals, games, or visual media. The objective is to redirect children's attention from a painful medical procedure. Some have speculated that distraction works because the technique can help the child "use up cognitive capacity" (MacLaren & Cohen, 2005, p. 387), simply leaving less of the child's awareness available to experience pain. While not all forms of distraction have been equally empirically supported, one method that does appear successful is breathing exercises, teaching children to use slow, deliberate, audible breaths (e.g., make an "ss–ss-ss" sound) while exhaling. Although not presented in the same way as traditional behavioral "relaxation breathing" (Benson, 1975), Jay, Elliott, Woody, et al. (1991) note that relaxation may be a by-product of the technique. Alternatively, breathing may also allow a simple feeling of being more detached from pain, allowing a focus on the child's breathing itself instead of the pain of a procedure.

Imagery

This technique, which is referred to in different studies also as visual or emotive imagery (Lazarus & Abramovitz, 1962) provides children with a story "stem" that they may creatively embellish with their own more specific detail. One typical example used in confronting pain is to introduce the character of a superhero with special skills. Jay, Elliott, Ozolins, et al. (1985) used a "Wonder Woman" story to "transform the meaning of pain" (p. 516), or "Superman," who is able to overcome pain through superior powers (Jay et al., 1991). The imagery technique is believed to be effective to the extent that it facilitates feelings of mastery and competence. Another way in which imagery has been used is with pleasant imagery (e.g., Jay, Elliott, FitzGibbons, et al., 1995) in the form of children's imagining a peaceful scene (e.g., a relaxing beach setting).

Modeling and Rehearsal

Filmed modeling components used in successful evidence-based treatments may provide either "information sharing" (described above) or opportunities for behavioral rehearsal. Brief (10–15 minutes long) videos depict a similarly aged child as the patient, who expresses anxiety over treatment and then uses self-statements (e.g., "I can do this."). The rationale is that allowing patients to watch a child actor on video admitting his or her anxiety—and then demonstrating coping skills to confront it—will encourage the child to try the same. Additionally, behavioral rehearsal may be combined with the modeling, giving the child real practice in what to expect via trial enactment of procedures (on film or with dolls) using artificial or actual medical equipment.

Combined Cognitive Behavioral Treatments

The work of Jay and colleagues (Jay, Elliott, Fitzgibbons, et al., 1995; Jay, Elliot, Katz, et al., 1987; Jay, Elliott, Ozolins, et al., 1985; Jay, Elliott, Woody, et al.,1991,) provides an impressive example of a combined treatment approach that works in alleviating distress during pediatric cancer procedures. A series of successful studies has been conducted by these investigators for pediatric leukemia patients facing the pain of bone marrow aspiration (BMA) or lumbar puncture (LP). The basic paradigm for these interventions is a combination package of filmed modeling, distraction breathing, visual–emotive imagery, and rehearsal. A fifth "positive incentive" component is also added in the form of a "trophy" children are offered (that they will earn for having successfully endured the procedure). An initial small sample study with five children aged 3½ through 7 (Jay, Elliott, Katz, et al., 1987) demonstrated effectiveness of the above techniques using a multiple baseline design that implemented the five elements of the intervention in sequence. Later replications over a 10-year period, with larger sample sizes and randomized controlled designs, found the combined CBT package to be superior to pharmacotherapy (e.g., oral Valium) alone (Jay, Elliott, Woody, et al., 1991). A comparison with general anesthesia (Jay et al., 1995) also found CBT effective in treating procedure-related distress, especially when children's parents' reports of their children's distress were taken into account. In interpreting the success of programs such as these, Kazak and colleagues (1996) note that combined interventions that add a pharmacological component (such as premedication with lidocaine) may augment the success of psychological interventions. However, medical professionals (Noonan, personal communication, May 18, 2006) and researchers alike (Jay, Elliott, Fitzgibbons, et al., 1995) caution that not all children gain relief from any intervention tested, and that cancer-related procedures remain stressful and upsetting. In fact, some children require physical restraint regardless of which procedures are implemented. When this occurs, the use of general anesthesia may indeed be indicated.

Hypnosis

Hypnosis has been used for several decades as a method of reducing children's pain in cancer-related medical procedures. Some studies have demonstrated effective use of hypnosis when administered to children by therapists (Gerik, 2005), and other studies have trained pediatric patients in self-hypnosis (e.g., Liossi & Hatira, 1999). One of the most recent reports of the technique's efficacy is that of Liossi, White, and Hatira (2006), who reported results of a randomized clinical trial of hypnosis in treating pain during lumbar puncture (LP) in 45 pediatric patients aged 6 through 16. This investigation paired hypnosis with administration of a pain-reducing ointment (EMLA) during LP and compared this combined condition with both EMLA administration only and also EMLA plus an attention control condition (in which patients were allowed to play and talk with an adult during the LP procedure). The hypnosis condition was a multistep protoool that included (1) discussing with children their ideas and beliefs about hypnosis; (2) hypnotic induction and "analgesic suggestions" (p. 310); and (3) a posthypnotic suggestion for use during the actual procedure (children were trained in standard self-hypnosis techniques). Results indicated that the EMLA plus hypnosis condition was significantly better than either the attention control or EMLA alone in reducing anxiety and procedure-related pain, and that children with that condition also showed less behavioral distress.

Wild and Espie (2004) reviewed eight studies that utilized hypnosis for alleviation of pain for bone marrow aspiration or lumbar puncture; the majority of the studies cited compared hypnosis either to standard presurgical preparation or to another mode of psychological treatment (such as distraction). Taken together, results were positive in indicating the effectiveness of hypnosis. For example, Smith, Barabasz, and Barabasz (1996) contrasted hypnosis with distraction in 27 3- to 8-year-olds and found hypnosis to be more effective than distraction for children who were rated more highly on hypnotic suggestibility. In contrast, children who were rated low on "hypnotizability" (p. 208) were aided more by distraction, which significantly reduced their anxiety but not their procedure-related pain. Wild and Espie's review provides a summary of important factors that influence the success of hypnosis when used this way. They note the importance of assessment of hypnotic suggestibility prior to implementing treatment; giving children adequate opportunity to practice hypnotic techniques; use of appropriate comparison conditions; and long-term follow-up to assess maintenance of pain control ability.

The Importance of Adequate Outcome Measures

Key among the characteristics of successful programs described above is that these programs use well-validated outcome measures. One example of this type of measure is the Observation Scale of Behavioral Distress (OSBD; Elliott, Jay, & Woody, 1987). The OSBD was designed to assess children's level of distress during bone marrow aspiration procedures, and consists of 11 dimensions assessing behavioral aspects of pain and discomfort. These aspects include seeking attention, screaming and crying, need for physical restraint, moving and flailing one's arms and legs, and having rigid muscles. The OSBD is a well-documented, effective measure of the efficacy of the treatment interventions described. Also, the Visual Analog Scale (Varni, Walco, & Katz, 1989), which allows patients to subjectively indicate their level of pain by drawing a line on a continuum, is a reliable, adaptable, and multiculturally appropriate outcome measure of pain.

It must be noted that in addition to the above psychotherapeutic interventions, there are other essential elements of treatment for pediatric cancer that must be provided if children are to have the full support they need. These elements, medical in nature, all relate to access to adequate treatment. For example, the availability of specialized pediatric oncology medical centers is absolutely vital (Bognar & Reichert, 2006).

Treatment Strategies That Might Work

A number of treatment methods exist (some of which also draw upon established therapies) that are not yet as well established as those described above. Differences in the effectiveness of these treatments lie primarily in the fact that these are more recently developed and have not yet been extensively replicated. Also, these procedures often draw upon newer technologies (such as the Internet or other computer-based media). Several examples are presented below.

Visual and Interactive Media

Several studies have utilized watching or playing video games or other interactive media to distract or inform children. For example, one of the first attempts at using video games to distract young patients was by Kolko and Rickard-Figueroa (1985). These authors found that access to playing video games was effective in reducing symptoms of anticipatory distress before chemotherapy with three male patients aged 11 to 17. Dragone et al. (2002) contrasted an interactive CD-ROM condition and bibliotherapy condition (book reading) for pediatric leukemia patients aged from 4 through 11 years old. After conducting focus group interviews with the children, their parents, and health care providers, a script was prepared that was developed into a CD-ROM program entitled *Kidz with Leukemia: A Space Adventure* (p. 297). The program allowed children to download and view information from each of three segments that presented information about the illness, medical tests, hospital stays, and other pertinent information. Findings indicated that the intervention was helpful, entertaining, and appropriate for patients, and was well accepted by parents and health care providers. The authors note that compared to the book reading, the CD-ROM condition yielded greater feelings of control for the child over her or his health.

MacLaren and Cohen (2005) compared interactive toys and DVDs as strategies for reducing venipuncture distress in a randomized study using two age-appropriate distraction devices. They contrasted the distress-reducing effects of toy robots (with buttons to push and lights that turned on, for children 3 years old and younger) and laptop computer games (such as tic-tac-toe, for children 4 and older) with movies shown on handheld, 7-inch DVD players. The effect of the movies was found superior to the interactive play opportunities, a finding that the authors reported as counterintuitive, but possibly due to the length of the movies presented (*Teletubbies* for younger children; *Toy Story 2* or *The Little Mermaid* for older children), or the fact that children became bored with the toys more quickly than expected.

Klosky et al. (2004) investigated the effectiveness of interactive video and other methods for juvenile cancer patients undergoing radiation therapy. These authors compared the *Starbright Hospital Pals* program utilizing a talking "Barney the Dinosaur" doll with a didactic video (also narrated by Barney) that informed children of the nature of their treatment. An attention control condition additionally allowed children to see a cartoon during the procedure. Results indicated that observations of behavioral distress across groups did not differ, but that the pulse rates of children in the interactive (*Starbright*) group were significantly lower than those of the other children.

Virtual Reality

Gershon, Zimand, Pickering, Rothbaum, and Hodges (2004) used a randomized control group design to investigate the effectiveness of a virtual reality intervention on the level of pain children experienced during subcutaneous needle insertions. Participants were pediatric cancer patients aged 7 to 19. Patients were assigned randomly to the experimental condition (virtual reality), a distraction condition involving use of computer imagery, or no intervention. The virtual reality condition (developed from interesting scenes obtained from an area zoo's promotional materials) allowed participants to enter in virtual reality a nature preserve and view it from the vantage point of a baby animal. Results showed that although children's reports of anxiety during the needle insertion was lower than authors expected, the virtual reality intervention proved successful as it had a significantly beneficial effect on pulse rate compared to both other conditions.

Use of the Internet

Tannert (1996, as cited by Mash & Wolfe, 1999) describes an Internet support group for children with cancer that allows children to place "video calls" to other children with cancer from their hospital rooms (p. 487). The interactive network, entitled *Starbright World* has the potential to link similarly aged cancer patients across the country for peer-based social support.

Social Skills Training

Children who have been treated for brain cancer may show neurocognitive, neuropsychological, or interpersonal difficulties that may affect their peer relationships (Mulhern, 1994). Barakat et al. (2003) designed a social skills training program that incorporated behavioral techniques of modeling and role playing to help 13 children aged 8 to 14 improve their peer conversation skills. Children rehearsed modeled strategies and received feedback, and a parent component was also incorporated to allow children to practice at home. The preliminary results indicated a positive effect.

Treatment Strategies That Do Not Work

It can safely be stated that many different types of supportive psychotherapy have been attempted with children with cancer. However, there are no good outcome studies that demonstrate that the provision of traditional, one-on-one verbal psychotherapy is effective in reducing the emotional distress associated with the diagnosis. Similarly, as noted, while educational and informational interventions have been found to be helpful, the way that these programs are implemented is the key. For example, routine provision of information by a medical staff member, without acknowledgment of developmental level or children's needs, may not be enough to moderate the distress felt by children undergoing painful medical procedures. This point is similar to many findings indicating that factual information provision alone may not be sufficient to prevent maladaptation—such as in education about the risks of drug and alcohol abuse. In this sense, this issue is similar to studies of Drug Abuse Resistance Education (DARE), which have consistently indicated that the primary objective of the program—increasing children's resolve to not try drugs—is not achieved (Ennett, Tobler, Ringwalt, & Flewelling, 1994). Eiser (2004) points to information provided by the International Society of Pediatric Oncology that recommends an awareness of the need to explain the disease, side effects, and possibility of cure, but also to keep in mind the child's developmental level. Finally, it is well documented that providing children with information that is too limited or even incorrect (e.g., trying to protect them by distorting, downplaying, or deemphasizing essential facts) is not at all helpful to them in understanding or coping with their cancer (Bearison, 1998).

The Promotion of Emotional Health for Children Experiencing Cancer

The development of strategies to promote emotional health and quality of life in children with cancer is a similarly twofold task in several senses. First, the topic must address both short- and long-term needs of children and adolescents; and second, any review must also relate to the dual tasks of children's need to (1) cope with the physical challenges of cancer itself (for example, by assisting them with treatment side effects), and (2) meet normal developmental needs as well as the social and emotional challenges that the illness brings to their everyday lives. Accordingly, effective interventions for children with cancer can also be thought of as falling into two categories. Relevant to the second task (promotion of overall quality of life), previous works in prevention by Cowen (1982, 1996) and others (e.g., Durlak & Wells, 1997; Institute of Medicine, 1994) provide a useful guide for two reasons. First, *primary prevention* (Cowen, 1980) as an intervention strategy refers to attempts to prevent emotional maladjustment *before* its development, including with "high-risk" populations (such as children at the time of their diagnosis to this unequivocally stressful life event). Second, efforts at *health promotion* (Durlak, 1997) further fit the example of pediatric cancer, in that efforts to help children maintain a high level of emotional health can have effects on their physical outcome and overall health as well. Children with cancer would in fact seem a near perfect example of Cowen's (1982) statement that primary prevention may target children who do not show emotional disturbance but who "may, because of their life situations or recent experiences, be at risk for such outcomes" (p. 132). It is important to keep in mind that a multilevel and multiple domain approach is vital. Durlak and Gillespie (2003) noted that "quality of life" (QOL) as a construct has multiple domains. They cited the World Health Organization's (1958) long-held definition of "total health" as reflecting more than the absence of disability or disease. Quality of life, they stated, "involves the degree to which a child's personal experiences...are excellent in four major domains, physical, psychological, cognitive, and social" (p. 184). Eiser (2004) noted that quality of life for children with cancer is an extremely complex issue. She proposes that for some children with cancer, their quality of life is reflected in the difference between that which they would *like to do* in their daily lives and that which they *can* do (as influenced by physical illness). To the extent that children can be helped to resume the "normal" life activities that they wish to experience and enjoy, their QOL is enhanced.

Promotion Strategies That Work

A review of the literature did not uncover a preventive intervention that met the criteria of three successful trials.

Promotion Strategies That Might Work

There is some evidence that peers, teachers, and school personnel might be successfully educated about the diagnosis of cancer in preparation for children's return to school.

Educating Teachers about Cancer

Prevatt et al. (2000) reviewed 13 different school reintegration strategies for juvenile cancer patients, addressing three types: (1) workshops aimed at preparing school personnel; (2) peer education programs that informed school children about characteristics of cancer and how it affected returning schoolmates; and (3) multimodal "comprehensive programs" (p. 460) designed to teach teachers, peers, and the child and his or her family as well. These investigators drew several conclusions. First, they indicated that workshops intended for school personnel *do* effectively and efficiently improve the knowledge level of school staff about pediatric cancer. However, they caution that more empirical proof is needed that indicates that this meaningfully translates to improved QOL for the children and recommend further study.

Educating Peers about Cancer

Results of the review (cited above) of peer-based programs were equivocal, and Prevatt et al.(2000) state "there is inconsistent evidence regarding the long-term effectiveness of peer programs as well as the relationship between knowledge and peer acceptance (p. 462). Finally, the six "comprehensive" programs, Prevatt et al. (2000) concluded, remain difficult to interpret, as data from outcome measures in these studies are frequently anecdotal or qualitative in nature.

Special Recreational Programs

A review of websites describing specialized summer camps for children with cancer indicated that approximately 75 such camps currently exist in the United States (Camps for Kids with Cancer, 2001). The popularity and success of these programs is thought to be the availability of a safe space for children who may be medically fragile, who require special care, and who need the company of other children who can empathize with their situation. A review of the literature revealed just two published studies of effects of summer camp programs for children with cancer (Bluebond-Langner, Perkel, Goertzel, Nelson, & McGeary, 1990; Smith, Gotlieb, Gurwitch, & Blotcky, 1987). Neither study utilized a randomized control group design. Nonetheless, these studies did report positive benefits for the children who attended. Bluebond-Langner et al. (1990) found significant changes in children's knowledge of their cancer after camp attendance, based on prepost ratings. Smith, Gotlieb, Gurwitch, and Blotcky (1987) examined possible changes in physical activity level and family interactions for 18 children enrolled in a one-week summer camp, and found that the camp experience was successful at both increasing children's physical activity and time spent with family in enjoyable activities. Not all effects, however, lasted beyond a short-term (two-week) follow-up to a later assessment one month after the camp ended.

Promotion of a Healthy Lifestyle

Donze and Tercyak (in preparation, as cited by Tercyak et al., 2006) describe the Survivor Health and Resilience Education (SHARE) program, a randomized controlled health promotion program for survivors of childhood cancer. The objectives of SHARE include use of a health education approach to promote healthy behaviors in pediatric survivors. While outcome data are not yet available, Tercyak et al. (2006) give as the elements of SHARE: (1) randomization to a health promotion intervention group or a waiting list control condition; (2) a three- to four-hour group session focusing upon discussion of personal behaviors relevant to cancer risk reduction (for example, nutrition, exercise, contact with health care providers, and avoidance of tobacco); and (3) follow-up evaluations of completion of health promotive behaviors at a 1- and 3-month intervals.

Hudson et al. (2002) reported results of The Protect Study, also a brief intervention for childhood cancer survivors that utilized an educational approach. Intervention topics were individually tailored to specific participants' needs, and could include modules that covered exercise, weight control, healthy diets, and avoidance of smoking. Information was presented to participants by group leaders who allowed the youth themselves to select their preferred areas of interest for health behaviors. For each topic, a module was prepared that included (1) discussion of advantages and disadvantages of the health-related behavior; (2) presentation of alternative solutions which indicated ways to strengthen a positive health behavior or decrease a negative behavior; (3) discussion of obstacles or barriers to health-promoting behaviors; and (4) asking participants to make a personal commitment to behavior change. Unfortunately, few positive health behavior effects were achieved, a finding that the authors note was likely due to the limited time period of the intervention (i.e., a single session).

There are other health promotion strategies that may benefit children with cancer, but these have not been investigated empirically. Other possible helpful methods may exist that assist in enhancing QOL for survivors of cancer. These methods include after- school recreational programs, specialized advocacy and cooperative care programs, and other family organizations that provide information, support, and referral to both children and families, and resources that help young adult survivors obtain and maintain access to long-term survivorship care. Collectively, the addition of these types of preventive efforts may be helpful, but the effectiveness of these based on actual data has not yet been provided.

Finally, the success of these aforementioned efforts will be the result of the use of all of prevention's technology and not just the use of education. Educational efforts alone increase knowledge, occasionally change attitudes, but rarely change behavior. When education is combined with social support, competency enhancement, and systems change, it is then that change is observed (Gullotta & Bloom, 2003).

Promotion Strategies That Do Not Work

The health promotion knowledge base supplies several key pieces of advice on preventive efforts that may also be applicable for children who have or who have survived cancer. First, much of the child prevention literature substantiates the idea that "fear appeals" do not work well in helping children or adolescents adhere to health promotive behaviors (e.g., Albino, 1984). Second, health promotion efforts that ignore the need for rehearsal of skills or the relevance of the skills and situations presented to the youth involved, do not tend to be successful (Botvin & Tortu, 1988). However, a review of the literature specific to children with cancer yielded few studies giving any precise advice on strategies to avoid. One possibility exists in qualitative data provided by Searle, Askins, and Bleyer (2003). Their interviews of 10 students who, after beginning cancer treatment, were returned to one of three possible educational settings indicated that the pupils found homebound schooling less satisfying than either enrollment in a hospital school or reentering the school they had left at the time of their diagnosis.

BEST PRACTICE

Summarizing best practice requires consideration of the multiple needs of children with cancer, the need for valid treatment and preventive interventions, and the importance of accurately assessing treatment effects. Each is described briefly.

Kazak (2005) described four clear areas that should be addressed in meeting the multiple needs of children with cancer. These are (1) finding ways to deal with the pain of treatment procedures; (2) appreciating both children's short- and long-term distress; (3) recognizing possible long-term emotional consequences of cancer; and (4) paying attention to social relationships.

Powers (1999), in a review on procedure-related pain in children, stressed the importance of evaluating intervention studies using the Chambless criteria for empirically supported treatments (Chambless & Ollendick, 2001; Chambless et al., 1996). In writing this chapter, the authors endeavored to select studies that met these criteria. These criteria include a clearly articulated treatment protocol and multiple successful between-group designs interventions.

Drotar, Crawford, and Ganofsky (1984) stressed that preventive interventions for chronically ill children will be most successful when principles include the active involvement of their health care providers; the participation of children's families; the use of advocacy to help facilitate access to care; and an acknowledgment of the importance of the developmental perspective. These recommendations are similar to some points provided by Durlak (1997), who (writing about prevention programs of all types) recommended that interventionists begin from a sound theoretical base, "abandon the use of information only programs" (p. 192), and incorporate parents' involvement whenever possible. In fact, Bearison and Mulhern (1994) noted that many children with cancer report that what helped "most" was simply having their parents present during as many aspects of the process as possible. Parents of children with cancer also need special support in all domains of their lives: emotional, financial, social, spiritual. The presence of Ronald McDonald Houses or involving parents as well as children in the summer camp programs mentioned earlier are examples of how to keep parents close to their children who need them.

NOTE

1.   The authors wish to thank Patricia Newcomb for her helpful comments on an earlier draft of this manuscript. This chapter is dedicated to the memory of Jamie A. Hulley.

REFERENCES

Albino, J. (1984). Prevention by acquiring health-enhancing habits. In M. C. Roberts & L. Peterson (Eds.), *Prevention of problems in childhood: Psychological research and applications* (pp. 200–231). New York: Wiley.

Altman, R., & Sarg, M. (1992). *The cancer dictionary* (2nd ed.). New York: Facts on File.

Barakat, L. P., Hetzke, J. D., Foley, B., Carey, M. E., Gyato, K., & Phillips, P. C. (2003). Evaluation of a social skills training group intervention with children treated for brain tumors: A pilot study. *Journal of Pediatric Psychology, 28*, 299–307.

Barlow, D. (1985). *Clinical handbook of psychological disorders: A step-by-step treatment manual.* New York: Guilford.

Beale, I. L. (2006). Scholarly literature review: Efficacy of psychological interventions for pediatric chronic illnesses. *Journal of Pediatric Psychology, 31*, 437–451.

Bearison, D. J. (1998). Pediatric psychology and children's medical problems. In W. Damon, I. E. Siegel, & K. A. Renninger, (Eds.), *Handbook of child psychology: Vol. 4. Child psychology in practice* (5th ed., pp 635–713). New York: Wiley.

Bearison, D. J., & Mulhern, R. K. (Eds.). (1994). *Pediatric psychooncology: Psychological perspectives on children with cancer.* New York: Oxford University Press.

Benson, H. (1975). *The relaxation response.* New York: HarperCollins.

Bluebond-Langner, M., Perkel, D., Goertzel, T., Nelson, K., & McGeary, J. (1990). Children's knowledge of cancer and its treatment: Impact of an oncology camp experience. *Pediatrics, 116*, 207–213.

Bognar, S. (Producer), & Reichert, J. (Producer). (2006). *A lion in the house.* [Motion picture]. (Available from Films Transit International, Inc., 252 Gouin Boulevard East, Montreal, Quebec H3L 1A8 Canada).

Botvin, G. J., & Tortu, S. (1988). Preventing adolescent substance abuse through life skills training. In R. H. Price, E. L. Cowen, R. P. Lorion, & J. Ramos-McKay (Eds.), *Fourteen ounces of prevention: A casebook for practitioners* (pp. 98–111). Washington, D.C.: American Psychological Association.

Bronfenbrenner, U. (1977). Toward an experimental ecology of human development. *American Psychologist, 52*, 513–531.

Butler, R. W., & Mulhern, R. K. (2005). Neurocognitive interventions for children and adolescents surviving cancer. *Journal of Pediatric Psychology, 30*, 65–78.

Camps for Kids with Cancer. (2001). Retrieved June 29, 2006 from: http://www.chemoangels.com/camps/htm

Canadian Association of Physicians for the Environment. (2000). Cancer and immunological effects: What do we know about children's cancer? Retrieved June 28, 2006 from: http://www.cape.ca/children/cancer.html

Canning, E. H., Canning, R. D., & Boyce, W. T. (1992). Depressive symptoms and adaptive style in children with cancer. *Journal of the American Academy of Child and Adolescent Psychiatry, 31*, 1120–1124.

Chambless, D. L., Sanderson, W. C., Shoham, V., Johnson, S. B., Pope, K. S., Crits-Christoph, P., et. al. (1996). An update on empirically validated therapies. *Clinical Psychologist, 49*, 5–18.

Chambless, D. L., & Ollendick, T. H. (2001). Empirically supported psychological intervention: Controversies and evidence. *Annual Review of Psychology, 52*, 685–716.

Chantada, G. L., & Schvartzman, E. (2005). Retinoblastoma. In P. A. Voute, A. Barrett, M. C. G. Stevens, & H. N. Caron (Eds.), *Cancer in children: Clinical management* (5th ed., pp. 384–395). New York: Oxford.

Cowen, E. L. (1980). The wooing of primary prevention. *American Journal of Community Psychology, 8*, 258–284.

Cowen, E. L. (1982). Primary prevention research: Barriers, needs, and opportunities. *Journal of Primary Prevention, 2*, 131–137.

Cowen, E. L. (1996). The ontogenesis of primary prevention: Lengthy strides and stubbed toes. *American Journal of Community Psychology, 24*, 235–249.

Davies, S. M., & Ross, J. A. (1998). Childhood cancer etiology: Recent reports. *Medical and Pediatric Oncology, 30*, 4–6.

Day, S. D., & Henry, D. W. (2002). Acute leukemias. In J. T. DiPiro, R. L. Talbert, G. C. Yee, G. R. Matzke, B. G. Wells, & L. M. Posey (Eds.), *Pharmacotherapy: A pathophysiologic approach* (5th ed., pp. 2373–2395). New York: McGraw-Hill.

DeClerq, B., DeFruyt, F. D., Koot, H. M., & Benoit, Y. (2004). Quality of life in children surviving cancer: A personality and multi-informant perspective. *Journal of Pediatric Psychology, 29*, 579–590.

Dragone, M. A., Bush, P. J., Jones, J. K., Bearison, D. J., & Kamani, S. (2002). Development and evaluation of an interactive CD-ROM for children with leukemia and their families. *Patient Education and Counseling, 46*, 297–301.

Drotar, D., Crawford, P., & Ganofsky, M. A. (1984). Prevention with chronically ill children. In M.C. Roberts & L. Peterson (Eds.), *Prevention of problems in childhood: Psychological research and applications* (pp. 232–265). New York: Wiley.

Durlak, J. A. (1997). *Successful prevention programs for children and adolescents.* New York: Plenum.

Durlak, J. A. (2000). Health promotion as a strategy in primary prevention. In D. Cicchetti, J. Rappaport, I. Sandler, & R. P. Weissberg (Eds.), *The promotion of wellness in children and adolescents* (pp. 221–241). Washington, D.C.: CWLA Press.

Durlak, J. A., & Gillespie, J. F. (2003). Quality of life in children. In D. Wertlieb, F. Jacobs, & R. M. Lerner (Eds.), *Handbook of applied developmental science: Promoting positive child, adolescent, and family development through research, policies, and programs: Vol. 3. Promoting positive youth and family development: Community systems, citizenship, and civil society* (pp. 183–204). Thousand Oaks, CA: Sage.

Durlak, J. A., & Wells, A. M. (1997). Primary prevention mental health programs for children and adolescents: A meta-analytic review. *American Journal of Community Psychology, 25*, 115–152.

Eiser, C. (1998). Practitioner review: Long-term consequences of childhood cancer. *Journal of Child Psychology and Psychiatry, 39*, 621–633.

Eiser, C. (2001). Cancer. In H. M. Koot & J. L. Wallander (Eds.), *Quality of life in child and adolescent illness: Concepts, methods and findings* (pp. 271–295). New York: Brunner-Routledge.

Eiser, C. (2004). *Children with cancer: The quality of life.* Mahwah, NJ: Erlbaum.

Elliott, C. H., Jay, S. M., & Woody, P. (1987). An observation scale for measuring children's distress during medical procedures. *Journal of Pediatric Psychology, 12*, 543–551.

Engel, G. (1977). The need for a new medical model: A challenge for biomedicine. *Science, 196*, 129–136.

Ennett, S. T., Tobler, N. S., Ringwalt, C. L., & Flewelling, R. L. (1994). How effective is drug abuse resistance education? A meta-analysis of Project DARE outcome evaluations. *American Journal of Public Health, 84*, 1394–1400.

Favara-Scacco, C., Smirne, G., Schiliro, G., & DiCataldo, A. (2001). Art therapy as support for children with leukemia during painful procedures. *Medical Pediatric Oncology, 36*, 474–480.

Fisher, C. B. (2005). Commentary: SES, Ethnicity, and goodness-of-fit in clinician–parent communication during pediatric cancer trials. *Journal of Pediatric Psychology, 30,* 231–234.

Fox, E., & Adamson, P. C. (2005). Future trends in cancer chemotherapy. In P. A. Voute, A. Barrett, M. C. G. Stevens, & H. N. Caron (Eds.), *Cancer in children: Clinical management* (5th ed., pp. 56–67). New York: Oxford University Press.

Gerik, S. M. (2005). Pain management in children: Developmental considerations and mind–body therapies. *Southern Medical Journal, 98*, 295–302.

Gershon, J., Zimand, E., Pickering, M., Rothbaum, B. O., & Hodges, L. (2004). A pilot and feasibility study of virtual reality as a distraction for children with cancer. *Journal of the American Academy of Child and Adolescent Psychiatry, 43,* 1243–1249.

Gullotta, T. P. & Bloom, M. (Eds.) (2003). Primary prevention at the beginning of the 21st century. In T. P. Gullotta & M. Bloom (Eds.), *The encyclopedia of primary prevention and health promotion* (pp. 116–120). New York: Kluwer/Academic.

Haas, O. A. (2005). Genetics of childhood malignancies. In P. A. Voute, A. Barrett, M. C. G. Stevens, & H. N. Caron (Eds.), *Cancer in children: Clinical management* (5th ed., pp. 17–33). New York: Oxford.

Hasle, H., Clemmensen, I. H., & Mikkelsen, M. (2000). Risks of leukemia and solid tumors in individuals with Down's syndrome. *Lancet, 355*, 165–169.

He, Z., Liu, H., & Rosenwaks, Z. (2003). Cryopreservation of nuclear material as a potential method of fertility preservation. *Fertility and Sterility, 79*, 347-354.

Holland, J. C. (2002). History of psycho-oncology: Overcoming attitudinal and conceptual barriers. *Psychosomatic Medicine, 64*, 206–221.

Houtzager, B. A., Oort, F. J., Hoekstra-Weebers, J. E. H. M., Caron, H. N., Grootenhuis, M. A., & Last, B. F. (2004). Coping and family functioning predict longitudinal psychological adaptation of siblings of childhood cancer patients. *Journal of Pediatric Psychology, 29*, 591–605.

Hudson, M. M., Tyc, V. L., Srivastava, D. K., Gattuso, J., Quargnenti, A., & Crom, D. B. (2002). Multi-component behavioral intervention to promote health protective behaviors in childhood cancer survivors: The Protect Study. *Medical and Pediatric Oncology, 39*, 2–11.

Institute of Medicine. (1994). *Reducing risks for mental disorders: Frontiers for preventive intervention research.* Washington, D.C.: National Academy Press.

Institute of Medicine. (2006). Childhood cancer survivorship: Improving care and quality of life. Retrieved May 20, 2006 from: http://iom.edu/CMS/28312/4931/14782.aspx

Jacobsen, P. B., Manne, S., Gorfinkle, K., Schorr, O., Rapkin, B., & Redd. W. (1990). Analysis of child and parent behavior during painful medical procedures. *Health Psychology, 9*, 559–576.

Jay, S. M., & Elliott, C. H. (1990). A stress inoculation program for parents whose children are undergoing painful medical procedures. *Journal of Consulting and Clinical Psychology, 58,* 799–804.

Jay, S. M., Elliott, C. H., Fitzgibbons, I., Woody, P., & Siegel, S. (1995). A comparative study of cognitive behavior therapy versus general anesthesia for painful medical procedures in children. *Pain, 62,* 3–9.

Jay, S. M., Elliott, C. H., Katz, E., & Siegel, S. E. (1987). Cognitive-behavioral and pharmacologic interventions for children's distress during painful medical procedures. *Journal of Consulting and Clinical Psychology, 55,* 860–865.

Jay, S. M., Elliott, C. H., Ozolins, M., Olson, R. A., & Pruitt, S. D. (1985). Behavioral management of children's distress during painful medical procedures. *Behavior Research and Therapy, 23,* 513–520.

Jay, S. M., Elliott, C. H., Woody, P. D., & Siegel, S. (1991). An investigation of cognitive-behavior therapy combined with oral valium for children undergoing painful medical procedures. *Health Psychology, 10,* 317–322.

Kazak, A. E. (1994). Implications of survival: Pediatric oncology patients and their families. In D. Bearison & R. Mulhern (Eds.), *Pediatric psychooncology: Psychological perspectives on children with cancer* (pp. 171–192). New York: Oxford University Press.

Kazak, A. E. (2005). Evidence-based interventions for survivors of childhood cancer and their families. *Journal of Pediatric Psychology, 30,* 29–39.

Kazak, A. E., Penati, B., Boyer, B. A., Himelstein, P. B., Waibel, M. K., Blackall, G. F., et al. (1996). A randomized controlled prospective outcome study of a psychological and pharmacological intervention protocol for procedural distress in pediatric leukemia. *Journal of Pediatric Psychology, 21,* 615–631.

Kazak, A. E., Barakat, L. P., Meeske, K., Christakis, D., Meadows, A. T., Casey, R., et al. (1997). Posttraumatic stress, family functioning, and social support in survivors of childhood leukemia and their mothers and fathers. *Journal of Consulting and Clinical Psychology, 65,* 120–129.

Kiltie, A. E., Lashford, L. S., & Gattamaneni, H. R. (1997). Survival and late effects in medulloblastoma patients treated with craniospinal irradiation under three years old. *Medical and Pediatric Oncology, 28,* 348–354.

Kliesch, S., Behre, H. M., Jurgens, H., & Nieschlag, E. (1996). Cryopreservation of semen from adolescent patients with malignancies. *Medical and Pediatric Oncology, 26,* 20–27.

Klosky, J. L., Tyc, V. L., Srivastava, D. K., Tong, X., Kronenberg, M., Booker, Z. J., et al. (2004). Brief report: Evaluation of an interactive intervention designed to reduce pediatric distress during radiation therapy procedures. *Journal of Pediatric Psychology, 29,* 621–626.

Knudson, A. G. (1971). Mutation and cancer: Statistical study of retinoblastoma. *Proceedings of the National Academy of Sciences USA, 68,* 820–823.

Kolko, D., & Rickard-Figueroa, J. L. (1985). Effects of video games on the adverse corollaries of chemotherapy in pediatric oncology patients. *Journal of Consulting and Clinical Psychology, 53,* 223–228.

Koocher, G. P., & O'Malley, J. E. (1981). *The Damocles syndrome: Psychosocial consequences of surviving childhood cancer.* New York: McGraw-Hill.

Krajinovic, M., Labuda, D., Richer, C., Karimi, S., & Sinnett, D. (1999). Susceptibility to childhood acute lymphoblastic leukemia: Influence of CYP1A1, CYP2D6, GSTM1, and GSTT1 genetic polymorphisms. *Blood, 93,* 1496–1501.

Kupst, M. J. (1992). Long-term family coping with acute lymphoblastic leukemia in childhood. In A. M. La-Greca, L. J. Siegel, J. L. Wallander, & C. E. Walker (Eds.), *Stress and coping in child health* (pp. 242–261). New York: Guilford.

Lanzkowsky, P. (2005). *Manual of pediatric hematology and oncology* (4th ed.). Burlington, MA: Elsevier.

Last, B. F., & Grootenhuis, M. A. (2005). Psychosocial issues. In P. A. Voute, A. Barrett, M. C. G. Stevens, & H. N. Caron, (Eds.), *Cancer in children: Clinical management* (pp 101–109). New York: Oxford.

Last, B. F., & van Veldhuizen, A. M. H. (1996). Information about diagnosis and prognosis related to anxiety and depression in children with cancer aged 8–16 years. *European Journal of Cancer, 32A,* 290–294.

Lazarus, A. A., & Abramovitz, A. (1962). The use of "emotive imagery" in the treatment of children's phobias. *Journal of Mental Science, 108,* 191–195.

Liossi, C., & Hatira, P. (1999). Clinical hypnosis versus cognitive behavioral training for pain management with pediatric cancer patients undergoing bone marrow aspirations. *International Journal of Clinical Hypnosis, 47,* 104–116.

Liossi, C., White, P., & Hatira, P. (2006). Randomized clinical trial of local anesthetic versus a combination of local anesthetic with self-hypnosis in the management of pediatric procedure-related pain. *Health Psychology, 25,* 307–315.

MacLaren, J. E., & Cohen, L. L. (2005). A comparison of distraction strategies for venipuncture distress in children. *Journal of Pediatric Psychology, 30,* 387–396.

Margolin, J. F., Steuber, C. P., & Poplack, D. G. (2001). Acute lymphocytic leukemia. In P. A. Pizzo & F. E. Alexander (Eds.), *Principles and practice of pediatric oncology* (pp. 489–544). Philadelphia: JB Lippincott.

Mash, E. J., & Wolfe, D. A. (1999). *Abnormal child psychology*. Belmont, CA: Wadsworth.

Masters, J. C., Burish, T. G., Hollon, S. D., & Rimm, D. C. (1987). *Behavior therapy: Techniques and empirical findings* (3rd ed.). San Diego, CA: Harcourt Brace Jovanovich.

Meichenbaum, D. (1985). *Stress inoculation training*. New York: Pergamon.

Melamed, R. G., & Siegel, L. J. (1975). Reduction of anxiety in children facing hospitalization and surgery by use of filmed modeling. *Journal of Consulting and Clinical Psychology, 43*, 511–521.

Mishell, D. R. (2001). Adult sequelae of fetal exposure to diethylstilbestrol. In M. A. Stenchever, W. Droegemueller, A. L. Herbst, & D. R. Mishell (Eds.), *Comprehensive gynecology* (pp. 71–124). St. Louis, MO: Mosby.

Moore, I. M. (2002). Cancer in children. In L. L. Hayman, J. R. Turner, & M. M. Mahon (Eds.), *Chronic illness in children: An evidence-based approach* (pp. 80–103). New York: Springer.

Mulhern, R. K. (1994). Neuropsychological late effects. In D. J. Bearison & R. K. Mulhern (Eds.), *Pediatric psychooncology: Psychological perspectives on children with cancer* (pp. 99–121). New York: Oxford University Press.

National Cancer Institute. (2005). Cancer health disparities fact sheet. Retrieved May 20, 2006 from: http://www.cancer.gov/newscenter/healthdisparities

Newcomb, P. M. (2003). Prevention of birth defects. In T. P. Gullotta & M. Bloom (Eds.), *Encyclopedia of primary prevention and health promotion* (pp. 229–233). New York: Kluwer Academic/Plenum.

Orford, J. (1992). *Community psychology: Theory and practice*. New York: Wiley.

Park, E.R., Li, F.P., Liu, Y., Emmons, K.M., Ablin, A., Robison, L.L., & Mertens, A.C. (2005). Health insurance coverage in survivors of childhood cancer: The Childhood Cancer Survivor Study. *Journal of Clinical Oncology, 23*, 9187-9197.

Peterson, C., & Seligman, M. (2004). *Character strengths and virtues: A handbook and classification*. Washington, D.C.: American Psychological Association; London: Oxford University Press.

Peterson, L. (1989). Coping by children undergoing stressful medical procedures: Some conceptual, methodological, and therapeutic issues. *Journal of Consulting and Clinical Psychology, 57*, 380–387.

Peterson, L., Reach, K., & Grabe, S. (2003). Health-related disorders. In E. J. Mash & R. A. Barkley (Eds.), *Child psychopathology* (2nd ed., pp. 716–749). New York: Guilford.

Phipps, S., Larson, S., Long, A., & Rai, S. N. (2006). Adaptive style and symptoms of posttraumatic stress in children with cancer and their parents. *Journal of Pediatric Psychology, 31*, 298–301.

Pinkerton, C. R., Cushing, P., & Sepion, B. (1994). *Childhood cancer management: A practical handbook*. London: Chapman & Hall.

Powers, S. W. (1999). Empirically supported treatments in pediatric psychology: Procedure-related pain. *Journal of Pediatric Psychology, 24*, 131–145.

Prevatt, F. F., Heffer, R. W., & Lowe, P. A. (2000). A review of school reintegration programs for children with cancer. *Journal of School Psychology, 38*, 447–467.

Searle, N. S., Askins, M., & Bleyer, W. A. (2003). Homebound schooling is the least favorable option for continued education of adolescent cancer patients: A preliminary report. *Medical and Pediatric Oncology, 40*, 380–384.

Seligman, M. E. P. (2002). *Authentic happiness*. New York: Free Press.

Shedler, J., Mayman, M., & Manis, M. (1993). The illusion of mental health. *The American Psychologist, 48*, 113–117.

Slavin, L. A., O'Malley, J. E., Koocher, G. P., & Foster, D. J. (1982). Communication of the cancer diagnosis to pediatric patients: Impact on long-term adjustment. *American Journal of Psychiatry, 139*, 179–183.

Smith, J. T., Barabasz, A., & Barabasz, M. (1996). Comparison of hypnosis and distraction in severely ill children undergoing painful medical procedures. *Journal of Counseling Psychology, 43*, 187–195.

Smith, K. E., Gotlieb, S., Gurwitch, R. H., & Blotcky, A. D. (1987). Impact of a summer camp experience on daily activity and family interactions among children with cancer. *Journal of Pediatric Psychology, 12*, 533–542.

Steingraber, S. (1997). *Living downstream: An ecologist looks at cancer and the environment*. New York: Addison-Wesley.

Stiller, C. (2002). Overview: Epidemiology of cancer in adolescents. *Medical Pediatric Oncology, 39*, 149–155.

Stiller, C. A., & Draper, G. J. (2005). The epidemiology of cancer in children. In P. A. Voute, A. Barrett, M. C. G. Stevens, & H. N. Caron (Eds.), *Cancer in children: Clinical management* (pp. 1–16). New York: Oxford.

Tannert, C. (1996, February/March). Star power: Starbright world enlivens the pediatric-healthcare experience. *Video*, 33–37.

Tercyak, K. P., Donze, J. R., Prahlad, S., Mosher, R. B., & Shad, A.T. (2006). Identifying, recruiting, and enroll-
ing adolescent survivors of childhood cancer into a randomized controlled trial of health promotion:
Preliminary experiences in the Survivor Health and Resilience Education (SHARE) program. *Journal of
Pediatric Psychology, 31*, 252–261.

Varni, J. W., Walco, G. A., & Katz, E. R. (1989). A cognitive-behavioral approach to pain associated with pediatric chronic diseases. *Journal of Pain and Symptom Management, 4*, 238–241.

Versteeg, R. (2005). Molecular biology of childhood tumors. In P. A. Voute, A. Barrett, M. C. G. Stevens, & H.
N. Caron (Eds.), *Cancer in children: Clinical management* (pp. 35–43). New York: Oxford.

Wicks-Nelson, R., & Israel, A. C. (2006). *Behavior disorders of childhood* (6th ed.). Upper Saddle River, NJ:
Pearson/Prentice Hall.

Wild, M. R., & Espie, C. A. (2004). The efficacy of hypnosis in the reduction of procedural pain and distress in
pediatric oncology: A systematic review. *Developmental and Behavioral Pediatrics, 25*, 207–213.

World Health Organization. (1958). *The first ten years: The health organization.* Geneva: Author.

Part IV

BEHAVIORAL HEALTH ISSUES

Chapter Eleven

Anxiety Disorders in Childhood

Patricia A. Graczyk and Sucheta D. Connolly

INTRODUCTION

Anxiety disorders are the most common type of psychiatric disorder in school-aged children, with estimated prevalence rates ranging from 4% to 19% (Ford, Goodman, & Meltzer, 2003; Shaffer et al., 1996). Anxiety disorders frequently co-occur with other anxiety disorders, depression, and disruptive behavior disorders (Ford et al., 2003). Children with anxiety disorders also face a heightened risk for subsequent anxiety disorders, depressive disorders, schizophrenia, substance abuse, suicide, and psychiatric hospitalization in adolescence and young adulthood (Kim-Cohen et al., 2003).

Anxiety disorders can interfere with a child's ability to function in a variety of settings (Ezpeleta, Keeler, Erkanli, Costello, & Angold, 2001), yet often go unrecognized by parents, teachers, and physicians. Fortunately, there have been major advances since the mid-1990s in understanding the development, treatment, and prevention of anxiety disorders.

DESCRIPTION OF ANXIETY DISORDERS

The *Diagnostic and Statistical Manual of Mental Disorders* (DSM-IV-TR; American Psychiatric Association, 2000) provides a comprehensive categorical system for classifying anxiety disorders. Each disorder has distinct features, yet they all share a common foundation of excessive, irrational fear and dread that significantly interferes with a child's ability to function in different situations. A brief synopsis of each major anxiety disorder follows.

Children with *separation anxiety disorder* (SAD) experience developmentally excessive fear and distress concerning separation from home or significant attachment figures. Frequently their worries center on their parents' well-being. These children often have difficulty sleeping without their parents, complain of stomachaches and headaches, and manifest school refusal.

Specific phobia (SP) represents an intense fear of a particular object or situation and frequently is accompanied by avoidance of the focal object or situation. Compared to normal fears, phobias are excessive, persistent, developmentally inappropriate, or maladaptive.

Generalized anxiety disorder (GAD) is characterized by chronic, excessive, and uncontrollable worry. Worries may relate to friends, family, health, safety, or the future. A diagnosis of GAD also requires that at least one somatic symptom be present, such as sleep problems or muscle tension.

Children with *social phobia* (SocP) experience excessive fear or discomfort in social or performance situations. They are especially fearful of negative evaluations from others and worry about doing something embarrassing or stupid in the presence of other people such as in a classroom, restaurant, or during a sports event.

Selective mutism (SM) is characterized by a failure to speak in certain social situations where speaking is expected (e.g., school, with unfamiliar adults or peers), while being able to speak in other social situations (e.g., home). Although the current DSM-IV nosology classifies SM as a disorder "usually first diagnosed in infancy, childhood, or adolescence" (APA, 2000, p. 125), several scholars have proposed that SM be considered an anxiety disorder (Black & Uhde, 1995), possibly a variant of SocP that is manifested by young children (Anstendig, 1999).

Panic disorder (PD) with or without *agoraphobia* (AG) involves recurrent and spontaneous attacks or episodes of intense fear accompanied by at least four somatic symptoms such as pounding or racing heart, sweating, shaking, difficulty breathing, or chest pain. Individuals with AG avoid or are extremely uncomfortable in places where they fear they will be unable to get help or escape, such as crowds, on public transportation, or in enclosed or open places. Although AG frequently accompanies PD, it can occur independently.

Other anxiety disorders include obsessive-compulsive disorder, posttraumatic stress disorder, and acute stress disorder. *Obsessive-compulsive disorder* (OCD) involves recurrent obsessions or compulsive acts that are time-consuming and cause significant impairment or distress for the individual. *Posttraumatic stress disorder* (PTSD) can occur in children exposed to an extremely traumatic event or who have learned that a significant person in their lives has had such an experience. Children with PTSD often experience difficulties sleeping or concentrating, irritability, reexperiencing of the event in dreams or flashbacks, emotional numbing (e.g., restricted range of affect), or avoidance of anything or anyone associated with the event. Children with *acute stress disorder* experience similar symptomatology to those with PTSD, but their symptoms typically occur immediately following a traumatic event and abate within four weeks or less.

The typical age of onset varies across the anxiety disorders and approximates the developmental progression of normal fears in childhood. SM often starts in the preschool years (Black & Uhde, 1995). SAD presents at ages 6 through 9, GAD at any age but most often at ages 10 to 12, and social phobia at age 12 and older (Albano & Kendall, 2002). PD with or without AG typically begins in late adolescence or young adulthood (American Psychiatric Association, 2000).

MAJOR THEORETICAL MODELS DRIVING TREATMENT AND PREVENTION EFFORTS

Numerous theories have been proposed since the early 20th century to explain the etiology and maintenance of anxiety disorders. The behavioral-learning, cognitive-behavioral, and biological models are reviewed here because they serve as the foundation for current effective treatment and preventative approaches (Weems & Stickle, 2005).

Behavioral-Learning Models

Behavioral-learning models describe anxiety as something that is learned through classical conditioning, operant conditioning, or observation. In *classical conditioning*, a nonaversive stimulus, the conditioned stimulus (CS), is repeatedly paired with a feared or aversive stimulus, the unconditioned stimulus (UCS), until the presentation of the CS alone evokes fear and fear-related behaviors. *Operant conditioning* emphasizes the role of consequences in reinforcing or extinguishing anxious behaviors.

Mowrer's two-stage theory (1960) is an example of a conditioning theory of anxiety. According to this theory, a child is classically conditioned to fear a previously nonaversive stimulus, the CS (e.g., dentist chair). Operant conditioning then occurs when the child experiences a reduction in anxiety by avoiding the CS. In other words, the drop in anxiety *reinforces* the child for engaging in avoidance behavior and increases the likelihood that avoidance behavior will occur whenever the CS is presented in the future. Mowrer's two-stage theory not only accounts for the genesis of fears but also the persistence of avoidance behavior in phobic individuals.

Conditioning models have their limitations, however. They cannot explain why all people who experience a traumatic event do not go on to develop a phobia. These models are unable to account for the role of observational learning in fear acquisition. To address these and other issues, social learning theory has proven useful with its emphasis on observational learning, modeling, self-efficacy, and perceived control as influential factors in the development and maintenance of anxiety.

According to social learning theory, children learn how to behave in different situations by observing how others behave. For example, if a child observes his mother scream and run when she sees a spider, he is more likely to fear spiders and avoid them, too. In other words, the child's mother modeled how to react to a spider. Modeling is a powerful form of learning and is considered one of the mechanisms by which anxious parents foster anxiety in their offspring. Social learning theory's emphasis on self-efficacy and perceived control are also relevant to anxiety disorders. *Self-efficacy* refers to children's beliefs in their ability to *control* themselves and events in their lives (Bandura, 2001). From a social learning perspective, anxious children experience low self-efficacy. That is, they perceive themselves as having limited, if any, control over their thoughts, feelings, behaviors, or their environment. For example, children with PTSD demonstrate low self-efficacy by doubting their ability to recover from the traumatic experience (Benight & Bandura, 2004).

As can be seen, social learning theory places a much greater emphasis on cognitive or thought processes in the development and maintenance of anxiety disorders than do classical and operant conditioning models. In that respect, the social learning model is more similar to the cognitive-behavioral model discussed next. In fact, elements of all three learning/behavioral models have been incorporated into the cognitive-behavioral perspective.

Cognitive-Behavioral Models

From a cognitive-behavioral perspective, anxiety can be adaptive or pathological (Albano & Kendall, 2002). Adaptive anxiety serves a protective function because it signals real dangers and motivates a person to take action to avoid stress or negative experiences.

Pathological anxiety develops in response to irrational or unrealistic fears and significantly compromises an individual's ability to function appropriately in circumstances perceived to be unsafe.

Anxiety is also conceptualized as consisting of three components: physiological, cognitive, and behavioral (Lang, 1968). The *physiological component* refers to the activity of the autonomic nervous system that prepares an individual to respond to a threatening situation with "fight or flight" behavior. Such responses include increased rate of respiration, increased heart rate, and blood flow to the muscles, and are activated to enable the person to respond quickly, if necessary. The *cognitive component* of anxiety refers to selective and focused attention, interpretations, and recall of information emphasizing threat and ways to protect oneself. *Behavioral reactions* (e.g., running away) are actions taken to avoid a negative event or encounter. Like behavioral-learning models, cognitive-behavioral approaches emphasize how maladaptive thoughts, feelings, and behaviors are learned through person–environment interactions in which anxious behaviors are reinforced, modeled, or both.

Biological Models

Biological models focus on the role of brain chemistry and structure, genes, and temperamental differences that serve to cause or maintain anxiety disorders. Models emphasizing brain chemistry highlight the role of neurotransmitters. These chemicals in the brain facilitate the transmission of electrical impulses from one neuron to another. Serotonin, dopamine, and noradrenaline are neurotransmitters implicated in anxiety and fear conditioning (Sweeney & Pine, 2004). Models emphasizing the role of the hypothalamic-pituitary-adrenal (HPA) axis and amygdala propose that anxiety disorders are due to an excess of normal anticipatory anxiety that in turn causes an exaggerated startle response, elevated neuroendocrine activity (e.g., production of cortisol), and heightened sympathetic arousal (Granger, Weisz, & Kauneckis, 1994). There is evidence to suggest that right prefrontal lobe activation could be associated with anxiety by its impact on emotional learning and threat assessment (Baving, Laucht, & Schmidt, 2002).

Genetic theories suggest that anxious symptomatology is transmitted genetically from parents to offspring. Twin studies find that approximately 33% of the variance in measures of childhood anxiety might be attributed to genetic factors (Eley, 2001). Moreover, multiple family studies suggest that offspring of parents with anxiety disorders are at increased risk of experiencing anxiety disorders. For example, Turner, Beidel, and Costello (1987) reported that 7- to 12- year-old offspring of anxious parents were seven times more likely to meet criteria for an anxiety disorder than the control group.

Temperament theories propose that anxiety disorders are due to biological predispositions toward certain patterns of behavior. Anxiety has been linked to two temperamental profiles, one characterized by behavioral inhibition (BI) and another characterized by high negative affect and neuroticism (NA/N) and low effortful control (EC). Because these temperamental profiles are often referred to as risk factors, they are covered in the next section.

The aforementioned theoretical perspectives provide key information relative to the etiology, prevention, and treatment of childhood anxiety disorders. These theories have helped to identify a variety of risk and protective factors associated with childhood anxiety disorders.

RISK AND PROTECTIVE FACTORS ASSOCIATED WITH ANXIETY DISORDERS

Risk factors for anxiety are those that place youth at increased risk of developing an anxiety disorder. *Protective factors* enhance a child's resilience in the presence of risk factors or emergent pathological anxiety. In this section, risk and protective factors for anxiety disorders are organized according to their reference to biological–genetic factors, characteristics of the individual, characteristics of the family, and characteristics of the broader social environment.

Biological–Genetic Factors Influencing Risk and Resiliency

Biological and genetic risk factors are derived from the biological models described above. They include physiological reactivity, parental anxiety, and temperament.

Physiological Reactivity

Exaggerated startle response, cortisol reactivity, and a lower threshold of reactivity in the HPA axis appear to be biological risk factors for anxiety. Evidence in support of these putative risk factors come primarily from studies of neuroendocrine reactivity in clinic-referred children (Granger et al., 1994) and studies comparing norepinephrine levels in behaviorally inhibited (BI) and non-BI children (Weems & Stickle, 2005).

Parental Anxiety

Parental anxiety disorder has been associated with increased risk of anxiety disorders in offspring (Merikangas et al., 1998) and high levels of functional impairment in children and adolescents with anxiety disorders (Manassis & Hood, 1998). Donovan and Spence (2000) proposed that parental anxiety might serve as an indirect risk factor in that its effects are moderated or mediated by other factors such as child temperament or parenting behaviors (to be discussed in a later section).

Temperament

As noted earlier, two temperamental profiles have been linked to anxiety. The first, behavioral inhibition (BI), refers to a tendency to respond negatively to new situations or stimuli (Garcia-Coll, Kagan, & Reznick, 1984). Physiological indicators of BI include high stable heart rates, low vagal tone, and other indicators of high sympathetic arousal or low parasympathetic arousal (Kagan, Reznick, & Snidman, 1987). Behavioral manifestations of BI include shyness, caution, and emotional restraint, particularly in novel situations (Kagan, 1997).

Lonigan and colleagues have proposed that two temperament characteristics, high negative affect-neuroticism (NA-N) and low effortful control (EC), place a child at increased risk for anxiety disorders (e.g., Lonigan, Vasey, Phillips, & Hazen, 2004). High NA-N can lead to maladaptive anxiety through its association with processing biases in favor of threat cues. When combined with low EC, a child's risk for anxiety is heightened because the child not only experiences greater anxiety but has difficulty managing it. High EC, on the other hand, can lower that risk to the extent that it diverts the child's automatic focus on threat cues. For example, a child with high NA-N and high EC could intentionally channel his or her attention away from threat cues that result in avoidance behaviors to coping strategies that allow him to successfully manage his anxiety. Evidence in support of this model is accruing and could lead to additional preventive and treatment approaches in the future.

Individual Factors Influencing Risk and Resiliency

For prepubertal children, behavioral characteristics and maladaptive information processing have been identified as risk factors for anxiety disorders. To date, only one child characteristic has been identified as a protective factor—problem-focused coping skills.

Anxious/Withdrawn Behavior

Children with elevated scores on the anxious-withdrawn dimension typically exhibit shy, withdrawn, inhibited, and fearful behavior. Anxious-withdrawn behavior at age 8 was associated significantly with major depression and anxiety disorders in adolescence and young adulthood, especially SocP and SP (Goodwin, Fergusson, & Horwood, 2004). However, it should be noted that only half of the children displaying the highest levels of anxious–withdrawn behavior in this study went on to develop a disorder by age 21. This last observation is important because it highlights the fact that the presence of a risk factor does not necessarily lead to disorder.

Maladaptive Information Processing

Maladaptive information processing refers to dysfunctional biases or processes relative to attention selectivity, meaning what information the individual attends to, how information is interpreted or remembered, or how judgments are made. Such cognitive biases and distortions can contribute to dysfunction. Of these processes, attention issues have been studied the most and two, threat biases and anxiety sensitivity, have been identified as risk factors for anxiety.

When presented with a myriad of stimuli, children at risk for anxiety disorders often manifest a proclivity to focus their attention on threatening stimuli (Ehrenreich & Gross, 2002; Hadwin, Garner, & Perez-Olivas, 2006). Anxiety sensitivity (AS) refers to a belief that physiological symptoms of anxiety (e.g., shortness of breath, trembling, increased heart rate) will result in severe physical, psychological, or negative consequences (Reiss, 1991). Such expectancies in turn can encourage higher levels of anxiety, more intense physical symptoms, and, eventually, panic. AS is noteworthy because it appears to be a risk factor specific to panic attacks and panic disorder (Kearney, Albano, Eisen, Allan, & Barlow, 1997).

Other forms of biases and information processing differences have been investigated in clinically anxious children and in community samples. However, results to date have been mixed (Hadwin et al., in press).

Coping Skills

Children cope with unpleasant experiences in a variety of ways, and those ways can influence the extent to which they experience anxiety, distress, and fear (Spence, 2001). Coping strategies can be categorized as *emotion focused, avoidant,* or *problem focused* (Donovan & Spence, 2000). *Emotion-focused strategies* target the level of distress and *avoidant strategies* emphasize efforts to escape or avoid the problem. In contrast, *problem-focused coping* refers to efforts to deal directly with a problem or to minimize its effect (e.g., seeking information, positive self-talk, doing something to change the situation that is creating stress). Several studies offer evidence of the benefits of problem-focused activities and the negative impact of emotion-focused and avoidant strategies for children and adolescents (Donovan & Spence, 2000), although others emphasize the benefits of being able to use problem- and emotion-focused coping strategies flexibly (Pincus & Friedman, 2004).

Family Factors Influencing Risk and Resiliency

Along with parental anxiety discussed earlier, family characteristics associated with childhood anxiety include parent–child relationships and parental behaviors.

Attachment

Attachment theory emphasizes the importance of the early caregiver–infant relationship to the child's emotional and social development. According to attachment theory (Bowlby, 1988), infants form a trusting and secure attachment when their caregivers are available and responsive to their basic needs for nurturance and support. Insecure attachments develop when parents are unresponsive, rejecting, or inconsistent. Insecurely attached infants show anxious fearfulness in difficult or unfamiliar situations because they doubt the availability of a caregiver's assistance. Findings from two studies provide evidence of the link between insecure attachment and anxiety disorders (Manassis, 2001; Warren, Huston, Egeland, & Sroufe, 1997), a link that is even stronger when a child is temperamentally predisposed to fearfulness and inhibition (Fox & Calkins, 1993).

Parental Behavior

Parental overcontrol and overprotectiveness have been implicated in the development and maintenance of anxiety disorders in children and adolescents (Wood, McLeod, Sigman, Hwang, & Chu, 2003). By excessively controlling their children's activities or solving problems for them, parents encourage avoidance behavior and limit their children's opportunities to learn effective coping strategies (Rubin, Burgess, Kennedy, & Stewart, 2003). Several observational studies confirm this explanation (Hudson & Rapee, 2001). However, there is evidence to suggest that anxious parents only display overprotective behavior in anxiety-provoking situations (Turner, Beidel, Roberson-Nay, & Tervo, 2003).

Children are at heightened risk for anxiety when their parents display rejecting behavior toward them; conversely, parental warmth and sensitivity demonstrate a negative relationship to childhood anxiety (Dadds, Barrett, Rapee, & Ryan, 1996; Leib et al., 2000). Retrospective studies of adults with anxiety disorders have revealed a link between lack of warmth in parent–child relations and anxiety (Wood et al., 2003).

Modeling and vicarious learning are two other processes in family interactions that can increase anxious cognitions in children. Several studies have revealed that parents of children with anxiety disorders are more likely to model anxiety or reinforce avoidance compared to parents of nonanxious children. For example, Gerull and Rapee (2002) reported that children whose mothers had earlier expressed negative affect toward a rubber snake were less willing to approach the snake compared to children whose mothers remained neutral. Finally, there is growing evidence that anxious children interpret ambiguous situations as threatening and prefer avoidant solutions to these situations if that is what their parents do (Barrett, Rapee, Dadds, & Ryan, 1996).

In summary, several family processes appear to play a role in childhood anxiety. This is particularly true when parents display high levels of anxiety (Albano, Chorpita, & Barlow, 2003). Parents can encourage anxious behaviors in children by attending to such behaviors, focusing selectively on negative outcomes and threat, modeling maladaptive coping skills such as avoidance, or by failing to reward their child's brave behaviors.

Social and Community Factors Influencing Risk and Resiliency

Events that occur outside the home, such as negative or traumatic life events, community violence, and problematic peer relationships can place a child at increased risk for anxiety disorders. However, social support can come from multiple individuals within the youth's environment and serve to buffer the effects of other risk factors that could be present.

Negative Life Events

Multiple studies have shown that children and adolescents with mental health needs experience more negative, stressful, or traumatic life events than their healthy counterparts (Boer et al., 2002), and these events increase risk for anxiety. Elevated rates of anxiety disorders have been found following natural disasters (Yule & Williams, 1990) and negative life events such as the death of a family member, divorce, or changes in school (Donovan & Spence, 2000). Youth with anxiety disorders appear to experience a higher incident of negative life events compared to nonanxious children, even when compared with siblings in the same household (Boer et al., 2002).

Community Violence

Research to understand the risk relationships between child anxiety disorders and broader environmental factors is limited (Spence, 2001), but suggests that minority and economically disadvantaged youth are at increased risk for anxiety disorders. Minority and disadvantaged youth report decreased feelings of safety (Schwab-Stone et al., 1995). They are exposed to high rates of community violence (Cooley, Turner, & Beidel, 1995), and are often victims of violence (Freeman, Mokros, & Poznanski, 1993). Violence exposure is linked consistently to symptoms of psychological trauma such as depression, anger, dissociation, anxiety, and posttraumatic stress (Berman, Kurtines, Silverman, & Serafini, 1996).

Peer Relationships

In social situations, children with anxiety disorders are likely to react with negative self-appraisals, social skill deficits, and elevated states of physiological arousal (Spence, Donovan, & Brechman-Toussaint, 2000). Beidel and Turner (1998) reported that approximately 40% of socially phobic children in their clinic expressed fear of speaking to peers. Such fears may be at least partially grounded in reality. Anxious and socially isolated children are more likely to be victimized (Olweus, 1993), rejected, or neglected by their peers (Strauss, Lahey, Frick, Frame, & Hynd, 1988), especially in the intermediate grades and beyond when withdrawn, inhibited, and submissive behaviors become viewed as deviant by other children (Waas & Graczyk, 2000).

Social Support

Social support appears to serve as a protective factor for anxious youth. Social support refers to children's beliefs about the availability of others to shield them from negative circumstances or help them be successful in life (Demaray & Malecki, 2002). Low levels of family and peer support have been associated with a variety of negative indicators including anxiety and stress (e.g., Demaray & Malecki, 2002). Conversely, multiple investigations provide evidence of the role of social support in promoting self-efficacy, psychological and physical well-being, social skills, adaptive skills, and academic competence (Benight & Bandura, 2004; Levitt, Guacci-Franco, & Levitt, 1994) and in shielding children from psychological and physical adversity (Dubow, Edwards, & Ippolito, 1997).

At the present time, more risk than protective factors for childhood anxiety disorders have been identified. It is highly probable that no one risk factor causes pathological anxiety or that any one protective factor prevents or mitigates it. Rather, anxiety disorders most likely are developed, maintained, ameliorated, or prevented by complex interactions among risk and protective factors within various developmental contexts (Weems & Stickle, 2005).

EVIDENCE-BASED TREATMENT INTERVENTIONS FOR ANXIETY DISORDERS

In our review of intervention and treatment studies, we focus primarily on information derived from carefully controlled investigations that randomly assigned participants to treatment or comparison conditions. These investigations are referred to as randomized control trials (RCTs). An additional criterion for inclusion in our review is that the studies include at least some children in the 5- to 12-year-old age group.

What Works

Multiple studies support the efficacy of behavioral therapies, cognitive-behavioral, and pharmacological interventions for the treatment of anxiety disorders.

Behavioral Therapies

Behavioral therapies are grounded in behavioral and learning models and frequently serve as the framework for interventions used to treat SP and SocP. Treatment strategies include contingency management, systematic desensitization, exposures, shaping, reinforcement, and modeling.

Contingency Management

Contingency management involves the utilization of various consequences contingent on the young person's behavior; for example, praise would be provided to a child with SocP for reading aloud to a group of peers. *Systematic desensitization* refers to a counterconditioning technique in which a classically conditioned response (CR), such as an avoidance of dogs, becomes unlearned through repeated pairings of a variety of dogs (CS) with a response that is incompatible with anxiety, such as deep muscle relaxation. During *exposure* activities youth are systematically presented with or exposed to feared stimuli, moving from least to most feared, while they are encouraged to use coping strategies to manage their anxiety. *Shaping* allows the child to be reinforced for completing each exposure activity that brings her closer to a goal behavior. In other words, reinforcement is not withheld until the goal behavior is attained (e.g., a child with dog phobia who eventually pets a dog). Exposures can be imagined or take place in real life. Modeling is an important component of the exposure process and can be provided in a variety of formats: live with the therapist, through videotapes, with assistance in approaching the feared stimulus (participant modeling), or with prompts to display a modeled behavior without assistance (Ollendick & King, 1998).

RCTs have demonstrated the efficacy of systematic desensitization and in vivo exposures for the treatment of phobias when compared to wait-list controls or alternative treatments (Barabasz, 1973; Kondas, 1967; Mann & Rosenthal, 1969; Muris, Merckelbach, Holdrinet, Sijsenaar, 1998; Ost, Svensson, Hellstrom, & Lindwall, 2001). RCTs have provided evidence for the efficacy of modeling, especially participant modeling in the treatment of SP (Bandura, Blanchard, & Ritter, 1969; Lewis, 1974; Ritter, 1968).

Social Skills Training

Social skills training (SST) is particularly helpful for children and adolescents with SocP because they often have significant social skills deficits (Beidel, Turner, & Tracy, 1999). SST is typically conducted in groups and covers a wide variety of skills including making eye contact, handling conflicts, conversational skills, assertion skills, giving corrective feedback, friendship skills, and group skills (Beidel, Turner, & Morris, 2000; Spence et al., 2000).

Beidel and colleagues (2000) have developed *Social Effectiveness Therapy for Children* (SET-C), a multicomponent group treatment for social phobia. SET-C consists of educating the children and parents about anxiety and providing children with social skills training, peer generalization activities, and individual in vivo exposures. Beidel et al. (2000) found that SET-C was superior to a nonspecific intervention in reducing social fears and associated psychopathology, and in enhancing social skills and social interactions. Recovery rates (i.e., percentage of participants who no longer met criteria for their primary disorder) immediately following the interventions were 67% for SET-C compared to 5% for the nonspecific intervention. Treatment effects were sustained at the six-month follow-up. At the three-year follow-up, 72% of the SET-C group continued to be free of SocP and had maintained the majority of posttreatment gains (Beidel, Turner, Young, & Paulson, 2005).

In summary, behavioral interventions have a relatively long history of demonstrated efficacy in the treatment of a variety of anxiety disorders. Many of these strategies have been incorporated into cognitive-behavioral treatment protocols.

Cognitive-Behavioral Therapy (CBT)

CBT has been found efficacious whether treatment is provided individually or in a group, in a clinic or in a school. Due to its relevance to multiple treatment and prevention efforts, a brief overview of Kendall's (1990) *Coping Cat* treatment protocol is presented next. A summary of CBT treatment outcome studies follows.

Coping Cat (Kendall, 1990) was the first CBT treatment protocol with demonstrated efficacy for the treatment of child and adolescent anxiety disorders (Kendall, 1994). Throughout treatment, the child and her family are provided with psychoeducation about anxiety, the child's symptoms, the rationale for treatment, and ways to cope or manage feelings. During the first half of treatment the therapist teaches the child how to identify and rate the intensity of her feelings. This is done by having the child use a feeling thermometer to rate how anxious or worried she is in various situations on a scale from, for example, 0 = "not at all" to 8 = "a lot." Therapy sessions also focus on managing somatic and cognitive coping strategies. For somatic symptoms, the child is taught ways to identify and relax tense muscle groups. For cognitive symptoms, the child is taught to identify and challenge her maladaptive thoughts (e.g., "If I try to go up those stairs, I'll fall and hurt myself."), and replace them with coping self-statements (e.g., "I walked up those stairs before and didn't fall. I can do it again."). Newly learned knowledge and skills are then consolidated and used to develop a FEAR plan. *FEAR* is an acronym that is used to remind the child of steps she needs to take when feeling anxious. The "F" refers to frightened feelings and reminds the child to use her physical symptoms of anxiety as signals to implement coping strategies. The "E" prompts the child to monitor and challenge maladaptive, anxious self-talk ("thinking traps") that could lead her to expect bad things to happen. The "A" serves as a reminder to employ attitudes (e.g., coping self-statements) and actions (e.g., problem solving, deep breathing) to counter anxiety. The "R" is intended to encourage the child to reflect on results and to reward herself for her efforts to cope with anxiety. Once the FEAR plan is developed, it is applied in graduated and controlled exposure activities, both in and outside of therapy sessions, until eventually the child is able to manage anxiety in response to her most feared or dreaded situations. Throughout treatment, the child is expected to do homework assignments called Show That I Can (STIC) tasks. STIC tasks involve practice of newly learned skills and exposures outside of the therapy session, and help facilitate a sense of self-mastery, generalization, and ultimately recovery. In the final session of therapy, relapse prevention plans are made with the family to insure that the child continues to generalize and maintain skills learned in therapy. The ultimate goal of treatment is to help anxious children perceive their world less from a "threat" template and more from a "coping" template (Kendall, Aschenbrand, & Hudson, 2003).

Studies by groups of researchers in four different countries offer evidence in support of the efficacy of cognitive-behavioral interventions for the treatment of childhood anxiety disorders. CBT has been found to be superior to a wait-list or no treatment control group in multiple studies (Flannery-Schroeder & Kendall, 2000; Mendlowitz et al., 1999; Muris,

Meesters, & van Melick, 2002; Nauta, Scholing, Emmelkamp, & Minderaa, 2003; Rapee, 2000; Shortt, Barrett, & Fox, 2001; Silverman et al., 1999a; Spence et al., 2000).

To illustrate, recovery refers to the percentage of participants no longer meeting the criteria for a disorder and represents an important way to determine the effectiveness of an intervention. Several studies using CBT to treat anxiety disorders have reported these rates (Barrett, 1998; Barrett , Dadds, & Rapee, 1996; Flannery-Schroeder & Kendall, 2000; Kendall, Flannery-Connor, et al., 1997; Shortt et al., 2001; Silverman et al., 1999a; Spence et al., 2000). The average recovery rate across studies for children receiving CBT was 65.1% compared to 13% for controls. Four studies reported recovery rates at one-year follow-up (Barrett, 1998; Barrett et al., 1996; Flannery-Schroeder, Choidhury, & Kendall, 2005; Spence et al., 2000). On average, 74.6% of CBT participants no longer met the criteria for their pre-treatment primary anxiety disorder one year following treatment. There is evidence to suggest that treatment gains for CBT can endure as long as six to seven years following treatment (Barrett, Duffy, Dadds, & Rapee, 2001; Kendall, Safford, Flannery-Schroeder, & Webb, 2004; Manassis, Avery, Butalia, & Mendlowitz, 2004).

This review suggests that there is ample evidence for the superiority of CBT over no treatment at all. However, less information is available regarding how CBT compares to other types of control groups or to alternative treatments. For example, Ginsburg and Drake (2002) compared group CBT to an attention control group. The latter consisted of group meetings in which participants shared their fears and worries with one another. Posttreatment recovery rates were 75% for the CBT group and 20% for the control group. These rates are similar to those obtained in studies comparing CBT with no-treatment. Muris, Meesters, et al. (2002) compared group CBT with a no-treatment control and a placebo treatment group. The placebo group participated in an emotional disclosure (ED) intervention requiring participants to keep a diary of anxiety-provoking situations and then share them in a supportive group context. At posttreatment, only the CBT group experienced a significant decrease in anxious and depressed symptomatology compared to the control and placebo treatment groups.

Two studies compared in vivo exposure to eye movement desensitization and re-processing (EMDR) to treat SP. EMDR is a treatment approach that requires the therapist to precipitate rapid, lateral eye movements while the patient imagines himself exposed him to the phobic object. The procedure is repeated until the individual habituates or becomes accustomed to the phobic object and no longer experiences negative affect in its presence. In one study spider phobic children participated in one session each of in vivo exposure and EMDR, with order of treatment randomly assigned (Muris, Merckelbach, Van Haaften, & Mayer, 1997). No significant differences were found between treatments on a physiological measure of fear. EMDR significantly decreased perceived distress and self-reported fear, but in vivo exposure was superior to EMDR on behavioral outcome measures. In the second study EMDR resulted in significant improvement on self-reported spider fear, but in vivo exposure resulted in significant improvement on all outcome measures (Muris, Merckelbach, Holdrinet, & Sijsenaar, 1998). Computerized exposures, also evaluated in this study, produced nonsignificant outcomes.

The majority of studies related to child and adolescent anxiety disorders have been conducted with Caucasian youth. Thus, a question might be raised as to the extent to which such findings are applicable to youth from other racial and ethnic groups. Encouragingly, studies of ethnic and racial differences revealed similar treatment effects across groups, whether comparing Caucasian youth to African-American youth

(Treadwell, Flannery-Schroeder, & Kendall, 1995) or to Hispanic/Latino youth (Pina, Silverman, Fuentes, Kurtines, & Weems, 2003), even at 12-month follow-up (Pina et al., 2003). Moreover, similar treatment effects have been found across these cultural-racial groups regardless of gender (Berman, Weems, Silverman, & Kurtines, 2000; Southam-Gerow, Kendall, & Weersing, 2001).

Results from studies of the effectiveness of a parent treatment component are mixed at this time but suggest that parental involvement in treatment for their anxiety appears to enhance treatment outcomes for their children (Barrett, Rapee et al., 1996; Cobham et al., 1998). Finally, it should be noted that treatment studies involving CBT have most frequently targeted SAD, GAD, and SocP. Fewer CBT studies have been conducted with children suffering from SP, Selective Mutism, Ag, PD, PTSD, and acute stress disorders.

What Might Work

Parent–Child Interaction Therapy (PCIT) and educational support (ES) are two psycho-social interventions that show promise in the treatment of anxiety disorders.

Parent–Child Interaction Therapy (PCIT)

PCIT is an evidence-based family treatment for disruptive behavioral disorders in children and is currently being evaluated for its efficacy in the treatment of SAD in young children (Pincus, Eyberg, & Choate, 2005). PCIT is grounded in social learning and attachment theory. The goal of treatment is to improve child behavior by helping parents build a supportive and caring relationship with their children and improve parenting skills. The standard protocol for PCIT consists of two components. During the Child-Directed Interaction (CDI) phase, the focus is on improving parent–child interactions by teaching parents how to increase positive interactions with their child during playtimes. The Parent Directed Interaction (PDI) phase focuses on helping parents learn age-appropriate and effective means of communicating with their child. For the treatment of SAD a Bravery Directed Interaction (BDI) phase has been added. During the BDI phase parents are provided with psychoeducation about anxiety, encouraged to apply PCIT techniques in separation situations, and directed to reflect on parenting behaviors that could be reinforcing their child's anxiety. Parents are also encouraged to conduct "separation practices" (similar to exposures) with their children. In the RCT currently in progress children in the treatment group are being compared to those waiting for services. The efficacy of the intervention will be determined through a variety of child- and parent-report measures and through systematic behavioral observations.

Educational Support

Two studies found that treatment effects for educational support (ES) were comparable to those for behavioral and CBT approaches for the treatment of specific phobias (Last, Hansen, & Franco, 1998; Silverman et al., 1999b). In both studies, the ES condition utilized a group format and involved information sharing and discussions about anxiety disorders. The findings from these two studies are particularly noteworthy because ES or psychoeducational support, is a major component of CBT interventions. Thus, another way to view these efforts is as "dismantling" studies. That is, studies in which the efficacy of a treatment package is compared to one or more of its parts to determine which specific components are driving treatment effects. Viewed in this light, the findings suggest that psychoeducation is an active ingredient of comprehensive CBT approaches and that more dismantling studies are warranted to determine if streamlined approaches involving fewer components would prove as effective as and more cost-effective than current, more comprehensive CBT models. Indeed, researchers have started to look at tailoring CBT interventions to a child's specific symptoms, social skills deficits, parental behaviors, motivation for treatment, or co-occurring conditions as ways to enhance treatment outcomes and recovery rates (Chorpita, Taylor, Francis, Moffitt, & Austin, 2004; Eisen & Silverman, 1998).

What Doesn't Work for Anxiety Disorders

A review of the literature did not identify any treatments that were studied in multiple RCTs and found to be ineffective.

PHARMACOLOGY AND ANXIETY DISORDERS

Since the mid-1990s, there have been significant advances in the pharmacological treatment of childhood anxiety disorders.

What Medications Work for Anxiety Disorders

Medication may be combined with CBT for several reasons, including acute reduction of symptoms in a severely anxious child, management of comorbid disorders, addressing risk factors that warrant different interventions, and augmentation of CBT when there is a partial response (March, 2002).

    Several RCTs have established selective serotonin reuptake inhibitors (SSRIs) as the first-line pharmacological treatment for the following anxiety disorders in children: OCD, GAD, SAD, SocP, and possibly selective mutism. SSRIs increase the level of serotonin available in the brain by inhibiting reuptake of serotonin. Side effects with the SSRIs are often transient and mild. The most common side effects in children include gastrointestinal symptoms (decreased appetite, nausea, stomachache, diarrhea), increased activity level, sleep difficulties (drowsiness or insomnia). Less common side effects include dry mouth, manic symptoms, disinhibition (uncharacteristic oppositionality, agitation, or apathy), or muscle twitching. In 2004 the FDA issued a black box warning about the increased risk for suicidal thinking and suicidal behavior that can occur in children and adolescents during the early phases of treatment with antidepressants. The FDA recommended that pediatric patients receiving treatment with antidepressants (including SSRIs) be monitored closely for worsening depression, agitation, or suicidality, particularly during the first few months of medication treatment, dosage changes, and discontinuation. The FDA black box also noted the serious impairments of untreated depression and called for more research on the long-term effectiveness of antidepressants in children and adolescents.

It is important to note that it may be necessary to consider pharmacological treatment of comorbid or co-occurring conditions as part of the treatment plan for children with anxiety disorders. For example, if severe depression is present along with the anxiety disorder, initiation of antidepressant treatment (preferably an SSRI) may be necessary before the child can benefit from CBT (Labellarte, Ginsburg, Walkup, & Riddle, 1999).

What Medications Might Work for Anxiety Disorders

Three types of pharmacological interventions, noradrenergic antidepressants, benzodiazepines, and buspirone, are sometimes used to treat childhood anxiety disorders. *Noradrenergic antidepressants* such as venlafaxine and tricyclic antidepressants are potential alternatives when SSRIs have not been successful. The FDA black box warning applies to all antidepressants and recommends close monitoring for increased risk of suicidal ideations or behavior. Prior to the development of SSRIs, *benzodiazepines* were commonly used to treat anxiety disorders such as GAD, severe SP, and PD. However, now they are typically used to reduce severe anxiety symptoms and avoidance only until SSRIs take effect. Because there is a risk for dependence after prolonged use, benzodiazepines are contraindicated for children with substance use disorders (Riddle et al., 1999). Side effects such as sedation, disinhibition, cognitive impairment, and difficulty with discontinuation, also need to be monitored closely (Labellarte et al., 1999). *Buspirone* is sometimes used alone by clinicians as an alternative to SSRIs for treatment of GAD and to augment other medications for anxiety disorders, but no controlled studies exist to support its efficacy in children. Unlike the benzodiazepines, buspirone has demonstrated no risk of dependence in the long-term. The most common side effects of buspirone in children are lightheadedness, headache, and upset stomach (Salazar et al., 2001).

PREVENTION OF ANXIETY DISORDERS

Primary prevention and health promotion encompass those planned activities that help participants prevent predictable problems, protect existing states of health and healthy functioning, and promote desired goals for a specified population. Prevention programs can be classified according to the population targeted for the preventive intervention (Institute of Medicine, 1994). *Universal* prevention activities are intended for all members of a general population. *Selective* prevention activities target subgroups of a population who may be at above-average risk for developing a disorder. Children at risk for anxiety disorders include those with anxious parents, an anxious–resistant attachment style, temperaments characterized by BI or high NA-N low EC, and those children exposed to traumatic or stress life events (Spence, 2001). *Indicated* prevention activities are designed for those individuals who are already demonstrating some characteristics of the disorder and are at enhanced risk of increased psychopathology.

What Works

A primary strategy for many prevention efforts is to target malleable risk and protective factors in order to eliminate or decrease identified risk factors for the targeted disorder or introduce or augment protective factors. Although some risk factors may influence a child's development at any point in time (e.g., traumatic life events, parental anxiety), still others may only be influential at particular points in time (e.g., start of formal schooling). Most prevention efforts targeting anxiety disorders have taken a developmental perspective, focus on malleable risk and protective factors, and take place in schools.

Cognitive-Behavioral Interventions

Current evidence suggests that cognitive-behavioral interventions are useful in preventing childhood anxiety disorders. RCT studies conducted in the United States and Australia have demonstrated the preventive benefits of three variations of a group CBT approach. These programs are: (1) *Coping Koala* as an indicated prevention program (Barrett, Rapee, et al., 1996); (2) the *FRIENDS* program as a universal and selective prevention intervention (Barrett, Lowry-Webster, & Holmes, 1999); and (3) *Cool Kids Program: School Version* as a selective intervention for children in low socioeconomic (SES) neighborhoods (Lyneham et al., 2003). These programs are variations of Kendall's (1990) *Coping Cat* program.

Coping Koala includes 10 group sessions and three parent sessions. The program covers a variety of topics and strategies, including psychoeducation about anxiety, relaxation skills to manage the physiological symptoms of anxiety, replacement of maladaptive thoughts with coping thoughts, problem-solving skills, exposures, self-rewards, and relapse prevention. The *Coping Koala* program was renamed the *FRIENDS* program in 1999. *FRIENDS* consists of 10 weekly sessions and two booster sessions, together with evening sessions for parents. The *FRIENDS* program has been used effectively with diverse groups of children in schools and community mental health clinics. The *Cool Kids* program consists of eight sessions and two parent information meetings. Like other CBT preventive interventions, *Cool Kids* includes psychoeducation about anxiety, cognitive strategies to challenge maladaptive thoughts and replace them with coping thoughts, and exposures to anxiety-provoking situations. It also includes a social skills component with an emphasis on assertiveness training and dealing with teasing.

Dadds, Spence, Holland, Barrett, and Laurens (1997) investigated the effectiveness of *The Coping Koala* program as an indicated prevention effort and early intervention program. Children and adolescents were assigned randomly to either a treatment or monitoring condition if they either met the criteria for a DSM-IV anxiety disorder with mild impairment in functioning or did not meet criteria for the disorder but had symptoms of anxiety or a "nonspecific sensitivity." Results were that both groups showed improvement with nonsignificant differences between groups. However, at the six-month follow-up continued improvement was seen in the treatment group but some backsliding was found in members of the control group who met the full criteria for an anxiety disorder. At the one-year follow-up treatment effects for both groups converged, but at the two-year follow-up the intervention group demonstrated significantly better outcomes (Dadds et al., 1999).

Lowry-Webster, Barrett, and Dadds (2001) investigated the *FRIENDS* program as a universal prevention program. Study participants included 594 6th grade children who were assigned randomly to the intervention or to a wait-list condition. At the completion of the program, both groups showed significant decreases in self-reported anxiety and depression. However, when highly anxious participants were compared between conditions, only the prevention group showed significant decreases in anxiety and depression. At the one-year follow-up, 85% of the prevention group and 31.2% of the control group originally scoring above the clinical cut-off for anxiety and depression were diagnosis-free (Lowry-Webster, Barrett, & Lock, 2003).

Other studies have evaluated the effectiveness of the *FRIENDS* program in reducing anxiety in children with subclinical anxiety (an indicated group). One school-based RCT compared the effectiveness of group CBT, group CBT plus parent training component, to a no-treatment control group (Bernstein, Layne, Egan, & Tennison, 2005). For children in each group with an initial anxiety disorder, recovery rates postintervention were 79% for the child-only CBT group, 67% for the CBT plus parent training group, and 38% for the control group.

Mifsud and Rapee (2005) studied the effectiveness of *Cool Kids* as a selective intervention for children from disadvantaged communities. Ninety-one high anxious children were assigned randomly to either a *Cool Kids* group or a wait-list control condition. Results were that children in the intervention group had significantly fewer self- and teacher-reported symptoms of anxiety than the control group at the conclusion of the intervention and at the four-month follow-up.

These findings suggest that CBT interventions are beneficial in preventing anxiety disorders and that symptom reductions can be sustained even for children demonstrating high risk or mild to moderate severity in diagnosable disorders.

PREVENTING ANXIETY DUE TO MEDICAL PROCEDURES

Children who undergo painful or stressful medical procedures are at greater risk for the development of phobias and other anxiety disorders. Selective prevention efforts include a number of techniques that are used widely to attenuate children's anxiety during medical procedures. These anxiety reduction techniques include sharing information about the procedure, modeling demonstrations, and training in such coping strategies as comforting self-talk, mental imagery, and cue-controlled relaxation (Spence, 2001).

What Might Work in the Prevention of Anxiety

Two promising preventive interventions for anxiety have been identified. One program targets social skills and the other coping skills.

Social Skills Training

The *Social Skills GRoup Interventions (S.S. Grin;* DeRosier, 2002) is a selective preventive intervention for children who have difficulties relating to peers, notably children characterized as socially anxious, bullied, or peer-rejected. The program employs cognitive-behavioral and social learning techniques and consists of eight weekly group sessions in schools. *S. S.Grin* was developed to help children improve peer relationships, develop basic behavioral and cognitive social skills, increase self-confidence in their ability to handling social situations, and learn adaptive coping strategies for peer problems such as teasing and responding to peer pressure (DeRosier, 2004).

To test the efficacy of *S. S. Grin,* DeRosier (2004) randomly assigned targeted third graders to an *S. S. Grin* or no-treatment control group. *S.S. Grin* was found to be equally effective for all three types of peer problems. Compared to controls, participants in the program showed a significant decrease in social anxiety and a significant increase in self-esteem, self-efficacy, and peer liking. At the one-year follow-up, intervention effects were sustained and additional effects were found (DeRosier & Marcus, 2005). These additional benefits included decreased social anxiety with new peers, increased leadership skills, and decreased depression. Although these results are promising, replication studies involving children of various ages are needed.

Coping Skills Training

The *I Can Do* program (Dubow, Schmidt, McBride, Edwards, & Merk, 1993) is a universal prevention program designed to teach children skills to manage stress. The program was evaluated in a RCT in which 88 fourth grade students were assigned randomly to either a treatment or wait-list control group. Treatment group participants demonstrated significant improvement in their ability to generate effective solutions to stressful situations as well as in their self-efficacy to implement effective solutions to two targeted stressors (i.e., loved one's death, parents' divorce). At follow-up, participants in the treatment condition maintained and generalized posttreatment gains in the ability to generate solutions to four out of five stressors. They also demonstrated continued improvement in self-efficacy. Although these findings are promising, they are based on self-report measures and reactions to hypothetical situations. Thus, this intervention warrants further study involving larger sample sizes, children of various ages, and multimethod assessment procedures.

In summary, preventive interventions for anxiety disorders are available and more are being developed. Some prevention efforts have been adapted from successful treatment protocols, while others are emerging from theoretical and empirical findings related to specific risk factors for anxiety disorders. Although the prevention of anxiety disorders is in its infancy, efforts to date provide an optimistic outlook for the continued success of future work.

CONCLUSIONS AND RECOMMENDATIONS FOR BEST PRACTICE

Anxiety disorders can interfere significantly with a child's current and future well-being. Numerous empirical studies support the efficacy of various treatment approaches and demonstrate the promise of others. In view of the information currently available, we propose the following:

- Given the high prevalence of anxiety disorders in children, mental health professionals, primary care physicians, and schools should routinely screen for anxiety disorders.

- Anxiety disorders often co-occur with other anxiety disorders, depression, and disruptive behavior disorders. These comorbid disorders need to be identified and treated along with the primary anxiety disorder.
- Behavioral and cognitive-behavioral treatments have the most evidence in support of their efficacy at this time and should be considered first line treatments for anxiety disorders. There is evidence to suggest that these treatments are efficacious for European-American, Latino-Hispanic, and African-American boys and girls.
- Peer groups represent a critical developmental context for school-aged children. Clinicians and educators should evaluate a child's peer relationships when developing a treatment plan.
- Social skills training appears to be a promising treatment component for children with SocP.
- Currently, there is limited and inconsistent information available as to the role of parents in the treatment and prevention of anxiety disorders. Parental involvement in treatment appears most beneficial for younger children, girls, and when parents also suffer from anxiety.
- Medication, especially SSRIs, may be combined with behavioral or cognitive-behavioral treatments when symptoms are severe, comorbid disorders are present, risk factors exist that require different interventions, or to supplement behavioral or cognitive-behavioral interventions when there is a partial response (March, 2002). The FDA black box warning recommends close monitoring for increased risk of suicidal thinking or behavior when antidepressants (including SSRIs) are used in children or adolescents.
- School-based prevention efforts at the universal, selective, and indicated levels have been developed and should be considered for adoption by school mental health professionals.
- Further work is needed to identify effective treatments for the approximately 25% to 30% of treated youth who do not respond well to current treatments.

Finally, it is important to note that treatment and prevention interventions for anxiety disorders can only be successful if anxious youth are identified and provided access to services. Results from the National Comorbidity Study revealed a 9- to 23-year delay on average from onset of an anxiety disorder to initial treatment contact (Wang et al., 2005). These findings underscore the fact that identification and accessibility represent two of the most pressing needs for children with anxiety disorders, especially children living in resource-scarce communities.

REFERENCES

Albano, A. M., Chorpita, B. F., & Barlow, D. H. (2003). Childhood anxiety disorders. In E. J. Mash & R. A. Barkley (Eds.), *Child psychopathology* (2nd ed., pp. 279–329). New York: Guilford.

Albano, A. M., & Kendall, P. C. (2002). Cognitive behavioural therapy for children and adolescents with anxiety disorders: Clinical research advances. *International Review of Psychiatry, 14*,129–134.

American Psychiatric Association. (2000). *Diagnostic and statistical manual of mental disorders* (4th ed., TR). Washington, D.C.: Author.

Anstendig, K. D. (1999). Is selective mutism an anxiety disorder? Rethinking its DSM-IV classification. *Journal of Anxiety Disorders, 13*, 417–434.

Bandura, A. (2001). Social cognitive theory: An agentic perspective. *Annual Review of Psychology, 52,* 1–26.

Bandura, A., Blanchard, E. B., & Ritter, B. (1969). Relative efficacy of desensitization and modeling approaches for inducing behavioral, affective, and attitudinal changes. *Journal of Personality and Social Psychology, 13,* 173–199.

Barabasz, A. F. (1973). Group desensitization of test anxiety in elementary school. *The Journal of Psychology, 83,* 295–301.

Barrett, P. M. (1998). Evaluation of cognitive-behavioral group treatments for childhood anxiety disorders. *Journal of Clinical Child Psychology, 27,* 459–468.

Barrett, P. M., Dadds, M. R., & Rapee, R. M. (1996). Family treatment of childhood anxiety: A controlled trial. *Journal of Consulting and Clinical Psychology, 64,* 333–342.

Barrett, P. M., Duffy, A. L., Dadds, M. R., & Rapee, R. M. (2001). Cognitive-behavioral treatment of anxiety disorders in children: Long-term (6-year) follow-up. *Journal of Consulting and Clinical Psychology, 69,* 135–141.

Barrett, P. M., Lowry-Webster, H., & Holmes, J. (1999). *Friends for children group leader manual* (2nd ed.). Brisbane, Australia: Australian Academic Press.

Barrett, P. M., Rapee, R. M., Dadds, M. M., & Ryan, S. M. (1996). Family enhancement of cognitive style in anxious and aggressive children. *Journal of Abnormal Child Psychology, 24,* 187–203.

Baving, L., Laucht, M., & Schmidt, M. H. (2002). Frontal brain activation in anxious school children. *Journal of Child Psychology and Psychiatry, 43,* 265–274.

Beidel, D., & Turner, S. (1998). *Shy children, phobic adults: Nature and treatment of social phobia.* Washington, D.C.: American Psychological Association.

Beidel, D. C., Turner, S. M., & Morris, T. L. (2000). Behavioral treatment of childhood social phobia. *Journal of Consulting and Clinical Psychology, 68,* 1072–1080.

Beidel, D. C., Turner, S. M., & Tracy, L. (1999). Psychopathology of childhood social phobia. *Journal of the American Academy of Child an Adolescent Psychiatry, 38,* 643–650.

Beidel, D. C., Turner, S. M., Young, B., & Paulson, A. (2005). Social effectiveness therapy for children: Three-year follow-up. *Journal of Consulting and Clinical Psychology, 73,* 721–725.

Benight, C. C., & Bandura, A. (2004). Social cognitive theory of posttraumatic recovery: the role of perceived self-efficacy. *Behaviour Research and Therapy, 42,* 1129–1148.

Berman, S. L., Kurtines, W. K., Silverman, W. K., & Serafini, L. T. (1996). The impact of exposure to crime and violence in urban youth. *American Journal of Orthopsychiatry, 66,* 329–336.

Berman, S. L., Weems, C. F., Silverman, W. K., & Kurtines, W. M. (2000). Predictors of outcome in exposure-based cognitive and behavioral treatment for phobia and anxiety disorders in children. *Behavior Therapy, 31,* 713–731.

Bernstein, G. A., Layne, A. E., Egan, E. A., & Tennison, D. M. (2005). School-based interventions for anxious children. *Journal of the American Academy of Child and Adolescent Psychiatry, 44,* 1118–1127.

Black, B., & Uhde, T. (1995). Psychiatric characteristics of children with selective mutism: A pilot study. *Journal of the American Academy of Child and Adolescent Psychiatry, 34,* 8847–8856.

Boer, F., Markus, M. T., Maingay, R., Lindhout, I. E., Borst, S. R., & Hoogendijk, T. H. (2002). Negative life events of anxiety disordered children: Bad fortune, vulnerability, or reporter bias? *Child Psychiatry & Human Development, 32,* 187–199.

Bowlby, J. (1988). *A secure base: Clinical applications of attachment theory.* London: Tavistock-Routledge.

Chorpita, B. E., Taylor, A. A., Francis, S. E., Moffitt, C., & Austin, A. A. (2004). Efficacy of modular cognitive behavior therapy for childhood anxiety disorders. *Behavior Therapy, 35,* 263–287.

Cobham, V. E., Dadds, M. R., & Spence, S. H. (1998). The role of parental anxiety in the treatment of childhood anxiety. *Journal of Consulting and Clinical Psychology, 66,* 893–905.

Cooley, M. R., Turner, S. M., & Beidel, D. C.(1995). Assessing community violence: The children's report of exposure to violence. *Journal of the American Academy of Child and Adolescent Psychiatry 34*(2), 201–208.

Dadds, M. R., Barrett, P. M., Rapee, R. M., & Ryan, S. (1996). Family processes and child anxiety and aggression: An observational study. *Journal of Abnormal Child Psychology, 24,* 715–734.

Dadds, M. R., Holland, D. E., Laurens, K,. R., Mullins, M., Barrett, P., & Spence, S. H. (1999). Early intervention and prevention of anxiety disorders in children: Results at 2-year follow-up. *Journal of Consulting and Clinical Psychology, 67,* 145–150.

Dadds, M. R., Spence, S. H., Holland, D. E., Barrett, P. M., & Laurens, K. R. (1997). Prevention and early intervention for anxiety disorders: A controlled trial. *Journal of Consulting and Clinical Psychology, 65,* 627–635.

Demaray, M. K., & Malecki, C. K. (2002). The relationship between perceived social support and maladjustment for students at risk. *Psychology in the Schools, 39,* 305–315.

DeRosier, M. E. (2002). *Group interventions and exercises for enhancing children's communication, coopera-tion, and confidence.* Sarasota, FL: Professional Resource Press.

DeRosier, M. E. (2004). Building relationships and combating bullying: Effectiveness of a school-based social skills group intervention. *Journal of Clinical Child and Adolescent Psychology, 33,* 196–201.

DeRosier, M. E., & Marcus, S. R. (2005). Building friendships and combating bullying: Effectiveness of S.S. Grin at one-year follow-up. *Journal of Clinical Child and Adolescent Psychology, 34,* 140–150.

Donovan, C. L., & Spence, S. H. (2000). Prevention of childhood anxiety disorders. *Clinical Psychology Review, 20,* 509–531.

Dubow, E. F., Edwards, S., & Ippolito, M. F. (1997). Life stressors, neighborhood disadvantage, and resources: A focus on inner-city children's adjustment. *Journal of Clinical Child Psychology, 26,* 130–144.

Dubow, E. F., Schmidt, D., McBride, J., Edwards, S., & Merk, F. L. (1993). Teaching children to cope with stressful experiences: Initial implementation and evaluation of a primary prevention program. *Journal of Clinical Child Psychology, 22,* 428–440.

Ehrenreich, J. T., & Gross, A. M. (2002). Biased attentional behavior in childhood anxiety: A review of theory and current empirical investigation. *Clinical Psychology Review, 22,* 991–1008.

Eisen, A. R., & Silverman, W. K. (1998). Prescriptive treatment for generalized anxiety disorder in children. *Behavior Therapy, 29,* 105–121.

Eley, T. C. (2001). Contributions of behavioral genetics research: Quantifying genetic, shared environmental and nonshared environmental influences. In M. Vasey & M. Dadds (Eds.), *The developmental psychopa-thology of anxiety* (pp. 45–59). London: University of London, Institute of Psychiatry.

Ezpeleta, L., Keeler, G., Erkanli, A., Costello, E. J., & Angold, A. (2001). Epidemiology of psychiatric disabil-ity in childhood and adolescence. *Journal of Child Psychology & Psychiatry & Allied Disciplines, 42,* 901–914.

Flannery-Schroeder, E., Choidhury, M. S., & Kendall, P. C. (2005). Group and individual cognitive-behavioral treatments for youth with anxiety disorders: 1-year follow-up. *Cognitive Therapy and Research, 29,* 253–259.

Flannery-Schroeder, E. C., & Kendall, P. C. (2000). Group and individual cognitive-behavioral treatments for youth with anxiety disorders: A randomized clinical trial. *Cognitive Therapy and Research, 24,* 251–278.

Ford, T., Goodman, R., & Meltzer, H. (2003). The British child and adolescent mental health survey 1999: The prevalence of DSM-IV disorders. *Journal of the American Academy of Child and Adolescent Psychiatry, 42,* 1203–1211.

Fox, N. A., & Calkins, S. (1993). Social withdrawal: Interactions among temperament, attachment, and regula-tion. In K. H. Rubin & J. B. Asendorpf (Eds.), *Social withdrawal, inhibition, and shyness in childhood* (pp. 81–100). Hillsdale, NJ: Erlbaum.

Freeman, L. N., Mokros, H., & Poznanski, E. O. (1993). Violent events reported by normal urban school-aged children: Characteristics and depression correlates. *Journal of the American Academy of Child and Adolescent Psychiatry, 32,* 419–423.

Garcia-Coll, C., Kagan, J., & Reznick, J. S. (1984). Behavioural inhibition in young children. *Child Develop-ment, 55,* 1005–1019.

Gerull, F. C., & Rapee, R. M. (2002). Mother knows best: The effects of maternal modeling on the acquisition of fear and avoidance in toddlers. *Behavior Research and Therapy, 40,* 169–178.

Ginsburg, G. S., & Drake, K. L. (2002). School-based treatment for anxious African-American adolescents: A controlled pilot study. *Journal of the American Academy of Child and Adolescent Psychiatry, 41,* 768–775.

Goodwin, R. D., Fergusson, D. M., & Horwood, L. J. (2004). Early anxious/withdrawn behaviours predict later internalising disorders. *Journal of Child Psychology and Psychiatry, 45,* 874–883.

Granger, D. A., Weisz, J. R., & Kauneckis, D. (1994). Neuroendocrine reactivity, internalizing behavior prob-lems, and control related cognitions in clinic-referred children and adolescents. *Journal of Abnormal Psychology, 103,* 267–276.

Hadwin, J. A., Garner, M., & Perez-Olivas, G. (2006). The development of information processing biases in childhood anxiety: A review and exploration of its origins in parenting. *Clinical Psychology Review,26, 876-894.*

Hudson, J. L., & Rapee, R. M. (2001). Parent–child interactions and anxiety disorders: An observational study. *Behaviour Research & Therapy, 39*(12), 1411–1427.

Institute of Medicine (1994). *Reducing risks for mental disorders: Frontiers for preventive intervention research.* Washington, D.C.: National Academy Press.

Kagan, J. (1997). Temperament and the reactions to unfamiliarity. *Child Development, 68,* 139–143.

Kagan, J., Reznick, J. S., & Snidman, N. (1987). The physiology and psychology of behavioural inhibition in children. *Child Development, 58,* 1459–1473.

Kearney, C. A., Albano, A. M., Eisen, A. R., Allan, W. D., & Barlow, D. H. (1997). The phenomenology of panic disorders in youngsters: An empirical study of a clinical sample. *Journal of Anxiety Disorders, 11,* 49–62.

Kendall, P. C. (1990). *Coping Cat workbook.* Ardmore, PA: Workbook.

Kendall, P. C. (1994). Treating anxiety disorders in children: Results of a randomized clinical trial. *Journal of Consulting and Clinical Psychology, 62,* 100–110.

Kendall, P. C., Aschenbrand, S. G., & Hudson, J. L. (2003). Child-focused treatment of anxiety. In A. Kazdin & J. Weisz (Eds.), *Evidence-based psychotherapies for children and adolescents* (pp. 81–100). New York: Guilford.

Kendall, P. C., Flannery-Schroeder, E., Panichelli-Mindel, S., Southam-Gerow, M., Henin, A., & Warman, M. (1997). Therapy for youths with anxiety disorders: A second randomized clinical trial. *Journal of Consulting and Clinical Psychology, 65,* 366–380.

Kendall, P. C., Safford, S., Flannery-Schroeder, E., & Webb, A. (2004). Child anxiety treatment: Outcomes in adolescence and impact on substance use and depression at 7.4 year follow-up. *Journal of Consulting and Clinical Psychology, 72,* 276–287.

Kim-Cohen, J., Caspi, A., Moffitt, T. E., Harrington, H., Milne, B. J., & Poulton, R. (2003). Prior juvenile diagnoses in adults with mental disorder: Development follow-back of a prospective-longitudinal cohort. *Archives of General Psychiatry, 60,* 709–717.

Kondas, O. (1967). Reduction of examination anxiety and "stage fright" by group desensitization and relaxation. *Behaviour Research and Therapy, 5,* 275–281.

Labellarte, M. J., Ginsburg, G. S., Walkup, J. T., & Riddle, M. A. (1999). The treatment of anxiety disorders in children and adolescents. *Biological Psychiatry, 46,* 1567–1578.

Lang, P. J. (1968). Fear reduction and fear behavior: Problems in treating a construct. In J. M. Schlien (Ed.), *The structure of emotion* (pp. 18–30). Seattle, WA: Hogrefe & Huber.

Last, C., Hansen, C., & Franco, N. (1998). Cognitive-behavioral therapy of school phobia. *Journal of the American Academy of Child and Adolescent Psychiatry, 37,* 404–411.

Leib, R., Wittchen, H., Hofler, M., Fuetsch, M., Stein, M., & Merikangas, K. (2000). Parenting psychopathology, parenting styles, and the risk of social phobia in offspring: A prospective, longitudinal community study. *Archives of General Psychiatry, 57,* 859–866.

Levitt, M. J., Guacci-Franco, N., & Levitt, J. L. (1994). Social support achievement in childhood and early adolescence: A multicultural study. *Journal of Applied Developmental Psychology, 15,* 207–222.

Lewis, S. (1974). A comparison of behavior therapy techniques in the reduction of fearful avoidance behavior. *Behavior Therapy, 5,* 648–655.

Lonigan, C. J., Vasey, M. W., Phillips, B. M., & Hazen, R. A. (2004). Temperament, anxiety, and the processing of threat-relevant stimuli. *Journal of Clinical Child and Adolescent Psychology, 33,* 8–20.

Lowry-Webster, H. M., Barrett, P. M., & Dadds, M. R. (2001). A universal prevention trial of anxiety and depressive symptomatology in childhood: Preliminary data from an Australian study. *Behaviour Change, 18,* 36–50.

Lowry-Webster, H. M., Barrett, P. M., & Lock, S. (2003). A universal prevention trial of anxiety symptomatology during childhood: Results at 1-year follow-up. *Behaviour Change, 20,* 35–43.

Lynehan, H. J., Abbott, M. J., Wignall, A., & Rapee, R. M. (2003). *The Cool Kids School Program: Therapist manual.* Sydney, Australia: Macquarie University Anxiety Research Unit.

Manassis, K. (2001). Child–parent relations: Attachment and anxiety disorders. In W. Silverman & P. Treffers (Eds.), *Anxiety disorders in children and adolescents: Research, assessment, and intervention* (pp. 255–272). New York: Cambridge University Press.

Manassis, K., Avery, D., Butalia, S., & Mendlowitz, S. (2004). Cognitive-behavioral therapy with childhood anxiety disorders: Functioning in adolescence. *Depression and Anxiety, 19,* 209–216.

Manassis, K., & Hood, J. (1998). Individual and familial predictors of impairment in childhood anxiety disorders. *Journal of the American Academy of Child & Adolescent Psychiatry, 37,* 428–434.

Mann, J., & Rosenthal, T. L. (1969). Vicarious and direct counter-conditioning of test anxiety through individual and group desensitization. *Behaviour Research and Therapy, 7,* 359–367.

March, J. S. (2002). Combining medication and psychosocial treatments: an evidence-based medicine approach. *International Review of Psychiatry, 14,* 155–163.

Mendlowitz, S. L., Manassis, K., Bradley, S., Scapillato, D., Miezitis, S., & Shaw, B. F. (1999). Cognitive-behavioral group treatments in childhood anxiety disorders: The role of parental involvement. *Journal of the American Academy of Child and Adolescent Psychiatry, 38,* 1223–1229.

Merikangas, K., Stevens, D. E., Fenton, B., Stolar, M., O'Malley, S., Woods, S. W., et al. (1998). Co-morbidity and familial aggregation of alcoholism and anxiety disorders. *Psychological Medicine, 28* (4), 773–788.

Mifsud, C., & Rapee, R. M. (2005). Early intervention for childhood anxiety in a school setting: Outcomes for an economically disadvantaged population. *Journal of the American Academy of Child and Adolescent Psychiatry, 44,* 996–1004.

Mowrer, O. (1960). *Learning theory and behaviour.* New York: Wiley.

Muris, P., Meesters, C., & van Melick, M. (2002). Treatment of childhood anxiety disorders: A preliminary comparison between cognitive-behavioral group therapy and a psychological placebo intervention. *Journal of Behavior Therapy and Experimental Psychiatry, 33,* 143–158.

Muris, P., Merckelbach, H., Holdrinet, I., & Sijsenaar, M. (1998). Treating phobic children: Effects of EMDR versus exposure. *Journal of Consulting and Clinical Psychology, 66,* 193–198.

Muris, P. Merckelbach, H., Van Haaften, H., & Mayer, B. (1997). Eye movement desensitisation and reprocessing versus exposure in vivo: A single-session crossover study of spider-phobic children. *British Journal of Psychiatry, 171,* 82–86.

Nauta, M. H., Scholing, A., Emmelkamp, P. M. G., & Minderaa, R. B. (2003). Cognitive-behavioral therapy for children with anxiety disorders in a clinical setting: No additional effect of a cognitive parent training. *Journal of the American Academy of Child and Adolescent Psychiatry, 42,* 1270–1278.

Ollendick, T. H., & King, N. J. (1998). Empirically supported treatments for children with phobic and anxiety disorders: Current status. *Journal of Clinical Child Psychology, 27,* 156–167.

Olweus, D. (1993). *Bullying at school: What we know and what we can do.* Oxford: Blackwell.

Ost, L., Svensson, L., Hellstrom, K., & Lindwall, R. (2001). One-session treatment of specific phobias in youth: A randomized clinical trial. *Journal of Consulting and Clinical Psychology, 69,* 814–824.

Pina, A. A., Silverman, W. K., Fuentes, R. M., Kurtines, W. M., & Weems, C. F. (2003). Exposure-based cognitive-behavioral treatment for phobic and anxiety disorders: Treatment effects and maintenance for Hispanic/Latino relative to European-American Youths. *Journal of the American Academy of Child and Adolescent Psychiatry, 42,* 1179–1187.

Pincus, D. B., Eyberg, S. M., & Choate, M. L. (2005). Adapting parent–child interaction therapy for young children with separation anxiety disorder. *Education and Treatment of Children, 28,* 163–181.

Pincus, D. B., & Friedman, A. G. (2004). Improving children's coping with everyday stress: Transporting treatment interventions to the school setting. *Clinical Child and Family Psychology Review, 7,* 223–240.

Rapee, R. M. (2000). Group treatment of children with anxiety disorders: Outcome and predictors of treatment response. *Australian Journal of Psychology, 52,* 125–129.

Reiss, S. (1991). Expectancy model of fear, anxiety, and panic. *Clinical Psychology Review, 11,* 141–153.

Riddle, M. A., Bernstein, G. A. Cook, E. H., Leonard, H. L., March, J. S., & Swanson, J. M. (1999). Anxiolytics, adrenergic agents, and naltrexone. *Journal of the American Academy of Child and Adolescent Psychiatry, 38,* 546–556.

Ritter, B. (1968). The group desensitization of children's snake phobias using vicarious and contact desensitization procedures. *Behaviour Research and Therapy, 6,* 1–6.

Rubin, K. H., Burgess, K. B., Kennedy, A. E., & Stewart, S. L. (2003). Social withdrawal in childhood. In E. J. Mash & R. A. Barkley (Eds.), *Child psychopathology* (2nd ed., pp. 372–408). New York: Guilford.

Salazar, D. E., Frackiewicz, E. J., Dockens, R., Kollia, G., Fulmor, I. E., Tigel, P. D., et al. (2001). Pharmacokinetics and tolerability of buspirone during oral administration to children and adolescents with anxiety disorder and normal healthy adults. *Journal of Clinical Pharmacology, 41,* 1351–1358.

Schwab-Stone, M. E., Ayers, T. S., Kasprow, W., Voyce, C., Barone, C. , Shriver, T., et al. (1995). No safe haven: A study of violence exposure in an urban community. *Journal of the American Academy of Child and Adolescent Psychiatry, 34,* 1343–1352.

Shaffer, D., Fisher, P., Dulcan, M. K., Davies, M., Piacentini, J., Schwab-Stone, M. E., et al. (1996). The NIMH Diagnostic Interview Schedule for Children Version 2.3 (DISC-2.3): Description, acceptability, prevalence rates, and performance in the MECA Study. *Journal of the American Academy of Child and Adolescent Psychiatry, 35,* 865–877.

Shortt, A. L., Barrett, P. M., & Fox, T. L. (2001). Evaluating the FRIENDS program: A cognitive-behavioral group treatment for anxious children and their parents. *Journal of Consulting and Clinical Psychology, 30,* 525–535.

Silverman, W. K., Kurtines, W. M., Ginsburg, G. S., Weems, C. F., Lumpkin, P. W., & Carmichael, D. H. (1999a). Treating anxiety disorders in children with group cognitive-behavioral therapy: A randomized clinical trial. *Journal of Consulting and Clinical Psychology, 67,* 995–1003.

Silverman, W. K., Kurtines, W. M., Ginsburg, G. S., Weems, C. F., Rabian, B., & Serafini, L. T. (1999b). Contingency management, self-control, and education support in the treatment of childhood phobic disorders: A randomized clinical trial. *Journal of Consulting and Clinical Psychology, 67,* 675–687.

Southam-Gerow, M. A., Kendall, P. C., & Weersing, V. R. (2001). Examining outcome variability: Correlates of treatment response in a child and adolescent anxiety clinic. *Journal of Clinical Child Psychology, 30,* 422–436.

Spence, S. H. (2001). Prevention strategies. In M. Vasey & M. R. Dadds (Eds.), *The developmental psychopathology of anxiety* (pp. 325–341). New York: Oxford University Press.

Spence, S. H., Donovan, C., & Brechman-Toussaint, M. (2000). The treatment of childhood social phobia: The effectiveness of a social skills based, cognitive-behavioral intervention, with and without parental involvement. *Journal of Clinical Psychology and Psychiatry, 41,* 713–726.

Strauss, C. C., Lahey, B. B., Frick, P., Frame, C. L., & Hynd, G. W. (1988). Peer social status of children with anxiety disorders. *Journal of Consulting and Clinical Psychology, 56,* 137–141.

Sweeney, M. J., & Pine, D. (2004). Etiology of fear and anxiety. In T. H. Ollendick & J. S. March (Eds.), *Phobic and anxiety disorders in children and adolescents: A clinician's guide to effective psychosocial and pharmacological interventions* (pp. 34–60). New York: Oxford University Press.

Treadwell, K. R. H., Flannery-Schroeder, E. C., & Kendall, P. C. (1995). Ethnicity and gender in relative to adaptive functioning, diagnostic status, and treatment outcome in children from an anxiety clinic. *Journal of Anxiety Disorders, 9,* 373–384.

Turner, S. M., Beidel, D. C., & Costello, A. (1987). Psychopathology in the offspring of anxiety disorders patients. *Journal of Consulting and Clinical Psychology, 55,* 229–235.

Turner, S. M., Beidel, D. C., Roberson-Nay, R., & Tervo, K. (2003). Parenting behaviors in parents with anxiety disorders. *Behavior Research and Therapy, 41,* 541–554.

Waas, G. A., & Graczyk, P. A. (2000). Child behaviors leading to peer rejection: A view from the peer group. *Child Study Journal, 29*(4), 291–306.

Wang, P. S., Berglund, P., Olfson, M., Pincus, H. A., Wells, K. B., & Kessler, R. C. (2005). Failure and delay in initial treatment contact after first onset of mental disorders in the National Comorbidity Survey replication. *Archives of General Psychiatry, 62,* 603–613.

Warren, S. L., Huston, L., Egeland, B., & Sroufe, L. A. (1997). Child and adolescent anxiety disorders and early attachment. *Journal of the American Academy of Child and Adolescent Psychiatry, 36,* 637–641.

Weems, C. F., & Stickle, T. R. (2005). Anxiety disorders in childhood: Casting a nomological net. *Clinical Child and Family Psychology Review, 8,* 107–134.

Wood, J. J., McLeod, B. D., Sigman, M., Hwang, W., & Chu, B. C. (2003). Parenting and childhood anxiety: Theory, empirical findings, and future directions. *Journal of Child Psychology and Psychiatry, 44,* 134–151.

Yule, W., & Williams, R. (1990). Post-traumatic stress reactions in children. *Journal of Traumatic Stress, 3,* 279–295.

Chapter Twelve

Depression and Bipolar Disorder in Childhood

Clare Roberts, Brian Bishop, and Rosanna Rooney

INTRODUCTION

This chapter focuses on mood disorders in children, major depressive disorder (MDD), which is episodic and recurrent, dysthymic disorder (DD), which involves more chronic mood disturbance, and bipolar disorder (BPD) involving depression and mania.

Definitions

Depression in children has been described as an unhappy or sad *mood*, or as a *syndrome* including other symptoms, such as, anhedonia, low self-esteem, worry, pessimism, guilt, and loneliness (Cicchetti & Toth, 1998). Depressive symptoms that occur for two weeks or more, and are associated with functional impairment are classified as *clinical disorders*. *The Diagnostic and Statistical Manual of Mental Disorders* (DSM-IV-TR; American Psychiatric Association, 2000) and the *International Classification of Diseases 10* (ICD-10; World Heath Organization, 2006) use similar criteria to diagnose depressive disorders in children, adolescents, and adults. For a diagnosis of MDD, children must experience a depressed or irritable mood and loss of pleasure, most days of the week for at least two weeks, plus at least four of the following symptoms, suicidal ideation, appetite change, sleep or weight changes, psychomotor agitation or retardation, decreases in energy or concentration, and feelings of worthlessness-guilt. They may also experience excessive crying. These symptoms must be severe enough to interfere with school, social, or family functioning to warrant a diagnosis of MDD. DD in childhood requires less severe symptomatology but is of a longer duration, lasting for at least one year. Depressed mood or irritability and two or more of the following symptoms—appetite increases or decreases, difficulty sleeping, difficulty concentrating and making decisions; low self-esteem and energy, plus feelings of hopelessness—must be present on more days than not, impacting on daily functioning.

BPD in children involves episodes of depressed or irritable mood and mania. Manic episodes may include irritability or euphoria, along with at least three other symptoms such as grandiosity, decreased need for sleep, pressured speech, flight of ideas, distractibility, increased goal-directed activity, and overinvolvement in pleasurable but risky activities (APA, 2005). A mixed episode is defined as lasting at least a week and includes symptoms that meet both criteria for a manic and a MDD episode nearly every day (APA). Bipolar I disorder involves one or more manic episodes possibly alternating with MDD episodes, while bipolar II involves at least one episode of MDD and hypo-mania. Difficulties in identifying bipolar disorder in children have occurred because of uncertainty about the length of time for a manic episode, and comorbidity between prepubertal onset of mania and ADHD (Kessler, Avenevoli, & Merikangas, 2001). Unique features of childhood BPD are chronicity, with long and predominately mixed episodes of rapid cycling, and irritability (Pavuluri, Birmaher, & Naylor, 2005).

Prevalence and Incidence

Hankin et al. (1998) found the first incidence rate for any depressive disorder at age 11 was 1.79% for males and 0.31% for females, compared to 0.56% for males and 4.39% for females at age 15, and 9.58% for males and 20.69% for females at age 18. Childhood MDD is a risk factor for reoccurrence in adolescence, and for BPD (Kovacs, 1996), which affects 20% to 40% of depressed children (Geller, Fox, & Clark, 1994). Depressive dis-orders have a six-month prevalence of 1% to 3% in children (Garber & Horowitz, 2002; Lewinsohn & Essau, 2002). However, these rates vary across studies, age groups, and gender. Costello, Mustillo, Erkanli, Keeler, and Angold (2003) found the three-month prevalence at 9 to 10 years to be 0.5%, 1.9% for 11-year-olds, 0.4% for 12-year-olds, and 2.6% for 13-year-olds. The lowest prevalence rate for depressive disorders was at 12 years, generally just prior to puberty, when many childhood disorders have low levels of prevalence. Sawyer et al. (2000) found Australian point prevalence rates of 3.7% for 6- to 12-year-old boys, and 2.1% for girls. The prevalence of MDD in school aged children is approximately 2% and 0.6% to 1.7% for DD (Son & Kirchner, 2000). However, children with DD often develop MDD in the following two- to three-year period (Kovacs, 1996). The median length of an MDD episode in children is approximately nine months, while the duration for DD has a median episode length of approximately 3.9 years (Kovacs, 1996). Follow-up studies suggest that depressive symptoms can persist in children for up to four years after an episode (Kumpulainen & Rasanen, 2002).

The prevalence rates for BPD disorder in children are less clear because the age at which this disorder begins is uncertain, and may differ in different countries (Reichart & Nolen, 2004). The lifetime prevalence for mania has been estimated at 1% to 2% by the end of adolescence (Lewinsohn, Klein, & Seeley, 1995; Kessler et al., 2001). Costello and colleagues (1996) reported no cases of BPD I over three months in a group of 9- to 13-year-olds, and only 0.1% of BPD II cases. BPD in childhood has a poor prognosis. Geller, Craney et al. (2002) followed 89, 10- to 11-year-olds diagnosed with mania for two or more weeks or hypomania for two or more months, six monthly for two years. After two years, 65.2% had recovered from their initial episode, but 55.2% had relapsed. Retrospective clinical studies have identified symptom onset as young as 2.8 to 4 years with a delay of approximately 7 years before diagnosis (Dilsaver & Akiskal, 2004; Faedda, Baldessarini, Glovinsky, & Austin, 2004).

BIOLOGICAL AND GENETIC FACTORS

Both biological and genetic factors play central roles in the genesis of depression and BPD in children and adolescents. The research indicates that biological and genetic factors that place children at risk may be different from those that impact on adults and adolescents, and that chronic stress and early childhood trauma may stimulate biological risk factors.

Biological Factors

Support for neuroendocrine system dysfunction related to hypothalamic–pituitary–adrenal (HPA) axis abnormalities and dysregulation of the sleep-onset mechanism in depressed adolescents, is less consistent in prepubertal children (Forbes et al., 2006; Ivanenko, Crabtree, & Gozal, 2005). Forbes and colleagues found elevated presleep-onset cortisol levels for depressed adolescents and anxious children and adolescents, but not depressed children. They hypothesized that dysregulation of the HPA axis for anxious children may lead to early onset depression at puberty, as anxiety serves as a chronic stressor. Depressed children may be more sensitive to stress, rather than displaying the chronic dysregulation or hyperarousal found in depressed adults (Birmaher, Ryan, et al., 1996). Rios, Miyatake, & Thase (2002) implicate a history of early childhood trauma and maltreatment in relation to increased sensitivity to stress and HPA axis involvement.

Birmaher et al., (1996) reviewed research on other potential biological markers, and found abnormal variations in growth hormone, prolactin secretion, and serotonergic functioning in response to psychopharmacological stressors in depressed children. They suggested that changes in growth hormone secretion and serotonergic regulation may be associated with earlier onset of depressive disorders. In support, Dahl et al. (2000) found that depressed 11-year-olds had a lower response to growth hormone-releasing hormone than nondepressed children. Other biological markers noted by Rosso et al. (2005) included structurally smaller left and right amygdala volumes compared to nondepressed children.

BPD in children is distinct from other psychiatric illnesses because of marked state fluctuations rather than a constant negative mood state. Geller and Luby (1997) and Pavuluri et al. (2005) reviewed neurobiological factors based on imaging studies and reported on enlarged ventricles and increased white matter hyperintensities in both cortical and subcortical areas of the brain, particularly in the frontal cortex of children and adolescents. Functional MRI studies indicated increased activation in frontal areas and the anterior cingulate gyrus, which may relate to either abnormal neuronal densities or compensatory recruitment of frontal areas to modulate subcortical areas. Child case studies suggest high levels of central nervous system activation coupled with reduced autonomic system arousal may lead to regulation difficulties in biological rhythms, affect, and behavior, and impairment in adapting to contextual demands (Bar-Haim et al., 2002). Misdiagnosis of MDD or ADHD and treatment with antidepressants or psychostimulants in younger children can also result in a manic episode switch and early onset of BPD (Reichart & Nolan, 2004).

Genetic Factors

Twin studies in children and adolescents have indicated that up to 50% of mood disorders could be attributed to genetic predispositions and that the genetic contributions increase with age (Eaves et al., 1997; Pike, McGuire, Hetherington, Reiss, & Plomin, 1996; Rice, Harold, & Thapar, 2002). However, adoption studies (e.g., Eley, Deater-Deckard, Fombonne, Fulker, & Plomin, 1998) find less evidence of heritability. In a study of twins aged 8 to 16 years, Thaper and McGuffin (1994) found heritability of depression symptomatology at 79%. However, symptoms in children could be explained by environmental factors alone, while in adolescents heredity was the main explanation. Rice, Harold, and Thapar (2005) found both shared family environmental and genetic factors impacted on depression in children aged between 8 and 17, but genetic risk was less apparent in children. Eley (1999) concluded that there is a genetic component to depression which increases with age, appears to be stronger in boys than girls, and explains approximately one third of the variance.

BPD is one of the most heritable disorders, with heritability estimates up to 85%. The risk of BPD among children of BPD parents is four times greater than children of typical parents, while children of BPD parents are also at risk for other disorders like ADHD (Miklowitz & Johnson, 2006). Olson and Pacheco (2005) looked at parent–child co-occurrence of BPD and found a 15% coincidence, and 30% of the children whose parent had BPD had mood disorders. Althoff, Faraone, Rettew, Morley, and Hudziak (2005) reviewed family, twin, adoption, and molecular genetic studies and found evidence for both environmental and genetic influences.

INDIVIDUAL FACTORS INFLUENCING RISK AND RESILIENCY

Gender, comorbidity, cognitive factors, poor physical and mental health, social and interpersonal factors, and negative life events, all influence risk and resiliency for childhood depression. Cognitive, social and life stressor risk factors appear to have a more direct impact on childhood depression, while such factors interact with genetic and biological for childhood BPD.

Gender

Few gender differences in rates of depression have been identified until adolescence (Sorensen, Nissen, Mors & Thomson, 2005). However, by 16 years of age, the rates of any depressive disorder are higher in females (11.7%) compared to males (7.3%) (Costello et al., 2003). Gender differences in the prevalence of depressive disorders in New Zealand adolescents favoring females, emerged between 13 and 15 years (McGee, Freehan, Williams, & Anderson, 1992). However, severity and reoccurrence rates are not gender related (Hankin et al., 1998). Wichstrøm's (1999), cross-sectional study of 12,000 Norwegian school children, reported few gender differences at age 13, but more girls with depressed mood at age 18. Boys showed relatively stable rates across adolescence. In childhood boys and girls are equally likely to suffer from depression.

A similar lack of gender differences have been reported for BPD (Biederman, Kwon et al., 2004; Geller et al., 2000). Geller et al. (2000) found gender differences when BPD and attention deficit hyperactivity disorder (ADHD) were comorbid, with more younger males experiencing both disorders. There were no gender differences after puberty.

Comorbidity

Depression in children and adolescents can be comorbid with anxiety and externalizing disorders such as ADHD, substance abuse, eating disorders, and disruptive behavior (Avenevoli, Stolar, Li, Dierker, & Merikangas, 2001). Angold, Costello, and Erkanli's (1999) meta-analysis found that depression was most commonly comorbid with anxiety, and conduct problems, including conduct disorder, and oppositional defiant disorder, followed by ADHD. Comorbidity of depression and anxiety is more common for girls, while boys are more likely to have depression and externalizing disorders (Kessler et al., 2001). In comorbid anxiety and depression, anxiety often occurs before depression (Cole, Peeke, Martin, Truglio, & Seroczynski, 1998). Avenevoli et al.'s eight-year longitudinal study found that depression was frequently comorbid with anxiety, and the onset of depression followed the onset of most anxiety subtypes.

ADHD is often comorbid with BPD (e.g. Biederman, Faraone et al., 2005; Masi et al., 2006; Post et al., 2004). BPD in childhood is also comorbid with conduct disorder, oppositional defiant disorder (Biederman, Faraone et al., 2004; Post et al. 2004; Wozniak et al., 2004); anxiety (Biederman et al., 2005); panic disorder (Birmaher et al., 2002); psychosis (Biederman, Faraone et al., 2004; Biederman et al., 2005); and impaired psychosocial functioning (Biederman et al., 2005). Wozniak et al. (2004) distinguished between unipolar and bipolar depression in children with ADHD, aged between 6 and 17 years and suggested that MDD was present prior to BPD.

Cognitive Factors

Cognitive factors such as information processing, attribution style, future expectations, and self-perceptions, are associated with childhood depression (Gibb & Coles, 2005). However, the relationship appears to be a more direct or moderating one compared to the mediational or diathesis–stress relationship seen in adolescents and adults. Depressed children show evidence of deficits in frontal lobe functioning demonstrated by impairments in problem solving, maintaining attention, and shifting mental set (Emerson, Mollet, & Harrison, 2005). Timbremont and Braet (2004) found that depressed children showed less positive information processing compared to the not depressed or remitted depressed children and a more negative recall bias. Muris and van der Heiden (2006) indicated that highly anxious 10- to 13-year-olds estimated future negative events as far more likely to occur, and this was associated with depression symptoms. Similarly, negative interpretations about the self in 7– to 9-year-olds were related to concurrent depressive symptoms (Dineen & Hadwin, 2004). Abela, Skitch, Adams, and Hankin (2006) found children's tendency to attribute negative events to global and stable causes, to catastrophize, and to view themselves as flawed, a depressogenic attribution style, were more adversely affected by parental depression. Gladstone and Kaslow's (1995) meta-analyses found moderate to large effect sizes for associations between children's pessimistic attributional style and depressive symptoms. However, the effect appears to be a direct one in younger children, with the proposed diathesis–stress effect found in older children just beginning adolescence. Cognitive risk factors such as cognitive style and negative self-perceptions develop during the childhood years as youngsters observe and interact with their environment. Their experiences shape their perceptions, cognitions, and sense of self into styles that are helpful or unhelpful to their emotional well-being (Abela et al., 2006).

For BPD a vulnerability-stress model suggests that psychosocial stressors interact with the individual's genetic and biological predisposition in eliciting episodes of the illness. Negative cognitive styles have been found in adult studies of BPD and are more related to depressive rather than manic phases. Also, negative cognitive styles and low self-esteem in adults with BPD predict increases in depression over time (Miklowitz & Johnson, 2006).

Poor Physical and Mental Health

Reinherz et al. (1993) identified serious preschool illness as a risk factor for MDD at age 18. Williamson, Walters, and Shaffer (2002) studied 59 chronically ill pediatric patients and their caregivers. Both child-reported pain and caregiver-reported depression predicted child-reported depression. Physical health problems, particularly those with functional impairments are risk factors for depression. A previous history of subclinical or clinical levels of depressive symptomatology has been associated with an increased risk for depression (Ge, Conger, Elder, & Simmons, 1994; Lewinsohn, Clarke, Seeley, & Rohde, 1994). Similarly, anxiety frequently occurs before depression in children (Cole et al., 1998). Reinherz et al. (1989) reported that anxiety at age 9 significantly increased the risk for depression at age 15.

Both Garno, Goldberg, Ramirez, and Ritzler (2005), and Leverich and Post (2006) have reported on the relationship between childhood abuse and early onset BPD in vulnerable children. Leverich and Post reported that early traumatic life events have a direct effect on age of onset and a more adverse course of BPD. In addition, Wozniak et al. (2004) found that in youth with BPD and ADHD, MDD was present prior to BPD.

Social and Interpersonal Factors

A variety of psychosocial difficulties have been associated with depression in young people, including insecure attachment and need for excessive reassurance (Abela, Zuroff, Ho, Adams, & Hankin, 2006); self-consciousness and low self-esteem (Piko & Fitzpatrick, 2003); lower levels of peer acceptance (Cole, 1990); more negative peer nominations (Cole & Jordan, 1995); and peer perceptions of incompetence (Seroczynski, Cole, & Maxwell, 1997); more friendship difficulties (Goodyer & Altham, 1991b); poorer social skills and poor social problem solving (Rudolph, Hammen, & Burge, 1994; Goodman, Gravitt, & Kaslow, 1995). Seroczynski et al. (1997) found that teacher, parent, and peer perceived incompetence in the social and academic spheres were related to depression. Children with multiple spheres of perceived incompetence had higher levels of depression, and negative evaluations in one sphere negated positive evaluations in others. Goodyer and Altham (1991b) found that friendship difficulties exerted a direct effect of similar magnitude to aversive life events, on the probability of emotional disorder in childhood, but were not specific to depression. Goodman et al. found that the effectiveness of solutions to peer conflict problems, not the number of solutions, acted as a moderator between negative life stress and depression in children. Abela, Vanderbilt, and Rochon (2004) and Abela, Brozina, and Haigh (2002) reported that ruminative response styles led to increased child depression. While older children who used more distractive or active problem solving responses to lower depressive symptoms were more effective, in younger children use of these problem-solving styles did not impact on depressed mood.

Children with BPD tend to have poor peer relationships and social impairment (Geller, Zimermann, et al., 2000). In a two-year follow-up study Geller, Craney, et al. (2002) found that more than half of the BPD children had social difficulties (e.g., no friends, experienced teasing, or had poor social skills). These children reported high levels of interpersonal conflict with parents and siblings, and their parents reported high levels of novelty-seeking.

Negative Life Events

Negative life events and chronic daily stress have been implicated as risk factors for a number of childhood disorders such as depression, anxiety, and phobic disorders (Bruce et al., 2006). Turner, Finkelhor, and Ormrod (2006) found that victimization such as sexual assault, maltreatment, and witnessing family violence, was a significant predictor of childhood depression in a large scale telephone survey of caregivers. Rice, Harold, and Thapar (2003) found a genetic covariation between negative life events and depression with stressors more strongly related in younger children. Genetic covariation may relate to temperament. Grant, Compas, Thurm, McMahon, and Gipson's (2004) review of 60 studies of stressful life events found evidence that stressful life events predict increases in both internalizing and externalizing problems in children after controlling for preexisting symptoms, and that these problems reciprocally create further stress for children. In addition, temperamental characteristics such as negative and positive emotionality and attentional control interact with stressful life events to promote automatic stress responses and effortful coping (Compas, Connor-Smith, & Jaser, 2004). Depressed children actually generate more stress in their lives in relation to interpersonal conflict (Rudolph et al., 2000).

Children and adolescents with BPD and their parents report high levels of novelty-seeking (Geller et al., 2002). These behaviors put them at risk for negative life events. Stressful life events, expressed emotion, and negative communication styles within families serve as "environmental provoking agents" that influence the course of pediatric BPD (Miklowitz, Goldstein, Nuechterlein, Snyder, & Mintz, 1988). In addition, conflict and low socioeconomic status in families of parents with BPD are associated with more negative life events for children with BPD (Pavuluri et al., 2005). Garno, Goldberg, Ramirez, and Ritzler (2005), and Leverich and Post (2006) have suggested a relationship between childhood abuse and early onset BPD. Leverich and Post reported that early traumatic life events have a direct effect on age of onset and a more adverse course of BPD.

Individual Resiliency Factors

Individual resilience factors are relevant to children with depressive and PBD disorders. Grant et al. (2006) reviewed the relationship between child and adolescent stressors and how children cope with stress. Resilience factors that have the most evidence for buffering children and adolescents against stress included cognitive factors such as positive attributions in response to stressors in older children, intelligence and academic achievement, and social competence in younger children. Efforts of children using both problem- and emotion-focused coping can have an effect in moderating the impact of stress. Baumgartner (2002) explored the role of hardiness in the choice of coping strategies in stressful situations. Hardy people were shown to prefer active coping solutions and reject avoidance in stressful situations. Also, children with higher IQs and greater educational aspirations are more resilient (Tiet et al., 1998). Social support and peer relationships have been found to buffer stress in approximately half of the studies reviewed by Grant et al. (2006). However, some studies have found that social support, particularly from peers in adolescence, can exacerbate depression if it promotes dysfunctional coping strategies like substance abuse. Positive life experiences and activities have been shown to directly buffer negative events as well as moderate the effects of stressors (Jackson & Warren, 2000).

FAMILY RISK AND RESILIENCY FACTORS

Sixty-one percent of the studies of family functioning reviewed by Grant and colleagues (2006) found evidence for the protective effects of family for childhood depression. Conversely, parent–child conflict, divorce and separation, untimely parental death, child maltreatment or physical abuse, and marital discord have been found to be associated with childhood depression. These factors create more psychosocial stressors and negative life events for children with BPD (Pavuluri et al., 2005). There is also evidence from case studies that the rapid cycling seen in pediatric BPD can create significant stressors for families (Bar-Haim et al., 2002).

Parental Depression

Parental depression that impacts on family functioning, health and climate can influence child depression (Verdeli et al., 2004). Children of parents with a history of major depression episodes are four to six times more likely to develop depression than other children (Beardslee, Keller, Lavori, Staley, & Sacks, 1993; Weissman, Warner, Wickramaratne, Moreau, & Olfson, 1997). Maternal depression has been singled out for investigation and maternal depression has been significantly related to offspring depression (Burke, 2003; Hammen, Burge, & Adrian, 1991; Hammen, Shih, & Brennan, 2004; Lyons-Ruth,

Eastbrook, & Cibelli, 1997; Warner, Mufson, & Weissman, 1995). Ferguson, Horwood, and Lynsky (1995) found that mothers' depression was more associated with depression in female than male children. This effect was moderated by socioeconomic status.

Parenting Style

Parenting styles are risk and resilience factors for depression. Lack of rewards and high criteria for maternal rewards were more common among children with depression than among controls (Cole & Rehm, 1986). However, this may differ in different cultural groups. Finkelstein, Donenberg, and Martinovich (2001) found that maternal control was not associated with depression for an ethnically mixed group of Caucasian, Latino, and African-American girls. However, high maternal control for African-American girls was associated with low levels of depressive symptoms. This study indicates the importance of not generalising studies across ethnic groups.

Family Functioning

The relationship of parental and offspring depression may be due to many factors. As noted earlier, genetic contributions may be substantial. Family functioning may also be a mediator. Downey and Coyne (1990) indicated that offspring of mothers with schizo-phrenia or depression were at greater risk, but argued that that the effect was mediated through marital discord. Parental marital dissatisfaction was related to depression in girls but not boys in a Ukrainian study (Drabick, Beauchaine, Gadow, Carlson, & Bromet, 2006). In addition, Richman and Flaherty (1987) demonstrated that parental overprotec-tion was associated with depression. Nilzen and Palmérus (1997) found that families of depressed compared to nondepressed children had a higher frequency of major family problems, life events, parent symptoms, and parental overprotection. Families of depressed children were less cohesive and there was less happiness. Finally, Rapee (1997) reviewed the vast literature of family dynamics. He concluded that rejection and control were associated with depression, particularly rejection, while control was more associated with anxiety.

Family context can be predictive of depression. Families with high levels of ex-pressed emotion, critical emotionality, overinvolved attitudes of key relatives and parents, were more likely to have children with depression (Asarnow, Thompson, Hamilton, & Goldstein, 1994; Schwartz, Dorer, Beardslee, & Lavori, 1990). The structure of families has been investigated in relation to childhood depression. Boyce-Rogers and Rose (2002) looked at intact and blended families, and single divorced families, and found that there was a small effect for children of intact families having fewer internalizing problems.

An early study of family risk factors for BPD in adolescents and adults (Miklowitz, Goldstein, Neuchterlein, Snyder, & Mintz, 1988), found that levels of family expressed emotion and affective style predicted the likelihood of relapse up to nine months follow-up. Family affective style predicted psychosocial functioning in the follow-up period, with patients living in families with a negative affective style having 5.9 times the risk of relapse as patients in families with a benign affective style. More recently, Geller et al. (2000) found impairment in mother–child warmth, and both mother–child and father–child tension for children with BPD. In addition, Chang, Blaser, Ketter, and Steiner (2001) found that poor family cohesion and organization, coupled with high conflict in the family environment created more aversive life events for BPD children.

Family Resiliency Factors

Grant and colleagues' (2006) review indicates that family variables, such as parent–child relationships and parenting practices, mediate the relationship between stressors and child psychopathology generally. In particular, Nilzen and Palmérus (1997) showed that higher levels of family cohesion in combination with lower levels of conflict are associated with less psychopathology, including depression, in children. Self-reported good relationships with parents (Sund & Wichstrøm, 2002), and good mother–child communication (Drabick et al., 2006) are related to lower levels of depression in offspring. Strong parental attachment can be a resilience factor for depression (Papini, Roggman, & Anderson, 1991), while insecure attachments are risk factors for depression (Sund & Wichstrøm, 2002). Boyce-Rogers and Rose's (2002) study of intact, blended, and single divorced families, reported that internalizing problems were buffered by parental support, parental monitoring, perceiving peers as supportive, high school attachment, and having a neighbor to confide in.

Walsh (2003) proposed a model of family resilience where stress was not seen simply in terms of the individual, but impacting on the entire family. Some of the key processes involved; family belief systems, where a positive shared construction of reality emerges through family and social transactions; making meaning of adversity; a positive outlook, learned optimism; transcendence and spirituality, which emphasizes the sense that life has more meaning and purpose beyond ourselves; and social support for families through their religious connections. Rituals and ceremonies associated with these provide support from the community and extended family. Walsh argues that flexibility in structure and adaptability in family organization is a resilience factor, in terms of connectedness, and social and economic resources.

SOCIAL AND COMMUNITY RISK AND RESILIENCY FACTORS

No studies of social and community risk and resilience factors that are specific to depression or BPD could be located so factors affecting child adjustment generally are reviewed.

Risk Factors

A number of risk factors have been identified as predictors of child psychopathology such as poverty (Luthar, 1991), war (Heskin, 1980), living in a high crime area (Felsman & Vaillant, 1987), experiencing a disaster (Reijneveld, Crone, Verhulst, & Verloove-Vanhorick (2003), poor family relationships, and exposure to violence (Grant et al., 2006). In a review, Wolkow and Ferguson (2001) argued the case for social and community factors being implicated in lack of well-being for vulnerable children, as well as having a warm and supportive caregiver as a protective factor. Environmental stressors and community risk factors generally exert their negative impact on children by disrupting significant family relationships and interactions (Grant et al., 2006; Hammen, Shih, & Brennan, 2004).

Resilience Factors

Wolkow and Ferguson (2001) argued that having a warm and supportive caregiver is a protective factor which buffers social and community factors for vulnerable children. A child's coping resources can also be expanded or limited by their family and community contexts (Grant et al., 2006). School connectedness has been investigated as a protective factor. Stewart, Sun, Patterson, Lemerle, and Hardie (2004) looked at the promotion of resilience in children aged 8 to 12 years in school, family, and community settings. Schools in which students reported more positive adult and peer social networks, feelings of connectedness to at least two adults and peers, and a strong sense of autonomy, were associated with high self-ratings of resilience in children. These results were supported by parents and caregivers perceptions.

EVIDENCE-BASED TREATMENTS FOR CHILDHOOD DEPRESSION AND BIPOLAR DISORDER

Psychosocial interventions have been developed specifically for childhood depressioon, however, the range and efficacy of these interventions is not as extensive or as advanced as that of interventions for adolescent depression. Treatments use mostly cognitive behavioural strategies targeted at children and familyh interactions. Treatments for childhood BPD are even more limited with few clinical trials. Early family-based interventions focus on reducing life stress within the family environment.

What Works: Depression

Psychosocial Treatments

Psychosocial treatments for childhood depression have been conducted primarily in community settings with school children experiencing elevated depressive symptoms (Compton, Burns, Egger & Robertson, 2002; Compton, March, Brent, Albano, Weersing & Curry, 2004; Curry, 2001). Michael and Crowley's (2002) meta-analysis identified nine controlled studies and three prepost uncontrolled studies of psychosocial interventions for depression in children. Large mean effect sizes of 0.65 (95% CI 0.34–0.94) for the controlled trials and 0.73 (95% CI 0.14–1.30) for the prepost studies were found. These effect sizes were slightly lower than those for psychosocial treatments for depressed adolescents (controlled 0.93; prepost 1.35), but larger than the small effects found for pharmacological treatments for depressed children (Mean ES = .15). Hence, psychosocial interventions for childhood depression work.

Cognitive Behavioral Therapy

Eight randomized controlled (RCT) studies of depression treatments that included children were identified. All interventions were based on behavioral (BT) or cognitive-behavioral therapy (CBT) (Compton, March, et al., 2002; Compton, Burns, et al., 2004; Curry, 2001). The interventions were group-based and provided to nonreferred school children with elevated depression symptoms. The one exception was Vostanis, Feehan, and Grattan's (1996) nine-session individual CBT treatment program. The 8- to 14-year-old clinically depressed participants in this study were recruited from community based outpatient clinics. No studies were identified that used other models of therapy. However, three studies included psychoeducational sessions for families that were adjunctive to the child therapy (Asarnow, Scott, & Mintz, 2002; Rehm & Sharp, 1996; Stark, Brockman, & Fraser, 1990). These were conducted in groups (Asarnow et al., 2002; Rehm & Sharp, 1996) or in the home setting (Stark et al., 1990).

The interventions included, symptom monitoring, cognitive restructuring, social skills training, social problem solving, coping skills, relaxation, and pleasant events scheduling, plus programming to generalize these skills across various settings. The format differed across studies. Strategies, such as psychoeducation, discussion, role modeling, self-monitoring, facilitator reinforcement, and homework practice were used. Family sessions were designed to increase positive parent–child interactions and pleasant family activities, and to help parents to encourage their child to use their new skills. Three studies compared different versions of active BT and CBT treatments (Butler, Miezitis, Friedman, & Cole, 1980; Kahn, Kehle, Jenson, & Clarke, 1990; Stark et al., 1987). For example, Kahn et al. compared a combined CBT intervention to relaxation alone, self-modeling, and wait-list control.

Of the eight RCTs, six studies using school-based samples reported significant postintervention reductions in depressive symptoms in the active CBT conditions when compared to a wait-list or no treatment control groups (Asarnow et al., 2002; Butler et al., 1980; Kahn et al., 1990; Stark et al., 1990; Stark, Reynolds, & Kaslow, 1987; Weisz, Thurber, Sweeney, Proffitt, & Legagnoux, 1997). Effect sizes were large to moderate, ranging from 1.68 (Kahn et al., 1990) to .48 (Weisz et al., 1997), and alternative CBT components tended to show similar effects at postintervention. Response rates for immediate remission of clinical levels of symptomatology ranged from 88% to 50% for combined CBT interventions compared to 11% to 38% for wait-list and no treatment control groups (Butler et al., 1980; Kahn et al., 1990; Stark et al., 1987; Weisz et al., 1997). Four studies (Kahn et al., 1990; Stark et al., 1990; Stark et al., 1987; Weisz et al., 1997) indicated maintenance of effects at follow-up periods ranging from four weeks (Kahn et al., 1990) to nine months (Weisz et al., 1997). Kahn et al., 1990 reported remission rates of 50% four weeks after CBT intervention, compared to 88% immediately after treatment, while Stark et al. (1987) found increased remission rates at the seven-month follow-up from 75% to 88% for their self-control treatment and 60% to 67% for their behavioral problem solving treatment. Group-based CBT treatments, with or without parental psychoeducation components, reduce depressive symptoms and decrease the proportion of children with clinical levels of symptomatology.

What Works: Bipolar Disorder

There are currently no psychosocial treatments that meet the criteria for interventions that work (Pavuluri et al., 2005).

What Might Work: Depression

School-Based Intervention

Stark (1990) published a CBT treatment for depression in children that has undergone a number of iterations. Stark et al. (1987) reported on a comparison between two group-based interventions, *self-control therapy* and *problem-solving therapy* and a wait-list control condition. Each program involved 12-, 45-, to 50-minute sessions completed over a five-week period, with younger and older children meeting in separate groups. Common elements included a rationale, information on the relationship between mood and participation in pleasant activities, and self-monitoring. Both programs resulted in significant decreases on child reported depressive symptoms compared to the wait-list condition. However, the *self-control* condition improved significantly more than the wait-list control at postintervention and had more improvements on the Children's Depression Rating Scale-Revised at two-month follow-up compared to the *problem-solving* group. Stark et al. (1990) reported on another RCT, of a 24- to 26-week program that combined the two interventions and added three family meetings over a 3.5-month intervention period. This treatment was compared against a nonspecific psychotherapy group. This CBT treatment was effective in reducing depressive cognitions and clinical symptomatology as measured by the Kiddie-Schizophrenia and Affective Disorders Schedule.

Rehm and Sharp (1996) evaluated the effectiveness of Stark's (1990) program with children nominated by school personnel, in an uncontrolled pretest-posttest study. Child group sessions were well attended, but family meetings were poorly attended. They found few changes on depressive symptoms at postintervention, however, for children with preintervention clinical diagnoses, decreases in depression, and improvements in social skills and optimistic attributions were observed at postintervention.

Stark's (1990) childhood depression school-based treatment has been evaluated in two RCTs and one uncontrolled trial by independent researchers. Versions of the program are effective in decreasing depressive symptoms and associated cognitions at postintervention, and two-month follow-up. Hence, this particular CBT program might work for children.

Family Therapy

Few studies have evaluated FT interventions for depressed children. No RCTs were identified. However, two uncontrolled trials of a psychoeducational family-based treatment have been conducted by Fristad and colleagues (Fristad, Arnett, & Gavazzi, 1998; Fristad, Gavazzi, & Soldano, 1998). Fristad, Arnett, and Gavazzi (1998) evaluated a 90-minute psychoeducational workshop for parents that focused on the symptoms, etiology, and course of depression, treatments, and family factors in treatment outcome. At postintervention, parents of inpatient depressed children reported a better understanding of their children's mood disorders; at four-month follow-up, there were decreased levels of negative emotion and emotional overinvolvement with their children. Fristad, Gavazzi, and Soldano (1998) then evaluated a six-session multifamily psychoeducational group program with expanded content. At postintervention, mothers and fathers were satisfied with the program, reported more positive attitudes toward their depressed children, and more positive attitudes and behavior from their depressed children. At four-month follow-up half of the measures were still improved.

Psychoeducational family therapy may promote more positive attitudes between parents and their depressed children, and reduce family risk factors for childhood depression. However, as yet there is no evidence that this results in decreased depressive symptoms or remission of depressive disorders in children.

What Works: Bipolar Disorder

Kowatch et al. (2005) in their treatment guidelines for pediatric BPD suggest that once a child with BPD is stabilized on medication, psychoeducation can be beneficial. Teaching parents and children about BPD, its symptoms, course, and treatment; skill building, including communication and problem solving about symptom management, emotion regulation, and impulse control, may be effective in managing symptoms for the child and family. Approaches that may work with medication include, child- and family-focused CBT (Fristad, Gavazzi, & Mackinaw-Koons, 2003; Miklowitz, George, & Axelson, 2004; Pavuluri et al., 2004).

Fristad and colleagues (2003) conducted psychoeducation groups for families with either depressed or BPD children. The content and outcomes of small controlled and uncontrolled trials of this program were reviewed earlier under family interventions for MDD. Results for families with BPD offspring included an increase in parental knowledge of child problems and greater ability to access services for their children, and increased parental social support for children. As yet, there are no published results relating to reductions in child symptoms or differential results for families of children with BPD. An uncontrolled trial of a 12-session family-focused CBT program conducted by Pavuluri et al. (2004) emphasised empathic validation of specific parental concerns, helped parents to manage their own unhelpful cognitions about their child's symptoms, and also helped them to serve as *coaches* for their children and adolescents. Postintervention evaluations indicated significant reductions in child symptom severity, and increased general functioning for the children. Treatment integrity was good and families were satisfied with the results. Miklowitz et al. (2004) developed a family-focused therapy that included 21 individual family sessions for parents and adolescents over nine months. The intervention aimed to help adolescents to make sense of their illness and accept it, as well as their medications. It also focused on managing stress, reducing negative life events, and promoting a positive family environment, using strategies such as psychoeducation, communication enhancement, and problem solving skills training. In an uncontrolled trial, 20 adolescents with BPD showed significant reductions in depressive and manic symptoms and reductions in behaviour problems over one year of intervention. Randomized controlled trials are proceeding.

Hence, psychoeducational family-focused interventions presented in group or individual family formats may be effective in changing the family environment to better support children with BPD, and by reducing child symptoms and symptom severity.

What Doesn't Work

Currently, there is no evidence that individual CBT treatment for children with depressive disorders works in clinical settings. The only published RCT of individual psychotherapy that included depressed children (Vostanis Feehan, Grattan, & Bickerton, 1996a, 1996b) indicated that a nine-session CBT intervention was as effective as a nonfocused intervention, therapist-attention condition. Both groups showed improvement in internalizing symtomatology, self-esteem, social functioning, and remission from depressive disorders after treatment and at 9- and 24-month follow-ups; however, 50% of the CBT patients dropped out before receiving the cognitive components.

Hence, clinic-based interventions for depressive disorders in children do not work at present. Further work is required to assist youngsters to remain in therapy, even when their symptoms begin to lift, and to identify components that are active over and above the effects of nonspecific therapist attention.

Bipolar Disorder

It is clear that early, brief versions of Fristad et al.'s (2003) multifamily psychoeducation groups did not result in significant changes in child symptoms, although they did result in changes in parents' knowledge and family expressed emotion levels from pre- to postintervention..

OVERALL CONCLUSION

Psychosocial treatments for childhood depression are not as advanced as interventions for adolescent depression. This may be related to lower prevalence rates in childhood, and difficulty in identifying depressive symptoms and disorders in children (Ryan, 2001). There is evidence only for the efficacy of CBT treatments (with or without adjunctive family psychoeducation) implemented in group formats, in school settings, with children with elevated depressive symptoms, but not necessarily clinical disorders (Compton, Burns, et al., 2002; Compton, March, et al., 2004; Curry, 2001; Michael & Crowley, 2002).

No specific CBT interventions meet the "What Works" criteria. However, Stark's (1990) school-based CBT intervention shows the most promise. Family-based psychoeducation in group or individual format is promising as an adjunctive component to promote better communication and positive affect between parent and child (Asarnow et al., 2002). Currently, no treatments for clinical disorders have proven efficacy.

The efficacy of psychosocial interventions for BPD is at a very early stage. Interventions that are promising include child- and family-focused therapies that aim to promote understanding of the illness and adherence to medical treatments, and change the family environments and management of psychosocial stressors (Pavuluri et al., 2005).

PSYCHOPHARMACOLOGY AND CHILDHOOD DEPRESSION AND BIPOLAR DISORDER

Much of the evidence for the efficacy for pharmacological treatments for childhood depression and BPD has come from adolescent and adult studies. However, children are regularly being prescribed psycho-pharmacological medications for depression and BPD, and the rates of prescriptions for childhood depression are increasing.

Depression

Pharmacological treatment of depression in childhood and adolescence is common. In a study conducted in the United States, Skaer, Robinson, Sclar, and Galin (2000) reported that 48.2% of physician office visits for depressed children or adolescents resulted in the prescription of an antidepressant medication, 50.1% receiving serotonin-selective reuptake inhibitors (SSRIs) and 41.9% receiving tricyclic antidepressants (TCAs). Also, Ma, Lee and Stafford. (2005) reported that the proportion of outpatient visits where antidepressants were prescribed to children or adolescents has risen slightly from 47% in 1995 to 1999 to 52% in 2001 to 2002. SSRIs represented 81% of all prescriptions in 2000 to 2001. Other drugs used include monoamine oxidase inhibitors (MAOIs), other nontricyclic antidepressants such as trazodone, bupropion, and nefazodone, venlafaxine, mirtazapine, and lithium (Findling, Feeny, Stansbrey, Delporto-Bedoya, & Demeter, 2002; Ryan, 2005).

What Works: Depression

Reviews, and placebo controlled trials of the effectiveness of pharmacological treatments for depression generally have not distinguished between children and adolescents (Emslie & Mayes, 2001; Findling et al., 2002; Ryan, 2005; Varley, 2003; Wagner, 2005; Wittington et al., 2004).

Serotonin-Selective Reuptake Inhibitors

SSRIs are antidepressant compounds that specifically and selectively inhibit the reuptake of serotonin at the synapse (Findling et al., 2002). These include fluoxetine (Prozac), sertraline (Zoloft), paroxetine (Paxil), fluvoxamine (Luxov), and citalopram (Celexa, Cipramil, Ciazil). These medications have been evaluated in a number of published double-blind placebo-controlled (DBPC) trials (Ryan, 2005; Vasa, Carlino, & Pine, 2006; Wagner, 2005; Wittington et al., 2004).

Fluoxetine

Of the SSRI drugs, fluoxetine (Prozac) is the only antidepressant approved for children and adolescents by the U.S. Food and Drug Administration (FDA) (Wagner, 2005). Four published DBPC trials have been completed on fluoxetine, two with children and adolescents (Emslie et al., 2002; Emslie et al., 1997) and two with adolescents alone (Simeon, Dinicola, Ferguson, & Copping, 1990; TADS, 2004). Simeon et al.'s small study of adolescent treatment with fluoxetine revealed no significant results. Emslie et al. found that 56% (1997) and 52% (2002) of children and adolescents treated with fluoxetine (20 mg daily) were very much improved on measures of clinical impression, compared to 33% (1997) and 37% (2002) of the placebo group. There were no significant group differences in aversive side effects in either study. In a 12-month follow-up of the 1997 study, Emslie et al. (1998) found that 85% of those who received acute treatment were recovered, but 39% of these had experienced a recurrence of MDD in the follow-up period, a rate higher than that found in adults. However, continued fluoxetine treatment delayed time to relapse by 181 days compared to 71 days for the placebo group (Emslie et al., 2001).

The Treatment of Adolescent Depression Study (TADS, 2004) found that fluoxetine (10–40 mg/day) alone and in combination with CBT was more effective than placebo or CBT alone. Treatment response rates on global improvement showed that 71% of the fluoxetine plus CBT condition and 61% of the fluoxetine alone groups improved, compared to 43% of the CBT group and 35% or the placebo group. The TADS study revealed that suicidal thinking decreased in all groups, but the greatest reduction occurred for the fluoxetine plus CBT group. CBT alone and with fluoxetine was associated with decreased suicidality, compared to other conditions. Other adverse events recorded for the fluoxetine groups included, gastric symptoms (5.5%), vomiting (3.74–1.83%), and insomnia (4.67–2.75%).

Conclusions

Fluoxetine is an effective acute treatment for child and adolescent depression. It may be better than CBT alone, or in combination with CBT for adolescents; however, trials have not yet been completed with children. Fluoxetine is the only drug that is recommended for children and adolescents by the FDA and the British Medicine and Healthcare Products Regularity Agency (Wagner, 2005).

What Works: Bipolar Disorder

There are few controlled trials or prospective studies of the efficacy and safety of pharmacological treatments for childhood BPD. Hence, no medications meet the criteria for a drug that works, and no medications have been recommended by the FDA for childhood BPD (Pavuluri et al., 2005).

Strategies That Might Work: Depression

Sertraline

Two multicenter DBPC studies with children and adolescents have been conducted. The pooled results of these studies indicated that flexible daily doses of sertraline (Zoloft) (50–200mg) resulted in significantly greater symptom reduction than placebo in 6- to 17-year-old outpatients (Wagner et al., 2003). Sixty-nine percent of treated patients responded compared to 56% of the placebo condition. Adolescents showed slightly greater symptom reduction than children. However, 9% of treated and 3% of placebo patients discontinued due to aversive side effects such as diarrhea, vomiting, anorexia, and agitation. In a follow-up 24-week open label trial, 62% of both treated and placebo patients experienced reduced symptomology (Ryan, 2005). Headaches, nausea, and insomnia were the most common side effects, occurring in 5% of treated patients, double the placebo rate.

Citalopram

Wagner (2005) reports on two DBPC studies, one positive and one negative, that have assessed the efficacy of this drug with depressed children and adolescents. Wagner et al. (2004) found that 36% of citalopram (Celexa) (20–40 mg/day) treated 7- to 17-year-olds responded with reduced depressive symptoms compared to 24% of placebo patients. However, more than 5% of treated patients reported adverse side effects such as influenzalike symptoms, nausea, abdominal pain, diarrhea, tiredness, and back pain. Citalopram treatment for adolescents with MDD, DD, or bipolar disorder was effective in 76% of cases investigated in a retrospective case review study from a community mental health center (Bostic, Prince, Brown, & Place, 2001). An unpublished report of a European DBPC trial (FDA, 2004) reported by Wagner (2005) found similar side effects and no significant group differences.

Conclusions

Currently, sertraline and citalopram have demonstrated superiority to placebo in at least one DBPC. Hence, these drugs may be effective treatments for acute childhood depression.

What Might Work: Bipolar Disorder

All studies have included more adolescents than children. The majority of pediatric trials are open trials with only six published placebo controlled trials (Pavuluri et al., 2005). This research indicates that a combination of mood stabilisers such as lithium or the anticonvulsant divalproex sodium (DVPX; Valproate) and second generation antipsychotics such as risperidone (Risperdal), olanzapine (Zyprexa), or quetiapine (Seroquel) have been found to be effective in placebo controlled trials for treating the acute symptoms of BPD and for stabilization of symptoms up to six months follow-up (Miklowitz & Johnson, 2006; Pavuluri et al., 2005). For children with comorbid ADHD, Scheffer and colleagues (Scheffer, Kowatch, Carmody, & Rush, 2005) found that DVPX and Adderall (mixed amphetamine salt) resulted in significantly greater global functioning compared to placebo. Findling, Youngstrom, et al. (2005) indicated that treatment with mood stabilisers led to maintenance of treatment effects for less than 4 months of an 18-month follow-up period. Of these drugs, only lithium carbonate is approved by the FDA for the treatment of BPD in adolescents (Pavuluri et al., 2005).

Treatment algorithms have recently been developed for acute phase treatment of children 6 to 17 years who meet DSM-IV criteria for BPD-I, manic or mixed episode, depending on whether the child presented with or without features of psychosis (Kowatch et al., 2005). These recommend that first stage treatment include monotherapy with any of the mood stabilisers or antipsychotic drugs noted above. If response is not adequate, then augmentation with an additional mood stabiliser, DVPX, or an antipsychotic drug should be added. For children with no response or aversive side effects an alternative monotherapy or augmentation should be added until a better response or fewer side effects are apparent. However, as the side effects of these drugs can be aversive to children and time to relapse is relatively short (Findling et al., 2005; Kowatch et al., 2005). Hence, it is clear that pharmacological treatments work for some children and not for others.

What Doesn't Work: Depression

Tricyclic Antidepressants (TCA)

TCAs that have been used with children and adolescents include imipramine (Tofranil), Amitriptyline (Elvil), nortriptyline (Pamelor, Aventyl), desipramine (Norpramin, Pertofrane), and clomipramine (Anafranil). These drugs impact on the noradrenergic system by blocking the reuptake of monamine neurotransmitters, or other neurotransmitter systems. TCAs are not superior to placebo in any DBPC trials with children, and there is little evidence for their efficacy with adolescents (Findling et al., 2002; Geller, Reising, et al., 1999; Ryan, 2005; Wagner, 2005). Also, meta-analyses (Hazell, O'Connell, Heathcote, Robertson, & Henry, 1995; Thurber, Ensign, Punnett, & Welter, 1995) indicated that the effect size for TCAs was not significant. TCA usage in adolescents has been associated with side effects such as dry mouth, cardiovascular problems, including reports of four unexplained sudden deaths of children receiving desipramine (Hazell et al., 1995). The sedation effects often associated with TCAs interfere with learning and school activities (Geller, Reising et al., 1999). Hence, TCAs do not work in children.

Paroxetine

Three multicenter DBPC trials of the SSRI paroxetine (Paxil) have found negative effects on the primary outcome variable for depression. Keller et al. (2001) conducted a large study of paroxetine (20–40 mg daily) compared to the TCA imipramine with adolescent outpatients who received paroxetine (20–40 mg/day). It showed no significant differences between groups on depressive symptoms; however, on global clinical impressions the paroxetine group was rated significantly better. However, discontinuation due to aversive events occurred in 9.7% of the paroxetine, 31.5% of imipramine, and 6.9% of the placebo groups. Eleven paroxetine patients experienced serious adversive events including; headaches, emotional lability, suicide ideation and gestures, worsening depression, conduct problems or hostility, and euphoria, compared to two placebo group patients. Hence, the FDA (2003) has recommended that paroxetine not be used for children or adolescents.

Nefazodone

This antidepressant (Serzone) blocks postsynaptic serotonin and inhibits the reuptake of both serotonin and norepinephrine. Wagner (2005) and Ryan (2005) report on two studies that involved children or adolescents, one unpublished. The unpublished study found no significant differences between treatment and placebo group adolescents. However, the adolescent study (Ryan et al., 2002) reported that 65% of the nefazodone group responded on the clinical global impression compared to only 46% of the placebo group, despite not finding significant group differences on response to the primary depression outcome.

Other Antidepressants

Other antidepressants found to be ineffective include, the SSRI excitalopram (Lexapro), mirtazapine (Remeron) a noradrenergic, and a specific serotonergic antidepressant, bupropion (Wellbutrin).

Overall Conclusion

The SSRIs have the strongest empirical support for the treatment of childhood and adolescent depression. Of these, fluoxetine (Prozac) appears to work for children and adolescents. The TADS study (2004) suggests that fluoxetine works even better when combined with CBT, however, such findings need to be replicated. Few studies have looked at the effects of various drugs on children as opposed to adolescents, and more studies of prepubertal children are required. Other pharmacological treatments that may work include sertraline (Zoloft) and citalopram (Celexa).

Evidence for effective treatment of childhood BPD is more limited. It is clear that monotherapy involving mood stabilisers or antipsychotic treatments is unlikely to be effective, and that a combination of drugs and psychosocial intervention for both children and parents may be required to manage this more complex disorder.

THE PREVENTION OF DEPRESSION

Studies of the prevention of depression have concentrated on school and/or family-based interventions. These interventions typically involve small groups or classes of children or adolescents who participate in skills and resilience building activities. Universal and targeted interventions have been developed and tested.

What Works

A Cochrane Review (Merry, McDowell, Hetrick, Bir, & Muller, 2005) has identified 21 studies and concluded that programs aimed at preventing depressive symptoms were effective in reducing depressive symptoms immediately after the program, with a standardized mean difference (SMD) of −0.26 (CI −0.36 −.0.15). This effect was driven primarily by targeted interventions (SMD = −0.26; CI −0.40 −0.13), while universal programs were not effective (SMD = −0.21; CI -0.48−0.06). At follow-up no significant effects were found for either universal or targeted programs. When depressive disorders was the primary outcome variable, preventive interventions showed effectiveness at postintervention (risk difference, RD = −0.10, CI −0.15–0.05). The effects for both targeted (RD = −0.13) and universal interventions (RD = −0.08) were significant. Effects were not significant at 3 to 6 months follow-up, but at a 12-month follow-up the pooled data from two of the available targeted studies reported a significant decrease in diagnoses of depressive disorders (RD = −0.12) while the two available universal studies did not. Merry et al. noted that the change in depression scores is small; however, when translated into *numbers needed to treat* (NNT) the results are encouraging. Based on the pooled results of all studies, 10 children would need to be treated to prevent one case of depression; eight for targeted and 13 for universal programs.

Horowitz and Garber's (2006) meta-analytic review of child and adolescent prevention programs included 13 related to samples of children. Effect sizes ranged from −0.62 to 1.51 at immediate postintervention, and −15 to 1.95 at follow-up. They concluded that selective programs for children and adolescents (0.29) achieved better postintervention effects than universal interventions (0.12), but that at follow-up, selective (0.56) and indicated programs (0.25) were showing better effects than universal interventions (0.02). Selective programs were more effective than indicated programs at follow-up. Gender and age were not associated with effect sizes, nor was the length of time to follow-up or the number of sessions included in the interventions. None of the universal intervention studies met the criteria for a prevention effect, defined as an increase in the control group symptoms accompanied by no increase or a decrease in the intervention group. Most selective studies showed a treatment effect with reduction in depressive symptoms in the intervention group. Indicated studies tended to show treatment effects. They suggested that indicated and selective interventions had larger effect sizes and may be more practical and beneficial. However, universal interventions prevent small numbers of cases of depression at a low level of cost per participant. Only four of the 30 studies showed a true prevention effect.

Conclusions

These reviews indicate that targeted interventions, in particular selective interventions, work. They are not moderated by gender or age, or the length of the individual programs.

The Penn Resilience Program (PRP)

This program is a 12-session group-based intervention program based on CBT, teaching skills to reduce cognitive errors, promote optimistic attribution styles, and enhance social problem-solving and coping skills (Reivich, Gillham, Chaplin, & Seligman, 2005). The program has been implemented with 10- to 13-year-olds.

In a targeted controlled trial of this intervention, significant intervention group differences in depressive symptoms were found at postintervention, six-month follow-up (Jaycox, Reivich, Gillham, & Seligman, 1994), and two-year follow-up (Gillham, Reivich, Jaycox, & Seligman, 1995), but not at three-year follow-up (Gillham & Reivich, 1999). Analysis of effects for children of divorce found that the program was effective, but effects diminished over time (Zubernis, Cassidy, Gillham, Reivich, & Jaycox, 1999). Targeted RCTs of this program have found significant intervention effects for depressive symptoms immediately after treatment, and at three- and six-month follow-ups, for low-income Latino children, but not African-American children (Cardemil, Reivich, & Seligman, 2002), and Chinese children with elevated depressive symptoms and parental conflict (Yu & Seligman, 2002). An Australian trial of PRP with rural school children with elevated levels of depression, found an effect on anxiety symptoms at postintervention and 6- and 30-month follow-ups, but no effects on depressive symptoms (Roberts, Kane, Bishop, Matthews, & Thomson, 2004). However, at the 30-month follow-up effects on anxiety mediated the impact on depressive symptoms. In an RCT of the PRP program implemented in a primary care setting, effects of depressive symptoms were apparent for girls but not for boys (Gillham, Hamilton, Freres, Patton, & Gallop, 2006). The program prevented depression, anxiety, and adjustment disorders in children with high initial symptom levels.

Two small RCTs of universal applications of PRP have been conducted in Australia. Pattison and Lynd-Stevenson (2001) found no immediate or follow-up effect of POP compared to an attention control condition. However, Quayle, Dziurawiec, Roberts, Kane, and Ebsorthy (2001) using a shorter eight-session adaptation of PRP showed six-month follow-up effects for depression and self-esteem in girls, compared to a no-treatment control.

Conclusions

PRP works to prevent depressive symptoms when run in small groups in schools with children targeted because of increased risk factors. PRP does not work for African Americans, or when used with nonselected groups of Australian children. It is effective for anxiety when implemented under regular service delivery conditions, and prevents internalizing disorders in children with high initial symptom levels.

What Might Work

Family-based prevention, anxiety prevention programs, and social and academic competence programs may work.

Family-Based Prevention

Gladstone and Beardslee's (2000) research targets children and adolescents whose parents have affective disorders. They compared a family-based CBT therapy and a psychoeducational approach. The 6- to 10-session individual family intervention helped families to develop a shared perspective of the depressive illness, to change parents' behavior toward their children, and to promote resilience in children by providing information about a parent's illness, ways of coping, and encouraging supportive relationships outside the home. The psychoeducational approach involved two short group lectures. Postintervention and at 18-month follow-up, family intervention parents reported significantly more changes in behavior and attitudes to their illness, compared to families that received the psychoeducational intervention only (Beardslee et al., 1993; Beardslee, Wright, et al., 1997). Children in the family intervention group experienced better understanding of their parent's disorder, improved communication with parents, and enhanced global functioning at 18-months follow-up (Beardslee, Salt, et al., 1997). Depressive disorders occurred in 9% of the children and adolescents in the family-based intervention, compared to 25% in the lecture-based condition at follow-up. This family-based intervention may work.

Anxiety Prevention Programs

The *Friends Program* (Lowry-Webster, Barrett, & Dadds, 2001) is an anxiety prevention program that has recently been used universally with children and young adolescents in schools. The program involves 10 sessions run in school and an adjunctive three-session parent program. Given that anxiety frequently coexists or predates depression, anxiety prevention may act as a prevention strategy for depression (Cole et al., 1998). Lowry-Webster et al. (2001) showed that children and adolescents with elevated anxiety scores at preintervention reported improvements in depression symptoms at postinterventions and 12-month follow-up (Lowrey-Webster, Barrett, & Lock, 2003). Hence, anxiety prevention programs that are implemented in late childhood period may prevent childhood and adolescent depression.

Social and Academic Competence Programs

Strategies targeting risk factors such as low social competence and poor academic achievement in the early and middle childhood years show promise. King and Kirschenbaum (1990) used a nine-session social skills and social problem solving intervention, plus a parent and teacher consultation service for fourth grade children who were at risk for depression because of poor social competence. The combined program showed decreased depressive symptoms compared to the parent–teacher consultation service only and a control group at posttest with social competencies improving for all groups.

Kellam, Bebok, Mayer, Ialongo, and Kalodner (1994) targeted pessimistic attribution style in association with poor academic mastery and implemented a universal school-based prevention strategy designed to enhance mastery of academic skills in first-grade children. It included an enriched reading curriculum and flexible, individualized correction procedures, implemented by teachers throughout the first year of school. Intervention group boys with high initial levels of depressive symptoms and good gains in reading achievement reported lower levels of symptoms at the end of first grade. However, girls with high initial levels of depressive symptoms who made gains in reading achievement, reported lower levels of symptoms regardless of whether they attended intervention or control group classes. These interventions show promise as prevention strategies, for reducing depressive symptoms in younger children.

What Doesn't Work?

Research related to interpersonal problem-solving strategies has not been effective in reducing mental health problems when implemented universally, although they are effective in increasing competence (Durlak & Wells, 1997). Brief classroom-based programs are not as effective as longer multiyear programs in producing stable effects in children's knowledge, attitudes, and behavior in social competence. Also, school-based programs that are focused only on the child or the environment are less effective than strategies that focus on both simultaneously (Durlak, 2000).

Overall Comment

School- and family-based programs have been effective in preventing depression as children move into adolescence. However, better effects have been achieved by targeted programs, The majority of outcomes have been treatment effects related to reduction of symptoms and prevalence of disorders rather than prevention of symptoms or reductions in the incidence of depressive disorders.

Depression

The Penn Resiliency Program remains the best depression prevention program for children. It has positive outcomes for depressive symptoms and for disorders in high risk children, in three separate RCTs, and has shown effects across different cultural groups. However, it has shown null effects for depression in trials with Australian children conducted by research teams other than the program developers. Research on the prevention of depression in children indicates that both school-based and family-based interventions targeted at children with known risk factors, such as elevated depressive symptoms, poor social competence, and parental affective disorder, result in reductions in risk factors for depression, reductions in depressive symptoms, and changes to family contexts.

Other promising strategies with sound theoretical underpinnings and some empirical support include school-based interventions targeting anxiety, social skills, and low levels of social competence, plus environment-centered strategies such as parent and teacher consultations, and enriched curriculum materials that promote academic mastery. Strategies that are yet to be tested include universal interventions for all children regardless of risk, multiyear interventions, and those that integrate child- and family-centered strategies.

Bipolar Depression

Pavuluri et al. (2005) indicate that prodromal symptoms and a positive family history for BPD could be used to identify children and families for prevention or early intervention in high risk populations. So far only pharmacological interventions such as DVPX monotherapy have been trialed, with mixed findings. Chang et al. (2003) found a 79% response rate based on Clinical Global Improvement scores, while another study by Findling, Feeny, et al. (2000) found no significant benefit of DVPX compared to a placebo, when used as a preventive approach in children with high levels of risk for BPD.

RECOMMENDED BEST PRACTICE

Cognitive behavioral interventions run in small groups in schools currently offers the best treatment and prevention strategy for childhood depression. It is unclear at this stage if any psychosocial or pharmacological intervention could prevent childhood BPD.

Depression

The evidence base for the treatment and prevention of childhood depression is promising. Psychosocial treatments, in particular group-based CBT when conducted in school groups holds the most promise. Of the intervention programs available, Stark's (1990) program has the best level of empirical validation for treating depressive symptoms in children, and the Penn Resiliency Program (Gillham, Hamilton, et al., 2006) works in preventing depression in selected groups of children. However, as yet, no interventions have been effective for the treatment of children with depressive disorders in community outpatient settings. There is a significant need to develop or adapt school-based treatments for children suffering from depressive disorders if we are to prevent the reoccurring cycles of depression that are frequently seen in adolescence.

The SSRI, fluoxetine (Prozac) may be the most effective pharmacological treatment. RCTs of promising interventions with large sample sizes and measurement of disorder as well as symptoms will be important in the future for both psychosocial and pharmacological interventions.

Bipolar Disorder

In contrast, the evidence base for treatment of BPD is limited with virtually no evidence for prevention. The use of psychosocial interventions for pediatric BPD is at an early stage with RCTs underway, but currently unpublished. However, practice guidelines are available that provide best practice clinical advice for working with these complex cases and supporting families (Mackinaw-Koons & Fristad, 2004). Promising psychosocial interventions include child- and family-focused therapies that aim to promote understanding of the illness and adherence to medical treatments, and change the family environments to reduce and manage psychosocial stressors (Pavuluri et al., 2005). As yet no pharmacological agent or combination or drugs has been found to work for this early onset BPD. It is clear that monotherapy involving mood stabilisers (e.g., lithium) or antipsychotic treatments (e.g., DVPX and risperidone) are unlikely to be effective, and that a combination of drugs and psychosocial interventions for both children and parents may be required to manage this more complex disorder.

REFERENCES

Abela, J. R. Z., Brozina, K., & Haigh, E. P. (2002). An examination of the response styles theory of depression in third- and seventh-grade children: A short-term longitudinal study. *Journal of Abnormal Child Psychology, 30,* 515–527.

Abela, J. R. Z., Skitch, S. A., Adams, P., & Hankin, B. L. (2006). The timing of parent and child depression: A hopelessness theory perspective. *Journal of Clinical Child and Adolescent Psychology, 35,* 253–263.

Abela, J. R. Z., Vanderbilt, E., & Rochon, A. (2004). A test of the integration of the response styles and social support theories of depression in third and seventh grade children. *Journal of Social & Clinical Psychology, 23,* 653–674.

Abela, J. R. Z., Zuroff, D. C., Ho, M. R., Adams, P., & Hankin, B. L. (2006). Excessive reassurance seeking, hassles, and depressive symptoms in children of affectively ill parents: A multiwave longitudinal study. *Journal of Abnormal Child Psychology, 34,* 171–187.

Althoff, R. R., Faraone, S. V., Rettew, D. C., Morley, C. P., & Hudziak, J. J. (2005). Family, twin, adoption, and molecular genetic studies of juvenile bipolar disorder. *Bipolar Disorders, 7*, 598–609.

American Psychiatric Association. (2000). *Diagnostic and statistical manual of mental disorders* (4th ed., TR). Washington, D.C.: Author.

Angold, P. R., Costello, E. J., & Erkanli, A. (1999). Comorbidity. *Journal of Child Psychology and Psychiatry, 40*, 57–87.

Asarnow, J. R., Scott, C. V., & Mintz, J. (2002). A combined cognitive-behavioral family education intervention for depression in children: A treatment development study. *Cognitive Therapy Research, 26*, 221–229.

Asarnow, J. R., Thompson, M., Hamilton, E. B., & Goldstein, M. J. (1994). Family expressed emotion, child-hood-onset depression and childhood-onset schizophrenia spectrum disorders: Is expressed emotion a nonspecific correlate of child pathology or a specific risk factor for depression? *Journal of Abnormal Child Psychology, 22*, 129–146.

Avenevoli, S., Stolar, M., Li, J., Dierker, L.. & Merikangas, K. R. (2001). Comorbidity of depression in children and adolescents: Models and evidence from a prospective high-risk family study. *Society of Biological Psychiatry, 49*, 1071–1081.

Bar-Haim, Y., Perez-Edgar, K., Fox, N. A., Beck, J. M., West, G. M., & Bhangoo, R. K., et al. (2002). The emergence of childhood bipolar disorder: A prospective study from 4 months to 7 years of age. *Applied Developmental Psychology, 23*, 431–450.

Baumgartner, F. (2002). The effect of hardiness in the choice of coping strategies in stressful situations. *Studia and Psychologica, 44*, 69–74.

Beardslee, W. R., Keller, M. B., Lavori, P. W., Staley, J. E., & Sacks, N. (1993). The impact of affective disorder on depression in offspring: A longitudinal follow-up in a non-referred sample. *Journal of the American Academy of Child and Adolescent Psychiatry, 32*, 723–730.

Beardslee, W. R., Salt, P., Veersage, M. A., Gladstone, T. R. G., Wright, E. J., & Rothberg, P. C. (1997). Sustained change in parents receiving preventive interventions for families with depression. *American Journal of Psychiatry, 154,* 510–515.

Beardslee, W. R., Wright, E. J., Salt, P., Drezner, K., Gladstone, T. R. G., Versage, E. M., et al. (1997). Examination of children's responses to two prevention intervention strategies over time. *Journal of the American Academy of Child and Adolescent Psychiatry, 36*, 196–204.

Biederman, J., Faraone, S. V, Wozniak, J., Mick, E., Kwon, A., & Aleardi, M. (2004). Further evidence of unique developmental phenotypic correlates of pediatric bipolar disorder: Findings from a large sample of clinically referred preadolescent children assess over the last 7 years. *Journal of Affective Disorders, 82* (Suppl.), S45–S54.

Biederman, J., Faraone, S. V., Wozniak, J., Mick, E., Kwon, A., Cayton, G. A., et al. (2005). Clinical correlates of bipolar disorder in a large, referred sample of children and adolescents. *Journal of Psychiatric Research, 39*, 611–622.

Biederman, J., Kwon, A., Wozniak, J., Mick, E., Markowitz, S., Fazio, V., et al. (2004). Absence of gender differences in pediatric bipolar disorder: Findings from a large sample of referred youth. *Journal of Affective Disorders, 83*, 207–214.

Birmaher, B., Kennah, B. S., Brent, D., Ehmann, M., Bridge, J., & Axelson, D. (2002). Is bipolar disorder specially associated with panic disorder in youths? *Journal of Clinical Psychiatry, 63*, 414–419.

Birmaher, B., Ryan, N. D., Williamson, D. E., Brent, D. A., Kaufman, J., Dahl, R. E., et al. (1996). Childhood and adolescent depression: A review of the past 10 years. Part 1. *Journal of the American Academy of Child and Adolescent Psychiatry, 35*, 1427–1439.

Bostic, J. Q., Prince, J., Brown, K., & Place, S. (2001). A retrospective study of citalopram in adolescents with depression. *Journal of Child and Adolescent Psychopharmacology, 11*, 159–166.

Boyce-Rogers, K., & Rose, H. A. (2002). Risk and resiliency factors among adolescents who experience marital transitions. *Journal of Marriage and Family, 64*, 1024–1037.

Bruce, A. E., Cole, D. A., Dallaire, D. H. Jacquez, F. M., Pineda, A. Q., & LaGrange, B. (2006). Relations of parenting and negative life events to cognitive diatheses for depression in children. *Journal of Abnormal Child Psychology, 34*, 321–333.

Burke, L. (2003). The impacts of maternal depression on family relationships. *International Review of Psychiatry, 15*, 243–255.

Butler, L., Miezitis, S., Friedman, R., & Cole, E. (1980). The effect of two school-based intervention programs on depressive symptoms in pre-adolescents. *American Education Research Journal, 17*, 111–119.

Cardemil, E. V., Reivich, K. J., & Seligman, M. E. P. (2002). The prevention of depressive symptoms in low-income minority middle school students. *Prevention and Treatment, 5*, Article 8, np.

Chang, K. D., Adleman, N., Dienes, K., Goraly-Barnea, N., Reiss, A., & Ketter, T. (2003). Decreased nacetylas-partate in children with familial bipolar disorder. *Biological Psychiatry, 53*, 1059–1065.

Chang, K. D., Blaser, C., Ketter, T. A., & Steiner, H. (2001). Family environment of children and adolescents with bipolar disorder parents. *Bipolar Disorder, 3,* 73–78.

Cicchetti, D., & Toh, S. L. (1998). The development of depression in children and adolescents. *American Psychologist, 53,* 221–241.

Cole, D. A. (1990). The relation of social and academic competence to depressive symptoms in childhood. *Journal of Abnormal Psychology, 99,* 422–429.

Cole, D. A., & Jordan, A. E. (1995). Competence and memory: Integrating psychosocial and cognitive correlates of child depression. *Child Development, 66,* 459–473.

Cole, D. A., Peeke, L. G., Martin, J. M., Truglio, R., & Seroczynski, A. D. (1998). A longitudinal look at the relation between depression and anxiety in children and adolescents. *Journal of Consulting & Clinical Psychology, 66,* 451–460.

Cole, D. A., & Rehm, L. P. (1986). Family interaction patterns and childhood depression. *Journal of Abnormal Child Psychology, 14,* 297–314.

Compas, B. E., Connor-Smith, J., & Jaser, S. S. (2004). Temperament, stress reactivity and coping: Implications for depression in children and adolescents. *Journal of Clinical Child and Adolescent Psychology, 33,* 21–31.

Compton, S. N., Burns, B. J., Egger, H. L., & Robertson, E. (2002). Review of the evidence base for treatment of childhood psychopathology: Internalizing disorders. *Journal of Consulting and Clinical Psychology, 70,* 1240–1266.

Compton, S. N., March, J. S., Brent, D., Albano, A. M., Weersing, V. R., & Curry, J. (2004). Cognitive-behavioral psychotherapy for anxiety and depressive disorders in children and adolescents: An evidenced-based medicine review. *Journal of the American Academy of Child and Adolescent Psychiatry, 43,* 930–959.

Costello, E. J., Angold, A., Burns, B. J., Stangle, D. K., Tweed, D. L., Erkanli, A., et al. (1996).The Great Smokey Mountains study of youth: Goals, design, methods, and the prevalence of DSM-III-R disorders. *Archives of General Psychiatry, 53,* 1129–1136.

Costello, E. J., Mustillo, S., Erkanli, A., Keeler, G., & Angold, A. (2003). Prevalence and development of psychiatric disorders in childhood and adolescence. *Archives of General Psychiatry, 60,* 837–844.

Curry, J. (2001). Specific psychotherapies for childhood and adolescent depression. *Biological Psychiatry, 49,* 1091–1100.

Dahl, R. E., Birmaher, B., Williamson, D. E., Dorn, L., Perel, J., Kaufman, J., et al. (2000). Low growth hormone response to growth hormone-releasing hormone in child depression. *Society of Biological Psychiatry, 48,* 981–988.

Dilsaver, S. C., & Akiskal, H. S. (2004). Preschool-onset mania: incidence, phenomenology and family history. *Journal of Affective Disorders, 82*(Suppl.), S35–S43.

Dineen, K. A., & Hadwin, J. A. (2004). Anxious and depressive symptoms and children's judgments of their own and others' interpretation of ambiguous social scenarios. *Journal of Anxiety Disorders, 18,* 499–513.

Downey, G., & Coyne, J. C. (1990). Children of depressed parents: An integrative review. *Psychological Bulletin, 108,* 50–76.

Drabick, D. A. G., Beauchaine, T. P., Gadow, K. D., Carlson, G. A., & Bromet, E. J. (2006). Risk factors for conduct disorder and depressive symptoms in a cohort of Ukrainian children. *Journal of Clinical Child and Adolescent Psychology, 35,* 244–252.

Durlak, J. A. (2000). Health promotion as a strategy in primary prevention. In D. Cicchetti, J. Rappaport, I. Sandler, & R. P. Weissberg (Eds.), *The promotion of wellness in children and adolescents* (pp. 221–242). Washington, D.C.: CWLA Press.

Durlak, J. A., & Wells, A. M. (1997). Primary prevention mental health programs for children and adolescents: A meta-analytic review. *American Journal of Community Psychology, 25,* 115–152.

Eaves, L., Silberg, J., Meyer, J. M., Maes, H. H., Simonoff, E., Pickles, A., et al. (1997). Genetics and developmental psychopathology: 2. The main effects of genetics and environment on behavioral problems in the Virginia twin study of adolescent behavioral development. *Journal of Child Psychology and Psychiatry, 38,* 965–980.

Eley, T. C. (1999). Behavioral genetics as a tool for developmental psychology: Anxiety and depression in adolescents. *Clinical Child and Family Psychology Review, 2,* 21–36.

Eley, T. C. Deater-Deckard, K., Fombonne, E., Fulker, D. W., & Plomin, R. (1998). An adoption study of depressive symptoms in middle childhood. *Journal of Child Psychology and Psychiatry, 39,* 337–345.

Emerson, C. S., Mollet, G. A., & Harrison, D. W. (2005). Anxious-depression in boys: An evaluation of executive functioning. *Archives of Clinical Neuropsychology, 20,* 539–546.

Emslie, G. J., & Mayes, T. L. (2001). Mood disorders in children and adolescents: psychopharmacological treatment. *Biological Psychiatry, 49,* 1082–1090.

Emslie, G. J., Heiligenstein, J. H., Wagner, K. D., Hoog, S. L., Ernest, D. E., Brown, E., et al. (2002). Fluoxetine for acute treatment of depression in children and adolescents: A placebo-controlled, randomized clinical trial. *Journal of the American Academy of Child and Adolescent Psychiatry, 41,* 1205–1215.

Emslie, G. J., Rush, A. J., Weinberg, W. A., Kowatch, R. A., Carmody, T., & Mayes, T. L. (1998). Fluoxetine in child and adolescent depression: Acute and maintenance treatment. *Anxiety Depression, 7,* 32–39.

Emslie, G. J., Rush, A. J., Weinberg, W. A., Kowatch, R. A., Hughes, C. W., & Carmody, T. (1997). A double-blind, randomized, placebo-controlled trial of fluoxetine in children and adolescents with depression. *Archives of General Psychiatry, 54,* 1031–103.

Faedda, G. L., Baldessarini, R, J., Glovinsky, I. P., & Austin, N. B. (2004). Pediatric bipolar disorder: phenomenology and course of illness. *Bipolar Disorder, 6,* 305–313.

Felsman, J. K., & Vaillant, G. E. (1987). Resilient children as adults: A 40 year study. In E. J. Anthony & B. J. Cohler (Eds.), *The invulnerable child* (pp. 289–314). New York: Guilford.

Ferguson, D. M., Horwood, L. J., & Lynsky, N. T. (1995). Maternal depressive symptoms and depressive symptoms in adolescents. *Journal of Child Psychology and Psychiatry, 36,* 1161–1178.

Findling, R. L., Feeny, N. C., Stansbrey, R. J., DelPorto-Bedoya, D., & Demeter, C. (2002). Somatic treatment for depressive illnesses in children and adolescents. *Child and Adolescent Psychiatric Clinics of North America, 11,* 555–578.

Findling, R. L., Gracious, B. L., McNamara, N. K., & Calabrese, J. R. (2000). The rationale, design and progress of two novel maintenance treatment studies in pediatric bipolarity. *Acta Neuropsychiatrica, 12,* 136–138.

Findling, R. L., Youngstrom, E. A., McNamara, N. K., Stansbrey, R. J., Demeter, C. A., Bedoya, D., et al. (2005). Early symptoms of mania and the role of parental risk. *Bipolar Disorders, 7,* 623–634.

Finkelstein, J. S., Donenberg, & Martinovich, Z. (2001). Maternal control and adolescent depression: Ethnic differences among clinically referred girls. *Journal of Youth and Adolescence, 30,* 155–171.

Forbes, E. E., Williamson, D. E., Ryan, N. D., Birmaher, B., Axelson, D. A., & Dahl, R. E. (2005). Peri-sleep-onset cortisol levels in children and adolescents with affective disorder. *Biological Psychiatry, 59,* 24–30.

Fristad, M. A., Arnett, M. M., & Gavazzi, S. M. (1998). The impact of psychoeducational workshops on families with mood-disordered children. *Family Therapy, 25,* 151–159.

Fristad, M. A., Gavazzi, S. M., & Mackinaw-Koons, B. (2003). Family psychoeducation: an adjunctive intervention for children with bipolar disorder. *Biological Psychiatry, 53,* 1000–1008.

Fristad, M. A., Gavazzi, S. M., & Soldano, K. W. (1998). Multi-family psychoeducation groups for childhood mood disorders: A program description and preliminary efficacy data. *Contemporary Family Therapy, 20,* 385–402.

Garber, J., & Horowitz, J. L. (2002). Depression in children. In I. H. Gotlib & C. L. Hammen (Eds.), *Handbook of depression* (pp. 510–540). New York: Guilford.

Garno, J. L., Goldberg, J. F., Ramirez, P. M. & Ritzler, B. A. (2005). The impact of childhood abuse on the clinical course of bipolar disorder. *British Journal of Psychiatry, 186,* 121–125.

Ge, X., Lorenz, F. O., Conger, R. D., Elder, G. H., & Simmons, R. L. (1994). Trajectories of stressful life events and depressive symptoms during adolescence. *Developmental Psychology, 30,* 467–483.

Geller, B., Craney, J. L., Bolhofner, K., Nickelsberg, M. J., Williams, M., & Zimerman, B. (2002). Two-year prospective follow-up of children with a prepubertal and early adolescent dipolar disorder phenotype. *American Journal of Psychiatry, 159,* 927–933.

Geller, B., Fox, L. W., & Clark, K. A. (1994). Rate and predictors of prepubertal bipolarity during follow-up of 6- to 12-year old depressed children. *Journal of the American Academy of Child and Adolescent Psychiatry, 33,* 461–468.

Geller, B., & Luby, J. (1997). Child and adolescent bipolar disorder: A review of the past 10 years. *Journal of the American Academy of Child and Adolescent Psychiatry, 36,* 1168–1176.

Geller, B., Reising, D., Leonard, H. L., Riddle, M. A., & Walsh, B. T. (1999). Critical review of tricyclic antidepressant use in children and adolescents. *Journal of the American Academy of Child and Adolescent Psychiatry, 38,* 513–516.

Geller, B., Zimerman, B., Williams, M., Bolhofner, K., Craney, J. L., Delbello, M. P., et al. (2000). Diagnostic characteristics of 93 cases of prepubertal and early adolescent bipolar disorder phenotype by gender, puberty and comorbid attention deficit hyperactivity disorder. *Journal of Child and Adolescent Psychopharmacology, 10,* 157–164.

Gibb, B. E., & Coles, M. E. (2005). Cognitive vulnerability-stress models of psychopathology: A developmental perspective. In B. L. Hankin & J. R. Z. Abela (Eds.), *Development of psychopathology: A vulnerability-stress perspective* (pp. 104–135). Thousand Oaks, CA: Sage.

Gillham, J. E., Hamilton, J., Freres, D. R., Patton, K., & Gallop, R. (2006). Preventing depression among early adolescents in the primary care setting: a randomized controlled study of the Penn Resiliency Program. *Journal of Abnormal Child Psychology, 34,* 203–219.

Gillham, J. E., & Reivich, K. J. (1999). Prevention of depressive symptoms in school children: Update. *Psychological Science, 10,* 461–462.

Gillham, J. E., Reivich, K. J, Jaycox, L. H., & Seligman, M. E. P. (1995). Prevention of depressive symptoms in school children: Two-year follow-up. *Psychological Science, 6*, 343–351.

Gladstone, T., & Kaslow, N. (1995). Depression and attributions in children and adolescents: A meta-analytic review. *Journal of Abnormal Child Psychology, 23*, 597–606.

Gladstone, T. R. G., & Beardslee, W. R. (2000). The prevention of depression in at-risk adolescents: Current and future directions. *Journal of Cognitive Psychotherapy: An International Quarterly, 14*, 9–23.

Goodman, S. H., Gravitt, G. W., & Kaslow, N. J. (1995). Social problem solving: A moderator of the relation between negative life stress and depression symptoms in children. *Journal of Abnormal Child Psychology, 23*, 473–485.

Goodyer, I. M., & Altham, P. M. (1991). Lifetime exit events and recent social and family adversities in anxious and depressed school-age children and adolescents: II. *Journal of Affective Disorders, 21*, 229–238.

Grant, K. E., Compas, B. E., Thurm, A. E., McMahon, S. D., & Gipson, P. Y., (2004). Stressors and child and adolescent psychopathology: Measurement issues and prospective effects. *Journal of Clinical Child and Adolescent Psychology, 33*, 412–425.

Grant, K. E., Compas, B. E., Thurm, A. E., McMahon, S. D., Gipson, P. Y., Campbell, A. J., et al. (2006). Stressors and child and adolescent psychopathology: Evidence of moderating and mediating effects. *Clinical Psychology Review, 26*, 257–283.

Hammen, C., Burge, D., & Adrian, C. (1991). Timing of mothers and child depression in a longitudinal study of children at risk. *Journal of Consulting and Clinical Psychology, 59*, 341–345.

Hammen, C., Shih, J. H., & Brennan, P. A. (2004). Intergenerational transmission of depression: test of an interpersonal stress model. *Journal of Consulting and Clinical Psychology, 72*, 511–522.

Hankin, B. L., Abramson, L. Y., Moffitt, T. E., Silva, P. A., McGee, R., & Angell, K. E. (1998). Development of depression from pre-adolescence to young adulthood: Emerging gender differences in a 10-year longitudinal study. *Journal of Abnormal Psychology, 107*, 128–140.

Hazell, P., O'Connell, D., Heathcote, D., Robertson, J., & Henry, D. (1995). Efficacy of tricyclic drugs in child and adolescent depression: A meta-analysis. *British Medical Journal, 3*, 897–901.

Heskin, K. (1980). *Northern Ireland: Psychological analysis.* New York: Columbia University Press.

Horowitz, J. L., & Garber, J. (2006). The prevention of depressive symptoms in children and adolescents: A meta-analytic review. *Journal of Consulting and Clinical Psychology, 74*, 401–415.

Ivanenko, A., Crabtree, V. M., & Gozal, D. (2005). Sleep and depression in children and adolescents. *Sleep Medicine Reviews, 9*, 115–129.

Jackson, Y., & Warren, J. S. (2000). Appraisal, social support, and life events: Predicting outcome behavior in school-age children. *Child Development, 71*, 1441–1457.

Jaycox, L. H., Reivich, K. J., Gillham, J., & Seligman, M. E. P. (1994). Preventing depressive symptoms in school children. *Behaviour Research and Therapy, 32*, 801–816.

Kahn, J. S., Kehle, T. J., Jenson, W. R., & Clarke, E. (1990). Comparison of cognitive behavioral, relaxation, and self-modeling interventions for depression amongst middle-school students. *School Psychology Review, 19*, 196–211.

Kellam, S. G., Bebok, G. W., Mayer, L. S., Ialongo, N., & Kalodner, C. R. (1994). Depressive symptoms over first grade and their response to a developmental epidemiologically based prevention trial aimed at improving achievement. *Development and Psychopathology, 6*, 473–481.

Keller, M. B., Ryan, N. D, Strober, M., Klein, R. G., Kutcher, S. P., Birmaher, B., et al. (2001). Efficacy of Paroxetine in the treatment of adolescent major depression: A randomized controlled trial. *Journal of the American Academy of Child and Adolescent Psychiatry, 40*, 762–772.

Kessler, R. C., Avenevoli, S., & Merkingas, K. R. (2001). Mood disorders in children and adolescents: An epidemiological perspective. *Biological Psychiatry, 49*, 1002–1014.

King, C. A., & Kirschenbaum, D. S. (1990). An experimental evaluation of a school-based program for children at risk: Wisconsin early intervention. *Journal of Community Psychology, 18*, 167–177.

Kovacs, M. (1996). Presentation and course of major depressive disorder during childhood and later years of the life span. *Journal of the American Academy of Child and Adolescent Psychiatry, 35*, 705–715.

Kowatch, R. A., Fristad, M., Birmaher, B., Wagner, K. D., Findling, R. L., & Hellander, M. (2005). Treatment guidelines for children and adolescents with bipolar disorder. *Journal of the American Academy of Child and Adolescent Psychiatry, 44*, 213–235.

Kumpulainen, K., & Rasanen, E. (2002). Symptoms of deviant behavior among eight-year-olds as predictors of referral for psychiatric evaluation by age 12. *Psychiatric Services, 53*, 201–206.

Leverich, G. S., & Post, R. M. (2006). Courses of bipolar illness after a history of childhood trauma. *The Lancet, 367*, 1040–1042.

Lewinsohn, P. M., Clarke, G. N., Seeley, J. R., & Rohde, P. (1994). Major depression in community adolescents: Age at onset, episode duration, and time to recurrence. *Journal of the American Academy of Child and Adolescent Psychiatry, 33*, 714–722.

Lewinsohn, P. M., & Essau, C. A. (2002). Depression in adolescence. In I. H. Gotlib & C. L. Hammen (Eds.), *Handbook of depression* (pp. 541–559). New York: Guilford.

Lewinsohn, P. M., Klein, D. N., & Seeley, J. R. (1995). Bipolar disorders in a community sample of older adolescents: Prevalence, phenomenology, comorbidity and course. *Journal of the American Academy of Child and Adolescent Psychiatry, 34,* 454–463.

Lowry-Webster, H., Barrett, P. M., & Dadds M. R. (2001). A universal prevention trial of anxiety and depression symptomatology in childhood: Preliminary data from an Australian Study. *Behaviour Change, 18,* 36–50.

Lowry-Webster, H., Barrett, P. M., & Lock, S. (2003). A universal prevention trial of anxiety symtomology during childhood: Results at 1-year follow-up. *Behaviour Change, 20,* 25–43.

Luthar, S. S. (1991). Vulnerability and resilience: A study of high risk adolescents. *Child Development, 62,* 600–616.

Lyons-Ruth, K., Eastbrook, M. A., & Cibelli, C. D. (1997). Infant attachment strategies, infant mental lag, and maternal depressive symptoms: Predictors of internalizing and externalizing problems at age 7. *Developmental Psychology, 33,* 681–692.

Ma, J., Lee, K., & Stafford, R. S. (2005). Depression treatment during outpatient visits by U.S. children and adolescents. *Journal of Adolescent Health, 37,* 434–442.

Mackinaw-Koons, B., & Fristad, M. A. (2004). Children with bipolar disorder: how to break down barriers and work effectively together. *Professional Psychology: Research and Practice, 35,* 481–484.

Masi, G., Perugi, G., Toni, C., Millepiedi, S., Mucci, M., Bertini, N., et al. (2006). Attention-deficit hyperactivity disorder—Bipolar comorbidity in children and adolescents. *Bipolar Disorders, 8,* 373–-381.

McGee, R., Freehan, M., Williams, S., & Anderson, J. (1992). DSM-III disorders from age 11–15 years. *Journal of the American Academy of Child and Adolescent Psychiatry, 31,* 50–59.

Merry, S., McDowell, H., Hetrick, S., Bir J., & Muller, N. (2005). Psychological and/or educational interventions for the prevention of depression in children and adolescents. *The Cochrane Database of Systematic Reviews, Issue 3* http://www.thecochranelibrary.com

Michael, K. D., & Crowley, S. L. (2002). How effective are treatments for child and adolescent depression? A meta-analytic review. *Clinical Psychology Review, 22,* 247–269.

Miklowitz, D. J., George, E. L., & Axelson, D. A., (2004). Family-focused treatment for adolescents with bipolar disorder. *Journal of Affective Disorders, 82S1,* S113–S128.

Miklowitz, D. J., Goldstein M., Nuechterlein K., Synder K., & Mintz J. (1988). Family factors and the course of bipolar affective disorder. *Archives of General Psychiatry, 45,* 225–231.

Miklowitz, D. J., & Johnson, S. L. (2006). The psychopathology of bipolar disorder. *Annual Review of Clinical Psychology, 2,* 199–235.

Muris, P., & van der Heiden, S. (2006). Anxiety, depression, and judgments about the probability of future negative and positive events in children. *Journal of Anxiety Disorders, 20,* 252–261.

Nilzen, K. R., & Palmérus, K. (1997). The influence of familial factors on anxiety and depression in childhood and early adolescence. *Adolescence, 32,* 935–943.

Olson, P. M., & Pacheco, M. R. (2005). Bipolar disorder in school-age children. *Journal of School Nursing, 21,* 152–157.

Papini, D. R., Roggman, L. A., & Anderson, J. (1991). Early-adolescent perceptions of attachment to mother and father: A test of emotional-distancing and buffering hypotheses. *Journal of Early Adolescence, 11,* 258–275.

Pattison, C., & Lynd-Stevenson, R. M. (2001). The prevention of depressive symptoms in children: The immediate and long-term outcomes of a school-based program. *Behaviour Change, 18,* 92–102.

Pavuluri, M. N., Birmaher, B., & Naylor, M. N. (2005). Pediatric bipolar disorder: a review of the past 10 years. *Journal of the American Academy of Child and Adolescent Psychiatry, 44,* 846–875.

Pavuluri, M. N., Graczyk, P. A., Henry, D. B., Carbray, J. A., Heidenreich, J., & Miklowitz, D. J. (2004). Child- and family-focused cognitive-behavioral therapy for pediatric bipolar disorder: Development and preliminary results. *Journal of the American Academy of Child and Adolescent Psychiatry, 43,* 528–539.

Pike, A., McGuire, S., Hetherington, E. M., Reiss, D., & Plomin, R. (1996). Early environmental and adolescent depressive symptoms and antisocial behavior: A multivariate genetic analysis. *Journal of Child Psychology & Psychiatry and Allied Disciplines, 37,* 695–704.

Piko, B. F., & Fitzpatrick, K. M. (2003). Depressive symptomatology among Hungarian youth: A risk and protective factors approach. *American Journal of Orthopsychiatry, 73,* 44–54.

Post, R. M., Chang, K. D., Findling, R. L., Geller, B., Kowatch, R. A., Kutcher, S. P., et al. (2004). Prepubertal bipolar I disorder and bipolar disorder NOS are separable from ADHD. *Journal of Clinical Psychiatry, 67,* 898–902.

Quayle, D., Dziurawiec, S., Roberts, C., Kane, R., & Ebsworthy, G. (2001). The effect of an optimism and life skills program on depressive symptoms in preadolescence. *Behaviour Change, 18,* 194–203.

Rapee, R. M. (1997). Potential role of childrearing practices in the development of anxiety and depression. *Clinical Psychology Review, 17*, 47–67.

Rehm, L. P., & Sharp, R. N. (1996). Strategies for childhood depression. In M. A. Reinecke, F. M. Dattilio, & A. Freeman (Eds.), *Cognitive therapy for children and adolescents: A case book for clinical practice* (pp. 103–123). New York: Guildford.

Reichart, C. G., & Nolen, W. A. (2004). Earlier onset of bipolar disorder in children by antiprepressants or stimulants? A hypothesis. *Journal of Affective Disorders, 78*, 81–84.

Reijneveld, S.A., Crone, M. R., Verhulst, F. C., & Verloove-Vanhorick, S P. (2003). The effects of severe disaster on the mental health of adolescents: a controlled study. *The Lancet, 362*, 691–696.

Reinherz, H. Z., Giaconia, R. M., Pakiz, B., Silverman, A. B., Frost, A. K., & Lefkowitz, E. S. (1993). Psychosocial risks for major depression in late adolescence: a longitudinal community study. *Journal of the American Academy of Child and Adolescent Psychiatry, 32*, 1159–1164.

Reinherz, H. Z., Stewart-Berghauer, G., Pakiz, B., Frost, A. K., Moeykens, B. A., & Holmes, W. M. (1989). The relationship of early risk and current mediators to depressive symptomatology in adolescents. *Journal of the American Academy of Child and Adolescent Psychiatry, 28*, 942–947.

Reivich, K. J., Gillham, J. E., Chaplin T. M., & Seligman, M. E. P. (2005). From helplessness to optimism: The role of resilience in treating and preventing depression in youth. In S. Goldstein & R. Brooks (Eds.), *Handbook of resilience in children* (pp. 223–237). New York: Kluwer Academic/Plenum.

Rice, F., Harold, G. T., & Thapar, A. (2002). Assessing the effects of age, sex and shared environment on the aetiology of depressive symptoms in childhood and adolescence. *Journal of Child Psychology and Psychiatry, 43*, 1039–1051.

Rice, F., Harold, G. T., & Thapar, A. (2003). Negative life events as an account of age-related differences in the genetic aetiology of depression in childhood and adolescence. *Journal of Child Psychology Psychiatry, 44*, 977–987.

Rice, F., Harold, G. T., & Thapar, A. (2005). The link between depression in mothers and offspring: An extended twin analysis. *Behaviour Genetics, 35*, 565–577.

Richman, J. A., & Flaherty, J. A. (1987). Adult psychosocial assets and depressive mood over time: Effects of internalized childhood attachments. *Journal of Nervous and Mental Disease, 175*, 703–712.

Roberts, C., Kane, R., Bishop, B., Matthews, H., & Thomson, H. (2004). The prevention of depressive symptoms in rural school children: A follow-up study. *The International Journal of Mental Health Promotion, 6*, 4–16.

Rosso, I. M., Cintron, C. M., Steingard, R. J., Renshaw, P. F., Young, A. D., & Yurgelun-Todd, D.A. (2005). Amygdala and hippocampus volumes in pediatric major depression. *Biological Psychiatry, 57*, 21–26.

Rudolph, K. D., Hammen, C., & Burge, D. (1994). Interpersonal functioning and depressive symptoms in childhood: Addressing the issues of specificity and comorbidity. *Journal of Abnormal Child Psychology, 22*, 355–371.

Rudolph, K. D., Hammen, C., Burge, D., Lindberg, N., Herzberg, D., & Daley, S. E. (2000). Toward an interpersonal life-stress model of depression: The developmental context of stress generation. *Development and Psychopathology, 12*, 215–234.

Ryan, M. A., Findling, R. L., Emslie, G. J., Marcus, R. N., Fernandez, L. A., D'Amico, M. F., et al. (2002, May 18–23). *Efficacy and safety of nefazodone in adolescents with MDD.* Poster session presented at the 155th Annual Meeting of the American Psychiatric Association, Philadelphia, PA.

Ryan, N. D. (2001). Diagnosing pediatric depression. *Biological Psychiatry, 49*, 1050–1054.

Ryan, N. D. (2005). Treatment of depression in children and adolescents. *The Lancet, 366*, 933–940.

Sawyer, M. G., Arney, F. M., Baghurst, P. A., Clark, J. J., Graetz, B. W., Kosky, R. J., et al. (2000). *Child and adolescent component of the national survey of mental health and wellbeing* (Government report). Canberra, Australia: Mental Health and Special programs Branch, Commonwealth Department of Health and Aged Care.

Scheffer, R., Kowatch, R., Carmody, T., & Rush, J. (2005). Randomized placebo-controlled trial of Dexedrine for symptoms of comorbid ADHD in pediatric bipolar disorder. *American Journal of Psychiatry, 162*, 58–64.

Seligman, M. E. P., Reivich, K., Jaycox, L., & Gillham, J. (1995). *The optimistic child: A revolutionary approach to raising resilient children.* Sydney, Australia: Random House.

Seroczynski, A. D., Cole, D. A., & Maxwell, S. E. (1997). Cumulative and compensatory effects of competence and incompetence on depressive symptoms in children. *Journal of Abnormal Psychology, 106*, 586–597.

Simeon, J. G., Dinicola, V. F., Ferguson, H. B., & Copping, W. (1990). Adolescent depression: A placebo-controlled fluoxetine treatment study and follow-up. *Progress in Neuropsychopharmacology & Biological Psychiatry, 14*, 791–795.

Skaer, T. L., Robinson, L. M., Sclar, D. A., & Galin, R. S. (2000). Treatment of depressive illness among children and adolescents in the United States. *Current Therapeutic Research, 61*, 692–705.

Son, S. E., & Kirchner, J. T. (2000). Depression in children and adolescents. *American Family Physician, 62*(10), 2297.

Sorensen, M. J. Nissen, J. B., Mors, O., & Thomson, P. H. (2005). Age and gender differences in depressive symtomatology and comorbidity: An incident sample of psychiatrically admitted children. *Journal of Affective Disorders, 84,* 85–91.

Stark, K. (1990). *Childhood depression: School-based intervention.* New York: Guildford Press.

Stark, K. D., Brockman, C. S., & Fraser, R. (1990). A comprehensive school-based treatment program for depressed children. *School Psychology Quarterly, 5,* 111–140.

Stark, K. D., Reynolds, W. M., & Kaslow, N. J. (1987). A comparison of the relative efficacy of self-control therapy and a behavioral problem-solving therapy for depression in children. *Journal of Abnormal Child Psychology, 15,* 91–113.

Stewart, D., Sun, J., Patterson, C., Lemerle, K., & Hardie, M. (2004). Promoting and building resilience in primary school communities: Evidence from a comprehensive "health promoting school" approach. *International Journal of Mental Health Promotion, 6,* 26–33.

Sund, A. M., & Wichstrøm, L. (2002). Insecure attachment as a risk factor for future depressive symptoms in early adolescents. *Journal of the American Academy of Child and Adolescence Psychiatry, 41,* 1478–1486.

Thurber, S., Ensign, J., Punnett, A. F., & Welter, K. (1995). A meta-analysis of antidepressant outcome studies that involved children and adolescents. *Journal of Clinical Psychology, 51,* 340–345.

Treatment for Adolescents with Depression Study (TADS) Team (2004). Fluoxetine, cognitive-behavioral therapy, and the combination for adolescents with depression. *Journal of the American Medical Association, 292,* 807–820.

Thaper, A., & McGuffin, P. (1994). A twin study of depressive symptoms in childhood. *British Journal of Psychiatry, 65,* 259–265.

Tiet, Q. Q., Bird, H. R., Davies, M., Hoven, C., Cohen, P., Jenson, P., et al. (1998). Adverse life events and resilience. *Journal of the American Academy of Child and Adolescent Psychiatry, 37,* 1191–1200.

Timbremont, B., & Braet, C. (2004). Cognitive vulnerability in remitted depressed children and adolescents. *Behavior Research and Therapy, 42,* 423–437.

Turner, H. A., Finkelhor, D., & Ormrod, R. (2006). The effect of lifetime victimization on the mental health of children and adolescents. *Journal Social Science and Medicine, 62,* 13–27.

U.S. Food and Drug Administration. (2003). FDA Statement regarding the antidepressant Paxil for pediatric depression. FDA Talk Paper. June 19, 2003. Retrieved from: http:/www.fda.gov/bbs/topics/AN-SWERS/2003/ANSO1230.html

Varley, C. K. (2003). Psychopharmacological treatment for major depressive disorder in children and adolescents. *Journal of the American Medical Association, 290,* 1091–1093.

Vasa, R. A., Carlino, A. R., & Pine, D. S. (2006). Pharmacotherapy of depressed children and adolescents: Current issues and potential directions. *Biological Psychiatry, 59,* 1021–1028.

Verdeli, H., Ferro, T., Wickramaratne, P., Greenwald, S., Blanco, C., & Weissman, M. M. (2004). Treatment of depressed mothers of depressed children: Pilot study of feasibility. *Depression and Anxiety, 19,* 51–58.

Vostanis, P., Feehan, C., & Grattan, E. (1996). Two-year outcome of children treated for depression. *European Child and Adolescent Psychiatry, 7,* 12–18.

Vostanis, P., Feehan, C., Grattan, E., & Bickerton, W. L. (1996a). A randomized controlled out-patient trial of cognitive-behavioral treatment for children and adolescents with depression: 9-month follow-up. *Journal of Affective Disorders, 40,* 105–116.

Vostanis, P., Feehan, C., Grattan, E., & Bickerton, W. L. (1996b). Treatment for children and adolescents with depression: Lessons from a controlled trial. *Clinical Child Psychology and Psychiatry, 1,* 199–212.

Wagner, K. D. (2005). Pharmacotherapy for major depression in children and adolescents. *Progress in Neuro-Psychopharmacology & Biological Psychiatry, 29,* 819–826.

Wagner, K. D., Ambrosini, P., Ryan, M., Wohlberg, C., Yang, R., Greenbaum, M. S., et al. (2003). Efficacy of sertraline in the treatment of children and adolescents with major depressive disorder. *Journal of the American Medical Association, 290,* 1033–1041.

Wagner, K. D., Robb, A. S., Findling, R. L., Jin, J., Gutierrez, M., & Heydorn, W. E. (2004). A randomized, placebo-controlled trial of citalopram for the treatment of major depression in children and adolescents. *American Journal of Psychiatry, 161,* 1079–1083.

Walsh, F. (2003). Family resilience: A framework for clinical practice: Theory and practice. *Family Process, 42,* 1–18.

Warner, V., Mufson, L., & Weissman, M. M. (1995). Offspring at high and low risk for depression and anxiety: Mechanisms of psychiatric disorder. *Journal of the American Academy of Child and Adolescence Psychiatry, 34,* 786–797.

Weissman, M. M., Warner, V., Wickramaratne, P., Moreau, D., & Olfson, M. (1997). Offspring of depressed parents: Ten years later. *Archives of General Psychiatry, 54,* 932–940.

Weisz, J. R., Thurber, C. A., Sweeney, L., Proffitt, V. D., & LeGagnoux, G. L. (1997). Brief treatment of mild-to-moderate child depression using primary and secondary control enhancement training. *Journal of Consulting and Clinical Psychology, 65,* 703–707.

Wichstrøm, L. (1999). The emergence of gender difference in depressed mood during adolescence: The role of intensified gender socialization. *Developmental Psychology, 35,* 232–245.

Williamson, G. M., Walters, A. S., & Shaffer, D. R. (2002). Caregiver models of self and others, coping and depression: Predictors of depression in children with chronic pain. *Health Psychology, 21,* 405–410.

Wittington, C. J., Kendall, T., Fonagy, P., Cottrell, D., Cotgrove, A., & Boddington, E. (2004). Selective serotonin reuptake inhibitors in childhood depression: Systematic review of published and unpublished data. *The Lancet, 363,* 1341–1345.

Wolkow, K. E., & Ferguson, H. B. (2001). Community factors in the development of resiliency: Considerations and future directions. *Community Mental Health Journal, 37,* 489–498.

World Health Organization. (2006). *International statistical classification of diseases and related health problems* (10th rev., 2nd ed.). Geneva: WHO.

Wozniak, J., Spencer, T., Biederman, J., Kwon, A., Monuteaux, M., Rettew, J., et al. (2004). The clinical characteristics of unipolar and bipolar major depression in ADHD youth. *Journal of Affective Disorders, 82S,* S59–S69.

Yu, D. L., & Seligman, M. E. P. (2002). Preventing depressive symptoms in Chinese children. *Prevention and Treatment, 5,* Article 9, np.

Zubernis, L. S., Cassidy, K. W., Gillham, J. E., Reivich, K. J., & Jaycox, L. H. (1999). Prevention of depressive symptoms in pre-adolescent children of divorce. *Journal of Divorce & Remarriage, 30,* 11–35.

Chapter Thirteen

ADHD in Childhood

Adam J. Schwebach, Miriam Mulsow,
and Derek J. Schwebach

INTRODUCTION

Attention deficit/hyperactivity disorder (ADHD) is one of the most common childhood disorders, reaching prevalence rates of 5% to 16% (American Psychiatric Association, 1994; Barbaresi et al., 2002). On average, these estimates place at least one child with ADHD in every classroom in America, making accurate assessment of the disorder and the use of effective interventions for reducing impairment characteristic of children with ADHD a significant issue for all school personnel (Fabiano & Pelham, 2003).

Children with ADHD display persistent problems with inattention, impulsivity, and hyperactivity relative to children of their same age and sex, which results in clinical impairment across multiple settings in the child's life. Factor analysis studies have repeatedly identified these two very distinct behavioral dimensions underlying the symptoms that characterize children with ADHD (Barkley, 2003). Furthermore, these domains have been identified across various ethnic and cultural groups (Beiser, Dion, & Gotowiec, 2000).

Specifically, these dimensions include symptoms related to impulse control and attention regulation. For example, children with ADHD have difficulty with excessive activity level and fidgetiness. Children with ADHD are more restless than children without ADHD (Barkley & Cunningham, 1978). They may talk excessively, interrupt others during activities, and be less able than others their age to wait in line. They may also act impulsively without considering the consequences of their actions (American Psychiatric Association, 1994). Children with ADHD are often described by their teachers or parents as acting as if they are driven by a motor or appear to always be on the go (Barkley, 2003).

Second, children with ADHD have difficulty sustaining attention to tasks, lacking persistence of effort or vigilance (Douglas, 1983). They may be easily distracted and have difficulty reengaging in tasks following disruption (Barkley, 1997a). They have trouble with following through on rules and instructions and may be easily distracted while doing so. They are often described as being disorganized, inattentive, and forgetful in routine activities, and they display carelessness in their work.

Although the symptoms of ADHD are often described in behavioral terms (e.g., poor impulse control or trouble remaining on task), Barkley (2003) has suggested children with ADHD most likely represent deficits in executive functions (e.g., planning and organization) and working memory. Barkley (1997b, 2003) defined "executive functions" as neuropsychological processes that permit or assist with human "self-regulation." Self-regulation has been defined as any behavior by a person that modifies the probability of a subsequent behavior by that person so as to alter the probability of a later consequence (Kanfer & Karoly, 1972). The role that cognitive actions play in shaping and modifying future behavior has led to the view that problems with ADHD most likely arise out of some dysfunction in the brain region associated with these functions (Barkley, 2003).

For example, children with ADHD have been shown to have difficulty with working memory tasks involving backward digit span, mental arithmetic, paced auditory serial addition, paired-associate learning, and many other tasks believed to reflect verbal working memory (Barkley, 1997b; Chang et al., 1999; Grodzinsky & Diamond, 1992; Kuntsei, Oosterlaan, & Stevenson, 2001). Children with ADHD have also been shown to have difficulty with a number of executive cognitive functions such as planning and anticipation (Grodzinsky & Diamond, 1992); developing, applying, and self-monitoring organizational strategies (Clark, Priori, & Kinsella, 2000; Zentall, 1988); and many other cognitive skills thought to be associated with the frontal cortex (Barkley, 2003, p. 80).

Although there has been much debate over the criteria outlined in the *Diagnostic and Statistical Manual* (DSM-IV-TR; APA, 2000) in relation to examining and diagnosing children with ADHD, the current criteria are based on a more comprehensive field trial conducted by Lahey and colleagues in 1994. Currently, the DSM-IV-TR outlines the following criteria when making a diagnosis of ADHD:

A. Either (1) or (2):

(1) Six or more of the following symptoms of **inattention** have persisted for at least 6 months to a degree that is maladaptive and inconsistent with developmental level:

Inattention

    a. often fails to give close attention to details or makes careless mistakes in schoolwork, work, or other activities

    b. often has difficulty sustaining attention in tasks or play activities

    c. often does not seem to listen when spoken to directly

    d. often does not follow through on instructions and fails to finish schoolwork, chores, or duties in the workplace (not due to oppositional behavior or failure to understand instructions)

    e. often has difficulties organizing tasks and activities

    f. often avoids, dislikes, or is reluctant to engage in tasks that require sustained mental effort (such as schoolwork or homework)

    g. often loses things necessary for tasks or activities (e.g., toys, school assignments, pencils, books or tools)

    h. is often easily distracted by extraneous stimuli

    i. is often forgetful in daily activities

(2) Six (or more) of the following symptoms of **hyperactivity-impulsivity** have persisted for at least 6 months to a degree that is maladaptive and inconsistent with developmental level:

Hyperactivity

    a. often fidgets with hands or feet or squirms in seat

      b. often leaves seat in classroom or in other situations in which remaining seated is expected

      c. often runs about or climbs excessively in situations in which it is inappropriate (in adolescents or adults, may be limited to subjective feelings of restlessness)

      d. often has difficulty playing or engaging in leisure activities quietly

      e. is often "on the go" or often acts as if "driven by a motor"

      f. often talks excessively

Impulsivity

      g. often blurts out answers before questions have been completed

      h. often has difficulty waiting turn

      i. often interrupts or intrudes on others (e.g., butts into conversations)

B. Some hyperactive-impulsive or inattentive symptoms that caused impairment were present before age 7 years

C. Some impairment from the symptoms is present in two or more settings (e.g., at school [or work] and at home)

D. There must be clear evidence of clinically significant impairment in social, academic, or occupational functioning

E. The symptoms do not occur exclusively during the course of a Pervasive Developmental Disorder, Schizophrenia, or other Psychotic Disorder and are not better accounted for by another mental disorder (e.g., Mood Disorder, Anxiety Disorder, Dissociative Disorder, or a Personality Disorder).

Types

- **Attention-Deficit/Hyperactivity Disorder, Combined Types:** if both Criteria A1 and A2 are met for the past 6 months
- **Attention-Deficit/Hyperactivity Disorder, Predominantly Inattentive Type:** if Criterion A1 is met but Criterion A2 is not met for the past 6 months
- **Attention Deficit/Hyperactivity Disorder, Predominantly Hyperactive-Impulsive Type:** if Criterion A2 is met but Criterion A1 is not met for the past 6 months
- **Coding note:** For individuals (especially adolescents and adults) who currently have symptoms that no longer meet full criteria, "In Partial Remission" should be specified.
- **Attention-Deficit/Hyperactivity Disorder Not Otherwise Specified**

This category is for disorders with prominent symptoms of inattention or hyperactivity-impulsivity that do not meet criteria for Attention-Deficit/Hyperactivity Disorder.

BIOLOGICAL–GENETIC FACTORS

Although recent attempts have been made to identify social causes of ADHD, research has consistently found that the heritability of ADHD is among the highest of any characteristic (Park et al., 2005; Price et al., 2005). In fact, Price and colleagues report longitudinal data indicating that "genetic influences underlie 91% of the stable variance in ADHD symptomatology" (2005, p. 121). Based on a review of neuropharmacological, genetic, and neuroimaging studies of ADHD, Dureton (2003) reports that ADHD is a neurobiological disorder linked to subtle differences in the circuitry within and connecting to frontal lobes as well as "subtle, widespread deficits in both grey and white matter" (p. 190), particularly in right cerebral volume (2003).

The presence of a strong genetic link to ADHD does not negate the possibility of environmental influences on the development or severity of the disorder. As Taylor and Rogers suggest, "many genes will act by modifying the organism's response to particular environmental influences" (2005, p. 451). For example, Amor and associates found a greater frequency of neonatal complications among children with ADHD compared to their unimpaired siblings (Amor et al., 2005). Other environmental factors that have been linked to ADHD are fetal alcohol exposure, maternal smoking during pregnancy, and the use of some medications during pregnancy (Taylor & Rogers, 2005). Factors that may be linked to the development of ADHD include lead exposure either prenatally or in childhood as well as prenatal exposure to mercury or some pesticides, and essential fatty acid deficiencies (Taylor & Rogers, 2005).

INDIVIDUAL FACTORS THAT INFLUENCE RISK AND RESILIENCY

Children with ADHD and their families face a variety of difficulties that can start long before ADHD is recognized and assessed. Andrea Greenblatt (1994) suggested that "life can be a continuous struggle if necessary interventions are not provided" (p. 93). Her research focused on the identification of ADD in children, with or without hyperactivity, and asked if gender played a role in the recognition and assessment of ADD. Her "study results support the hypothesis that the gender of a child affects the likelihood of an accurate ADD assessment [where hyperactivity is present].... Girls with ADD appear to have a much greater chance of being overlooked than do boys with the disorder" (Greenblatt, 1994, p. 92). "ADD without hyperactivity resulted in an altogether different situation, [with] neither gender [receiving] an adequate level of correct assessments" (Greenblatt, 1994, p. 92). Greenblatt believed that in part these findings were based on the false assumption that hyperactivity was still a key ingredient in the diagnosis of ADD. Obviously, children who are not properly assessed can have ongoing difficulties stretching all the way through the life span, including family, social, and academic environments.

FAMILY FACTORS INFLUENCING RISK AND RESILIENCY

Johnston and Mash (2001) felt that the "family environment remains an important consideration in the development, manifestation, and outcome of the disorder." Parental responses to "high stress, lack of support, low parental quality of life, family functioning difficulties, low parenting satisfaction and parental psychological health problems" may contribute to a vicious cycle: the families displaying such characteristics lead to the child with ADHD becoming "chronic," which in turn increases the families' reactions, which then "maintains" the child's symptoms (Lange, Sheerin, & Carr, 2005, p. 93). Peris and Hinshaw (2003) identify "expressed emotion [as] a measure of parental attitudes that [can be] used to assess the climate of the home environment [such as] the level of criticism and emotional over involvement of parents (p. 1178)." Their paper suggests the following results:

1. Negative maternal emotion appears to have a more negative influence on boys than girls;
2. Ethnicity, age or parent education level did not affect EE scores;
3. Parents of girls with ADHD appear to struggle more with the frustrations of their parenting role, which could be a result of the "gender atypical behaviors associated with ADHD" in girls;
4. Expressed emotion makes an incremental contribution above and beyond that of parental depression in predicting ADHD;
5. Parental criticism tends to be a higher predictor for diagnosis than parental involvement (p. 1184).

In addition to problems at home, children with ADHD often struggle with their peers.

> Interpersonal difficulties with peers, adults, and family members often result in rejection and subsequent social neglect due to the inappropriate pattern of behavior resulting from an impulsive manner of dealing with thoughts, feelings, and others.... [This, in turn,] leads to reduced opportunity to develop appropriate social interaction, self-esteem, coping skills, academic progress, and likely resilience process. (Goldstein & Rider, 2005, p. 209)

SOCIAL–COMMUNITY FACTORS INFLUENCING RISK AND RESILIENCY

In addition to problems at home, children with ADHD often struggle with their peers.

> Interpersonal difficulties with peers, adults, and family members often result in rejection and subsequent social neglect due to the inappropriate pattern of behavior resulting from an impulsive manner of dealing with thoughts, feelings, and others.... [This, in turn,] leads to reduced opportunity to develop appropriate social interaction, self-esteem, coping skills, academic progress, and likely resilience process. (Goldstein & Rider, 2005, p. 209)

Reid, Riccio, and Kessler (2000) found that in academic settings, girls were "referred more for learning problems rather than behavior problems" (p. 38). They noted that "behavior rating scales are 'simply quantifications of adult opinions'" (p. 48) that could be impacted by such things as "halo effects.'" Further academic stressors were identified by Goldstein and Rider (2005) as problems involving persistence, motivation, organization, and behavior.

> Because elementary experience provides the basic foundation skills necessary to learn, including achievement, study, test-taking, and organizational skill, many youth with ADHD enter the middle school years ill-prepared for the increasing demands of autonomy required by the upper grades. (Goldstein & Rider, 2005, p.209)

The teen years see further progress in this developmental process, including

adverse personality styles...social disability...mood, anxiety, disruptive, and substance abuse disorder, [thus limiting] the ability to connect and maintain satisfying reciprocal relationships with others, achieve in school, and maintain mental health to facilitate resilience. (Goldstein and Rider, 2005, p. 210)

Many suggestions have been made to increase resilience and positive outcomes in children with ADHD. Lange and her colleagues suggest that assessments and interventions target the family as well as the child with ADHD, and that such interventions for families could focus on helping parents build a support system, problem-solve "life stresses," "enhance parental quality of life," increase the ability of family members to work together on problems and life stresses, and create "an emotionally warmer and more responsive family climate" (Lange, Sheerin, & Carret, 2005, p. 93).

Sam Goldstein and Richard Rider (2005) proposed nine strategies for helping youth develop resilience, including helping them to

learn to rewrite negative scripts; develop stress management skills; nurture and develop the capacity for empathy; [learn] effective communication [that teaches] an appreciation for both understanding as well as seeking to be understood; accept themselves without feeling inadequate; serve as teachers for others; view mistakes as challenges to appreciate and overcome; experience success and an island of competence [others have an opportunity to see]; and, develop self-discipline and self-control. (pp. 216–217)

Resilience and success in the school environment appears to be impacted by class size and teacher responsiveness. Studies have shown that

when independent work is closely supervised, children with ADHD are able to produce a greater quantity and a higher quality of output relative to minimal supervision situations. Children with ADHD are also more likely to complete tasks that are stimulating and interesting to them, as well as those that are within their range of skills. (DuPaul & Stoner, 2003, p. 16)

Children with ADHD also do better when able to choose between tasks, receive instructions that are direct and "straightforward," have few distractions when receiving instructions, have close supervision for a brief time after receiving instructions, receive "immediate and frequent reinforcement," and receive "reprimands" away from peers (DuPaul & Stoner, 2003, p. 17). Naturally, class size and restraints on teachers' time will impact the frequency and effectiveness of such interventions.

In an alternate pathway, it is possible that there are extremely responsive, sensitive family [social and academic] environments that [serve] as protective factors [to] facilitate the development of self regulation and may attenuate or even terminate ADHD symptoms in children with a biological predisposition for the disorder. Interestingly, children in this developmental pathway will not be represented in clinical or even community samples of children who are identified on the basis of ADHD symptomatology. As such, this developmental pathway, while offering promise for prevention or early intervention in ADHD, remains only a hypothetical possibility. (Johnston & Mash, 2001, p. 185)

EVIDENCE-BASED TREATMENT INTERVENTION FOR ADHD

Treatment of ADHD must be multidisciplinary, multimodal, and maintained over a long period (Goldstein & Teeter-Ellison, 2002). By far, the most effective short-term interventions for ADHD reflect the combined use of medical, behavioral, and environmental techniques. Medication has demonstrated the ability to reduce the severity of impairment resulting from the core symptoms of ADHD. Behavior management increases the salience of behaving in a way consistent with environmental expectations. The manipulation of the environment (e.g., making tasks more interesting and payoffs more valuable) reduces the risk of problems within the natural setting.

Regardless of the treatment modality employed, the basic underlying premise in managing problems of ADHD involves increasing the child's capacity to inhibit before acting, lending to consistent, predictable, and functional behavior. This axiom fits with the theoretical construct that the core problem for ADHD reflects an inability to permit sufficient time to think or respond consistently to consequences.

What Works

Typically, interventions focus on alleviating symptoms associated with ADHD. Such interventions include helping to improve social skills, assisting with academic problems (e.g., disorganization), cognitive problems (e.g., inattention), or behavior problems (e.g., hyperactivity, noncompliance). However, medication intervention has dominated the literature as the most effective symptom relief intervention for ADHD. The MTA Cooperative Group (1999) study funded by the National Institute of Mental Health, clearly demonstrated that impairments related to ADHD (e.g., poor attention, hyperactivity, etc.) are dramatically reduced through education about the condition, medication intervention, and parent training and behavior management. Further analysis of the data reveals that the most robust effects when treating ADHD come when closely monitored medication and behavior management interventions are used collaboratively instead of using medication alone. Furthermore, adolescents with ADHD who were treated with a combination of medication and behavior management interventions improved performance on academic tasks such as note taking, daily assignments, and quiz scores (Evans et al., 2001). Other interventions specifically focused on helping children with ADHD to develop appropriate social skills is also necessary given the fact that children with ADHD who demonstrate poor social relatedness often carry such behaviors into their adolescents in turn becoming even more socially rejected (Bagwell, Molina, Pelham, & Hoza, 2001).

What Might Work

Neurobiofeedback is among popular treatment approaches that have shown some benefit to children with ADHD (Lubar & Lubar, 1984; Monastra et al., 2005). Early results suggest that some of these effects may be maintained over time. However, further research is needed to show whether the effects that are measured in the laboratory translate into important practical improvements in function, and which children with ADHD are likely to benefit from this type of treatment.

Such interventions may help to reduce impairments with children having ADHD, but is simply reducing symptoms enough to help such individuals? Some children who may respond well to a symptom-focused treatment approach do not necessarily become well functioning. Brooks and Goldstein (2002) propose that more has to be done than just alleviating the symptoms of ADHD.

First, Brooks and Goldstein (2002) purpose that the treatment for young people having ADHD must include research validated interventions such as medication, behavior management, and classroom interventions. Such interventions are critical because of their usefulness in helping young people function better in daily life. However, the second component to treating youth with ADHD is providing such individuals with the opportunity to develop a resilient mindset. Young people who possess a resilient mindset are empathetic, they communicate well with others, can problem solve, have a social conscience, and are self-disciplined. By working with parents and teachers, these skills can be reinforced and modeled helping the youth with ADHD incorporate their usefulness in daily life. These skills may in turn help youth as they transition into adolescence and later, adult life. If a young people with ADHD are better able to see their strengths rather than their weaknesses they may in turn be able to function more effectively in their future lives.

What Doesn't Work

There have been a number of treatments proposed to help children with ADHD which have not demonstrated effective treatment results when evaluated in large, well-controlled group studies. These include dietary treatments such as removal of food additives (red dye) or even removal of sugar from the child's diet. Some have argued that taking supplements such as herbs, vitamins, or minerals may improve the symptoms and impairment associated with ADHD, but no well-controlled study has proven these interventions to be effective (Barkley, 1998). Other better researched approaches to ADHD have also shown little benefit. For example, well-controlled studies assessing the effectiveness of cognitive therapy in children with ADHD have yielded minimal results (Baer & Nietzel, 1991; Dush, Hirt, & Schroeder, 1989). Since children with ADHD often exhibit impaired or limited social skills, training in this area has been thought of as an effective intervention. However, most studies have demonstrated little benefit for these types of interventions (Hinshaw & Erhardt, 1992, 1991; Whalen & Henker, 1991).

PSYCHOPHARMACOLOGY AND ADHD

By far the most common approach to treating ADHD is the use of medications. In the late 1930s, the use of *dl*-amphetamine was found to be effective in reducing disruptive behaviors in children (Bradley, 1937). Bradley initially reported that the use of this amphetamine improved compliance, academic performance, and subsequently reduced motor activity in hyperkinetic children. Further reports by Bradley and others continued to demonstrate that stimulant medication decreased oppositional behavior in boys with conduct disorders (Eisenberg et al., 1961) and also showed improvements in target symptoms of ADHD on a standardized rating form completed by parents and teachers (Conners, Eisenberg, & Barcai, 1967). Since these initial observations, stimulant medications have become the most commonly prescribed medication for children and adolescents having ADHD (American Academy of Child and Adolescent Psychiatry, 2002).

Today there are a variety of commonly used stimulant medications such as methylphenidate (Ritalin), amphetamine (Dexedrine and Adderall) and pemoline (Cylert) to treat symptoms related to ADHD. Over the past decade, there has been a dramatic increase in the rate of prescriptions for stimulant medication. Individuals receiving outpatient care by a primary practitioner for ADHD related symptoms increased from 1.6 to 4.2 million per year during the years 1990 to 1993 (Swanson, Lerner, & Williams, 1995). During these visits 90% of the children received a prescription, 71% of which were for methylphenidate. More than 10 million prescriptions for methylphenidate were written in 1996 (Vitiello & Jensen, 1997) and epidemiological surveys estimate that 12-month prescription rates range from 6% in urban Baltimore (Safer, Zito, & Fine, 1996) to 7.3% in rural North Carolina (Angold, Erkanli, Egger, & Costello, 2000). One survey found up to 20% of white boys in the fifth grade in one location were receiving medication for ADHD (LeFever, Sawson, & Morrow, 1999), and another study reported a 2.5-fold increase in methylphenidate use between 1990 and 1995 (National Institute of Mental Health, 2000).

Many speculate that the increase in stimulant use may be related to individuals requiring longer periods of medication for symptom relief. Others hypothesize that the increased usage of stimulant medication may be related to more girls and adults receiving medication treatment for ADHD, improved awareness of the condition by physicians, or an increase in prevalence rates of the disorder (Goldman, Genel, Bezman, & Slanetz, 1998). Regardless, the increased use of stimulant medication raises concern by both parents and professionals and has been highly scrutinized by the media.

Although psychostimulant medications are the primary treatment for individuals having ADHD, little is known about the central mechanisms of these medications. However, sufficient data is available demonstrating that stimulant medications primarily impact central dopamine and norepinephrine neurotransmitters in the prefrontal cortex. Stimulants act on the striatum by binding to the dopamine transporter resulting in an increase in synaptic dopamine. This reaction may enhance the functioning of executive control processes, overcoming deficits in inhibitory control and working memory reported in children with ADHD (Barkley, 1997; Douglas, Barr, Amin, O'Neill, & Britton, 1988). Psychostimulants are absorbed rapidly in the gut usually within the first 30 minutes following ingestion, thus, effects on behavior are quick and noticeable by both parents and teachers.

There has been extensive research conducted on the short-term effectiveness of stimulant medications in the treatment of ADHD. However, the primary focus of this research involved investigating stimulant use with school aged children with little emphasis being placed on stimulant use with adolescents, preschoolers, and adults. A review by Spencer et al. (1996) reported 161 randomized control studies investigating the effectiveness of psychostimulants. The studies encompassed five for preschool age children, 140 with school-age children, seven with adolescents, and nine with adults.

All of the studies demonstrated robust short-term improvements in ADHD symptoms when treated with stimulant medication. Improvement occurred in 65% to 75% of the 5,899 patients assigned stimulant treatment when compared to only 4% to 30% of those assigned placebo. Other short term and well-controlled double-blind studies have further demonstrated improvements in inattentive and hyperactive symptoms when treated with stimulants. Several meta-analyses have also demonstrated robust effects of stimulant use with effect sizes on behavior of .8 to 1.0 standard deviations (Kavale, 1982; Ottenbacher & Cooper, 1983; Thurber & Walker, 1983).

Perhaps the most well-known study in investigating the effectiveness of stimulant medication in the treatment of ADHD is the NIMH Collaborative Multisite Multimodal Treatment Study of Children with Attention-Deficit/Hyperactivity Disorder (MTA study), which concluded that stimulant medication (when taken either alone or in combination with behavioral treatments) leads to stable improvements in ADHD symptoms as long as the medication continues to be taken. Similar results that indicated stimulant medications can be beneficial for many groups of children were replicated across six sites located in various geographical locations involving diverse groups of individuals.

Besides the MTA study, there have been three other long-term randomized controlled studies on the effectiveness of stimulant medications for the treatment of ADHD (Abikoff & Hechmann, 1998; Gillberg et al., 1997; Schachar & Tannock, 1993). Although various findings were observed, in general all of these studies continued to demonstrate superior benefits of medication treatment lasting more than a 12-month period.

Although little research has been done on stimulant medication use in adolescent populations, the benefits of stimulants in children is well documented. In general, stimulant medications are beneficial in ameliorating disruptive ADHD behaviors across multiple settings (e.g., classroom, home, playground) when taken throughout the day (Greenhill, 2002). Stimulants are beneficial in inhibiting impulsive responses on cognitive tasks, and they increase accuracy of performance,; improve short-term memory, reaction time, seatwork completion, and attention. Improvement in behavior and attention has been demonstrated with greater improvements being noted with behavior affects (Greenhill, 2002).

Stimulant medication treatment may pose greater challenges with adolescent populations. Adolescents are more aware of the effects stimulants have on them and can report the benefits of their use. However, only some adolescents may report benefits of taking stimulant medication where others may rebel against frequent administration or the social stigma associated with such treatment. Compliance in taking the medication is no longer the sole responsibility of the parent. Now the adolescent is responsible for complying with treatment. It may be vitally important to work directly with the adolescent and parent together in regard to medication management to ensure optimal compliance. Adolescents should be informed about the risks and benefits of the medication and the importance of compliance. If the adolescent is concerned about taking multiple doses of medication throughout the day, a longer lasting or extended release medication may be beneficial to increase compliance. Concerta may be a good selection because it cannot be ground or snorted and has longer lasting effects (AACAP, 2002).

Although there are a number of stimulant medications available to treat ADHD in adolescents, there have also been promising results shown for the usefulness of nonstimulant interventions. Some children and adolescents may not tolerate stimulant medications well or may have a condition that is contraindicated for the use of stimulants (e.g., cardiovascular defects, or Tourette's disorder; AACAP, 2002). Tricyclic antidepressants (TCAs) have been the most widely researched nonstimulant medication for the treatment of ADHD. Their long half-life (approximately 12 hours) and decreased potential for abuse make TCAs a positive alternative for treating children with ADHD. There are a number of randomized controlled studies demonstrating that TCAs, such as imipramine and desipramine, are effective in eliminating various ADHD symptoms in children and adolescents (Biederman & Spencer, 2002). Beta-blockers have also been well studied and have demonstrated robust effects for the treatment of ADHD. In contrast, however, little benefit has been shown for the use of traditional antidepressants affecting serotonin, such as Prozac and Zoloft, in treating ADHD (Biederman & Spencer, 2002). Pharmaceutical companies appear to have recognized the need for developing a nonstimulant medication for the treatment of ADHD. Eli Lilly, for example, has released Straterra as a new nonstimulant intervention for the treatment of ADHD.

THE PREVENTION OF ADHD

Strategies for preventing ADHD have received little attention in the literature. Since there is no definitive method of preventing ADHD, the goal of "prevention" is seen as a process the may involve parent and teacher education on the signs, symptoms and prognosis of children with ADHD. Parents should be educated on the importance of avoiding alcohol, cigarettes or other harmful substances during pregnancy.

What Works

A review of the literature did not uncover any intervention that met the criteria of three successful trials.

What Might Work

Few research studies have been conducted to determine factors that may actually prevent the onset of ADHD in childhood. An extensive review of the literature for this chapter yielded only one study that reviewed whether early intervention might reduce the incidence of ADHD in a group of preschool children at risk for developing this disorder (Rappaport, Ornoy, & Tenenbaum, 1998). Rappaport and his colleagues conducted a study of 51 children who at the age of 2 to 4.5 years displayed inattention, speech delay, or motor delay with or without hyperactivity. The children in this study were involved in "nonmedicinal" interventions including speech, language, and occupational therapy. Rappaport et al. reported that in children with a family history of this syndrome, early intervention reduced the incidence of ADHD at school age. The authors cautioned that the small sample size limited study conclusions, and further replication was needed.

Because children with ADHD often have other comorbid issues like social skill deficits, many studies have focused on preventing the onset of these problems. For example, parent training that focuses on the etiology of ADHD and assists parents in developing effective management programs has shown promise. Danforth, Harvey, Ulaszek, and

McKee (2006) demonstrated that a guided parent training program focusing on educating parents about ADHD and comorbid problems enabled parents to develop consistent practices that reduced their child's hyperactive, defiant, and aggressive behavior. This intervention not only improved parenting management behavior but reduced parent stress.

What Doesn't Work

A review of the literature did not uncover any intervention that should not be used at the present time.

RECOMMENDED BEST PRACTICE

Due to the pervasive, multisetting nature of problems related to ADHD and its high comorbidity with other childhood disorders, accurately determining whether a child has ADHD can be challenging. The ADHD assessment should involve a thorough emotional, cognitive, and behavioral evaluation. This involves gathering appropriate information from parents, teachers, and the child. In 1997, the American Academy of Child and Adolescent Psychiatry published practice parameters for the assessment and treatment of children, adolescents, and adults with ADHD. These guidelines suggest:

(a) An interview with the parents of the child and when necessary the child to obtain a developmental history, psychiatric history and past treatments, present and past DSM-IV-TR ADHD symptoms, impairment history (including the domains of school work, family and peers), differential diagnosis of alternate and/or comorbid DSM-IV-TR disorders, an assessment of strengths, talents and abilities and mental status examination;
(b) standardized rating scales completed by the child's parent and teacher;
(c) medical history;
(d) family history;
(e) interview with significant other or parent (if available);
(f) physical evaluation (if not completed within the past year);
(g) School related information (e.g., performance, complaints etc.); and
(h) referral for additional evaluations if indicated, such as psycho educational or neuropsychological. (p. 102).

Psychologists are encouraged to complete a psychoeducational and neuropsychological evaluation as part of the evaluation process (Barkley, 1998). Originally, these procedures were recommended to address diagnostic concerns beyond simple symptom count. That is, conducting cognitive measures was not viewed as necessary to diagnose a child with ADHD, but completing these measures aided in ruling out other comorbid conditions such as learning disabilities. Also assessing cognitive functioning in children with ADHD can be useful in developing an effective treatment protocol. Because ADHD is viewed as a neurological disorder with deficits in frontal and prefrontal functioning, there are increasing arguments that assessing cognitive processes in children with ADHD should be included as part of the diagnostic process. Naglieri and Das (2005) argue that the evaluation of cognitive processes should play an important role in the assessment and diagnosis of ADHD so that children who are identified have characteristics that are consistent with the definition of the disorder.

Once an evaluation has been completed, a multimodal treatment approach focusing on the individual needs of the child is necessary. While a very few children with ADHD may require only medication to function successfully, other children will require additional services. In this regard behavioral interventions show the most promise. Despite the growing public popularity of neurobiofeedback, more research is necessary to support claims of its success. Regardless of the level of intervention, parent and teacher support is necessary.

While few studies have been undertaken to assess preventive interventions for children with ADHD, developing the behavior management skills of parents and teachers to address the issues the child with ADHD presents is advised. By establishing a consistent, fair, and nurturing environment for the child with ADHD, the probability of increasing the child's skills to successfully manage home life, school life, and life with peers is increased.

REFERENCES

Abikoff, H., & Hechmann, L. (1998). *Multimodal treatment for children with ADHD: Effects on ADHD and social behavior and diagnostic status.* Unpublished manuscript.

American Psychiatric Association. (1994). *Diagnostic and statistical manual of mental disorders* (4th ed.). Washington D.C: Author.

American Academy of Child and Adolescent Psychiatry (AACAP). (2002). Practice parameters for the use of stimulant medications in the treatment of children, adolescents and adults. *Journal of the American Academy of Child and Adolescent Psychiatry, 41*(2,Suppl.), 27S–49S.

Amor, L. B., Grizenko, N., Schwartz, G., Lageix, P., Baron, C., Ter-Stepanian, M., et al. (2005). Perinatal complications in children with attention deficit hyperactivity disorder and their unaffected siblings. *Journal of Psychiatry and Neuroscience, 30,* 120–126.

Angold, A., Erkanli, A., Egger, H., & Costello, J. (2000). Stimulant treatment for children: A community perspective. *Journal of the American Academy of Child and Adolescent Psychiatry, 39,* 975–983.

Baer, R. A., & Nietzel, M. T. (1991). Cognitive and behavioral treatment of impulsivity in children: A meta-analytic review of the outcome literature. *Journal of Clinical Child Psychology, 20,* 400–412.

Bagwell, C. L., Molina, D. S., Pelham, W. E., & Hoza, B. (2001). ADHD and problems in peer relations: Predictions from childhood to adolescence. *Journal of the American Academy of Child and Adolescent Psychiatry, 40,* 1285–1299.

Barbaresi, W. J., Katusic, S. K., Colligan, R. C., Pankratz, S., Weaver, A. L., Webber, K. J., et al. (2002). How common is ADHD? *Archives of Pediatric and Adolescent Medicine, 156,* 217–224.

Barkley, R. A. (1997). Attention-deficit/hyperactivity disorder, self-regulation, and time: Toward a more comprehensive theory. *Developmental and Behavioral Pediatrics, 18,* 271–279.

Barkley, R. A. (1997b). *ADHD and the nature of self-control.* New York: Guilford.

Barkley, R. A. (1998). Attention-deficit/hyperactivity disorder. In E. J. Marsh & R. A. Barkley (Eds.), *Treatment of childhood disorders* (pp. 55–110). New York: Guilford.

Barkley, R. A. (2003). Attention deficit hyperactivity disorder. In E. Marsh & R. Barkley (Eds), *Child psychopathology* (2nd ed.). New York: Guilford.

Barkley, R. A., & Cunningham, C. E. (1978). Do stimulant drugs improve the academic performance of hyperkinetic children? A review of outcome research. *Journal of Clinical Pediatrics, 17,* 85–92.

Beiser, M., Dion, R., & Gotowiec, A. (2000). The structure of attention-deficit and hyperactivity symptoms among Native and non-Native elementary school children. *Journal of Abnormal Child Psychology, 28,* 425–537.

Biederman, J., & Spencer, T. J. (2002). Nonstimulant treatment for ADHD. In P. S. Jensen & J. R. Cooper (Eds.), *Attention deficit hyperactivity disorder. State of the science. Best practices.* Kingston, NJ: Civic Research Institute.

Bradley, C. (1937). The behavior of children receiving benzedrine. *American Journal of Psychiatry, 94*, 577–585.

Brooks, R., & Goldstein, S. (2002). *Raising resilient children*. Chicago: Contemporary Books.

Chang, H. T., Lorma, R., Shaywitz, S. E., Fletcher, J. M., Marchione, K. E., Holahan, J. M., et al. (1999). Paired associate learning in attention-deficit/hyperactivity disorder as a function of hyperactivity-impulsivity and oppositional defiant disorder. *Journal of Abnormal Child Psychology, 27*, 237–245.

Clark, C., Priori, M., & Kinsella, G. J. (2000). Do executive function deficits differentiate between adolescents with ADHD and oppositional defiant/conduct disorder? A neuropsychological study using the Six Elements Test and Hayling Sentence Completion Test. *Journal of Abnormal Child Psychology, 16*, 1–15.

Conners, C. K., Eisenberg, L., & Barcai, A. (1967). Effect of dextroamphetamine on children: Studies on subjects with learning disabilities and school behavior problems. *Archives of General Psychiatry, 17*, 478–485.

Danforth, J., Harvey, E., Ulaszek, W. R., & McKee, T. E. (2006). The outcome of group parent training for families of children with attention-deficit hyperactivity disorder and defiant/aggressive behavior. *Journal of Behavior Therapy and Experimental Psychiatry, 37*, 188–205.

Douglas, V. I. (1983). Attention and cognitive problems. In M. Rutter (Ed.), *Developmental neuropsychology* (pp. 280–329). New York: Guilford.

Douglas, V. I., Barr, R. G., Amin, K., O'Neill, M. E., & Britton, B. G. (1988). Dose effects and individual responsivity to methylphenidate in attention deficit disorder. *Journal of Child Psychology and Psychiatry, 29*, 453–475.

DuPaul, G. J., & Stoner, G. (2003). *ADHD in the schools: Assessment and intervention strategies* (2nd ed.). New York: Guilford.

Durston, S. (2003). A review of the biological bases of ADHD: What have we learned from imaging studies? *Mental Retardation and Developmental Disabilities Research Reviews, 9,* 184–195.

Dush, D. M., Hirt, M. L., & Schroeder, H. E. (1989). Self-statement modification in the treatment of child behavior disorders: A meta-analysis. *Psychological Bulletin, 106*, 97–106.

Eisenberg, L., Lachman, R., Molling, P., Lockner, D., Mizelle, J., & Conners, C. (1961). A psychopharmacologic experiment in a training school for delinquent boys: Methods, problems and findings. *American Journal of Orthopsychiatry, 33*, 431–437.

Evans, S. W., Pelham, W. E., Smith, B. H., Bukstein, O., Gnagy, E. M., Greiner, A. R., et al. (2001). Dose-response effects of methylphenidate on ecologically valid measures of academic performance and classroom behavior in adolescents with ADHD. *Experimental and Clinical Psychopharmacology, 9*, 163–175.

Fabiano, G. A., & Pelham, W. E. (2003). Improving the effectiveness of behavioral classroom interventions for attention-deficit/hyperactivity disorder: A case study. *Journal of Emotional and Behavioral Disorders, 11*, 122–128.

Gillberg, C., Melander, H., von Knorring, A., Janols, L. O., Thernlund, G., Hagglof, B., et al. (1997). Long-term central stimulant treatment of children with attention-deficit hyperactivity disorder. A randomized double-blind placebo-controlled trial. *Archives of General Psychiatry, 54*, 857–864.

Goldman, L., Genel, M., Bezman, R., & Slanetz, P. (1998). Diagnosis and treatment of attention-deficit/hyperactivity disorder. *Journal of the American Medical Association, 279*, 1100–1107.

Goldstein, S., & Rider, R. (2005). Resilience and the disruptive disorders of childhood. In S. Goldstein & R. B. Brooks (Eds.), *Handbook of resilience in children*. 203-222. New York: Kluwer Academic/Plenum.

Goldstein, S., & Teeter-Ellison, A. (2002). (Eds.). *Clinical Interventions for adult ADHD: A comprehensive approach*. New York: Academic Press.

Greenblatt, A. P. (1994). Gender and ethnicity bias in the assessment of attention deficit disorder. *Social Work in Education, 16*(2), 89–95.

Greenhill, L. (2002). Stimulant medication treatment of children with attention deficit hyperactivity disorder. In P. S. Jensen & J. R. Cooper (Eds.), *Attention deficit hyperactivity disorder. State of the science. Best practices*. Kingston, NJ: Civic Research Institute.

Grodzinsky, G. M., & Diamond, R. (1992). Frontal lobe functioning in boys with attention-deficit hyperactivity disorder. *Developmental Neuropsychology, 8*, 427–445.

Hinshaw, S. P., & Erhardt, D. (1991). Attention deficit hyperactivity disorder. In P. C. Kendall (Ed.), *Child and adolescent therapy: Cognitive behavioral procedures* (pp. 9–128). New York: Guilford.

Hinshaw, S. P., & Erhardt, D. (1992). Interventions for social competence and social skill. *Child and Adolescent Psychiatric Clinics of North America, 1*(2), 539–552.

Johnston, C., & Mash, E. J. (2001). Families of children with attention-deficit/hyperactivity disorder: Review and recommendations for future research. *Clinical Child and Family Psychology Review, 4* (3). 183-207

Kanfer, F. H., & Karoly, P. (1972). Self-control: A behavioristic excursion into the lion's den. *Behavior Therapy, 3*, 398–416.

Kavale, K. (1982). The efficacy of stimulant drug treatment for hyperactivity: A meta-analysis. *Journal of Learning Disabilities, 15,* 280–289.

Kuntsei, J., Oosterlaan, J., & Stevenson, J. (2001). Psychological mechanisms in hyperactivity: Response inhibition deficit, working memory impairment, delay aversion, or something else? *Journal of Child Psychology and Psychiatry, 42,* 199–210.

Lahey, B. B., Applegate, B., McBurnett, K., Biederman, J., Greenhill, L., Hynd, G., et al. (1994). DSM-IV field trials for attention deficit hyperactivity disorder in children and adolescents. *American Journal of Psychiatry, 151,* 1673–1685.

Lange, G., Sheerin, D., & Carr, A. (2005). Family factors associated with attention deficit hyperactivity disorder and emotional disorders in children. *Journal of Family Therapy, 27,* 76–96.

LeFever, G., Sawson, K. V., & Morrow, A. L. (1999). The extent of drug therapy for attention deficit-hyperactivity disorder among children in public schools. *American Journal of Public Health, 89,* 1359–1364.

Lubar, J., & Lubar, J. (1984). Electroencephalographic biofeedback of SMR and beta for treatment of attention deficit disorders in a clinical setting. *Biofeedback and Self-Regulation, 9,* 1–23.

Monastra, V. J., Lynn, S, Linden, M, Lubar, J. F., Gruzelier, J, & LaVaque, T. J. (2005). Electroencephalographic biofeedback in the treatment of attention-deficit/hyperactivity disorder. *Applied Psychophysiology and Biofeedback, 30,* 95–114.

MTA Cooperative Group. (1999). 14-month randomized clinical trial of treatment strategies for attention deficit hyperactivity disorder. *Archives of General Psychiatry, 56,* 1073–1086.

Naglieri, J. A., & Das, J. P. (2005). *Are intellectual measures important in the diagnosis and treatment of ADHD?* Unpublished manuscript.

National Institute of Mental Health. (2000). Diagnosis and treatment of attention-deficit/hyperactivity disorder. *NIH Consensus Conference Statement, 16*(2), 9.

Ottenbacher, J., & Cooper, H. (1983). Drug treatment of hyperactivity in children. *Developmental Medicine and Child Neurology, 25,* 358–366.

Park, L., Nigg, J. T., Waldman, I. D., Nummy, K. A., Huang-Pollock, C., Rappley, M., & Friderici, K. H. (2005). Association and linkage of a-2A adrenergic receptor gene polymorphisms with childhood ADHD. *Molecular Psychiatry, 10,* 572–580.

Peris, T. S., & Hinshaw, S. P. (2003). Family dynamics and preadolescent girls with ADHD: The relationship between expressed emotion, ADHD symptomatology, and comorbid disruptive behavior. *Journal of Child Psychology and Psychiatry, 44* (8), 1177–1190.

Price, T. S., Simonoff, E., Asherson, P., Curran, S., Kuntsi, J., Waldman, I., et al. (2005). Continuity and change in preschool ADHD symptoms: Longitudinal genetic analysis with contrast effects. *Behavior Genetics, 35,* 121–132.

Rappaport, G. C., Ornoy, A., & Tenenbaum, A. (1998). Is early intervention effective in preventing ADHD? *Israel Journal of Psychiatry and Related Sciences, 35,* 271–279.

Reid, R., Riccio, C. A. & Kessler, R. H. (2000). Gender and ethnic differences in ADHD as assessed by behavior ratings. *Journal of Emotional and Behavioral Disorders, 8*(1), 38–49.

Safer, D., Zito, J., & Fine, E. (1996). Increased methylphenidate usage for attention deficit hyperactivity disorder in the 1990s. *Pediatrics, 98,* 1084–1088.

Schachar, R. J., & Tannock, R. (1993). Childhood hyperactivity and psychostimulants: A review of extended treatment studies. *Journal of Child and Adolescent Psychopharmacology, 3,* 81–89.

Spencer, T., Biederman, J., Wilens, T., Harding, M., O'Donnell, D., & Griffin, S. (1996). Pharmacotherapy of attention-deficit hyperactivity disorder across the life cycle. *Journal of the American Academy of Child and Adolescent Psychiatry, 35,* 409–432.

Swanson, J., Lerner, M., & Williams, L. (1995). More frequent diagnosis of attention deficit hyperactivity disorder. *New England Journal of Medicine, 333,* 944.

Taylor, E., & Rogers, J. W. (2005). Practitioner review: Early adversity and developmental disorders. *Journal of Child Psychology and Psychiatry 46,* 451–467.

Thurber, S., & Walker, C. (1983). Medication and hyperactivity: A meta-analysis. *Journal of General Psychiatry, 108,* 79–86.

Vitiello, B., & Jensen, P. (1997). Medication development and testing in children and adolescents. *Archives of General Psychiatry, 54,* 871–876.

Zentall, S. S. (1988). Production deficiencies in elicited language but not in the spontaneous verbalizations of hyperactive children. *Journal of Abnormal Child Psychology, 16,* 657–673.

Chapter Fourteen

Posttraumatic Stress Disorder in Children

Theresa Kruczek, Stephanie Vitanza, and Jill Salsman

INTRODUCTION

The detrimental impact of severe emotional trauma on the development and functioning of children has long been recognized (i.e., A. Freud, 1936/1966). Most current discussions of childhood trauma begin by distinguishing between traumatic events and traumatic reactions. Traumatic events are adverse life experiences and include war, disasters (i.e., natural and technological), interpersonal violence (e.g., sexual and physical abuse), community violence, and life-threatening illness, injury, or medical procedures (Pynoos, 1994). Terr (1991) suggests traumatic stressors can be classified as type I and type II events. Type I events are single incident stressors which are unexpected, short duration experiences. Typically, less severe stress reactions follow type I events. However, type I events with an associated significant loss (e.g., death of a loved one or loss of physical functioning) can lead to a more severe stress reaction. In contrast, type II events involve chronic or repetitive exposure (e.g., a series of natural disasters or repeated sexual molestation). More severe stress reactions and adjustment difficulty are likely with type II trauma.

Traumatic reactions in children can be moderated not only by the type of trauma experienced, but by a host of biopsychosocial factors. Current biological models of trauma are broadly based on a diathesis–stress perspective (Flouri, 2005) and more narrowly on stress reaction theory or the "fight or flight" response (Selye, 1952). Selye noted that both humans and animals display a characteristic behavioral and physiological response to threats in the environment. He based his general adaptation syndrome (described in more detail in the "Biological/Genetic Factors" section of this chapter) on this response pattern. In addition, the diathesis–stress perspective suggests certain children are predisposed (either via temperament factors or genetic predisposition) to develop a posttraumatic stress disorder (PTSD) following exposure to traumatic life events. However, the specific reaction of a given child will likely be moderated by the social context within which the trauma occurs (including cultural and familial factors) as well as a host of personal factors such as cognitive ability, cognitive appraisal, and dissociation (Flouri, 2005).

While each child's traumatic reaction will be idiosyncratic, there are three broad symptom clusters typical in PTSD (American Psychiatric Association [APA], 2000). The first symptom cluster involves reexperiencing the trauma. Specific manifestations of this cluster include nightmares (can be nonspecific in children), intrusive thoughts (can be posttraumatic or compulsive repetitive play in children), psychological distress or physiological reactivity. Some children experience dissociation which may or may not include flashbacks or trauma-specific behavioral reenactments. The second symptom cluster includes avoiding stimuli related to the trauma and numbing. Avoidance can include any specific stimuli associated with the trauma as well as thoughts and discussions about the trauma. Those with numbing symptoms may appear detached or estranged from others. They may demonstrate a loss of pleasure in activities they previously enjoyed or display generally constricted affect. They may have an inability to remember the traumatic event and have a "foreshortened" sense of the future. The third symptom cluster involves hyperarousal. Children expressing these symptoms can be irritable, hypervigilant, and display exaggerated startle responses. They may display sleep and concentration disturbances. Sleep disturbances can include increased difficulty going to sleep and frequent nocturnal awakening,

Although posttraumatic reactions and symptoms have been described since the mid-20th century (i.e., Kardiner, 1941), posttraumatic stress disorder (PTSD) did not emerge as a diagnostic category until the third version of the *Diagnostic and Statistical Manual of Mental Disorders* (DSM-III; APA, 1980), It was not until the next version that the diagnosis was specifically applied to children (DSM-III-R; APA, 1987). In order to receive a diagnosis of PTSD, children must have first been exposed to a traumatic event in which they either directly experienced or witnessed a threat to their own or someone else's life or person. According to the DSM-IV-TR (APA, 2000) diagnostic criteria, their response to the event must include an intense anxious–helpless affective reaction that in children can be manifest as agitation or disorganized behavior. Children must display one symptom from the reexperiencing cluster, three or more from avoidance-numbing, and two or more from the hyperarousal cluster. The onset of PTSD symptoms is typically sometime within three months following the trauma, however, there can be a delay in symptom onset. Acute stress disorder (ASD) is diagnosed if the symptoms both begin and resolve within four weeks of the traumatic event. For symptoms that either begin or extend one month postevent, PTSD should be diagnosed (APA, 2000).

While the symptoms of PTSD in adolescents seem to be fairly consistent with adult symptomatology (Amaya-Jackson & March, 1995), the impact of trauma on young children may not be fully recognized if researchers and practitioners rely exclusively on the current DSM-IV- TR (APA, 2000) diagnostic criteria. The DSM-IV-TR criteria for PTSD may not be sensitive or specific enough for accurate diagnosis in children (Scheeringa, Zeanah, Drell, & Larrieu, 1995). One of the difficulties with the current diagnostic criteria may arise from the fact that children and teens appear to alternate between periods of reexperiencing and avoidance-numbing symptoms (American Academy of Child and Adolescent Psychiatry [AACAP], 1998). To meet the DSM-IV-TR criteria an individual must simultaneously display symptoms from all three clusters. Further, certain manifestations of the symptom clusters may not be developmentally relevant. For example, avoidance symptoms in children may manifest as avoiding anxiety producing experiences in general (vs. trauma specific stimuli) or experiencing separation difficulties with significant caregivers. Sleep disturbance in children can include secondary nocturnal enuresis. Time perspective and memory is less well developed in children than adults and therefore ability to remember and communicate about the traumatic event may be related to developmental capability versus trauma specific repression. Additionally, this less developed time perspective may make the sense of a "foreshortened" future developmentally irrelevant in children. Finally, children may appear asymptomatic when they use avoidance and numbing to cope or their symptoms of PTSD may be masked (AACAP, 1998). Scheeringa et al. (1995) suggest altering the diagnostic criteria for PTSD to take into account these age and developmental aspects of children's trauma response. Specifically, they recommend requiring only one developmentally adjusted symptom from each of the three symptom clusters as well as adding the onset of one postevent symptom of fear and aggression (i.e., aggressive acting out, separation anxiety, fear of toileting/dark/new situations/etc.). Any developmental regression can be part of a child's trauma reaction.

This difficulty with applying the current DSM IV-TR diagnostic criteria to children may explain why there are no large scale prevalence studies of PTSD in children. However, Reinherz, Giaconia, Lefkowitz, Pakiz, and Frost (1993) estimate 6.3% of adolescents in the general population have PTSD. According to the DSM-IV-TR, one-third to one-half of all those exposed to a traumatic life event will go on to develop PTSD. Most studies of PTSD prevalence in children are traumatic event specific or conducted within the context of risk and resiliency research. Yule, Perrin, and Smith (1999) estimate that approximately one third of children involved in life-threatening accidents will develop PTSD; "high risk" groups (i.e., children exposed to war, violent crime, sexual abuse, and natural disasters) may even be as high as two thirds.

BIOLOGICAL/GENETIC FACTORS

The biological bases of stress reactions have been long recognized. However, recent research has begun to identify the biological and genetic factors contributing to the development of post traumatic stress symptomatology.

Biological Factors

In order to understand the biological basis for trauma reactions in children, it is necessary to first review the body's normal reaction to stress. Hans Selye (1952) proposed one of the earliest stress theories. He described the general adaptation syndrome (GAS) in which our bodies demonstrate a physiologically predictable response to stress, commonly referred to as the "fight or flight response." The physiological changes which accompany this response prepare our bodies to deal with impending threat. He further proposed that chronic exposure to stress results in adverse health outcomes.

Modern stress theory and research has built on Selye's work and focuses on several psychobiological systems. Neuroendocrine, neurotransmitter, and immune systems are all affected by exposure to stress. The three major neurobiological stress response systems include the sympathetic nervous system (SNS), the hypothalamic-pituitary-adrenal (HPA) axis (sometimes referred to as the limbic-hypothalamic-pituitary axis (LHPA), and the serotonin system (DeBellis, 2005). These systems influence not only the stress response, but also the regulation of behavior and emotion, arousal, and neurodevelopment. It is not surprising then that these systems are implicated in many of the symptoms of PTSD as well as the impaired neurobiological development of children exposed to trauma (van der Kolk, 2003). Children may be more vulnerable than adults to maladjustment following trauma exposure because the neurobiological systems regulating their stress response are probably not fully developed or adaptive (Perry, 1994). Children exposed to trauma often display an increased vulnerability to physical illness as well as deficits in learning and memory, social relationships, and emotional self-regulation (van der Kolk, 2003).

Life experiences which precipitate intense anxiety activate the locus coeruleus and the sympathetic nervous system (SNS). This activation leads to the biological changes accompanying the "fight or flight" reaction, including arousal and vigilance (Cohen, Perel, DeBellis, Friedman, & Putnam, 2002). The locus coeruleus is the primary site for production of the neurotransmitter norepinephrine (NE). NE is part of a class of neurotransmitters known as the catecholamines, which also includes dopamine (DA). The catecholamines and indolamines, or Serotonin (5-HT), belong to a family of neurotransmitters known as the monoamines. This group of neurotransmitters shows the strongest evidence of involvement in PTSD symptoms (Donnelly, Amaya-Jackson, & March, 1999). While the specific action of DA is not entirely clear, stress leads to enhanced DA function in the prefrontal cortex, resulting initially in heightened attention and cognitive function. However, prolonged elevations in prefrontal DA may ultimately impair prefrontal cortical function and lead to inattention, hypervigilance, learning problems, or paranoia in children (DeBellis, 2005). Some research has associated low 5-HT levels with PTSD symptoms in adults (Spivak et al., 1999). Low 5-HT is also associated with aggression, suicidality, obsessions, compulsions, and depression (Cohen et al., 2002), often part of the posttraumatic response in children. However, it is the adrenergic system (NE and EPI) that appears to play a key role in trauma reactions (Cohen et al., 2002). Specifically, increased NE output from the locus coeruleus precipitates activation of the LHPA via the amygdala and hypothalamus.

The limbic system modulates emotional behavior, particularly aggressive or defensive behavior in response to perceived environmental threat. More specifically, the amygdala integrates sensory input from the environment (directly from the olfactory system and indirectly via the thalamus) so the information from life experiences can be encoded in and retrieved from memory. The amygdala also appears to play a role in assigning emotional valence to these life experiences and memories (Eichenbaum & Cohen, 2001). When an organism perceives a situation as threatening, it is neurochemical action in the amygdala that triggers the body's stress response via the HPA axis. These automatic physiological and psychological stress reactions are minimally influenced by higher cortical functions (van der Kolk, 2003) and seem to precipitate a "fear conditioning" response (LeDoux, 1996). This fear conditioning response appears to be a classically conditioned fear reaction to environmental stimuli associated with the traumatic event (Foa, Zinbarg, & Rothbaum, 1992).

Activation of the HPA axis initiates the automatic physiological stress reactions associated with the fight or flight response (Cicchetti, 2003). This physiologic stress reaction is mediated by the SNS and hypothalamus, which controls the neuroendocrine system. Under stress, the hypothalamus is activated by increased NE output as earlier described. The hypothalamus then releases corticotrophin factor (CRF) which signals the pituitary gland to release adrenocorticotrophic hormone (ACTH). The ACTH then stimulates the adrenal glands (located on top of the kidneys) to release cortisol, sometimes referred to as the "stress hormone" and epinephrine (EPI). Cortisol is involved in regulating such bodily functions as blood pressure, cardiovascular and immune systems, and metabolism. Higher levels of cortisol secretion during stressful situations facilitate the break down of fatty acids and proteins to assist with increased energy production. While the temporary elevation of cortisol helps an individual successfully manage stressful experiences, chronic elevations have detrimental effects on both the neurophysiological and neuropsychological functioning of children (Cicchetti, 2003). Further, a hyperfunctioning of CRF has been implicated in stress disorders as well as anxiety and depression (Kehne, Hoffman, & Baron, 2005).

The medial prefrontal cortex also is connected to the amygdala via neural pathways. The prefrontal cortex is involved in organization and planning, motivation, and working memory (Knight, Grabowecky, & Scabini, 1995). The anterior cingulate, part of the medial prefrontal cortex, plays a role in extinguishing learned fear responses (Cohen et al., 2002). In a functional stress reaction the medial prefrontal cortex releases catecholemines in a way that provides negative feedback to the amygdala, resulting in an inhibitory (vs. excitatory) effect on the LHPA axis, thus returning the system to homeostasis. In PTSD the amygdala appears to be overreactive and the medial prefrontal cortex underreactive, thus exacerbating fear conditioning responses (Cohen et al., 2002). This heightened limbic system sensitivity is known as kindling and has been associated with chronic illness in adults with PTSD (Lubit, 2006)

It is the fear conditioning response that likely underlies the reexperiencing symptom cluster of PTSD, particularly intrusive memories and nightmares (Cohen, 2001). Environmental stimuli or "triggers" associated with the trauma initiate a classically conditioned physiological and psychological fear reaction in the child. In children this process may be largely "unconscious" in that the reactivity to environmental triggers happens outside his or her cognitive awareness. The fear conditioning response may contribute also to avoidance symptoms when the child has a greater awareness of specific triggers. Further, there is evidence that traumatized children show a heightened physiological reactivity to stress when they are exposed to subsequent stressors. Research has found that these children have increased levels of NE, EPI, or their metabolites in 24-hour urine samples (DeBellis et al., 1999; Perry, 1994). Traumatized children also show hypersecretion of cortisol (DeBellis et al., 1999). This physiological reactivity to future stressors may underlie many of the hyperarousal symptoms in children with PTSD. Yehuda (1997) further suggested the symptoms of numbing and avoiding may result from the long-term inhibitory effect of corticosteroids on the brain.

Genetic Factors

The role of genetics in the etiology of PTSD is not yet clear. Two twin studies conducted with the Vietnam Era Twin Registry found genetics accounted for 13.6% (Chantarujika-pong et al., 2001) and 30% (True & Lyons, 1999) of the variability in PTSD symptoms. While children who have a parent with PTSD are five times more likely to develop PTSD themselves (Sack, Clarke, & Seeley, 1995), at this time it is impossible to determine whether this increased vulnerability to PTSD is due to genetic or environmental factors.

It may be that the genetic underpinnings of disease-associated traits (e.g., proneness to startle) will be easier to determine (Farkas, 2004). It is likely that certain children are temperamentally more vulnerable to develop PTSD following trauma exposure. However, even children born with genetically "normal" brains may be adversely affected by traumatic experiences because their developing brain may be more vulnerable to the neurophysiological insult of trauma (Cicchetti, 2003).

INDIVIDUAL FACTORS INFLUENCING RISK AND RESILIENCY

There has been an increased focus since the mid-1990s on examining both risk and resiliency factors in children and adolescents who experience traumatic life events. Resiliency in children has been investigated in terms of both protective and resource factors. Protective factors are those traits which provide a buffering effect in situations of high risk. In contrast, resource factors have a beneficial effect regardless of whether or not the situation is one of low or high risk (Tiet et al., 1998). Tiet and her colleagues noted that it is the absence of protective factors which likely results in increased vulnerability to development of PTSD. In addition to resiliency factors, several risk factors exacerbating the likelihood for development of PTSD have been identified. A review of those risk and resiliency factors most commonly researched in children who have experienced trauma follows. However, it is important to note that others have been suggested (i.e., biological factors, psychological traits, spiritual factors, social skills, and environmental factors), but not yet been thoroughly explored (APA, 2004).

Age and Developmental Factors

While many assume trauma does not have a significant effect on young children, even preschool age children can be affected by adverse events (Osofsky, 1995; Pfefferbaum, 1997). Most traumatologists consider age and developmental stage crucial considerations in the assessment and treatment of PTSD in children (APA, 2004; Clark & Miller, 1998). In fact, the child's experience of subjective threat is determined by her or his developmental level (Schwarz & Perry, 2002; Yule, Perrin, & Smith, 1999). Some researchers argue that age may be a protective factor for younger children in that a very young child may not have the depth of cognitive understanding to process the danger he or she was in, as compared to a teen or young adult who might fully appreciate the severity of the circumstances (Davis & Siegel, 2000; Keppel-Benson & Ollendick, 1993; Schwarz & Perry, 2002; Yule et al., 1999). Most agree children's response to trauma is a complex combination of factors which are related to how they perceive the event(s) (Pandit & Shah, 2000; Yule et al., 1999). While overall the literature appears to be mixed in this area, several studies report that even if very young children do not have the cognitive capacity to recognize and perceive threat, they are greatly affected by their parents' response and thus, can experience secondary traumatization (Pynoos, 1994; Silverman & LaGreca, 2002).

While there is little argument that cognitive development contributes to a child's awareness and assessment of the severity of the situation, there is less consensus about whether or not age affects a child's development of symptoms of PTSD. Some authors have concluded the age at which an adverse or traumatic event occurs has not been linked definitively with a child's subsequent development of PTSD (Foa, Keane, & Friedman, 2000), while others disagree (Davidson & Smith, 1990). For example, not all studies with child survivors of sexual abuse have found a correlation between age at onset of the abuse and PTSD (Boney-McCoy & Finkelhor, 1995). However, the age at which the traumatic experience occurs has been linked more generally with adverse developmental outcomes (Schwarz & Perry, 2002). It appears the earlier and more extensive the trauma, the greater the adverse developmental impact (van der Kolk, 2003). Although the child's age or developmental level may not result in diagnosable PTSD, posttraumatic symptomatology often disrupts a child's subsequent development (Davis & Siegel, 2000; DiNicola, 1996). Those developmental processes most likely to be affected include a capacity for trust, initiative, positive worldview, intimate relationships, positive self-esteem, and impulse control (DiNicola, 1996).

Gender

Research is somewhat mixed with regard to whether there are gender differences in the development of symptoms of PTSD (AACAP, 1998; Silverman & LaGreca, 2002). On the one hand, Tiet and colleagues (1998) found that being a female served as a resource effect for girls who experience a significant degree of adverse life events *and* have mothers with a history of psychopathology. In contrast, the APA Practice Guidelines (2004) for the treatment of ASD and PTSD indicate that while it is not apparent why, prevalence rates of PTSD in adolescent or adult women are significantly higher than for adolescent or adult men. Some research suggests the prevalence for both adolescent and adult females may be twice as high as for men (Davis & Siegel, 2000; Foa et al., 2000; Norris, Foster, Weisshar, 2002; Rojas & Pappagallo, 2004). Norris et al. (2002) reports prevalence rates for childhood PTSD with an even greater gender discrepancy, where rates for females may be high as 35% versus 10% for males. Overall, these gender differences appear across cultures and types of traumatic events with the prevalence for females ranging from two to five times higher than males (Davis & Siegel, 2000; Norris, et al., 2002; Yule, et al., 1999).

These findings are consistent with the literature on general psychological functioning related to PTSD. Girls have significantly higher scores than their male peers on measures of depression, anxiety, and intrusive thoughts (Davis & Siegel, 2000; Rojas & Pappagallo, 2004; Silva & Kessler, 2004). Several factors appear related to the varied responses by boys and girls on these measures of psychopathology. Those factors include the type of traumatic events experienced (i.e., females are more likely to experience sexual abuse, males physical abuse) and their perception of the event after the trauma (Tolin & Foa, 2002). Female trauma survivors are more likely to describe feelings of shame, guilt and responsibility following a traumatic event. They also are more likely than males to evaluate the world more negatively and as less safe. Most authors agree the specific nature of the gender differences in response to trauma needs further clarification.

Additional Protective Factors

With regard to other individual variables, the literature consistently supports higher cognitive functioning as a protective factor (Silva & Kessler, 2004; Silva et al., 2000;

Silverman & La Greca, 2002; Tiet et al., 1998), especially for those who may be at a higher risk due to other family or community factors. Good psychological adjustment (i.e., having no psychiatric diagnosis) is related to better physical health and higher educational aspirations for those children who have experienced an adverse life event (Tiet et al., 1998). Temperament, coping skills, and positive self-esteem are also individual protective factors (Clark & Miller, 1998; Davis & Siegel, 2000; Harvey & Delfabbro, 2004).

Individual Risk Factors

Experiences of adversity, abuse, violence, and trauma are risk factors for the development of PTSD in children. The type and intensity along with the acute versus chronic nature of the traumatic experience interact with individual risk factors to influence a child's adjustment (Silva & Kessler, 2004). Other individual variables influencing the development of PTSD in children include learned helplessness and excessive emotionality or passivity in coping with daily stressors (Davis & Siegel, 2000; O'Donohue, Fanetti, & Elliott, 1998). In children with a history of sexual abuse, those with higher levels of anxiety arousal or dissociative symptoms at the time of disclosure are more likely to develop symptoms of ASD or PTSD (Kaplow, Dodge, Amaya-Jackson & Saxe, 2005; O'Donohue et al., 1998; Pfefferbaum, 1997; Saxe et al., 2005). It is possible children who demonstrate these same symptoms at or around the experience of other traumatic life events are at increased risk.

FAMILY FACTORS INFLUENCING RISK AND RESILIENCY

Family is the means through which children learn about themselves, relationships, and life. Therefore, it is not surprising that those child trauma survivors who live with two parents, have positive relationships with their parents, and have a higher socioeconomic status demonstrate more adaptive coping than those who have fewer of those advantages (Davis & Siegel, 2000; Tiet et al., 1998). Family support has long been recognized as vital to minimizing the adverse impact of trauma in children. Research has consistently shown that family support moderates the negative impact of traumatic life events (AACAP, 1998; Davis & Siegel, 2000; Pynoos, Steinberg, & Wraith, 1995; Rabalais, Ruggerio, & Scotti, 2002; Rojas & Pappagallo, 2004). Family support does not have to occur within the context of a traditional nuclear family but can include a broader spectrum of familial support including extended family members and even a wider network of caregivers, family friends, or foster parents (di Silva, 1999).

Conversely, numerous studies have documented a correlation between parental psychopathology (especially mothers or a parent with a diagnosis of PTSD) and subsequent risk for the development of PTSD (Aisenberg, 2001; Davis & Siegel, 2000; Pfefferbaum, 1997; Silverman & LaGreca, 2002; Tiet et al., 1998; Yehuda, Schmeidler, Giller, Siever, & Binder-Brynes, 1998). Interestingly, in the case of a natural disaster, it is not the severity of the event that is most predictive of the development of symptoms in children. Parental response to the event (immediate and long term) and family functioning after the event (i.e., disruption to day-to-day routines) are more predictive of the child's posttraumatic symptomatology than the actual event (AACAP, 1998; Davis & Siegel, 2000;

McFarlane, 1987; Silva & Kessler, 2004). Silverman and LaGreca (2002) also found that PTSD symptoms are strongly linked to the loss of a loved one, a loss of belongings, and a disruption to a child's everyday life (e.g., school, activities, displacement from home environment).

Exposure to or witnessing of family violence, living with parents who have alcohol or drug problems, and being a member of a low income family are considered high risk factors for the later development of posttraumatic symptoms in children (Clark & Miller, 1998; McCloskey & Walker, 2000; Osofsky, 1995, 2004; Rojas & Pappagallo, 2004; Widom, 1999). As with other traumatic events, the effects of family violence on the development of PTSD are moderated by variables such as whether the violence exposure is a single incident versus chronic exposure, the violence results in a loss, and the violence is directly experienced or witnessed (Silva & Kessler, 2004; Wasserstein & LaGreca, 1998).

SOCIAL AND COMMUNITY FACTORS INFLUENCING RISK AND RESILIENCY

Cultures exposed to natural disaster, war, terrorism, extreme poverty, and genocide have high rates of PTSD among their citizens (Davis & Siegel, 2000). For children living in urban environments in the United States, estimates for the rates of traumatic exposure range from 59% to 67% (Horowitz, Weine, & Jekel, 1995; Silva et al., 2000). However, not all these children go on to receive a diagnosis of PTSD and estimates of prevalence in urban children, range from 24% (Breslau, Davis, Andeski, & Peterson, 1991) to 34.5% (Berman, Kurtines, Silverman, & Serafini, 1996). While these prevalence rates are high, the fact that not all these high risk children go on to develop PTSD speaks to the strength of protective factors promoting resilience in some of these children. Just as parental support is key to a child's successful adjustment, community support and level of responsiveness is key to a parent's adaptive functioning in response to trauma (Aisenberg, 2001; Pynoos et al., 1995). Lack of community support and new immigration status contribute to high percentages of PTSD in immigrant populations (Aisenberg, 2001; Jaycox et al., 2002). Finally, it is important to note that preschool children (less than 5 years) appear to be particularly vulnerable to the adverse effects of community violence (Aisenberg, 2001). These young children have an increased incidence of insecurity, fears, nightmares, regressive behaviors (including clinging and separation anxiety), and bedwetting (Osofsky, 1995, 2004; Scheeringa et al., 1995) following exposure to community violence.

Ethnicity

Again, researchers have documented that PTSD can occur in children across all cultures and ethnic groups (AACAP, 1998). Native American, Hispanic, and African-American children seem to be at greater risk than nonminority children for the development of PTSD (APA, 2004; Rabalais, Ruggerio, & Scotti, 2002). While research on PTSD in children who are minorities is in the early stages, minority teens often report an increase in symptoms of PTSD and increased difficulty recovering from traumatic or adverse life events (Silverman & LaGreca, 2002).

It may not be that ethnicity or culture per se affects the prevalence or incidence of

PTSD, but differences may lie instead in how PTSD is expressed depending on a child's ethnicity or culture (Osofsky, 2004). Cultural norms, values, or beliefs may contribute to a child's view of the event as traumatic (APA, 2004; DiNicola, 1996; Pfefferbaum, 1997). Longstanding feelings of powerlessness, helplessness, disenfranchisement, and poverty may interact with a current stressful life event to intensify the negative outcome of the experience. Further, minority groups' posttraumatic cultural responses can even be misinterpreted and the victims villanized, as evidenced in the United States recently with Hurricane Katrina and historically with Native Americans. Current cultural experiences such as ongoing prejudice and discrimination are also risk factors. It is important to consider both a culture's history of oppression and current cultural experiences when interpreting community responses to traumatic events. For children who experience longstanding prejudice or discrimination in their community, traumatic events may overburden their coping resources. On the other hand, a strong cultural identity, a sense of safety and belonging, and a network of community support, can help these children cope more effectively with current traumatic events (Rabalais et al., 2002). The APA Practice Guidelines (2004) suggest that culture provides a system of social support as well as helping define one's identity. This strong sense of cultural identity can result in a broader and more positive sense of self. Both a strong cultural and general sense of self are critical buffers against the negative effects of adverse life events, including traumatic experiences (Rabalais et al., 2002). Many culturally based practices, such as rituals or traditions associated with loss as well as dancing and storytelling, provide meaning and context for traumatic events and therefore aid the healing process (Osofsky, 2004). The rituals and structure of specific religious practices and spirituality in general it appears can serve as positive cultural moderating variables (di Silva, 1999; Rabalais et al., 2002). As with other risk and resiliency factors, research on the impact of ethnicity and culture has not yet fully explained the nature of these relationships (Rojas & Pappagallo, 2004).

EVIDENCE-BASED TREATMENT INTERVENTIONS FOR PTSD IN CHILDREN

Although there is some empirical research on the treatment of PTSD in childhood, the evidence-based literature is limited primarily to one treatment approach (i.e., cognitive behavioral therapy) with one group of trauma survivors (i.e., sexually abused children). Research support for the efficacy of PTSD treatments varies in terms of methodological rigor, with most investigations utilizing case reports of children being treated for the disorder rather than randomized trials with control groups (Yule, 2001; Yule, Perrin, & Smith, 2001). While there are extensive recommendations and guidelines for treating symptoms of posttraumatic stress in children (i.e., AACAP, 1998; Cohen, Berliner, & March, 2000; Vernberg & Vogel, 1993), the degree of empirical support for these recommendations and guidelines varies. The recommendations for treatment of PTSD in children in this chapter are based on the following definitions of efficacy. Interventions that "work" are those supported by a minimum of three empirical investigations of efficacy which used an experimental design. In addition, interventions that "might work" are those well grounded in theory or supported by less than three empirical investigations.

What Works

Cognitive behavioral therapy (CBT) is the most studied treatment modality when investigating PTSD interventions with children. CBT has been subjected to the most empirical investigations because this modality is amenable to standardized manual-based treatment, making it easier to operationalize therapeutic variables under investigation as well as ensuring reliability of study findings (Schechter & Tosyali, 2001). As such, CBT is most often recommended (e.g., Cohen, Berliner, & March, 2000; Perrin, Smith, & Yule, 2000) as the preferred treatment for PTSD in childhood when used alone or in combination with other approaches.

Trauma-focused cognitive-behavioral interventions for children typically involve a combination of controlled exposure to stimuli associated with a traumatic event, stress/anxiety management, skill development, and cognitive restructuring techniques (Cohen, Berliner, & March, 2000). However, the complexity and degree of CBT interventions should be modified based on the child's developmental level (Myerson et al., 2000), with simplified activities being preferred with children who are younger. For example with younger children cognitive restructuring may involve having the therapist make anxiety-reducing statements to the child that are related to the traumatic event, such as "You're o.k. now" or "You're safe now" (Myerson et al., 2000). There is some controversy about the appropriateness of exposure techniques with children and exposure-based treatment is probably most relevant when specific memories or situational triggers cause distress for the child (AACAP, 1998). Controlled exposure in younger children may be achieved by having him or her act as a "story-teller". In this case, the child is encouraged to gradually generate "the story" of the traumatic event over a series of sessions until the narrative of the child's traumatic experience is completed and "telling the story" can be tolerated by the child. The child should first develop anxiety and stress reduction skills to facilitate her or his capacity to tolerate exposure to recall of "the story." These skills can then be simultaneously practiced while telling the story.

Six controlled-trial studies have been conducted evaluating the efficacy of CBT in treating posttraumatic symptoms in children. Four of the six studies were conducted with school aged sexually abused children (Berliner & Saunders, 1996; Cohen & Mannarino, 1998; Deblinger, Lippman, & Steer, 1996; King et al., 2000) and one with sexually abused preschoolers (Cohen & Mannarino, 1996). The sixth study evaluated a school-based CBT intervention following a natural disaster (Goenjian et al., 1997). Traumatized children participating in individual or family (King et al., 2000) and group CBT (Goenjian et al., 1997) showed a greater reduction in PTSD symptoms than traumatized children in a non-treatment control group. Further, trauma focused CBT (TF-CBT) was more effective than nondirective, supportive therapy (Cohen & Mannarino, 1996, 1998; Deblinger, Lippman, & Steer, 1996) in reducing PTSD symptoms. Berliner and Saunders (1996) found that an intervention combining trauma focused activities and coping skill development was superior to an intervention utilizing trauma focused activities alone.

Outcome research on CBT with traumatized children seems to generally support the efficacy of this approach in reducing symptoms of posttraumatic stress disorder. Further, cognitive-behavioral interventions are adaptable because they have been implemented successfully with children in a wide variety of community-based settings and with different cultural populations (DeArellano et al., 2005). Nevertheless, more research on the use of TF-CBT with children is needed. Most studies of cognitive behavioral interventions in children with PTSD have been conducted on children who were victims of sexual trauma. Therefore, the generalizability of these findings to samples of children experiencing other types of trauma (i.e., war, other forms of interpersonal violence or disasters) is not known. It is also unclear which specific elements of the CBT interventions contribute to efficacy. Finally, clear guidelines for recommended "frequency" and "dosage" of CBT are not yet available (Cohen, Berliner, & March, 2000).

What Might Work

While CBT is the most rigorously researched approach to treatment of PTSD and trauma in children, it is certainly not the only approach to treatment. Unfortunately, other modalities commonly recommended for treatment of PTSD have not been subjected to controlled systematic investigations. At present, other treatment modalities lack sufficient empirical evidence to clearly support their efficacy and therefore are considered treatments for childhood PTSD that "might" be effective. The alternative individual approaches most commonly used include play therapy, creative arts therapies, psychoanalytic therapy, and eye movement desensitization and reprocessing (EMDR). Group and family therapy approaches also are commonly recommended.

Historically, play therapy has been the most commonly recommended approach for treatment of trauma in children (Gil, 1991). In play therapy the child uses representational, often fantasy-based play to rework the trauma in order to gain a sense of mastery and understanding of the event as well to develop mechanisms to cope with the traumatic experience. Since children have not developed a capacity for abstract reasoning it is frequently difficult for them to directly communicate and process their thoughts, feelings, and behaviors. Fantasy and make-believe are integrated naturally as part of a child's play and used to communicate, learn, regulate emotion, practice life roles, and develop ego strength (O'Connor, 2000). Children typically use play to enact conflicts and situations that they do not have the cognitive capacity to express in words (O'Connor, 2000). Further, a child is often less defensive during play and therefore more likely to express negative affect via play (Hall, Kaduson, & Schaefer, 2002). A play therapist identifies the cognitive and affective processes being expressed through the child's representational play and then helps the child develop the language and skills to describe these processes (Russ, 2004).

Trauma-focused play therapy techniques are seen as a developmentally appropriate modality because they use the child's naturally occurring, nonverbal methods of communication (i.e., play) to convey her or his subjective experience related to the trauma (Scheidlinger & Batkin Kahn, 2005). Further, play therapy can serve to increase a child's comfort with expressing emotions related to the trauma (Cohen, Berliner, & March, 2000) and assist children in gaining a sense of control over the traumatic experience (Scheidlinger & Batkin Kahn, 2005). Specific therapeutic goals that enhance effective coping via trauma focused play therapy include: promoting a sense of safety, externalizing the trauma, developing a sense of mastery over the negative affect associated with the trauma, being able to remain present focused when thinking about the trauma (versus dissociating or engaging in posttraumatic play), developing a healthy sense of self, and maintaining healthy relationship boundaries

Few studies are available that examine the efficacy of play therapy techniques. Frick-Helms (1997) used a qualitative research methodology to record the content and process of client-centered play-therapy sessions with children who had symptoms of posttraumatic stress after exposure to domestic violence. The play therapy appeared to serve as an effective mechanism for children to reenact the traumatic event in a way that enabled the emotions associated with the trauma (e.g., tension, anxiety, fear, anger, and sadness) to be adaptively experienced and processed.

Creative therapies which incorporate artistic expression, movement, poetry, drama, or music are often integrated into treatment with children experiencing posttraumatic stress. As with play therapy, some empirical support for creative therapies is available in the form of clinical reports and case studies. However, few outcome-based studies examining the efficacy of these therapies have been conducted. One of the few research studies evaluating the efficacy of art therapy with children and adolescents (Chapman, Morabito, Ladakakos, Schreier, & Knudson, 2001) failed to identify a significant reduction in PTSD following an art therapy treatment intervention. However, these authors did find that children who participated in the art therapy intervention showed a reduction in symptoms of acute stress. Further investigation of the efficacy of creative therapies is needed because these approaches can facilitate the therapeutic process, particularly the exploration of feelings, for children who struggle with talking abstractly about the traumatic event (Read Johnson, 2000).

Similarly, support for psychoanalytic therapy with children exposed to trauma is available through case studies (McElroy & McElroy, 1989; Seinfeld, 1989; Van Leeuwen, 1988). Case studies also offer some support for the use of hypnotherapy with children suffering from posttraumatic stress. Hypnotic techniques can include therapeutic storytelling when processing trauma with children (Rhue & Lynn, 1991). Friedrich (1991) found a significant reduction in symptoms between pre- and posthypnosis treatment assessments, in two case studies of children with posttraumatic stress.

More recently, eye movement desensitization and reprocessing (EMDR) has been recommended as an approach to treat PTSD. In EMDR a clinician assists the child with generating an image or memory associated with the traumatic event. The child then simultaneously follows the clinician's hand with his or her eyes in order to regulate his or her physiological response to the image and memories associated with the trauma (Schechter & Tosyali, 2001; Yule, 2001). EMDR is often described as a potential treatment for PTSD in children, although the treatment is considered controversial (Perrin, Smith, & Yule, 2000).

There have been two controlled trials which offer some empirical support for the use of EMDR with children. Chemtob, Nakashima, and Carlson (2002) conducted a randomized study involving lagged-groups with children exposed to a hurricane disaster. These authors found a significant reduction in PTSD symptoms among those children who had not responded to previous psychotherapy, following three sessions of EMDR. These same children showed a modest reduction in anxiety and depression following the EMDR treatment. Soberman, Greenwald, and Rule (2002) conducted a controlled study with male children and adolescents participating in a day or residential treatment program. EMDR effectively reduced these children and teens symptoms of posttraumatic stress. Additional support for EMDR is available in the form of case studies (Coco & Sharpe, 1993; Greenwald, 1994; Muris & de-Jongh, 1996, Tinker & Wilson, 1999). This emerging outcome literature suggests EMDR might be an effective approach to treating PTSD with children, particularly when other interventions fail.

Although lacking clear empirical validation (Riggs, 2000), conceptually based family therapy models with traumatized children have been proposed (e.g., Figley, 1988; Harris, 1991). Such models involve the therapist establishing trust and building rapport with family members, assessing maladaptive coping skills, developing adaptive coping skills, and increasing communication and support among family members. Trauma focused family systems therapy focuses on reorganizing the family's maladaptive interaction and communication patterns around the traumatic event *and* increasing familial support so the child feels safe and protected following trauma exposure (Faust, 2001). Published research utilizing family systems therapy to treat PTSD has predominantly been conducted with adult populations. Limited support for the use of family systems therapy with children experiencing posttraumatic stress is available in an unpublished study by Faust, Ransom, Weiss, and Phelps-Doray (1999). Children who participated in trauma focused family therapy showed significant symptom reductions in depression and anxiety. While these initial findings are promising, further empirical validation is needed for the use of family systems therapeutic approaches with traumatized children.

Nevertheless, the risk and resiliency literature suggests it is important to include parents when conducting interventions for childhood PTSD. Cohen, Berliner, and March (2000) recommend that children practice coping techniques learned in individual therapy at home with parents between sessions. Parents can assist in identifying signs of symptom relapse in their children (Kruczek, in press). Family interventions also may help reduce the emotional distress experienced by parents due to secondary trauma. By reducing parental emotional distress, parents can be more attentive and responsive to the emotional needs of their children (Burman & Allen-Meares, 1994). This family support is important when treating children with PTSD because research has consistently found that the level of emotional distress experienced by parents is correlated with treatment outcome in sexually abused children, regardless of type of intervention (Cohen & Mannarino, 1996; Davis & Siegel, 2000; McFarlane, 1987; Silva & Kessler, 2004).

Group therapy is commonly used with child trauma survivors. Some empirical support for group treatments of PTSD with the child population is available. Galante and Foa (1986) found children who participated in a group therapy program exhibited significant reductions in the frequency of fears related to surviving an earthquake and were less likely to be at risk for subsequent antisocial and neurotic problems. March, Amaya-Jackson, Murray, and Schulte (1998) used a group intervention combining psychoeducation and cognitive-behavioral techniques to reduce posttraumatic stress symptoms in child trauma survivors.

A few researchers have attempted to determine whether individual or group interventions are superior in reducing symptoms of PTSD in children with trauma exposure. Chemtob, Nakashima, and Hamada (2002) found a reduction in posttraumatic symptoms for children participating in both individual and group trauma focused treatment compared to those assigned to a control condition. However, one treatment context did not appear to be superior to the other. Similarly, Trowell et al. (2002) failed to find a significant difference between individual therapy and a psychoeducational group in reducing general psychopathology or improving global functioning of sexually abused girls. However, those participating in the psychoeducational group did evidence significantly greater reduction in PTSD symptoms than those receiving individual therapy.

While research comparing the efficacy of individual and group therapy in treating childhood PTSD is limited (AACAP, 1998), group therapy continues to be recommended for many child trauma survivors. It is thought that group treatment can combat the sense of alienation and isolation that often follows trauma exposure, especially abusive experiences (Kruczek & Vitanza, 1999). Further, clinicians may be able to reach large numbers of children exposed to the same traumatic event through short-term group interventions (AACAP, 1998). In contrast, children experiencing severe distress or meeting full criteria for PTSD may benefit more from long-term individual treatment. At present, the majority of clinical cases of PTSD in children are treated using individual therapy (Cohen, Berliner, & March, 2000). Short term CBT (i.e., 12–20 sessions) can result in significant improvement for most children who experience a single incident exposure with an uncomplicated stress reaction (McKnight, Compton, & March, 2004).

What Doesn't Work

Currently, there is not a sufficient evidence to identify treatment interventions that "do not work" and thus should be avoided.

Overall Comment

CBT clearly has received the most empirical support to date for the treatment of PTSD in child trauma survivors. However, there currently is not sufficient evidence to support which specific CBT techniques are most efficacious with a given type of trauma exposure. Historically, play therapy has been the treatment of choice with traumatized children, and there is strong theoretical but not empirical support for this treatment approach. EMDR has been used extensively with the adult trauma survivor population and more recently investigated with child trauma survivors. There is some preliminary evidence to support the efficacy of EMDR with traumatized children. There is no clear evidence to support individual versus group approaches to intervention. While there is strong theoretical and related research to support trauma focused family therapy, there again is not clear empirical support for this treatment approach.

Children with a strong capacity for verbal expression and processing (either because of age or cognitive developmental level) are most likely to benefit from trauma focused CBT. Those children less able to express themselves verbally may benefit more from a combination of behaviorally based anxiety/stress management skill development and play or creative arts therapies. Trauma focused family therapy may be necessary when family members are struggling themselves with the traumatic event or experiencing secondary trauma.

It may be that certain types of trauma exposure are more amenable to individual versus group interventions. Single incident, uncomplicated stress reactions can likely be treated with group CBT. Longer term trauma exposure (i.e., abuse, war, chronic community-based violence) with more extensive PTSD symptoms may require more intensive individual therapy in combination with group or family therapy. At present, interventions for any given child should be based on a thorough assessment of that child's unique treatment needs and guided by the available research.

Psychopharmacology and PTSD

Limited empirical data is available to guide medication interventions of PTSD with child survivors of trauma. There has been only one randomized, double blind, control group trial and several open trial studies. One of the problems with open trial studies is that all participants (child, physician, and family) know which medication the child is receiving. Thus, it is impossible in open trial studies to distinguish between gains due exclusively to the medication or gains due to a placebo effect. With the placebo effect gains occur simply because the participants *expect* a positive result from treatment with medication. Current medication recommendations for treating PTSD in children are based on rational pharmacotherapy (Friedman, 1990). When using this approach, medication interventions are based on what is known about the physiological mechanisms of the disorder and the neurobiological action of the medication.

The class of neurotransmitters collectively referred to as the catecholamines (NE, EPI, and DA) are most implicated in PTSD symptoms. The adrenergic system in particular (NE and EPI) plays a key role in PTSD symptomatology. The severity of PTSD symptoms is also correlated positively with DA elevations. Both child and adult trauma survivors demonstrate elevated DA levels (DeBellis et al., 1999). The mood regulation symptoms which are often comorbid with PTSD (i.e., anxiety, aggression, impulsivity, obsessions and compulsions, and suicidality) are influenced by serotonin (5-HT) (Friedman, 1990).

Rational pharmacotherapy would suggest drugs affecting the catecholamines and serotonin as the treatment of choice for PTSD in children. Indeed, the selective serotonin reuptake inhibitors (SSRIs) are currently the medication of choice for PTSD (Lubit, 2006). The SSRIs are used to manage the re-experiencing and avoidance symptoms as well as anxiety and depression. The SSRIs most often used with child survivors include fluox-etine (Prozac), sertraline (Zoloft), paroxetine (Paxil), fluvoxamine (Luvox) and citaloram (Celexa). Of these medications, only two (fluoxetine and sertraline) have received U.S. Food and Drug Administration (FDA) approval for use with children. Sertraline is approved for treatment of obsessive-compulsive disorder (OCD) in children older than 6, and fluoxetine is approved for depression in children and adolescents. To date, there has only been one open trial investigation of the efficacy of an SSRI with child trauma survivors. Seedat et al. (2002) investigated the efficacy of citalopram to reduce PTSD symptoms in children and adolescents. This open trial study suggested the children's PTSD symptoms were decreased to a level comparable to adults. One advantage of the SSRIs is their benign side effect profile. However, in 2003 the FDA issued a public health advisory, and the United Kingdom's Medicines and Healthcare Products Regula-tive Agency (MHRA) (2003) issued a precautionary statement about use of this class of medications with children and teens, due to the potential increased risk for self-harm and suicidal behaviors. The MHRA specifically banned the use of paroxetine with chil-dren and teens due to the high risk for self-harm behaviors, but concluded fluoxetine has a positive risk-benefit ratio when treating depression in children and teens. Simon, Savarino, Operskalski, and Wang (2006) recently conducted a wide scale study of sui-cide risk and antidepressant medications (including SSRIs). These authors found that while the overall prevalence of suicide attempts was significantly higher in children and adolescents (as compared to adults), the risk of suicide attempts for all age groups was actually highest in the month preceding antidepressant intervention and declined steadily after starting medication. Further, there was no increased risk of suicide attempt with the newer antidepressant medications. That said, the FDA's "black box" warning for use of the SSRIs with children and adolescents remains in effect.

The most investigated medication interventions for PTSD in children have been with those drugs affecting the catecholamine system. Antihypertensive medications (adrenergic agents) were originally developed to treat high blood pressure, but are frequently used to remediate the physical sequelae of anxious symptoms in child trauma survivors. Beta-blockers such as propranolol (Inderal) are used to treat symptoms of hyperarousal. Alpha adrenergic agonists such as clonidine (Catapres) and guanfacine (Tenex) reduce arousal and reexperiencing symptoms as well as decrease the neuropsychological kindling associated with chronic illness (Lubit, 2006). Clonidine is not FDA approved for use in children but is commonly used with this population. The FDA does not recommend use of guanfacine in children less than 12 years of age. The efficacy of these medications in treating childhood symptoms of PTSD has been demonstrated in several open-trial studies (i.e., Famularo, Kinscherff, & Fenton, 1988; Harmon & Riggs, 1996; Perry, 1994). However, while these medications appear to have some benefits, the potential for severe adverse side effects, especially the risk of cardiovascular crisis with abrupt discontinuation of the alpha-adrenergic agonists, suggest extreme caution should be utilized when using them with children (Lubit, 2006).

Additionally, the antipsychotic medications also affect the catecholamine system as DA agonists. This class of medications has been regularly used to treat PTSD in adults (Donnelly et al., 1999). Recently the lower risk of adverse side effects with the atypical antipsychotics such as risperidone (Risperdal), olanzapine (Zyprexa), and quetiapine (Seroquel) has lead to their increased use (Friedman, 1998). In an open trial investigation, Horrigan & Barnhill (1999) evaluated the efficacy of risperidone in a small sample of boys with severe PTSD and a high rate of comorbid psychiatric disorders (i.e., attention deficit hyperactivity disorder, oppositional defiant disorder, bipolar disorder, conduct disorder, psychosis, and major depression). Half of these children demonstrated significant improvement in PTSD symptoms with another 22% showing moderate improvement and 11% mild improvement. Again caution should be exercised when using this class of medications given their negative side effect profile (Cohen, 2001), including increased risk for developing diabetes (Koller, Malozowski, & Doraiswamy, 2001).

The monoamine oxidase inhibitors (MAOIs) and tricyclic antidepressants (TCAs) act on both the adrenergic and seratonergic systems. These classes of medications have been used successfully to treat the symptoms of PTSD in adults (Cohen, 2001). In adults, MAOIs, such as phenelzine (Nardil), have been successful in treating all three symptom clusters of PTSD (Friedman, Davidson, Mellman, & Southwick, 2000). TCAs, including imipramine (Tofranil), desipramine (Norpramine), and amitriptyline (Elavil) also have been used successfully with adults (Cohen, 2001). There has been one double-blind, randomized trial of imipramine (one of the TCAs) with children. In this investigation children on an acute burn unit were treated with either imipramine or chloral hydrate in an attempt to prevent the development of PTSD. The children receiving imipramine were significantly less likely to develop subsequent symptoms of PTSD than those treated with chloral hydrate (Roberts, Blackeney, Villareal, Rosenbert, & Meyer, 1999). The efficacy of this medication with other types of trauma has not been established. Further, these two classes of medication have significant and potentially dangerous side effect profiles. There are considerable food and medication interactions with the MAOIs that can be fatal. While rare, TCAs can result in sudden cardiac arrest and death. These medications are not recommended as a first line treatment due to their potentially life threatening side effects (Cohen, 2001).

In adults, anticonvulsants, also known as mood stabilizers, have been used to successfully treat the symptoms of hyperarousal, impulsivity, and kindling in chronic PTSD (Lubit, 2006). Again, in adults carbamazepine (Tegretol) has been shown to decrease reexperiencing and avoidant symptoms while valproic acid (Depakote and Depakene) decreased reexperiencing and hyperarousal (Friedman & Southwick, 2000). Valproic acid can be helpful in managing impulsivity and dissociation (Lubit, 2006). While these medications are approved for the treatment of seizure disorders in children, there have been no empirical investigations of the efficacy of the mood stabilizers to treat PTSD in children.

THE PREVENTION OF PTSD

The best way to prevent PTSD in children is to limit exposure to traumatic life experiences. However, once exposed to trauma, the available prevention research tends to focus on early intervention for children in an attempt to prevent subsequent development of PTSD symptoms (APA, 2004). Theoretical models of developmental psychopathology suggest if traumatized children do not receive early intervention following an adverse life event, then they are at increased risk for maladjustment as they progress through later developmental phases. Untreated posttraumatic symptoms, negative coping behaviors, and taxed resources can combine to eventually result in deleterious adjustment and long-standing psychopathology (Bosquet, 2004). Therefore, early intervention with children exposed to traumatic life events is critical to prevent not only later adult posttraumatic symptoms, but to promote positive development in these children.

What Works

Primary prevention of PTSD often includes psychoeducational interventions as an effective part of the acute crisis intervention (AACAP, 1998). While psychoeducational groups can be conducted with traumatized children, they are more typically provided for parents and teachers. When the psychoeducational group is conducted with the children, there are two overarching goals. The first is to help the child understand a normal stress reaction and the second is to help the child develop adaptive coping strategies to minimize the likelihood of future reenactment and risk taking (Nader, 2001). The first goal of psychoeducational groups with parents and teachers is learning about typical stress reactions at the child's corresponding developmental level. These adults are then alerted to the signs and symptoms of maladaptive coping in an attempt to enable them to identify the need for early intervention (Kruczek, in press). Finally, these psychoeducational interventions help identify the ways that parents and teachers can best support children's adaptive response to trauma. Preventive psychoeducational groups have been successfully implemented in schools (Blom, 1986; LaGreca, Silverman, Vernberg, & Prinstein, 1996; Rigamer, 1986) and hospitals (Butler, Rizzi, & Handwerger, 1996).

Psychological debriefing is the specific form of psychoeducation that is used directly with traumatized children to prevent the development of PTSD. The objective of psychological debriefing is to facilitate the recovery process for children following trauma exposure, and to prevent rather than treat posttraumatic symptomatology (Yule & Canterbury, 1994). Psychological debriefing can help children correctly understand the traumatic event that occurred. Children experiencing traumatic events may not fully comprehend what they experienced, and in an effort to make sense of the event they may incorrectly fill in memory gaps or misperceptions with fantasy based interpretations. Because many young children still hold egocentric worldviews, they often display "magical thinking" with regard to their own culpability or role in the event. Psychological debriefing can correct these misperceptions and misunderstandings about the actual event and the child's role in the event. Additionally, psychological debriefing can be used to normalize and express thoughts and feelings the child may be experiencing as well as to develop coping skills for dealing with trauma reactions.

Several researchers (Stallard & Law, 1993; Vila, Porche, & Mouren-Simeoni, 1999; Yule, 1992; Yule & Udwin, 1991) have studied psychological debriefing in children or teens exposed to traumatic events. This preventive intervention has been shown to be effective in reducing symptoms of posttraumatic stress following a variety of community-based traumatic events. Psychological debriefing appears to be particularly effective in reducing intrusive thoughts and avoidance behaviors (Stallard & Law, 1993; Yule, 1992).

Three studies have been conducted utilizing psychological debriefing with children or adolescents. Yule and Udwin (1991) evaluated the efficacy of psychological debriefing with a group of youth who had experienced a ferryboat sinking. Identified through initial screenings as being at high risk for development of PTSD, these youth were more likely to seek help after the event and to participate in voluntary group sessions. However, at a five-month follow-up, these "high risk" youth reported higher levels of depression, anxiety, intrusive thoughts, and avoidant behavior compared to lower risk peers. Further, while those "high risk" youth who participated in the psychological debriefing had lower levels of intrusive thoughts than those who did not, they remained constant in levels of anxiety and depression.

Stallard and Law (1993) also examined the effect of psychological debriefing. They investigated the effect of a two-session group psychological debriefing with adolescent survivors of a minibus accident. Again, the debriefing resulted in significant reductions of intrusive thoughts and avoidance. However, in this study participants also displayed a reduction in anxiety and depression at three-month follow-up. Finally, Vila et al. (1999) provide the only known empirical evaluation of debriefing with children only. These authors compared levels of posttraumatic distress in those children who did and did not receive psychological debriefing after having been held hostage. Those children who participated in the psychological debriefing received lower follow-up ratings of posttraumatic distress than did the children who did not participate in the debriefing intervention.

Generally speaking, debriefing should occur within 72 hours following the traumatic event (Mitchell, 1983). However, psychological readiness is particularly important when conducting psychological debriefing with children (Stallard & Satler, 2003). It is important to reestablish the child's sense of safety before administering psychological debriefing interventions (Wraith, 2000). Similarly, children need to have worked through the immediate shock and numbness associated with the traumatic event in order to address the cognitive and affective tasks of debriefing (Chemtob, 2000; Yule, 1994).

Psychological debriefing can be offered in an individual or group format and should be tailored to the client's developmental level (Stallard & Satler, 2003). Nonverbal materials like dolls, toys, and art supplies may help to facilitate discussions when using debriefing with younger children. Elementary school aged children are capable of focusing on observable behaviors and factual information related to the trauma. However, children at this age will have difficulty exploring abstract ideas (e.g., danger or threat to self) related to the traumatic event and understanding the long-term ramifications of their traumatic experience, as this is a feature of formal operations. As previously discussed, blame reduction is also important for children falling within this age range given that they often believe they in some way caused or are responsible for the traumatic event.

What Might Work

As with treatment interventions, psychological debriefing can include collateral family involvement. The collateral debriefing sessions with parents are designed to teach them how to reduce their own distress while providing support to their children. Psychological debriefing is particularly important in situations where both the child and parent(s) experienced the traumatic event. To date, no research has examined the effectiveness of joint psychological debriefings in reducing PTSD symptoms in children. However, psychological debriefing is commonly used to reduce PTSD symptoms in adult trauma survivors (Stallard & Satler, 2003).

Pynoos and Nader (1988) proposed psychological first aid, a prevention program that while similar in therapeutic goals to psychological debriefing, is recommended for use with children more broadly exposed to community violence (e.g., sniper attacks, shootings, murders). Psychological first aid can be provided to children individually, with their families, or in a group context near or on the site where the violence occurred (particularly if the violence occurred at or near a school). Psychological first aid shares similar objectives with psychological debriefing including: assessing the degree of risk for experiencing posttraumatic stress, clarifying cognitive misperceptions related to the trauma, reinforcing supportive relationships with parents or school staff (e.g., teachers, school counselors, school nurses), encouraging adaptive emotional expression and help-seeking behavior, and providing psychoeducation about posttraumatic symptoms (with parents in the case of younger children). Currently, there are no published studies substantiating the efficacy of psychological first aid with children. Given the similarity to psychological debriefing, the technique should be considered one that "might work" in preventing PTSD in children.

As discussed earlier in this section, the best way to prevent posttraumatic symptoms in children is to limit trauma exposure. The RAND Corporation reviewed intervention programs for children and youth and provided several specific recommendations with regard to childhood trauma. Those recommendations included: developing zero tolerance for abuse, early intervention and prevention with at risk youth, focusing on children's development of "emotional intelligence" to facilitate adaptive coping with stressors, and improving children's access to mental health care professionals with expertise in traumatology (Stien & Kendall, 2004). The Violence Intervention Program (VIP) is a good example of one such community-based prevention program. This program for children was developed in an attempt to ameliorate the negative effects of witnessing domestic violence (Osofsky, Hammer, Freeman, & Rovaris, 2004). These authors found that a combination of crisis intervention, traditional psychological treatment, and community support was effective in reducing the development of posttraumatic symptoms and future victimization in high risk children. The program provided trauma focused education to law enforcement individuals, families, professionals, and the community at large. Collaboration between these groups and prompt referral to additional community resources was encouraged.

What Doesn't Work

Sufficient research is not yet available to identify preventive interventions that do not work.

Overall Comment

Psychoeducational intervention is the most commonly used preventive intervention for posttraumatic symptoms. There is sufficient evidence to support the use of psychological debriefing techniques with child trauma survivors. Psychological first aid has been suggested as an intervention to minimize the development of trauma symptoms in those exposed to community violence. While there is no direct evidence to support this preventive intervention, its similarity to psychological debriefing suggests it might be an effective intervention. There is no clear evidence to support individual over group prevention strategies; however, most preventive strategies described in this section were offered in a group format.

Wraith (2000) suggests the need for ongoing stress management for those children who have experienced traumatic events. As traumatized children grow older, it is advisable to monitor their long term coping and adjustment. For some of these young people future stressful events may serve to exacerbate trauma reactions and trigger a reemergence of posttraumatic symptoms. Likewise, previously asymptomatic youth may display later posttraumatic symptoms as they encounter future stressful life events.

RECOMMENDED BEST PRACTICE

Best practice with PTSD in children starts with the accurate identification of posttraumatic reactions in this population. While children appear to display symptoms from all three clusters comprising the DSM-IV-TR diagnostic criteria, they frequently do not display sufficient numbers of symptoms to meet the current criteria. Further, some symptoms are not developmentally relevant and others not included in the current diagnostic criteria seem more developmentally indicative of a posttraumatic disorder in children. Assessment recommendations are:

- Children displaying one or more developmentally adjusted symptoms from each cluster (reexperiencing, avoidance/numbing, and hyperarousal) are likely displaying a posttraumatic stress disorder.

- Children displaying posttrauma onset of fear and aggression symptoms (i.e., aggressive acting out, separation anxiety, fear of toileting/dark/new situations, etc.) in addition to the above symptom clusters may be experiencing a posttraumatic stress disorder.
- Children may alternate between periods of reexperiencing and avoidance/numbing symptoms versus displaying these symptoms concurrently.
- Children may have difficulty verbally identifying and articulating thoughts or feelings associated with their trauma response. These experiences are more likely to be manifest via posttraumatic play, nightmares, and generalized fear/anxiety reactions.

Treatment of PTSD must occur within an appropriate cultural context for the children being treated. While there are extensive recommendations for treating PTSD in children, there is little outcome research to support most intervention approaches. Available literature suggests the following best practices when treating children with PTSD:

- Trauma focused CBT (TF-CBT) is currently a first line treatment for PTSD in children. However, even though TF-CBT has received the most empirical support to date, there is not sufficient evidence to identify which CBT techniques are most efficacious with different types of trauma exposure. Most of this research has been done with sexual abuse survivors. Therefore, this approach is clearly best practice with this population.
- Children with a strong capacity for verbal expression and processing (due to their level of cognitive developmental level) are likely to benefit most from TF-CBT.
- Single incident, uncomplicated stress reactions probably can be treated effectively with group TF-CBT and may not require individual treatment.
- Children with a less well developed capacity for verbal expression may benefit from a combination of behaviorally based anxiety/stress management skill development and play or creative arts therapies as opposed to TF-CBT.
- EMDR may be an effective treatment of PTSD, particularly in those children who have not responded to more traditional interventions.
- Trauma focused family therapy can be a useful adjunct to individual and group interventions with traumatized children. Trauma focused family therapy should promote adaptive interaction and communication patterns around the traumatic event while increasing familial support to help the child feel safe and protected. Trauma focused family therapy may be particularly important when family members are experiencing secondary PTSD or struggling with successful coping themselves.
- Children experiencing longer term trauma exposure (i.e., abuse, chronic community-based violence, war) and more extensive PTSD symptoms may require a combination of intensive individual, group, or family therapy.

Given the dearth of controlled trial studies of medication interventions for PTSD in children, current recommendations for pharmacological treatment of PTSD in children are based on rational pharmacotherapy. This approach uses what is known about the physiological mechanisms of the disorder and the neurobiological action of the medication to guide medication choices. Thus:

- When psychotherapy interventions are not sufficient to manage the symptoms of PTSD in children, the SSRIs are considered the first line medication choice. Of the SSRIs only fluoxetine (Prozac) and sertraline (Zoloft) have received FDA approval for use in children. However, this approval is for psychiatric disorders other than PTSD. Children treated with an SSRI should be closely monitored for risk of self-harm and suicidal behaviors.
- Caution should be exercised when using other classes of medication to treat PTSD in children. The risk-benefit ratio of alternative medications should be closely evaluated given the significant negative side effect profiles of most other medications *and* a lack of empirical support for their efficacy in treating this disorder in children.

Ideally, children's exposure to traumatic life events would be limited, thereby preventing PTSD in this population. Unfortunately many children do have traumatic life experiences and once exposed these children may need both short term, immediate preventive interventions to minimize acute stress reactions, and longer term preventive interventions to reduce the risk of PTSD. The following are recommendations for best practices in the prevention of PTSD:

- Psychoeducational interventions are the most commonly used and best supported preventive interventions for stress disorders. Psychoeducational interventions should be provided directly to child survivors, to their parents, and to their teachers-caregivers.
- Psychological debriefing is a specific form of psychoeducation provided to child trauma survivors that can effectively be used to help children understand normal stress reactions, express their thoughts and feelings about the experience, and develop adaptive coping skills to deal with the traumatic event. Debriefing should also be used to dispel any misconceptions the child has about the traumatic event and his or her role in the event. Typically debriefing should occur within 72 hours of the event. However the child's sense of safety must clearly be reestablished before attempting the debriefing. As with all child trauma interventions, nonverbal materials can be used to facilitate the debriefing and should match the developmental level of the child.
- Psychological first aid is similar to psychological debriefing, but should be used more broadly with children exposed to community violence.
- Psychoeducational and debriefing preventive interventions with parents, teachers, and caregivers should focus on providing information about stress reactions at the children's developmental level and ways to promote the children's adaptive coping. Adults can then aid in the early identification of those children requiring more intensive treatment interventions.
- Collateral psychological debriefing is important when parents and family experienced the traumatic event, are experiencing secondary posttraumatic stress, or are struggling with effective coping. The goal of this collateral debriefing is to reduce the family member's own distress while enabling her or him to provide support to the child.
- Children who experience a traumatic life event should be monitored as they grow older. Future stressors and normal developmental transitions can precipitate later

posttraumatic reactions, even in children who were previously asymptomatic. Early identification and intervention can minimize the severity of these later posttraumatic reactions.

• Community-based prevention programs should include the education of and collaboration between law enforcement individuals, families, professionals, and the community at large. These programs should offer a combination of crisis intervention services, traditional psychological interventions, and community support.

REFERENCES

Aisenberg, E. (2001). The effects of exposure to community violence upon Latina mothers and preschool children. *Hispanic Journal of Behavioral Sciences, 23*(4), 378–398.

Amaya-Jackson, L., & March, J. (1995). Posttraumatic stress disorder in adolescents: Risk factors, diagnosis, and intervention. *Adolescent Medicine, 6,* 251–269.

American Psychiatric Association. (1980). *Diagnostic and statistical manual of mental disorders* (3rd ed.). Washington, D.C.: Author.

American Psychiatric Association. (1987). *Diagnostic and statistical manual of mental disorders* (3rd ed., rev.). Washington, D.C.: Author.

American Psychiatric Association. (2000). *Diagnostic and statistical manual of mental disorders* (4th ed., TR). Washington, D.C.: Author.

American Psychiatric Association. (2004). Practice guidelines for the treatment of patients with acute stress disorder and posttraumatic stress disorder. *American Journal of Psychiatry* [On-line]. Available: www.psych.org/psych_pract/treat/pg/PTSD-PG-PartsA-B-C-New.pdf

American Academy of Child and Adolescent Psychiatry. (1998). Practice parameters for the assessment and treatment of children and adolescents with posttraumatic stress disorder. *Journal of the American Academy of Child and Adolescent Psychiatry, 37*(10), 4S–26S.

Berliner, L., & Saunders, B. E. (1996). Treating fear and anxiety in sexually abused children: Results of controlled 2-year follow-up study. *Child Maltreatment, 1,* 294–309.

Berman, S. L., Kurtines, W. M., Silverman, W. K., & Serafini, L. T. (1996). The impact of exposure to crime and violence on urban youth. *American Journal of Orthopsychiatry, 66,* 329–336.

Blom, G. E. (1986). A school disaster: Intervention and research aspects. *Journal of the American Academy of Child Psychiatry, 25,* 336–345.

Boney-McCoy, S., & Finkelhor, D. (1995). Prior victimization: A risk factor for child sexual abuse and for PTSD related symptomatology among sexually abused youth. *Child Abuse and Neglect, 19,* 1401–1421.

Bosquet, M. (2004). How research informs clinical work with traumatized young children. In J. Osofsky (Ed.), *Young children and trauma: Intervention and treatment* (pp. 301–325). New York: Guilford.

Breslau, N. Davis, C. G., Andeski, P., & Peterson, E. (1991). Traumatic events and posttraumatic stress disorder in an urban population of young adults. *Archives of General Psychiatry, 48,* 216–222.

Burman, S., & Allen-Meares, P. (1994). Neglected victims of murder: Children's witness to parental homicide. *Social Work, 39*(1), 28–34.

Butler, R. W., Rizzi, L. P., & Handwerger, B. A. (1996). Brief report: The assessment of posttraumatic stress disorder in pediatric cancer patients and survivors. *Journal of Pediatric Psychology, 21*(4), 499–504.

Chantarujikapong, S. I., Scherrer, J. F., Xian, H., Eisen, S. A., Lyons, M. J., Goldberg, J., et al. (2001). A twin study of generalized anxiety disorder symptoms, panic disorder symptoms and post-traumatic stress disorder in men. *Psychiatry Research, 103*(2–3), 133–145.

Chapman, L., Morabito, D., Ladakakos, C., Schreier, H., Knudson, M. (2001). The effectiveness of art therapy interventions in reducing post traumatic stress disorder (PTSD) symptoms in pediatric trauma patients. *Art Therapy, 18*(2), 100–104.

Chemtob, C .M. (2000) Delayed debriefing: After a disaster. In B. Raphael & J. P. Wilson (Eds.), *Psychological debriefing: Theory, practice and evidence* (pp. 145–160). Cambridge, UK: Cambridge University Press.

Chemtob, C. M., Nakashima, J., & Carlson, J. G. (2002). Brief treatment for elementary school children with disaster-related posttraumatic stress disorder: A field study. *Journal of Clinical Psychology*, 58(1), 99–112.

Chemtob, C. M., Nakashima, J. P., & Hamada, R. S. (2002).Psychosocial intervention for postdisaster trauma symptoms in elementary school children: A controlled community field study. *Archives of Pediatric and Adolescent Medicine, 156*(3), 211–216.

Cicchetti, D. (2003). Neuroendocrine functioning in maltreated children. In D. Cicchetti & E. Walker (Eds.), *Neurodevelopmental mechanisms in psychopathology* (pp. 345–365). New York: Cambridge University Press.

Clark, D. B., & Miller, T. W. (1998). Stress response and adaptation in children: Theoretical models. In T. W. Miller (Ed.), *Children of trauma: Stressful life events and their effects on children and adolescents* (pp. 3–27). Madison, CT: International Universities Press.

Coco, N., & Sharpe, L. (1993). An auditory variant of eye movement desensitization in a case of childhood post-traumatic stress disorder. *Journal of Behavior Therapy and Experimental Psychiatry, 24,* 373–377.

Cohen, J. A. (2001). Pharmacologic treatment of traumatized children. *Trauma, Violence, and Abuse, 2(2),* 155–171.

Cohen, J. A., Berliner, L., & March, J. S. (2000). Treatment of children and adolescents. In. E. B. Foa, T. M. Keane, & M. J. Friedman (Eds.), *Effective treatments for PTSD: Practice guidelines from the International Society for Traumatic Stress Studies* (pp. 106–138). New York: Guilford.

Cohen, J. A., & Mannarino, A. P. (1996). A treatment outcome study for sexually abused preschool children: Initial findings. *Journal of the American Academy of Child and Adolescent Psychiatry, 35,* 42–50.

Cohen, J. A., & Mannarino, A. P. (1998). Factors that mediate treatment outcome in sexually abused preschool children: Six and 12-month follow-up. *Journal of the American Academy of Child and Adolescent Psychiatry, 37,* 44–51.

Cohen, J. A., Perel, J. M., DeBellis, M. D., Friedman, M. J., & Putnam, F. W. (2002). Treating traumatized children: Clinical implications of the psychobiology of posttraumatic stress disorder. *Trauma, Violence, & Abuse, 3(2),* 91–108.

Davidson, S., & Smith, R. (1990). Traumatic experiences in psychiatric outpatients. *Journal of Traumatic Stress Studies, 3,* 459–475.

Davis, L., & Siegel, L. J. (2000). Posttraumatic stress disorder in children and adolescents: A review and analysis. *Clinical Child and Family Psychology Review, 3(3),* 135–154.

DeArellano, M. W., Waldrop, A. E., Deblinger, E., Cohen, J. A., Kmett Danielson, C., & Mannarino, A. R. (2005). Community outreach program for child victims of child victims of traumatic events. *Behavior Modification, 29(1),* 130–155.

DeBellis, M. D. (2005). The psychobiology of neglect. *Child Maltreatment, 10(2),* 150–172.

DeBellis, M. D., Baum, A. S., Birmaher, B., Keshavan, M. S., Eccard, C. H., Boring, A. M. et al. (1999). Developmental traumatology, part I: Biological stress systems. *Biological Psychiatry, 45,* 1259–1270.

Deblinger, E., Lippman, J., & Steer, R. (1996). Sexually abused children suffering post-traumatic stress symptoms: Initial treatment findings. *Child Maltreatment, 1,* 310–21.

DiNicola, V. F. (1996). Ethnocultural aspects of PTSD and related disorders among children and adolescents. In A. J. Marsella, M. J. Friedman, E. T. Gerrity, & R. M. Scurfield (Eds.), *Ethnocultural aspects of posttraumatic stress disorder* (pp. 389–414). Washington, D.C.: American Psychological Association.

di Silva, P. (1999). Cultural aspects of posttraumatic stress disorder. In W. Yule (Ed.), *Posttraumatic stress disorders: Concepts and therapy* (pp. 116–137). New York: Wiley.

Donnelly, C. I., Amaya-Jackson, L., & March, J. S. (1999). Psychopharmacology of pediatric posttraumatic stress disorder. *Journal of Child and Adolescent Psychopharmacology, 9(3),* 203–220.

Eichenbaum, H., & Cohen N. J. (2001). *From conditioning to conscious recollection: Memory systems of the brain.* Oxford: Oxford University Press.

Famularo, R., Kinscherff, R., & Fenton, T. (1988). Propranolol treatment for childhood PTSD acute type. *American Journal of Diseases of Childhood, 142,* 1244–1247.

Farkas, B. (2004). Etiology and pathogenesis of PTSD in children and adolescents. In R. R. Silva (Ed.), *Posttraumatic stress disorders in children and adolescents* (pp. 123–140). New York: W.W. Norton.

Faust, J. (2001). Post traumatic stress disorder in children and adolescents: Conceptualization and treatment. In H. Orvaschel, J. Faust, & M. Hersen (Eds.), *Handbook of conceptualization and treatment of child psychopathology* (pp. 239–265). Amsterdam, Netherlands: Pergamon/Elsevier.

Faust, J., Ransom, M., Weiss, D., & Phelps-Doray, D. (1999). *Comparison of two treatments for sexually abused children with PTSD.* Paper presented at the annual meeting of the American Psychological Association: Boston.

Figley, C. R. (1988). A five-phase treatment of post-traumatic stress disorder in families. *Journal of Traumatic Stress, 1,* 127–141.

Flouri, E. (2005). Post-traumatic stress disorder (PTSD): What we have learned and what we still have not found out. *Journal of Interpersonal Violence, 20(4),* 373–379.

Foa, E. B., Keane, T. M., & Friedman, M. J. (2000). Introduction. In E. B. Foa, T. M. Keane, & M. J. Friedman (Eds.), *Effective treatments for PTSD: Practice guidelines from the International Society for Traumatic Stress Studies* (pp. 106–138). New York: Guilford.

Foa, E. B, Zinbarg, R., & Rothbaum, B. O. (1992). Uncontrollability and unpredictability in post-traumatic stress disorder: An animal model. *Psychological Bulletin, 112*(2), 218–238.

Friedrich, W. N. (1991). Hypnotherapy with traumatized children. *International Journal of Clinical and Experimental Hypnosis, 39*, 67–81.

Freud, A. (1966). *The ego and the mechanisms of defense.* In *The Writings of Anna Freud* (Vol. 2). New York: International Universities Press. (Original work published 1936)

Frick-Helms, S. B. (1997). "Boys cry better than girls": Play therapy behaviors of children residing in a shelter for battered women. *International Journal of Play Therapy, 6*(1), 73–91.

Friedman, M. J. (1990). Interrelationships between biological mechanisms and pharmacotherapy of posttraumatic stress disorder. In M. E. Wolfe & A. D. Mosnian (Eds.), *Posttraumatic stress disorder: Etiology, phenomenology, and treatment* (pp. 204–225). Washington, D.C.: American Psychiatric Press.

Friedman, M. J. (1998). Current and future drug treatment for posttraumatic stress disorder patients. *Psychiatric Annals, 28*, 461–468.

Friedman, M. J., Davidson, J. R., Mellman, T. A. & Southwick, S. M. (2000). Pharmacotherapy. In E. B. Foa, T. M. Keane, & M. J. Friedman (Eds.), *Effective treatment for PTSD* (pp. 84–105). New York: Guilford.

Friedman, M. J., & Southwick, S. M. (2000). Towards pharmacotherapy for posttraumatic stress disorder. In M. J. Friedman, D. S. Charney, & Y. A. Deutsch (Eds.), *Neurobiological and clinical consequences of stress: From normal adaptation to PTSD* (pp. 465–481). Philadelphia: J.B. Lippincott.

Galante, R., & Foa, D. (1986). An epidemiological study of psychic trauma and treatment effectiveness for children after a natural disaster. *Journal of the American Academy of Child Psychiatry, 25*(3), 357–363.

Gil, E. (1991). *The healing power of play: Therapy with abused children.* New York: Guilford.

Goenjian, A. K., Karayan, I., Pynoos, R. S., Minassian, D., Najarian, L. M., Stienberg, A. M., et al. (1997). Outcome of psychotherapy among early adolescents after trauma. *American Journal of Psychiatry, 154*, 536–542.

Greenwald, R. (1994). Applying eye movement desensitization and reprocessing (EMDR) to the treatment of traumatized children: Five case studies. *Anxiety Disorders Practice Journal, 1*, 83–97.

Hall, T. M., Kaduson, H. G., & Schaefer, C. E. (2002). Fifteen effective play therapy techniques. *Professional Psychology: Research and Practice, 33*, 515–522.

Harris, C. J. (1991). A family crisis-intervention model for the treatment of posttraumatic stress reaction. *Journal of Traumatic Stress, 4*, 195–207.

Harmon R. J. & Riggs, P. D. (1996). Clinical perspectives: Clonidine for PTSD in preschool children. *Journal of the American Academy of Child and Adolescent Psychiatry, 35*, 1247–1249.

Harvey, J., & Delfabbro, P. H. (2004). Psychological resilience in disadvantaged youth: A critical overview. *Australian Psychologist, 39*(1), 3–13.

Horrigan, J. P., & Barnhill, L. J. (1999). Risperidone and PTSD in boys. *Journal of Neuropsychiatry and Clinical Neuroscience, 11*, 126–127.

Horowitz, K., Weine, S., & Jekel, J. (1995). PTSD symptoms in urban adolescent girls. *Journal of the American Academy of Child and Adolescent Psychiatry, 34*(10), 1353–1361.

Jaycox, L. H., Stein, B. D., Kataoka, S. H., Wong, M., Find, A., Escudero, P..et al. (2002). Violence exposure, posttraumatic stress disorder, and depressive symptoms among recent immigrant schoolchildren. *Journal of the American Academy of Child and Adolescent Psychiatry, 41*(9), 1104–1110.

Kaplow, J. B., Dodge, K. A., Amaya-Jackson, L., & Saxe, G. N. (2005). Pathways to PTSD, part II: Sexually abused children. *American Journal of Psychiatry, 162*(7), 1305–1310.

Kardiner, A. (1941). *The traumatic neurosis of war.* New York: Hoeber.

Kehne, J. H., Hoffman, D., & Baron, B. (2005). CRF$_1$ receptor antagonists for the treatment of anxiety, depression, and stress disorders: An update. In C. M. Velotis (Ed.), *Anxiety disorder research* (pp. 89–112). Hauppauge, NY: Nova Science.

Keppel-Benson, J. M., & Ollendick, T. H. (1993). Posttraumatic stress disorders in children and adolescents. In C. F. Saylor (Ed.), *Children and disasters* (pp. 29–43). New York: Plenum.

King, N., Tonge, B. J., Mullen, P. Myerson, N., Heyne, D., Rollings, S., et al. (2000). Treating sexually abused children with posttraumatic stress symptoms: A randomized clinical trial. *Journal of the Academy of Child and Adolescent Psychiatry, 39*(11), 1347–1355.

Knight, R. T., Grabowecky, M. F., & Scabini, D. (1995). Role of human prefrontal cortex in attention control. *Advances in Neurology, 66*, 21–34.

Koller, E., Malozowski, S., & Doraiswamy, M. P. (2001). Atypical antipsychotic drugs in adolescents. *Journal of the American Medical Association, 286*, 2547–2548.

Kruczek, T. (In press). Family involvement in school-based treatment of childhood trauma. *Proceedings of the 2005 Oxford Symposium in School-Based Family Counseling, UK, 3.*

Kruczek, T., & Vitanza, S. (1999). Treatment effects with an adolescent abuse survivor's group. *Child Abuse & Neglect, 23*(5), 477–485.

LaGreca, A. M., Silverman, W. K., Vernberg, E. M., & Prinstein, M. J. (1996). Symptoms of posttraumatic stress in children after Hurricane Andrew: A prospective study. *Journal of Consulting and Clinical Psychology, 64*, 712–723.

LeDoux, J. E. (1996). *The emotional brain: The mysterious underpinnings of emotional life.* New York: Simon & Schuster.

Lubit, R. (2006). Posttraumatic stress disorder in children. *eMedicine.* Retrieved May 11, 2006 from: http://www.emedicine.com/ped/topic3026.htm

March, J. S., Amaya-Jackson, L., Murray, M. C., & Schulte, A. (1998). Cognitive-behavioral psychotherapy for children and adolescents with posttraumatic stress disorder after a single incident stressor. *Journal of the American Academy of Child and Adolescent Psychiatry, 37*, 585–593.

McCloskey, L. A., & Walker, M. (2000). Posttraumatic stress in children exposed to family violence and single-event trauma. *Journal of the American Academy of Child and Adolescent Psychiatry, 39*(1), 108–115.

McElroy, L. P., & McElroy, R. A. (1989). Psychoanalytically oriented psychotherapy with sexually abused children. *Journal of Mental Health Counseling, 11*(3), 244–258.

McFarlane, A. C. (1987). Posttraumatic phenomena in a longitudinal study of children following a natural disaster. *Journal of the American Academy of Child and Adolescent Psychiatry, 26*, 764–769.

McKnight, C. D., Compton, S. N., & March, J. S. (2004). Posttraumatic stress disorder. In T. L. Morris & J. S. March (Eds.), *Anxiety disorders in children and adolescents* (2nd ed., pp. 241–262). New York: Guilford.

Mitchell, J. I. (1983). When disaster strikes….The critical incident stress debriefing process. *Journal of Emergency Medical Services, 8*, 36–38.

Muris, P., & de-Jongh, A. (1996). Eye movement desensitization and reprocessing: Een nieuwe behandelingstechniek voor trauma-gerelateerde angstklachten. Over de toepassing bij kinderen [Eye movement desensitization and reprocessing: A new treatment method for trauma-related anxiety complaints]. *Kind en Adolescent, 17*, 190–199.

Myerson, N. N., King, N. J., Tonge, B. J., Heyne, D. A., Young, D. A., & Papadopoulos, H. (2000). Cognitive-behavioral treatment for young people who have been sexually abused: Developmental considerations. *Behaviour Change, 17*(1), 37–47.

Nader, K. (2001). Treatment methods for childhood trauma. In J. P. Wilson, M. J. Friedman, & J. D. Lindy (Eds.), *Treating psychological trauma and PTSD* (pp. 278–334). New York: Guilford.

Norris, F. H., Foster, J. D., & Weisshar, D. L. (2002). The epidemiology of sex differences in PTSD across developmental, social, and research contexts. In R. Kimmerling, P. Ouimette, & J. Wolfe (Eds.), *Gender and PTSD* (pp. 3–42). New York: Guilford.

O'Connor, K. J. (2000). *The play therapy primer.* New York: Wiley.

O'Donohue, W., Fanetti, M., & Elliott, A. (1998). Trauma in children. In V. M. Follette, J. I. Ruzek, & F. R. Abueg (Eds.), *Cognitive behavioral therapies for trauma* (pp. 355–383). New York: Guilford.

Osofsky, J. D. (1995). The effects of exposure to violence on young children. *American Psychologist, 59*(9), 782–788.

Osofsky, J. D. (2004). Introduction. In J. D. Osofsky (Ed.), *Young children and trauma: Intervention and treatment* (pp. 3–9). New York: Guilford.

Osofsky, J., Hammer, J. H., Freeman, N., & Rovaris, J. M. (2004). How law enforcement and mental health professionals can partner to help traumatized children. In J. Osofsky (Ed.), *Young children and trauma: Intervention and treatment* (pp. 285–298). New York: Guilford.

Pandit, S., & Shah, L. (2000). Post-traumatic stress disorder: Causes and aetiological factors. In K. Dwivedi (Ed.), *Post-traumatic stress disorder in children and adolescents* (pp. 25–38). London: Whurr.

Perrin, S., Smith, P., & Yule, W. (2000). Practitioner review: The assessment and treatment of post-traumatic stress disorder in children and adolescents. *Journal of Child Psychology and Psychiatry, 41*(3), 277–289.

Perry, B. D. (1994). Neurobiological sequelae of childhood trauma: PTSD in children. In M. M. Murburg (Ed.), *Catecholamine function in posttraumatic stress disorder:Emerging concepts* (pp. 223–255). Washington, D.C.: American Psychiatric Press.

Pfefferbaum, B. (1997). Posttraumatic stress disorders in children: A review of the past 10 years. *Journal of the American Academy of Child and Adolescent Psychiatry, 36*, 1503–1511.

Pynoos, R. S. (1994). Traumatic stress and developmental psychopathology in children and adolescents. In R. S. Pynoos (Ed.), *Posttraumatic stress disorder: A clinical review* (pp. 64-98). Lutherville, MD: Sidran Press.

Pynoos, R. S., & Nader, K. (1988). Psychological first aid and treatment approach to children exposed to community violence: Research implications. *Journal of Traumatic Stress, 1*, 445–473.

Pynoos, R. S., Steinberg, A. M., & Wraith, R. (1995). A developmental model of childhood traumatic stress. In D. Chicchetti & D.J. Cohen (Eds.), *Developmental psychopathology* (Vol. 2, pp. 72–95). New York: Wiley.

Rabalais, A. E., Ruggerio, K. J., & Scotti, J. R. (2002). Multicultural issues in the response of children to disasters. In A. M. La Greca, W. K. Silverman, E. M. Vernberg, & M. C. Roberts (Eds.), *Helping children cope with disasters and terrorism* (pp. 73–100). Washington, D.C.: American Psychological Association.

Read Johnson, D. (2000). Creative therapies. In E. B. Foa, T. M. Keane, & M. J. Friedman (Eds.), *Effective treatments for PTSD: Practice guidelines from the International Society for Traumatic Stress Studies* (pp. 302–314). New York: Guilford.

Reinherz, H. Z., Giaconia, R. M., Lefkowitz, E. S., Pakiz, B., & Frost, A. K. (1993). Prevalence of psychiatric disorders in a community population of older adolescents. *Journal of the American Academy of Child and Adolescent Psychiatry, 32,* 369–377.

Rhue, J., & Lynn, S. J. (1991). Storytelling, hypnosis and the treatment of sexually abused children. *International Journal of Clinical and Experimental Hypnosis, 39,* 198–214.

Rigamer, E. F. (1986). Psychological management of children in a national crisis. *Journal of the American Academy of Child Psychiatry, 25,* 364–369.

Riggs, D. (2000). Marital and family therapy. In. E. B. Foa, T. M. Keane, & M. J. Friedman (Eds.), *Effective treatments for PTSD: Practice guidelines from the International Society for Traumatic Stress Studies* (pp. 280–301). New York: Guilford.

Roberts, R., Blackeney, P. E., Villareal, C., Rosenbert, L., & Meyer, W. J. (1999). Imipramine treatment in pediatric burn patients with symptoms of adult stress disorder. *Journal of the American Academy of Child Psychiatry, 38,* 873–882.

Rojas, V. M., & Pappagallo, M. (2004). Risk factors for PTSD in children and adolescents. In R. R. Silva (Ed.), *Posttraumatic stress disorders in children and adolescents* (pp. 38-59). New York: W.W. Norton.

Russ, S. W. (2004). *Play in child development and psychotherapy: Toward empirically supported practice.* Mahwah, NJ: Lawrence Erlbaum.

Sack, W. H., Clarke, G. N., & Seeley, J. (1995). Posttraumatic stress disorder across two generations of Cambodian refugees. *Journal of the American Academy of Child and Adolescent Psychiatry, 34*(9), 1160–1166.

Saxe, G. N., Stoddard, F., Hall, E., Chawla, N., Lopez, C., Sheridan, R., et al. (2005). Pathways to PTSD, part I: Children with burns. *American Journal of Psychiatry, 162*(7), 1299–1304.

Schechter, D. S., & Tosyali, M. C. (2001).Posttraumatic stress disorder. In C. A. Essau & F. Peterman (Eds.), *Anxiety disorders in children and adolescents: Epidemiology, risk factors and treatment* (pp. 285–322). New York: Brunner-Routledge.

Scheeringa, M. S., Zeanah, C. H., Drell, M. J., & Larrieu, J. (1995). Two approaches to the diagnosis of posttraumatic stress disorder in infancy and early childhood. *Journal of the American Academy of Child and Adolescent Psychiatry, 34,* 191–200.

Scheidlinger, S., & Batkin Kahn, G. (2005). In the aftermath of September 11: Group interventions with traumatized children revisited. *International Journal of Group Psychotherapy, 55*(3), 335–354.

Schwarz, E. D., & Perry, B. D. (2002). The post-traumatic response in children and adolescents. Retrieved July 16, 2002 from: http://www.childtrauma.org/ptsdchildadoles.htm.

Seedat, S., Stein, D. J., Ziervogel, C., Middleton, T., Kaminer, D., Emsley, R. A., et al. (2002). Comparison of response to a selective serotonin reuptake inhibitor in children, adolescents and adults with PTSD. *Journal of Child and Adolescent Psychopharmacology, 12,* 37–46.

Seinfeld, J. (1989). Therapy with a severely abused child: An object relations perspective. *Clinical Social Work Journal, 17*(1), 40–49.

Selye, H. (1952). *The story of the adaptation syndrome.* Montreal, Canada: Acta.

Silva, R. R., Alpert, M., Munoz, D. M., Singh, S., Matzner, F., & Dummit, S. (2000). Stress and vulnerability to posttraumatic stress disorder in children and adolescents. *American Journal of Psychiatry, 157*(8), 1229–1235.

Silva, R. R., & Kessler, L. (2004). Resiliency and vulnerability factors in childhood PTSD. In R. R. Silva (Ed.), *Posttraumatic stress disorders in children and adolescents* (pp. 18-37). New York: W.W. Norton.

Silverman, W. K., & LaGreca, A. M. (2002). Children experiencing disasters: Definitions, reactions, and predictors of outcomes. In A. M. LaGreca, W. K. Silverman, E. M. Vernberg, & M. C. Roberts (Eds.), *Helping children cope with disasters and terrorism* (pp. 11–34). Washington, D.C.: American Psychological Association.

Simon, G. E, Savarino, J., & Operskalski, B, & Wang, P. S. (2006). Suicide risk during antidepressant treatment. *The American Journal of Psychiatry, 163*(1), 41–47.

Soberman, G. B., Greenwald, R., & Rule, D. L. (2002). A controlled study of eye movement desensitization and reprocessing (EMDR) for boys with conduct problems. In R. Greenwald (Ed.), *Trauma and juvenile delinquency: Theory, research, and interventions* (pp. 217–236). Binghamton, NY: Haworth Press.

Spivak, B., Vered, Y., Graff, E., Blum, I., Mester, R., & Weizman, A. (1999). Low platelet-poor plasma concentrations of serotonin in patients with combat-related posttraumatic stress disorder. *Biological Psychiatry, 45,* 840–845.

Stallard, P., & Law, F. D. (1993). Screening and psychological debriefing of adolescent survivors of life-threatening events. *British Journal of Psychiatry, 163,* 660–665.

Stallard, P., & Satler, E. (2003). Psychological debriefing with children and young people following traumatic events. *Clinical Child Psychology and Psychiatry, 8*(4), 445–457.

Stien, P. T., & Kendall, J. (2004). *Psychological trauma and the developing brain: Neurologically based interventions for troubled children.* Binghamton, NY: Haworth Press.

Terr, L. C. (1991). Childhood traumas: An outline and overview. *American Journal of Psychiatry, 148,* 10–19.

Tiet, Q. Q., Bird, H. R., Davies, M., Hoven, C., Cohen, P., Jensen, P. S., et al. (1998). Adverse life events and resilience. *Journal of the American Academy of Child and Adolescent Psychiatry, 37,* 1191–1200.

Tinker, R. H., & Wilson, S. A. (1999). *Through the eyes of a child: EMDR with children.* New York: W.W. Norton.

Tolin, D. F., & Foa, E. B. (2002). Gender and PTSD: A cognitive model. In R. Kimmerling, P. Ouimette, & J. Wolfe (Eds.), *Gender and PTSD* (pp. 76–97). New York: Guilford.

Trowell, J., Kolvin, I., Weeramanthri, T., Sadowski, H., Berelowitz, M., Glaser, D., et al. (2002). Psychotherapy for sexually abused girls: Psychopathological outcome findings and patterns of change. *British Journal of Psychiatry, 180,* 234–247.

True, W. R., & Lyons, M. J. (1999). Genetic risk factors for PTSD: A twin study. In R. Yehuda (Ed.), *Risk factors for posttraumatic stress disorder* (pp. 68–71). Washington, D.C.: American Psychiatric Press.

U.K. Medicines and Healthcare Products Regulative Agency. (2003). *Use of selective serotonin reuptake inhibitors (SSRIS) in children and adolescents with major depressive disorder (MDD).* Retrieved January 13, 2004, from: http://www.mhra.gov.uk/news/2003.htm#ssri

U.S. Food and Drug Administration. (2003). *Reports of suicidality in pediatric patients being treated with antidepressant medications for major depressive disorder.* Retrieved January 13, 2004, from: http://www.fda.gov/cder/drug/advisory/mdd.htm

van der Kolk, B. A. (2003). The neurobiology of childhood trauma and abuse. *Child and Adolescent Psychiatric Clinics of North America, 12,* 293–317.

Van Leeuwon, K. (1988). Resistances in the treatment of a sexually molested 6-year-old girl. *International Review of Psycho-Analysis, 15*(2), 149–156.

Vernberg, E. M., & Vogel, J. M. (1993). Task force report, part 2: Interventions with children after disasters. *Journal of Clinical Child Psychology, 22,* 485–498.

Vila, G., Porche, L. M., & Mouren-Simeoni, M. C. (1999). An 18 month longitudinal study of posttraumatic disorders in children who were taken hostage in their school. *Psychosomatic Medicine, 61,* 746–754.

Wasserstein, S. B., & LaGreca, A. M. (1998). Hurricane Andrew: Parent conflict as a moderator of children's adjustment. *Hispanic Journal of Behavioral Sciences, 20*(2), 212–224.

Widom, C. S. (1999). Posttraumatic stress disorder in abused and neglected children grown up. *American Journal of Psychiatry, 158*(8), 1223–1229.

Wraith, R. (2000). Children and debriefing: Theory, interventions, and outcomes. In B. Raphael & J. P. Wilson (Eds.), *Psychological debriefing: Theory, practice, and evidence* (pp. 195–212). Cambridge, UK: Cambridge University Press.

Yehuda, R. (1997). Hypothalamic-pituitary-adrenal in PTSD. In R. Yehuda & A. C. McFarlane (Eds.), *Psychobiology of posttraumatic stress disorder* (pp. 437–441). New York: New York Academy of Science.

Yehuda, R., Schmeidler, J., Giller, E. L., Jr., Siever, L. J., & Binder-Brynes, K. (1998). Relationship between posttraumatic stress disorder characteristics of Holocaust survivors and their adult offspring. *American Journal of Psychiatry, 155,* 841–843.

Yule, W. (1992). Post-traumatic stress disorder in child survivors of shipping disasters: The sinking of the "Jupiter." *Psychotherapy and Psychsomatics, 57,* 200–205.

Yule, W. (1994). Posttraumatic stress disorders. In M. Rutter, E. Taylor, & L. Hersov (Eds.), *Child and adolescent psychiatry: Modern approaches* (3rd ed., pp. 392–406). Oxford: Blackwell Science.

Yule, W. (2001). Post-traumatic stress disorder in children and adolescents. *International Review of Psychiatry, 13,* 194–200.

Yule, W., & Canterbury, R. (1994). The treatment of posttraumatic stress disorder in children and adolescents. *International Review of Psychiatry, 6,* 141–151.

Yule, W., Perrin, S., & Smith, P. (1999). *Post-traumatic stress reactions in children and ado.* New York: Wiley.

Yule, W., Perrin, S., & Smith, P. (2001). Traumatic events and post-traumatic stress disorder. In W. K. Silverman & P. D. A. Treffers (Eds.), *Anxiety disorders in children and adolescents: Research, assessment and intervention* (pp. 212–234). New York: Cambridge University Press.

Yule, W., & Udwin, O. (1991). Screening child survivors for post-traumatic stress disorders: Experiences from the "Jupiter" sinking. *British Journal of Clinical Psychology, 30,* 131–138.

Chapter Fifteen

Oppositional Defiant Disorder and Conduct Disorder in Childhood

Thomas L. Sexton, Heather M. Pederson,
and Rachael A. Schuster

INTRODUCTION

Since the mid-1990s, attention has focused primarily on the behavior problems of adolescents (Elliott, 1998; Sexton, Alexander, & Mease, 2004). The behavior problems of children have become an increasing concern in schools, within families, and for communities who must provide treatment services (Webster-Stratton, 1996). Conduct problems of adolescents and children are the most common referrals to mental health clinics in the western hemisphere (Frick, 1998). Youth who fall into the broader category of externalizing problems account for between one third and half of all child and adolescent clinic referrals (Kazdin, Siegel, & Bass, 1992; Robins, 1981; Sexton, Gilman, & Johnson-Erickson, 2005). The two major types of behavior problems, oppositional defiant disorder (ODD) and conduct disorder (CD), comprise the majority of these referrals. The prevalence rates of these two forms of behavior disorders are significant. Between 9% and 16% of all youth are diagnosed with either ODD or CD (Russo & Beidel, 1994; American Psychiatric Association, 2000). These types of behavior problems also have the poorest prognosis for adult adjustment of any childhood disorder (Kohlberg, Ricks, & Snarey, 1984).

Chronic externalizing problems are already present in the preschool years, particularly in boys (Bates, Bayles, Bennett, Ridge, & Brown, 1991; Pianta & Caldwell, 1990). Data suggest that the percentage of preschool and early school-age children meeting the criteria for the clinical diagnoses of ODD and early onset CD ranges from 7% to 25%, depending on the population surveyed (Campbell & Ewing, 1990; Crowther, Bond, & Rolf, 1981). Developmental theorists have suggested that these "early starters"—children who develop conduct problems in the preschool and kindergarten years—are at high risk for continuing on a trajectory toward further conduct problems, including CD, delinquency, school dropout, and interpersonal violence during adolescence (Loeber, 1991; White, Moffitt, Earls, Robins, & Silva, 1990). Because of the high costs to society as well as to individuals and their families, it is important to understand factors that predict the development of conduct problems (from McCabe, Lucchini, Hough, Yeh, & Hazen, 2005). Furthermore, given the significant number of children who become chronically antisocial and delinquent during the preschool years (Loeber, 1991), there is a compelling need to identify these children early and to understand the specific predictors related to escalating externalizing behavior problems.

Current conceptualizations suggest that a developmental perspective with an emphasis on the patterns of behavior of the youth over the life course provides the most comprehensive understanding of these difficult problems (U.S. Surgeon-General, 2000). Furthermore, these views suggest that successful interventions require the identification, interpretation, and treatment of problematic externalizing behavior of children to be based on assessments across multiple sources and contexts. Multisystemic assessment allows for elements of the child's multiple environments involved to be improved in consistent and systematic ways. The data on childhood conduct problems suggests that successful interventions require specific treatment methods that work to help overcome the problems of youth in ways that are responsive to the individual differences of families. Accordingly, the treatment provider addresses the significant risk and protective factors that are likely to result in problems. The process of identifying appropriate treatment methods for children can build upon the well-developed knowledge base for the treatment of adolescent conduct problems. Thus, while specific treatments for children and adolescents may vary (to match the different family and youth development variables), the core principles of understanding problems and identifying treatments still apply.

Our goals in this chapter are threefold. First, we present a multidimensional way of understanding the symptoms of childhood conduct and behavior problems that goes beyond diagnostic labels (i.e., DSM labels). Although DSM labels are useful in the sense that they describe disorders, a multidimensional lens indicates points of entry for treatment via a more comprehensive understanding of behavior, its context, and the meaning of particular behaviors in regard to where they may serve to put youth at risk or protect youth from becoming at risk. Looking at specific clinical problems from a more holistic and "functional" perspective is a way to integrate the multiple systems involved in childhood behavior (biological, psychological, and social). This way of looking at problems illuminates how specific behavior problems "fit" or "function" in the context of the family, school, and community. Second, we discuss the role of evidence-based prevention and treatment programs and identify the most promising evidence-based options for these problems. Finally, we make some suggestions for future developments in this difficult category of behavior problems.

It is a challenging task to identify and describe youth behavior problems because to a certain extent, externalizing behaviors are part of the normal developmental trajectory of youth. For example, part of normal adolescent development includes fighting, withdrawing, disagreeing, and standing up to authority figures. Oftentimes these children are simply labeled as having "dysfunctional" behavior. However, it should be recognized that they actually have very complex behavioral profiles and are undoubtedly experiencing a wide range of developmental, emotional, and behavioral problems. Kazdin (2004) distinguishes between psychiatric disorders (diagnosable disorders such as anxiety, mood, substance-related, adjustment, and disruptive behavior disorders), problem or at-risk behaviors (such as drug and alcohol use or school suspension and truancy), and delinquency (committing unlawful acts) as adolescent problems that may require intervention. These problem areas can also be described using the extensive diagnostic systems (e.g., DSM-IV) that assist in differentiation from other labels and diagnostic categories. At yet another level, the child's problem behaviors are inexorably intertwined with the relational and social context around and within which it functions. We examine the diagnostic definition as well as a multisystemic approach that considers the "functioning" of individual, family, and social risk factors. A comprehensive understanding of these clinical problems aids in both the initial identification of at-risk youth as well as forming the basis of treatment and prevention programs for youth with externalizing behavior problems.

According to the DSM-IV, the distinguishing feature of CD is a repetitive and persistent pattern of behavior in which either the basic rights of others or major age-appropriate norms or rules are violated in a way that significantly impairs functioning in academic, social, or work settings. The major behavioral domains of importance in CD include: aggression toward people or animals, destruction of property, deceitfulness or theft, and serious violation of rules. To warrant a diagnosis of CD, a child must exhibit at least three conduct problem behaviors during the past year, with at least one conduct problem behavior present in the past six months. Oppositional defiant disorder (ODD) is a secondary conduct disorder characterized by a pattern of negativistic, hostile, and defiant behavior lasting at least six months. To meet the criteria for ODD, the child must display at least four of the following behaviors more frequently than is typically observed in individuals of comparable age and developmental level. The child often: loses temper, argues with adults, actively defies or refuses to comply with requests or rules, deliberately annoys people, blames others for his or her mistakes or misbehavior, is touchy or easily annoyed by others, is angry and resentful, and is spiteful or vindictive. The range of these problems is significant. Epidemiological studies report that approximately 2% of girls and 9% of boys are diagnosed with CD (Russo & Beidel, 1994), and onset is later in girls. Prevalence rates for ODD range from 2% to 16% (APA, 2000), with three times more boys than girls diagnosed before puberty.

Externalizing behavior problems are commonly seen along with other learning, behavior, and mental health problems. For example, CD and ODD are viewed as comorbid disorders, and are most often associated with ADHD, mood disorders, and depression. The age of onset for ODD is earlier than that of CD, often as early as preschool. These authors note that ODD has been associated with CD, but research does not emphatically tie the two. Oppositional Defiant Disorder does not lead to CD; however, it has been pointed out that almost all children with CD have had an earlier ODD diagnosis (Markward & Bride, 2001, p. 74).

Despite these differences, there is a developmental relationship between the two categories of behavior problems. Youth meeting the criteria for Conduct Disorder often present symptoms of Oppositional Defiant Disorder, ADHD, and anxiety disorders. There is a great degree of overlap among the characteristics of CD, ODD, ADHD, emotional disturbances, and other classifications of mental health problems. Due to their interrelatedness, the distinctions become blurred and these definitions continue to evolve (Forness & Kavale, 2000).

While the acting out behaviors exhibited by these children appear quite similar, each case is unique in that the behaviors occur at very different times in the biological development of the youth and within very different environmental and family contexts. There seem to be two well-documented developmental trajectories for the emergence of youth violence and other behavior problems, one characterized by an early onset of violence and one by a late onset. Children who commit their first serious violent act before puberty are in the early-onset group, whereas youth who do not become violent until adolescence are in the late-onset group (U.S. Surgeon-General, 2000). In the early-onset trajectory, problem behavior that begins in early childhood gradually escalates, culminating in serious problems before adolescence. The problems of between 65% and 80% of children in this early-onset group are corrected by natural supports, such as family and community, along with the developmental growth of the youth (Huizinga, 1995; Nagin & Tremblay, 1999; Patterson & Yoerger, 1997; Stattin & Magnusson, 1996). In the late onset group, the system around the youth and the family begins to strain the individual's and family's capacity to manage outside stressors. The decline of these abilities results in changes in the relational systems that develop around and maintain the chronic nature of the specific behaviors of the youth. Those who do not improve become the adolescents who commit the most serious violent acts, and who continue their violent behavior beyond adolescence and into early adulthood (Loeber, Farrington, Stouthamer-Loeber, & Van Kammen, 1998; Moffitt, 1993; Tolan, 1987; Tolan & Gorman-Smith, 1998).

A MULTISYSTEMIC APPROACH TO UNDERSTANDING CHILDHOOD BEHAVIOR PROBLEMS

The diagnostic labels of CD and ODD serve several key functions: they help improve the precision of communication among professionals, they help organize the epidemiological and treatment studies, and they help direct clients to the treatment that might benefit them most. Diagnostic labels represent a *nomothetic* approach and there are disadvantages to utilizing this avenue. Diagnostic labels do describe the externalizing behaviors that fit into respective diagnostic categories; however, they do not provide a comprehensive and individualized understanding of the youth's behavior within the relational context of the family and the surrounding social context. What practitioners need is a means to go beyond the nomothetic view of diagnostic criteria to incorporate a more *ideographic* perspective that may lead to enhanced treatment choices and clinical decisions. According to Sexton, Gillman, and Johnson (2005), when it comes to problems that are highly embedded in relational systems. Diagnostic categories and processes are important to consider and understand for the purposes of epidemiology and for communication; however, they are simply incomplete when it comes to treatment. In fact, these authors suggest that for effective treatment to take place, therapists need a conceptual map that incorporates the multi-axial and descriptive qualities of the DSM and ICD-9 frameworks as a base. The therapist then works to build upon that foundation by developing a schema for understanding the functioning of the youth within the multiple relational systems in which he or she lives.

> We suggest that a multisystemic approach aids in identifying and implementing treatments that address the ideographic family-specific factors, which are the key to improving the youth's functioning. A multisystemic approach views the factors from individual sources, along with those from family, social, and environmental contexts, which disrupt the normal resiliency of a child and result in difficult behavioral patterns amongst youth and their parents, teachers, and

peers. To accomplish this goal, our multisystemic approach to understanding and assessing childhood behavior problems specifically considers the biological, family, and social factors that help explain both the origins and the facilitating features of these chronic behavioral problems.

We suggest that a risk and protective factors approach, based on an established body of etiological research, has the potential to integrate the epidemiological research into a developmental and multisystemic perspective that enhances successful intervention. Risk and protective patterns describe alterable behavior, rather than "labeling" the youth or family with characteristics that become stable and enduring. This model helps organize the complex information from the multiple systems (individual, family, and social). It is a useful way of thinking about problems because it describes them through a "probability lens" (determining the likelihood of problems), rather than in terms of causal relationships. The risk and protective factor model can be helpful in organizing critical information, such as how the multiple systems function in regards to difficulties as well as strengths. It allows the interventionist to identify which factors to develop, which to work around, and which to attempt to decrease. The process is completed in an ideographic (as opposed to a nomothetic) manner, which helps match individuals to efficacious treatments that fit the unique context of the child. Finally, the risk and protective factor approach helps define the outcomes of prevention and therapy for children with these types of problems. Many risk factors are not changeable (e.g., unemployment, biological predisposition, and relational histories). Thus, successful intervention with children with behavior problems involves building protective factors to overcome some of the more static risk factors. In this way, intervention focuses on building the resiliency of the child, parents, and family.

A comprehensive approach identifies the most reliable risk and protective factors in each of the three areas: individual factors, family factors, and social factors. Together these domains comprise a complete picture of the child's functioning that will assist in providing more accurate assessments, identifying potential treatments, and developing goals that are specific to the family as a result of addressing their unique and specific systemic factors. Child characteristics are typically considered the biological influences in the development of conduct disorders, while parent characteristics, particularly those of adopted parents, are considered closer to a social context or environmental influences (Lytton, 1990). Lytton noted that there is a continuum of influences on psychopathology, where most effects fall interactively within the extremes of child and environment effects. This is not unlike the suggestion of Webster-Stratton (1996) who categorized risk factors into three groups. These are: (1) child risk variables, including a difficult temperament or high rate of disruptive, impulsive, inattentive, and aggressive behaviors (Campbell & Ewing, 1990); (2) parenting variables, including ineffective parenting strategies and negative attitudes (Patterson & Stouthamer-Loeber, 1984); (3) family variables, apart from the parent–child relationship, which include parental psychopathology, marital factors, socioeconomic factors, and other stressors (Webster-Stratton, 1990). Consistent with these findings, in the following sections, we review the risk and protective factors in the following three domains: biological–individual factors, family factors, and social–community factors.

Biological–Genetic Factors

Biological factors include biochemical, temperament, and genetic (i.e., preexisting biological parent characteristics) factors. Biological factors can be conceptualized as stable risk factors, or relatively fixed diatheses that render children vulnerable in certain stressful environments. To date, biological factors alone are insufficient when it comes to either conceptualization or treatment of childhood behavior problems. In fact, it is often difficult to decipher what is purely biological from what may stem from a particular interaction with external features of the environment. Nevertheless, evidence shows that individual factors do moderate some effects of the environment, which highlights the complexity of childhood behavior and further indicates the need for a multimodal approach to child mental health (Nakamura, 2005).

Biological factors serve as distal predictors of childhood conduct problems. At the broadest level, biological factors (e.g., gender) imply both divergent physiological and socialization processes that in some combinations, not understood, result in more boys than girls developing behavior problems (Webster-Stratton, 1996). Twin adoption studies are the standard way of teasing apart the more specific genetic influences from the environmental ones. These studies investigate the interactive effects of an adverse adoptive environment (including marital problems, adoptee parent psychopathology, substance abuse, or legal problems) as well as genetic factors. In one important study, a biological background of antisocial personality disorder, indicated by both hospital and prison record diagnosis of a biological parent, amplified the effects of an adverse environment (Cadoret, Yates, Troughton, Woodworth, & Stewart, 1995). The outcome of this study was the first time (to the researchers' knowledge) that the environmental influences on aggressiveness and conduct problems depended on the genetic background. Other adoption studies have substantiated some genetic–environmental interaction on the genesis of conduct disorder (Cadoret, 1981, 1983; Crowe, 1974).

The pathway through which genetics influences child psychopathology is not well understood. Some research has focused on the influence of genetics on CD through child personality factors. For instance, researchers found that genetics influences temperament, which in turn relates to behavior problems over time (Gjone & Stevenson, 1997). Another study narrowed down the risk factor to a specific genotype. Caspi and colleagues (2002) were curious as to why some children who are maltreated or abused develop conduct problems, whereas other children do not. There must be some implicit individual factors that leave some children vulnerable, and others protected. Caspi and colleagues (2002) did find some evidence that genotype moderates children's diathesis to abrasive environments. Psychopathology research has only recently become more biologically driven, so much of the current evidence of predisposition to psychopathology tends to be a measurement of parent characteristics that precede child characteristics. For example, Frick et al. (1992) noted that two of the best indicators for early-onset conduct problems for male children in particular are paternal antisocial behavior and maternal depression. The next section highlights the overarching biological findings on behavior disorders up to date. Some of the most salient protective factors include high intelligence, female sex, positive social orientation, competence at one skill, anxiety, and worry (Bassareth, 2001).

Biochemical factors represent the relationship between basic biological functions (i.e., neurohormones, neurotransmitter) and behavior problems (Mpofu, 2002; Shapiro &

Hynd, 1993). Hormones in the endocrine system such as testosterone and cortisol have been studied in an attempt to measure individual responses to stress. This research is driven by an underlying assumption that conduct disordered individuals have relatively low levels of fear, deduced from their apparent insensitivity to consequences of their behavior (see van Goozen & Fairchild, 2006, for a detailed review). Thus, children with behavior problems should show less physiological arousal to stress. Due to various difficulties that arise from measuring and interpreting the levels of testosterone and cortisol (e.g., unknown effects of the differences in age and gender, timing of sample, and the standard, indirect method for measurement through bodily fluids), suggested hormonal contributions to childhood conduct disorders are not yet well-accepted (Mpofu, 2002; Shapiro & Hynd, 1993; Van de Wiel, Van Goozen, Matthys, Snoek, & Van Engeland, 2004).

There is some clearer evidence to support theories of underarousal in the autonomic nervous system (ANS) for behavior problem children and adolescents, such as correlated lower heart rate and skin conductance (for a review, Mpofu, 2002; Lytton, 1990a; e.g., Crowell et al., 2006). Moreover, limited research has tracked the impact of thr neurotransmitters serotonin and norepinephrine levels in children diagnosed with disruptive behavior disorders (typically, comorbid ADHD and CD or ODD). Serotonin is generally believed to regulate, inhibit emotional behavior, and in adult and adolescent studies, has been negatively related to aggressive behavior. Norepinephrine, on the other hand, is believed to excite behavior, and circulating norepinephrine metabolites have been positively correlated with aggressiveness in adult males (Mpofu & Conyers, 2003; van Goozen & Fairchild, 2006).

Children with aggression and hyperactivity have had lower levels of urine-measured norepinephrine, but the marker seemed more related to hyperactivity (Mpofu, 2002). Reviewers of this research (Shapiro & Hynd, 1993) contended that the current evidence connecting norepinephrine and behavior problems in children is weak at best. There is also some evidence that ties aggressiveness to low levels of serotonin (van Goozen & Fairchild, 2006). In the few studies of children with DBD or ADHD, there are mixed results for negative and positive correlations between serotonin and aggressiveness (Mpofu, 2002). Kruesi, Hibbs et al. (1992) and Kruesi, Rapoport et al. (1990) found at two-year follow-up that initial concentration of serotonin predicted the severity of physical aggression. These studies suggest a relation between serotonin and aggression is stable over time, and the assessment of serotonin may inform the clinical prediction of later aggression (as described in Shapiro & Hynde, 1993; van Goozen & Fairchild, 2006). Interestingly in a review of comorbidity between CD and ADHD, obsessive-compulsive disorder, and other personality disorders in childhood and adolescence, deficits or abnormalities in serotonin and norepinephrine were considerable markers of risk (Mpofu & Conyers, 2003).

Some psychopharmacological treatment findings support a link between serotonin and the increasing and lowering of aggression in children and adolescents (see "Treatment" section of this chapter). The primary justification for using pharmacological agents to treat children with CD is that these medications enhance the transmission of serotonin or norepineprine, which ideally leads to less aggressive or conduct disordered behaviors (Mpofu, 2002). Current intervention studies tend to combine behavior modification and psychotropic drugs, as well as taking into consideration variation of treatment effects across environments/activities, in order to address the interactive constellation of risk factors that effect childhood conduct disorder behaviors (Kolko, Bukstein, & Barron, 1999).

Individual Factors Influencing Risk and Resiliency

Temperament is a biological–individual factor that generally refers to inherited "differences in behavior style that are visible from the child's earliest years" (Sanson, Hemphill, & Smart, 2004, p. 143). Rende and Plomin (1992) found that the effects of stress on externalizing behavior problems were exacerbated if children had a more difficult temperament (e.g., one that was more emotional, more active, or less sociable). Although the study could not decipher causation, certain aspects of temperament could partially contribute to the way children respond to stressful events. As in this study, temperamental characteristics may function as either protective or risk factors under stressful conditions. However, researchers have emphasized the importance of noting that protective factors do not consist simply of the absence or opposite of risk factors (Bassareth, 2001). A large scale longitudinal study found that children who had difficult temperaments at age 1.5 were between 6 and 10 times more likely to have clinically significant aggressive behavior problems during childhood. Interestingly, the fact that most of the children who had difficult temperaments did not eventually have conduct problems stipulates that early difficult temperament is only one of many significant risk factors that may precipitate the full onset of conduct problems. For instance, "poorness of fit" between parental caregiving and childhood temperament may increase the probability of developing behavior problems (Wright-Guerin, Gottfried, & Thomas, 1997, p. 86). Additionally, there is a wealth of research on the moderating effects of parental sensitivity to children's needs in terms of children's healthy development (Stams, Juffer, & Ijzendoorn, 2002).

Sanson, Hemphill, and Smart (2004) reviewed the literature on the relationship between temperament and externalizing behavior problems, finding that factors such as negative emotionality (a "predisposition for angry and aggressive behavior"), impulsivity, and high activity predicted behavior problems (p. 147). Interestingly, Sanson et al. also clarified that temperament and behavior problems were mediated by aspects of self-control, such as maladaptive coping styles and novelty seeking. Protective factors included early childhood inhibition, low emotional reactivity, high social engagement, and being affectionate, responsive, and moderately active as an infant. Identifying these insulating factors is a good start to understanding childhood resiliency to conduct problems, but the child exists within a family and that family, within the larger society that also influence the child's development. There is a wealth of literature that positions the effect of parenting on the continuum between other interacting child and environmental factors (Patterson, DeBaryshe, & Ramsey, 1989).

Family Factors Influencing Risk and Resiliency

Research on familial risk and protective factors provides a useful environmental lens from which to conceptualize child behavior problems. As noted by Masten and Shaffer (2006), this lens can be used to increase awareness of the precise ways in which "families count" in contributing to risk and resiliency models of child development. The system around the youth and the family begins to strain the individual's and family's capacity to manage outside stressors. The decline of these abilities results in changes in the relational systems that develop around the specific behaviors of the youth. Finally, these crystallized relationships are connected to the chronic nature of the youth's conduct problems.

Families are a child's primary social context, and parents are highly implicated in children' mastery of social competence, including interpersonal and self-regulatory skills. It is well-accepted that families characterized by conflict (anger and aggression), deficient parenting, and family interactions that are cold, unsupportive, or neglectful, contribute to childhood psychopathology (Knutson, DeGarmo, & Reid, 2004). Furthermore, family dynamics that are unresponsive or rejecting of children likely exacerbate children's genetic or temperamental diathesis to the development of conduct disorders and aggression (Repetti, Taylor, & Seeman, 2002). Protective parenting factors include the quality of maternal instructions, frequent joint activities, monitoring, structuring the child's time and constructive discipline strategies (Hutchings & Lane, 2005).

Some researchers believe strongly that antisocial behavior begins with a predisposition (temperamental or biological), evolves and is maintained through social interaction (Reid & Patterson, 1989). Thus, parents who raise their children in aversive environments have difficulty practicing effective discipline and supervision. Maternal stress has been connected with unemployment, poverty, marital problems or divorce, negative life events, health problems, all of which have been found to predict aggression and antisocial behavior in children. The theme here is that situational factors "undermine [parents'] practice of discipline and supervision" and exacerbate children's chances of developing conduct problems. Reid and Patterson's view is palpably blameful because it contends that parents not only provoke children with their own irritation, but also follow up with inappropriate discipline tactics. Some studies have investigated the process that follows deficient discipline. For instance, one study found that parents who more frequently used physical punishment, exercised lower levels of warmth, and provided nonexplicated discipline practices (not providing warnings or rationale) would have children with less developed consciences (moral regulation), and of course, higher levels of conduct problems (Kerr, Lopez, Olsen, & Sameroff, 2004). In the eyes of the clinician, the fact is that if the behavior is learned, it can be unlearned. Parental behavior is therefore an important target for conduct problem interventions.

The most compelling evidence that parental behavior exerts causal influence in changing children's behavior comes from intervention studies, whereby changes in behavior of parents results in changes in behavior of untreated children (Collins, Maccoby, Steinberg, Hetherington, & Bornstein, 2000). Similarly persuasive evidence showing that parent behavior is not just a response to child behavior comes from longitudinal studies that show how parent behavior over time affects children's behavior. Nevertheless some researchers argue that parent behavior should not be viewed as having a *deterministic* effect on childhood behavior (Collins et al., 2000). Parental influence is complicated by an interaction of individual characteristics of the child, the way that the family system functions, and the factors that exist outside of the family unit.

Raine, Brennan, Mednick, and Mednick (1996) found evidence to support the common assumption that individuals with both biological and social deficits increase the likelihood of antisocial behaviors. Children who had early neuromotor deficits as well as unstable family environments were at greater risk for criminality. Unstable families were indicated by a greater number of marriages for the mother in the child's first 18 years, a greater number of changes in the family constellation of the household, and a lower number of years the biological father lived in household. The structure of the family—whether intact or broken into single parents—has received a lot of attention with regard to childhood conduct disorder due to repeated findings that aggressive children tend to be reared in single-parent homes (Loeber & Hay, 1997). Again, family structure is simply one of many influential factors. Brannigan, Gemmell, Pevalin, and Wade (2002) tested the effects of family structure, hyperactivity (lack of self-control/ prosocial behavior at each continuum), and social control processes (family processes and parenting strategies) on the development of conduct problems. Family structure did affect conduct disorder and aggression. Individual level traits (hyperactivity) and social factors such as hostile parenting also contributed to misconduct and aggression throughout early childhood. Brannigan et al. (2002) noted appropriately that, "What is significant is that the models are not mutually exclusive. Structure, control factors and individual characteristics retain their significance when tested together and yield a stronger model together than any model tested individually" (p. 131).

SOCIAL AND COMMUNITY FACTORS THAT INFLUENCE RISK AND RESILIENCY

As we have highlighted, the genetic predisposition of a child may render that child more vulnerable to risky social environments. The amount and type of support provided by the family could also pose as risk or protective factors in the child's behavioral response patterns in and outside of the family context. In addition to individual and family dynamics, there are a multitude of factors outside the family circle which interact in different ways to affect a child's behavior. Neither the child nor the family exists in isolation, and consideration must be given to the specific context or community in which the child and family live. The literature shows that high rates of childhood conduct problems correlate with a multitude of social and community factors including low socioeconomic status and high levels of residential instability, urbanization, and exposure to community violence (Elze, Stiffman, & Doré, 1999; McCabe, Lucchini, Hough, Yeh, & Hazen, 2005; Offord, Alder, & Boyle, 1986). Rowe and Liddle (2002) described social disadvantage and six related factors as follows: (1) income below the federal poverty line; (2) impoverished home environment; (3) one or both parents unemployed; (4) one or more parents without a high school degree; (5) neighborhood; and (6) school perceived to be dangerous by parent or child. Utting and Pugh (2004) identified demographic trends of the 21st century including fewer marriages, increased cohabitation, high divorce rates, and the growing divide between rich and poor families. Caspi, Taylor, Moffitt, and Plomin (2000) maintain that children who are in deprived neighborhoods are at increased risk of behavioral problems. High-risk communities and living environments include those with high crime rates, residential instability, poor housing, and single-parent homes. There is clearly a growing number of social and environmental stress factors associated with child well-being and the development of problem behaviors. However, labeling isolated community factors as "predictors" of childhood conduct problems may be an oversimplification of the complex interaction among community environment, family, and individual risk or promotive factors. The majority of research on social and community factors associated with child externalizing behaviors recognizes a multitude of mediating and moderating factors. Thus, researchers widely endorse an approach that emphasizes an in-depth assessment and analysis of the complexity of immediate interacting risk and protective factors.

For instance, McCabe and colleagues (2005), found that exposure to community violence predicted conduct disorder and externalizing problems two years later. Elze, Stiffman, and Doré (1999) similarly concluded that exposure to violence in the community is a significant risk factor for conduct problems. Yet the authors stress the importance of addressing the interplay between the community environment and the family environment. Exposure to community violence could very likely be linked to influential family factors such as lower parental monitoring or single-parent homes. In fact, researchers are beginning to explore the precise point of influence for factors identified as putting children at increased risk of developing conduct problems. It has been suggested that many social and environmental stress factors that increase the likelihood of children's risk of conduct problems mainly do so through their impact on parenting (Knutson, DeGarmo, & Reid, 2004; Patterson & Forgatch, 1995).

The influence of parenting can be more significant under certain conditions under which the child is particularly vulnerable (e.g., genetic predisposition, disadvantaged neighborhood). In the same vein, social and community factors (e.g., exposure to community violence, interaction with deviant peers) vary in impact depending on the quality of family functioning. On one hand, the family could serve to buffer the individual child from exposure to adverse circumstances and would thus provide an island of safety and security for the child (Richters & Martinez, 1993). On the other, parenting could serve to exacerbate the effects of negative contexts in which the child lives. Children with a predisposition for conduct problems, in combination with an unstable child-rearing environment, would be put at increased risk. Galambos, Barker, and Almeida (2003), for example, found that the influence of peers in the community environment is dependent on parenting factors. It appears that deviant peers can be less influential in the context of positive parental behaviors (Galambos et al., 2003; Pettit, Bates, Dodge, & Meece, 1999).

Adverse social and community factors could impact children and families in a variety of ways. The premise of resilience or "protective factors" is based on the individual variation of response to similar experiences. Because quality of parenting has been recognized as one of the most influential moderating variables (Dishion & McMahon, 1998; Repetti, Taylor, & Seeman, 2002), it is often utilized as a point of entry in treatment of children with conduct behavior problems. While clinicians legitimately may feel unable to effect change on a number of social and community factors (e.g., socioeconomic status, stability of residential community), they would do well to promote parenting strategies which take into account the influence of contributing environmental factors.

EVIDENCE-BASED PREVENTION AND TREATMENT INTERVENTIONS FOR CHILDHOOD BEHAVIOR PROBLEMS

There are myriad prevention and treatment programs available for childhood behavior disorders. Our focus in the following section is on evidence-based programs that either prevent children from beginning or continuing along a trajectory into behavior difficulties or programs that intervene to stop an existing pattern of behavior disorder. Historically, prevention and treatment programs have been considered as distinct intervention approaches. While there are considerable concerns about evidence-based approaches, there do seem to be a number of approaches with clinical improvements that are consistent, lasting, and generalizable to different populations—in other words they "work." There are other approaches that have some evidence and thus might be better classified as ones that "might work." Our classification is based on existing reviews of the prevention and treatment literature. Our summaries focus exclusively on prevention and treatment programs or comprehensive models of intervention. To date, the best evidence to support successful outcomes emanates from these comprehensive programs rather than individual techniques. These evidence-based programs are those practices that integrate the best research evidence with clinical experiences, the most current and clinically relevant psychological theory, and patient values (Institute of Medicine, 2001; Sexton & Alexander, 2002).

In the sections below we separate prevention, treatment, and psychopharmacological approaches and programs that "work," "might work," and "don't work." While this approach allows for a systematic presentation, we suggest that the traditional separation between treatment as therapy, and prevention as education, no longer holds true (Alexander, Sexton, & Robbins, 2001). Many programs traditionally viewed as "therapeutic" are now being used as prevention interventions aimed at interrupting the trajectory of youth and preventing them from becoming more deeply involved in the justice system, involved in drug use, or preventing the escalation of family conflict such that less severe mental health problems develop in the future (Alexander et al., 2001). Similarly, pharmacological interventions are often included with other treatment programs for a comprehensive approach. Linking evidence-based programs is a complex issue that in part, holds the future of prevention and intervention in this area.

There are a number of conditions that place a child at risk for disruptive behavior disorders, including low socioeconomic status, parenting difficulties, parental psychopathology, marital disharmony, inconsistent parenting, single parenting, and a high risk living environment (Burke, Loeber, & Birmaher, 2002; McGee & Williams, 1999). Many of these particular risk factors make it very challenging for individuals and families to obtain and successfully complete treatment. In fact, years ago, the prognosis for a child with CD was poor—about 50% of those referred to clinics would exhibit antisocial behavior as adults (Robins, 1966, 1978). Much of the research from the past decade has focused on treatment interventions. Strong efforts in process research have advanced our understanding of the critical and central mechanisms of change that result in successful outcomes. These impressive outcomes have been identified not just by model developers but as a result of a number of systematic efforts to carefully scrutinize the scientific evidence to ensure that programs work, the outcomes last, and these outcomes are replicable in local communities (Elliott, 1998; U.S. Surgeon-General, 2000). Since the early 21st century, many evidence-based programs have been successfully implemented, with impressive results, in local communities, and some across entire statewide systems of care (Barnoski, 2004).

What Works: CD and ODD

The EBP literature and accompanying meta-analytic research identifies three treatment modalities that have demonstrated effectiveness with children who have conduct behavior problems. Points of intervention are at the individual, family, and community levels. Corresponding treatments include cognitive problem-solving skills training (CPSST; Kazdin, Bass, Siegel, & Thomas, 1989), parent management training (PMT; Firestone, Kelly, & Fike, 1980), and the Incredible Years Program (Webster-Stratton, 2001).

Intervention at the individual level involves problem-solving and social skills training. Youth are taught cognitive and behavioral techniques and strategies that are useful in solving interpersonal problems. Cognitive social skills training programs typically teach a combination of problem-solving skills, anger-control skills, social skills, coping skills, and assertiveness skills (CCST; Shure, Spivack, & Gordon, 1972). This combination seeks to address the aspect of temperament and behavior problems that may be mediated by adaptive modes of self-control, such as coping style.

Because parenting behaviors have a vital influence on children's self-regulatory skills, and changes in behavior of parents have shown changes in behavior of children exhibiting CD, parent management training (PMT; Firestone et al., 1980) is often considered one of the most effective treatment options (Serketich & Dumas, 1996). PMT coaches parents in discouraging child problem behaviors and encouraging child prosocial behaviors. PMT programs teach parents skills in the areas of positive reinforcement, nonviolent and consistent discipline, effective monitoring and supervision, and constructive family problem solving. For young children in particular, parent–child interactive training (PCIT) is another option that warrants further consideration. Burke, Loeber, and Birmaher (2002) noted that PCIT leads to "clinically significant improvement in children with Oppositional Defiant Disorder" (p. 1286).

Not all parenting interventions demonstrate effectiveness with children exhibiting disruptive behavior problems. Hutchings, Gardner, and Lane (2004) identified six essential components of parenting interventions for the treatment of CD: (1) the rehearsal of new parenting skills; (2) the teaching of management principles rather than techniques; (3) the practice of new parenting strategies at home; (4) the teaching of both (nonviolent) sanctions for negative behavior and strategies to build positive relationships; (5) the addressing of difficulties in the parental relationship; and (6) the early delivery of interventions because later interventions are less effective. Hutchings and Lane (2005) identified the Incredible Years Program (Webster-Stratton, 2001) as a blueprint program and suggest that it is possibly the best evidence-based parenting program in the world.

The Incredible Years Program teaches parents about child-directed play, how to increase positive behavior, nonviolent discipline techniques (such as time-out), and problem-solving techniques. The Incredible Years Program has also been identified as one that targets hard-to-engage families. The Webster-Stratton interventions have been shown to reduce conduct problems and improve parenting interactions for approximately two-thirds of families whose children have conduct disorders and who have been treated in clinics, and improvements were sustained for up to three years (Webster-Stratton, 1990). Additionally, there is a classroom version of the Incredible Years program called "Dinosaur School" which has established efficacy as a treatment program and demonstrated significant improvements in classroom behavior and social and peer group skills (Webster-Stratton & Hammond, 1997; Webster-Stratton, Reid, & Hammond, 2001).

What Might Work

The Mellow Parenting Program (Puckering, Rogers, Mills, Cox, & Mattsson-Graf, 1994) uses structured practice in parenting skills with a focus on the parent–child relationship alongside psychotherapeutic support to parents. It provides a whole day program for 14 weeks that utilizes video and hands-on practice. While the evidence base for this program is not as robust as that of the Incredible Years program, it addresses how to engage high-risk families and appears to be effective in recruiting and retaining high-risk parents.

Day treatment programs for children with conduct behavior problems appear to be a promising treatment modality (Grizenko, Papineau, & Sayegh, 1993); however, further research is required to determine optimal methods of service delivery (Tse, 2006). Typical day treatment program allow the youth to be in treatment during the majority of the day yet stay at home in the evening. Unlike "outpatient" treatment, these program are extensive day long treatments that utilize a multimodal approach, it is difficult to identify which particular interventions contribute to positive outcomes. Many children are referred to day treatment centers when their needs cannot be met with family, community, or outpatient resources (Ware, Novotny, & Coyne, 2001). It has been shown that youth are less likely to recidivate when treated in a more normalized (as opposed to institutionalized) setting (Coates, Alden, & Olin, 1978; Winsberg, Bailer, Kupietz, Botti, & Balka, 1980). Unlike outpatient treatment, day treatment is an intensive intervention that, for severely affected children, cuts down on treatment time and thus reduces the risk of dropouts. As compared with a residential treatment environment, day treatment offers the advantages of community location and preservation of links to the family and peer group (Grizenko et al., 1993). Multimodal day treatment interventions often occur at numerous levels: individual, family, school, and community. The interventions typically utilized in day treatment emphasize child-problem-solving skills, parent management training, attention to families' basic needs, improved access to care, and provision of education.

Multidimensional treatment foster care (MTFC; Chamberlain, 1994, 2003; Chamberlain & Reid, 1998; Eddy & Chamberlain, 2000) has been identified as an evidence-based treatment intervention that might work in residential settings. The MDTFC program involves placing youth with foster parents who have received extensive training in parent management training (PMT) skills and who receive ongoing and intensive support. Preservice training is provided by case managers and by experienced MTFC foster parents. Foster parents can be supervised during weekly case manager-led foster parent group meetings as well as through weekday telephone calls.

Foster parents are trained in behavior management methods focused on establishing and maintaining a structure, supervised, and consistent living environment. MTFC parents are responsible for delivering treatment on a moment-by-moment basis using a daily behavior management system (i.e., the point-and-level system) that requires frequent and consistent use of reinforcement (earned points) and sanctions (lost points) to alter and shape youth behavior (Rimm & Masters, 1974). MTFC parents provide consequences to teach and reinforce prosocial behaviors across multiple contexts (e.g., home, school, community). Recent research has identified four key components of the MTFC models as mediators of the effect of treatment: supervision, discipline, positive adult–youth relationship, and decreased association with delinquent peers (Eddy & Chamberlain, 2000).

Some of the evidence-based family intervention programs for adolescents may also work for younger children. For example, multisystemic therapy (MST; Henggeler, Melton, & Smith, 1992) focuses on factors that might pertain to individual characteristics of the youth (e.g., poor problem-solving skills), family relations (e.g., inept discipline), peer relations (e.g., association with deviant peers), and school performance (e.g., academic difficulties). It is an individualized case management program that often incorporates many aspects of parent management training and cognitive social skills training. MST is designed for youth with serious behavior disorders who are at risk for out of home placement. It utilizes a home-based model of service delivery, which helps to remove barriers of access to care and provide the high level of intensity needed for successful outcomes within this target population. Functional Family Therapy (FFT; Sexton & Alexander, 2002) focuses on the multiple family systems by adopting a traditional family therapy approach. The three phases of FFT (engagement/motivation, behavior change, and generalization) are aimed at reducing within family risk factors and building family based protective factors to empower families to successfully manage the behavior of their youth.

What Does Not Work

Two such modalities are deterrence programs (e.g., shock incarceration, "Scared Straight") and peer-group interventions. Deterrence programs such as Scared Straight involved organized visits to prison facilities by juvenile delinquents or at-risk children, with the intention that their frightening observations will deter them from delinquency. Despite reviews questioning the effectiveness of these programs, many are still in place today. Meta-analytic research has indicated that these types of interventions on average are more harmful to juveniles than no intervention (Petrosino, Turpin-Petrosino, & Buehler, 2003). Recent research has also demonstrated that group programs often introduce youth to new opportunities for negative–delinquent peer influences and participation in rule-breaking activities. Dishion, McCord, and Poulin (1999) provided data that showed iatrogenic effects and poorer outcomes for peer-group interventions. Barcalow (2006) reported that peer-group interventions should be used with extreme caution, if used at all because they have been shown to reinforce deviant behaviors. Lastly, the following forms of treatment have not been shown to be useful in reducing disruptive behaviors: overcorrecting, physical punishment, verbal reprimands, and extinction procedures (Kavale, Forness, & Walker, 1999).

PSYCHOPHARMOCOLOGY AND OPPOSITIONAL DEFIANT DISORDER AND CONDUCT DISORDER

There are currently no formally approved psychotropic medications for treating conduct disorder; however, there is evidence to suggest that psychopharmacology is appropriate and useful with some specific symptom sets, as with comorbid disorders (Searight, 2001).

What Works

There are currently no formally approved psychotropic medications for treating conduct disorder; however, there is evidence to suggest that psychopharmacology is appropriate and useful with some specific symptom sets, as with comorbid disorders (Searight, 2001). Particularly because of a strong history of clinical improvements with childhood ADHD symptoms, as well as a high prevalence of comorbid ADHD and conduct disorders, psychostimulants are a first choice drug treatment for children with CD. Dextroamphetamine (Dexedrine; for children age 3 years and older) and methylphenidate (Ritalin; for children age 6 years and older) are considered the most effective psychostimulants for treating conduct disorder (Searight, 2001). Research that suggests psychostimulants are effective with CD is based on studies of ADHD and comorbid conduct disorders, and so psychostimulants seem to be helpful with a specific constellation of behavior problems related to manifest inattention and hyperactivity. On the other hand, methylphenidate has demonstrated effectiveness with milder cases of CD with *and without* ADHD symptoms (see Mpofu, 2002 for a review). Psychostimulants may have undesirable side effects such as stunted growth, weight loss, and social withdrawal, although compared to all other current psychotropic drugs for treating childhood CD, side effects are of lesser concern.

What Might Work

Due to another specific constellation of symptoms, as when conduct disorder occurs with depressive symptoms, antidepressants such as bupropion (Wellbutrin; for children age 6 years and older) and fluoxetine (Prozac; for children age 5 years and older) may be helpful. Antidepressants are currently only advisable treatments when CD is comorbid with diagnosed childhood depressive disorder, but not for a CD diagnosis alone (Searight, 2001). Neuroleptics have a strong history with adults and severe psychiatric disorders, and less but some base for use with children (Mpofu, 2002). Neuroleptics such as haloperidol and lithium may help to restore normal levels of circulating neurotransmitters such as serotonin and norepinephrine. Haloperidol is most studied with an adolescent and child population and has been shown as comparable to lithium in reducing fighting, bullying, and explosiveness in children with CD (Searight, 2001; Mpofu, 2002). Although lithium has mixed results for treating children and adolescents with CD, low doses of lithium and other neuroleptics are sometimes used to reduce disruptive behaviors (Searight, 2001; Mpofu, 2002).

What Does Not Work

A diagnosis of CD foremost indicates practical interventions such as family therapy and behavior modification, and only potentially adjunct pharmacotherapy, depending on the severity of the child's aggressive or impulsive behavior, the age of the child, and other relatively stable risk factors in the child's rearing environment (e.g., psychopathology in the parents). For a less severe diagnosis such as ODD, for example, pharmacotherapy is not widely recommended. In sum, medication may be a necessary intervention, but it is considered insufficient for effective treatment of conduct problems (Searight, 2001).

Moreover, experts of psychopharmacological treatment for childhood CD caution practitioners to examine how unreliable courses of treatment may come in conflict with the ethics of proper care (Mpofu, 2002). Particularly for children, the potential developmental and physiological repercussions of psychotropic medications are not well understood. Not all children respond to pharmacotherapy, and the health related costs are difficult to predict with consistency. Furthermore, Mopfu (2002) raises the credible concern that since parents are highly implicated in the development and maintenance of CD, medication may just be a circuitous way to subdue symptoms and not causes. Current treatment practices are leaning more toward combined approaches when considering the use of medications, such as combined behavior modification and psychopharmco-therapy, especially given some evidence that behavioral interventions are enhanced by biochemical interventions (e.g., Kolko, Bukstein, & Barron, 1999).

THE PREVENTION OF OPPOSITIONAL DEFIANT DISORDER AND CONDUCT DISORDER

The premise for using prevention efforts for conduct disorders is that early antisocial behavior, as early as in preschool years, has been considered one of the best predictors of later socially costly antisocial behavior (White et al., 1990). White and colleagues (1990) found clear evidence to the effect that behavior problems are stable throughout lifetime and children who are behavior problematic at young ages (e.g., parent-reported behavior problems at age 5, and difficult to manage or externalizing behaviors at age 3) are to a degree at risk for continuing the same pathway. Second, oppositional and defiant behaviors in school and home settings are generally believed to impair the overall quality of relationships with parents, teachers, and peers. Thus, early problem child behavior likely self-perpetuates, putting children at risk for lower academic achievement, as well as being at greater risk for physical injury (Kalb & Loeber, 2003). Prevention efforts are thus well indicated at young ages in order to impede the maintenance of stable and pervasive conduct problems into adolescence.

What Works

Prevention studies require longitudinal designs in order to show empirically that in-terventions during early ages account for the variation in clinical outcomes. Given the time-consuming nature of carrying out long-term prevention programs, there are few programs that have repeated outcome studies. Nonetheless, certain evidence-based prevention programs have repeatedly demonstrated the critical importance of acting on the child-rearing environment. Sometimes these kinds of programs are referred to as "behavioral family interventions" because the key to adjusting children's behavior is to change the behavior of the parents. Prevention efforts during the infancy period as well as preschool years have demonstrated a considerable reduction in *adolescent* behavior problems, particularly for families at greater social risk, such as low SES and unmarried mothers, weak parental involvement, low educational attainment, and marital discord (Bor, 2004; Olds, et al., 1998). Two best practices for the prevention of adoles-cent conduct problems are early childhood home visitation and the Triple P ("Positive Parenting Program").

Nurse home visitation program (0–2 years). For over 20 years, the nurse home visitation program has evolved as an evidence-based prevention program, particularly due to the demands by government funders for convincing support of the program's effectiveness with young mothers and their children (Olds & Korfmacher, 1997). For the program developer's detailed account of the theoretical underpinnings that guide the home visitation practice, see Olds, Kitzman, Cole, and Robinson (1997). Home visitation was designed both to promote maternal health related behaviors early in the child's life, as well as to promote maternal long term self-development through family planning, educational achievement, and participation in the work force. Ultimately, the support for the maternal figure, including connecting her with community resources, involving friends and family, teaching her sensitivity and responsiveness to her infant's needs, was hoped to have an enduring positive impact on caregiving and thus, child outcomes. Several randomized clinical trials of nurse home visitation in New York, Tennessee, and Colorado provide evidence that greater chances of positive clinical outcomes with parental caregiving, child and mother's health and development are mediated by these factors: following families at high risk at least through the child's second year, and training nurses to implement the comprehensive service (Olds & Korfmacher, 1997; Olds et al., 1998).

From a risk factors perspective, intervention efforts of the nurse home visitation program from birth to 2 years improved maternal health-related behavior, thereby reducing potentially aggravating factors of their child's antisocial behavior development. These maternal factors include fewer child problems due to substance abuse, fewer pregnancies, lower incidence of child abuse and neglect, less criminal behavior on part of low income unmarried mothers, more mothers returning to work (Olds, Henderson, Tatelbaum, & Chamberlin, 1986; Olds et al., 1998). At 15-year follow up, child outcomes (in adolescence) of the nurse home visitation program were observable: fewer episodes of running away from home, fewer arrests and convictions (e.g., recurrent truancy, destroying parents property), fewer violations of probation, fewer sexual partners, and less frequent engagement in smoking and alcohol consumption (Olds et al., 1998). Given these clinical outcomes, it is arguable that insulating the mother from risk by extension insulates children from poor early rearing and from certain later antisocial behaviors. Future directions of nurse home visitation mirror the evidence-based practices movement, gravitating toward refining theoretical and clinical practice through continued research, examining the effect of fidelity to their model, deciphering the adaptability of the program to more significantly at-risk communities, and identifying the core components of the program that enhance change (Olds & Korfmacher, 1997).

Triple P (3–4 years). Triple P ("Positive Parenting Program") is an Australia-based prevention effort that aims to "equip parents in their child-rearing role" with competence and confidence, and the ultimate goal, to provide preschool age children with a less risk-laden environment. For nearly three decades as a behavioral family intervention, Triple P has repeatedly shown that a focus on enhancing parents' skills, knowledge, and mental health results in less disruptive and oppositional behaviors in their children (Sanders, 1999). The program has demonstrated clinically meaningful success with many family types that may be considered a risk for CD, such as single-parent families, stepfamilies, maternally depressed families, maritally discordant families (Sanders, 1999 for a comprehensive review). Consistent with the current clinical view that basic psychoeducational interventions are less potent when used with high-risk families, the enhanced level of the Triple P intervention, or the highest level of parental support and skills training, has shown more reliable short-term positive changes in parenting practices and child behavior outcomes (Sanders, Markie-Dadds, Tully, & Bor, 2000).

Certain characteristics of Triple P make it a viable program in multiple communities. First, Triple P is meant to be cost-effective, given that the intervention can be tailored to the minimum level of support and resources that parents need to manage their children. And second, the intervention can be delivered in various formats (e.g., individual, group, by telephone), as well as by professionals within various disciplines (e.g., community nurses, family doctors, pediatricians, teachers, mental health professionals, police officers). Third, Triple P has a nationally coordinated system of training that promotes appropriate program use (fidelity to the model) through access to consultation support and research updates. To date, Triple P has demonstrated comparable success with families in one non-Western cultural context (Leung, Sanders, Leung, Mak, & Lau, 2003). The implementation in Hong Kong exemplifies both that a group-administered Triple P program is effective in reducing disruptive child behavior problems in the short-term, and that these changes are associated with changes in parenting and family risk factors. Short-term outcomes like these from Triple P are promising; however, a continuous look at long-term follow-up data ultimately will discern the impact of parent-centered prevention programs on the course of conduct disorders.

What Might Work

The future of prevention is a multisystemic approach, based on the stance that child conduct problems are determined by multiple interacting risk and protective factors. Although the quality of child rearing is centrally implicated in the development and maintenance of child behavior problems, child factors, peer relationships, and school experiences are significant elements of the developmental terrain. Studies have demonstrated the benefits of combining parent skills training with child skills training (e.g., Kazdin, Siegel, & Bass, 1992), including improvements in antisocial behavior and prosocial competencies. Thus, due to infinite individual differences in families, current practices consider and target the child's entire ecology. Prevention interventions are geared to be intensive (interwoven in the child's family life), long-term, and to target multiple risk and protective factors. As you can imagine, these types of cutting edge prevention efforts are large in scale, and require sound planning and ample resources for implementation. Two promising programs for addressing the multiple ecologies of children are the Fast Track and EARLY ALLIANCE prevention trials.

The Fast Track Prevention Trial (5–6 years). Fast Track is an "integrated model of prevention" programs, including a skills-building curriculum (the PATHS or "Promoting Alternative Thinking Strategies"), parent training groups, child "friendship" or social skills groups, parent–child cooperative activity time, home visitation (generalization efforts), child–peer pairing, and academic tutoring for reading (Conduct Problems Prevention Research Group, 1999). Compared to no-intervention peers, the intervention-group children showed initial improvements in prosocial behaviors and coping skills and indices of reading ability, and moderately less aggressive and disruptive behavior problems. Furthermore, intervention-group parents demonstrated more warm parenting behaviors and parental involvement in school and less harsh and inconsistent discipline. Fast Track is an exemplary prevention trial that hypothesizes changes in child, family and school-based risk repertoires are key to curtailing development of childhood and adolescent CD.

Importantly, Fast Track is a large-scale, long-term (from 1st to 10th grade), manualized intervention that requires the reciprocal efforts of researchers, teachers, parents, and community to implement. As Fast Track gains more evidence for its effectiveness, attention must be paid to the various practicalities necessary for transporting the intervention to other sites. Although it may be difficult to anticipate the feasibility, cost-effectiveness, and relative benefit of such comprehensive prevention programs, the one-year follow-up for the Fast Track prevention trial suggests some urgency for changes in the child's whole ecology to reach the long-term goal of reducing the likelihood of CD in adolescence.

The EARLY ALLIANCE prevention trial (5–8 years). Dumas, Prinz, Phillips-Smith, and Laughlin's (1999) EARLY ALLIANCE prevention trial is another promising multifaceted effort to curtail the development of childhood conduct disorder, as well as substance abuse and school failure in the long-term. The program lays distinctive emphasis on the promotion of prosocial competencies, and the hypothesis that an increase in affect, social, and achievement-related coping mechanisms within the family, peer group, and school settings will account partly for resiliency to developing CD. Thus, *protective* factors as well as risk factors are identified and manipulated for successful clinical outcomes. For these ends, interventions begin at school entry, and include a classroom program, a peer intervention, reading mentoring, and a family intervention.

The classroom program involves teacher training, an emphasis on school- and home-based recognition for daily "successes" (the "Good News Note system"), a classroom management program that reduces aggressive behavior (the "Good Communication Game"), and finally, ongoing weekly consultation for teachers. To further promote positive school experience, the peer intervention teaches children in culturally sensitive ways how to be assertive and communicative with peers and adults. The biweekly reading mentoring, too, is meant to protect children from school failure experiences. As do preceding prevention program developers, EARLY ALLIANCE developers recognize the role of parents as the primary "socializing agents" (p. 48). The family intervention includes parent skills building and connecting families to necessary community resources to support competent caregiving. For detailed procedures as well as discourse on the intended impact of these modalities, see Dumas et al. (1999). EARLY ALLIANCE is currently implemented and is being compared annually to a universal conflict management intervention for use with 1st and 2nd grade students in 12 participating schools. At the time of this publication, there are not yet any available outcome publications.

What Does Not Work

Dumas, Prinz, Phillips-Smith, and Laughlin (1999) summarized several characteristics of interventions that do not help reduction of risk for CD in the early years. First, interventions that focus on a single factor (individual, familial, social) in risk reduction ignore the general consensus that CD is determined by multiple and cumulative (interacting) variables. Second, interventions aiming at risk factors while not promoting competencies, or starting "too late" in development when antisocial behavior is a stable trait, are not promising prevention efforts. Rigid interventions that are insensitive to variations in families or cultures are likely inert. Lastly, interventions that pivot on inaccurate models of developmentally appropriate prosocial and antisocial behavior are not advocated (p. 40). These are helpful ways of thinking about the nature of childhood conduct problems, and the fact that disruptive behavior will likely not be averted with unidimensional or unaccommodating efforts with respect to the family.

RECOMMENDATIONS

Externalizing behavior problems in children are a significant concern for parents, teachers, and mental health professionals. There is little question that the behavior problems of children are complex. Both proximal and distal risk factors in the youths' biology, family, and social context interact with other more protective factors in the same areas to lead to a course of conduct problems. The status of the research suggests that a multidimensional approach to both understanding and intervening with these youth is the most effective approach to either prevention efforts or treatment of problem behavior with these youth. Evidence-based prevention and intervention programs currently offer the most reliable way to help children with these problems. There are a number of comprehensive programs for intervening early and later, to treat behavioral difficulties. The current EBP provides a constructive framework for making decisions about what works, what might work, and what does not work.

Given the nearly unthinkable number of variables that may contribute to the maintenance of behavior problems across the lifespan, what we do know is that prevention and treatment interventions that target multiple risk and protective factors do work. We also know, given that parent behavior and nurturing practices are the primary social environment of children, interventions that support parents with resources and enhance parenting skills provide children with perhaps the strongest backbone with which to withstand an antisocial life course. The future of intervention is less reliant on one factor, however, such as marital discord or lack of secure attachment, as culprits in the onset of CD: family counts; context counts; individual factors count; and so on. Thus, a multifaceted approach is indicated. Next, we know that the intensity, or face-to-face nature of the intervention, is critical. Handing out pamphlets with little or no involvement with the parental figures does not have comparable impact on later outcomes with children. Community intervention is less about disseminating information than it is about changing the interactive experience of the parents, children, and family unit and community as a whole.

Notwithstanding, it will continue to be critical to develop a range of evidence-based practices in order to address the complexity of problems within children's ecologies. Second at the forefront of treatment and prevention science is the need for systematic strategies to mobilize these practices to communities where they are needed. Despite their great potential, the future of evidence-based prevention and intervention programs for children lies in the ability of interventionists and model developers to devise successful strategies to transport programs from development into community settings. To better move to community settings EBP need to retain standards of practice that are high, while focusing on better dissemination and systematic attention to successful implementation and quality assurance and improvement (Sexton, Gillman, & Johnson, 2005).

REFERENCES

Alexander, J. F., Sexton, T. L., & Robbins, M. (2001). The developmental status of family therapy in family psychology intervention science. In H. Liddle, D. Santisteban, R. Levant, & J. Bray (Eds.), *Family psychology science-based interventions* (pp. 17-40). Washington, D.C.: American Psychiatric Press.

American Psychiatric Association (2000). *Diagnostic and statistical manual of mental disorders* (4th ed., TR). Washington, D.C.: Author.

Barcalow, K. (2006). Oppositional defiant disorder: Information for school nurses. *Journal of School Nursing, 22*, 9–16.

Barnoski, R. (2004). Outcome Evaluation of Washington State's Research-based Programs for Juvenille Offender. *Washington State Institute for Public Policy*. http://www.wsipp.wa.gov (retrieved September 19, 2006).

Bassareth, L. (2001). Conduct disorder: A biopsychosocial review. *Canadian Journal of Psychiatry, 46*(7), 609–615.

Bates, J. E., Bayles, K., Bennett, D. S., Ridge, B., & Brown, M. M. (1991). Origins of externalizing behavior problems at eight years of age. In D. J. Pepler, & K. H. Rubin (Eds.), *Earlscourt symposium on childhood aggression, jun 1988, toronto, canada* (pp. 93–120). Hillsdale, NJ: Lawrence Erlbaum.

Bor, W. (2004). Prevention and treatment of childhood and adolescent aggression and antisocial behavior: A selective review. *Australian and New Zealand Journal of Psychiatry, 38*, 373–380.

Brannigan, A., Gemmell, W. Pevalin, D. J., & Wade, T. J. (2002, April). Self-control and social control in childhood misconduct and aggression: The role of family structure, hyperactivity, and hostile parenting. *Canadian Journal of Criminology, 44*(2), 119–142.

Burke, J. D., Loeber, R., & Birmaher, B. (2002). Oppositional defiant disorder and conduct disorder: A review of the past 10 years, part II. *Journal of the American Academy of Child and Adolescent Psychiatry, 41*(11), 1275–1293.

Cadoret, R. J. (1981). Environmental and genetic factors in predicting adolescent antisocial behavior in adoptees. *Psychiatric Journal University of Ottawa, 6*, 220–225.

Cadoret, R. J. (1983). Evidence for gene-environment interaction in the development of antisocial behavior. *Behavior Genetics, 13*, 301–310.

Cadoret, R. J., Yates, W. R., Troughton, E., Woodworth, G., & Stewart, M. (1995). Genetic-environmental interaction in the genesis of aggressivity and conduct disorders. Archives of *General Psychiatry, 52*(11), 916–924.

Campbell, S. B., & Ewing, L. J. (1990). Follow-up of hard-to-manage preschoolers—Adjustment at age 9 and predictors of continuing symptoms. *Journal of Child Psychology and Psychiatry and Allied Disciplines, 31*(6), 871–889.

Caspi, A., & Henry, B., McGee, R. O., Moffitt, T. E., & Silva, P. A. (1995). Temperamental origins of child and adolescent behavior problems: From age three to age fifteen. *Child Development, 66*, 55–68.

Caspi, A., Moffitt, T. E., Mill, J., Martin, J., Craig, I. W., Taylor, A. Resou, & Poulton, R. (2002). Role of genotype in the cycle of violence in maltreated children. *Science, 297*, 851–854.

Caspi, A., Taylor, A., Moffitt, T. E., & Plomin, R. (2000). Neighbourhood deprivation affects children's mental health: Environmental risks identified in a genetic design. *Psychological Science, 11*, 338–342.

Chamberlain, P. (1994). *Family connections: Treatment foster care for adolescents with delinquency.* Eugene, OR: Northwest Media.

Chamberlain, P. (2003). *Treating chronic juvenile offenders: Advances made through the Oregon multidimensional treatment foster care model.* Washington, D.C.: American Psychological Association.

Chamberlain, P., & Reid, J. (1998). Comparison of two community alternatives to incarceration for chronic juvenile offenders. *Journal of Consulting and Clinical Psychology, 6*, 624–633.

Coates, R. B., Alden, D. M., & Ohlin, L. E. (1978). *Diversity in a youth correctional system.* Cambridge, MA: Ballinger.

Collins, W. A., Maccoby, E. E., Steinberg, L., Hetherington, E. M., & Bornstein, M. (2000). Contemporary research on parenting: The case for nature and nurture. *American Psychologist, 55*, 218–232.

Conduct Problems Prevention Research Group. (1999). Initial impact of the Fast Track prevention trial for conduct problems: I. High-risk sample. *Journal of Consulting and Clinical Psychology, 67*(5), 631–647.

Crowe, R. R. (1974). An adoption study of antisocial personality. *Archive of General Psychiatry, 31*, 785–791.

Crowell, S. E., Beauchaine, T. P., Gatzke-Kopp, L., Sylvers, H. M., Mead, H., & Chipman-Chacon, J. (2006). Autonomic correlates of attention-deficit/hyperactivity disorder and oppositional defiant disorder in preschool children. *Journal of Abnormal Psychology, 115*(1), 174–178.

Crowther, J. H., Bond, L. A., & Rolf, J. E. (1981). The incidence, prevalence, and severity of behavior disorders among preschool-aged children in day care. *Journal of abnormal child psychology, 9*(1), 23–42.

Dishion, T. J., McCord, J., & Poulin, F. (1999). When interventions harm: Peer groups and problem behavior. *American Psychologist, 54*(9), 755–764.

Dishion, T. J., & McMahon, R. J. (1998). Parental monitoring and the prevention of child and adolescent problem behavior: A conceptual and empirical formulation. *Clinical Child and Family Psychology Review, 1*(1), 61–75.

Dumas, J. E., Prinz, R. J., Phillips-Smith, E., & Laughlin, J. (1999). The EARLY ALLIANCE Prevention Trial: An integrated set of interventions to promote competence and reduce risk for conduct disorder, substance abuse, and school failure. *Clinical Child and Family Psychology Review, 2*(1), 37–53.

Eddy, J. M., & Chamberlain, P. (2000). Family management and deviant peer association as mediators of the impact of treatment condition on youth antisocial behavior. *Journal of Consulting and Clinical Psychology, 5,* 857–863.

Elliott, D. S. (Series Ed.). (1998). *Blueprints for violence prevention.* University of Colorado, Center for the Study and Prevention of Violence. Boulder, CO: Blueprints.

Elze, D. E., Stiffman, A. R., & Doré, P. (1999). The association between types of violence exposure and youths' mental health problems. *International Journal of Adolescent Medicine and Health, 11*(3), 221–255.

Firestone, P., Kelly, M. J., & Fike, S. (1980). Are fathers necessary in parent training groups? *Journal of Clinical Child Psychology, 9*(1), 44–47.

Forness, S. R., & Kavale, K. A. (2000). Emotional or behavioral disorders: Background and current status of the E/BD terminology and definition. *Behavioral Disorders, 25*(3), 264–269.

Frick, P. J. (1998). *Conduct disorders and severe antisocial behavior.* New York: Plenum.

Frick, P. J., Lahey, B. B., Loeber, R., Stouthamer-Loeber, M., Christ, M. A., & Hanson, K. (1992). Familial risk factors to oppositional defiant disorder and conduct disorder: Parental psychopathology and maternal parenting. *Journal of Consulting and Clinical Psychology, 60,* 49–55.

Galambos, N. L., Barker, E. T., & Almeida, D. M. (2003). Parents do matter: Trajectories of change in externalizing and internalizing problems in early adolescence. *Child Development, 74,* 578–594.

Gjone, H., & Stevenson, J. (1997). A longitudinal twin study of temperament and behavior problems: Common genetic or environmental influences? *American Academy of Child and Adolescent Psychiatry, 36*(10), 1448–1456.

Grizenko, N., Papineau, D., & Sayegh, L. (1993). Effectiveness of a multimodal day treatment program for children with disruptive behavior problems. *Journal of the American Academy of Child & Adolescent Psychiatry, 32*(1), 127–134.

Henggeler, S. W., Melton, G. B., & Smith, L. A. (1992). Family preservation using multisystemic therapy: An effective alternative to incarcerating juvenile offenders. *Journal of Consulting and Clinical Psychology, 60(6),* 953-961.

Hutchings, J., & Lane, E. (2005). Parenting and the development and prevention of child mental health problems. *Current Opinion in Psychiatry, 18*(4), 386–391.

Hutchings, J., Gardner, F., & Lane, E. (2004). Making evidence-based interventions work. In C. Sutton, D. Utting, & D. Farrington (Eds.), *Support from the start: Working with young children and their families to reduce the risks of crime and antisocial behaviour* (pp. 69–79). Nottingham, UK: Department for Education and Skills. *Collaborative.*

Huizinga, D. (1995). Developmental sequences in delinquency: Dynamic typologies. In L. J. Crockett & A. C. Crouter (Eds.), *Pathways through adolescence: Individual development in relation to social contexts* (pp. 15–34). Hillsdale, NJ: Lawrence Erlbaum.

Institute of Medicine (2001). *Crossing the quality chasm: A new health system for the 21st century.* (Executive Summary). Washington, D.C.: National Academy Press.

Kalb, L. M., & Loeber, R. (2003). Child disobedience and noncompliance: A review. *Pediatrics, 111*(3), 641–652.

Kavale, K. A., Forness, S. R., & Walker, H. M. (1999). Interventions for oppositional defiant disorder and conduct disorder in the schools. In H. C. Quay & A. E. Hogan (Eds.), *Handbook of disruptive behavior disorders* (pp. 441–454). New York: Plenum.

Kazdin, A. E. (2004). Psychotherapy for children and adolescents. In M. Lambert (Ed.), *Bergin and Garfield's handbook of psychotherapy and behavior change* (5th ed., pp. 543–589). Hoboken, NJ: Wiley.

Kazdin, A. E., Bass, D., Siegel, T., & Thomas, C. (1989). Cognitive-behavioral therapy and relationship therapy in the treatment of children referred for antisocial behavior. *Journal of Consulting and Clinical Psychology, 57,* 522–535.

Kazdin, A. E., Siegel, T. C., & Bass, D. (1992). Cognitive problem-solving skills training and parent management training in the treatment of antisocial behavior in children. *Journal of Consulting and Clinical Psychology, 60*(5), 733–747.

Kerr, D. C., Lopez, N. L., Olsen, S. L., & Sameroff, A. J. (2004). Parental discipline and externalizing behavior problems in early childhood: The roles of moral regulation and child gender. *Journal of Abnormal Child Psychology, 32*, 369–383.

Knutson, J. F., DeGarmo, D. S., & Reid, J. B. (2004). Social disadvantage and neglectful parenting as precursors to the development of antisocial and aggressive child behavior: Testing a theoretical model. *Aggressive Behavior, 30*, 187–205.

Kohlberg, L., Ricks, D., & Snarey, J. (1984). Childhood development as a predictor of adaptation in adulthood. *Genetic Psychology Monographs, 110*(1), 91–172.

Kolko, D. J., Bukstein, O. G., & Barron, J. (1999). Methylphenidate and behavior modification in children with ADHD and comorbid ODD or CD: Main and incremental effects across settings. *American Academy of Child and Adolescent Psychiatry, 38*(5), 578–586.

Kruesi, M. J., Hibbs, E. D., Zahn, T. P., Keysor, C. S., Hamburger, S. D., Bartko, J. J., & Rapoport, J. L. (1992). A 2-year prospective follow-up study of children and adolescents with disruptive behavior disorders. *Archives of General Psychiatry, 49*, 429–435.

Kruesi, M. J., Rapoport, J. L., Hamburger, S., Hibbs, E., Potter, W. Z., Lenane, M., et al. (1990). Cerebrospinal fluid monoamine metabolites, aggression, and impulsivity in disruptive behavior disorders of children and adolescents. *Archives of General Psychiatry, 47*, 419–426.

Leung, C., Sanders, M. R., Leung, S., Mak, R., & Lau, J. (2003). An outcome evaluation of the implementation of the Triple P-Positive Parenting Program in Hong Kong. *Family Process, 42*(4), 531–544.

Loeber, R. (1991). Antisocial behavior: More enduring than changeable? *Journal of the American Academy of Child & Adolescent Psychiatry, 30*(3), 393–397.

Loeber, R., Farrington, D. P., Stouthamer-Loeber, M., & Van Kammen, W. B. (1998). *Antisocial behavior and mental health problems: Explanatory factors in childhood and adolescence.* Mahwah, NJ: Lawrence Erlbaum.

Loeber, R., & Hay, D. (1997). Key issues in the development of aggression and violence from childhood to early adulthood. *Annual Review of Psychology, 48*, 371–410.

Lytton, H. (1990a). Child and parent effects in boys' conduct disorder: A reinterpretation. *Developmental Psychology, 26*(5), 683–697.

Lytton, H. (1990b). Child effects: Still unwelcome? Response to Dodge and Wahler. *Developmental Psychology, 26*(5), 705–709.

Markward, M. J., & Bride, B. (2001). Oppositional defiant disorder and the need for family-centered practice in schools, *Children and Schools, 23*(2), 73–82.

Masten, A. S., & Shaffer, A. (2006). How families matter in child development: Reflections from research on risk and resilience. In A. Clarke-Stewart & J. Dunn (Eds.), *Families count: Effects on child and adolescent development* (pp. 5–25). New York: Cambridge University Press.

McCabe, K. M., Lucchini, S. D., Hough, R. L., Yeh, M., & Hazen, A. (2005). The relation between violence exposure and conduct problems among adolescents: A prospective study. *American Journal of Orthopsychiatry, 75*(4), 575–584.

McGee, R., & Williams, S. (1999). Environmental risk factors in oppositional defiant disorder and conduct disorder. In H. C. Quay & A. E. Hogan (Eds.), *Handbook of disruptive behavior disorders* (pp. 419–440). New York: Plenum.

Moffitt , T. E. (1993). Adolescent-limited and life-course-persistent antisocial behavior: A developmental taxonomy. *Psychological Review, 100*, 674–701.

Mpofu, E. (2002). Psychopharmacology in the treatment of conduct disorder children and adolescents: Rationale, prospects, and ethics. *South African Journal of Psychology, 32*(4), 9–21.

Mpofu, E., & Conyers, L. (2003). Neurochemistry in the comorbidity of conduct disorder with other disorders in childhood and adolescence: Implications for counseling. *Psychology Quarterly, 16*(1), 37–41.

Nagin, D., & Tremblay, R. E. (1999). Trajectories of boy's physical aggression, opposition, and hyperactivity on the path to physically violent and nonviolent juvenile delinquency. *Child Development, 70*(5), 1181–1196.

Nakamura, R. (2005). Outreach Partnership Program 2005 Annual Meeting. *NIMH Science Update.* Retrieved September 5, 2006 from http://www.nimh.nih.gov/outreach/partners/nakamura2005.cfm

Offord, D. R., Alder, R. J., & Boyle, M. H. (1986). Prevalence and sociodemographic correlates of conduct disorder[Special issue]. *American Journal of Social Psychiatry 6*(4), 272–278.

Olds, D., Henderson, C. R., Cole, R., Eckenrode, J., Kitzman, H., Lucky, D., et al. (1998). Long-term effects of nurse home visitation on children's criminal and antisocial behavior: 15 year follow-up of a randomized controlled trial. *Journal of the American Medical Association, 280*(14), 1238–1244.

Olds, D., Henderson, C., Tatelbaum, R., & Chamberlin, R. (1986). Preventing child abuse and neglect: a randomized trial of nurse home visitation. *Pediatrics, 78*, 65–78.

Olds, D., Kitzman, H., Cole, R., & Robinson, J. (1997). Theoretical and empirical foundations of a program of home visitation for pregnant women and parents of young children. *Journal of Community Psychology, 25*, 9–25.

Olds, D., & Korfmacher, J. (1997). The evolution of a program of research on prenatal and early childhood home visitation [Special issue].*Journal of Community Psychology, 25*, 1–7.

Patterson, G. R., DeBaryshe, B. D., & Ramsey, E. (1989). A developmental perspective on antisocial behavior. *American Psychologist, 44*(2), 329–335.

Patterson, G. R., & Forgatch, M. S. (1995). Predicting future clinical adjustment from treatment outcome and process variables. *Psychological Assessment, 7*, 275–285.

Patterson, G. R., & Stouthamer-Loeber, M. (1984). The correlation of family management practices and delinquency. *Child Development, 55*(4), 1299–1307.

Patterson, G. R., & Yoerger, K. (1997). *A developmental model for late-onset delinquency.* In D. W. Osgood (Ed.), *Motivation and delinquency: Nebraska Symposium on Motivation* (Vol. 44, pp. 119–177). Lincoln: University of Nebraska Press,.

Petrosino, A., Turpin-Petrosino, C., & Buehler, J. (2003). Scared straight and other juvenile awareness programs for preventing juvenile delinquency: A systematic review of the randomized experimental evidence. *The Annals of the American Academy, 589*, 41–62.

Pettit, G. S., Bates, J. E., Dodge, K. A., & Meece, D. W. (1999). The impact of after-school peer contact on early adolescent externalizing problems is moderated by parental monitoring, perceived neighborhood safety, and prior adjustment. *Child Development, 70*(3), 768–778.

Pianta, R. C., & Caldwell, C. B. (1990). Stability of externalizing symptoms from kindergarten to first grade and factors related to instability. *Development and Psychopathology, 2*(3), 247–258.

Puckering, C., Rogers, J., Mills, M., Cox, A. D., & Mattsson-Graf, M. (1994). Process and evaluation of a group intervention for mothers with parenting difficulties. *Child Abuse Review, 3*(4), 299–310.

Raine, A., Brennan, P., Mednick, B, & Mednick, S. A. (1996). High rates of violence, crime, academic problems, and behavioral problems in males with both early neuromotor deficits and unstable family environments. *Archives of General Psychiatry, 53*(6), 544–549.

Reid, J. B., & Patterson, G. R. (1989). The development of antisocial behavior problems in childhood and adolescence. *European Journal of Personality, 3*, 107–119.

Rende, R. D., & Plomin, R. (1992). Relations between first grade stress, temperament, and behavior problems. *Journal of Applied Developmental Psychology, 13*, 435–446.

Repetti, R. L., Taylor, S. E., & Seeman, T. (2002). Risky families: Family social environments and the mental and physical health of offspring. *Psychological Bulletin, 128*(2), 330–366.

Richters, J. E., & Martinez, P. E. (1993). Violent communities, family choices, and children's chances: An algorithm for improving the odds. *Development and Psychopathology, 5*(4), 609–627.

Rimm, D. C., & Masters, J. C. (1974). *Behavior therapy: Techniques and empirical findings.* New York: Academic Press.

Robins, L. (1966). *Deviant children grown up: A sociological and psychiatric study of sociopathic personality.* Baltimore: Williams & Wilkins.

Robins, L. N. (1978). Sturdy childhood predictors of adult antisocial behaviour: Replications from longitudinal studies. *Psychological Medicine, 8*(4), 611–622.

Robin, L. (1981). Epidemiological approaches to natural history research—Antisocial disorders in children. Journal of the American Academy of Child and Adolescent Psychiatry, 20(3), 566-580.

Rowe, C. L., & Liddle, H. A. (2002). *Substance abuse..* In D. Sprenkle (Ed.), *Effectiveness research in marriage and family therapy* (pp. 53-87). Alexandria, VA: American Association for Marriage and Family Therapy.

Russo, M. F., & Beidel, D. C. (1994). Comorbidity of childhood anxiety and externalizing disorders: Prevalence, associated characteristics, and validation issues. *Clinical Psychology Review, 14*(3), 199–221.

Sanders, M. (1999). Triple P-Positive Parenting Program: Towards an empirically validated multilevel parenting and family support strategy for the prevention of behavior and emotional problems in children. *Clinical Child and Family Psychology Review, 2*(2), 71–90.

Sanders, M. R., Markie-Dadds, C., Tully, L. A., & Bor, W. (2000). The Triple P-Positive Parenting Program: A comparison of enhanced, standard and self-directed behavioral family intervention for parents of children with early onset conduct problems. *Journal of Consulting and Clinical Psychology, 68*(4), 624–640.

Sanson, A., Hemphill, S. A., & Smart, D. (2004). Connections between temperament and social development: A review. *Social Development, 13*(1), 142–170.

Searight, R. (2001). Conduct disorder: Diagnosis and treatment in primary care. *American Family Physician, 63*(8), 1579–1588.

Serketich, W. J., & Dumas, J. E. (1996). The effectiveness of behavioral parent training to modify antisocial behavior in children: A meta-analysis. *Behavior Therapy, 27*(2), 171–186.

Sexton, T. L., & Alexander, J. F. (2002). Family based empirically supported interventions. *The Counseling Psychologist, 30*(2), 1–8.

Sexton, T. L., Alexander, J. F., & Mease, A. L. (2004). Levels of evidence for the models and mechanisms of therapeutic change in couple and family therapy. In M. Lambert (Ed.), *Handbook of psychotherapy and behavior change* (5th ed., pp. 590–646). New York: Wiley.

Sexton, T. L., Gillman, L., & Johnson, C. (2005). Evidence based practices in the prevention and treatment of adolescent behavior problems. In T. P Gullotta & A. Gerald, (Eds.), *Handbook of adolescent behavioral problems: Evidence-based approaches to prevention and treatment,* (pp. 101-128). New York: Springer.

Shure, M. B., Spivack, G., & Gordon, R. (1972). Problem-solving thinking: A preventive mental health program for preschool children. *Reading World, 4*(4), 259–273.

Shapiro, S. K., & Hynd, G. W. (1993). Psychobiological basis of conduct disorder. *School Psychology Review, 22*(3), 386–402.

Stams, G. J., Juffer, F., & Ijzendoorn, M. H. (2002). Maternal sensitivity, infant attachment, and temperament in early childhood predict adjustment in middle childhood: The case of adopted children and their biologically unrelated parents. *Developmental Psychology, 38*, 806–821.

Stattin, H., & Magnusson, D. (1996). Antisocial development: A holistic approach. *Development and Psychopathology, 8*(4), 617–645.

Tolan, P. H. (1987). Implications of age of onset for delinquency risk. *Journal of Abnormal Child Psychology, 15*(1), 47–65.

Tolan, P. H., & Gorman-Smith, D. (1998). Development of serious and violent offending careers. In R. Loeber & D. P. Farrington (Eds.), *Serious & violent juvenile offenders: Risk factors and successful interventions* (pp. 68–85). Thousand Oaks, CA: Sage.

Tse, J. (2006). Research on day treatment programs for preschoolers with disruptive behavior disorders. *Psychiatric Services, 57*(4), 477–486.

U.S. Surgeon-General (2000). *Mental health: A report of the surgeon-general.* Washington, D.C.: Government Printing Office.

Utting, D., & Pugh, G. (2004). The social context of parenting. In M. Hoghughi & N. Long (Eds.), *Handbook of parenting: Theory and research for practice* (pp. 110–129). London: Sage.

Van de Wiel, N. M. H., Van Goozen, S. H. M., Matthys, W., Snoek, H., & Van Engeland, H. (2004). Cortisol and treatment effects in children with disruptive behavior disorders: a preliminary study. *Journal of the American Academy of Child and Adolescent Psychiatry, 43*, 1011–1118.

Van Goozen, S. H., & Fairchild, G. (2006). Neuroendocrine and neurotransmitter correlates in children with antisocial behavior. *Hormones and Behavior, 50*(4), 647–654.

Ware, L. M., Novotny, E. S., & Coyne, L. (2001). A therapeutic nursery evaluation study. *Bulletin of the Menninger Clinic, 65,* 522–548.

Webster-Stratton, C. (1990). Stress: A potential disruptor of parent perceptions and family interactions. *Journal of Clinical Child Psychology, 19*, 302–312.

Webster-Stratton, C. (1996). Early-onset conduct problems: Does gender make a difference? *Journal of Consulting and Clinical Psychology, 64*(3), 540–551.

Webster-Stratton, C. (2001). The incredible years: Parents, teachers, and children training series [*Special Issue*]. *Residential Treatment for Children & Youth 18*(3), 31–45.

Webster-Stratton, C., & Hammond, M. (1997). Treating children with early-onset conduct problems: A comparison of child and parent training interventions. *Journal of Consulting and Clinical Psychology, 65,* 93–108.

Webster-Stratton, C., Reid, J., & Hammond, M. (2001). Social skills and problem-solving training for children with early-onset conduct problems: Who benefits? *Journal of Child Psychology and Psychiatry, 42*(7), 943–952.

White, J. L., Moffitt, T. E., Earls, F., Robins, L., & Silva, P. A. (1990). How early can we tell? Predictors of childhood adolescent delinquency. *Criminology, 28* (4), 507–533.

Winsberg, B. G., Bailer, I., Kupietz, S., Botti, E., & Balka, E. (1980). Home vs. hospital care of children with behavior disorders: A controlled investigation. *Archives of General Psychiatry, 37*(4), 413–418.

Wright-Guerin, D., Gottfried, A. W., & Thomas, C. W. (1997). Difficult temperament and behaviour problems: A longitudinal study from 1.5 to 12 years. *International Journal of Behavioral Development, 21*(1), 71–90.

Chapter Sixteen

Autism Spectrum Disorders in Childhood

David S. Mandell, Aubyn C. Stahmer, and Edward S. Brodkin

INTRODUCTION

Autism spectrum disorders (ASD) comprise a group of similar developmental disorders that manifest in the first three years of life and are characterized by impairments in reciprocal social interaction and communication, and the presence of restricted behaviors, interests and activities (American Psychiatric Association, 2000). The disorder was first described by (Kanner, 1943); higher functioning children with similar social impairments and restricted behaviors were described almost concurrently by Asperger (Wing, 1981).

The Diagnostic and Statistical Manual of Mental Disorders (DSM IV-TR; APA, 2000) criteria for autistic disorder, the most impairing manifestation of the spectrum, include:

A. A total of six (or more) items from (1), (2), and (3), with at least two from (1), and one each from (2) and (3):
  1. qualitative impairment in social interaction, as manifested by at least two of the following:
     a. marked impairment in the use of multiple nonverbal behaviors such as eye-to-eye gaze, facial expression, body postures, and gestures to regulate social interaction
     b. failure to develop peer relationships appropriate to developmental level
     c. a lack of spontaneous seeking to share enjoyment, interests, or achievements with other people (e.g., by a lack of showing, bringing, or pointing out objects of interest)
     d. lack of social or emotional reciprocity
  2. qualitative impairments in communication as manifested by at least one of the following:
     a. delay in, or total lack of, the development of spoken language (not accompanied by an attempt to compensate through alternative modes of communication such as gesture or mime)

      b. in individuals with adequate speech, marked impairment in the ability to initiate or sustain a conversation with others

      c. stereotyped and repetitive use of language or idiosyncratic language

      d. lack of varied, spontaneous make-believe play or social imitative play appropriate to developmental level

  3. restricted repetitive and stereotyped patterns of behavior, interests, and activities, as manifested by at least one of the following:

      a. encompassing preoccupation with one or more stereotyped and restricted patterns of interest that is abnormal either in intensity or focus

      b. apparently inflexible adherence to specific, nonfunctional routines or rituals

      c. stereotyped and repetitive motor manners (e.g., hand or finger flapping or twisting, or complex whole-body movements)

      d. persistent preoccupation with parts of objects

B. Delays or abnormal functioning in at least one of the following areas, with onset prior to age 3 years: (1) social interaction, (2) language as used in social communication, or (3) symbolic or imaginative play.

C. The disturbance is not better accounted for by Rett's Disorder or Childhood Disintegrative Disorder. (p. 71)

The DSM requires that children exhibit abnormal functioning in at least one of the above areas prior to 3 years of age. It is important to note that the Autism Diagnostic Observation Schedule (Lord et al., 1989), often considered the gold standard diagnostic instrument, measures this last category of behavior, but does not require its presence for children to meet diagnostic criteria.

Asperger's disorder is characterized by impairments in social interaction and restricted and repetitive behaviors and interests, but language acquisition is typical or accelerated. Individuals with pervasive developmental disorder—not otherwise specified (PDD-NOS)—do not meet criteria for autistic or Asperger's disorders, but still exhibit many of these symptoms. Symptoms are typically less severe and do not meet criteria in one or more of the three areas listed above. In childhood disintegrative disorder children have a period of clearly typical development for at least two to four years and then gradually exhibit symptoms similar to autistic disorder. The course of childhood disintegrative disorder, which is extremely rare, is often worse than the other ASDs. The presentation of ASD can vary widely among affected individuals and within an individual over the lifespan (Volkmar & Pauls, 2003; Wing, 1997).

There is increasing concern over the rising rates of individuals diagnosed with ASD. Fombonne's (2003) survey of epidemiologic studies from 1966 to 2001 showed a dramatic rise in prevalence from approximately 2 per 10,000 in the 1960s to 30 per 10,000 in the 1990s, and more recent studies suggest an even higher proportion of approximately 60 per 10,000 (Yeargin-Allsopp et al., 2003). Considerable debate has ensued regarding whether this increase is due to changes in diagnostic criteria (Byrd, 2003; Croen, Grether, Hoogstrate, & Selvin, 2002; Fombonne, 2001; Wing & Potter, 2002), better differentiation from other disorders (Croen et al., 2002), the decreasing age of diagnosis (Wing & Potter, 2002), increased attention to this puzzling disorder in the popular press, or increases in community prevalence (Mandell, Thompson, Weintraub, DeStephano, & Blank, 2005). Most evidence suggests that the bulk of this increase is due to changes in diagnostic practices and increased awareness and recognition, especially at the ends of the continuum among individuals who are either severely affected or higher functioning (Fombonne, 2005). Increase in community prevalence cannot be ruled out, however. There have been no observed differences in the community prevalence of ASD among cultural, ethnic, or racial groups, with studies conducted in different groups and countries with the same birth cohorts and diagnostic criteria finding similar results.

Individuals with ASD are at increased risk for a number of other conditions. Meta-analyses suggest that mental retardation occurs in 50% to 70%, seizure disorders in 30%, tuberous sclerosis in 5%, and hearing impairment in 10% to 20% of children with autistic disorder (Gillberg & Billstedt, 2000). Lower proportions of these conditions have been found among children with other disorders on the spectrum.

BIOLOGICAL–GENETIC FACTORS

Abnormalities of brain development, structure, and function underlie the behavioral symptoms of ASD and underlie associated features, such as seizures (in up to 30% of individuals with ASDs) (Muhle, Trentacoste, & Rapin, 2004). Moreover, susceptibility to ASD is highly influenced by particular gene variants (alleles) or mutations.

Brain imaging studies have revealed several macroscopic abnormalities of brain structure in ASD. At birth, head circumferences and brain sizes of infants who go on to develop autism are, on average, normal or slightly small (Dementieva et al., 2005; Redcay & Courchesne, 2005). In the first two years of life, however, there is often an abnormal acceleration of brain growth so that, by toddlerhood, brains of children with ASD are, on average, larger and heavier than those of other children (Bauman & Kemper, 1994; Courchesne, Carper, & Akshoomoff, 2003; Dementieva et al., 2005; Herbert, 2005; Herbert, Ziegler, Deutsch, et al., 2003; Lainhart et al., 1997; Nicolson & Szatmari, 2003; Piven, Arndt, Bailey, & Andreasen, 1996; Redcay & Courchesne, 2005). Large brain size has been found in adults with ASD as well (Hardan, Minshew, Mallikarjuhn, & Keshevan, 2001; Hazlett et al., 2005; Piven, Arndt, et al., 1996), although not as consistently as in children with ASD, which suggests that some individuals with ASD may undergo an abnormal deceleration of brain growth from when they are toddlers to adulthood (Courchesne, Redcay, Morgan, & Kennedy, 2005).

There is evidence that brain enlargement is due to enlargements of both gray and white matter, with a disproportionate enlargement of subcortical white matter (Courchesne, Redcay, Morgan, & Kennedy, 2005; Herbert, Ziegler, Makris, et al., 2004). The deeper brain white matter is not as enlarged, and major sagittal white matter tracts (Herbert, Ziegler, Makris, et al., 2004), such as the corpus callosum, have been found to be abnormally small, relative to total brain size, in many studies (Eggas, Courchesne, & Saitoh, 1995; Hardan, Minshew, & Keshavan, 2000; Herbert, 2005; Piven, Bailey, Ransom, & Arndt, 1997; Vidal et al., 2006; Waiter et al., 2005). It has been proposed that the increased brain size, together with white matter abnormalities, may lead to underconnectivity in the brains of individuals with ASD, which may underlie impairments in functional integration of various brain regions, as well as the psychological phenomena of impaired complex information processing and "weak central coherence" in ASD (Happe & Frith, 2006; Herbert, 2005; Just, Cherkassky, Keller, & Minshew, 2004; Vidal et al., 2006).

Postmortem neuropathological studies of autistic brains have consistently revealed a reduction in numbers of Purkinje cells in cerebellum, primarily in posterolateral neo-cerebellar cortex and adjacent archicerebellar cortex of the cerebellar hemispheres (Arin, Bauman, & Kemper, 1991; Bailey, Luther, et al., 1998). Some studies have revealed small, densely packed neurons bilaterally in the hippocampus, subiculum, entorhinal cortex, medial amygdala, mammillary body, anterior cingulate gyrus, and medial septal nucleus (Bauman & Kemper, 1994, 2005). Brains of autistic individuals also show abnormalities in minicolumn structure in the cerebral cortex, with smaller and more numerous minicolumns, and with less compact cellular configuration (Casanova, Buxhoeveden, Switala, & Roy, 2002). There is compelling evidence suggesting these various neuro-anatomical phenotypes are due to prenatal brain developmental anomalies (Bauman & Kemper, 2005).

Approximately 25% of individuals with ASD have elevated levels of blood serotonin (Cook & Leventhal, 1996). It also has been demonstrated that these individuals show developmental abnormalities in brain serotonin synthesis capacity, with abnormally low brain serotonin synthesis capacity in childhood, and somewhat elevated brain serotonin synthesis capacity in adulthood (Chugani et al., 1999). The precise mechanisms by which these neuroanatomical and neurophysiological anomalies might mediate the behavioral manifestations of autism are not well understood.

Individuals with ASD have abnormalities of information and social-emotional processing in the brain, as demonstrated by functional brain imaging. Relative to con-trols, individuals with ASD show decreased activation of the fusiform face area of the brain during tasks involving perception of faces (Schultz, 2005). Compared to controls, individuals with ASDs show significantly less amygdala activation and poorer perfor-mance on tasks that require them to judge facial emotions (Adolphs, Sears, & Piven, 2001; Baron-Cohen et al., 1999; Baron-Cohen, Wheelwright, Hill, Raste, & Plumb, 2001; Critchley et al., 2000).

ASDs are highly heritable. The large difference in concordance rates between monozygotic twins vs. dizygotic twins (92% concordance of monozygotic twins vs. 10% concordance of dizygotic twins for ASD) suggests a very high level of heritability (Bailey, Le Couteur, et al., 1995). Less than 10% of cases of ASD are associated with known genetic mutations or chromosomal abnormalities, including maternally inherited chromosome 15q11-q13 duplications, Fragile X syndrome (caused by a trinucleotide expansion in the *FMR1* gene), Rett syndrome (caused by loss-of-function mutations in the *MECP2* gene), Tuberous sclereosis complex (due to mutations of the *TSC1* or *TSC2* genes), or deletions and translocations that affect chromosome 13q13, chromosome Xp22, chromosome 7q22-q33, and other chromosomal regions (Veenstra-VanderWeele, Christian, & Cook, 2004).

Approximately 90% of cases of ASD are not associated with single gene mutations or single chromosomal locus anomalies. Rather, the common forms of ASD appear to be largely due to the effects of multiple, as yet unidentified, gene variants on brain devel-opment and behavior. Efforts to identify the susceptibility genes have been impeded by the genetic heterogeneity of ASD. For this reason, genome scans in ASDs have tended to reveal relatively weak linkages, and suggestive or significant loci identified in one study are often not replicated by subsequent studies. Despite these difficulties, a few areas of the genome have been identified in more than two or more linkage studies, including regions on chromosomes 2q, 3q, 7q, 13q, 16p, and 17q (Veenstra-VanderWeele et al., 2004). Candidate genes in these linkage regions are being tested for association with ASDs. In the chromosome 7q linkage region, for example, there is some evidence of association between *RELN* and *FOXP2* polymorphisms and ASDs (Perisco et al., 2001).

INDIVIDUAL FACTORS INFLUENCING RISK AND RESILIENCY

There are few individual factors that influence an individual's risk of having ASD. Most prominently, males are three to four times more likely than females to meet diagnostic criteria for ASD (Bryson & Smith, 1998; Fombonne, 2003; Yeargin-Allsopp et al., 2003). There is some preliminary evidence regarding factors associated with long term outcome, although longitudinal studies of individuals with ASD have found contradictory results, perhaps because of the heterogeneity of subjects and differences in outcomes measures (Howlin & Goode, 1998). With notable exceptions (Seltzer et al., 2003), most studies have found that most adults with ASD continue to require considerable supports, and most do not live independently (Howlin, Goode, Hutton, & Rutter, 2004). Systematic treatment and supports appear to improve functioning, even if symptoms are not ameliorated (Howlin, 1997). These and other studies discussed in the evidence-based treatment section of this chapter have found that children with higher intelligence quotients and greater communication skills show greater gains in behavioral treatment, with 15% of individuals diagnosed with autistic disorder achieving independence as adults, and another 20% able to function well in the presence of community-based support (Howlin, Goode, et al., 2004).

FAMILY FACTORS INFLUENCING RISK AND RESILIENCY

As discussed previously, the genetic component of ASD is not fully understood, although it is clear that ASD and related conditions are highly heritable. The probability of having a second child with autism is one in 10, compared with a community prevalence of one in 200 (Bolton et al., 1994; Constantino et al., 2006; Constantino & Todd, 2003). The risk of having a second child with some broader communication or cognitive deficit is even higher (Le Couteur, Bailey, et al., 1996). There is also evidence for the intergenerational transmission of symptoms, with parents of children with ASD more likely than other adults to exhibit subthreshold autistic behavior (Constantino & Todd, 2005).

With regard to this last point, there is a limited literature regarding schizotypal personality traits among mothers of children with ASD (Wolff, 1995; Wolff, Narayan, & Moyes, 1988). Larsson and colleagues (2005) found that 17% of children diagnosed with ASD in Denmark had mothers who had been diagnosed with schizophrenia. While this finding is provocative, it is difficult to determine whether this association is driven by conferred risk or by selection bias (Berkson, 1946).

SOCIAL AND COMMUNITY FACTORS INFLUENCING RISK AND RESILIENCY

Because the heritability of ASD is less than 100%, and because of the possibility of increased community prevalence of ASD, it is possible that particular biological environmental factors may contribute to the etiology or pathophysiology of ASD. A number of hypotheses are under investigation, the most prominent one being the association between vaccines and mercury and autism. Two possible pathways have been posited. The first mechanism posited is that the measles-mumps-rubella (MMR) vaccine results in gastrointestinal abnormalities that are, in turn, associated with developmental delays (Wakefield et al., 1998), perhaps through the opiod system (Wakefield et al., 2002). The original case series that sparked considerable controversy regarding this pathway (Wakefield et al., 1998) has since been retracted by 10 of the 12 original authors (Murch et al., 2004). The second posited mechanism is through thimerosal, the mercury-containing preservative that, until recently, was used in many vaccines. There are some theoretical reasons to assume a biomechanism of action between mercury and autism (Aschner & Walker, 2002; Bernard, Enayati, Redwood, Roger, & Binstock, 2001; Palomo, Beninger, Kostrzewa, & Archer, 2003) and at least one ecological study has shown such a link (Palmer, Blanchard, Stein, Mandell, & Miller, 2006). Large scale, carefully conducted epidemiological studies have found no association between vaccines and autism, however (Demicheli, Jefferson, Rivetti, & Price, 2005; DeStefano & Chen, 2000; Madsen et al., 2002), leading the Institute of Medicine (2004) to conclude that there is no association.

Perinatal insults are another commonly studied set of environmental factors associated with ASD. For example, prenatal exposure to valproic acid, thalidomide, rubella, and alcohol has been found to increase the risk for ASD (Arndt, Stodgell, & Rodier, 2005). Low birth weight, low Apgar scores, prematurity, breech presentation, and older maternal age have also been show to increase risk for ASD (Larsson et al., 2005).

EVIDENCE-BASED TREATMENT INTERVENTIONS FOR AUTISM SPECTRUM DISORDERS

Recent research in the field of autism has heavily emphasized the importance of early intervention (i.e., treatment before the age of 4 years). This emphasis may be attributed in part to results of treatment studies suggesting substantial gains may be achieved when treatment is provided at a very early age (Dawson & Osterling, 1997; Lord & McGee, 2001; Lovaas, 1987; McGee, Daly, & Jacobs, 1994; Rogers, 1998; Strain & Cordisco, 1994). Gains made by children with autism in early intervention programs may result in a cost savings of nearly $1 million over the course of their lifespan (Columbia Pacific Consulting, 1999; Jacobson, Mulick, & Green, 1998). Although early intervention is critical for optimizing outcome, intervention should not end after age 5. It is also important to note that if a child receives no intervention prior to age 5, behavioral and educational services can still result in positive outcomes.

What Works

A review of the literature did not uncover any intervention that met the criteria of three successful randomized clinical trials.

What Might Work

Although no treatment method completely ameliorates the symptoms of ASD and no specific treatment has emerged as the established standard of care for all children with ASD, several methods have been demonstrated to be efficacious with some children in research settings. Thus far, direct comparison of specific treatment methods has not been systematically conducted. Therefore, no one program can claim to be more effective than another, nor are we able to predict efficacy of individual treatment methods for specific children (Feinberg & Vacca, 2000; Lord, Wagner, et al., 2006). Researchers are beginning to compare methods directly; however, this has proved difficult due to differences in assessment procedures and populations served. Additionally, parents are hesitant to allow their child to be randomly assigned to a specific treatment method at such a critical stage in development.

The most well-researched programs are based on the principles of applied behavior analysis (Dunlap, 1999). Treatments based on behavioral principles represent a wide range of early intervention strategies for children with autism, from highly structured programs conducted in one-on-one settings to behaviorally based inclusion programs that include typically developing children. The first types of behavioral treatment programs developed and examined were highly structured, intensive, one-on-one programs called *discrete trial training,* which were highly effective for as many as half of children enrolled in one of the only randomized clinical trials for autism (Lovaas, 1987; McEachin, Smith, & Lovaas, 1993). Results have been positive but less dramatic in studies enrolling children with autism who may be lower functioning, or older than those in the original study (Anderson, Avery, Dipietro, Edwards, & Christian, 1987; Smith, 1999; Smith, Groen, & Wynn, 2000).

These intensive programs are very expensive and children often have difficulty generalizing the information they learn within highly structured programs to group and community settings. To remedy these limitations, researchers began using less structured, more naturalistic, behavioral programming in both individual and school settings. Examples of naturalistic behavior programs with some research evidence include *pivotal response training* (Koegel, Koegel, Harrower, & Carter, 1999; Schreibman & Koegel, 1996, 2005; Stahmer, 1995); *incidental teaching* (McGee, Krantz, & Mcclannahan, 1985; McGee, Morrier, & Daly, 1999) and *embedded learning opportunities* (Horn, Lieber, Li, Sandall, & Schwartz, 2000). Children may exhibit greater generalization of skills than those participating solely in discrete trials training, and these programs are more easily adapted for use in parent education and training programs (Baker-Ericzen, Stahmer, & Burns, 2007; Schreibman, Kaneko, & Koegel, 1991; Stahmer & Gist, 2001). Numerous single subject and nonrandomized group studies find that, approximately half of the children have good outcomes in these types of programs (Humphries, 2003; Schreibman & Koegel, 2005). Currently, even structured behavioral programs typically include naturalistic methods for increasing generalization and maintenance as part of the intervention. Recently, a combination of these behavioral methods has been shown to be more effective than usual care (in this case, community special education classrooms) in improving outcomes for children with autism (Howard, Sparkman, Cohen, Green, & Stanislaw, 2005).

Studies of inclusion models (educating children with autism alongside typically developing peers) using naturalistic behavioral techniques also report positive results. Prepost studies of inclusion programs find that as many as 50% of children are mainstreamed into regular education programs upon conclusion of the intervention (McGee, Daly, et al., 1994; McGee, Morrier, & Daly, 1999; Strain & Cordisco, 1994). Other behavioral techniques developed to target specific behaviors are also reporting promising results. For example, an augmentative communication system designed specifically for children with autism, the *picture exchange communication system* increases communication and initiation in many children (Bondy & Frost, 1994). *Positive behavioral support* techniques are now required in many school settings for addressing behavioral difficulties due to their proactive strategies and strong evidence base (Horner et al., 2005).

Parent education has been shown, in controlled studies, to be an important aspect of ASD intervention. Early behavioral intervention research found that generalization and maintenance of behavior changes were improved when parents were trained in highly structured behavioral methods (Koegel, Schreibman, Britten, Burke, & O'Neill, 1982; Lovaas, Koegel, Simmons, & Long, 1973). As behavioral programming for children with autism evolved from teaching single behaviors to a broader focus of increasing general motivation and responsivity (Koegel, O'Dell, & Koegel, 1987), parent education also began to change. Parents were taught more naturalistic strategies that were easier to use in the home, required fewer hours of training, increased both leisure and teaching time, and increased parent satisfaction and enjoyment of the treatment (Schreibman & Koegel, 1996). Parents are now considered important collaborators in all levels of programming, from assessment through goal development and treatment delivery (Albin, Lucyshyn, Horner, & Flannery, 1996).

A few techniques that are not behavioral in nature are beginning to demonstrate effectiveness as well; however, little controlled research has been conducted. Some of these are functional techniques that use structured environments, such as visual cueing and other strategies to assist children with autism in navigating their environments. These strategies are based on the assumption that intervention focusing on the visual strengths of children with ASD can increase attention and independence. An example of a comprehensive program utilizing these techniques is *treatment and education of autistic and related communication handicapped children* (TEACCH; see Mesibov, Shea, & Schopler, 2004). Case studies and dismantling designs support the treatment efficacy of these techniques (e.g., Ozonoff & Cathcart, 1998; Panerai, Ferrante, & Zingale, 2002; Schopler, Mesibov, & Baker, 1982).

Developmental/social pragmatic models, such as *developmental, individual-difference, relationship-based)/floortime* (DIR; Greenspan & Wieder, 1997, 1999), the *SCERTS model* (Prizant, Wetherby, Rubin, & Laurent, 2003), and the *Denver model* (Rogers & Dilalla, 1991; Rogers & Lewis, 1989) have shown some promising results in case review or quasi-experimental studies, and again, about half of the children respond positively. These models derive from research on typical development showing a relationship between social relationships and communicative development. Although the theory underlying these models differs greatly from learning theory, many techniques used in naturalistic behavioral interventions are common to developmental approaches. Systematic studies provide preliminary support for a developmental approach (Ingersoll, Dvortcsak, Whalen, & Sikora, 2005). A new developmental method called *relationship development intervention* (RDI) has recently been suggested as a promising technique, however research to date is very limited (Gutstein & Sheely, 2002).

In order to address the fact that multiple treatments appear to be effective, as well as the possibility that a combination of treatments may be most effective, researchers have delineated some elements common to different treatments by reviewing programs and techniques through published descriptions and intake and outcome data (Dawson & Osterling, 1997; Hurth, Shaw, Izeman, Whaley, & Rogers, 1999; Lord & McGee, 2001; Rogers, 1998). Because a majority of research has been conducted in younger children, Iovannone, Dunlap, Huber, & Kincaid (2003) examined those reviews and expanded them to include recommendations for school age children. Elements common to most comprehensive treatment methods include: (1) the earliest possible start to treatment; (2) high intensity of engagement; (3) use of a functional approach to behavior problems; (4) ongoing, systematic assessment, which leads to intervention choices; (5) strategies to promote generalization of learned skills; (6) use of developmentally appropriate practice; (7) structured environment with a predictable routine; (8) high levels of staff education and training; (9) active, sustained engagement of the child; (10) individualized treatment programs designed to meet a child's needs; (11) specific curriculum content with a focus on communication, social/play skills, cognitive, self-help and behavioral issues; (12) high parent involvement; and (13) planned transitions between kindergarten and first grade (Dawson & Osterling, 1997; Dunlap, 1999; Hurth et al., 1999; Iovannone et al., 2003; Lord & McGee, 2001; Rogers, 1996). Some researchers also report that inclusion with typically developing peers is important (Robbins, Giordano, Rhoads, & Feldman, 1996; Lord & McGee, 2001; Tsai, 1998) as well as a high adult-to-child ratio (Dawson & Osterling, 1997; Lord & McGee, 2001; Tsai, 1998). These structural elements of early intervention programs may be as important as specific intervention techniques in improving care for children with autism. However, research has not yet isolated the key ingredients for effective treatment.

Some researchers believe that combining efficacious treatments in a systematic way may be best practice (e.g., Rogers, 1996; Sheinkopf & Siegel, 1998), as the exclusive use of one treatment method may ignore important aspects of social, emotional, communicative, or preacademic development. Early studies indicate that combining methods, such as behavioral and developmental interventions, is a promising avenue to pursue (Rogers, Hall, Osaki, Reaven, & Herbison, 2000; Stahmer & Ingersoll, 2004); however, some researchers have argued that this eclectic approach may be detrimental to learning, confuse children, and reduce the fidelity with which any one treatment is administered (e.g., McGee et al., 1999). A recent study found one-on-one structured behavior therapy to be superior to an eclectic model that combined behavioral methods and other methods such as sensory integration, visual strategies, developmental strategies and general special education techniques (Howard et al., 2005). Community programs typically report using more than one method, therefore continued research on the efficacy of treatment combinations is imperative (Stahmer, Collings, & Palinkas, 2005).

Some methods widely used to treat children with autism have not been empirically tested and do not have evidence to support or refute their use. For example, early intervention providers unanimously reported using Sensory Integration Training (SIT) in their community programs (Stahmer et al., 2005), but research is not yet available to support its use. Sensory difficulties have been described as part of the course of autism;

however related symptoms vary greatly by child and are not necessarily specific to autism. Children with autism may exhibit over- or underresponsiveness to the environment; for example, not responding to their name being called, but clearly hearing the soft sound of a treat being opened (e.g., Kientz & Dunn, 1997; Le Couteur, Rutter, et al., 1989). Children with autism may also have unusual responses to sensory stimuli, such as fear of specific sounds, difficulty with particular textures, and unusual attention to specific types of visual stimuli. *Sensory integration therapy* (SIT), attempts to improve functioning by providing specific sensory experiences to the child (Ayres, 1972). Several different types of SIT have been developed and include activities, such as providing the child with deep pressure, brushing the child with a soft brush, playing with unusual textures, or engaging in specific types of movement. There have been few empirical studies of SIT. A review of the current literature concluded that there may be some effect of treatment for certain children in psychoeducational and motor areas compared with those in a no treatment condition, but there appeared to be no effect when SIT was compared with other alternative treatments (Baranek, 2002). In general, research is needed in this area to both clarify the nature of the theory behind the treatment and link specific changes in sensory functioning to behavioral changes.

Another possible avenue for treatment is through diet. Some studies provide limited evidence of a link between gastrointestinal symptoms and the behavioral symptoms of autism (e.g., Jyonouchi, Geng, Ruby, & Zimmerman-Bier, 2005). Specifically, children with autism may develop antibodies against casein and gluten (Vojdani, Pangborn, Vojdani, & Cooper, 2003). This has led to proliferation of the use of a *gluten-free casein-free diet* (GFCF) in the treatment of autism. Although this approach is widely used (Levy, Mandell, Merhar, Ittenbach, & Pinto-Martin, 2003), few controlled studies have tested its effectiveness. Preliminary studies indicate some improvement for some children when the diet is used (Knivsberg, Reichelt, Hoien, & Nodland, 2003; Knivsberg, Wiig, Lind, Nodland, & Reichelt, 1990); however, other studies have not found differences between diet and nondiet groups (Elder et al., 2006). Because children with autism exhibit heterogeneity in their symptoms, nutritional methods, such as a controlled diet, may only be effective for a subset of children. Clarifying which subset, and which symptoms, if any, are improved with diet is needed.

What Doesn't Work

There has been a proliferation of treatments that do not have an evidence base (Levy & Hyman, 2005; Schreibman, 2005). Perhaps due to the limited understanding of the disorder, the heterogeneity of the children, or the splinter skills often seen in this population, hope for a miracle treatment among parents and some professionals has been extremely high. Promoters of specific treatments often report dramatic results in a few children, but do not have scientific data to support their claims. Often extensive media coverage and the enthusiasm of families looking for a cure provide an avenue for dissemination of unproven methods.

While a few alternative methods have not yet been tested with children who have autism, some alternative methods have been examined and have been found to be ineffective. For example, *facilitated communication* (FC), an augmentative communication system involving the provision of physical support to children as they point to pictures or letters in order to communicate, was once thought to help children with autism. Proponents of this method reported that children who had previously been labeled severely mentally retarded or autistic were able to use this method to communicate not only daily needs but also higher level emotions and thoughts. Families, clinicians, and the popular media began to tout this new method as a miracle before any rigorous testing was conducted. Once the methodology was tested, it became clear that the facilitator was (albeit unknowingly) communicating for the child (e.g., Bligh & Kupperman, 1993; Mostert, 2001; Shane & Kearns, 1994). It rapidly became clear that facilitated communication did not help individuals with autism to communicate and may have caused unintentional harm.

Psychodynamic therapies are not effective in addressing the core deficits associated with autism. Psychotherapy has been used to treat both children with autism and their families, who were once thought to be the cause of the autistic symptoms. This often led to separation from family members and institutionalization of individuals with autism, which proved ineffective and often iatrogenic. As early as 1975 the National Institute of Mental Health (1975) reported that psychotherapy has not proven effective for this population.

Auditory integration training (AIT) purports to address the auditory processing problems found in children with autism. Headphones are used to present music filtered for certain frequencies over a short, intensive treatment period. The theory behind this strategy is that the altered music reduces hypersensitivity to specific frequencies and increases attention and social skills. AIT is one of the most highly researched of the alternative treatments. Well-controlled studies have not found any positive or lasting effects of treatment (Baranek, 2002).

There are also several methods in which no empirically sound studies have been conducted, but are considered unlikely to have a positive effect. For example, *Holding therapy* (Welch, 1988) is based on the theory that a child can be forced out of social withdrawal though social contact with a parent. It involves holding a child in an embrace until he becomes calm and engages in eye contact. There have been no empirically sound studies of this intervention, and it can be stressful for both parent and child (Schreibman, 2005). *Options therapy* (Kaufman, 1976) involves having the parent join the child by following the child's actions and imitating the child. It is highly intensive and there is no evidence to its effectiveness except anecdotal reports supplied by the developers of the program.

Clinicians and families are advised to proceed with caution when examining methods that promise a "cure" for all children on the autism spectrum. Each method must be examined with a specific child's symptoms in mind. Additionally, any possible harm which may come from an alternative treatment must be discussed along with any possible benefit.

OVERALL COMMENT ON AUTISM INTERVENTION

The heterogeneity and developmental nature of autism make it unlikely that one specific treatment will be best for all children, or will work for any one child throughout his or her educational career. Because a subset of children do not respond favorably to each of studied treatment methods, many researchers recognize the need for the individualization of treatment based on specific characteristics of the individual child and family (Anderson & Romanczyk, 1999; Bristol, McIlvane, & Alexander, 1998; Pelios & Lund, 2001; Prizant & Wetherby, 1998; Levy et al., 2003). The goal, then, is not to find the perfect treatment, but to identify the important variables that influence the effectiveness of specific interventions for each child (Gabriels, Hill, Pierce, Rogers, & Wehner, 2001; Kazdin, 1993; Schreibman, 2000). Research that furthers our understanding of how to match clients with efficacious treatments will enable consumers to make better choices between procedures (Prizant & Wetherby, 1998), decrease the outcome variability that characterizes early intervention research at present, and provide for the most efficient allocation of resources during the critical early intervention period (Ozonoff & Cathcart, 1998; Sherer & Schreibman, 2005). This type of research is in its infancy, but is imperative if we are to determine a priori which treatment method will be most effective for a specific child.

In summary, while positive results have been reported for many treatment methods, there are no autism treatments that currently meet criteria for well-established or probably efficacious, empirically supported treatment (Lonigan, Elbert, & Johnson, 1998; Rogers, 1998). Additionally, due to the heterogeneity of the disorder and the changing needs of children with autism as they develop, it is unlikely that one specific treatment will emerge as the treatment of choice for all children. Currently, researchers and clinicians must use their judgment and training to choose the most suitable methodology for a specific child. Critical elements have been defined which can assist in the development of treatment programs. Eventually, a prescriptive method of choosing treatment based on child and family characteristics may be developed.

PSYCHOPHARMACOLOGY AND AUTISM SPECTRUM DISORDERS

Despite the fact that medication is not considered a first line treatment, its use is quite common among children with ASD and is increasing. A 1995 survey found that 30% of children with ASD were using some psychotropic medication; follow-up studies six years later found 46% using some psychotropic medication in both this sample (Langworthy-Lam, Aman, & Van Bourgondien, 2002) and another sample (Aman, Lam, & Collier-Crespin, 2003). Neuroleptics were the most commonly used medication in two out of three studies (Aman, Lam, & Collier-Crespin, 2003; Aman, Van Bourgondien, Wolford, & Sarphare, 1995), with antidepressants the most common in the third (Langworthy-Lam, Aman, & Van Bourgondien, 2002). In 2003, 21% were using more than one drug, compared with 8% in 1995. A study of high-functioning adolescents and adults with autism found that 55% were currently taking a psychotropic medication, with 24% taking more than one (Martin, Scahill, Klin, & Volkmar, 1999).

To date, there are no medications that address the core deficits associated with ASD (Findling, 2005; Volkmar, 2001). Psychotropic medications may be helpful, however, in addressing related symptoms, such as hyperactivity, mood instability, depression, irritability, stereotypies, and aggression. Given the many behavioral domains in which children with ASD can experience impairment, it should not be surprising that a plethora of psychotropic agents have been tried as strategies to ameliorate symptoms. Few have been tested using randomized controlled trials. There are three notable exceptions. In a trial of 45 children and adolescents, the antidepressant fluoxetine was found to result in decreased stereotypies and repetitive behaviors (Hollander, Phillips, & Chaplin, 2005). Three randomized trials have found that the atypical antipsychotic, Risperidone, was effective in reducing irritability and aggression, as well as global clinical impressions. Side effects included increased appetite and weight gain. Secretin has also been tested using randomized trials, based on a case series reported in 1998 (Horvath, Stephantos, & Sokolski, 1998). Randomized trials found no effect of the medication, however (Chez, Buchanan, & Bagan, 2000; Roberts, Weaver, & Brian, 2001; Sandler, Sutton, & DeWeese, 1999).

There are many other reports of case studies, case series and open label trials of medications to address behavioral impairments in ASD. Several excellent reviews provide specific information on the results from these studies (Filipek et al., 2000; Findling, 2005; Volkmar, 2001; Volkmar, Cook, Pomeroy, Realmuto, & Tanguay, 1999). In general, stimulants have shown mixed results in reducing hyperactivity and tend to be associated with a number of side effects, including increased stereotypies and irritability. Clomipramine has similarly been found to have mixed results in improving behavioral symptoms and may cause seizures. Other selective serotonin reuptake inhibitors, while not as well studied as fluoxetine, have shown some positive effects, although some, especially mirtazapine, have been associated with considerable side effects. Mood stabilizers and anticonvulsants are generally well tolerated, but have shown mixed results in open label and retrospective studies. Similar studies of antipsychotics other than risperidone have shown generally positive results in reducing irritability and aggression, although weight gain was a common side effect.

THE PREVENTION OF AUTISM SPECTRUM DISORDERS

A review of the literature did not uncover any intervention that met the criteria of three successful trials. Until the etiology or etiologies of autism are better understood, prevention of the disorder is not likely. However, there are strategies that can help children with autism successfully reach their highest developmental potential.

As mentioned above, intensive early intervention results in improved outcomes for children with ASD (Dawson & Osterling, 1997; Filipek et al., 1999; Hurth et al., 1999; Lord & McGee, 2001; Rogers, 1996, 1998). Early identification of children at high risk for ASD or developmental delays is critical if a child is to benefit from early intervention and treatment.

Currently, even though symptom presentation before 36 months is mandatory according to the DSM-IV (APA, 2000), children with ASD are rarely diagnosed before the age of 36 months. In fact it is only in recent years that most children are identified in the preschool period (Baird et al., 2001; Charman & Baird, 2002; Filipek et al., 2000; Scambler, Rogers, & Wehner, 2001). Part of the improvements in diagnosis is due to improvements in the recognition of the early features of autism among primary healthcare providers and other professionals who interact with very young children, the development of appropriate screening tools, and the availability of early intervention services (Baird, Charman, Baron-Cohen, et al., 2000; Robins, Fein, Barton, & Green, 2001; Siegel, 1999).

Concerns regarding stability of diagnosis have been one barrier to using screening for early identification. Cox et al. (1999) prospectively assessed children at both 20 and 42 months of age. Their data indicate that the diagnosis of autism was sensitive and stable as young as 20 months of age, yet children are rarely diagnosed this young. Research has demonstrated that the use of standardized test instruments by experienced clinicians results in a relatively stable early diagnosis in children as young as 2 (Lord, 1995).

Parents of all socioeconomic groups with concerns about their child's development typically seek advice from a primary care physician (De Giacomo & Fombonne, 1998). Physicians, therefore, have great potential to identify and refer children with developmental concerns such as autism when they conduct routine well-child examinations. Parents of children with ASD, however, continue to express frustration with lack of pediatrician awareness and limited early identification of ASD (Mandell, Novak, & Zubritsky, 2005; Sperry, Whaley, Shaw, & Brame, 1999). In a study of parental concerns, the mean age at which parental developmental concerns arose was 18 months and parents first sought assistance from a medical professional when the child was age 2 (De Giamcomo & Fombonne, 1998). However, many parents were told not to worry, or a referral for a more comprehensive evaluation was delayed until up to 40 months of age. Educating physicians regarding appropriate screening methods and appropriate early intervention referrals may be the best way to ensure the best possible outcomes for children with ASD.

What Might Work

A review of the literature did not uncover any promising preventive intervention for autism spectrum disorders. However, the intervention strategies described above currently hold the most promise for improving functioning for individuals with autism. For example, early studies of individuals with autism reported that approximately 50% of people with autism gain functional communication (c.f. Schreibman, 2005). More recent studies have reported that upwards of 80% of children with autism are using functional language by age 5 (e.g., Lovaas, 1987; McGee et al., 1994; Strain & Cordisco, 1994). The best prevention for autism at this point is early, intensive, quality intervention.

What Doesn't Work

The only preventive strategy that has been proposed for autism spectrum disorders is the withholding of vaccines. To date, there is no evidence from any type of study (case study, case control, cohort, or randomized controlled trial) suggesting the effectiveness of this strategy.

RECOMMENDED BEST PRACTICE

While there are promising interventions for children with autism that show efficacy in research settings, there is a paucity of evidence regarding the effectiveness of different treatment modalities. Perhaps because of the lack of a clear intervention protocol, a myriad of complementary and alternative treatments have proliferated, some with potentially harmful effects. Families and practitioners may have conflicting views regarding the best treatment strategy, and even the most efficacious treatments may result in improvements for only half of children with ASD. Below we present a brief outline of strategies in line with our current understanding of best practice. We urge practitioners to consult treatment guidelines and consensus statements developed by experts in the field (Filipek, Steinberg-Epstein, & Book, 2006; Lord & McGee, 2001; Volkmar, Cook, et al., 1999).

Treatment

Assessment, treatment choices, measuring progress, and negotiating treatment modalities with parents are all very important.

Assessment

A careful assessment using standardized instruments is critical for treatment planning. Frequently co-occurring conditions, such as seizure disorders, hearing impairment, and anxiety (among higher-functioning children) should be assessed. Depending on the chronological and developmental age of the child, practitioners should consider using the Autism Diagnostic Observation scale (Lord et al., 2000) and the Autism Diagnostic Interview (Rutter, LeCouteur, & Lord, 2003), which are considered the gold standard diagnostic tools. Measures of IQ and adaptive functioning are also necessary for good treatment planning.

Treatment Choices

The intervention modalities found most efficacious in research settings appear to show large effects with only a subset of children with autism. Still, interventions in the applied behavior analysis family have shown the best results in research settings. These interventions, including discrete trial training, pivotal response training, incidental teaching, and embedded learning opportunities, vary primarily as a function of the amount of structured activities versus more naturalistic teaching strategies. Other intervention strategies, based primarily on a more developmental or social pragmatic model, are also popular, although evidence regarding their efficacy is more limited. Developmental, Individual-Difference, Relationship-Based Treatment is the most popular of these strategies; others include the SCERTS Model, the Denver Model, and Relationship Development Intervention. It is interesting to note that while the theory driving these interventions is markedly different from that underlying ABA-based intervention, many of the techniques look similar in practice. A growing number of clinicians and researchers advocate for some mix of these developmental and behavioral approaches, but there is little rigorous evidence regarding this eclectic approach (Howard et al., 2005; Stahmer, 2006).

Measuring Progress

Given the lack of evidence regarding treatment effectiveness in autism, careful measurement of progress at regular intervals is critical. A number of challenges to measuring change in children with autism have been noted, with most researchers finding little sensitivity to change among diagnostic instruments and more sensitivity to change using measures of adaptive skills (Charman, Howlin, Berry, & Prince, 2004; Matson, 2006; Wolery & Garfinkle, 2002). Clinicians therefore might consider using the Vineland Adaptive Behavior scales, the Social Responsiveness scale (SRS) (Constantino, 2005), the Childhood Autism Rating scale (CARS) (Schopler, Reichler, DeVellis, & Daly, 1980), or the Child Behavior Checklist for Ages 6–18 (CBCL/6-18) (Achenbach, 1991; Achenbach & Rescorla, 2001) at regular intervals to measure the effects of treatment. In addition, clinicians should consider identifying caregiver-nominated symptoms at treatment initiation. Careful measurement of and change in these symptoms may improve adherence and engagement in treatment.

Negotiating Treatment

Caregivers' beliefs regarding autism may profoundly affect what treatment modalities are acceptable to families. Clinicians should ask families about their beliefs and their use of specific treatments prior to treatment planning. Levy, Mandell, et al. (2003) suggest beginning with a series of questions adapted from (Kleinman, 1980):

- What do/did you call your child's problem before it was diagnosed?
- What do you think caused it?
- Why do you think it started when it did?
- What do you think autism does? How does it work?
- How severe is it? Will it have a short or long course?
- What are the chief problems your child's autism has caused?
- What do you fear most about it?
- What kind of treatment do you think your child should receive? What do you expect from this treatment?

A second set of questions, developed by (Pachter, Cloutier, & Bernstein, 1995), is designed specifically to help clinicians discern the use of CAM and negotiate related treatment decisions. The authors suggest initiating the following dialogue:

Some of my patients have told me that there are ways of treating autism that are known in the community that physicians don't know about or use. Have you heard of any of these treatments?

If a parent responds in the affirmative, the clinician should then ask, "Are you using or have you ever used this treatment with your child?" If the answer is yes, and the clinician determines that the treatment is not toxic, the clinician might respond with, "I am not sure if this treatment is effective for treating autism, but I know that if used/taken as directed, it will not be harmful. If you believe it is effective, you can continue to use it. But I think that your child will show greater improvement if you use the treatments I have prescribed in addition to this other treatment."

Pachter and colleagues also present methods for discussing potentially harmful treatments with parents. They point out that any harmful practice must be discouraged, but can be replaced with acceptable substitutes. For example, clinicians can negotiate lower concentrations of substances like some vitamins that may be toxic at high doses. Other potentially harmful practices such as withholding vaccines can be switched with more acceptable replacements, such as changing the timing and spacing of vaccines.

It is important to remember that the goal of many of these treatments is most likely not to treat autism per se, but rather to address some of the associated problems faced by children with autism. For example, melatonin is given to treat the sleep disturbances that affect many children with autism. Likewise, gastrointestinal medicines are given to many children with autism who experience gastrointestinal distress, although many parents use these drugs because they believe them to affect autism-specific symptoms. If parents feel that clinicians do not respect their beliefs and decisions, or are unwilling to negotiate around the use of addition treatment strategies, these strategies may become alternative rather than complementary.

Pharmacology

It is important to remember that the purpose of medications in autism is to address ancillary behaviors, rather than the core symptoms of autism per se. Volkmar (2001) recommends extreme caution in the use of psychotropic medications with children under 5 years. For older children, atypical antipsychotics have been found to be useful in decreasing aggressive and self-injurious behaviors, as well as irritability. Findings regarding stimulants and antidepressants in this population have been decidedly mixed. Anticonvulsants and mood stabilizers may show greater benefit for certain subgroups. Anecdotal evidence suggests that children with autism may be particularly sensitive to medications, so small doses may be warranted to start, titrating up as necessary. Monitor carefully for side effects with all medications.

Prevention

To date there are no effective preventive interventions for autism spectrum disorders. Early intervention is critical, however. As previously discussed, early intensive interventions can result in profound improvements in functioning for children with autism. Regular developmental screening, with autism-specific screening if warranted, should be combined with immediate referral to early intervention services for children not meeting developmental milestones.

REFERENCES

Achenbach, T. M. (1991). *Manual for the Child Behavior Checklist/4-18 and 1991 Profile*. Burlington, VT: University of Vermont, Department of Psychiatry.

Achenbach, T. M., & Rescorla, L. A. (2001). *Manual for the ASEBA school-age forms and profiles*. Burlington, VT: University of Vermont, Research Center for Children, Youth, & Families.

Adolphs, R., Sears, L., & Piven, J. (2001). Abnormal processing of social information from faces in autism. *Journal of Cognitive Neuroscience, 13*, 232–240.

Albin, R. W., Lucyshyn, J. M., Horner, R. H., & Flannery, K. B. (1996). Contextual fit for behavioral support plan: A model for "goodness of fit." In L. K. Koegel, R. L. Koegel, & G. Dunlap (Eds.), *Positive behavioral support: Including people with difficult behavior in the community* (pp. 81–98). Baltimore, MD: Paul II. Brookes.

Aman, M., Lam, K., & Collier-Crespin, A. (2003). Prevalence and patterns of use of psychoactive medicines among individuals with autism in the Autism Society of America. *Journal of Autism and Developmental Disorders, 33*(5), 527–533.

Aman, M., Van Bourgondien, M., Wolford, P., & Sarphare, G. (1995). Psychotropic and anticonvulsant drugs in subjects with autism: Prevalence and patterns of use. *Journal of the American Academy of Child & Adolescent Psychiatry, 34*(12), 1672–1681.

American Psychiatric Association. (2000). *Diagnostic and statistical manual of mental disorders* (4th ed., TR). Washington, D.C.: Author.

Anderson, S. R., Avery, O. L., Dipietro, E. K., Edwards, G. L., & Christian, W. P. (1987). Intensive home-based early intervention with autistic children. *Education and Treatment of Children, 10*, 352–366.

Anderson, S. R., & Romanczyk, R. G. (1999). Early intervention for young children with autism: Continuum-based behavioral models. *Journal of the Association for Persons with Severe Handicaps, 24*(3), 162–173.

Arin, D. M., Bauman, M. L., & Kemper, T. L. (1991). The distribution of Purkinje cell loss in the cerebellum in autism. *Neurology, 41* (Suppl. 1), 307.

Arndt, T., Stodgell, C., & Rodier, P. (2005). The teratology of autism. *International Journal of Developmental Neuroscience, 23*(2–3), 189–199.

Aschner, M., & Walker, S. (2002). The neuropathogenesis of mercury toxicity. *Molecular Psychiatry, 7*(Suppl. 2), S40–S41.

Ayres, a. J. (1972). Improving academic scores through sensory integration. *Journal of Learning Disabilities, 5*(6), 338–343.

Bailey, A., Le Couteur, A., Gottesman, I., Bolton, P., Simonoff, E., Yuzda, E., et al. (1995). Autism as a strongly genetic disorder: Evidence from a British twin study. *Psychological Medicine, 25*, 63–77.

Bailey, A., Luther, T., Dean, A., Harding, B., Janota, I., Montgomery, M., et al. (1998). A clinicopathological study of autism. *Brain, 121*, 889–905.

Baird, G., Charman, T., Baron-Cohen, S., Cox, A., Swettenham, J., Wheelwright, S., et al. (2000). A screening instrument for autism at 18 months of age: A six-year follow-up study. *Journal of the American Academy of Child and Adolescent Psychiatry, 39*, 694–702.

Baird, G., Charman, T., Cox, A., Baron-Cohen, S., Swettenham, J., Wheelwright, S., et al. (2001). Screening and surveillance for autism and pervasive developmental disorders. *Archives of Diseases in Childhood, 84*, 468–475.

Baker-Ericzen, M., Stahmer, A. C., & Burns, A. (2007). Association of child demographics with child outcomes in a community-based pivotal response training program. *Journal of Positive Behavior Interventions, 9*(1), 52-60.

Baranek, G. T. (2002). Efficacy of sensory and motor interventions for children with autism. *Journal of Autism & Developmental Disorders, 32*(5), 397–422.

Baron-Cohen, S., Ring, H. A., Wheelwright, S., Bullmore, E. T., Brammer, M. J., Simmons, A., et al. (1999). Social intelligence in the normal and autistic brain: An fMRI study. *European Journal of Neuroscience, 11*, 1891–1898.

Baron-Cohen, S., Wheelwright, S., Hill, J., Raste, Y., & Plumb, I. (2001). The "reading the mind in the eyes" test revised version: A study with normal adults, and adults with Asperger syndrome or high-functioning autism. *Journal of Child Psychology and Psychiatry, 42*, 241–251.

Bauman, M. L., & Kemper, T. L. (1994). Neuroanatomic observations of the brain in autism. In M. L. Bauman & T. L. Kemper (Eds.), *The neurobiology of autism* (pp. 119–145). Baltimore: Johns Hopkins University Press.

Bauman, M. L., & Kemper, T. L. (2005). Neuroanatomic observations of the brain in autism: a review and future directions. *International Journal of Developmental Neuroscience, 23*, 183–187.

Berkson, J. (1946). Limitation of the application of fourfold table analysis to hospital data. *Biomedical Bulletin, 2*, 47–53.

Bernard, S., Enayati, A., Redwood, L., Roger, H., & Binstock, T. (2001). Autism: A novel form of mercury poisoning. *Medical Hypotheses, 56*, 462–471.

Bligh, S., & Kupperman, P. (1993). Facilitated communication evaluation procedure accepted in a court case. *Journal of Autism and Developmental Disorders, 23*(3), 553–557.

Bolton, P., Macdonald, H., Pickles, A., Rios, P., Goode, S., Crowson, M., et al. (1994). A case-control family history study of autism. *Journal of Child Psychology & Psychiatry & Allied Disciplines, 35*(5), 877–900.

Bondy, A. S., & Frost, L. A. (1994). The picture exchange communication system. *Focus on Autistic Behavior, 9*(3), 1–19.

Bristol, M., McIlvane, W. J., & Alexander, D. (1998). Autism research: Current context and future direction. *Mental Retardation and Developmental Disabilities Research Reviews.* [Special Issue]. *Autism, 4*(2), 61–64.

Bryson, S., & Smith, I. (1998). Epidemiology of autism: Prevalence, associated characteristics, and implications for research and service delivery. *Mental Retardation and Developmental Disabilities Research Reviews, 4,* 97–103.

Byrd, R. (2003). *Autistic spectrum disorders. Changes in the California caseload. An update: 1999–2002.* Sacramento, CA: California Health and Human Services Agency.

Casanova, M. F., Buxhoeveden, D. P., Switala, A. E., & Roy, E. (2002). Minicolumnar pathology in autism. *Neurology, 58,* 428–432.

Charman, T., & Baird, G. (2002). Practitioner review: Diagnosis of autism spectrum disorder in 2- and 3-year-old children. *Journal of Child Psychology & Psychiatry, 43*(3), 289–305.

Charman, T., Howlin, P., Berry, B., & Prince, E. (2004). Measuring the developmental progress of children with autism spectrum disorder on school entry using parent report. *Autism, 8*(1), 89–100.

Chez, M., Buchanan, C., & Bagan, B. (2000). Secretin and autism: A two-part clinical investigation. *Journal of Autism & Developmental Disorders, 30,* 87–94.

Chugani, D. C., Muzik, O., Behen, M., Rothermel, R., Janisse, J. J., Lee, J., et al. (1999). Developmental changes in brain serotonin synthesis capacity in autistic and nonautistic children. *Annals of Neurology, 45,* 287–295.

Columbia Pacific Consulting (1999). *Preliminary report: Cost-benefit analysis of Lovaas treatment for autism and autism spectrum disorder (ASD).* Vancouver, BC: Columbia Pacific.

Constantino, J. (2005). *The social responsiveness scale.* Los Angeles: Western Psychological Services.

Constantino, J., Lajonchere, C., Lutz, M., Gray, T., Abbacchi, A., McKenna, K., et al. (2006). Autistic social impairment in the siblings of children with pervasive developmental disorders. *American Journal of Psychiatry, 163*(2), 294–296.

Constantino, J., & Todd, R. (2003). Autistic traits in the general population, a twin study. *Archives of General Psychiatry, 60,* 524–530.

Constantino, J., & Todd, R. (2005). Intergenerational transmission of subthreshold autistic traits in the general population. *Biological Psychiatry, 57*(6), 655–660.

Cook, E., & Leventhal, B. (1996). The serotonin system in autism. *Current Opinion in Pediatrics, 8,* 348–354.

Courchesne, E., Carper, R., & Akshoomoff, N. (2003). Evidence of brain overgrowth in the first year of life in autism. *Journal of the American Medical Association, 290,* 337–344.

Courchesne, E., Redcay, E., Morgan, J. T., & Kennedy, D. P. (2005). Autism at the beginning: Microstructural and growth abnormalities underlying the cognitive and behavioral phenotype of autism. *Development and Psychopathology, 17,* 577–597.

Cox, A., Klein, K., Charman, T., Baird, G., Baron-Cohen, S., Swettenham, J., et al. (1999). Autism spectrum disorders at 20 and 42 months of age: stability of clinical and ADI-R diagnosis. *Journal of Child Psychology and Psychiatry and Allied Disciplines, 40*(5), 719–732.

Critchley, H., Daly, E., Phillips, M., Brammer, M., Bullmore, E., Williams, S., et al. (2000). Explicit and implicit neural mechanisms for processing of social information from facial expressions: A functional magnetic resonance imaging study. *Human Brain Mapping, 9*(2), 93–105.

Croen, L., Grether, J., Hoogstrate, J., & Selvin, S. (2002). The changing prevalence of autism in California. *Journal of Autism and Developmental Disorders, 32*(3), 207–215.

Dawson, G., & Osterling, J. (1997). Early intervention in autism: Effectiveness and common elements of current approaches. In M. J. Guralnick (Ed.), *The effectiveness of early intervention: Second generation research* (pp. 307–326). Baltimore: Paul H. Brookes.

De Giacomo, A., & Fombonne, E. (1998). Parental recognition of developmental abnormalities in autism. *European Child & Adolescent Psychiatry, 7*(3), 131–136.

Dementieva, Y. A., Vance, D. D., Donnelly, S. L., Elston, L. A., Wolpert, C. M., Ravan, S. A., et al. (2005). Accelerated head growth in early development of individuals with autism. *Pediatric Neurology, 32,* 102–108.

Demicheli, V., Jefferson, T., Rivetti, A., & Price, D. (2005). Vaccines for measles, mumps and rubella in children. *Cochrane Database of Systematic Reviews,* (4), CD004407.

DeStefano, F., & Chen, R. (2000). Autism and measles, mumps, and rubella vaccine: No epidemiological evidence for a causal association. *Journal of Pediatrics, 136*(1), 125–126.

Dunlap, G. (1999). Consensus, engagement, and family involvement for young children with autism. *Journal of the Association for Persons with Severe Handicaps, 24,* 222–225.

Eggas, B., Courchesne, E., & Saitoh, O. (1995). Reduced size of corpus callosum in autism. *Archives of Neurology, 52,* 794–801.

Elder, J. H., Shankar, M., Shuster, J., Theriaque, D., Burns, S., & Sherrill, L. (2006). The gluten-free, casein-free diet in autism: Results of a preliminary double blind clinical trial. *Journal of Autism and Developmental Disorders.* 36(3), 413-20.

Feinberg, E., & Vacca, J. (2000). The drama and trauma of creating policies on autism: Critical issues to consider in the new millennium. *Focus on Autism and Other Developmental Disabilities, 15*(3), 130–137.

Filipek, P., Accardo, P., Ashwal, S., Baranek, G., Cook, E., Dawson, G., et al. (2000). Practice parameter: Screening and diagnosis of autism. *Neurology, 55*, 468–479.

Filipek, P., Accardo, P., Baranek, G., Cook, E., Dawson, G., Gordon, B., et al. (1999). The screening and diagnosis of autistic spectrum disorders. *Journal of Autism and Developmental Disorders, 29*(6), 439–484.

Filipek, P., Steinberg-Epstein, R., & Book, M. (2006). Intervention for autistic spectrum disorders. *The Journal of the American Society of Experimental NeuroTherapeutics, 3*, 207–216.

Findling, R. (2005). Pharmacologic treatment of behavior symptoms in autism and pervasive developmental disorders. *Journal of Clinical Psychiatry, 66*(Suppl. 10), 26–31.

Fombonne, E. (2001). Is there an epidemic of autism. *Pediatrics, 107*(2), 411–413.

Fombonne, E. (2003). Epidemiological surveys of autism and other pervasive developmental disorders: An update. *Journal of Autism and Developmental Disorders, 33*(4), 365–382.

Fombonne, E. (2005). Epidemiology of autistic disorder and other pervasive developmental disorders. *Journal of Clinical Psychiatry, 66*(Suppl. 10), 3–8.

Gabriels, R. L., Hill, D. E., Pierce, R. A., Rogers, S. J., & Wehner, B. (2001). Predictors of treatment outcome in young children with autism [Special issue]. *Autism: Early Interventions, 5*(4), 407–429.

Gillberg, C., & Billstedt, E. (2000). Autism and Asperger syndrome: Coexistence with other clinical disorders. *Acta Psychiatrica Scandinavica, 102*(5), 321–333.

Greenspan, S. I., & Wieder, S. (1997). Developmental patterns and outcomes in infants and children with disorders in relating and communicating: A chart review of 200 cases of children with autistic spectrum diagnoses. *Journal of Developmental and Learning Disorders, 1*, 87–141.

Greenspan, S. I., & Wieder, S. (1999). A functional developmental approach to autism spectrum disorders. *Journal of the Association for Persons with Severe Handicaps, 24*(3), 147–161.

Gutstein, S. E., & Sheely, R. K. (2002). *Relationship development intervention with young children: Social and emotional development activities for Asperger syndrome, autism, and PDD-NOS.* Philadelphia: Jessica Kingsley.

Happe, F., & Frith, U. (2006). The weak coherence account: Detail-focused cognitive style in autism spectrum disorders. *Journal of Autism and Developmental Disorders, 36*, 5–25.

Hardan, A. Y., Minshew, N. J., & Keshavan, M. S. (2000). Corpus callosum size in autism. *Neurology, 55*, 1033–1036.

Hardan, A. Y., Minshew, N. J., Mallikarjuhn, M., & Keshevan, M. S. (2001). Brain volume in autism. *Journal of Child Neurology, 16*, 421–424.

Hazlett, H. C., Poe, M., Gerig, G., Smith, R. G., Provenzale, J., Ross, A., et al. (2005). Magnetic resonance imaging and head circumference study of brain size in autism: Birth through age 2 years. *Archives of General Psychiatry, 62*, 1366–1376.

Herbert, M. R. (2005). Large brains in autism: The challenge of pervasive abnormality. *The Neuroscientist, 11*, 417–440.

Herbert, M. R., Ziegler, D. A., Deutsch, C. K., O'Brien, L. M., Lange, N., Bakardjiev, A., et al. (2003). Dissociations of cerebral cortex, subcortical and cerebral white matter volumes in autistic boys. *Brain, 126*, 1182–1192.

Herbert, M. R., Ziegler, D. A., Makris, N., Filipek, P. A., Kemper, T. L., Normandin, J. J., et al. (2004). Localization of white matter volume increase in autism and developmental language disorder. *Annals of Neurology, 55*, 530–540.

Hollander, E., Phillips, A., & Chaplin, W. (2005). A placebo controlled crossover trial of liquid fluoxetine on repetitive behaviors in childhood and adolescent autism. *Neuropsychopharmacology, 30*, 582–589.

Horn, E., Lieber, J., Li, S., Sandall, S., & Schwartz, I. (2000). Supporting young children's IEP goals in inclusive settings through embedded learning opportunities. *Topics in Early Childhood Special Education, 20*(4), 208–223.

Horner, R. H., Dunlap, G., Koegel, R. L., Carr, E. G., Sailor, W., Anderson, J., et al. (2005). Toward a technology of "nonaversive" behavioral support. *Research and Practice for Persons with Severe Disabilities, 30*(1), 3–10.

Horvath, K., Stephantos, G., & Sokolski, K. (1998). Improved social and language skills after secretin administration in patients with autistic spectrum disorders. *Journal of the Association of Academic Minority Physicians, 9*, 9–15.

Howard, J., Sparkman, C., Cohen, H., Green, G., & Stanislaw, H. (2005). A comparison of intensive behavior analytic and eclectic treatments for young children with autism *Research in Developmental Disabilities, 26*(4), 359–383.

Howlin, P. (1997). Prognosis in autism: Do specialist treatments affect long-term outcome? *European Child & Adolescent Psychiatry, 6*(2), 55–72.

Howlin, P., & Goode, S. (1998). Outcome in adult life for individuals with autism. In F. Volkmar (Ed.), *Autism and developmental disorders.* 201-222, New York: Cambridge University Press.

Howlin, P., Goode, S., Hutton, J., & Rutter, M. (2004). Adult outcome for children with autism. *Journal of Child Psychology and Psychiatry, 45*(2), 212–237.

Humphries, T. L. (2003). Effectiveness of pivotal response training as a behavioal intervention for young children with autism spectrum disorders. *Bridges: Practice-Based Research Syntheses, 2*(4), 1–9.

Hurth, J., Shaw, E., Izeman, S. G., Whaley, K., & Rogers, S. J. (1999). Areas of agreement about effective practices among programs serving young children with autism spectrum disorders. *Infants and Young Children, 12*, 17–26.

Ingersoll, B., Dvortcsak, A., Whalen, C., & Sikora, D. (2005). The effects of a developmental, social-pragmatic language intervention on rate of expressive language production in young children with autistic spectrum disorders. *Focus on Autism and Other Developmental Disabilities, 20*(4), 213–222.

Institute of Medicine. (2004). *Vaccines and autism.* Washington, D.C.: National Academies Press.

Iovannone, R., Dunlap, G., Huber, H., & Kincaid, D. (2003). Effective educational practices for students with autism spectrum disorders. *Focus on Autism & Other Developmental Disabilities, 18*, 150–165.

Jacobson, J. W., Mulick, J. A., & Green, G. (1998). Cost-benefit estimates for early intensive behavioral intervention for young children with autism—General model and single state case. *Behavioral Interventions, 13*(4), 201–226.

Just, M. A., Cherkassky, V. L., Keller, T. A., & Minshew, N. J. (2004). Cortical activation and synchronization during sentence comprehension in high-functioning autism: Evidence of underconnectivity. *Brain, 127*, 1811–1821.

Jyonouchi, H., Geng, L., Ruby, A., & Zimmerman-Bier, B. (2005). Dysregulated innate immune responses in young children with autism spectrum disorders: Their relationship to gastrointestinal symptoms and dietary intervention. *Neuropsychobiology, 51*(2), 77–85.

Kanner, L. (1943). Autistic disturbances of affective contact. *Nervous Child, 2*, 217–250.

Kaufman, B. N. (1976). *Son-rise.* New York: Harper & Row.

Kazdin, A. E. (1993). Evaluation in clinical practice: Clinically sensitive and systematic methods of treatment delivery. *Behavior Therapy, 24*(1), 11–45.

Kientz, M. A., & Dunn, W. (1997). A comparison of the performance of children with and without autism on the sensory profile. *American Journal of Occupational Therapy, 51*(7), 530–537.

Kleinman, A. (1980). *Patients and healers in the context of culture.* Berkeley: University of California Press.

Knivsberg, A.-M., Reichelt, K.-L., Hoien, T., & Nodland, M. (2003). Effect of a dietary intervention on autistic behavior. *Focus on Autism and Other Developmental Disabilities, 18*(4), 247–256.

Knivsberg, A. M., Wiig, K., Lind, G., Nodland, M., & Reichelt, K. L. (1990). Dietary intervention in autistic syndromes. *Brain Dysfunction, 3*(5–6), 315–327.

Koegel, L. K., Koegel, R. L., Harrower, J. K., & Carter, C. M. (1999). Pivotal response intervention I: Overview of approach. *Journal of the Association for Persons with Severe Handicaps, 24*(3), 174–185.

Koegel, R. L., Schreibman, L., Britten, K., Burke, J. C., & O'Neill, R. E. (1982). A comparison of parent training with direct child treatment. In R. L. Koegel, A. Rincover, & A. L. Egel (Eds.), *Educating and understanding autistic children* (pp. 260–279). San Diego, CA: College-Hill Press.

Koegel, R. L., O'Dell, M. C., & Koegel, L. K. (1987). A natural language teaching paradigm for nonverbal autistic children. *Journal of Autism & Developmental Disorders, 17*(2), 187–200.

Lainhart, J. E., Piven, J., Wzorek, M., Landa, R., Santangelo, S. L., Coon, H., et al. (1997). Macrocephaly in children and adults with autism. *Journal of the American Academy of Child and Adolescent Psychiatry, 36*, 282–290.

Langworthy-Lam, K., Aman, M., & Van Bourgondien, M. (2002). Prevalence and patterns of use of psychoactive medicines in individuals with autism in the Autism Society of North Carolina. *Journal of Child & Adolescent Psychopharmacology, 2*(4), 311–321.

Larsson, H., Eaton, W., Madsen, K., Vestergaard, M., Olesen, A., Agerbo, E., et al. (2005). Risk factors for autism: Perinatal factors, parental psychiatric history, and socioeconomic status. *American Journal of Epidemiology, 161*(10), 916–925.

Le Couteur, A., Bailey, A., Goode, S., Pickles, A., Robertson, S., Gottesman, I., et al. (1996). A broader phenotype of autism: the clinical spectrum in twins. *Journal of Child Psychology & Psychiatry & Allied Disciplines, 37*(7), 785–801.

Le Couteur, A., Rutter, M., Lord, C., Rios, P., Robertson S., Holdgrafer M., & McLennan, J. (1989). Autism diagnostic interview: A standardized investigator-based instrument. *Journal of Autism and Developmental Disorders, 19*(3), 363–387.

Levy, S. E., & Hyman, S. L. (2005). Novel treatments for autistic spectrum disorders. *Mental Retardation and Developmental Disabilities Research Reviews, 11*(2), 131–142.

Levy, S. E., Mandell, D. S., Merhar, S., Ittenbach, R. F., & Pinto-Martin, J. A. (2003). Use of complementary and alternative medicine among children recently diagnosed with autistic spectrum disorder. *Journal of Developmental and Behavioral Pediatrics, 24*(6), 418–423.

Lonigan, C. J., Elbert, J. C., & Johnson, S. B. (1998). Empirically supported psychosocial interventions for children: An overview [Special issue]. *Journal of Clinical Child Psychology, 27*(2), 138–145.

Lord, C. (1995). Follow-up of two-year-olds referred for possible autism. *Journal of Child Psychology and Psychiatry, 36*(8), 1365–1382.

Lord, C., & McGee, J. (Eds.). (2001). *Educating children with autism.* Washington, D.C.: National Academy Press.

Lord, C., Risi, S., Lambrecht, L., Cook, E. J., Leventhal, B., DiLavore, P., et al. (2000). The autism diagnostic observation schedule-generic: A standard measure of social and communication deficits associated with the spectrum of autism. *Journal of Autism & Developmental Disorders, 30*(3), 205–223.

Lord, C., Rutter, M., Goode, S., Heemsbergen, J., Jordan, H., Mawhood, L., et al. (1989). Autism diagnostic observation schedule: A standardized observation of communicative and social behavior. *Journal of Autism & Developmental Disorders, 19*(2), 185–212.

Lord, C., Wagner, A., Rogers, S., Szatmari, P., Aman, M., Charman, T., et al. (2006). Challenges in evaluating psychosocial interventions for autistic spectrum disorders. *Journal of Autism and Developmental Disorders.* 35(6), 695-708.

Lovaas, O. I. (1987). Behavioral treatment and normal educational and intellectual functioning in young autistic children. *Journal of Consulting & Clinical Psychology, 55*, 3–9.

Lovaas, O. I., Koegel, R., Simmons, J. Q., & Long, J. S. (1973). Some generalization and follow-up measures on autistic children in behavior therapy. *Journal of Applied Behavior Analysis, 6*, 131–166

Madsen, K., Hviid, A., Vestergaard, M., Schendel, D., Wohlfahrt, J., Thorsen, P., et al. (2002). A population-based study of measles, mumps, and rubella vaccination and autism. *New England Journal of Medicine, 34*, 1477–1482.

Mandell, D., Novak, M., & Zubritsky, C. (2005). Factors associated with the age of diagnosis among children with autism spectrum disorders. *Pediatrics, 116*(6), 1480–1486.

Mandell, D., Thompson, W., Weintraub, E., DeStephano, F., & Blank, M. (2005). Trends in diagnosis rates for autism and ADHD at hospital discharge in the context of other psychiatric diagnoses. *Psychiatric Services, 51*(1), 56–62.

Martin, A., Scahill, L., Klin, A., & Volkmar, F. (1999). Higher functioning pervasive developmental disorders: Rates and patterns of psychotropic drug use. *Journal of the American Academy of Child & Adolescent Psychiatry, 38*(7), 923–931.

Matson, J. (2006). Determining treatment outcome in early intervention programs for autism spectrum disorders: A critical analysis of measurement issues in learning based interventions. *Research in Developmental Disabilities*

McEachin, J. J., Smith, T., & Lovaas, O. I. (1993). Long-term outcome for children with autism who received early intensive behavioral treatment. *American Journal of Mental Retardation, 97*(4), 359–391.

McGee, G. G., Daly, T., & Jacobs, H. A. (1994). The Walden preschool. In S. L. Harris, & J. S. Handleman (Eds.), *Preschool education programs for children with autism* (pp. 127–162). Austin, TX: Pro-Ed.

McGee, G. G., Krantz, P. J., & Mcclannahan, L. E. (1985). The facilitative effects of incidental teaching on preposition use by autistic children. *Journal of Applied Behavior Analysis, 18*(1), 17–31.

McGee, G. G., Morrier, M. J., & Daly, T. (1999). An incidental teaching approach to early intervention for toddlers with autism. *Journal of the Association for Persons With Severe Handicaps, 24*, 133–146.

Mesibov, G. B., Shea, V., & Schopler, E. (2004). *The TEACCH approach to autism spectrum disorders.* New York: Springer.

Mostert, M. P. (2001). Facilitated communication since 1995: A review of published studies. *Journal of Autism and Developmental Disorders, 31*(3), 287–313.

Muhle, R., Trentacoste, S., & Rapin, I. (2004). The genetics of autism. *Pediatrics, 113*(5), e472–486.

Murch, S., Anthony, A., Casson, D., Malik, M., Berelowitz, M., Dhillon, A., et al. (2004). Retraction of an interpretation. *Lancet, 363*(9411), 750.

National Institute of Mental Health. (1975). *Research in the service of mental health*, Rockville, MD: U.S. Government Printing Office.

National Research Council. (2001). *Educating children with autism.* Washington, D.C.: National Academy Press.

Nicolson, R., & Szatmari, P. (2003). Genetic and neurodevelopmental influences in autistic disorder. *Canadian Journal of Psychiatry, 48*, 526–537.

Ozonoff, S., & Cathcart, K. (1998). Effectiveness of a home program intervention for young children with autism. *Journal of Autism and Developmental Disorders, 28*(1), 25–32.

Pachter, L., Cloutier, M., & Bernstein, B. (1995). Ethnomedical (folk) remedies for childhood asthma in a mainland Puerto Rican community. *Archives of Pediatrics & Adolescent Medicine, 149*(9), 982–988.

Palmer, R., Blanchard, S., Stein, Z., Mandell, D., & Miller, C. (2006). Environmental mercury release, special education rates, and autistic disorder: An ecological study of Texas. *Health and Place, 12*(2), 203–209.

Palomo, T., Beninger, R., Kostrzewa, R., & Archer, T. (2003). Brain sites of movement disorder: Genetic and environmental agents in neurodevelopmental perturbations. *Neurotoxological Research, 5*(1–2), 1–26.

Panerai, S., Ferrante, L., & Zingale, M. (2002). Benefits of the treatment and education of autistic and communication handicapped children (TEACCH) programme as compared with a non-specific approach. *Journal of Intellectual Disability Research, 46*(4), 318–327.

Pelios, L. V., & Lund, S. K. (2001). A selective overview of issues on classification, causation, and early intensive behavioral intervention for autism [Special issue, part 1]. *Behavior Modification, 25*(5), 678–697.

Perisco, A., D'Agruma, L., Maiorano, N., Totaro, A., Militerni, R., Bravaccio, C., et al. (2001). Reelin gene alleles and haplotypes as a factor predisposing to autistic disorder. *Molecular Psychiatry, 6*, 150–159.

Piven, J., Arndt, S., Bailey, J., & Andreasen, N. (1996). Regional brain enlargement in autism: A magnetic resonance imaging study. *Journal of the American Academy of Child and Adolescent Psychiatry, 35*, 530–536.

Piven, J., Bailey, J., Ransom, B., & Arndt, S. (1997). An MRI study of the corpus callosum in autism. *American Journal of Psychiatry, 154*, 1051–1056.

Prizant B. M., & Wetherby, A. M. (1998). Understanding the continuum of discrete-trial traditional behavioral to social-pragmatic developmental approaches in communication enhancement for young children with autism/PDD. *Seminars in Speech and Language, 19*(4), 329–353.

Prizant, B. M., Wetherby, A. M., Rubin, E., & Laurent, A. C. (2003). The SCERTS Model: A transactional, family-centered approach to enhancing communication and socioemotional abilities of children with autism spectrum disorder. *Journal of Infants and Young Children, 16*(4), 296–316.

Redcay, E., & Courchesne, E. (2005). When is the brain enlarged in autism? A meta-analysis of all brain size reports. *Biological Psychiatry, 58*, 1–9.

Robbins, F. R., Giordano, S., Rhoads, S., & Feldman, R. S. (1996). Preschool children with autism: Current conceptualizations and best practices. In R. S. Feldman (Ed.), *The psychology of adversity* (pp. 63–90). Amherst, MA: University of Massachusetts Press.

Roberts, W., Weaver, L., & Brian, J. (2001). Repeated dose of porcine secretin in the treatment of autism: A randomized, placebo-controlled trial. *Pediatrics, 107*, E71.

Robins, D. L., Fein, D., Barton, M. L., & Green, J. A. (2001). The modified Checklist for Autism in Toddlers: An initial study investigating the early detection of autism and pervasive developmental disorders. *Journal of Autism and Developmental Disorders, 31*, 131–144.

Rogers, S. J. (1996). Early intervention in autism. *Journal of Autism and Developmental Disorders, 26*, 243–246.

Rogers, S. J. (1998). Empirically supported comprehensive treatments for young children with autism. *Journal Clinical Child Psychology, 27*, 168–179.

Rogers, S. J., & Dilalla, D. L. (1991). A comparative study of the effects of a developmentally based instructional model on young children with autism and young children with other disorders of behavior and development. *Topics in Early Childhood Special Education, 11*(2), 29–47.

Rogers, S. J., Hall, T., Osaki, D., Reaven, J., & Herbison, J. (2000). The Denver model: A comprehensive, integrated educational approach to young children with autism and their families. J. S. Handleman & S. L. Harris (Eds.), *Preschool education programs for children with autism* (2nd ed., pp. 95–133). Austin, TX: Pro-Ed.

Rogers, S. J., & Lewis, H. (1989). An effective day treatment model for young children with pervasive developmental disorders. *Journal of the American Academy of Child & Adolescent Psychiatry, 28*, 207–214.

Rutter, M., LeCouteur, A., & Lord, C. (2003). *Autism Diagnostic Interview—Revised manual.* Los Angeles: Western Psychological Services.

Sandler, A., Sutton, K., & DeWeese, J. (1999). Lack of benefit of a single dose of synthetic human secretin in the treatment of autism and pervasive developmental disorder. *New England Journal of Medicine, 341*, 1801–1806.

Scambler, D., Rogers, S., & Wehner, E. (2001). Can the checklist for autism in toddlers differentiate young children with autism from those with developmental delays? *Journal of the American Academy of Child & Adolescent Psychiatry, 40*(12), 1457–1463.

Schopler, E., Mesibov, G., & Baker, A. (1982). Evaluation of treatment for autistic children and their parents. *Journal of the American Academy of Child Psychiatry, 21*(3), 262–267.

Schopler, E., Reichler, R., DeVellis, R., & Daly, K. (1980). Toward objective classification of childhood autism: Childhood Autism Rating Scale (CARS). *Journal of Autism & Developmental Disorders, 10*(1), 91–103.

Schreibman, L. (2000). Intensive behavioral/psychoeducational treatments for autism: Research needs and future directions. *Journal of Autism and Developmental Disorders, 30*(5), 373–378.

Schreibman, L. (2005). *The science and fiction of autism.* Cambridge, MA: Harvard University Press.

Schreibman, L., Kaneko, W. M., & Koegel, R. L. (1991). Positive affect of parents of autistic children: A comparison across two teaching techniques. *Behavior Therapy, 22*(4), 479–490.

Schreibman, L., & Koegel, R. L. (1996). Fostering self-management: Parent-delivered pivotal response training for children with autistic disorder. In E. D. Hibbs & P. S. Jensen (Eds.), *Psychosocial treatments for child and adolescent disorders: Empirically based strategies for clinical practice* (pp. 525–552). Washington, D.C.: American Psychological Association.

Schreibman, L., & Koegel, R. L. (2005). Training for parents of children with autism: Pivotal responses, generalization, and individualization of interventions. In E. D. Hibbs & P. S. Jensen (Eds.), *Psychosocial treatments for child and adolescent disorders: Empirically based strategies for clinical practice* (2nd ed., pp. 605–631). Washington, D.C.: American Psychological Association.

Schultz, R. T. (2005). Developmental deficits in social perception in autism: The role of the amygdala and fusiform face area. *International Journal of Developmental Neuroscience, 23*, 125–141.

Seltzer, M., Krauss, M., Shattuck, P., Orsmond, G., Swe, A., & Lord, C. (2003). The symptoms of autism spectrum disorders in adolescence and adulthood. *Journal of Autism and Developmental Disorders, 33*(6), 565–581.

Shane, H., & Kearns, K. (1994). An examination of the role of the facilitator in "facilitated communication." *American Journal of Speech-Language Pathology, 3*, 48–54.

Sheinkopf, S. J., & Siegel, B. (1998). Home based behavioral treatment of young children with autism. *Journal of Autism and Developmental Disorders, 28*, 15–23.

Sherer, M. R., & Schreibman, L. (2005). Individual behavioral profiles and predictors of treatment effectiveness for children with autism. *Journal of Consulting and Clinical Psychology, 73*(3), 525–538.

Siegel, B. (1999). *Detection of autism in the 2nd and 3rd years: The Pervasive Developmental Disorders Screening Test (PDDST).* Paper presented at the biennial meeting of the Society for Research in Child Development, Albuquerque, NM.

Smith, T. (1999). Outcome of early intervention for children with autism. *Clinical Psychology: Science and Practice, 6*(1), 33–49.

Smith, T., Groen, A. D., & Wynn, J. W. (2000). Randomized trial of intensive early intervention for children with pervasive developmental disorder. *American Journal of Mental Retardation, 105*(4), 269–285.

Sperry, L., Whaley, K., Shaw, E., & Brame, K. (1999). Services for young children with autism spectrum disorder: voices of parents and providers. *Infants and Young Children, 11*, 17–33.

Stahmer, A. (2006). The basic structure of community early intervention programs for children with autism: Provider descriptions. *Journal of Autism & Developmental Disorders.* http://www.springerlink.com/content/2817066341658h1w/?p=f8a7c9ac1000492fbd6be2431c31f211&pi=3

Stahmer, A. C. (1995). Teaching symbolic play skills to children with autism using pivotal response training. *Journal of Autism and Developmental Disorders, 25*(2), 123–141.

Stahmer, A. C., Collings, N. M., & Palinkas, L. A. (2005). Early intervention practices for children with autism: Descriptions from community providers. *Focus on Autism & Other Developmental Disabilities, 20*, 66–79.

Stahmer, A. C., & Gist, K. (2001). The effects of an accelerated parent education program on technique mastery and child outcome. *Journal of Positive Behavior Interventions, 3*(2), 75–82.

Stahmer, A. C., & Ingersoll, B. (2004). Inclusive programming for toddlers with autism spectrum disorders: Outcomes from the children's toddler school. *Journal of Positive Behavior Interventions, 6*(2), 67–82.

Strain, P., & Cordisco, L. (1994). LEAP Preschool. In S. L. Harris & J. S. Handleman (Eds.), *Preschool education programs for children with autism* (pp. 225–244). Austin, TX: PRO-ED.

Tsai, L. Y. (1998). *Pervasive developmental disorders briefing paper.* Washington, D.C.: NICHCY.

Veenstra-VanderWeele, J., Christian, S. L., & Cook, E. H., Jr. (2004). Autism as a paradigmatic complex genetic disorder. *Annual Review of Genomics and Human Genetics, 5*, 379–405.

Vidal, C. N., Nicolson, R., DeVito, T. J., Hayashi, K. M., Geaga, J. A., Drost, D. J., et al. (2006). Mapping corpus callosum deficits in autism: An index of aberrant cortical connectivity. *Biological Psychiatry, 60*(3), 218–225.

Vojdani, A., Pangborn, J. B., Vojdani, E., & Cooper, E. L. (2003). Infections, toxic chemicals and dietary peptides binding to lymphocyte receptors and tissue enzymes are major instigators of autoimmunity in autism. *International Journal of Immunopathology and Pharmacology, 16*(3), 189–199.

Volkmar, F. (2001). Pharmacological interventions in autism: Theoretical and practical issues. *Journal of Clinical Child Psychology, 30*(1), 80–87.

Volkmar, F., Cook, E., Pomeroy, J., Realmuto, G., & Tanguay, P. (1999). Practice parameters for the assessment and treatment of children, adolescents and adults with autism and other pervasive developmental disorders. *Journal of the American Academy of Child & Adolescent Psychiatry, 38*(Suppl. 12), 32S–54S.

Volkmar, F., & Pauls, D. (2003). Autism. *Lancet, 362*(9390), 1133–1141.

Waiter, G. D., Williams, J. H. G., Murray, A. D., Gilchrist, A., Perrett, D. I., & Whiten, A. (2005). Structural white matter deficits in high-functioning individuals with autistic spectrum disorder: A voxel-based investigation. *Neuroimage, 24*, 455–461.

Wakefield, A., Murch, S., Anthony, A., Linnell, J., Casson, D., Malik, M., et al. (1998). Ileal-lymphoid-nodular hyperplasia, non-specific colitis, and pervasive developmental disorder in children. *Lancet, 351*(9103), 637–641.

Wakefield, A., Puleston, J., Montgomery, J., Anthony, A., O'Leary, J., & Murch, S. (2002). The concept of entero-colonic encephalopathy, autism and opiod receptor ligands. *Alimentary Pharmacology & Therapeutics, 16*(4), 663–674.

Welch, M. G. (1988). *Holding time.* New York: Simon & Schuster.

Wing, L. (1981). Asperger's syndrome: A clinical account. *Psychological Medicine, 11*, 115–130.

Wing, L. (1997). The autistic spectrum. *The Lancet, 350*, 1761–1766.

Wing, L., & Potter, D. (2002). The epidemiology of autistic spectrum disorders: Is the prevalence rising? *Mental Retardation & Developmental Disabilities Research Reviews, 8*(3), 151–161.

Wolery, M., & Garfinkle, A. (2002). Measures in intervention research with young children who have autism. *Journal of Autism & Developmental Disorders, 32*(5), 463–478.

Wolff, S. (1995). *The life path of unusual children.* London: Routledge.

Wolff, S., Narayan, S., & Moyes, B. (1988). Personality characteristics of parents of autistic children: A controlled study. *Journal of Child Psychology & Psychiatry, 29*, 143–153.

Yeargin-Allsopp, M., Rice, C., Karapurkar, T., Doernberg, N., Boyle, C., & Murphy, C. (2003). Prevalence of autism in a U.S. metropolitan area. *Journal of the American Medical Association, 289*(1), 49–55.

Chapter Seventeen

Pervasive Developmental Delay and Autistic Spectrum Disorder in Childhood

Raymond W. DuCharme and Kathleen A. McGrady

INTRODUCTION

This chapter examines Asperger's syndrome and related disorders. After reviewing definitional issues, incidence, and possible influencing factors, we describe interventions to improve the lives of young people experiencing this issue.

Definitional Issues

A literature search produced 385 studies, articles, and other references with 166 studies pertaining to diagnosis. The researchers attempting to clarify definitional issues related to Asperger syndrome (AS) are the primary source of information for the following discussion. Their articles examined the factors that differentiated autism from Asperger syndrome, high functioning autism, pervasive developmental delay, not otherwise specified, and nonverbal learning disability (see Table 17.1). Raja and Azzoni (2001) discussed the autistic condition described almost simultaneously by Dr. Asperger in Vienna (1944) and Dr. Kanner (1943) in Baltimore. Both men were medically trained in Vienna at nearly the same time. Dr. Kanner (1943) described the characteristics of children that he diagnosed as having infantile autism, while Dr. Asperger (1944) made observations of children in his hospital unit in Vienna that he characterized as "autistic psychopathy" (Frith, 1991). Dr. Kanner's diagnosis of infantile autism was more severe than Dr. Asperger's label. Together, their work has inspired decades of research attempting to clarify the differences and similarities between these two clinical descriptions.

In recent years Asperger syndrome (AS) was considered a pervasive developmental disorder and included as a new diagnosis in the World Health Organization (1992) *International Classification of Diseases* (ICD-10) and the American Psychiatric Association's *Diagnostic and Statistical Manual of Mental Disorders* (DSM-IV, 1994) (see Table 17.2). Eisenmajer et al. (1996) note that the DSM-IV criteria for Asperger's

Table 17.1 Comparison of Autistic spectrum diagnostic criteria

Diagnosis	Onset of symptoms	Gender	Social skills	Head Circumference	Language skills	Cognitive functioning	Motor Skills
Autism	Prior to age 3 years. Symptoms in infancy are subtle.	Males (8 times greater than females)	Social skill deficits	Delay, or lack of development	75% have mental retardation	Repetitive and stereotyped	
Rett's disorder	Five months normal development; diagnosed between 5–48 months	Females	Loss of social interaction early; may develop later	Decelerates between 5 - 48 months	Expressive and receptive language problems	Severe to profound mental retardation	"Hand-wringing"; gait and truck coordination problems
Childhood disintegrative disorder	Two years normal development; diagnosed before age 10	Males - more common	Loss of social skills (after age 2 years)	Expressive or receptive (after age 2 years)	Severe mental retardation (usually)	Loss of motor skills after age 2 years	
Asperger syndrome	Recognition and diagnosis later (e.g., school age, between ages 7–11 years)	Males (8 times greater than females)	Social skill deficits	No general delay in language; but pragmatic language deficits. Theory of mind– Subvocal speech	Normal IQ verbal performance deviation	Motor delays and clumsiness: Absence of research	
PDD, NOS	Does not meet criteria for any of the above, but has some of the behaviors	Does not meet criteria for any of the above, but has some of the behaviors	Does not meet criteria for any of the above, but has some of the behaviors	Does not meet criteria for any of the above, but has some of the behaviors	Does not meet criteria for any of the above, but has some of the behaviors	Does not meet criteria for any of the above, but has some of the behavior	Does not meet criteria for any of the above, but has some of the behaviors

Source: The Learning Clinic, Inc. January 16, 2004

disorder (now called Asperger syndrome), is the same as that for autism disorder (AD) with three exceptions:

1. Communication and imagination impairment criteria for autism disorder are not listed for AS.
2. The child with an AS diagnosis is described as not suffering from a clinically significant general delay in language (e.g., single words by age 2 years and phrases by age 3).
3. The child with AS does not have a clinically significant delay in cognitive development, the development of age appropriate self-help skills, adaptive behavior, or curiosity about the environment.

Research suggests that a dimensional view of the autism spectrum is more appropriate than the categorical approach represented by the ICD-10 and DSM-IV. A dimensional view considers patterns of symptoms, or characteristics, and degrees of severity.

For example, Ozonoff et al. (2000) compared 23 children with high functioning autism with 12 children who were diagnosed with AS. Both groups were matched for chronological age, gender, and intellectual ability. The sources of difference between the groups were categorized as cognitive functions, current symptoms, and early history. The authors concluded that high functioning autism and AS involve the same symptomatology differing only in degree of severity.

Klin and his colleagues (1995) reported on the validity of neuropsychological characterization of AS and the convergence of AS with nonverbal learning disability using the ICD-10 diagnostic criteria. The authors compared neuropsychological profiles of AS and high functioning autism and the assets and deficits described by the term *nonverbal learning disability* reported by Rourke (1995). This comparison showed that the two groups differed significantly in 11 neuropsychological areas. Schopler, Mesibov, and Kunce (1998) identified similar characteristics of high functioning autism and AS supporting the notion of "symptom overlap" between autism, high-functioning autism, and AS. Manjiviona and Prior (1999) reported that higher IQ scores among Asperger

Table 17.2 Asperger syndrome criteria

	DSM-IV	ICD-10
Qualitative impairment in social interaction	X	X
Restricted repetitive and stereotyped patterns of behavior, interests		
and activities	X	X
No general language delay	X	X
No delay in cognitive development	X	X
Normal general intelligence (most)		X
Markedly clumsy (common)		X
No delay in development of: age appropriate self-help skills adaptive behavior (excluding social interaction) curiosity about environment	X	

syndrome students accounted for the differences. Klin et al. (1995) reported that although the AS and high functioning autism groups did not differ in full-scale IQ, the
verbal–performance differentials (VIQ–PIQ) were significantly different. The Asperger
syndrome group demonstrated a higher verbal IQ and lower performance IQ in comparison to the high functioning autism group.

The degree of overlap between the psychiatric diagnoses AS, high functioning autism, and the neuropsychological characterization of nonverbal learning disability (NLD),
indicates a high degree of concordance between AS and NLD. The neuropsychological
description of NLD assets and deficits is a model for AS, but not for high functioning autism. Thus, it is *not* useful to identify NLD as a separate diagnostic group apart from AS.

PREVALENCE

Ehlers and Gillberg (1993) reported the prevalence of Asperger syndrome to be 26 to 36
per 10,000 school age individuals. Paul Shattuck in his 2002 presentation at the Gatlin-
berg Conference for Research on Mental Retardation and Developmental Disabilities
detailed prevalence data of autism in public schools. He reported an increase of 24%
from 1994 to 2000 (Blacher, 2002). Other researchers from Queens College and the Texas
Center for Autism Research and Treatment reported similar trends in prevalence data
(Blacher, 2002).

INDIVIDUAL FACTORS: CHARACTERISTICS OF CHILDREN
WITH ASPERGER SYNDROME

The individual factors include such issues as motor development, speech and prosody,
language and meaning, and cognitive processes.

Motor Development

It is reported that delayed motor milestones and the presence of motor clumsiness are
Asperger syndrome characteristics. But there is a paucity of research to corroborate
a clear association between motor delay and other AS characteristics (Ghaziuddin &
Butler, 1998). Motor development and "clumsiness" were investigated by Ghaziuddin
and Butler (1998), and Ghaziuddin et al. (1994). The authors found no significant relationship between coordination scores and diagnostic category after adjusting scores for
intelligence. Weimer, Schatz, Lincoln, Ballantyne, and Trauner (2001) suggest that the
motor clumsiness reported by Green et al. (2002) and Miyahara et al. (1997) may be the
result of the proprioceptive deficits that underlie the cases of coordination difficulties
observed in some children with AS.

Speech and Prosody

Shriberg, Paul, McSweeny, Klin, and Cohen (2001) investigated the speech and prosody
characteristics of adolescents and adults with high functioning autism and AS. Prosody

includes phrasing, variability in speech production, same word duration in sentences, and grammatical placement of stressed and unstressed syllables and words. Voice loudness, pitch, and quality also were compared. There were minor differences in volubility differences and articulation errors between AS and high functioning autism subjects. AS subjects used higher volume, and there was a high prevalence of speech–sound distortion in both groups. Findings associated with prosody and voice analyses identified significant differences between clinical and control groups in the areas of phrasing, stress, and nasal resonance. Two-thirds of the AS speakers were coded as having nonfluent phrasing on more than 20% of their utterances. It was speculated that individuals with AS use repetition and revision to compensate for formulation difficulties. There was also a suggestion that increasing length of utterance was associated with increased phrasing errors. Higher levels of grammatical complexity were also associated with increased phrasing errors and length of utterance.

Gilchrist et al. (2001) compared adolescent AS, high functioning autism, and conduct disorder (CD) diagnoses to behavioral and speech abnormalities. The findings for the group with AS were: (1) demonstrated less severe behavioral abnormalities than the autism group; (2) were unlikely to have speech abnormalities; (3) had other communication and social behavior difficulties similar to high functioning autism; (4) did better in structured one-to-one conversation than other groups.

Language and Meaning

Joliffe and Baron-Cohen (2000) examined linguistic processing in high functioning adults with autism or AS. The ability to establish causal connections and to interrelate "local chunks"[1] into higher-order "chunks" so that most linguistic elements are linked together thematically was defined as "global coherence." The authors hypothesized that adults on the autism spectrum, including AS, would have difficulty integrating information so as to derive meaning. Results showed that the clinical groups were less able to arrange sentences coherently and to use context to make a global inference. The findings of the study on the abilities called "global coherence" are inconsistent with the classroom experience of adolescent high functioning autism and AS student performance with the authors research at The Learning Clinic (TLC)—a private nonprofit school for young people with special learning needs (DuCharme & McGrady, 2003).

For example, 30 TLC students were assigned a task with directions for writing a news story. They were given seven statements of instruction and 10 individual descriptive informational statements, six of which were relevant to a theme, and four that were not. The assignment was to create a news story that had a main point by selecting relevant information from the sentences provided. All 30 students successfully completed the task set but demonstrated an inability to select information less relevant or irrelevant to the main theme.

Joliffe and Baron-Cohen (2000) required an inference and use of connotative meaning to demonstrate comprehension. Global coherence may be different from inference. TLC student behavior demonstrated the ability to identify a main theme and related, supporting data that were "coherent." No inference was required. But students were not able to differentiate the relative importance of information provided.

The "global coherence" requirement of the Joliffe and Baron-Cohen (2000) study to interpret and infer within the context of a story is different from combining facts into a

coherent statement or conclusion. The definition of their task has connotative implications. Both connotative and denotative meaning derives from linguistic processes that
may differ from the processes used to infer meaning from factual content. Frith and
Happe (1994), and Minshew, Goldstein, and Siegel (1995) describe linguistic difficulties present when an AS person is given complex interpretive language tasks. Deficits
were found in complex information processing abilities. However, linguistic basic skills
were preserved.

Channon, Charman, Heap, Crawford, and Rios (2001) presented videotaped real-life
problems to 30 preteen and adolescent youth. Fifteen were diagnosed with Asperger
syndrome and 15 were placed in a control group. The AS group differed in their ability to
provide socially appropriate solutions to the problems as compared to the control group.
This inability to draw inferences and assign appropriate attribution to key factors present
in social situations is also discussed by Barnhill (2001; Barnhill & Myles, 2001).

Cognitive Processes

The cognitive flexibility required to solve a novel problem, or a familiar problem in a
novel situation is absent for AS persons to a degree beyond what their normal to superior
IQ scores should predict. Shulman, Yirmiya, and Greenbaum (1995) have reported that
individuals on the autism spectrum have difficulties with tasks that necessitate internal
manipulation of information.

This relates to a concept known as Theory of Mind (TOM). TOM is understood as
the ability to perceive mental states, including beliefs, intentions, and thoughts (Perner
& Wimmer, 1985). Happe (1995) describes these internalized manipulations of information as mentalizing. How "mentalizing" is related to "global coherence" and theory of
mind is unclear. But these processes suggest an interface among auditory processing,
language, cognition, and the "load" of factors present in any situation.

Preliminary evidence from Dunn, Myles, and Orr (2002) supports a view that differences exist in the sensory processing patterns of children with AS when compared
with nonclinical peers. Asperger syndrome students are reported to have difficulty with
auditory processing. They demonstrate poor ability to modulate their responses from one
situation to another. The authors advocate for a student to receive a sensory measurement
that will yield a profile that reflects the assessment of sensory processing, modulation
of behavioral-emotional responses, and level of response to "sensory events." Sensory
processing deficits may alter the ability to cognitively manipulate data accurately.

The observations by Frith (1991) and Frith and Happe (1994) that children with AS
are limited in their ability to demonstrate pretend play, imagination, and creativity has
some support in the research literature (Craig and Baron-Cohen, 1999). This apparent
restricted ability to predict future events by manipulating past experience, as part of
problem solving, may be related to measures of limited creativity and theory of mind
factors identified early in child development (Baron-Cohen, O'Riordan, Stone, Jones, &
Plaisted 1999; Joliffe & Baron-Cohen, 2000).

Ehlers et al. (1997) compared the cognitive profiles of AS, autism disorder, and
attention deficit disorder students 5 to 15 years old. Using the Swedish version of the
WISC-III Kaufman Factors of Verbal Comprehension, Perceptual Organization and Freedom from Distractibility measurements, the AS and autism disorder groups differed in

respect to "fluid" and "crystallized" cognitive ability, with the AS group scoring higher in both areas. They also reported that the Kaufman Factor scores accounted for more variance than WISC-III Verbal or Performance IQ scores.

De Leon, Munoz, and Pieo (1986), Courchesne et al. (1994), Schultz, Romanski, and Tsatsanis (2000), and Morris et al. (1999) investigated brain hemisphere function associated with developmental prosopagnosia and visual-perceptual functions involved in face recognition. While evidence was inconclusive regarding the ability to perceive emotion in facial cues as a neurocognitive dysfunction of visual perception (Grossman, Klin, Carter, & Volkmar, 2000), this conclusion does not imply that there is no evidence of cortical neuropathology present in AS (Aman, Roberts, & Pennington, 1998; Casanova, Buzhoeveden, Switala, & Roy, 2002; Rourke, Fisk, & Strang, 1983).

ASPERGER SYNDROME PROFILE

Barnhill (2001) provides a synthesis of research conducted by the Asperger Syndrome Project, which provides an "empirically valid profile of individuals with Asperger Syndrome" (p. 300). Those characteristics are:

1. IQs similar to the general population, ranging from deficient to very superior.
2. Significantly less capable written than oral language skills.
3. Limited ability to problem solve in contrast to verbal fluency skill.
4. Measured emotional difficulties not endorsed by the Asperger syndrome students themselves.
5. Problems with inferential comprehension.
6. Attributions that parallel a learned helplessness approach.
7. Sensory problems similar to a cognitively deficient person.

The cluster of factors associated with socialization, social skill development, and social reality testing are important discriminate variables associated with AS. The tendency to prefer aloneness, to avoid peers in preference to adult interaction, other avoidant behaviors, and marginal independent living skills are also related to diagnosis and prognosis for persons with AS (Dewey, 1991; Dyer, Kneringer, & Luce, 1996; Matthews, 1996; Mawhood & Howlin,1999; Nesbitt, 2000; Tantam, 2000;).

The inability to draw inferences, to interpret connotative meaning, and to apprehend relationships between factual knowledge and higher order thinking also need to be included as Asperger syndrome characteristics worthy of investigation. Evidence of over- and underreactivity to ordinary stimuli, and attentional shift problems are important characteristics (Courchesne et al., 1994). Level of cognitive rigidity in the presence of anxiety-producing stimuli reported anecdotally has heuristic value in future researches.

Asperger syndrome is a complex continuum of symptoms and these problematic symptoms of communication and language, cognition, adaptability, lack of generalization of skill, socialization, and sensory processing are more evident in the interactions that are part of the daily activities in the natural environment than the testing room. The clarity of the diagnostic nosology that fits the child's environment is important. And the need to assess children with AS as part of the natural daily routine is important in order to obtain a valid assessment of their competencies.

ASSOCIATED CO-OCCURRING CONDITIONS

It is usually not a straightforward process to obtain an accurate diagnosis and treatment for a child with AS. Asperger syndrome is a multifaceted disorder with subtle deficits (Mesibov, Shea, & Adams 2001). The diagnostic process is often complicated by co-occurring conditions. These may include difficulties with attention and concentration, anxious behaviors, depression, motor or vocal tics, obsessive-compulsive acts, non-compliant or aggressive behaviors, or learning disabilities (Klin, Volkmar, & Sparrow, 2000). Behaviors associated with these conditions tend to be disruptive, and therefore become the focus of treatment and diagnosis. Before it is recognized that a youngster has Asperger syndrome, the child may be given one or more of the following diagnostic labels: attention-deficit/hyperactivity disorder (ADHD), depression, anxiety disorder, obsessive-compulsive disorder (OCD), oppositional-defiant disorder, or schizophrenia. In some cases the child may have a co-occurring condition, which warrants the diagnosis. In other cases, the behaviors are a manifestation of one of the many features of AS, and do not meet the criteria for a second diagnosis.

To illustrate, of 24 children at The Learning Clinic who were diagnosed with AS or PDD, NOS (using DSM-IV criteria), 24 students revealed a pattern of co-occurring diagnoses: 54% were diagnosed with two or more conditions and 25% with three or more conditions (R = 0–4) (mode = 2) (DuCharme & McGrady, 2004).

Attention-Deficit/Hyperactivity Disorder

Difficulties with attention and concentration are common with AS children, especially younger children (Klin et al., 2000). According to Klin and Volkmar (1997) 28% of AS children have a co-occurring diagnosis of ADHD. However, although the child with AS can present with impaired attention, he or she may do so without having ADHD. Some features of AS that interfere with attention include sensory overload, and fixated attention. With sensory overload, the child with AS has difficulty filtering out irrelevant stimuli, and can become overloaded with sensory input. Instead of focusing attention on what is relevant, he is distracted by too much sensory input, failing to attend to what is important.

Anxiety Disorders and Depression

Anxiety and depression are more common among older AS children and adults (Klin et al., 2000). As AS children mature, they increasingly become aware of how they differ from their peers, and the difficulty they have in social relationships. They are aware of standards of behavior and achievement that are difficult for them to attain. Frequently, the child with AS becomes the victim of peer teasing or ostracizing. In response to these very real differences, taunting, and social consequences, the child may become depressed. Adolescent depression tends to manifest differently than in adults. Instead of expressed sadness or withdrawn behaviors, it is manifested through acting-out or an irritable demeanor.

If the child with AS responds with anxious behaviors, it could manifest as nail-biting, tugging at clothing, hair pulling, avoidance of school or other social situations. In some cases, the anxious behaviors may meet the criteria of an anxiety disorder such as social anxiety, or school phobia. Similarly, if the depression becomes chronic and significantly interferes with daily life, it may meet the criteria for a mood disorder. In a study by Klin et al. (2000), 15% of AS children had a coexisting mood disorder. At The Learning Clinic (TLC), in 2006, the percentage of Asperger and PDD NOS students with a coexisting mood disorder was 66.7%.

Obsessive-Compulsive Disorder

Although obsessive-compulsive disorder does occur in some individuals with AS (19% according to Klin et al., 2000), features of AS can be mistaken for obsessive-compulsive disorder: cognitive rigidity, rigid adherence to routines and schedules, and a restricted range of interests. For example, it is common for children with AS to have a consuming interest in a specific limited topic (for example, trains, elevators, dinosaurs). They typically develop extensive knowledge about their specific area of interest. What distinguishes behaviors associated with these interests from obsessive-compulsive disorder is that the child with AS does not feel compelled to read about trains or ride a train as a means of reducing feelings of anxiety—they simply find pleasure in pursuing their area of interest.

Another feature of the child's restricted range of interests is ego-syntonic behavior. That is, the child with AS does not see anything wrong with engaging in the absorbing interest. An obsessive-compulsive disorder youngster is generally bothered by the obsessive thoughts and compulsive behaviors, and experiences them as intrusive and disruptive to his or her life. Not so for the child with AS.

Oppositional-Defiant Disorder

Children with AS can be difficult to manage and may exhibit noncompliant behaviors. However, an important difference between a child with AS and an oppositional-defiant child is volition. The oppositional-defiant child will planfully disobey the "rules," but the child with AS generally will make an effort to follow the rules, *as he understands them*. However, his understanding of the rules may be impaired either because of a miscommunication (comprehension or language pragmatics), sensory overload, misreading of contextual (nonverbal) cues, inattention, or because he acted impulsively. Additionally, when children with AS learn a rule in one environment, this learning does not generalize to the next setting. In the new setting the contextual cues are different, and the child with AS perceives the situation as entirely different, much to the frustration of his teachers, parents, and others around him.

Schizophrenia

Several aspects of AS can be confused with psychotic behavior. An untreated AS child can present as a solitary individual, uninterested in social interaction, and intensely preoccupied with internal thoughts. Poor language pragmatic skills can contribute to a child verbalizing tangential thoughts that are loosely related to ongoing discussions.

SOCIAL AND COMMUNITY FACTORS

A syndrome is defined as a group of signs and symptoms that occur together (Merriam-Webster, 1990). The term *Asperger disorder* was changed to *Asperger syndrome* to reflect the reality that it is characterized by a group of symptoms on a continuum. Many of these symptoms require specific interventions to help the child succeed. Among the special services that may be needed are: social skills training, special education, occupational therapy, physical therapy, speech and language therapy, psychiatric and psychological interventions, neurological and neuropsychological assessments, and social and ultimately employment opportunities. The resiliency of children is enhanced when these resources are readily available through social networks and community services and preplanned transition services are provided at the appropriate time and not as an afterthought.

Encouraging Resilience

Focusing on those characteristics and circumstances that enable individuals with pervasive development disorder, pervasive development disorder-not otherwise specified, and autism spectrum disorders to perform skills under stress and reduced structure are more productive than focusing on etiology, psychopathology, and deficits associated with the disorders. There is evidence that individuals with pervasive developmental disorder and autism diagnosis such as AS benefit from well-designed behavioral treatment in conjunction with medication therapy and psychoeducational interventions.

It is our experience that well-designed communities (whether residential or transitional in the sense that the individual's capacity dictates the living arrangement) that include specialized education, preparation for and participation in vocational experience, self-regulation training, self-medication training, and other mentoring for social skills and post high school (transition), produce positive, sustainable outcomes.

Resiliency depends upon ongoing affiliation with caring family members, competent adult mentors, and connection with an integrated network of supportive services including social clubs, special education, and employment preparation. Self-regulation, motivation, and self-confidence depend upon the focus of treatment and supportive services toward independent living and learning skills.

The individuals' appropriate level of community living and social independence are also factors in resiliency. Flexible levels of responsive intervention are necessary to buffer the overstimulation, anxiety, social demands, and skill adjustment experienced in the community by the child with AS.

FAMILY FACTORS INFLUENCING RISK AND RESILIENCY

While many family factors have been examined, no direct etiology has been identified. That said, there is anecdotal evidence that AS is linked to male family members. The evidence suggests that male AS characteristics are genetically linked to male children and the age of paternal fathers or paternal grandfathers. There are more male than female individuals identified with AS (ratio 8:1). And, if one child is born with characteristics of autistic symptoms, then there is a higher probability of siblings being diagnosed with symptoms on the autism spectrum. One study by Reichenberg et al. (2006) found it 5.75 times more likely that men over 30 years of age would father children with an autistic spectrum diagnosis than the children of men under that age.

Additionally, there have been other circumstances identified that may help to determine the etiology of these disorders. Beversdorf and his colleagues (2005) found a significant increase in prenatal stressors reported among mothers with children who were diagnosed with autism, especially during the 21- to 32-week gestation period. Studies suggest that pervasive developmental disorders are inheritable, and are more common where there is a family history of pervasive developmental disorders (Dixon-Salazar, Keeler, Trauner, & Gleeson, 2003; Lauritsen, Pedersen, & Mortensen, 2005; Ronald et al., 2006; Williams, Oliver, Allard, & Sears, 2003). Familial intelligence levels may play into the development of pervasive developmental disorders. For instance, an older study found that fathers of children with autism were of significantly above-average intelligence (Dor-Shav & Horowitz, 1984). A more recent study indicated that children with autism had mothers with higher levels of education and a higher frequency of paternal relatives with mental retardation (Williams et al., 2003).

Children with lower IQs diagnosed with autism have higher than expected medical histories involving maternal rubella and Goldenhar syndrome (Barton & Volkmar, 1998). Children with pervasive developmental disorders have been shown to have differences in their brain functioning (Oktem, Diren, Karaagaoglu, & Anlar, 2000; Salmond et al., 2005). Recent research has shown that children with autism also tend to display gastrointestinal symptoms more often than other children with other developmental delays and with typical development (Valicenti-McDermott et al., 2006).

GENETICS

With advances in medical research, there have been investigations into possible genetic contributions to the pervasive developmental disorders. While many studies have implicated specific genes as being somehow related to the disorders and some genes have been ruled out as being related, no direct causal link between any gene and pervasive developmental disorders has been made (Coutinho et al., 2004; Engstrom et al., 2003; Gharani, Benayed, Mancuso, Brzustowicz, & Millonig, 2004; Molloy, Keddache, & Martin, 2005; Michaelis et al., 2000; Nurmi et al., 2003; Rogers et al., 1999; Serajee, Nabi, Zhong, & Huq, 2003; Sigirci, Alkan, Kutlu, & Gulcan, 2005; Skaar et al., 2005).

A relationship has been made between autistic disorders and chromosomal abnormalities, particularly, facial dysmorphia (Konstantareas & Homatidis, 1999). Another study observes that the parents of children with autistic spectrum pervasive developmental disorders often display autisticlike traits in social and communication skills (Bishop et al., 2004). Miles, Takahashi, Haber, and Hadden (2003) report that in families where there are children diagnosed with infantile autism, there are higher than normal rates of alcoholism.

Finally, recent advances in genetics further support the growing belief that autism is a genetic disorder (DeNoon, 2007). It is claimed that heritability accounts for greater than 90% of diagnosed cases. DeNoon, reporting the work of Pat Levitt at the Vanderbilt Center for Research on Human Development, writes that the variant gene is called MET, and its effects are linked to brain, gut, and multiple body systems. The significance of this research is that the study links other findings of brain development, immune function, and environmental factors with a common gene, MET. Whether this finding proves valid awaits further testing.

EVIDENCE-BASED TREATMENT INTERVENTIONS

What Works

A review of the literature did not reveal an intervention that met the criteria of three successful trials for "What Works."

What Might Work

The following interventions are worthy of further testing because they appear promising in helping children with AS and PDDs lead more successful lives.

Behavioral Interventions

In one study, 71 children aged 10 to 12 years with anxiety and AS participated in a cognitive behavioral treatment (CBT) intervention. Parent reported results suggested that the program was effective in reducing anxiety. In this study active parental involvement yielded the best results (Sofronoff et al., 2005). Also, White (2004) found evidence that CBT is a feasible treatment option in high-functioning children with AS. Some children experienced improvements in coping strategies for anxiety promoting situations, behavior, and social interaction after CBT.

Using applied behavior analysis (ABA), Jensen and Sinclair (2002) reported behavioral interventions offered moderate to possibly significant gains in functioning for young children. ABA showed significant benefits for an overall increase in functioning skills, cognitive performance, and decrease in autistic symptoms after two to three years of intervention and maintained these gains at a seven-year follow-up. Jensen and Sinclair stress the importance of actively addressing maintenance.

A randomized control trial of ABA by Smith, Groen, and Wynn compared two groups of 15 children who were randomly assigned to either a year of 24 hours a week of ABA carried out by skilled therapists plus follow-up, or three to nine months of parent training several hours a week. The children who received ABA showed greater gains than the children in the parent training control group. Children with PDD-NOS and higher IQs at entry made greater gains than children with autism diagnoses (cited in Volkmar, Lord, Bailey, Schultz, & Klin, 2004).

Parental Support

On rare occasions, the authors have observed a family demonstrating unusually high tolerance for the symptoms of the AS family member. Specifically, if the father of the child with AS is diagnosed with AS then it may increase the family's resistance to treatment and obstruct the identification of the child's need for special education, possibly medication, and other help. In these situations, the father may not value social-skill training and may not perceive the clinical aspects of the child's behavior. Understanding the family system and family patterns of experience and interaction is important for the effective treatment of the child with AS. More frequently, the situation exists where the family is in utter turmoil over the inability of the child to fulfill family and school expectations. An adaptation of Beardslee's program described in the entry on depression may be helpful in increasing family understanding of this issue (Beardslee et al., 1993).

Social Skills

While the literature provides little evidence-based information about specific social skills training for children with AS, social skills training is generally accepted as an appropriate treatment for children with AS (DuCharme & McGrady, 2003; Klin et al., 2000; Mesibov et a.l, 2001). For students enrolled at The Learning Clinic, an intervention plan begins with an analysis of pragmatic skills strengths and weaknesses, and an adult mentor is used to facilitate these skills with peers. An example of a treatment plan for integrating pragmatic language and social skills follows.

Skill Building Strategies
1. Provide an adult mentor to:
    a. *interpret* social situations: What behavior is being asked for? What is the appropriate verbal or behavioral response to this particular situation?
    b. *role model* the appropriate verbal or behavioral response.
2. Role model perspective-taking
    Interpret for student the other person's intent, feelings, etc.
3. Role model the following:
    a. The *entry* and *exit* statements of social communication
    b. Competitive vs. aggressive behaviors
    c. Assertive vs. rude statements/behaviors
    d. Assertive vs. threatening statements/behaviors
4. Provide opportunity for student to practice the following. Initially with adult mentor; then with peers (one at a time, then small groups):
    a. *Entry* and *exit* statements of social communication
    b. Voice modulation
    c. Competitive vs. aggressive behaviors
    d. Assertive/polite vs. rude statements/behaviors
    e. Assertive vs. threatening statements/behaviors
5. Videotape role-playing scenarios for all of the above, and provide video feedback.
6. Videotape role-playing of common social dilemmas, and provide video feedback.
7. Provide opportunity for practice in "real life" settings, and provide feedback

What Doesn't Work

There is no evidence to support an introspective approach to counseling young people with AS.

PHARMACOLOGICAL INTERVENTIONS

Like other issues discussed in this volume, there is limited research on the efficacy of psychotropic medications for children with AS, pervasive developmental disorder, not otherwise specified, or autistic spectrum disorders. This despite the fact that in 2006 1.6 million children and adolescents in the United States were administered a minimum of two psychiatric drugs in combination. The number of children under 10 years old numbered 280,000 (http://www.medcohealth.com/medco/consumer/home).

Currently, there are no medications to specifically treat autistic spectrum disorders. There is no medication that is going to "cure" or eliminate the disorder. However, there are medications used to treat some of the symptoms associated with these disorders. These behaviors include irritability, aggression, stereotypy, hyperactivity, inattention, anxiousness, and mood lability. Co-occurring conditions are not unusual with PDD.

Medication Therapy

Medications do not treat the disorder itself. However, the newer generation antipsychotics have been found helpful in decreasing severe tantrums, aggression, and self-injurious behavior in children with AS (Hilt, 2006). Research has shown risperidone did not improve impairment of social interaction or communication impairment. However, repetitive and stereotyped patterns of behavior, interests, and activities did improve (McDougle et al., 2005). A study by Gagliano et al. (2004) concluded that risperidone was effective in treating aggressiveness, hyperactivity, irritability, stereotyped patterns of behavior, social withdrawal, and lack of interests. Despite the symptomatic improvement, Santosh and Baird (2001) caution that long-term use of psychotropics occasionally can worsen behavior and produce iatrogenic symptoms.

Masi, Cosenza, Mucci, and Brovedani (2003) conducted a three-year study of preschool children with pervasive developmental disorders treated with risperidone. Behavioral disorders and affect dysregulation were more sensitive to treatment than interpersonal functioning. Social skills were not affected. These findings suggest that low-dose risperidone may have a positive effect on the clinical outcome in young children with PDD in the short-term as well as long-term.

Hollander et al. (2003) also evaluated the use of risperidone with preschoolers who had severe behavior problems. This study concluded that risperidone was effective in reducing irritability, repetitive movements, and hyperactivity. They noted there were no significant improvements in social withdrawal or inappropriate speech. Another atypical antipsychotic, olanzapine (Zyprexa) produced a modest decrease in disruptive behaviors (Hollander, Phillips, & Yeh, 2003). The main side effect reported for these atypical antipsychotics was weight gain.

Hollander et al. (2003) also reported the effectiveness of other categories of prescription medications for autism: mood stabilizers, and SSRIs. The mood stabilizers, valproate

(Depakene) and levetiracetam (Keppra) were found to decrease aggression, labile mood, and impulsive behaviors. In patients diagnosed with mild autism and a family history of manic depression, lithium was reported beneficial.

In noncontrolled and retrospective studies, some of the SSRIs were associated with a reduction in symptoms (Hollander et al., 2003). For example, in adult autistic patients, fluvoxamine (Luvox) and sertraline (Zoloft) were associated with improvement in repetitive thoughts and behavior, aggression, social skills, and language. Decreased inattention, hyperactive and repetitive behaviors, and social skill deficit, along with improved communication skills, were associated with low doses of venlafaxine (Effexor). Overall, the SSRIs were found to be more effective in reducing symptoms associated with the mood disorders and obsessive-compulsive disorder.

To summarize, while there are no medications designed to specifically treat pervasive developmental disorders, there are medications that are used to treat many of the "symptoms," or behavioral manifestations associated with these disorders. The following summarizes the typical categories of medications for behavioral and psychiatric problems:

Hyperactivity, Inattention, and Impulsivity
Psychostimulants
Alpha-adrenergics
Atypical antipsychotics

Aggression and Irritability
SSRIs
Alpha-adrenergics
Beta blockers
Mood stabilizers
Atypical antipsychotics

Preoccupations, Rituals, Compulsions
SSRIs

Depression
SSRIs
TCAs

Alternative Treatments

Levy and Hyman (2002) reviewed alternative medicine options used to address symptoms of AS. Complementary and alternative medicines have not been validated through research. However, there is popular belief and widespread use of alternative treatments. For example, several vitamins are commonly used. Secretin, alkaline salts, Bethanecol, Pepcid, and other medications are used despite objective data disproving their effectiveness.

To illustrate, a gastrointestinal dysfunction theory for AS and PDD suggests a possible yeast overgrowth resulting in probiotic therapy where bacteria living in the gastrointestinal tract are replaced with other benign organisms or treated with antibiotics to eliminate a large number of gut bacteria. The use of antifungals has not been examined for efficacy in clinical trials. The gluten-free/casein-free diet may be the most commonly used nonmedication treatment attempted. However, families often do not implement the diet correctly with total elimination of gluten and casein. Since many AS children have gastrointestinal symptoms, and many parents report changes in affect and attention, it is hard to disregard these claims. However, efficacy studies are flawed due to lack of valid outcome measures, presence of confounding treatments, and no placebo controls.

The theory supporting chelation suggests that heavy metal intoxication, especially mercury, is responsible for the regressive form of autism. Protocols for chelation treatment in children with AS have been proposed and are being implemented by practitioners without controlled scientific studies to measure their efficacy for changes in symptoms of AS. Recent studies have not confirmed chelation's efficacy in producing changes in developmental function in children with documented lead intoxication. Nonbiologic treatments are also used despite the lack of evidence-based studies to support or disprove their efficacy. These treatments include auditory integration, facilitated communication, and craniosacral manipulation.

EVIDENCE-BASED PREVENTION APPROACHES

With our current understanding of AS and PDD, it is doubtful that in the near future we will be able to prevent AS/PDD. Rather, our interest in this section is focused on promoting conditions in which these young people may lead healthy, fulfilling, and productive lives. For children between the ages of 5 and 12 this objective involves focusing on school and home environments.

What Works

No program was identified that met the inclusion criteria of three successful trials.

What Might Work

Success in the classroom promotes a child's healthy development. The instructional methods that follow were tested at The Learning Clinic with students diagnosed with according to DSM-IV criteria, male and female in a ratio of 8 to 1, of adolescent age, and demonstrating a dual diagnosis that included attention deficit disorder, depression, anxiety disorder, specific learning disability, obsessive-compulsive disorder, and aggressive patterns of behavior. All the students demonstrated normal to gifted intelligence quotients as measured by the WISC-R.[2]

Instructional Setting

The "open" vs. "closed" environmental influence on social learning and compliant behavior is described by Tharpe and Wetzel (1969) in their examination of the variables connected to behavior modification in the natural environment. Open environments require self-regulation of transitions, interactions with others, and movement in space. Closed environments provide external control over behavioral options, number and type of transitions, preplanned schedules, social and instruction prompts, and degrees of personal freedom earned through reinforcement menus based on standards for performance.

Optimal Teaching Environment

Behavioral standards and choices designed for students with AS and PDD should be limited, precise, and based on self-regulation ability. A closed environment is more effective for instruction and social skill development than an open environment.

Class size. TLC students report a relationship between the task, the size of the instructional group, and the rate of learning with an increase in difficulty as the group size increases (DuCharme & McGrady, 2002).

Optimal teaching environment. Our experience suggests that the optimal group size is over three students but under 10. One-on-one instruction, in tutorial format is preferable to introduce new, complex cognitive material, and to monitor the acquisition rate and retention of skills.

Environmental Structure

The student with an AS diagnosis requires a cohesive, precise educational structure. The student's success depends on the way in which the structure of the child's experience at school is defined and communicated. A whole school approach is designed to coordinate expectations, standards of conduct, sanctions, and student-staff roles across settings. This appears beneficial when designed on the basis of the student's developmental needs (Grace, 1998).

Optimal teaching environment. Cues and prompts are needed to maintain the student's perception of the structure designed for him. Guided instruction is optimal for successful task completion.

- Daily plans and standards for self-monitoring their performance during and at the completion of an academic task is reported as helpful by students.
- Checklists and digital devices (organizers) provide prompts and reminders that assist students in keeping schedules.
- Assigned work stations, individual computers, prewritten daily plans, and schedules for each student serve as prompts.
- Peer-coaching or tutorial guide student performance with text or script for additional guidance.
- Icons and ideograms illustrate steps needed to perform tasks.

Discipline

The need for a reliable system of discipline is important. It is our experience that students with AS want to know the rules. They want rules to be consistently applied. They want the whole school to have the same rules, standards, and sanctions. These young people often are described as the junior attorneys of the school. They quickly recognize violations of rules in others that go unpunished but can explain how their behavior doesn't quite fit the description of a violation. The authors have developed and employed a behavior management flow chart that is used in all parts of the TLC program (school, residence, and home environments). A written manual explains the use of the flow chart for staff, students, and parents.

The effectiveness of a flow chart is noted in the clarity of direction given to students, the time allowed to understand the direction, and the consequences. The clarity of direction states what the student is to do. The direction is precise, brief, and within the response repertoire of the child. Then, at least 10 seconds are given for the student to process the request and to respond. This 10-second time for response is based on work that measured response latencies for children of different development ages when given verbal learning tasks (DuCharme, 1972). The use of the flow chart results in consistent improvement in compliance and decreases the need for negative consequences.

The teacher's ability to wait a sufficient amount of time for a student to process a request and to respond is critical to the student's ability to comply with the request. We have observed students who had been defined as "elective mute". The mute behavior is indicative of the student's inability to respond within the time allowed by the teacher. The child may require more time to formulate and express a response than is allowed. In such cases, the child is not mute. He simply requires more time than the teacher typically allows him to answer.

Optimal teaching environment. A precise, reliable, school wide behavior management system in combination with clear verbal directions and sufficient time allowed for response is best for students with AS.

Student Classroom Mix

The mix of other students in the classroom is important. The diagnosis of Asperger syndrome, even with comorbidity, is compatible with some diagnostic groups and not others. First, the comorbidity associated with an AS diagnosis determines inclusion criteria. Analysis of the mix of AS students with students who have other disabilities raises certain questions. Is the ratio of diagnosed to nondiagnosed students discernable to the teacher? If so, is the teacher able to teach children within the range of diagnoses? Can students who have medical issues be served given the mix of clinical issues? Is the student intelligence quotient a factor for inclusion or exclusion in the class?

Students with AS are diagnosed within a normal to gifted intellectual range. The instructional methods and curricula for a student with an IQ of 70 are profoundly different from those for students with a 136 quotient. Students with AS do not perform well socially or academically in classes with students diagnosed with conduct disorders, disruptive, or aggressive behaviors. The student with AS is intimidated or exploited by students who are prone to victimize their more vulnerable peers.

Optimal teaching environment. The absence of students who have below average IQ, conduct disorder, acting out/aggressive behavior is optimal for a student with an AS diagnosis in the classroom.

Teacher-to-Student Ratio

The teacher-to-student ratio depends upon a number of variables such as type, size, and kind of task, number of classroom distractions, clinical issues, and level of skill that the student is able to demonstrate. The range of options for instructional ratios also depends upon school resources. The optimal group size for general instruction is over three and under 10 students. But within that range, it must be noted, that the preferred ratio is one-to-one when new information, instructional strategy, or novel application is to be taught.

Optimal teaching environment. One-to-one tutorial instruction is best for the student with AS in the classroom in new situations. At other times a three to 10 class of students is ideal.

Instructional Methods

The tendency to misread social cues makes students with AS vulnerable to teaching methods using collaboration. These students best benefit from methods that are consistent, reliable, impersonal, individually paced, and interesting. This approach accounts for the absence of desire for social interaction and avoidance of social interaction with many children with AS—the misperception of social cues; the pragmatic deficits and decrease in competence with complex and abstract levels of language processing requirements; the preference for picture cues and ideograms; the restricted, repetitive patterns of behavior; the language processing difficulties; and expressive language response latency; the resistance to criticism and performance evaluation by teachers and others; the sensory overload response to loud noise, too much verbal information, textual material with a "dense" level of content, unregulated pace of questioning, and short time interval in response requirement; the negative responses to personal judgments of correct-incorrect performance; and the deficits in short-term memory and recall of previously learned material.

Optimal teaching environment. The methodology to best address the issues listed above is academic task presentation through computer-assisted instruction (CAI). Such instruction provides:

- Consistent format
- Reliable mode and pace of presentation of tasks
- Progressive increases in task complexity based on
- Performance evidence
- Rapid, contingent, correct-incorrect response feedback and scoring
- Controlled learning pace
- Impersonal presentation and assessment
- Motivation based on interests of AS students
- A controlled pace for reading text to the student

The computer-assisted tutorial format has been effective for students with AS over a 20-year period at TLC based on individual (single subject) performance reviewed weekly and quarterly as measured by an 80% criterion.

Academic Curricula Strategies

Jordan (2005) discusses several school barriers and ways in which professionals can better meet the needs of AS children. Sarcasm should be avoided because children with AS often take comments for the face value and do not look for an alternative meaning. "Street language" and appropriate slang should be included in the curriculum, since this is a requirement if AS children are to understand and interact with peers. Many children with AS are visual learners and are more compliant when provided with visual stimuli.

Maione and Mirenda (2006) found video modeling effective in increasing social language in two of three activities. In the third activity, video, feedback, and prompting was required. A study by Hagiwara and Myles (1999) revealed that overall the social story intervention using a multimedia social story program for three boys with autism was effective. However, there was no consistent effect between participants of the multimedia social story intervention. The use of computer activity schedules can be helpful in teaching how to manage work, play, and skill building independently (Stromer, Kimball, Kinney, & Taylor, 2006).

Teacher's Behavior

The teacher's interpersonal style clearly is related to the student's success in the classroom. Asperger syndrome students benefit from teachers who are calm, clear, and positive in their communication. Such teachers demonstrate the following:

Directness in communicating expectations and performance results avoids the problem of misunderstanding. Directness also decreases the need to revise messages, repeat directions, or correct student responses.

A *nonjudgmental* approach to student behavior is critical. Students with AS often react negatively to being told what they do wrong. The focus on "what to do" rather than "what was done wrong" is most productive. A calm, low-key personal demeanor has a reassuring and calming effect on student behavior. The teacher who is precise, relevant to the student's interests, organized, and consistent has fewer problems with students with AS. Further, student productivity rises in nonjudgmental settings.

The most effective teachers are those who focus on positive behavior and on behaviors that, if demonstrated by the student, will compete with or replace problem behaviors. Allowing negative or task-irrelevant behavior to occur is risky for both teacher and student. Learning a replacement behavior or corrective action is more difficult than practicing a correct response from the start.

Optimal. Much better, in our experience, is a "backward" chain task analysis. Demonstrate the correct answer, solution, or sequence of steps from the desired result to the first step. Provide the student with a model of the correct answer and then teach the components.

Task Design and Academic Risk

The complexity of the task and the requirements of answering questions are variables that risk the student's success. Noncompliance and symptoms of perseveration, rigidity, oppositionality, and "anxiety" may be a response to a transition, especially if the transition is out of the ordinary routine and is not well rehearsed in advance.

Optimal. Take the needed time to rehearse the student by explaining the need for a transition. State precisely how and when the transition will be made. Allow sufficient time for rehearsal prior to the transition. Maintain continuity during rehearsal, the transition, and the completion of the transition. A staff "coach" should have the role to support transitions with rehearsal.

Before presenting a question the teacher should consider: What are the parts of a multilevel question? What is the cognitive level required by the vocabulary in the question? What is the student to infer that the answer requires? The cognitive "load" of the question is important and must fit the student's level of ability (Bloom, 1964). The structure of the question, the student's preassessed knowledge, and exposure to evaluation and judgment are risk factors to control and to gradually increase. Response modes available to the student may add or detract from risk. If a written response is required, and a time limit is placed on the answer, the risk is increased. If the student must read an answer aloud, additional risk is present.

Too much risk will prevent a student from demonstrating skills and abilities. The lack of an answer may not signify a lack of knowledge, but rather the student's inability to answer a question with the level of risk present. The manner in which the teacher enables the student to develop a tolerance for academic risk may vary. But the principle is the same: Taking academic risks is a skill and can be taught.

The teacher's level of sensitivity and creativity cannot be overestimated as an influence on the student's success. To illustrate, we once observed a teacher speaking quietly, almost secretly, with a student who had a distressed look on his face. The child stated that a scary movie about two girls would not leave his mind. The child said that he could not do his work. The teacher took an empty plastic container that had previously held a cookie and calmly said, "When the scary thought comes into your mind, then blow it into this box and cover it with the lid." The boy blew into the box and calmly reported to his teacher that, "It works!" How blessed that child was to have that instructor.

Optimal. Control the level of academic risk in task design. When matching a teacher to a student with an AS diagnosis, stress the importance of an organized, calm, reliable, and creative approach.

Classroom Routine

At TLC the expectation is that each student, given an appropriate task and curricula, will complete 26 graded assignments to a minimum standard of 80% correct each academic quarter. Academic performance is self-paced and governed by the completion of designated objectives, not by time spent in class.

With the teacher's help, each student establishes a daily schedule of academic subjects with time allotted and specific objectives for each subject. Academic performance is assessed by the end of each day, and a plan for the next day is started.

The number of assignments to be completed each day is recorded as well as the number of assignments that are incomplete and do not meet the 80% standard criterion. Higher-level cognitive material requires a higher standard of 90%. The number of assignments and number of times assignments are redone to meet criteria is also recorded. The teacher adjusts the number of assignments per subject each day to ensure a practical expectation for performance. Assignments are adjusted according to ability level.

The student is given time in the schedule to select topics and tasks of interest. Opportunity for collaborative activity with selected peers and other adults is part of the student schedule. No homework is required other than reading or independent nongraded researches based on student interest. Note taking in class is rarely a requirement.

A balance is necessary between tutorial instruction and collaborative learning. Most important is the teacher's opportunity to schedule focused dialogues with each student. Talking about their writing, music, and art are important to students who are developing a pattern to externalize their thought and to consider the responses of others.

Optimal. Classrooms should provide the flexibility essential to establishing a climate of achievement success for the student with AS.

Transitions

Transitions are the changes in locations, attention, and responses to tasks that are required of a student. Consider the transitions required by using a different course textbook, work books, teachers' interpersonal styles, methods, and daily movements of students between classes. It reveals hundreds of changes each day. If a child's symptom profile includes decreases in competencies and self-regulation during these transitions, then we have created too many changes for the child. Programs with significant numbers and types of transitions are not easily negotiated by many children with AS.

The teacher should assess the degree of self-regulation expected of the student in the classroom. Expectations may change from one setting to another during and after transitions. Consider expectations of self-regulation along a continuum of supervision by staff, from continuous supervision to 90% supervision, then 80%, 70%, 50%, 25%, and finally none. The behavior of the student at different locations, during different activities, and at different times with different instructional groups provides the information needed to select the right level of supervision.

Optimal. During transitions the teacher must provide 80% to 90% supervision unless the data indicate that it is not needed. The decision about the level of supervision is best made by direct staff observation during various activities at different times. Such decisions should not be based solely on the student's report of incidents. It should be noted that noncompliance and symptoms of perseveration, rigidity, oppositionality, and "anxiety" may be a response to a request for a transition, especially when the transition is not well rehearsed. Teachers must take the time to rehearse the student by explaining the need for a transition and the steps to follow. Allow sufficient time prior to the transition for rehearsal, but maintain continuity in time from the rehearsal through the transition to its completion. A staff "coach" should have the role of easing transitions by necessary rehearsal.

Family Assistance

Earlier we referenced the work of Beardslee and his associates (1993) with easing the distress of families with a seriously mentally ill family member. For many families the child with AS is very stressful. Understanding the disorder and finding social support within and outside the family not only is beneficial for child with AS but for other family members as well.

What Doesn't Work

No program met the criteria for inclusion.

SUGGESTED BEST PRACTICE

Asperger syndrome and pervasive developmental disorders are lifelong conditions. The effects of specific symptom manifestation at different developmental stages are important to identify because early identification is essential for early diagnosis and treatment. The corresponding treatment, environmental modification, education, and medication adjustment to changing symptom profiles are important because AS is not a static condition. As changes occur in the performance and abilities of the child with AS appropriate service and treatment options need to be available to the child and his family.

Currently, treatment approaches using CBT or ABA show promising results. While medications cannot cure AS or PDD, they can provide relief from troubling behaviors that interfere with the child's ability to reach his full potential.

At the present time there is no preventive intervention for AS or the PDDs. Rather, attention is directed at promoting environmental conditions at home and in the school that maximize the child's ability to succeed.

NOTES

1. Chunking. The process of reorganizing materials in working memory to increase the number of items successfully recalled.
2. During a 10-year period 150 Asperger students were referred for services because of school failure, school avoidance, and clinical issues. All the students were identified through the IDEA procedures and standards in order to be eligible for special services and meet section 504 criteria.

REFERENCES

Aman, C. J., Roberts, Jr., R. J., & Pennington, B. F. (1998). A neuropsychological examination of the underlying deficit in attention deficit hyperactivity disorder: Frontal lobe versus right parietal lobe theories. *Developmental Psychology, 34*(5), 956–969.

American Psychiatric Association. (1994). *Diagnostic and statistical manual of mental disorders* (4th ed.). Washington, D.C.: Author.

Asperger, H. (1991). In U. Frith (Trans. & Ed.), *Autism and Asperger syndrome* (pp. 37–92). Cambridge: Cambridge University Press. (Translation of Die "autistischen Psychopathen" im Kindesalter. *Archiv fur Psychiatric und Nervenkrankheiten, 117*, 76–136; original work published 1944)

Baron-Cohen, S., O'Riordan, M., Stone, V., Jones, R., & Plaisted, K. (1999). Recognition of faux pas by normally developing children and children with Asperger syndrome or high-functioning autism. *Journal of Autism and Developmental Disorders, 29*(5), 407–418.

Barnhill, G. P. (2001). What's new in AS research: A synthesis of research conducted by the Asperger Syndrome Project. *Intervention in School and Clinic, 36*(5), 300–305.

Barnhill, G. P., & Myles, B. S. (2001). Attributional style and depression in adolescents with Asperger syndrome. *Journal of Positive BehaviorInterventions, 3*(3), 175–182.

Barton, M., & Volkmar, F. (1998). How commonly are known medical conditions associated with autism? *Journal of Autism and Developmental Disorders, 28*(4), 273–278.

Beardslee, W. R., Salt, P., Porterfield, K., Rothberg, P. C., van der Velde, P., Swatling, S., et al. (1993). Comparison of preventative interventions for families with parental affective disorder. *Journal of the American Academy of Child and Adolescent Psychiatry, 32*, 254–263.

Beversdorf, D. Q., Manning, S. E., Hillier, A., Anderson, S. L., Nordgren, R. E., Walters, S. E., et al. (2005). Timing of prenatal stressors and autism. *Journal of Autism and Developmental Disorders, 35*(4), 471–478.

Bishop, D. V. M., Maybery, M., Maley, A., Wong, D., Hill, W., & Hallmayer, J. (2004). Using self-report to identify the broad phenotype in parents of children with Autistic Spectrum Quotient. *Journal of Child Psychology and Psychiatry,* Nov *45*(8) 1431-6.

Blacher, J. (2002). Autism rising: Delivering services without draining parents and school systems. *Exceptional Parent Magazine, 32*(10), 94–97.

Bloom, B. S. (1956). *"Taxonomy of Educational Objectives."* Handbook I: Cognitive Domain. New York: David McKay.

Bloom, B. S. (ed.) (1964) *"Taxonomy of Educational Objectives"* (For measurement of awareness, values, etc.) Handbook II: Affective Domain. New York: David McKay.

Casanova, M. F., Buzhoeveden, D. P., Switala, A. E., & Roy, E. (2002). Asperger's syndrome and cortical neuropathology. *Journal of Child Neurology, 17*(2),142–145.

Channon, S., Charman, T., Heap, J., Crawford, C., & Rios, P. (2001). Real-life-type problem-solving in Asperger's syndrome. *Journal of Autism & Developmental Disorders, 3*(5), 461–469.

Courchesne, E., Townsend, J., Akshoomoff, N. A., Saitoh, O., Yeung Courchesne, R., Lincoln, A., et al. (1994). Impairment in shifting attention in autistic and cerebellar patients. *Behavioral Neuroscience, 108*(5), 848–865.

Coutinho, A. M., Oliveira, G., Morgadinho, T., Fesel, C., Macedo, T. R., Bento, C., et al. (2004). Variants of the serotonin transporter gene (SLC6A4) significantly contribute to hyperserotonemia in autism. *Molecular Psychiatry, 9,* 264–271.

Craig, J., & Baron-Cohen, S. (1999). Creativity and imagination in autism and Asperger syndrome. *Journal of Autism & Developmental Disorders, 29*(4), 314–326.

de Leon, M. J., Munoz, R. J., & Pieo, S. E. (1986). Is there a right-hemisphere dysfunction in Asperger's syndrome? *British Journal of Psychiatry, 148,* 745–756.

DeNoon, D. (2007). New autism gene doubles risk. *WebMD Medical News.* http://www.webmd.com

Dewey, M. (1991). Living with Asperger's syndrome. In U. Frith (Ed.), *Autism and Asperger syndrome* (pp. 184–206). New York: Cambridge University Press.

Dixon-Salazar, T. J., Keeler, L. C., Trauner, D. A., & Gleeson, J. G. (2003). Autism in several members of a family with generalized epilepsy with febrile seizures. *Journal of Child Neurology, 19*(8), 597–603.

Dor-Shav, N. K., & Horowitz, Z. (1984). Intelligence and personality variables of parents of autistic children. *The Journal of Genetic Psychology, 144,* 39–50.

DuCharme, R. W. (1972). *Sight word acquisition program.* Unpublished doctoral dissertation, University of Connecticut, Storrs, CT.

DuCharme, R. W., & McGrady, K. (2002). Social skill training and pragmatic skill assessment for Asperger's disorder or high functioning autism. Paper presented at the International Child & Adolescent Conference XI, Miami, FL.

DuCharme, R. W., & McGrady, K. (2003). *Promoting the healthy development of children with Asperger syndrome: Education and life skills issues.* New London, CT: Connecticut College,

DuCharme, R. W., & McGrady, K. (2004). What is Asperger syndrome? In *Asperger syndrome: A guide for professionals and families* (pp. 1–20). New York: Kluwer Academic/Plenum.

Dunn, W., Myles, B. S., & Orr, S. (2002). Sensory processing issues associated with Asperger syndrome: A preliminary investigation. *The American Journal of Occupational Therapy, 56*(1), 97–102.

Dyer, K., Kneringer, M. J., & Luce, S. C. (1996). An efficient method of ensuring program quality for adults with developmental disabilities in community-based apartments. *Consulting Psychology Journal: Practice & Research, 48*(3), 171 [summary].

Ehlers, S., Gillberg, C. (1993). The epidemiology of Asperger syndrome: A total population study. *Journal of Child Psychology & Psychiatry & Allied Disciplines, 34*(8), 1327–1350.

Ehlers, S., Nyden, A., Gillberg, C., Sandberg, A., Dahlgren, S., Hjelmquist, E., et al. (1997). Asperger syndrome, autism and attention disorders: A comparative study of the cognitive profiles of 120 children. *Journal of Child Psychology & Psychiatry & Allied Disciplines, 38*(2), 207–217.

Eisenmajer, R., Prior, M., Leekam, S., Wing, L., Gould, J., Welham, M., et al. (1996). Comparison of clinical symptoms in autism and Asperger's disorder. *Journal of the Academy of Child & Adolescent Psychiatry, 35*(11), 1523–1531.

Engstrom, H. A., Ohlson, S., Stubbs, E. G., Maciulis, A., Caldwell, V., Odell, J. D., et al. (2003). Decreased expression of CD95 (Fas/APO-1) on CD4+ T-lymphocytes from participants with autism. *Journal of Developmental and Physical Disabilities, 15*(2), 155–163.

Frith, U. (1991). *Autism and Asperger syndrome.* New York: Cambridge University Press.

Frith, U., & Happe, F. (1994). Autism: Beyond "theory of mind." *Cognition, 50,* 115–132.

Gagliano, A., Germano, E., Pustorino, G., Impallomeni, C., D'Arrigo, C., Calamoneri, F., et al. (2004). Risperidone treatment of children with autistic disorder: Effectiveness, tolerability, and pharmacokinetic implications. *Journal of Child Adolescent Psychopharmacology,* Spring *14*(1), 39–47.

Gharani, N., Benayed, R., Mancuso, V., Brzustowicz, L. M., & Millonig, J. H. (2004). Association of the homeobox transcription factor, ENGRAILED 2, 3, with autism spectrum disorder. *Molecular Psychiatry, 9,* 474–484.

Ghaziuddin, M., & Butler, E. (1998). Clumsiness in autism and Asperger syndrome: A further report. *Journal of Intellectual Disability Research, 42*(1), 43–48.

Ghaziuddin, M., Butler, E., Tsai, L., & Ghaziuddin, N. (1994). Is clumsiness a marker for Asperger syndrome? *Journal of Intellectual Disability Research, 38*(5), 519–527.

Gilchrist, A., Green, J., Cox, A., Burton, D., Rutter, M., & Le Couteur, A. (2001). Development and current functioning in adolescents with Asperger syndrome: A comparative study. *Journal of Child Psychology & Psychiatry & Allied Disciplines, 42,* 227–240.

Grace, D. (1998, May). The inclusion of students with emotional or behavioral disorders: What we know about effective and non-effective practices. Paper presented at the Council for Children with Behavior Disorders, South East Regional Conference, Gulf Shores, AL.

Green, D., Baird, G., Barnett, A. L., Henderson, L., Huber, J., & Henderson, S. E. (2002). The severity and nature of motor impairment in Asperger's syndrome: A comparison with specific developmental disorders of motor function. *Journal of Child Psychology & Psychiatry & Allied Disciplines, 43*(5), 655–668.

Grossman, J. B., Klin, A., Carter, A. S., & Volkmar, F. R. (2000). Verbal bias in recognition of facial emotions in children with Asperger syndrome. *Journal of Child Psychology & Psychiatry & Applied Disciplines*, 41:369-379.

Gupta, A. R., & State, M. W. (2007). Recent Advances in the Genetics of Autism. *Biological Psychiatry, 61*(4), 429–437.

Hagiwara, T., & Myles, B. S. (1999). A multimedia social story intervention: Teaching skills to children with autism. *Focus on Autism and Other Developmental Disabilities, 14*(2), 82–95. [Summary]

Happe, F. G. E. (1995). The role of age and verbal ability in the theory of mind task performance of subjects with autism. *Child Development, 66*, 843–855.

Hilt, R. J. (2006). Autistic spectrum disorders. Retrieved from: http://www.emedicine.com/med/topic3202.htm

Hollander, E., Phillips, A., & Yeh, C. (2003, August 30). Targeted treatments for symptom domains in child and adolescent autism. *Lancet*; *362*, 732–734.

Jensen, V. K., & Sinclair, L. V. (2002). Treatment of autism in young children: Behavioral intervention and applied behavior analysis. *Infants and Young Children, 14*(4), 42–52.

Joliffe, T., & Baron-Cohen, S. (2000). Linguistic processing in high-functioning adults with autism or Asperger's syndrome. Is global coherence impaired? *Psychological Medicine, 30*, 1169–1187.

Jordan, R. (2005). Managing autism and Asperger's syndrome in current educational provision. *Pediatric Psychology Review, 28*(4), 576–594.

Kanner, L. (1943). Autistic disturbance of affective contact. *Nervous Child, 2*, 217–250.

Klin, A., & Volkmar, F. R. (1997). Asperger's syndrome. In D. J. Cohen & F. R. Volkmar (Eds.), *Handbook of autism and pervasive developmental disorders* (2nd ed., pp. 94–112). New York: Wiley.

Klin, A., Volkmar, F., & Sparrow, S. (2000). *Asperger syndrome.* New York: Guilford.

Klin, A., Volkmar, F. R., Sparrow, S. S., & Cicchetti, D. V. (1995). Validity and neuropsychological characterization of Asperger Syndrome: Convergence with nonverbal learning disabilities syndrome. *Journal of Child Psychology & Psychiatry & Applied Disciplines, 36*(7), 1127–1140.

Konstantareas, M. M., & Homatidis, S. (1999). Chromosomal abnormalities in a series of children with autistic disorder. *Journal of Autism and Developmental Disorders, 29*(4), 275–285.

Lauritsen, M. B., Pedersen, C. B., & Mortensen, P. B. (2005). Effects of familial risk factors and place of birth on the risk of autism: A nationwide register-based study. *Journal of Child Psychology and Psychiatry, 46*(9), 963–971.

Levy, S., & Hyman, S. (2002). Alternative/complementary approaches to treatment of children with autistic spectrum disorders. *Infants and Young Children, 14*(3),33–42.

Maione, L., & Mirenda, P. (2006). Effects of video modeling and video feedback on peer-directed social language skills of children with autism. *Journal of Positive Behavior Interventions, 21*(1), 14–24.

Manjiviona, J., & Prior, M. (1999). Neuropsychological profiles of children with Asperger syndrome and autism. *Autism, 3*(4), 327–356.

Masi, G., Cosenza, A., Mucci, M., & Brovedani, P. (2003, September). A 3-year naturalistic study of 53 preschool children with pervasive developmental disorders treated with resperidone. *Journal of Clinical Psychiatry, 64*, 1039–1047. (From the Scientific Institute of Child Neurology and Psychiatry, Calambrone, Italy.)

Matthews, A. (1996). Employment training and the development of a support model within employment for adults who experience Asperger syndrome and autism: The Gloucestershire Group Homes Model. In H. Morgan (Ed.), *Adults with autism: A guide to theory and practice* (pp. 163–184). New York: Cambridge University Press.

Mawhood, L., & Howlin, P. (1999). The outcome of a supported employment scheme for high-functioning adults with autism or Asperger syndrome. *Autism, 3*(3), 229–254.

McDougle, C. J., Scahill, L., Aman, M. G., McCracken, J. T., Tierney, E., Arnold. L. E., et al. (2005). Risperidone for the core symptom domains of autism: results from the study by the Autism Network of the Research Units on Pediatric Psychopharmacology. *American Journal of Psychiatry, 162*, 1142–1148.

Merriam-Webster (1990). *Webster's ninth new collegiate dictionary.* Springfield, MA: Author.

Mesibov, G. B., Shea, V., & Adams, L.W. (2001). *Understanding Asperger syndrome and high functioning autism.* New York: Kluwer Academic/Plenum.

Michaelis, R. C., Copeland-Yates, S. A., Sossey-Alaoui, K., Skinner, C., Friez, M. J., & Longshore, J. W. (2000). The HOPA gene dodecamer duplication is not a significant etiological factor in autism. *Journal of Autism and Developmental Disorders, 30*(4), 355–358.

Miles, J. H., Takahashi, T. N., Haber, A., & Hadden, L. (2003). Autism families with a high incidence of alcoholism. *Journal of Autism and Developmental Disorders,33*(4), 403–415.

Minshew, N. J., Goldstein, G., & Siegel, D. J. (1995). Speech and language in high-functioning autistic individuals. *Neuropsychology, 9*(2) 255–261.

Miyahara, M., Tsujii, M., Hori, M., Nakanishi, K., Kageyama, H., & Sugiyama, T. (1997). Motor incoordination in children with Asperger syndrome and learning disabilities. *Journal of Autism & Developmental Disorders, 27*(5), 595–603.

Molloy, C. A., Keddache, M., & Martin, L. J. (2005). Evidence for linkage on 21q and 7q in a subset of autism characterized by development regression. *Molecular Psychiatry, 10,* 741–746.

Morris, R. G., Rowe, A., Fox, N., Feigenbaum, J. D., Miotto, E. C., & Howlin, P. (1999). Spatial working memory in Asperger's syndrome and in patients with focal frontal and temporal lobe lesions. *Brain & Cognition, 41*(1), 9–26.

Nesbitt, S. (2000). Why and why not? Factors influencing employment for individuals with Asperger syndrome. *Autism, 4*(4), 357–369.

Nurmi, E. L., Amin, T., Olson, L. M., Jacobs, M. M., McCauley, J. L., Lam, A.Y., et al. (2003). Dense linkage disequilibrium mapping in the 15q11-q13 maternal expression domain yields evidence for association in autism. *Molecular Psychiatry, 8,* 624–634.

Oktem, F., Diren, B., Karaagaoglu, E., & Anlar, B. (2000). Functional magnetic resonance imaging in children with Asperger's syndrome. *Journal of Child Neurology, 16*(4), 253–256.

Ozonoff, S., South, M., & Miller, J. (2000). DSM-IV defined Asperger syndrome: Cognitive, behavioral and early history differentiation from high-functioning autism. *Autism: The International Journal of Research and Practice, 4,* 29–46.

Perner, J., & Wimmer, H. (1985). "John thinks that Mary thinks that...." Attribution of second-order beliefs by 5–10 year old children. *Journal of Experimental Child Psychology, 39,* 437–471.

Raja, M. & Azzoni, A. (2001). Asperger's disorder in the emergency psychiatric setting. *General Hospital Psychiatry, 23,* 285–293.

Reichenberg, A., Gross, R., Weiser, M., Bresnahan, M., Silverman, J., Harlap, S., et al. (2006). Advancing paternal age and autism. *Archives of GeneralPsychiatry, 53,* 1026–1032.

Rogers, T., Kalaydjieva, L., Hallmayer, J., Petersen, P.B., Nicholas, P., Pingree, C., et al. (1999). Exclusion of linkage to the HLA region in ninety multiplex sibships with autism. *Journal of Autism and Developmental Disorders, 29*(3), 195–201.

Ronald, A., Happé F., Bolton, P., Butcher, L. M., Price, T. S., Wheelwright, et al. (2006). Genetic heterogeneity between the three components of the autism spectrum: A twin study. *Journal of the American Academy of Child and Adolescent Psychiatry, 45*(6), 691–699.

Ronald, A., Happé, F., & Plomin, R. (2005). The genetic relationship between individual differences in social and nonsocial behaviours characteristic of autism. *Developmental Science, 8*(5), 444–458.

Rourke, B. P. (1995). *Syndrome of nonverbal learning disabilities.* New York: Guilford.

Rourke, B. P., Fisk, J. L., & Strang, J. D. (1983). *Child neurophyschology: An introduction to theory, research, and clinical practice.* New York: Guilford.

Salmond, C. H., Ashburner, J., Connelly, A., Friston, K., Gadian, D. G., & Vargha-Khadem, F. (2005). The role of the medial temporal lobe in autistic spectrum disorders. *European Journal of Neuroscience, 22,* 764–772.

Santosh, P. J., & Baird, G. (2001). Pharmacotherapy of target symptoms in autistic spectrum disorders. *Indian Journal of Pediatrics, 68*(5), 427–431.

Schopler, E. Mesibov, G. B., & Kunce, L. j. (1998). *Asperger syndrome or high-functioning autism?* New York: Plenum Press.

Schultz, R. T., Romanski, L. M., & Tsatsanis, K. D. (2000). Neurofunctional models of autistic disorder and Asperger syndrome: Clues from neuroimaging. In A. Klin & F. R. Volkmar (Eds.), *Asperger syndrome* (pp. 172–209).

Serajee, F. J., Nabi, R., Zhong, H., & Huq, A. H. M. M. (2003). Polymorphisms in xenobiotic metabolism genes and autism. *Journal of Child Neurology, 19*(6), 413–417.

Shriberg, L. D., Paul, R., McSweeny, J. L., Klin, A., & Cohen, D. J. (2001). Speech and prosody characteristics of adolescents and adults with high-functioning autism and Asperger syndrome. *Journal of Speech, Language, & Hearing Research, 44*(5), 1097–1115.

Shulman, C., Yirmiya, N., & Greenbaum, C. W. (1995). From categorization to classification: A comparison among individuals with a retardation, and normal development. *Journal of Abnormal Psychology, 104*(4), 601–609.

Sigirci, A., Alkan, A., Kutlu, R., & Gulcan, H. (2005). The human secretin gene in children with autistic spectrum disorders: Screening for polymorphisms and mutations. *Journal of Child Neurology, 20*(8), 701–704.

Skaar, D. A., Shao, Y., Haines, J. L., Stenger, J. E., Jaworski, J. Martin, E. R., et al. (2005). Analysis of the RELN gene as a genetic risk factor for autism. *Molecular Psychiatry, 10,* 563–571.

Sofronoff, K., Attwood, T., & Hinton, S. A. (2005). A randomized controlled trial of a CBT intervention for anxiety in children with Asperger syndrome. *Journal of Child Psychology and Psychiatry, 46*(11), 1152–1160.

Stromer, R., Kimball, J. W., Kinney, E. M., & Taylor, B. A. (2006). Activity schedules, computer technology, and teaching children with autism spectrum disorders. *Focus of Autism and Other Developmental Disabilities, 21*(1), 14–24.

Tantam, D. (2000). Adolescence and adulthood of individuals with Asperger syndrome. *Asperger Syndrome,* 367–399.

Tharpe, R. G. & Wetzel, R. J. (1969). *Behavior modification in the natural environment.* New York: Academic Press.

Valicenti-McDermott, M., McVicar, K., Rapin, I., Wershil, H. C., Cohen, H., & Shinnar, S. (2006). Frequency of gastrointestinal symptoms in children with autistic spectrum disorders and association with family history of autoimmune disease. *Journal of Developmental & Behavioral Pediatrics, 27*(Suppl. 2), S128-S136.

Volkmar, F. R., Lord, C., Bailey, A., Schultz, R. T., & Klin, A. (2004). Autism and pervasive developmental disorders. *Journal of Child Psychology and Psychiatry, 45*(1), 135–170.

Weimer, A. K., Schatz, A. M., Lincoln, A., Ballantyne, A. O., & Trauner, D. A. (2001). "Motor" impairment in Asperger syndrome: Evidence for a deficit in proprioception. *Journal of Developmental & Behavioral Pediatrics, 22*(2), 92–101.

White, A. (2004). Cognitive behavioural therapy in children with autistic spectrum disorders. In Bazian Ltd. (Ed.), *STEER: Succinct and timely evaluated evidence reviews, 4*(5). University of Southampton: Bazian Ltd and Wessex Institute for Health Research & Development.

Williams, G., Oliver, J. M., Allard, A., & Sears, L. (2003). Autism and associated medical and familial factors: A case control study. *Journal of Developmental and Physical Disabilities, 15*(4), 335–349.

World Health Organization. (1992). *International Classification of diseases* (10th ed.). Geneva, Switzerland: Author.

Epilogue

Thomas P. Gullotta and Gary M. Blau

A book is a journey. The preface, like a guide, introduces the subjects you'll visit, the perspectives you'll experience, and the accommodations that have been made to make your reading more profitable. The chapters are excursions for the reader into lands of varying familiarity. Some chapters are baffling to the uninitiated. Other chapters are exceedingly painful, like an ever-present emotional sunburn, to those who as parents, siblings, or other loved ones have seen a son, brother, or friend strive to overcome seemingly insurmountable issues every waking hour of their lives. In this, the epilogue, we conclude this book's journey and reflect on certain themes that appeared and reappeared to us.

First among these, is that we live in a hopeful time. Imperfect as it is, this book would not have been possible a decade ago. The simple question, "Does it work?" is changing the face of helping services. But before we become overly intoxicated with our own success, we need to remember that this book well documents the enormous shortcomings in the field. Certain issues, such as depression, are better understood than others, such as autism. The reason for this is funding. Over the past half-century plus, governments and private foundations have invested significant funds into areas like depression and conduct disorders. The results of these investments are evident in the material found in this volume. There are treatment and preventive interventions that work. Remember, these are not panaceas. Remember also that one intervention will not work for all. But we can intervene and matter for good. It now rests on us to expand the scope of our efforts to attend to those issues that have been overlooked.

The advent of psychopharmacology has brought major advancements to the helping field. By breaking a cycle of behavior, whether sadness, aggression, or delusional thought, new medications allow for greater possibility. Parents, siblings, family members, and the practitioner can now be heard and responded to. No longer trapped in depression or lost in anger and aggressive feelings controlled by fear and other feelings, a child can now view the world and those who would help in a different or less threatening manner. However, this advancement has not come without its costs. The most visible of these is the black box warnings that the FDA requires with antidepressants. Less visible are side effects like weight gain that complicate lives already complex enough. The need for understanding the benefits and costs of medications with young people must be addressed immediately. Improvements to reduce side effects are eagerly awaited. Further, as this book has clearly and repeatedly indicated, medications alone are inadequate to effectively help a child in need. To help requires a human touch and invariably a group of people who are committed to the child and family.

While this book documents a variety of interventions that work or hold promise to improve certain conditions, such specificity may not be enough. Rather, it is not unusual to need a caring team of people who are working closely together. There is a need for a coordinated network of mental health services and supports, where families and youth work in partnership with public and private organizations to address mental health challenges. In essence, practitioners and families must be part of an overall system of mental health care. This approach, systems of care, was established over 20 years ago (Stroul & Friedman, 1986, 1996), and data over the past two decades clearly indicate that this model, in which coordination and partnerships are paramount, improves the likelihood that children and youth will reach their full potential at home, at school, and in their communities (Huang et al., 2005).

The importance of early intervention is a recurrent theme found in this handbook. Whether one chooses a social learning perspective that seeks to discourage unprofitable behaviors before they become too habituated or seeks to capitalize on the early brain's malleability or some other explanation, early intervention is good.

Prevention is also good. In a strange twist of events due in part to the early reluctance of the treatment community to embrace prevention's promise, the research of prevention's effectiveness is often better than that available for treatment interventions. We know more about effective prevention programming than we do about treatment. Still, the search for effective preventive and health promotion interventions with diverse populations needs to be undertaken. Further, developing interventions that can withstand field tinkering and still be effective are needed. This volume makes clear a message that children's mental health must be viewed as a public health issue, and that we must understand the factors that are responsible for creating and sustaining mental health disorders so that we can develop and implement broad-scale prevention and intervention efforts (Holden & Blau, 2006).

So, in the final analysis, does treatment work? The answer to that question is a qualified yes. This volume clearly documents the value of a variety of social learning approaches to many of the issues discussed in this volume. But social learning approaches are but a small portion of the treatments that have been developed over the last century and are in use today. Certainly, some techniques, like bloodletting of yesteryear, need to be retired. Others, like the amorphous phrase "play therapy" need definition. Most need to be evaluated because we have no clue, save antidotal reports, that they have any positive effect. This, of course, requires lots of funding. Or does it?

Our last thought turns to the multitude of doctoral students in clinical psychology, marriage and family therapy, and social work laboring away on dissertations that will remain forever hidden in some dusty corner of some ill-lit library to someday be digitized and remain forever hidden in cyberspace. Like our colleagues in physical medicine, we need to improve our efforts to help children lead more fulfilling lives. So, why not focus attention on determining the effectiveness of Gestalt, Rogerian counseling, logotherapy, play therapy in its many permutations, and the four score and one other techniques in use. Imagine graduate schools establishing centers to rigorously evaluate clinical practice cooperatively. Imagine graduate students within these centers focused not on some esoteric problem but making a contribution toward building an international database to determine whether an intervention works, how it works, and with whom it works best.

Come to think of it, prevention and health promotion research could equally benefit from such an arrangement. What new life this would bring to this field, and we imagine what new discoveries this would bring in custom tailoring approaches to best help children and their families in need. We close this epilogue with the wish that this day arrives soon.

REFERENCES

Holden, E. W., & Blau, G. M. (2006). An expanded perspective on children's mental health. *American Psychologist, 61*, 642–643.

Huang, L., Stroul, B., Friedman, R., Mrazek, P., Friesen, B., Pires, S., et al. (2005). Transforming mental health care for children and their families. *American Psychologist, 60*, 615–627.

Stroul, B. & Friedman, R. (1986). *A system of care for children and youth with serious emotional disorders.* Washington, D.C.: Georgetown University Child Development Center, National Technical Assistance Center for Children's Mental Health.

Stroul, B., & Friedman, R. (1996). The system of care concept and philosophy. In B. Stroul (Ed.), *Children's mental health: Creating systems of care in a changing society* (pp. 3–21). Baltimore: Paul H. Brookes.

Index

Page numbers in italics refer to Figures or Tables.